THE SPIRITUAL OUT-OF-BODY EXPERIENCE

THE PRACTICE OF OBES & LUCID DREAMING
IN THE ANCIENT RELIGION OF THE SUN

MARK ATWOOD & LARA ATWOOD

SŪRA ONDRÚNAR
PUBLISHING

The Spiritual Out-of-Body Experience:
The Practice of OBEs and Lucid Dreaming in the Ancient Religion of the Sun

Copyright © 2024 Mark Atwood and Lara Atwood

All rights reserved. No part of this book may be reproduced, modified, incorporated, or transmitted in any form or by any means, electronic, mechanical, or otherwise, including photocopying, recording, or by any information storage and retrieval system without permission in writing from the copyright holder, except where permitted by law, which allows for the use of brief quotations accompanied by proper attribution to the copyright holder. Requests for permission to reproduce copyrighted material may be emailed to the publisher Sura Ondrunar Publishing, visit suraondrunar.org for contact details.

Mark Atwood and Lara Atwood assert their moral right to be identified as the authors of The Spiritual Out-of-Body Experience.

First Edition, Published June 2024

ISBN 978-0-6487565-4-5

Sura Ondrunar Publishing

Every reasonable effort has been made by the publisher to locate and acknowledge copyright owners, and obtain any necessary clearances. Please refer to the Copyright Acknowledgments section at the end of this book for the full list of works. If any works requiring clearance have unwittingly been included, or any corrections need to be made, the publisher will be pleased to do so at the earliest opportunity.

NON-PROFIT PRINCIPLES

The authors do not receive any money for the writing or sale of this book, as they follow the ancient principle that spiritual knowledge should not be profited from. This book is sold by a not-for-profit publisher with the same principles who set its price to cover the cost of production, with any surplus going back into their operating expenses.

DISCLAIMER

This book contains general information on the topic of religion for educational use only. Neither the authors nor the publisher are providing any service or advice to the individual reader.

While we endeavor to keep the information in this book up-to-date and correct, we make no representations or warranties of any kind, express or implied, about the completeness, accuracy, reliability, or suitability for any purpose. Any reliance you place on such information is therefore strictly at your own risk. You need to make your own inquiries to determine if the information is appropriate for your intended use.

The information in the book should not be used to diagnose, prevent, treat, or cure any sickness, disease, health or medical condition and is not meant to substitute medical or health advice or treatment. If you have any mental health concerns, you should consult with a qualified medical professional before acting upon or using any information in the book. Never disregard professional medical advice or delay in seeking it because of something that you have read in this book.

NOTE TO READER

Having willed out-of-body experiences, also known as astral projection, is an ancient religious practice. It is practiced while going to sleep normally. It should never be attempted through stressing, endangering, or harming the physical body in any way, including through inducing death or near-death states. This book only recommends having OBEs naturally by using meditative-style exercises.

CONTENTS

Preface   1

CHAPTER ONE
Introduction   5

PART 1
★ HISTORY ★

CHAPTER TWO
Ancient Otherworldly Experiences   13

CHAPTER THREE
Ancient Out-of-Body Experiences   17
   The Different Kinds of Ancient OBEs   18
   Egyptian   21
   Hermetic   63
   Hindu   66
   Ancient Sites and Other Dimensions   85
   Norse/Germanic   110
   Celtic   118
   Maltese   134
   Göbekli Tepe   137
   Zoroastrian   142
   Gnostic and Christian   147
   Taoist   159
   Tibetan Buddhist and Bon Dream Yoga   167
   Greek   173
   Shamanism   177
   North American   184
   Other   193
   OBEs to Heaven   193
   OBEs to the Source   198
   OBEs in the Cosmology of the Ancient Religion of the Sun   204
   Ancient Sites Used for OBEs   214
   Ancient Portal Sites   215

CHAPTER FOUR
Ancient Dreams   219
   Sumerian   219
   Egyptian   221
   Ancient Dream Books   226

Ancient Dream Incubation	228
Hindu	232
Jain	234
Chinese	234
Native North American	236
Maya	236
Inca	236
Celtic	238
Norse/Germanic	239
Greek	239
Roman	240
Gnostic	240
Christian	242
Conclusion	243

CHAPTER FIVE
Ancient Near-Death Experiences — 245

Greek	247
Egyptian	248
Sumerian	249
Inca	250
Maya	252
Roman	253
Christian	254
Hindu	256
Chinese	259
Tibetan	259

PART 2
AN OVERVIEW OF
✭ OUT-OF-BODY EXPERIENCES ✭

CHAPTER SIX
Evidence for Out-of-Body Experiences Being Real — 263

Twelve Points That Indicate OBEs and NDEs Are Real	264
The Limits of Material Science	268
Having OBEs as Proof for Oneself	270

CHAPTER SEVEN
An Outline of Out-of-Body Experiences — 273

The Different Kinds of OBEs	273
Where We Go in OBEs	274
Some of the Benefits of Having OBEs	275

My First OBEs	278
Subjectivity and the Influence of the Mind	280

CHAPTER EIGHT
Different Realms and Dimensions — 283

Other Realms in Ancient Religion	283
Is It Another Dimension?	285
Other Dimensions in Science	288
What Realms Exist?	290
Our Bodies in Other Realms	294
The Nonphysical Parts of Our Psyche	296

CHAPTER NINE
Near-Death Experiences — 301

Experiences in NDEs	302
OBEs as a Way to Learn about the Afterlife	305

CHAPTER TEN
Looking at the Evidence Presented by Materialist Science That OBEs Aren't Real — 309

Defining OBEs	309
Experiments on Reading While Out of the Body	311
Seeing Tunnels	313
Comparisons to Psychedelics	314
The Central Scientific Explanation for What OBEs Are	314
Another Explanation – The Brain Limiter Theory	316
Current Scientific Studies on OBEs	321
Concluding Thoughts	327

PART 3
DREAMS AND
✯ LUCID DREAMING ✯

CHAPTER ELEVEN
Dreams — 333

Different Kinds of Dreams	334
Why We Dream	337
Dreams as an Insight into Our Psyche	338
Symbols in Dreams and OBEs	339
Dream Guides	341
Premonitions in Dreams and OBEs	343
Using Common Sense	344

CHAPTER TWELVE
How to Remember Dreams   345
- Bedtime and Morning Exercises   345
- Daytime Exercises   347

CHAPTER THIRTEEN
Dream Incubation   349
- The Elements of Ancient Dream Incubation   350
- An Ancient Dream Incubation Ritual   357
- Dream Incubation at Sacred Places   360

CHAPTER FOURTEEN
Lucid Dreaming   363
- The Astral Jump   364
- Pulling a Finger and It Stretches   364
- Questioning Which Dimension We're In   365
- Reminders   366
- Awareness   367
- Going Back into a Dream to Learn More about It   369
- Watching Dream Images While Falling Asleep   369

PART 4
✯ TECHNIQUES FOR HAVING CONSCIOUS OUT-OF-BODY EXPERIENCES ✯

CHAPTER FIFTEEN
Preparing for Conscious Projection   373
- A Relaxation Exercise   373
- The Ancient Practice of Concentration   375
- Why Concentration Is Important for OBEs   376
- How to Train in Concentration   379
- Visualization   380
- Practicing Sitting Concentration and Visualization   381
- The Problem of Chattering Thoughts   382
- Concentration and Visualization on an Object   383
- Concentration and Visualization on an Object with Imagination   385
- Imaginative Visualization   386
- Summary   388

CHAPTER SIXTEEN
The Process of Conscious Projection   389
- Asking for Spiritual Assistance   389
- The Process of Splitting from the Body   390

Stepping out into Another Realm 392
Nine Main Steps for Conscious Projection 393

CHAPTER SEVENTEEN
Summary of Ancient OBE Techniques — 395
The Seven Key Components of Ancient OBE Exercises 395
The Use of Sound and Binaural Beats 396
A List of Ancient OBE Techniques 399
Ancient Techniques Used in This Book 403

CHAPTER EIGHTEEN
Kayotsarga — 405
How to Practice Kayotsarga 406
Kayotsarga OBE Exercise 407
The Flame of Consciousness 408

CHAPTER NINETEEN
Concentrating on the Heart — 411
Concentrating on Heartbeats 411
Visualization of the Physical Heart 412
Visualizing the Heart in Stages 413
Visualizing the Heart as a Spiritual Place 414
When to Know We're Out of the Body 414

CHAPTER TWENTY
Mantras — 417
An Ancient Egyptian Mantra 418
Mantras of the Sun 420
Projecting with Mantras 422

CHAPTER TWENTY-ONE
Astral Travel — 425
Traveling to Different Places in the Astral Plane 425
When We Can't See Clearly in the Astral Plane 427
The Problem of Creating One's Own Reality 428
Tips When Astral Traveling 429
Checking Whether Your OBE Is Real 429

CHAPTER TWENTY-TWO
Projection to a Place in an OBE — 433
An Exercise to Consciously Project to a Place 433
Projecting to a Room in Your House 434
Discovering a Mystery Object in a Room 435

Projecting to a Sacred Place — 435
Meeting Other Projectors at a Sacred Place — 437

CHAPTER TWENTY-THREE
Ancient Visualizations — 439
Preparation — 440
Starlight Energy — 440
Sun Heart — 443
Star Travel — 445
Mountain Peak Energy — 446
Fire in the Lotus — 449
Complete Light — 452

CHAPTER TWENTY-FOUR
Further Considerations for OBE Practice — 455
Technique — 455
Preparation — 456
The Ability to Concentrate — 456
Having a Suitable Inner State — 457
Practical Considerations — 458
Spiritual Considerations — 459
Programs for Having Out-of-Body Experiences — 460

PART 5
✦ TYPES OF BEINGS AND EXPERIENCES ✦

CHAPTER TWENTY-FIVE
The Different Beings We Meet in OBEs — 465
People Awake in the Physical World — 465
Other People Dreaming or Conscious in the Fifth Dimension — 466
The Deceased — 466
Spiritual Beings — 470
Demons — 473
Nature Spirits/Fairies — 481
Extraterrestrials — 482
One's Higher Being — 484
The Source — 486
Jungian Archetypes — 488

CHAPTER TWENTY-SIX
Experiences of Dark Entities and Places — 491
Bad Dreams — 491
Nightmares — 492

Sleep Paralysis	493
Incubi and Succubi	496
Alien Abduction	497
Demons in Dreams	503
Experiences in Hellish Regions	505

CHAPTER TWENTY-SEVEN
Protection against Demonic Entities — 511

Ancient Examples of Protection	512
Protective Objects	513
Circles of Protection	516
Incantations	518
Talismans and Symbols	523
Using Ancient Forms of Protection Today	527
Invocations and Incantations	527
The Incantation of the Spiritual Son/Sun	529
Casting a Circle of Protection	532
Using the Protective Incantation and Circle	535
Using Symbols	538

CHAPTER TWENTY-EIGHT
Psychedelics — 539

Our Perception of the Dimensions	539
Breaching the Interdimensional Barrier	540
The Influence of the Subconscious	544
Negative Experiences	548
Demonic Contact	548
Schizophrenia	553
After Effects	555
Mystical vs. Psychedelic Experiences	555
The Ancient Use of Psychedelics	561

CHAPTER TWENTY-NINE
Spiritual Practice and the Misconception of Supernatural Powers — 567

CHAPTER THIRTY
Having Out-of-Body Experiences for a Spiritual Purpose — 571

References and Copyright Acknowledgments — 575

Text References	575
Text Copyright Acknowledgments	613
Image Credits - References and Copyright Acknowledgments	617

Preface

For those interested, this is some background as to how this book came about.

In 2011, my wife Lara and I embarked upon a project that would have huge implications for us—and perhaps will, one day, for some of the world. It began as a simple look at what spiritual meaning the solstices and equinoxes held to ancient peoples. We knew these times of year were incredibly important to them, as they had aligned their massive megalithic structures to the sun on these days with remarkable accuracy, such as the Great Pyramids and Sphinx of Egypt, Stonehenge, the Ziggurat of Ur, Angkor Wat, and the statues of Easter Island.

Although some would argue these times of year mark the turning points in the seasons so important for agriculture, the sites that are aligned to them were used for religious purposes, and so these dates clearly had a spiritual rather than purely mundane significance.

As we researched, we discovered that not only had numerous ancient civilizations and peoples across the world built their most important sites aligned to the sun at these times, but their sites, beliefs, practices, cultures, civilizations, and artifacts also shared similarities—so many, and often so alike, as to be statistically out of the question to assign to coincidence.

It became inescapably clear that the great ancient civilizations of the world, who had all once worshiped the sun as their primary divinity, did so not because the sun was the obvious choice, but because they shared the same religion, which had spread across the world in prehistory and branched off into many traditions over time. This is how pyramids, dynasties of sacred kings said to descend from the sun, beliefs about the afterlife centered around the stars, and a founding myth of seven sages, among many, many other things, can be found across the ancient world.

Since this religion had never formally been identified, it had never been given any name—and so we called it the Religion of the Sun. We present all the evidence for it in our books *Ancient Solstice* and *The Ancient Religion of the Sun*. We have embraced this religion as our own, and uncovering it has become part of each of our own spiritual journeys.

After spending years uncovering the history of the Religion of the Sun, and the cultural, archaeological, genetic, and linguistic evidence for its existence, as well as some of its central beliefs, the next step was to find out how it was practiced.

This is difficult as there is no one complete corpus of texts that describes what the Religion of the Sun was nor how to practice it; this religion broke off into many traditions that later developed independently from each other, and none have survived completely intact and unmodified until today. Additionally, the ancient civilizations that practiced the Religion of the Sun fell, and so many records of the past have been destroyed.

To find out how the Religion of the Sun was originally practiced requires piecing together the many fragments in different traditions that can be retraced back to it. And, since it's a spiritual practice, it has also required having an understanding of the kinds of spiritual experiences those who practiced it had.

I began doing spiritual practices to have out-of-body experiences (OBEs) in 1990, and have had many OBEs since then. I also dedicated my life to spiritual practice at that time, and started what I call the path of the Spiritual Sun soon afterward, which I continued on and have found was central to the ancient Religion of the Sun. As I explain in this book, as part of this I experienced numerous things while out of my body depicted in ancient religions, sometimes before I had ever heard about them—discovering their reality and meaning—and this is what enabled us to recognize the ancient stream of knowledge stemming from the Religion of the Sun in so many different texts and sites. I knew then that some ancient peoples must have seen the same things that I had out of the body—that is, I knew they must have been having OBEs themselves, and that this was an important area of research.

And indeed it turned out to be—what we've uncovered has astonished us. Having OBEs was so central to the ancient Religion of the Sun that many of their sacred sites were built and used for having them, including the Great Pyramids of Egypt, pyramids in other parts of the world, and ancient sites across Europe. Seeking guidance from spiritual beings through OBEs and dreams was also incredibly important. And there are a number of explicit references to having OBEs consciously in ancient texts, and to the techniques ancient peoples used to have them. This has been time-consuming and difficult to uncover as the knowledge of how to have OBEs was often guarded with great secrecy—either being not allowed, or unable to be written down (due to fear of persecution), for long periods of time.

I began working on this book solidly around May 2021 (Lara around December 2021)—so it has taken us over two and a half years of consistent work to produce it (along with another forthcoming book), though I already had a lot of experience in having OBEs that I brought to it. It kept expanding, as we never anticipated that OBEs would be so fundamental to ancient sites and beliefs, and so widespread.

Lara did most of the research on ancient texts and traditions. She co-wrote all the chapters in part 1, most of them in part 5, and wrote in the sections on ancient history elsewhere, such as in the ancient ritual for dream incubation. She also helped edit the entire book.

Although we present here a comprehensive look at OBEs, there's still so much to learn. For instance, we've only just begun to understand how an ancient form of "technology" worked to induce OBEs. The exact process of the "astral split" is something that needs much more study, both using science and personal out-of-body experience. As we better understand these things, we want to further develop and refine techniques for conscious projection. This is what we intend to continue investigating.

We've worked so hard on this book, not for personal gain, but because we wish to see the ancient knowledge within it restored for the good it can bring to everyone who's interested. We know, however, there are some people who will see our unique ideas and research as an opportunity for themselves—wanting to present our hard work as their own, without crediting or referencing us as the source, in order to bolster their own following and profit. By using another's work and presenting it as though it's their own, they're stealing. It's called plagiarism, which can involve taking someone's ideas and how they're expressed, through words, images, point structure, etc. It's fraudulent and can be against the law.[1] My work has suffered from it for decades. Our publisher keeps a watch for plagiarists, and follows up on them.

This book forms part of a series of books about the ancient Religion of the Sun and the revival of its practices, and we'll be uncovering many more aspects of it in forthcoming books.

CHAPTER ONE

Introduction

Although we rarely hear about out-of-body experiences (OBEs) in media, entertainment, education, or academia, they are a huge part of human experience, and always have been. Their lack of representation in mass, popular discourse might have given the impression they are somehow a fringe topic, perhaps belonging to certain obscure aspects of the New Age. But this couldn't be further from the truth.

Out-of-body experiences are a natural function of the body and are much more common than most people think. In different surveys, anywhere between 8 to 50 percent of people said they had experienced at least one OBE[1] (in which they felt themselves outside of their bodies), and 55 percent at least one lucid dream[2] (which is an OBE that happens when we become aware of being in a dream). That's a lot of people.

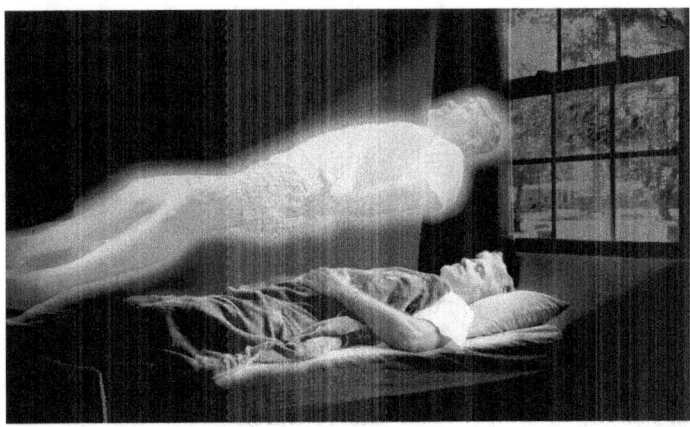

Depiction of an out-of-body experience.

OBEs are common to all of humanity, and have been recorded ever since we've had writing—accounts of them are found in some of the oldest texts in the world. Beliefs in out-of-body experiences can be found in about 95 percent of all cultures worldwide, and despite the distances between them, their beliefs about OBEs are remarkably similar, indicating they are based on real experiences.[3]

Sixteenth century painting of the rapture of the Christian Apostle Paul, which is widely considered an out-of-body experience.

Accounts of OBEs can be found in the texts of some of the world's largest religions, including Christianity, Hinduism, Buddhism, and Taoism, and also in the texts of the most ancient, like those of Egypt and Sumer.

Today, countless thousands of people from all faiths and walks of life share their out-of-body experiences on social media platforms like YouTube. Christians tell of life-changing OBEs where they have talked with Jesus; while Germanic pagans relate the many ways they have encountered Odin; those in the New Age often relate their experiences with astral projection; and atheists, Buddhists, Christians, and more, relate how they left their bodies when they died and entered a nonphysical world—coming back to tell the tale in what are called near-death experiences (NDEs).

Around 10 to 20 percent of those who come close to death recall having an NDE, which is about 5 percent of the overall population.[4] One study that surveyed people from thirty-five countries found it was as many as one in ten people generally, but the study counted the OBEs of those surveyed who were not close to death as though they were NDEs, which would have increased the number.[5] But again, this is a lot of people.

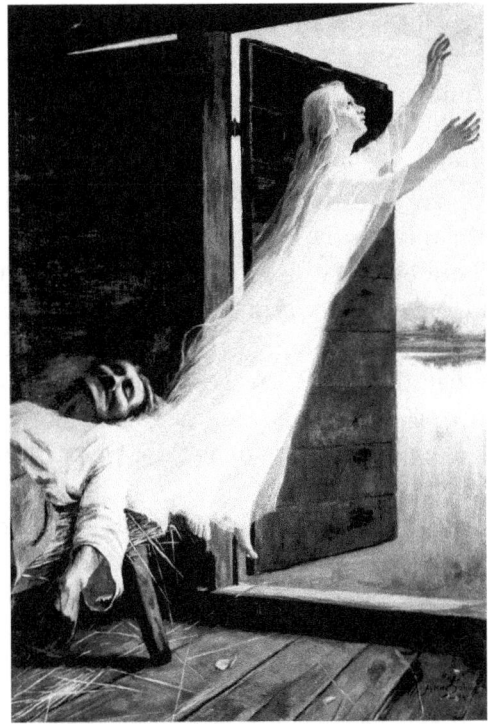

The painting *Passage* by Anna Sahlsten, 1894, depicting the soul/consciousness leaving the body at death.

Many who've had an OBE describe it in different ways, which means they often don't appear in searches for "out-of-body experience" or "astral projection," as the experiencer may not even recognize it as such.

But once you understand what these experiences are, how, and why they happen, as I hope you will by the end of this book, you'll be able to recognize them for what they are, and begin to see that they are an intrinsic part of human experience.

In fact, you, or someone close to you, may have already experienced an OBE—maybe as a dream in which you realized you were dreaming, or a very clear dream that felt as though you really traveled somewhere, or in which you had a premonition and saw something that later came true, or an experience where you felt yourself float up and away from your body, or the common feeling of "sleep paralysis" in which one can't move while transitioning into or out of sleep, or even a near-death experience.

OBEs are so common because every night when we sleep we leave our body and travel in another dimension where we normally dream.

The deceased also travel there too as they leave this world, and a few revive to tell the tale—these are called near-death experiences (NDEs).

Though sometimes it happens spontaneously, we can learn to travel to this dimension consciously, as a number of ancient peoples did, by consciously projecting there or by lucid dreaming.

This dimension is described in the cosmologies of numerous ancient religions, and there is quite a lot of scientific evidence that supports its existence. I explain why I use the term dimension to refer to it (specifically the fifth dimension) in chapter 8.

To make it easier to navigate, this book is divided into five parts, as it attempts to cover the breadth and depth of OBE phenomena—in ancient history and religion, in science, our everyday lives, and the practice of how to have them.

Part 1 is dedicated to the accounts of OBEs in history—covering the different types of OBEs, including dreams and near-death experiences. We look at the most ancient references to them in the world, and detail their many accounts across the ancient texts of numerous traditions, revealing how ancient people viewed them—traversing the records of ancient Egypt, Mesopotamia, China, Tibet, Iran, India, Europe, and more.

Then in part 2 I give an overview of what OBEs are, their different kinds, what happens during them, and the benefits of having them. I look at what science is able to tell us about them, and cover some of the most compelling scientific and anecdotal evidence that supports they are real. Not only that, but I address some of the scientific studies and explanations used to claim they aren't real. I also explore the existence of other dimensions, according both to ancient peoples and to science, and the multidimensional nature of the human psyche, and devote a chapter to near-death experiences, which are the most scientifically studied and compelling OBEs of all.

In part 3 I look at the type of OBE most are familiar with—dreams. I outline the different types of dreams we can have, and explain the appearance of symbols in them, and how to interpret them. I then give simple techniques for remembering dreams better, and an ancient ritual for incubating a dream, to try and invoke a divine-sent dream just as ancient peoples did. There is then a chapter on lucid dreaming—what it is, and techniques for how to lucid dream.

In part 4 we outline techniques for having OBEs that are based on methods used by ancient peoples, and how to train in them to have regular experiences. I describe how these techniques work and provide information on how to be successful with them. I also explain how to travel once out of the body and seek out meaningful experiences.

Then part 5 is for everything else, covering a lot of extra information. I list the different beings we can meet in OBEs, including those commonly depicted in ancient religions, broadly known as angels and demons. Not all OBEs are positive, and so there is a chapter devoted to experiences of dark entities and places, like nightmares and sleep paralysis. In answer to this, I outline the many forms of spiritual protection ancient people used. Another chapter addresses the relationship between OBEs and psychedelics, looking at the latest scientific discoveries. Then finally, I conclude with how to use OBEs for a spiritual purpose as they were in ancient times.

We've created a number of exercises in this book based on ancient practices and what we know to be effective. We've also included exercises that I've learnt during my time practicing which I've found to work best; I don't know where they originated from, though some are essentially the same as those found in ancient sources.

This book contains, what we feel, are numerous groundbreaking discoveries that have the potential to change the way we understand OBEs, as well as ancient history, religion, sacred sites, and psychedelic experiences. We propose several new theories, these being our Giza OBE Theory, Pyramid Portal Theory, Ancient Europe OBE Theory, Jesus Twice Born Theory, Ancient Portal Site Theory, Brain Limiter Theory, and Psychedelic Brain Barrier Theory.

Specifically, this book deals with OBEs from the perspective of the ancient Religion of the Sun, and in this book we present some of its major practices—those of dream incubation and having OBEs. This is the religion I belong to, which is why I have written this book; I wish to bring the knowledge of this religion back so that it can once more contribute to the collective knowledge of humanity—whether that be common, academic, or religious.

Ancient people in the Religion of the Sun used OBEs for a spiritual purpose, and as a practitioner of this religion, that's how I use them too, and why I give the methods for OBEs in this context—and why this book is called *The Spiritual Out-of-Body Experience*. I use the word spiritual in the sense of relating to divinity, rather than as referring to just any nonphysical phenomenon.

There are other traditions which OBEs are a part of—namely Shamanism and the dark occult/Satanism. I briefly touch on how these traditions are different to that of the Religion of the Sun. Because they are different, I don't include the methods used for having OBEs in them. This book is about the methods used in the ancient Religion of the Sun.

The teachings of the past can inspire and direct us today to do greater things. Just like ancient people, we too can meditate under the stars, receive messages in our dreams, meet the same spiritual beings out of the body as they did, perceive the divinity in creation, feel the presence of the spiritual in the sun and the life around us, and do spiritual practices in sacred places. In rediscovering the lost knowledge of the ancients, we re-awaken our sense of the mystical in life, and learn from a wisdom that had become lost.

Much of what is explained in this book was never intended to be shared publicly like this. But things are different now; the old ways and mystery schools of light are gone. Many of their surviving records have been brought out into the open for the whole world to see, after being discovered buried in tombs or in the ground, in private collections, or traded in antiquities markets. Now we have a rare opportunity to make sense and use of them. This is an attempt to bring some of their knowledge back.

PART I
HISTORY

CHAPTER TWO

Ancient Otherworldly Experiences

Dreams, OBEs, and NDEs are as old as humankind, as they are a natural part of human experience, and because of this, they have played a part in virtually every religion in one form or another and accounts of them can be found in almost every culture. There are references to people being "in the spirit" and of being "taken up" into otherworldly realms; of seeing heavens and hells; of encountering supernatural beings in dreams, visions, and mystical experiences; and of the person, soul, or spirit traveling to distant, otherworldly places.

Most people who had OBEs in ancient times would have left no trace for us to see today, but a few have been recorded where the means of the time allowed. The most common type of visit to the otherworld recorded in ancient sources are dreams, which is to be expected as they are how we experience the fifth dimension (the dimension we go to in OBEs) on a daily basis. Ancient sources referring to otherworldly experiences don't always directly state their origin—whether a dream, an OBE, or an NDE—but these are usually the most likely explanations, or the only viable ones.

What people experienced in OBEs, NDEs, and dreams formed the basis of much of the symbolic artwork and writings of ancient cultures, like those of ancient Egypt. These have often been misinterpreted as myths and the attempts of primitive peoples to understand their world, but some have their origin in the fifth dimension and accurately illustrate what people see in NDEs and OBEs today, as we'll see in part one of this book.

Though they are expressed through the culture of the individual, these otherworldly experiences often share the same core elements, irrespective of time and place, as all people can essentially have the same experiences out of the body. People today commonly experience heavens in NDEs, for example.[1]

The highly symbolic artwork of ancient Egypt largely
depicts the realms and beings that exist out of the body.

We can better understand ancient spiritual beliefs by taking into account the existence of other dimensions, and by knowing that ancient peoples experienced them. The fifth dimension is the source of some of these beliefs and provides a context for ancient cosmologies.

However, there is one religion in particular in which dreams and OBEs were used specifically for spiritual purposes and were central to its practice. This religion is what Lara and I have called the ancient Religion of the Sun.

The Religion of the Sun influenced and gave rise to many of the religions of the ancient world that were centered around the veneration of the sun as the greatest manifestation of light and the creator, including religions in ancient Egypt, Mesopotamia, Iran, India, Europe, China, the Americas, and other places, and this is why they share numerous cultural, spiritual, and cosmological themes.

What we've discovered is that many of the greatest ancient sites in the world, which had been part of the Religion of the Sun—such as pyramids, chambered mounds, ziggurats, stone circles, earthworks, and megalithic temples—symbolized some of the structure of nonphysical realms as part of their design, and among other purposes, had been used for helping to facilitate OBEs and contact with higher realms. They were all part of a massive worldwide effort of building structures based on the same basic principles and beliefs. In addition to this, there were ancient temples that were built and used for dream incubation, like the hundreds across Egypt, Greece, and the Roman Empire including the serapeum at the Library of Alexandria. This reveals that for thousands of years, having OBEs and incubating dreams were major religious practices.

OBEs were so central to the Religion of the Sun that the out-of-body realms formed the basis of the underlying symbolic design of the Great Pyramids, which was the most important site of the ancient Religion of the Sun, and we believe indicates that it was from here that much of the ancient knowledge about OBEs originates and then spread to other parts of the world.

We believe that understanding the history and beliefs of the Religion of the Sun is essential to understanding the many ancient cultures and civilizations it had a major influence upon, and that any historical study of NDEs, OBEs, and dreams should take it into account.

What we find in the surviving ancient texts from this religion is the use of dreams and OBEs for spiritual purposes. In ancient times, dreams were a common source of spiritual guidance and were seen as a form of communication with the otherworld, used particularly for obtaining guidance from divine beings. OBEs were used likewise, but also for going through initiations. An initiation involving an OBE was central to the ancient mysteries of the Religion of the Sun that spread across much of the world, which at times even kings had to undergo.

Some of the greatest figures in the ancient Religion of the Sun, such as Odin, Krishna and Arjuna, Hermes Trismegistus, Jesus, and the priests of Atlantis (including Osiris), were recorded as having OBEs and used them for these spiritual purposes. The disciples of Jesus had dreams in which they were given spiritual messages, sometimes by Jesus out of the body, who would then also later interpret their experiences in waking life—revealing that they were an important part of their interactions together.

These experiences informed the cosmology of the Religion of the Sun with its detailed descriptions of the multidimensional structure of creation and the human body, the realms of the afterlife, and of the gods, demons, angels, the dead, and other beings who inhabit them, as well as their supreme source.

The NDE accounts of today share many similarities with this cosmology, even though the people who have these NDEs are in most cases completely unfamiliar with ancient religion. That the NDEs of people living in modern Western civilization, for example, share commonalities with what's sometimes described in ancient Egyptian, Celtic, or Hindu texts produced thousands of years earlier in a completely foreign culture is a testament to their underlying reality, and to the ability of people in the ancient Religion of the Sun to use OBEs to objectively explore spiritual realities.

People still today have OBEs, sometimes in which they are taken out of their bodies and shown things found in ancient texts, such as the existence of hell and heaven, so that they will come back and tell people what they saw.

Through my own OBEs I've also experienced things portrayed in the ancient texts of those traditions derived from the ancient Religion of the Sun. For example, I've seen people who've died entering the gateway into hell/the underworld, what people call demons and angels, and Beings who were known as great spiritual teachers, including Jesus. These are common sights in NDEs today. But as I've been through the actual initiations on the path of the Spiritual Sun, I've also seen things only revealed to the initiated, such as being with figures who became known as gods in ancient Egypt, including Anubis, who oversaw an initiation I went through while out of the body in the Great Pyramid.

In the ancient Religion of the Sun, OBEs were generally used for very serious and specific spiritual purposes, and so understanding them requires some background knowledge of their context. That's why the following chapter is not just a simple rundown of ancient accounts, but discusses the cosmology that surrounds them and the ancient sites used for having them.

This means touching upon subjects that are obscure, and so before going further there are a couple of terms used throughout the book that I'll clarify briefly. I can only say a little about them here, as they need much more explanation, which can be found in some of my other books.

The path of the Spiritual Sun is the phrase we use to describe what has been called the path to enlightenment. We use a slightly different term to distinguish it from strictly Eastern ideas. This path was central to the ancient Religion of the Sun; the key events upon it like inner death, resurrection, and ascension, correspond to the apparent annual journey of the sun, which was used in ancient times to illustrate it (hence its name), as I explain in my book *Ancient Solstice*.

Initiation is another term we use frequently, as many ancient OBEs occurred as part of a system of initiation. This system was central to the ancient Religion of the Sun and formed the basis of mystery schools in different parts of the world. It required the initiate met certain standards, and would have inducted them into a more advanced level of the religion. They are different, however, to what were and still are an even more secret set of initiations that take place on the path of the Spiritual Sun, which are given by spiritual beings to someone while they are out of the body; this is a completely secret process that happens personally to someone when they meet the standards set in higher dimensions. The initiations conducted in the mystery schools of the ancient Religion of the Sun were based on these secret initiations of the path of the Spiritual Sun, and used the same symbols and knowledge, but were more like an enactment of them mostly for those who had not met the grade set in the higher dimensions. Instead, they were part of a teaching that encoded the knowledge of the path of the Spiritual Sun within it. I will discuss these initiations in more detail in another book.

Following are the ancient accounts of OBEs, dreams, and NDEs, that Lara and I have found in our research.

CHAPTER THREE

Ancient Out-of-Body Experiences

In this chapter we detail the surviving accounts of out-of-body experiences in ancient sources that we've found.

As far as we know, this is the most comprehensive study of ancient OBEs ever done. Many of the ideas and conclusions we've come to in this chapter are being given for the first time, and some now form the basis of new theories we're putting forward.

In terms of understanding ancient OBEs, we started from zero. Although we've been practicing and having OBEs for a long time (myself for more than thirty years, and Lara for more than twenty), we had no idea how ancient people had, saw, or used them. It's taken us more than two years of trawling through ancient texts and information about ancient sites to form a coherent picture. What we've now discovered is that ancient people (in traditions derived from the ancient Religion of the Sun):

- Used practices to still and focus the mind to overcome the brain's limitations and consciously leave the body in OBEs.

- Attempted to harness the energy of the sun and stars for having OBEs, both in its physical form as electromagnetic energy, and in its nonphysical form.

- Built numerous sites that were used for having OBEs, some of which have special acoustic and electromagnetic properties that were likely intended to help facilitate OBEs.

- Used OBEs for seeing the afterlife firsthand, and for preparing for the journey to heaven after death.

- Sought particularly to travel through the portal to heaven commonly seen in NDEs as existing in the sky and leading through the stars to the Source/Spiritual Sun. This type of OBE was part of an initiation that became central to many ancient mysteries.

All this and more will become clear in what follows.

THE DIFFERENT KINDS OF ANCIENT OBES

Few realize there were different types of OBEs that people had in ancient times. We've identified three types they had in the Religion of the Sun, which led to three different dimensions or regions. These types are explained in much more detail throughout the book, but are mentioned here to give a context to the ancient OBE accounts that follow.

1. To the fifth dimension (usually the astral plane): This first type is called astral travel today and is what people are usually referring to when they talk about OBEs. It includes astral projection and lucid dreaming. This is the most common type of OBE because it's the easiest to have, since it happens in the place we go to when we sleep—the astral plane of the fifth dimension. The astral plane was referred to as the Duat and Land of the Horizon in Egypt, *bhuva* and the sky of ether/*akasa* in Hinduism, Svavaland in Norse tradition, and *bardo* in Tibet.

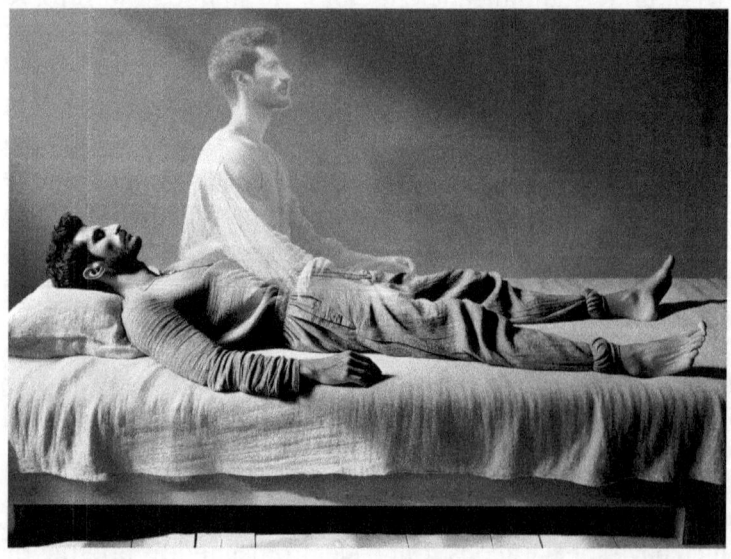

Depiction of an out-of-body experience to the astral plane.

Those recorded as having experienced astral travel within traditions that are part of the Religion of the Sun are the priests of Atlantis, those from among an esoteric order in ancient Egypt (the Enlightened Ones / Twice Born), Hermes Trismegistus, Jesus, the Hindu goddess Saraswati, the Hindu god Krishna and his disciple Arjuna, the Norse god Odin, the legendary Chinese immortal Han Xiangzi and Taoists of the "Highest Clarity" school, a Greek Pythagorean called Hermotimus, and another Greek called Timarchus.

Tibetan practitioners of dream yoga have maintained an ancient tradition of lucid dreaming. However, as we'll discuss, there are dark elements in it, making it different to the Religion of the Sun. There are indications that lucid dreaming was also practiced in Hinduism, though no tradition of it survived.

This entire book is dedicated to explaining and learning how to have this kind of OBE in the fifth dimension naturally using ancient meditative exercises.

2. To heaven: Heaven is usually only accessed by those who've died; it's not somewhere people ordinarily go in an OBE. It's the place that countless people who've had NDEs say they've visited. They typically describe firstly leaving their bodies (entering into the fifth dimension), but are then pulled upward to the sky, through a portal that leads into a dark tunnel with a light at the end of it, which they travel along, arriving to the end where it opens out into a beautiful realm, usually a garden or natural landscape—this realm is likely the first of a number of heavenly regions.

The near-death experience of Philip Siracusa describes what people typically see, which will be important to remember as we look at how people in the ancient Religion of the Sun symbolized this realm and the entrance to it in their ancient texts, sites, and rituals, as it was absolutely central to their beliefs:

> "I found myself starting to float out of my body upward toward the ceiling [...] and then I was pulled through the ceiling [...]. I started to go up into the sky and into this portal, this energy, this vortex, this tunnel of some sort. And when I was pulled in it, it was dark, very dark in there, and huge. I was going very, very fast. [...] I reached the end of the tunnel and a tremendous, beautiful light opens up into the sky, this magnificent sky, that we don't have here [...] we don't have this perfection of beauty that I've seen. There was a brightness that was overwhelming with love and energy. And I saw these tremendous gates [...] these golden gates [...] and then I'm being pulled through this garden [...]. It's as if my spirit body, my soul had taken back its true essence of form and went back home. And I'm drifting now through these fields, and the fields are beautiful, they're immense, they're perfection [...] the trees, the leaves, the roses, the flowers [...] and I'm feeling at the same time now this vibrational energy of pureness thing, I'm connected to everything. There's no such thing as a negative thought, a low vibration. This was home, heaven, I would call it heaven. And this angelic being [...] she was

able to pull me through vibration [...] into a garden [...]. The garden is second to none, the garden is euphoric. [...] [Then] I was pulled back [...] through the sky, through this open portal that's tremendous and not visible to the eye, only to the spirit eye, and through the ceiling of a hospital and right back into the body as if I slipped into a glove."[1]

People who have NDEs commonly describe heaven as a beautiful garden with a bright light shining, sometimes accessed through a gate at the end of a dark tunnel.

People were said to have once been able to easily reach this realm without dying, and without having to go through the "portal" or tunnel. This ability was lost, and so the order known as the Twice Born of ancient Egypt developed a method to reach heaven by inducing an NDE, which involved putting their bodies under certain conditions and taking a blend of substances (the knowledge of which is now lost). This ritual became central to the ancient mysteries that spread across large parts of the world. Because of the risk of death or injury, I totally recommend against doing anything like this.

It's interesting that the OBEs Jesus is attributed as having sound more like experiences of heaven and even of the Source of creation, than of the astral plane, as he passes through the gates of the firmament, visits "great and holy generations," travels the "Holy Light Stream" and enters the "Sea of Light." It's possible that he had or gained the ability to go into heaven out of the body naturally, without being near death.

Taoists of the "Highest Clarity" school also seem to have preserved OBE techniques for reaching heaven naturally without being near death, and these share notable similarities with practices used in Egypt (in the Pyramid Texts) and by Jesus to reach heaven out of the body—indicating that there were ancient methods for reaching heaven that were substance and near-death free.

3. To the Source: In the Vedic texts of India there are descriptions of an even rarer kind of OBE. In this kind, rather than feeling that one leaves their bodies, they have the sense of collapsing into their heart. Instead of going into the fifth dimension, they go into the Source or an aspect of it, but can only be there for a very short time. There was clearly a long yogic tradition of having this kind of OBE, and what is experienced during it is expressed in many of the most fundamental Hindu beliefs. However, the understanding of it seems to have been lost.

In ancient Hindu texts, there are descriptions of having an OBE to the Source, which is described as a place of vast and immense light, like the sun.

EGYPTIAN

The oldest accounts that describe OBEs come from ancient Egypt. OBEs and the astral plane formed a fundamental part of ancient Egyptian religious beliefs.

The religion of ancient Egypt is one of the oldest historically documented religions in the world and its veneration of the sun is well-known. Its beginnings are conventionally dated to the fourth millennium BC along with the emergence of Egyptian civilization. However, there are indications its religion (and civilization) is much older. A number of sources from among the ancient Egyptians themselves state that their religion originated as far back as tens of thousands of years ago, to a time when the gods manifested in human form and lived in a long-lost civilization.[2] This civilization is commonly known today as Atlantis.

The fifth dimension and the nonphysical body one used to travel there was extensively detailed in ancient Egyptian texts; the oldest religious texts of Egypt clearly describe OBEs; the Great Pyramids symbolize aspects of the fifth dimension, and were likely used for having OBEs; and there are records that the greatest teacher and god of Egypt, Osiris, taught about the fifth dimension. I'll cover all this and more in the following sections.

THE ASTRAL PLANE AND ASTRAL BODY

The ancient Egyptians knew of the astral plane. They called it the Duat—it was a parallel world where people went to dream, where everyone went after death, and where many gods resided.[3][4] It was also the place from which one traveled into heaven.

The hieroglyph for the Duat is a five-pointed star in a circle,[5] and in the oldest Egyptian texts, the Pyramid Texts, the Duat was associated with the sky and stars,[6] which is interesting, as the word astral means "pertaining to the stars." Although the use of the word astral in relation to OBEs is modern, the association between the astral and the sky and stars is very ancient. That the Duat hieroglyph is five-pointed is also interesting, as the astral plane is part of the fifth dimension and was associated with a fifth element (being the first of five) called ether.

Egyptian hieroglyph for the Duat, or astral plane (the star in the circle), as found in the Pyramid Texts.

Perhaps the oldest surviving depiction of the Egyptian five-pointed star (without the circle) was inscribed onto the ceiling of the burial chamber of the Step Pyramid of Djoser, dated to the twenty-seventh century BC. Painting/inscribing these stars onto the ceilings of burial chambers became a long tradition in ancient Egypt.[7] Pictured above is the funerary temple of the female Pharaoh Hatshepsut. The stars represented the night sky, which the Egyptians associated with the Duat, and so likely also signified the out-of-body realm the king entered after death.

Ancient Egyptian religion became focused on the preparation for the afterlife. Most of its surviving literature describes the afterlife journey each person had to make through the Duat, where they would face a divine judgment that determined, based on their actions in life, whether they would go on to live in a higher, heavenly realm, or be handed over to be swallowed by the jaws of a monstrous goddess and face annihilation. As numerous NDE accounts reveal, this judgment is sometimes part of the process that happens after we die.

Some say the Egyptians depicted the astral body as either what they called the Ka or the Ba. However, it appears they didn't write about the astral body as something distinct; this is because when we go into the astral plane we carry all parts of our psyche with us, minus our physical body (and its vital sheath), not just our astral body.

The Ka was essentially the vital essence or life-force of the body, and seems to correspond to what's been called the vital/pranic sheath in Hinduism, while the Ba was everything of a person that lives on after the death of their physical body (minus their Ka), and would have included the astral body. There was also the Sah, which was a spiritual body that only those worthy could form. And only those worthy became transformed into a being of light, called an Akh (which is one's higher Being).[8]

THE OLDEST RECORDS OF OBES IN THE WORLD

The oldest written records of OBEs from anywhere in the world are found in the Pyramid Texts of Egypt, which are among the world's oldest religious texts, dating to about 2400 BC. They were found inscribed into the walls inside some of the better preserved pyramids at Saqqara, which were built as tombs for pharaohs/kings, providing the first written records of ancient Egyptian religious beliefs. The texts are believed to be hymns that were

A section of the Pyramid Texts.

chanted inside the pyramid after the pharaoh had died as certain ritual acts were performed, such as incensing. They detail what would happen to the king in the afterlife, describing the OBE the king has within his pyramid after his death. The pyramid acted as a kind of miniature model of the Duat, which he traveled through while undergoing different spiritual processes before his soul's final transformation into a being of light, an Akh. This transformation occurred as he joined with his father, the sun, and traveled from the Duat through the portal on the eastern horizon (the place of the sun's rising, the Akhet) to the heavenly region of the northern circumpolar stars. He was thought to travel through this portal as his Akh/spirit left his pyramid.[9] The pyramid's use as a portal into higher dimensions is something we will return to shortly.

The Pyramid Texts contain explicit references to OBEs—the following excerpts are taken from Susan Brind Morrow's 2015 translation, though they contain more references to OBEs than listed here. Morrow has attempted to provide a reading of the Pyramid Texts based on her understanding that they contain a complex religious philosophy that was linked to the cycles of nature (of the sun, stars, and seasons) expressed poetically with puns, riddles, and metaphors, rather than the texts being superstitious and primitive spells as is commonly believed.

While we feel much still remains to be understood about ancient Egyptian language, Morrow's insightful attempt offers remarkable glimpses into the spiritual meaning of the Pyramid Texts. These glimpses are enough to demonstrate the ancient Egyptians knew about the out-of-body realm and the ability to travel there in a nonphysical body, and that it was central to their religion. The name Unis in these excerpts is the name of the king in whose pyramid they were inscribed.

"[...] he moves into his light body [...]
the light body goes to heaven as the corpse goes to the earth
What men receive when they are buried:
a thousand bread, a thousand beer
On the offering table, is a poor inheritance
As it cannot be eaten.[10]

He [Osiris] wipes away the flesh from the life force of Unis, [...]
He leads the life force of Unis from his body in the tomb.[11]

Thus not residing in his mummy or with it
Unis has absorbed the mind of pervasive holiness. [...]
The body that is this, his mummy,
That he so loved, is made hateful to him
For it does not function within the realm of light.
What is eternal is the soul.[12]

Come rise, come climb,
Come climb, come float.
It is the floating up that is the rising of Unis [...].[13]

As Unis passes away may he rise on this day
In the true form of a living light body.[14]

Then moving outside the bonds, he is free
Then moving on he is given his pervasive true nature.[15]

Unis comes out, the shining falcon.[16]

He was made for the earth
But leaves it as a falcon,
As his legs become wings.
As a falcon you are free, as a baby hawk.
His light body carries him, though he perish,
His life force is reassembled.
You open your place in heaven
Among the stars of the sky.[17]

To the end of the earth
To the end of the limits of space
Unis travels as the wind."[18]
~ THE PYRAMID TEXTS

Depiction of the king having left his body in the pyramid to travel
to the stars in his light body, as described in the Pyramid Texts.

The Pyramid Texts also include what seems like a kind of mantra and phrase used as part of inducing an OBE, which I include in chapter 20, Mantras.

And so we have clear references to out-of-body travel after death in Egypt, and these passages reveal it was the soul—the immortal, internal, and spiritual part of someone—that was the focus of ancient Egyptian religion, not the body or mummy.

Most of the texts that survived in ancient Egypt were the ones people were buried with in their tombs to guide them through the afterlife, which is not surprising, since they were hidden and sealed away, sometimes for thousands of years, thus preserving them. It's also not surprising they only refer to after-death OBEs, since they were written for a specific funerary purpose. But there would have been many other texts, and some of these may have survived too and contain more information about ancient Egyptian OBEs, including those they had in life.

The Kolbrin is such a collection of texts. Published in 1994 for the first time, it claims to be a set of ancient Egyptian texts that had been brought to Britain by refugees from Egypt and then added to by ancient Britons, who contributed a number of their own texts to the collection. It was passed down for centuries in secrecy in Britain, until being handed over for publication by an elderly man from Wales who'd attended a Druidic organization and been a member of a Hermetic one.[19] Their authenticity is being vindicated by researchers like Yvonne Whiteman, who are finding correlations between the texts and archaeological and genetic finds, some of which have only come to light after the Kolbrin was published.[20] The accuracy of the information found in the Kolbrin has led Lara and I to believe it contains authentically ancient material from Egypt (and Britain).

The texts of the Kolbrin describe OBEs that a secret order in Egypt consisting of initiates called Enlightened Ones (and among them a further class of initiates, the Twice Born) had while alive, which we'll discuss shortly. It also says that the funerary texts of Egypt had a hidden meaning, and that they weren't really intended for the dead, but for the living.

> "Men read the Great Book of the Master of the Hidden Temple. They die and take it with them, but there is no power in their words, and who but we, the Enlightened Ones, know the hidden meanings? It is not for those dead to the Earth, who step forth in the Netherworld, but for those who died and remain with us." [21]
> ~ THE KOLBRIN

The way the Great Book of the Master of the Hidden Temple is described sounds like it's referring to the Egyptian Book of the Dead (a later incarnation of the Pyramid Texts). It says there is no power in the words of those who die and take it with them, as the texts were meant to be recited, which surely refers to those who think it's about a physical death, but that the Enlightened Ones know its real meaning. The uninitiated die and leave their physical bodies, but the Enlightened Ones have died inwardly to their vices (which I call egos, and explain in chapter 8) and, through a process, have been reborn to eternal life. This inner process is the origin of the themes of death and resurrection in the ancient Religion of the Sun.

There is evidence that the Pyramid Texts are based on much older material,[22] [23] and that the pyramids of Saqqara they were found in are poor imitations of the Great Pyramids of Giza, which are far older than the dates given to them in mainstream Egyptology and were built and used for initiatory rites, rather than as tombs.[24] [25]

Left: The pyramids of Saqqara. Right: The Great Pyramids of Giza. It seems not only like the Saqqara pyramids are later copies of the Great Pyramids, but that the Pyramid Texts they were inscribed with detail a ritual that used to be conducted in the Great Pyramid.

It looks to us like the Pyramid Texts were not originally, or at least not only, to do with the process of death, but described the initiations of the path of the Spiritual Sun, and were probably derived from the OBEs of people who had gone through that path, with other things added at later times. We believe they originate from a far more ancient teaching that was preserved in the Religion of the Sun and became adapted for funerals by the time of the historical pharaonic dynasties.

OSIRIS' TEACHING ABOUT THE FIFTH DIMENSION

The Egyptian texts of the Kolbrin also reveal more about the origins of ancient Egyptian beliefs and their meaning, and include texts that record the teachings of Osiris, who was the most popular god of Egypt.

The knowledge of the fifth dimension, the multidimensional parts of a person, and much of what became ancient Egyptian religion, appears to trace back to Osiris. Indeed, in ancient Egyptian texts, Osiris was said to preside over the Duat—he was known as the "Lord of the Duat" and the Duat was known as "the Kingdom of Osiris,"[26] making him the lord of the astral. He was the most important deity of the Pyramid Texts (alongside Ra, the Spiritual Sun), and is strongly associated with the Great Pyramids and Sphinx. He was the ancient Egyptian equivalent of Jesus—offering all those who followed him the hope of resurrection and eternal life.

In ancient sources, Osiris was recorded as being a real person who came to Egypt in the distant past to teach people religion and the arts of civilization, and was later deified as a god. Specifically, he taught the Religion of the Sun; he is what Lara and I call a wisdom bringer, and she writes much about Osiris in her book *The Ancient Religion of the Sun*.

Osiris, the most famous god and great teacher of ancient Egyptian religion.

In the following excerpt from the Kolbrin, Osiris describes what would become known as the Ba, which he called the Lord of the Body, and how it experiences the fifth dimension. His description may have been the basis for the Ba being depicted in ancient Egyptian artwork with the head of the deceased person but the body (and wings) of a bird, which it used to fly away from the tomb and enter the realm of the afterlife. This is why in the excerpt from the Pyramid Texts earlier the king's legs are transformed into wings as he leaves his body and takes flight as a bird. I'd say the soul being depicted as having wings was meant to explain how we can fly in the astral plane, and how some in NDEs say they have experienced spending a short while coming to realize they are dead before flying to their heavenly destination in the sky, but generally cease flight once through the portal to heaven (thus shedding their "wings"). Osiris may have also been the source of the belief that the life of a person was associated with their breath—entering the mouth at first breath, and leaving at its last, leading to the ancient Egyptian "Opening of the Mouth" funeral ceremony.

> "[Osiris] taught that within each man resides a little man who is the Lord of the Body, and this is the life of men. While man sleeps the

little man wanders abroad to journey as it will, at death departing from him forever.

The Lord of the Body cannot be seen by mortal eyes, but it is not hidden from all seeing eyes of the Twice Born. When departing at death it comes out from the mortal mouth, waiting awhile until it grows celestial wings. Then it flies away to the Western Kingdom where the wings are shed."[27]

~ THE WAY OF YOSIRA, THE KOLBRIN

An illustration of the Ba hovering over the body of the deceased, from the ancient Egyptian Book of the Dead.

Osiris also taught about the astral plane, which he calls the Land of the Horizon.

"[Osiris said] Before the gates of Heaven is the Land of the Horizon, whence go all who depart from their earthly body. From here there are two great gates, one leads to the Place of Light and the other to the Place of Darkness, and the Lord of the Body is admitted into its appointed place according to its likeness."[28]

~ THE TEACHINGS OF YOSIRA, THE KOLBRIN

In Egypt, the Duat/astral plane was associated with the horizon, as the horizon is the plane or point of crossing over between day and night, light and darkness, and as Osiris states in the quote above, the Land of Horizon (or Duat/astral plane) is the place where those who die first go when they leave their physical bodies, before crossing over through one of the two great gates— either to the place of light (heaven), or through the other to the place of darkness (hell). In ancient Egyptian religion, the gate leading to heaven (Aaru), and the celestial realm of light that the king ascended to, was in the east, at the point where the sun rises on the horizon;[29] this gate to heaven was called Akhet.[30] The gate leading to the underworld, the place of darkness, was in the west where the sun set[31] (likely entered through the crocodile jaws of the goddess Ammit, which was later depicted in Christian artwork as the mouth of hell).

Top: Jesus overseeing the judgement of the dead, as they are either sent through the mouth/portal to hell (on the right side of the image) or ascend through the entrance/portal to heaven in the sky (in the left of the image). Bottom: Osiris overseeing the judgement of the dead, where it's decided whether they will go on to a heavenly realm or be swallowed by the jaws of the crocodile-headed goddess Ammit who waits between the scales. There are obvious similarities between these scenes though they are separated by more than a thousand years.

These gates/portals really exist, and have been seen by countless people in near-death experiences as I'll discuss later in the book. Specifically, based on our interpretation of ancient Egyptian texts and sites, we believe these gates were located due east and west, where the sun rises and sets twice each year at the equinoxes. For instance, the Great Sphinx gazes due east at the rising sun on the equinox, and was the guardian of the gateway to heaven, which I'll discuss in more depth shortly. I explain the meaning of these gates and the equinoxes in ancient Egypt, and in other ancient traditions, in my book *Ancient Solstice*.

The astral plane/Duat with its two gates was encoded in the symbol of Aker (a symbol with multiple meanings[33]). It contains the hieroglyph for horizon, which is a sun setting/rising on the horizon between two mountains, and this rests on the shoulders of two lions facing opposite directions. We believe the horizon hieroglyph symbolizes the Land of the Horizon spoken of by Osiris, which is the Duat/astral. In ancient Egyptian, the word for lion and gate are the same, and so the lions signify the two gates of the astral—one leading to the place of darkness, the other to light.

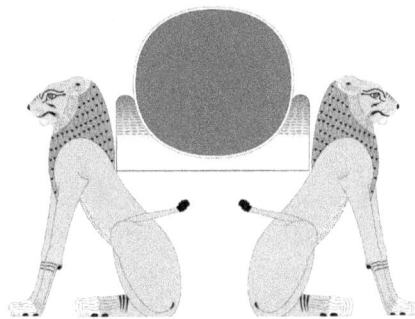

The symbol of Aker, which depicts the hieroglyph for horizon held between two lions facing opposite directions. Among other things, it symbolizes the astral plane with its two gates (and guardian lions[32])—one leading to the realms of darkness, the other to the realms of light.

Something of this meaning was preserved in languages containing related words, as in Arabic the word Akher means "the edge of the earth" and "the end," and in Greek the word Acheron is the name for the gate of hell.[34]

THE GREAT PYRAMIDS AND SPHINX AS SYMBOLS OF THE FIFTH DIMENSION

The symbol of Aker turns up in an astonishing place—it is physically depicted on a massive scale using the Great Pyramids and Sphinx. And this is where it all came together for us, and we realized that the structures on the Giza Plateau in Egypt were built to replicate the Land of the Horizon—the astral plane of the fifth dimension—as well as the portal leading from it to heaven (and more, as we discuss further on in the chapter).

Artist's impression of the summer solstice alignment at the Great Pyramids and Sphinx, which is when the sun sets almost exactly between the two largest pyramids while creating a halo of light around the head of the Sphinx. It also makes the hieroglyph for horizon, revealing this site was seen as the symbolic "Land of the Horizon," i.e. the Duat (the astral plane).

On the summer solstice the sun sets almost exactly between the two largest of the three pyramids, forming a halo of light around the head of the Great Sphinx and the hieroglyph for horizon as it does.[35][36] The Sphinx was known as the guardian of the site, and faces due east—to sunrise on the equinox, making it the guardian of the gateway to heaven. It has the body of a lion, but there is much evidence to show that it once took the form of Anubis, who was known as the judge of the dead and the guardian of the gateway to heaven. I discuss the symbolism of the Sphinx in detail in *Ancient Solstice* as part of my Sphinx Resurrection Theory.[37] There's evidence there was another sphinx that is so far undiscovered or has already been destroyed, which faced due west—to sunset on the equinox,[38][39] thus guarding the gateway to hell.

Left: Artist's impression of what the Great Sphinx once looked like.
Right: An actual Anubis sphinx from the Ramesseum in Egypt dated to 1,279–1,212 BC.

That a symbol of the Duat is made by the Great Pyramids and Sphinx indicates this site was seen as the physical representation of the astral/Duat (though it was also built to symbolize much more than this as we'll explain further on). The layout of the Great Pyramid and Sphinx, with their hidden chambers and passageways, corresponds to the illustrations of the Duat in the ancient Egyptian text the Amduat as its name suggests, as it literally translates to "the book of what is in the Duat."[40]

The Amduat's extended title provides a further description of its content, being "the positions of the Ba-souls, the gods, the shadows, the Akh-spirits, and what is done," referring to the role that different beings have in the out-of-body realm in the events on the path of the Spiritual Sun. And also, "To know the Ba-souls of the Duat, [...] to know their spiritualization for Re, [...] to know what is in the hours and their gods, [...] to know the gates, and the ways upon which the great god passes," describing the way or path that Re (the sun god, the Spiritual Sun) takes through the hours and gates (or stages of initiation), which the Ba (or initiate out of their body) follows in order to be spiritually transformed to the higher state of being Re epitomizes.[41]

In particular, its illustration of the fifth division/region of the Duat appears to portray the Giza Plateau as it depicts the giant double lion-god called Aker that looks (at least half) like the Great Sphinx, above which is a large pyramid. Aker seems to act as a guardian protecting "the Land of Sokar" (Sokar was an

Egyptian god identified with Osiris); this land seems to be the Giza complex, indicating the Sphinx may have guarded the gateway initiates used to enter it. The fifth division details the passages and chambers found in the Land of Sokar, which look like those inside the Great Pyramid.[42]

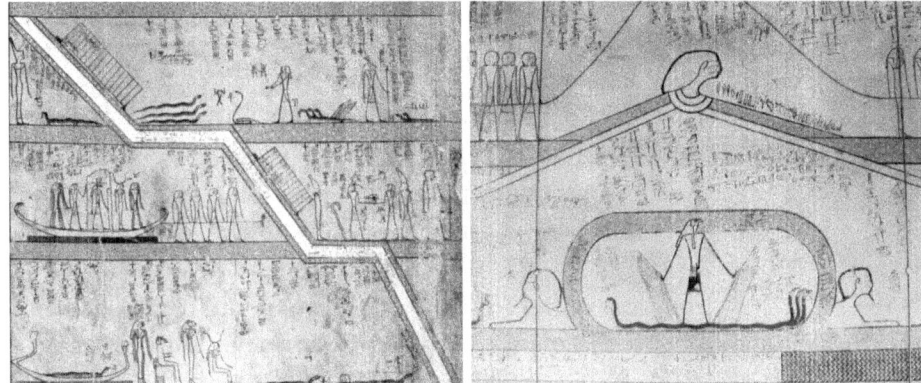

Left: Illustration of the fourth region of the Duat with a passage through it that looks similar to the ascending and descending passages inside pyramids. Right: Illustration of the fifth region of the Duat, in which a giant double fore-bodied sphinx is below a human-headed pyramid.

Additionally, the three Great Pyramids align with the three belt stars of Orion,[43] and the Duat was particularly associated with the constellation of Orion, which was seen as the celestial representation of Osiris—further indicating the site's intended connection to the Duat.

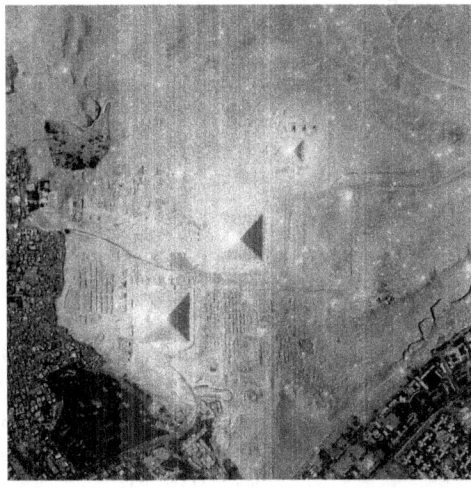

The belt stars of Orion superimposed over the three Great Pyramids, showing they form an approximate match.

We are in no way the first to recognize that the Giza Plateau was meant to represent the Duat. For example, Graham Hancock and Robert Bauval in their book *The Message of the Sphinx* correlate numerous lines in the ancient Egyptian Pyramid Texts with the astrological alignments of the Great Pyramids and Sphinx, and conclude that the whole site was a master plan of the Duat, saying:

> "Indeed the resemblance is so close that it is permissible to wonder whether one of the functions of the Pyramid may have been to serve as a kind of model or 'simulation' of the afterworld in which initiates underwent trials and ordeals intended to prepare them intellectually and spiritually for the terrifying experiences and judgements that the soul was believed to confront after death."[44]
> ~ GRAHAM HANCOCK AND ROBERT BAUVAL, THE MESSAGE OF THE SPHINX

We think, however, that rather than being used as a site to prepare initiates for death (or as tombs as mainstream Egyptology believes), the builders saw the Duat as the out-of-body realm, the astral plane, and built the site to facilitate the initiations that occur in that realm on the path of the Spiritual Sun in life.

As Wim van den Dungen, who has written a commentary on the Amduat, explains:

> "The presence of this remarkable book, with its unseen fusion of visual and textual meanings, also underlines *the accessibility of the Duat by those still living on Earth*. Although found in royal tombs and belonging to the privilege of the divine king, these texts are not exclusively funerary, but speak of a this-life ritual of rejuvenation (regeneration—cf. Osiris) & (royal?) illumination (Re). Repeatedly, the Amduat states: 'It is good for the dead to have this knowledge, but also for a person on Earth; a remedy—a million times proven!'"[45]

The initiations on the path of the Spiritual Sun occur in the fifth dimension where they are administered by spiritual beings, and so it follows that the layout of the site would be based on the fifth dimension and the structure of these initiations.

Given that everything in the physical world has a fifth-dimensional/etheric/astral component which exists and can be seen while in the fifth dimension, the entire Giza Plateau including the pyramids exists in the fifth dimension in their etheric component, which is why we can travel to the pyramids and see them in OBEs. This means they could have been used in the fifth dimension by spiritual beings, and the esoteric order while they were out of the body, to conduct rituals and initiations—there are accounts of this we'll explore further on. They still serve as places for initiation out of the body today, as I've experienced.

MY OUT-OF-BODY EXPERIENCES IN THE GREAT PYRAMID

I've had two experiences out of the body inside what I sensed was the Great Pyramid. The first occurred about two years after I had begun practicing astral projection. In it I became aware of walking in a corridor made of stone. There were life-sized statues of what appeared to be Egyptian deities, and the light was subdued but I could still see clearly. Directly in front of me was a door; a figure wearing a ceremonial headdress opened it for me and I walked in.

Inside I was astonished to be in a room where, like the corridor, the walls were unmarked and unadorned, and made of perfectly fitted stone, but the light was brighter, and there were statues and symbols around. Sitting up against a wall were spiritual beings wearing Egyptian ceremonial outfits. Each sat with their legs together and knees up—the same position the "Assessors of Maat" are seated in, which is unlike the Oriental cross-legged position. I recognized some but not all of them from artwork I'd seen from ancient Egypt. They sat motionless and in silence. It was a beautiful and serene environment.

The Egyptian Assessors of Maat, seated with their legs up and knees together, as I saw in my experience.

Another figure, a spiritual being, came up to me and took me to a granite pedestal, which had a bowl carved out of the top of it. There was water in the bowl. He gestured toward an opening in the wall near the bowl—it was a small, long passageway that had been carved through the stone, which went upward at an angle for a long way, and as I looked up into it I could see stars in the night sky.

I looked into the water and contemplated; the stars were reflected in the water and I felt an invitation to meditate upon them. I stilled my body and looked at them intensively and they began to take on a magical quality as though they were animated, and the water seemed to swirl as though in a spiral of creation. At that moment I lost consciousness of my surroundings and flew backward at high speed as though in a vortex and suddenly came back to my body and merged into it.

Many years later I read there are shafts in the Great Pyramid, and that some have theorized they were built to align to significant stars,[46] which I hadn't known at the time. While it's not possible to see to the stars through these shafts as they are in the physical world, in my experience it was possible to see stars through one of them while I was out of my body. This particular experience was my initiation into the path of the Spiritual Sun.

Years later, in another experience, I found myself lying in the sarcophagus of the King's Chamber inside the Great Pyramid. It was cold, dark, and eerily silent in the stone chamber, but I could see a light coming in through the entrance, and the figure of Anubis was silhouetted against it, though I could still see him clearly. This experience occurred when I was going through the initiatory stage of death before resurrection on the path of the Spiritual Sun.

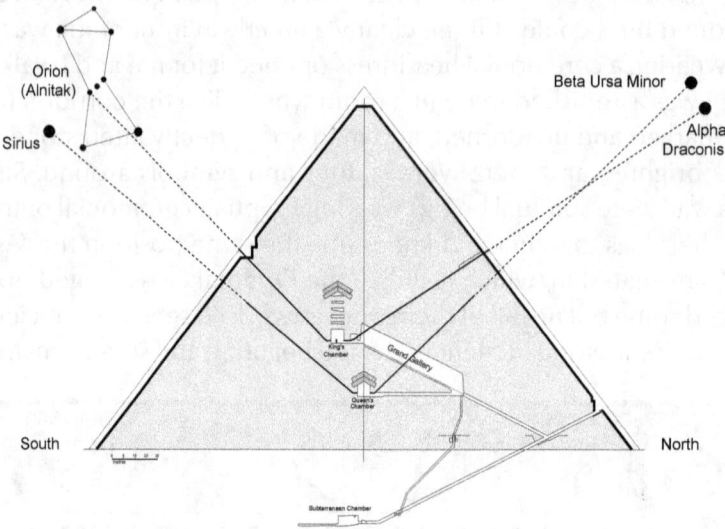

Diagram of the proposed alignments of the shafts of the Great Pyramid to certain stars between approximately 2,400 - 2,500 BC, which is when mainstream Egyptology believes it was built. However, there are problems with the proposed alignments and their dating, which is too much to get into here. And we (and numerous other researchers) believe there's evidence to indicate the Great Pyramid dates from a much earlier time; it's possible the shafts aligned to significant stars at earlier dates, but as far as we know this hasn't been explored.

These experiences confirmed to me that the Great Pyramids were used as places of spiritual practice and initiation.

THE PYRAMID AS A PORTAL TO OTHER DIMENSIONS?

But there is even more to the connection between Giza and the fifth dimension. As we've already seen, the Great Pyramids and Sphinx represent aspects of the Duat and the gateway to heaven beyond it. And as I'll explain in following sections, they were used for rites in which people had OBEs. Additionally, there are indications that the Great Pyramid in particular was somehow used as a gateway or portal to higher dimensions as part of the initiatory process. The two smaller of the three Great Pyramids were likely used for similar rituals that also involved OBEs, though maybe for different kinds and/or for people going through different stages of initiation.

There is also evidence outside of Egypt that further suggests this was their purpose, as pyramids were remembered as having this same function in other parts of the world too. Pyramids were built in numerous places as part of the spread of the ancient Religion of the Sun. Aside from their physical similarities, they also share remarkable similarities in the way they were viewed—as places which connected to the higher and lower other-dimensional realms. We'll look at some of these other pyramids further on in the chapter; here we'll look at how pyramids were viewed in ancient Egypt.

Pyramids were called "Mer" by the ancient Egyptians, which has been translated as "place of ascension,"[47] indicating they were used to ascend to higher realms. The Pyramid Texts are the first texts in Egypt to describe the use and purpose of pyramids, and state that a portal is opened up from within the pyramid to send the king into the heavenly region of the sky:

> "O Horus, this king is Osiris, this Pyramid of the king is Osiris, this construction of his is Osiris, betake yourself to it[48]
>
> The gate of the earth is open for you ... may a stairway to the Duat be set up for you to the place where Orion is[49]
>
> The celestial portal to the Horizon is open to you ... may you remove yourself to the sky[50]
>
> The Duat guides your feet to the Dwelling-place of Orion[51]
>
> The aperture of the sky window is opened for you[52]
>
> The doors of iron which are in the starry sky are thrown open for me, and I go through them."[53]
>
> ~ THE PYRAMID TEXTS

Although the Pyramid Texts were inscribed into pyramids at Saqqara (not the Great Pyramids of Giza, which are blank), the "sky window" and "doors of iron" sound like they could be describing the shafts in the King's Chamber, one of which was found with an iron plate near its interior opening.[54] These shafts are design features only found in the Great Pyramid and no other, indicating that the Pyramid Texts are based on earlier rituals conducted in the Great Pyramid that were modified for later pyramids.

The Pyramid Texts describe a spiritual process that lay at the very heart of ancient Egyptian religion and would continue to throughout the course of its thousands of years long history. This journey was seen as being expressed by and mystically connected to the sun and stars, so that the movements of certain constellations and the sun were tied to the journey and transformation of the soul.

As mentioned, they were found inscribed onto the walls of pyramids at Saqqara. These pyramids were all based on the same design, each with an inner tomb and a specific layout of chambers and passages that led from the tomb at the heart of the pyramid to the outside. The texts inscribed into the walls of each of these areas describes what happens to the king's spirit as he moves through them after death before leaving his pyramid.

The texts state how the Ba/soul of the king left his body at death and entered the Duat/astral plane, which was also the womb of the great mother goddess Nut (the Spiritual Mother), located in the region of the sky beneath the horizon (though could also be the Milky Way, and there is a reason it could be either, as we'll explain further on). The inner rooms of the pyramid represented the Duat and the womb, though the sarcophagus in which his body was laid to rest was especially seen as the Mother's womb (from which the king would be spiritually reborn as the sun).[55] Though the sarcophagus, tomb, and pyramid were all part of the Mother, they each played a slightly different role, as it says in the Pyramid Texts:

> "You have been given to your mother Nut in her identity of the burial place [the sarcophagus], she has collected you in her identity of the burial chamber, and you have been elevated to her in her identity of the tomb's super-structure [the pyramid]."[56]
> ~ THE PYRAMID TEXTS

That is, the king entered the Mother's womb when laid in the sarcophagus, was made whole as Osiris (symbolizing the Spiritual Son) by the Mother once he was out of the body in the inner chamber, and then was elevated to her sky realm by the pyramid.

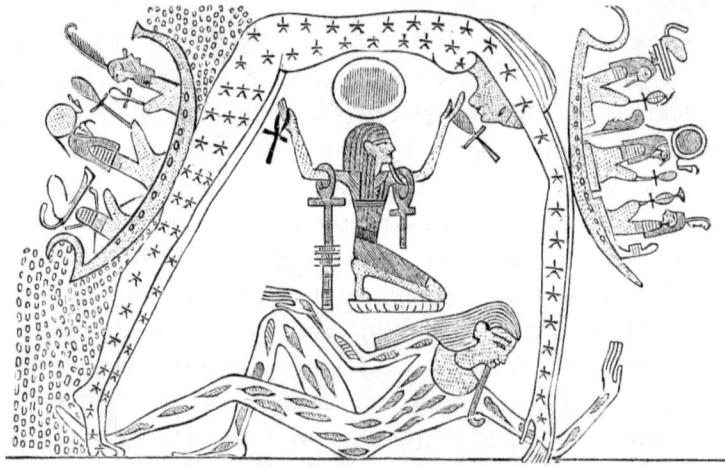

The ancient Egyptian goddess Nut, with her body stretched across the sky and painted with five-pointed stars, symbolized the land of the Duat/astral that was hidden beneath the horizon, and which the sun traveled through each night on its boat. As we'll see further on, her arched body of stars was also intended to mimic the arch of the Milky Way.

While out of the body in the Duat (with his physical body still lying in the sarcophagus), the Ba of the king was joined with Osiris as the constellation Orion, giving him the power to resurrect/be reborn. At the time the Pyramid

Texts were written, Orion was below the horizon (in the symbolic Duat) before dawn at the summer solstice, and so on the solstice in the starry Duat the king was said to merge with Osiris as Orion.[57]

The constellation of Orion was often portrayed as the figure of a man—in Egypt it represented Osiris, whom the king merged with while out of the body.

From here, the king's Ba floated/flew away from the sarcophagus and tomb due east into the antechamber of his pyramid. The antechamber represented the Akhet, which was the exit of the Duat and the portal/entrance to the tunnel to heaven. It was located due east where the sun rose above the horizon. As the king left the antechamber and Akhet, he was reborn with the sun, and transformed into a being of light (an Akh).

This occurred at the end of the fifth hour of the night, which was portrayed in the fifth division of the Duat in the text Amduat, which as we saw, was illustrated using giant sphinxes and a pyramid. At his emergence from the Akhet, the king (merged with Osiris and the sun) became known as Horus of the Akhet/Duat,[58] which is the oldest recorded name of the Great Sphinx, being Hor-em-akhet, meaning Horus of the Horizon.[59] What this reveals is that the Sphinx—specifically the sculpture of what would have been Osiris at its chest (though some megalomaniac king later re-carved the head of the Sphinx as his own[60])—symbolized the spiritually reborn initiate.

As mentioned earlier, the Sphinx in its form as Anubis was seen as the guardian of the site. Yet it was also referred to in the Pyramid Texts as Atum,[61] the Spiritual Father sun.[62] The Great Sphinx likely acted both as the guardian to the site and the symbolically reborn initiate ascending in the embrace of his

Spiritual Father. The Great Sphinx was a symbol, and as symbols often do, it appears to have had multiple meanings. There are good reasons why it could be Anubis, have the head of the king, and be part lion (and maybe even fully lion at some point), so no wonder it has taken these forms over its long history.

Yet even though the initiate was portrayed as having emerged symbolically with the Sphinx as Atum (having become a Twice Born, as we'll explain shortly, an event connected with the spring equinox), the king continued his journey within the pyramid. After passing through the antechamber and the portal Akhet, the king's Ba made a sharp turn inside his pyramid, now moving into the long corridor that ascends due north out of it—here he traveled along the "birth canal" leading from the Duat/astral to heaven that people commonly experience as the tunnel leading into the light in NDEs. The king was to ascend with that light, the sun, his Spiritual Father Atum, and finally exit his pyramid into the northern circumpolar region of the sky to the "imperishable" stars that never set beneath the horizon[63] (an event connected to the summer solstice).

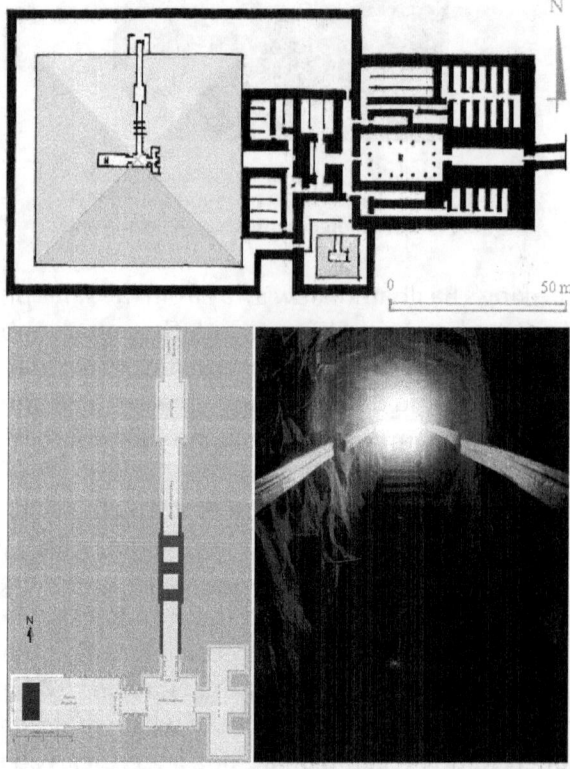

Top: Layout of the pyramid of Unis/Unas at Saqqara showing the inner burial chamber and passage exiting the pyramid's north side. The oldest rendition of the Pyramid Texts are inscribed on its interior walls. Bottom left: A closer look at the layout of the chambers and passage inside the pyramid of Unis. The black rectangle is the sarcophagus, which is within the burial chamber. The king traveled east from there to the antechamber, before heading north along the passage out of the pyramid. Bottom right: Looking up along a passage exiting a pyramid (this one is at Meidum), which recreated the visual of traveling along the dark tunnel into the light commonly seen in NDEs.

The Pyramid Texts seem to have been written around 3,400 BC, when Orion rose just before the sun (heliacally) at the summer solstice, which was seen as the king rising as Osiris with his Father Atum the sun before being eternally united with him—being embraced as Orion into, and engulfed by, the sun's post-dawn glow.[64] We believe, as do other researchers, that although the Pyramid Texts as we know them may have been written then, they incorporate, and were based on far older texts that were updated to reflect the movements of the sun and stars current at the time. It's well-known that the Pyramid Texts were recycled and reused for the pyramids of different kings, often by just changing a few personal details like the king's name;[65] there's no reason why this kind of adaptation couldn't have been going on earlier. It would explain why they seem to contain what appear to be sometimes contradictory astrological references. It would also explain why they seem to contain references to features that exist only in the Great Pyramid, i.e. the "star shafts" or "sky doors" as they are called. And as we'll explain shortly, they relate to the record of a ritual conducted in the Great Pyramid, which follows the same essential journey of the king, but in an OBE had while alive.

We suspect they are based on material that was first composed when the Great Pyramids and Sphinx were built—which seems to have been when the constellation of Leo rose just before the sun (heliacally) at the spring equinox at around 36,500 BC. The form of Leo matches that of the Sphinx, and so at 36,500 BC the Sphinx would have gazed directly at its own astronomical counterpart. At the heart of Leo is the "king star" Regulus, which is mirrored by a mysterious bulge at the heart of the Sphinx that we believe would have once been the carving of the king of kings, Osiris, or equivalent deity. The Pyramid Texts describe the Sphinx as having the body of Atum (the Spiritual Father and sun), and state that the king as Osiris rises in the embrace of his father Atum, just as Regulus is embraced between the imaginary forepaws of Leo as it rises together with the sun on the equinox. These may be the traces of older astrological references, and I describe them further in my book *Ancient Solstice*.

The constellation of Leo superimposed over the Great Sphinx, showing how it matches its form. Its brightest star, Regulus, corresponds to the chest where there is a bulge in the Sphinx that's likely to have once been a carving of Osiris or equivalent deity.

> "You come into being with your father Atum, you are high with your father Atum, you rise with your father Atum. The wants (of the Netherworld) are severed from you [...] you have become a spirit! [...] Atum! Elevate to you Osiris, enfold him in your embrace! This is your son of your body, eternally."[66]
> ~ THE PYRAMID TEXTS

The Egyptologist James P. Allen, who has translated the Pyramid Texts, concluded that the pyramids of Egypt functioned to send kings through the portal of the Akhet, the place of the sun's rising on the eastern horizon, to the celestial region of the sky.[67] What the texts reveal is that the ancient Egyptians believed that pyramids were a means to travel through the portal to heaven out of the body.

The "star shafts" of the King's Chamber are generally thought to have served as exits for the soul of the deceased king to travel to his afterlife destination in the stars, as the Pyramid Texts indicate. Specifically, the shaft that exits the north face of the pyramid is directed toward the northern circumpolar region of the sky, which was the king's final afterlife destination. The southern shaft has been theorized as targeting one of the three belt stars of Orion, or the sun at noon on certain dates each year, possibly allowing its light to have entered the King's Chamber.[68] Along with the northern circumpolar stars, the sun and Orion were very important in the king's afterlife journey. However, it's possible the shafts served a purpose like this, but for OBEs had during life. Lara has tried to travel to a specific destination in the sky while out of the body, and found it very difficult to orient herself. Stars can all start to look the same, particularly once traveling, and so it would be helpful to have some sort of guide. A shaft directed toward a specific star/sky location where the portal to heaven was believed to exist may have served to orient and direct someone out of the body to it, like a bullet along the shaft of a gun. The shafts wouldn't need to be big enough for a person to physically fit through, as it's possible to reduce our size out of the body, which could explain why they are small. They also wouldn't need to be straight for their entire length (although that probably would have been ideal), just for a certain length at the end, which may explain why the shafts start horizontally and even change angle before straightening out.

THE ANCIENT USE OF ACOUSTIC AND ELECTROMAGNETIC ENERGY TO INDUCE OBES

It would make sense that if the pyramid was intended to send the king through the portal to heaven, it would surely have been specifically designed to do so, and not just symbolically, but as a kind of device that facilitated this process. The Great Pyramid is taller, far more complex, and precise than any other pyramid, and it especially appears to have had some kind of "technological" function. Understanding what this function was and how it worked would help explain its strange and unique features. In this section we speculate a lot about why the ancient Egyptians saw it as a portal and how it could have functioned as one, as exactly how it did is unknown.

As noted by a number of researchers and Egyptologists, the Great Pyramid seems to have a kind of utilitarian, almost machine-like feel to it. The Egyptologist James P. Allen has described Egyptian pyramids as "resurrection machines,"[69] while Hancock and Bauval liken them to a "stargate."[70] The engineer Christopher Dunn recounts his impression of the Great Pyramid, saying, "While I was studying the inner chambers and passages of the Great Pyramid, I became convinced that I was looking at the prints for an extremely large machine, except this machine had been relieved of its inner components for some inexplicable reason."[71] The basic sense that some researchers across different fields have is that the Great Pyramid was built as a device of some sort, rather than as your average temple or tomb.

Dunn took his suspicions further, and after twenty years of research, proposed a model of how he thinks the Great Pyramid could have functioned like a machine for the purpose of generating power. He theorizes it did this by tapping into the energy of the earth by creating a harmonic resonance with it, saying "For the power plant to function, the designers and operators had to induce vibration in the Great Pyramid that was in tune with the harmonic resonant vibrations of the earth." This, he says, would explain why the Great Pyramid is built to scale to replicate Earth's measurements, and why the King's Chamber, which would have been the heart of the power plant, incorporates thousands of tons of granite with a high content of crystal, so that it could act as a resonator. He speculates that when operating, this chamber would have filled with a combination of acoustic and electromagnetic energy. He proposes it resonated harmonically with the frequency of hydrogen, which it used and excited to higher energy levels.[72] This is intriguing given that hydrogen is the primary component of stars and is what fuels them, and the Pyramid Texts repeatedly affirm the king's release from the earth and transformation into a star, and even state that he harnessed their energies.

Ten years after Dunn published his theory, some scientific evidence emerged to support the basic principle behind it. In 2018 a study using theoretical modeling suggested that when the Great Pyramid resonates due to naturally occurring conditions, it concentrates electromagnetic energy in its chambers[73] as Dunn had predicted.

It's not only electromagnetic energy that naturally concentrates in the King's Chamber, it's also low frequency sound that is often inaudible, but nevertheless can have psychological effects. In 1996 an acoustic analysis was conducted in the King's Chamber by NASA consultant and acoustic engineer Tom Danley, where he spent several nights taking measurements. Danley discovered the King's Chamber has a number of acoustic properties. He found it produced low frequency sounds within the range of a few Hz to around 20 Hz. These sounds were produced even when the people present were completely silent. He also found the sarcophagus had several resonances that directly corresponded to the resonances of the chamber, suggesting there was some intended acoustic connection between them. Danley also made the general observation that the chamber's dimensions, materials, and sarcophagus, were designed to enhance whatever sounds were made inside the chamber. Additionally, a musicologist who was part of the staff was sent the results of Danley's measurements, and discovered that many (though not all) of the frequencies that the King's Chamber resonated at formed an F# chord repeating over many octaves, indicating the King's Chamber was roughly tuned to F#. Danley concludes his observations by saying:

> "Anyone who has been in the Great Pyramid and chanted or hummed will tell you that it feels weird, and that the acoustic effect is powerful.
>
> [...] If, as some suggest, these pyramids were constructed as a 'temple' or for an initiation ritual rather than a tomb, then the LF [low frequency] sounds may be deliberate and have served a sacred purpose — with the sound triggering and even forcing changes in brain wave state (i.e., one's level of consciousness)."[74]
>
> ~ TOM DANLEY

Another acoustic engineer, Howard Vawter, who has collaborated with Dunn, has claimed that the dimensional features he had studied in the King's Chamber indicate it was a resonant chamber designed to resonate specific frequencies.[75]

It seems likely to us that harmonic ritual chanting was used in the rites conducted in the King's Chamber, and that the chamber's acoustics were designed to enhance it, particularly at specific musical intervals. As mentioned earlier, the Pyramid Texts are believed to have been sung as hymns inside the chambers of the pyramids they were inscribed into, and it's likely they would have been a continuation of hymns sung inside the Great Pyramids. Christian cathedrals have been designed to enhance the sound of religious singing inside them, and it's possible ancient people had also developed architectural acoustics for similar purposes.

Scholars generally believe that some ancient Egyptian ritual music may still survive today in the guise of Coptic chant, having been preserved by descendants of the ancient Egyptians that converted to Christianity and became the Coptic Christians. It's possible that an ancient Egyptian style of chanting, and even tracts of music from ancient Egypt have been preserved in Coptic chant, though converted to Christian themes. Some instruments that resemble those depicted in ancient Egyptian frescos and reliefs are still used to accompany Coptic chanting today. Coptic chants were never written down, but were passed down as part of an oral tradition for over a thousand years.[76] They use a seven vowel musical scale, which evidence indicates the ancient Egyptians used in their chanting too, as the Athenian orator and early librarian at Alexandria, Demetrius of Phaleron (circa 350-280 BC), recorded his impressions of ancient Egyptian ritual hymns, writing, "in Egypt the priests, when singing hymns in praise of the gods, employ the seven vowels, which they utter in due succession; and the sound of these letters is so euphonious that men listen to it in preference to [the] flute and lyre."[77]

Although the ancient Greek philosopher Pythagoras is generally credited with inventing the seven note musical scale, and of discovering the mathematics of musical intervals, given the evidence that indicates their use in ancient Egypt, it seems more likely he learned these during his sojourn with the priests of Egypt and/or his following time with the Persian Magi in Babylon. Pythagoras also theorized that the planets (that were known at the time) and fixed stars emitted sounds based on musical intervals in what would later be called "the music of the spheres."[78] While it's now known the model of the planets and stars Pythagoras based his theory on is wrong, and these celestial bodies have not been found to make noises at the intervals he predicted, it's possible he was transmitting a garbled version of knowledge he picked up in Egypt.

The F# chord produced in the King's Chamber would include a fifth interval, and since it's said to be produced over a number of octaves, would also include a fourth interval as well as an octave (as long as the F# root note and F# of the next octave up is produced at the same time). A perfect fourth and fifth interval is also expressed in the underlying geometry of the Giza site.[79] It seems almost certain that ancient Egyptian ritual chanting employed these intervals (they being the most harmonious after the unison and octave), and that they were used to sing the Pyramid Texts. Given that the Pyramid Texts were so focused on the sun and stars, we wonder therefore, if these intervals were seen as somehow connected to them.

Coptic and later Gregorian chant uses repeated vowels sung in succession, as ancient Egyptian chant was said to. Particularly the organum style of Gregorian Chant is based on the harmonic intervals of fourth, fifth, and octave. Although Gregorian and other types of Christian chanting are believed to have developed in Europe,[80] we wonder if they have much older roots that stretch back into Egypt.

These intervals (of fourth, fifth, and octave) are also produced "inaudibly" in the King's Chamber, where the initiate sought to journey out of their body to the stars. Could it be that these intervals were used to bring one into resonance with the stars in order to elevate one to them?

As we'll see further on, there are other ancient sites which were used for having OBEs that have similar acoustic properties, and it looks very likely that the purpose of these frequencies was to help induce OBEs.

Dunn has examined a number of artifacts and buildings in ancient Egypt that show machines, including powered tools, must have been used to produce them, including on the Giza Plateau.[81] For example, the coffers in the Great and second-largest pyramids show evidence of being precisely cut with powered saws,[82] indicating they date to a time when such an advanced, but now vanished civilization existed in Egypt. Dunn has worked for nearly fifty years "at every level of high-tech manufacturing."[83] His experience in creating precision artifacts has allowed him to assess, and essentially reverse engineer, how the ancient Egyptians manufactured theirs.[84] He concludes that some we could only replicate by using computer guided machines.[85] He says that it's not just that cuts were made into extremely hard stone, but these are accompanied by evidence of high-speed cut rates and levels of accuracy that cannot be achieved by hand.

Recently, in 2023, a number of ancient Egyptian artifacts were subjected to highly precise scanning, measurement, and computer analysis by a team including the professional metrologists Alex Dunn (Christopher Dunn's son) and Nick Sierra. To our knowledge, they are the only Egyptian artifacts that have been analyzed this way. The artifacts studied were six stone vases, made in a similar style and carved from granite, which is a very hard stone. They were found to have been made with extraordinary precision (often to within six thousandths of an inch); one of them was scanned using 3D laser technology (LiDAR) and found to have been made according to an astonishingly intricate geometrical design. We could only make vases like this today using highly advanced computer-guided machines. Stone vases in a similar style have turned up in many ancient Egyptian burials, some of which predate the historical beginnings of Egyptian civilization (one dating possibly as far back as 12,500 BC), showing they are at least more than five thousand years old. Exactly how old the analyzed vases are is unknown.[86] [87] They bear the same hallmark style as some of the Giza monuments. Both are unadorned, extremely precise, use granite, and have been made according to a unified, grand, sacred geometrical design (incorporating values like pi, phi, and golden ratios). This style seems wholly unlike anything else in the historical record of Egypt, and it appears to us that both the Giza monuments and vases belong to the same very ancient lost civilization.

Dunn ascribes a mundane function to the Great Pyramid as a generator of electricity used to power the machines and appliances of its ancient builders,[88] however we believe that given all the other evidence of its sacred function, whatever technology the Great Pyramid harnessed, it served a spiritual purpose. There are many original features of the Giza structures, such as astronomical alignments, the incorporation of highly advanced sacred geometry, and spiritual symbolism, which would be superfluous to a power plant (we have discussed many of these features in *Ancient Solstice*), and there is no evidence to suggest the Egyptians ever saw the Great Pyramid as a power plant only (that we have come across).

While there may be problems with Dunn's theory (which we're not qualified to assess), we do think it comes the closest to explaining how the Great Pyramid could have worked technologically. But we think the idea of the pyramid involving energy now needs developing further, so that the technology of the pyramid is applied to the purpose the ancient Egyptians described it as having—not as a power plant, but as a place for sending someone out of the body through the portal to heaven. So far, what's apparent is that electromagnetic energy was involved as the 2018 study suggests, as well as acoustics as the 1996 analysis indicates.

Passages in the Kolbrin support the idea of electricity/energy being harnessed by the Great Pyramid, but make clear its purpose was spiritual:

> "Now the Great House of Hidden Places [the Great Pyramid] stands in Kahemu. It is built to last forever and stands up strongly towards Heaven, high above the heads of men. It is covered with white stones [...] and above it is topped with copper. It is not the copper of men, but the copper of God. Within it lies the Womb of Rebirth [the King's Chamber] used by the Twice Born of the Enlightened Ones. Men enter its portals to die and come out restored to life, reborn as gods. Beside it stands the Temple of the Radiant Ones [likely the Sphinx and/or Valley Temple], many pillared and walled about. Here is the Great Portal of Entry into Life, and above it, on a great stone, these words may be seen: 'From the Children of God to the Children of Men. Behold, we found you in bondage to mortal bodies and bestowed upon you the gift of everlasting life.'"[89]
> ~ THE KOLBRIN

The white stones this passage refers to seem to correspond to the white limestone that once covered the Great Pyramid, and being topped with copper sounds like a reference to its missing capstone being made of copper. Or, it may refer to electrum, which was used in ancient Egypt to coat the capstones/pyramidions of pyramids and obelisks.[90] Electrum is a naturally occurring alloy of gold and silver, which can contain trace amounts of copper and other metals, although sometimes having a high enough component of copper to give it a reddish tint. Silver, followed by copper, and then gold, have the highest thermal and electrical conductivity of all elements, indicating the pyramidion had an electrical function.

The Great House of Hidden Places is directed toward heaven, was considered a portal, and was used repeatedly for initiations of resurrection for the living. The Kolbrin indicates the site was built by the Children of God (whom we refer to as the Children of the Sun) as an immense gift to humans (the Children of Men) to help us attain spiritual things that were, and are, much harder for us to reach. Perhaps this is why such a machine was needed.

Illustration of the Great Pyramid covered in white limestone and capped with electrum.

It almost sounds as though the Children of the Sun possessed advanced technology, which they used to build the Great Pyramid, but designed it so it could be operated by humans who didn't have advanced technology and were never given it. It may have also been designed to function at a simple level of technology that could continue to operate through civilization-destroying cataclysms, which the Children of the Sun knew afflicted Earth with some regularity, and this may also be why it was built to last. Thus when smaller machines are lost, destroyed, or stop working, the Great Pyramid may have been made to continue functioning by harnessing things like naturally occurring Earth resonance and electromagnetic energy. This might explain why such seemingly "out of place" evidence for technology having been used to build the Great Pyramids exists, and the Great Pyramid incorporates astronomical numbers only a technologically advanced civilization could obtain (as we'll see next), yet seems to have operated without the need for advanced tools. It would also explain why the Great Pyramids are made to human sized proportions even though the Children of the Sun were often remembered in ancient sources as giants.

Although this all sounds too outlandish to even consider, as we mention later in the book, the Pentagon has now admitted that there are UFOs on Earth using highly advanced technology,[91] and numerous government whistleblowers have stated Earth is being visited by UFOs of nonhuman origin.[92] UFOs of nonhuman origin would necessarily be crossing vast distances in space to get here, which would require traveling faster than the speed of light, so it's likely they have technology that can manipulate space, and perhaps even transport physical objects interdimensionally. There is a growing body of evidence in ancient records that the founders of the ancient Religion of the Sun (whom we refer to as the Children of the Sun) were of extraterrestrial origin, and that they had established a technologically advanced civilization on Earth that had coexisted with humans at some time in the distant past, but that this civilization was destroyed by a global cataclysm (which Lara discusses in her book *The Ancient Religion of the Sun*). Yet perhaps some knowledge of its technology survived and was utilized in the Great Pyramid.

Given its size, the Great Pyramid was built with an extraordinary level of precision both in its dimensions and alignment to astronomical bodies (like the sun and certain constellations), and incorporates astronomical numbers that could only be ascertained by an advanced civilization, such as the speed of light. These correspond to key concepts found in the Pyramid Texts, revealing just how connected the contents of this text are to the Great Pyramids. We don't believe for a moment this is coincidence—these numbers seem to have been incorporated both because they were symbolically important, and perhaps also because they played a part in facilitating the OBEs and other spiritual rites and practices that occurred within the pyramid using a kind of "spiritual technology" we as yet don't understand.

For instance, the Great Pyramid is located at the center of Earth's landmass. The estimated weight of the pyramid is about 6 million metric tons,[93] and the estimated weight of Earth is about 5.97 billion trillion metric tons,[94] which means the weight of the Great Pyramid times 10^{15} is approximately that of Earth's. The earth's equatorial longitude, circumference, and radius are incorporated in the Great Pyramid's dimensions,[95] as well as its rate of rotation.[96] It's almost like a mini replica of the earth, which in the Pyramid Texts, the king is said to be set free from.

The Great Pyramid incorporates the mathematical value of pi into its shape;[97] in the Pyramid Texts the king's light "rises pi for all eternity." Susan Brind Morrow, who has offered this translation, says that the word pi has no direct translation, though speculates it may be related to the mathematical constant known as pi.[98] The surrounding context of this excerpt from the Pyramid Texts suggests that the mathematical pi is indeed intended, as when expressed as a decimal number pi is infinite, never settling into a repeating pattern of digits,[99] thus expressing the concept of infinity or eternity, which would be why the king's light is said to rise pi for eternity.

The latitude of the Great Pyramid north of the equator matches the speed of light to six significant digits;[100] the king is said to travel in his body of light into the regions of light, where he is transformed into a star.

The height of the Great Pyramid corresponds mathematically to the sun's mean distance from Earth (the sun being symbolically positioned at its summit), and the perimeter of its base to the sun's annual cycle,[101] [102] while twice the perimeter of the bottom of the coffer in the King's Chamber times 10^8 is the sun's mean radius; in the Pyramid Texts, the king joins with the sun, and rises with him into the heavenly realm in the sky.

The peaks of the three Great Pyramids closely match the layout of the three belt stars of the constellation of Orion, which the ancient Egyptians saw as Osiris, whom the king was said to join with out of the body. Additionally, the peaks closely match the layout of three wing stars of the Cygnus constellation, which at certain dates could also have been viewed from ground level as setting into the peaks of the Great Pyramids.[103] In ancient Greek mythology Cygnus was a swan, based on an ancient tradition of it being viewed as a bird, and in ancient Egypt it was possibly seen as a falcon-headed god.[104] Cygnus essentially looks like a bird of light in flight in the northern region of the stars. This looks to be connected to an ancient Egyptian belief, which saw the annual northern migration of birds as symbolic of the Akhs, the spirits of the dead, emerging from the Duat.[105] In the Pyramid Texts, the king takes flight out of his body toward the northern stars as a falcon of light.

Left: The Cygnus constellation, depicted as a bird of stars in flight along the Milky Way. Right: An ancient Egyptian illustration of the northern constellations (as they saw them) dated to 1300 BC. The falcon-headed man labeled "'nw" may have been Cygnus, the bull was Ursa Major, and the hippo was Draco.[106]

The Great Pyramid is aligned to true north within a tenth of a degree,[107] and both its descending passage (which exits the pyramid), and one of the shafts that extends from the King's Chamber to the exterior of the pyramid, point to the northern circumpolar stars,[108] [109] which was the king's final destination.

These are just a small handful of the vast array of sacred and astronomical numbers and alignments found in the dimensions of the Giza monuments and their overall layout, which are truly mind-blowing.[110] [111] [112] [113] [114]

So as we've seen, alignments and numbers to do with the sun and stars are interwoven into the entire design of the Great Pyramids and Sphinx which are directed entirely toward them; the Pyramid Texts are likewise riddled with references to the sun and stars, and the king is likewise directed entirely toward them.

Although the contents of the Pyramid Texts are essentially spiritual, could these following lines be a reference to an ancient technology that was used in the Great Pyramid? The sun and stars radiate electromagnetic energy, and this is the energy that the chambers of the Great Pyramid appear to collect and concentrate. Now consider this passage in the Pyramid Texts:

> "Unis [the king] becomes a thing in motion,
> He sets out with the light,
> He embraces the constellations,
> Unis harnesses their energies.
> The energies seize him
> They make him wake
> For he sleeps."[115]
> ~ PYRAMID TEXTS

This passage indicates the king harnessed the energies of the stars so that he awakened in some way. Perhaps this waking refers to the feeling so many have described in NDEs and clear OBEs, of things being more real out of the body than they are in the physical world, so that the physical world seems illusory and dreamlike in comparison to the out-of-body world. The king's waking then, quite possibly refers either to him consciously astral projecting and leaving his body, or to him entering a more lucid/perceptive state while already out of the body. In both cases, it sounds as though this waking was induced by star energy.

As we'll see further on, the nonphysical/astral component of starlight was harnessed in Taoist OBE practices that may trace their origin to Egypt. But could it be that the physical component of star energy was also harnessed in the Great Pyramid in its form as electromagnetic energy? As I discuss further on, some of the most common sensations of "the astral split," when someone's astral body separates from their physical one, are the feeling of an electric current passing through their body, vibrations, and a humming or whirring noise, all of which seem to be related to electricity and electromagnetic energy.

By concentrating electromagnetic energy and bringing it into resonance with the astral body, the Twice Born may have been able to induce the astral split. They may have even energetically elevated the initiate while out of their body so that they could enter heaven. Being at a high enough energetic level sounds as though it's a prerequisite to enter heaven, as there have been a number of NDEs where the deceased have been told by spiritual beings that they had to be purified and energetically raised up before they were able to enter heaven, and were put through procedures out of the body, sometimes involving light, to do this.[116] In NDEs, the deceased are raised energetically through the help of spiritual beings. Perhaps the Great Pyramid enabled it "mechanically" in some way.

It seems the Great Pyramid harnessed resonance, sound, and electromagnetic energy (perhaps with an additional device) to induce OBEs, and that the knowledge of how to do this may have been utilized at other ancient sites, though on a much smaller and simpler scale. This may be why, as some researchers have noted, there are ancient sites that appear to have been purposefully built at places high in natural electromagnetic energy. It may also be why the chambers of some ancient sites in Europe have been found to resonate at certain frequencies of sound (as discussed further on). It may also be why so many of these sites were designed so that the sun or a star would shine into their inner chamber at an astronomically significant time, like a solstice or equinox.[117] Apart from symbolic reasons, could it have been done to harness earthly and celestial electromagnetic energy? Could these energies have been captured or amplified in some way with the use of huge stones of high crystal composition—perhaps providing a reason why the builders went to such lengths to mine, transport, and erect such difficult to work with megalithic materials? The electromagnetic energy radiating from stars is very weak compared to that from the sun, so it's unclear how it could have been amplified physically; star energy does have astral as well as higher-dimensional components that produce spiritual effects, and perhaps this is what their light was used for as Taoist OBE practices indicate.

The Twice Born ritual may have been conducted within the Great Pyramid at certain times when the electromagnetic energy of the sun and a certain star or stars were at their peak or in alignment with the pyramid—like for example at the summer solstice, which is when the king was said to travel to heaven out of his body in the Pyramid Texts. Or it may simply have been that the electromagnetic energy that concentrated in the chambers of the Great Pyramid was understood as being fundamentally the same energy that radiates from the sun and stars, which may be how the king came to be recorded as harnessing star energy.

There are two pieces of modern evidence we've come across that support the idea that electromagnetic energy can be used to induce OBEs. There are scientific studies that have found that at least the sense of being out of the body (as it's uncertain whether they were real OBEs) was induced in patients when part of their brain was stimulated with electricity (I discuss these studies in chapter 10). A second piece comes from Robert Monroe, who popularized the term "out-of-body experience" in the 1970s; he developed sounds called Hemi-Sync that were meant to be listened to through headphones to help with entering meditative states. Tests conducted on Hemi-Sync by the University of Virginia in 2002 found that it created measurable changes in the electrical activity of the brain (EEG) only when Monroe's electromagnetic headphones were used, and not air conduction headphones, suggesting the brain changes were caused by electromagnetic energy rather than sound.[118]

That the Great Pyramid could induce an OBE in itself may have been viewed as opening a portal to the Duat/astral plane. However, the Pyramid Texts are quite specific about the location of the portal—it was seen as taking someone from the Duat/astral plane to heaven—making it more likely the Great Pyramid could have functioned in some way to open the portal to heaven and send the initiate through it out of their body. The reason a "portal opening device" such as the Great Pyramid may have been needed is because I suspect that the portals leading to heaven and hell are not always open; people can't just wander in and out of them freely while out of the body. This is why people in NDEs can't escape hell without divine intervention, or stumble into heaven in an OBE. Rather, when people travel through these portals, which is most often in NDEs, it would be because spiritual beings open them even if they are not seen. Rod Pickens had an OBE, which I quote in chapter 26, in which he saw these portals opening and closing at "God's" command. These portals are often referred to as gates in ancient Egyptian texts, and gates are things that open and shut.

In ancient texts there are sometimes references to portals and gateways to the otherworlds, particularly to heaven, opening at the solstices and equinoxes. Perhaps there is truth to this, and these other-dimensional portals do open at certain times related to the sun, which could be another reason why ancient peoples chose to align their portal sites to the sun on these dates. Or it may be that because these ancient portal sites were aligned to the solstices and equinoxes, and were used for having OBEs at these times, a belief developed that the portals to otherworlds were open during them.

It's intriguing that much later somewhat similar practices are found in Taoism; they are among the few surviving references to practices of astral projection in ancient traditions. In them the practitioner attempts to astral project, particularly on the solstices and equinoxes, into the region of the northern circumpolar stars to absorb their energies, which sounds reminiscent of the Egyptian king's embrace and harnessing of star energy on the summer solstice. We discuss these practices further on in the chapter.

The Kolbrin later describes how the Great Pyramid was infiltrated by those with malicious intent, led by Setshra (who may have had some connection to the dark, adversarial god Set), who wanted to unlock the secrets of the King's Chamber for himself, and caused a mass of energy to build up, saying:

> "The twin powers drawn down entwined about themselves and grew ever stronger. Even as waters are dammed to be drawn upon, so was the united power built up into a reserve of force. A storehouse of strange energy was prepared. The thoughts of Setshra ever turned about within himself and, behold, the day came when he believed the secret key to be his, the key that would open the inner chamber of Sacred Mysteries."[119]
>
> ~ THE KOLBRIN

The adversarial relationship between Horus (son of Osiris) and Set in ancient Egyptian religion may have been distantly based on a conflict between the followers of Horus (who included the Twice Born) and someone who tried to destroy them and take over their sacred sites, like the Great Pyramid.

It's possible this or some other buildup of energy inside the Great Pyramid is connected to the evidence of an explosion, which shows signs of having involved extreme temperatures in the King's Chamber (beyond what could be caused by the dynamite used to explore it), and that Dunn believes was the result of a malfunction in the operation of the pyramid, which among other things, caused the walls of the chamber to be pushed out and the ceiling beams to crack.[120]

Whatever happened to how the Great Pyramid was used is unknown; later intrusive burials were made into the other two pyramids of Giza, though apart from a few scant objects, nothing was found inside the Great Pyramid. In any case, the knowledge of how it worked became lost (or hidden), though people retained a memory of pyramids as being places that bridged the dimensions during initiatory rites, producing them for the same purpose, though likely without the same level of technological function, but perhaps still effective to some degree. Without the knowledge of how it worked, or the ability to get it working again, it seems they developed a blend of substances that initiates ingested to induce OBEs instead, as detailed in the next section. It seems the knowledge of the Great Pyramid's functioning was lost at least by the time pyramids at Saqqara were built and inscribed with the Pyramid Texts (around 2400 BC), as by this time pyramids were built as tombs in which it seems the king relied more on the hymns written on the walls than on any kind of technology.

In the ancient Religion of the Sun, pyramids appear to have been used as places to access other dimensions by inducing OBEs to heaven as part of an initiation. They may have achieved this by somehow harnessing and directing electromagnetic energy and sound to energetically separate the initiate's astral body from their physical one, and maybe even then open the portal to heaven and elevate the initiate to a higher state to enable them to enter. We call this our Pyramid Portal Theory.

OBES IN LIFE

What the knowledge of Egypt, and the layout the Great Pyramids reveals, is that there had to have been people who were proficient at having OBEs involved in their origins. While no clear references to OBEs can be found in the funerary texts of ancient Egypt that are not part of the process of death, clear references to OBEs had by people in life are found in the Egyptian texts of the Kolbrin.

They state that the religion of ancient Egypt came from a lost civilization that had once flourished on an island in the ocean to its west, but which had been destroyed in a devastating natural disaster. Survivors from this lost civilization then made their way to Egypt.

This same story is preserved on the walls of an ancient temple in Egypt (still standing), and both narratives share many similarities with the story of Atlantis narrated by Plato, which had originally been told by an ancient Egyptian priest.[121]

A text in the Kolbrin says that the ancient priests who came to Egypt from Atlantis (called "the Land of Copper") were able to leave their bodies and return. However, those who witnessed these priests confused their out-of-body travels with resurrecting from death, and so developed the technique of mummification:

> "The priests who came from the Land of Copper could make their soul depart from the body at their command and return as they willed. Then ignorant men saw seemingly dead bodies return to life when the soul came back into them, they thought the same could happen to a dead body if kept long enough. Even this superstition stays with us. Later [...] they used every art to prevent the body falling apart and entering decay."[122]
>
> ~ THE KOLBRIN

This would explain how such a detailed and accurate knowledge of the fifth dimension came to Egypt, and how this knowledge became misinterpreted. These OBEs sound strange, as with an OBE the body normally seems asleep and not dead. Instead, they sound as though they were the particular type of OBE had by the Twice Born.

The ability to have OBEs was said to have been possessed by the Twice Born of the Enlightened Ones, who were a secret, initiatory order established in Egypt that knew the hidden meaning behind its funerary texts.[123] They sound as though they were established by and a continuation of the order of the priests of Atlantis. They were described as being able to have OBEs, as they could "free the spirit from the shackles of the body at will." Such abilities were said to require "moral self-discipline and courage" and were among the teachings that "remain within the higher circle of those who travel the Right Hand Path and not disclosed to the uninitiated."[124]

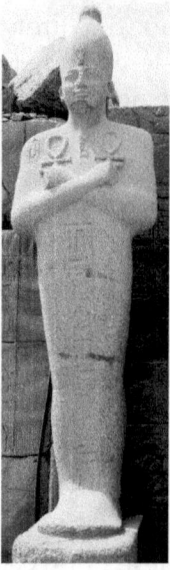

This ancient Egyptian statue fits well the description of a Twice Born who was called an Enwrapped One (Osiris was almost always shown wrapped in white linen), who traveled the Right Hand Path (indicated by their right arm crossed over their left), who had a connection to heaven (indicated by the ankhs they hold), and had risen their serpent of light (kundalini, indicated by the serpent on their brow). It's located at the Karnak Temple Complex, where some of the initiatory chambers of the Twice Born may have been located.

The OBEs they are described as having sound as though they took them not just to the astral plane, but from there through the portal/gate leading into heaven, described as the "Portal of Death." This is usually only experienced by people in NDEs, who travel through the portal as the famous tunnel into the light that opens out into heaven. The Kolbrin describes how the Twice Born used a lengthy ritual to induce what sounds like an NDE, thereby enabling themselves to go through the process of death and return. The preparation for it is described as involving a long bath in cold water, pledging to bear a burden of suffering for the good of others on one's return, and three days of enduring tests (in addition to more than twenty years of preparation before this). A similar, but somewhat different sounding ritual is described in another text of the Kolbrin, by which someone became a Reborn One and Enlightened One. In the ritual of the Twice Born, there is no mention of the use of substances, and the candidate lies so still they appear dead, whereas in the ritual of the Reborn One, a special blend of substances is used, and at times the candidate becomes covered with sweat, writhes, shouts, and struggles.[125] Reborn is really another way of saying Twice Born, and so at some point the ritual may have changed, or perhaps details were omitted from earlier accounts.

By inducing an NDE, the Twice Born were able to visit heaven, which gave them complete faith in their continued existence after death, and the knowledge of their fate in the afterlife. But they also say that after their experience they could recross the border to heaven almost at will, which indicates their experience opened some kind of permanent connection to heaven within themselves, which they continued to access for the rest of their lives. It's interesting that people who visit heaven in NDEs sometimes describe feeling like they have maintained a connection with it in some way—typically saying they have retained some aspect of the heightened spiritual perceptions they had during their NDE, which is what the Twice Born are similarly described as experiencing.

The ritual of the Twice Born was said to be a highly serious and dangerous procedure that could lead to actual death, though being only one of the lesser mysteries of initiation.

> "[...] the final ordeal brought earthly life as close as possible to extinction, without complete severance of the spiritual umbilical cord. Before this went more than twenty years arduous preparation. [...] Only the older men who had completed the three cycles of seven years were accepted. They had to be men with wisdom and courage, with the strength and fortitude to survive. Other essentials were absolute purity and complete self-discipline. The ability for self-sacrifice and a strict sense of duty were demanded. Only men possessing all these qualities could cross the border in consciousness and return. [...] For long years he who aspired to become one of the Twice Born had to practice the awakening of his spirit and bring his body under complete control. [...] It is a ceremony to regain spiritual vigour and to restore spiritual power [...]. It is a grim undertaking fraught with danger. [...] in the last small Cavern [...] the Lord of the Twice Born released his spirit. The Enwrapped One was then placed within the Womb of Rebirth and there, within the tomb of stone, he was left seven days. Here came complete liberation of the spirit. It floated out through the confining stone and went as it willed. No words of men, however learned, can ever describe this experience. The spirit of the Enwrapped One returned to the body at the behest of the Lord of the Twice Born, and he who had survived became a Twice Born One. [...] Once the mysterious border has been crossed it remains open ever after and can be recrossed almost at will."[126]
>
> ~ THE KOLBRIN

This and any procedure bringing the body close to death to enable an NDE or OBE is something I completely recommend against; there is no justification for risking anyone's life like this. It's not part of the path of the Spiritual Sun, but appears to be a distortion of the knowledge about it. This practice or something similar may have originated with priests from Atlantis, and may explain why they seemed to look dead during their out-of-body travels in the excerpt quoted earlier, rather than asleep. We're explaining it because it's part of the history of OBEs in the ancient Religion of the Sun.

It's interesting that in the accounts of the Twice Born ritual, the candidate's spirit is released from and returns to its body at the command of the Lord of the Twice Born. Another line in the Kolbrin appears to explain this further, as it suggests Osiris (who was a Lord of the Twice Born) had this ability, where it says he "placed a staff of power upright into the ground and danced around it, singing the song for drawing forth the spirit." Kolbrin researcher Yvonne Whiteman interprets this as meaning Osiris had the ability to "draw a human spirit out of its body—that is, induce catalepsy or trance."[127] I'm not aware of how this ability would work, as it's part of an ancient knowledge now lost, but if it were possible, it could explain why the Kolbrin refers to the Lord of the Twice Born as being able to induce an OBE in others. It may also partly explain why Osiris came to be known as Lord of the Duat/astral, and why, as described later on, he was seen as the one who stood by the portal to heaven (as the Orion constellation), granting access to it.

The soul of Osiris on the Erica tree.   Osiris of Hermopolis of Lower Egypt rising from his bier at the command of Horus.

> This image and others like it could well be related to the ritual in which the initiate (the Enwrapped One who took the role of Osiris) returned from their OBE in heaven at the behest of the Lord of the Twice Born as in the excerpt just quoted. The Ba/soul/consciousness of Osiris is shown as part bird at the top of a tree. As we'll see later, this may have been symbolic of Cygnus at the "top" of the Milky Way in the nothern circumpolar stars where heaven was believed to be located.

It's possible the Great Pyramid existed long before the survivors of Atlantis made their way to Egypt, and by then was perhaps no longer functioning as it once had, which could be why substances were used. The Kolbrin describes the ritual of the Twice Born being performed in a few different locations. One sounds as though it was within the Great Pyramid (as mentioned earlier). But others are described as hidden beneath temples or concealed within them. Yvonne Whiteman has potentially identified one of these as the Sphinx Temple (in front of the Great Sphinx), where the candidate entered the portal to Rostau (an ancient name for the site of the Great Pyramids), and another beneath the center of the Precinct of Amun-Ra (the Spiritual Sun) at the Temple Complex of Karnak in Egypt,[128] which is the largest religious site ever built and was the most important in Egypt for a long time, the beginnings of which date back to at least 2,000 BC. There is no mention of using any kind of technology or natural energies in the rituals of the Twice Born. Certainly by the time their rituals were conducted beneath temples, the functioning of any pyramid portal was no longer necessary to the ritual conducted, which is when it sounds as though it largely became induced by substances.

Area of the Karnak Temple Complex, within the Precinct of Amun-Ra, lined with statues of Osiris who is said to have been the first of the Twice Born of Egypt.

This experience is not to be confused with taking psychedelics, which I discuss in chapter 28. The blend of substances that seems to have been used by the Twice Born was not designed to induce "visions" or hallucinations, but was part of a procedure to put someone into a near-death state so they could leave their bodies and enter the heavenly region above the astral plane, which is usually only accessible to those who've died. By putting their physical body in a near-death state, they would have stopped their body (particularly their brain) from influencing their consciousness during their experience as much as possible (something I explain further at the end of chapter 7) without actually dying, allowing them to have a lucid experience as those in NDEs do, rather than just dreaming. This is totally different to taking a psychedelic in which someone usually does not have an OBE, but sees hallucinations sometimes mixed with fifth-dimensional experiences while remaining in their physical body.

Neither did it simply involve going through a procedure and taking substances, as physically rigorous as this procedure sounds. It was said that someone had to go through a process of preparation within the esoteric order lasting years and even decades. The procedure itself was then undertaken under the guidance of the order over a period of days to weeks, and the person going through it had knowledge of what they would encounter out of the body, and how to navigate it. It sounds like once they were out of their bodies they weren't guided through the portal to heaven as people in NDEs are, but had to cross it themselves after overcoming many obstacles and passing tests. It's possible there was even a long program of training in OBEs to be able to go through such an experience. The knowledge of this entire process has been lost.

It's remarkable that this same essential experience the Twice Born had within the Great Pyramid is found in the Pyramid Texts. Both describe an OBE in which one traveled firstly into the Duat/astral plane and then through the portal into heaven. This confirms what the Kolbrin records the Enlightened Ones as saying—that they knew the hidden meaning of the funerary literature of Egypt as being not for the dead who leave the earth, but for those who die and remain here. Rather than being reborn as the Spiritual Son/Sun, as the king was believed to be after death, those in the esoteric order of Egypt were said to be reborn during life.

I believe the term Twice Born would have originally referred to those who had been born again spiritually, when the part of their Being called the Spiritual Son/Sun incarnated/was born within them; this is an inner, spiritual process gone through by those worthy, and something I write about at length.[129] But this seems to have been misinterpreted by some to mean those who had gone through an induced physical death, then resurrected, and thus been "reborn."

I believe at least one of the reasons this practice was brought about was because there were people who knew their ancestors had lost their psychic faculties, and were attempting this dangerous procedure to restore them, and were basing what they were doing on a misunderstanding of the path of the Spiritual Sun. The Kolbrin essentially says the same thing.

> "[...] it was not an ordeal required to obtain something man has never possessed, it was to regain something he had lost."[130]

> "Once men could pass easily from one sphere to another, then came the misty veil. Now men must pass a grim portal to span the spheres and, as the generations pass, this, too, will be closed to men. The secret of the substances which, compounded together, become the horse which can bear men here [to heaven], will remain with those who know the mysteries, but these will become even harder to reach. As the ages roll by there will be many false mysteries and perhaps the path will become closed or the way lost."[131]
>
> ~ THE KOLBRIN

Those who could "pass easily from one sphere to another" would surely have been those we refer to as the Children of the Sun, who were said to have had greater psychic faculties, and, according to ancient legends, whose descendants lived on Atlantis. They were remembered as the original practitioners of the Religion of the Sun and as the builders of ancient megalithic sites aligned to the sun.[132]

Evidence for the existence of similar ancient myths has been found among the traditions of diverse peoples. These myths essentially state that in a distant, paradisiacal age people had been able to travel easily to the realms of the sky where they maintained direct relations with the gods, and also to the underworld, but that some catastrophe had brought this ability to an end, so that now only spiritually trained individuals could make such journeys to the otherworld.[133]

It sounds like the Children of the Sun were naturally able to have OBEs, even to heaven (which is normally only accessed through a portal at death or during an NDE), without the use of substances, and were the origin of much of the knowledge about other dimensions, the afterlife, and OBEs. In places like ancient Egypt, where the Religion of the Sun and its sites were preserved, those who came after them remembered them as gods and wished to emulate them, but many misunderstood the knowledge they left behind. It also sounds like those who came after them began using substances in an attempt to emulate their OBEs, as it seems they were increasingly less able to have them naturally, as false mysteries arose and the way became lost.

THE OLDEST EVIDENCE FOR OBES IN THE WORLD

So how old is the evidence for out-of-body experiences? We believe it's as old as the Great Pyramids themselves. There is compelling evidence that some of the structures on the Giza Plateau, as well as at other ancient Egyptian sites, are far older than the dates currently ascribed to them by mainstream Egyptology. This evidence is detailed in Lara's book *The Ancient Religion of the Sun*, but briefly, the oldest structures at Giza, like the pyramids and sphinx, were built to align to certain stars, and according to researcher Armando Mei, these alignments were most accurate (within the last one hundred thousand years) at 36,500 BC,[134] and according to researcher Randall Carlson, the weathering on the Great Sphinx and its enclosure, as well as other areas around the Great Pyramids, indicate that it could be at least twenty to forty thousand years old.[135] This is around the time when some ancient records in Egypt state that Egyptian civilization was founded.[136]

What this means is that the knowledge of the fifth dimension and of OBEs could trace back to at least this time. Scientists have recently discovered that a global catastrophe occurred at 40,000 BC,[137] which may have wiped out structures even older than the pyramids, and so this knowledge probably derives from an even earlier civilization that gave rise to ancient Egypt. The evidence we've collected indicates this civilization belonged to the Children of the Sun, who as noted earlier, were said to have been able to pass easily from one dimension to another, and who we believe gave rise to the knowledge of OBEs in the ancient Religion of the Sun and the many traditions that stem from it.

Notice the deep fissures in the bedrock surrounding the Great Sphinx and the apparent depth of them in comparison to the people, indicating the Sphinx was originally carved at a time long enough ago for such extreme weathering to have occurred.

THE GREATEST MONUMENTS TO OBES IN THE WORLD

Putting all the evidence together we believe reveals that the Great Pyramids are the greatest surviving monuments to OBEs in the world, and we call this our Giza OBE Theory. They are also the greatest monuments of the ancient Religion of the Sun, and were used to facilitate people's progress on the path of the Spiritual Sun.

To recap, this evidence includes:

- The depiction of the symbol of Aker made by the Great Pyramids and Sphinx, representing the Land of the Horizon and Duat (the astral plane) with its two portals to the higher and lower dimensions.

- The alignments of Giza monuments to the solar and stellar components of the Duat and Akhet, which include Orion, the rising equinox sun, the constellation of Leo, the northern circumpolar stars, etc.

- The king's out-of-body journey described in the Pyramid Texts.

- The teachings of Osiris about the fifth dimension and OBEs (in the Kolbrin), his central role in the OBE of the king in the Pyramid Texts (and all subsequent funerary texts and rituals), and his association with the Great Pyramids.

- The accounts of the OBEs that the priests of Atlantis and ancient Egypt are said to have had, as found in the Kolbrin, and the statement that the secret meaning of Egypt's funerary texts is that they were really for the living.

- The illustrations in the Amduat depicting elements of the Giza monuments and its statements that it was a guidebook to the Duat (the astral plane) for the living.

- The function that pyramids are known to have had in ancient Egypt (and in other parts of the world) as portals to the heavenly realm.

- The measurements encoded into the Great Pyramid and their correlation with the king's OBE in the Pyramid Texts.

- The evidence for some kind of technological function to the Great Pyramid that likely involved electromagnetic energy and sound, and the part these may play in inducing OBEs.

- The focus of the Great Pyramids and Pyramid Texts on the sun and stars, and the reference in the Pyramid Texts to the king harnessing star energy in his OBE.

- My own initiatory OBEs in the Great Pyramid.

The great legacy of spiritual knowledge bequeathed by the Children of the Sun, the Atlantean priesthood, and Osiris to what became the civilization of Egypt, became distorted under many layers of religious misinterpretation down the passage of so many thousands of years, but is still palpable in its enigmatic and awe-inspiring texts, artifacts, and monuments—the greatest ancient testaments to OBEs in the world.

HERMETIC

What's likely to be an account of an OBE is found in ancient Hermetic texts, which derive at least partially from ancient Egyptian religion.

Hermeticism is a spiritual philosophy said to have taken shape during the first few centuries after Christ in the ancient city of Alexandria, which was founded by Greeks in Egypt. It's believed to have been born out of the melting pot of spiritual traditions and ideas that mingled there, particularly those of the Greek and Egyptian religions. Indeed, the whole system of philosophy is attributed to a god and teacher called Hermes Trismegistus, who is an amalgamation of the Egyptian god Thoth with the Greek god Hermes.

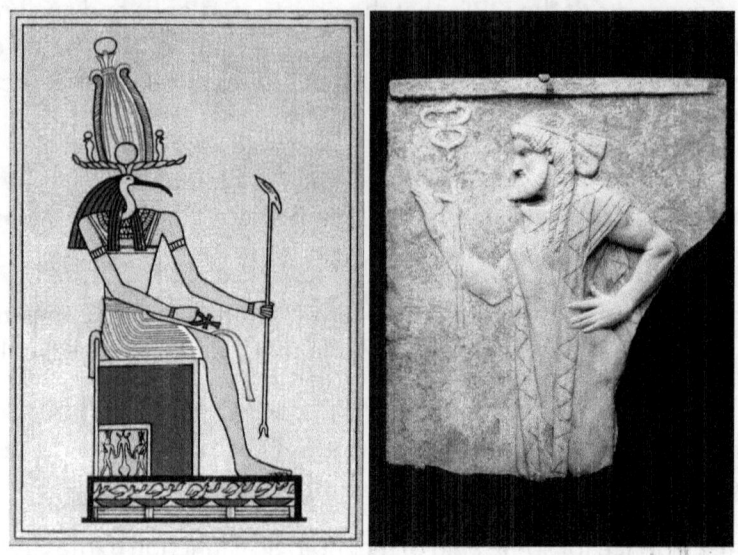

Left: The Egyptian god Thoth. Right: The Greek god Hermes.

The very first Hermetic texts have been dated to approximately 300 BC, around the time Alexandria was founded.[138] However, it's been speculated for as long as these texts have been around that the teachings of Hermes Trismegistus date from long before their Greek copies appeared—to the time before the great flood, which may refer to the great global flood that occurred at the end of the Ice Age around 9,700 BC and destroyed Atlantis.

In this version of events, a "first Hermes" wrote the sacred teachings down in hieroglyphics at some unspecified time before the flood. Then after the flood a "second Hermes" transferred these teachings to books, which were eventually translated from Egyptian to Greek—the language Hermetic texts surfaced in. Based on ancient sources, it was believed there were once tens of thousands of books by Hermes Trismegistus. However, only around two dozen survive today.[139]

Essentially, Hermetic texts claim to derive from the great antiquity of Egyptian religion, and both Egyptian and Greek religions were derived from the Religion of the Sun. This comes through in Hermetic texts, where the sun is described as the manifestation of God and object of veneration.

In the following excerpt, Hermes Trismegistus has what sounds like an OBE—it begins the Corpus Hermeticum, which is the most famous collection of Hermetic texts.

"Once, when my mind had become intent on the things which are, and my understanding was raised to a great height, while my bodily senses were withdrawn as in sleep, when men are weighed down by too much food or by the fatigue of the body, it seemed that someone immensely great of infinite dimensions happened to call my name and said to me:

'What do you wish to hear and behold, and having beheld, what do you wish to learn and know?'

[...] When he had thus spoken, he changed in form and forthwith, upon the instant, all things opened up before me; and I beheld a boundless view."[140]

~ HERMES TRISMEGISTUS IN THE CORPUS HERMETICUM

Poimandres appearing to Hermes Trismegistus, who is depicted as sleeping, though he is having an OBE or at least a very clear dream.

The great being who appears to Hermes Trismegistus in his OBE is called Poimandres, as is the text in which this experience appears. This name is derived from the Egyptian phrase "the Knowledge/Understanding of Re"[141]— Re being the ancient Egyptian sun god (the Spiritual Sun). Within the text, Poimandres tells Hermes Trismegistus that he's the *nous* (translated as the awareness, mind, or pure faculty of spiritual apprehension[142]) of God, which is another way of saying he is the intelligence of the Spiritual Sun.

The account of Hermes Trismegistus' OBE closes with him reflecting upon his experience, saying:

> "I was deeply happy because I was filled with what I wished, for the sleep of my body became sobriety of soul, the closing of my eyes became true vision [...]. This happened to me because I was receptive of mind – of Poimandres [...]. Therefore, I give praise to god the father from my soul and with all my might."[143]
> ~ HERMES TRISMEGISTUS IN THE CORPUS HERMETICUM

Being "receptive of mind" perhaps has the double meaning that his mind remained aware while he slept, and was itself also aware of Poimandres (the intelligence of God, the Spiritual Sun). This is another way of putting how he first explained his experience: "when my mind had become intent on the things which are, and my understanding was raised to a great height." Being in this state of mind while his eyes were closed and his body slept, he was given an OBE by the divine in which he was taught spiritual knowledge.

In another text, Hermes Trismegistus tells his disciple that he has an immortal body which cannot be seen with physical eyes.

> "I have come out of my former self into an immortal body. I am not now what I was before. For I have been born in *Nous*. Such a thing is not taught, nor can it be seen by the physical body." [144]
> ~ HERMES TRISMEGISTUS IN THE CORPUS HERMETICUM

The disciple is utterly confused by this, to which Hermes Trismegistus replies:

> "I wish you had now stepped out of yourself, my son, like those who dream in sleep and yet are awake." [145]
> ~ HERMES TRISMEGISTUS IN THE CORPUS HERMETICUM

And so it sounds like Hermes Trismegistus is saying that if his disciple was consciously out of his body, in the astral plane, he would be able to see the immortal body that he, Hermes Trismegistus, possesses.

In ancient Egypt, Thoth was said to have been one of the survivors of the lost island to the west of Egypt, which shares so many similarities with Atlantis—likely making Thoth a priest of Atlantis who came to Egypt.[146] Thus, the references to Hermes Trismegistus having OBEs in Hermetic texts may be distantly based on OBEs that Thoth was said to have had, making it another possible reference to the ability of the priests of Atlantis to have OBEs.

HINDU

There are a few clear accounts of OBEs in ancient Hindu texts—some undertaken by the most famous figures and gods of the religion. The astral body and astral plane also form part of its cosmology.

Hinduism is one of the oldest known continually practiced religions in the world, and is also the third largest. Hinduism has its roots in the ancient Religion of the Sun; in its oldest texts the supreme creator is frequently identified with the sun as the greatest source of light. Like ancient Egyptian religion, it claims it originates much earlier than conventionally thought, and its founding story shares many similarities with that of ancient Egypt, indicating that the two share a very ancient common origin.[147]

THE ASTRAL BODY

The texts of Hinduism clearly state that each person is comprised of far more than their physical body, and detail these other-dimensional parts, including what is likely to be the astral body.

For example, the Brihadaranyaka Upanishad, which is believed to have been composed in the seventh to sixth century BC, and appears in the Yajur Veda, considered among the oldest of the Hindu texts, says:

> "When a person dies, it is only the physical body that dies; that person lives on in a nonphysical body [...]."[148]
> ~ BRIHADARANYAKA UPANISHAD

This nonphysical body is first described in the Taittirya Upanishad, which was composed around the sixth century BC, and is also considered part of the Vedas. It lists the different "sheaths" that comprise both the physical and nonphysical bodies that each person has.

The physical body is called the "gross body" and is composed of the physical sheath made of food, but is also comprised of a nonphysical vital sheath made of prana or "living breath" (likely the same as the Egyptian Ka). Higher, or more subtle than these is the subtle body, which is comprised of the "mental sheath" and the "knowledge/wisdom sheath." The subtle body is described as being able to separate from the physical one and travel in nonphysical realms, and sounds very much like the astral body. Finally, there is a causal body, which is composed of the "bliss sheath," associated with the heart.[149]

THE ASTRAL PLANE

The cosmology of Hinduism describes many different nonphysical worlds existing parallel to our own. In the earliest known references to them, they include lower hellish underworlds of darkness (*naraka*), a sky world midway between our physical world and heaven above (*bhuva*), heavenly realms of light (*svarga*), and the abode of Brahman as the region of the sun and source (*maha*). These worlds are the places where people go when they sleep and have OBEs, where the deceased go, and gods and evil beings reside.[150]

A Hindu king tells his soldiers about heaven, which he indicates is above, and hell, below. The entrance to hell is symbolized using crocodile jaws, just as it was in ancient Egypt, and then as the mouth of a beast in Christian artwork.

In the OBEs found in Hindu texts, the traveler enters "the sky of ether." Ether, called *akasa* in Sanskrit, is considered the first of five elements in Hinduism and is associated with sky and space.[151] It corresponds to the midway sky world called *bhuva*, which is the most likely candidate for the astral plane. Both in Hinduism and ancient Egyptian religion, the astral plane was associated with the sky.

OBES

As far as we've found, there are two clear accounts of OBEs described in Hindu texts—one found in the Yoga Vasistha and the other in the Mahabharata. Both are very popular and influential Hindu texts.

In the Yoga Vasistha, the separation of the subtle body from the physical one and its ability to journey out of the body is described very clearly. The text is attributed to the legendary Indian poet Valmiki, and purportedly recounts the teachings of one of the oldest and most revered Vedic sages (one of the seven sages), Vasishtha, whom the text is named after. The text is structured as a discourse between the sage Vasishtha and prince Rama. However, it's unknown whether any of them are the real authors. The text was modified over a long period of time, incorporating Hindu, Buddhist, and Jain ideas, which even though can be contradictory, were brought together in this syncretic work, and the original lost. It's said to mainly espouse the philosophy of the branch of Hinduism known as Advaita Vedanta, particularly its drishti-srishti offshoot. Its final date of composition/modification is estimated to be sometime between the sixth to fifteenth century AD.

There are two versions of it—one is known as the Brihat, meaning big, and the other the Laghu, meaning small, as it's about a quarter of the length of the Brihat. There are different theories about how these versions came to exist. One is that the Laghu text was created in the tenth century AD as an abridged form of the Brihat text. Another theory reverses this, proposing that first there had been a small text containing the original teachings of Vasishtha, which was expanded into the Laghu version, the original text then being lost. The Laghu text was added to and modified over the centuries by different authors, until becoming the Brihat version as it's known today. This kind of expansion of Indian texts is apparently typical, and so we lean toward the theory that the Brihat text is a later expansion.[152]

The OBE is described in "The Story of Lila" as purportedly told by Vasishtha to Rama, as a kind of allegory in order to impart spiritual teachings to him on the nature of reality, and the way to achieve liberation. It appears in both the Laghu and Brihat versions, though greatly expanded or abridged in the different versions, depending on which way you look at it. We've included excerpts from both.

In the story, a lady named Lila is distraught as her husband has just died. She wishes to see him again, and so prays to the goddess Saraswati who comes to her aid. Saraswati helps Lila to leave her body, go see her husband in the realm of "spiritual *akasa*/ether" (Cidakasa), and travel to different places there, while imparting spiritual teachings to her. The story reveals an ancient method for astral projecting along with descriptions of astral travel and the astral plane and the ideas the authors held about them.

In the following excerpt taken from the Laghu text, Saraswati describes how to have a conscious OBE. She says that by quieting all one's thoughts, one's consciousness is allowed to manifest. Saraswati also tells Lila that to leave her body she must understand that all form is transient and illusory, including her physical body. With divine grace, Saraswati then helps Lila to leave her physical body to travel in her subtle body, and see her deceased husband.

> "Saraswati said: 'Of the three kinds of Akasa, namely Cidakasa, (Spiritual Akasa), Citta-kasa, (or mental Akasa) and Bhutakasa (elemental Akasa), Cittakasa is that intermediate state in which the mind is when it flits from one object to another in the elemental Akasa of objects. When the hosts of Samkalpa-s [thoughts] in us perish, then the light of Cit [consciousness], which is quiescent and immaculate and manifests itself as the universe, will shine in us. If one becomes convinced of the unreality of visible objects, then,

through that Jnana [knowledge], he will attain Cidakasa at once. May you attain through my grace that Cidakasa.'

Through this blessing, Lila went into Nirvikalpa Samadhi and was able to escape, like a bird from its cage, out of the body which is generally replete with stains and desires through the longing of the mind. There in the heart of Jnanakasa (Cidakasa), she saw, in a large town, a much beloved, valiant prince, sixteen years old [...]. Having recognized him to be her dear lord [husband], she entered the king's assembly [...]. Then, having visited many fertile tracts of earth, hills, cities, towns, holy rivers, etc. she, sparkling like lightning, returned to her abode and entered her body; lying entranced [...]."[153]

~ LAGHU YOGA VASISTHA

Illustration of Lila and Saraswati traveling out of the body together.

After returning, they go on a second out-of-body journey together. Saraswati explains to Lila that the gross/physical body is an impediment to acquiring knowledge of other realms. She says that as an enlightened being it's easy for her, as she no longer has a gross body, and has transformed her subtle body. But she says that Lila, with her physical body and lunar (untransformed) subtle body, who has not attained spiritual liberation/enlightenment, will instead have to keep her physical body still, and perceive through her lunar subtle body.

"This gross body of yours, bred out of Karman-s [karma], is an impediment in the way of you getting such knowledge. If you should become entirely oblivious of your body and know yourself as distinct from it and then become of the nature of the pure Bliss Enjoyer which is also Jnana light and Sat, after being cleansed of all Maya impurities, then you shall be able to reach the hallowed state. [...] Persons like myself can easily enter into the pure Brahman. But those who are like you have a subtle (lunar) body of the nature of mind, replete with desire, and it, in turn, generates the gross body. [...] Therefore you will have to perceive the former creation through your original, subtle body (of Ativahika), after stilling (or entrancing) this body of yours. [...]

Saraswati and Lila who thus conferred together that night, went into Svarupa Samadhi, free from the trammels of their body and remained motionless. In this state, Saraswati shining with her former Jnana body [transformed subtle body], along with Lila with her newly assumed Jnana one, rose up high in the Akasa [...].

Having penetrated far into the Akasa, which is like a great ocean at the time of deluge, they observed there the following. In the immeasurable, transparent and subtle Cidakasa, there were to be found the hosts of Siddha-s [those who have attained enlightenment] who journeyed fleeter than wind.

Then they passed through diverse places for ten Ghatika-s' distance, some full of gloom, inaccessible to any, and others, radiant with the lustre of Agni (fire) or the Sun journeying on his swift car. Thus passed they through the Akasa of the three worlds, wherein abode the myriads of Jiva-s [souls] created by Brahma buzzing like the swarms of flies collected on a ripe fig fruit."[154]

~ LAGHU YOGA VASISTHA

In the Brihat text this OBE is described quite differently. Instead of lying down, Lila leaves her body while standing up; this depiction was likely influenced by a standing method of Jain concentration. Perhaps it may be possible, but usually we need to be in a position to sleep to astral project; I've never met anyone who has had an OBE while standing, as I would imagine that once someone fell asleep and left their body, they would fall over. Despite this difference, a similar method for leaving the body is described. Saraswati and Lila astral project by holding their bodies totally still, keeping their minds quiet and concentrated, and by understanding the ephemeral nature of the physical world. This is actually a very detailed ancient description of astral projection:

"[Saraswati and Lila] then went to the cemetery and stood motionless on the spot, as if they were sculptures engraven on marble columns, or as pictures drawn upon the wall. They shook off all their thoughts and cares, and became as contracted as the faded blossoms of the lotus at the decline of the day, when their fragrance has fled from

them. They remained still, calm and quiet and without any motion
of their limbs, like a sheet of clouds hanging on the mountain top
in the calm of autumn. They continued in fixed attention without
any external sensation, like some lonely creepers shrivelled for want
of the moisture of the season. They were fully impressed with the
disbelief of their own existence, and that of all other things in the
world, and were altogether absorbed in the thought of an absolute
privation of every thing at large. They lost the remembrance of the
phantom of the phenomenal world, which is as unreal as the horn of
a hare. [...] The two ladies then became as quiet as inert nature herself,
and as still as firmament before the luminous bodies rolled about in
its ample sphere. They then began to move with their own bodies,
the goddess of wisdom in her form of intelligence, and the queen in
her intellectual and meditative mood. With their new bodies they
rose as high as one span above the ground, then taking the forms of
the empty intellect, they began to mount in the sky. [...] Then they
flew higher and higher by force of their intellect, and arrived at a
region stretching millions of leagues in length. Here the pair in their
etherial forms, looked about [...]."[155]
~ BRIHAT YOGA VASISHTHA

Flying by using willpower (the force of the intellect) to cross vast distances is an accurate description of how it's possible to travel in the astral plane by willing where we want to go. But the physical world is not unreal or a phantom as it says here. The text also describes the ability to travel wherever one wants in the earth or sky in the astral plane, without restriction:

"Hence Lílá and Sarasvatí, being in their vacuous intellectual bodies,
were led by the pure desire of their souls, to every place without any
obstruction or interruption. The intellectual spirit has the power, to
present itself wherever it likes, on earth or in the sky, and before
objects known or unknown and wished to be known by it. [...] This
is known as the spiritual and unconfined body (Átiváhika), whose
course cannot be obstructed by any restriction whatever."[156]
~ BRIHAT YOGA VASISHTHA

It describes how it's possible in the astral plane to pass through objects, to see them from the inside and outside, and to become very large or small.

"It [the intellectual body] moves at pleasure in the vast firmament,
and penetrates through the solid mountains. Its body bears no break
in it, and is as minute as an atom. Yet it becomes as big as a mountain
lifting its head to heaven, and as large as the earth, which is the fixed

and firm support of all things. It views the inside and outside of every thing, and bears the forests like hairs on its body."[157]

~ BRIHAT YOGA VASISHTHA

Rather than traveling in their subtle bodies as in the Laghu version, in the Brihat text Saraswati and Lila travel in "new bodies" that are said to be nothing but the creation of their intellects. This idea, that instead of having an astral body we create a new body with our minds each time we project, is also found in Shaivism and Tibetan Buddhism (explained shortly).

Additionally, the Brihat text says that the out-of-body realm of *akasa* is insubstantial and merely the creation of the intellect. I and many others who've had verifiably real experiences in OBEs and NDEs have found this to be incorrect; these experiences show that there are nonphysical realms of existence that have been independently corroborated by others, across time and culture. With this mistaken view, the text goes on to say that the OBEs of Saraswati and Lila occurred in their own minds, going so far as to say that the physical world and all that happens in it likewise occurs within one's mind:

> "Ráma said: Tell me sir, in what manner the goddesses broke out of the strongholds of their bodies, and the prison-house of this world (where their souls were pent up), and passed through infinite space, to survey the scenes beyond its confines. (i.e. How does the mind and the flight of imagination, reach to regions unknown and unseen before).
>
> Vasishtha replied: Where is the world and where is its support or solidity? They were all situated in the region within the minds of the goddesses. [...] All that she saw was mere vision and void; there was no world nor earth, nor a house nor the distance thereof. It was the mind which showed them these images, as it presents the objects of our desire to our view; or else there was neither any world nor earth in actuality. [...] He who understands rightly, views the world to be as unsubstantial as air; but whoso is misled by his wrong judgment takes it to be as a solid mountain. As a house and a city are manifested to us in our dream, so is this unreal world presented as a reality to our understandings."[158]
>
> ~ BRIHAT YOGA VASISHTHA

The text also says that what someone sees after death, as in an NDE, is really all just the creation of their imagination.

> "Soon after the insensibility occasioned by one's death is over, there appears to him (soul) the sight of the world, as he viewed it with his open eyes when he was living. It presents before him the circle

of the sky and its sides with the cycle of its seasons and times, and shows him the deeds of his pious and secular acts, as they were to continue to eternity. Objects never seen nor thought of before, also offer themselves to his view, as the sight of his own death in a dream, and as they were the prints in his memory. But the infinity of objects, appearing in the empty sphere of the immaterial intellect, is mere illusion, and the baseless city of the world, like an aerial castle, is but the creation of imagination."[159]

~ BRIHAT YOGA VASISHTHA

Modern accounts of NDEs in which people have seen things while dead and out of their bodies, such as details of what was happening in the hospital where they died, that later proved to be true, show that what's seen after death is not the product of imagination. The properties of the astral plane, such as the ability to fly, to travel to distant places, to pass through objects, and to imagine and then see whatever one wants, have been used in the text to support the idea that there is nothing real about it. No distinction is made in the Yoga Vasistha between seeing what is subjective and what is objective in the astral plane, that is, between seeing the projections of one's own mind versus seeing something verifiably real there (such as meeting someone else astral traveling at the same time, or seeing something you had no knowledge of and then verifying it was real back in the physical world). I discuss this in much more detail in following chapters.

The belief in Buddhism and in some branches of Hinduism that the universe isn't real, but an illusion, is essentially similar to the "brain in a vat" theory, which is the idea that you could just be a brain in a vat of a mad scientist and nothing of what you see is actually real, but is just his creation. There's no way to disprove this idea, but there's no way to prove it either. You can't just walk through a wall for example, no matter how hard you try to think it's an illusion. And I know that at the smallest level everything becomes energy and apparent nothingness, but the person who is in creation has to take what they ordinarily experience as real, or they will conflict with the reality of creation, like hurting themselves if they try to walk through a wall. Followers of this religious idea wouldn't be studying themselves, but maintaining an idea of nothingness throughout their lives—one they can never verify. We would not exist as individuals if everything became nothingness (or if there was just one universal mind), yet those who have NDEs and OBEs and experience the Source clearly do still have an individual existence. So the idea that everything is a creation of one's mind is an impractical and unproven theory that conflicts with reality. Those who believe in it will not be able to use their life properly if they follow it.

It's apparent that in the Yoga Vasistha the astral plane became viewed through the particular philosophy it espouses, which is that of Advaita

Vedanta. This philosophy states that "the whole world of things is the object of the mind."[160] Yet it's likely the knowledge of astral projection contained within it is older than the text itself.

The most famous Hindu epic, the Mahabharata, describes another OBE—this time undertaken by the great warrior Arjuna together with his spiritual guide Krishna. The Mahabharata is attributed to the Vedic sage Vyasa, whose biographical details are legendary. The text is believed to have reached the form it's in today around AD 400, though parts of it are known to have existed as far back as around 400 BC.[161]

In their OBE, Arjuna and Krishna travel to the fantastically beautiful residence of the god Shiva to seek his aid in dealing with a personal problem. It implies that Arjuna used a mantra to astral project, which is a practice I learned, taught for decades, and include in this book.

Arjuna and Krishna go on an out-of-body journey together.

Once out of the body, Krishna directs himself toward the rising sun and tells Arjuna to concentrate on the god Shiva in order to go to him. Concentrating on where you want to go is a method for traveling to that place in the astral plane, and so having concentrated on Shiva, Arjuna finds himself traveling at the speed of thought with Krishna to the other-dimensional residence of Shiva. Krishna holds Arjuna's arm, as this is a way people can remain together while astral traveling. Anyone who has had an OBE will recognize the speed and sensation of traveling in the astral plane as it's described in this account.

> "[Arjuna] recollected the mantras (given to him by Vyasa). And soon he was lulled in the arms of sleep. Unto that [...] hero, [Krishna] appeared in a dream. [...] [Arjuna] then said these words of grave import: '[...] O [Krishna]! How can a person like me live, having failed to accomplish his vow? [...]' Krishna hearing this cause of [Arjuna's] grief, touched water and sat with face turned to the east. And then [Krishna] said '[...] adore within thy heart the god having the bull for his mark. Thinking of that god in thy mind, remember him [...]! Thou art his devotee. [...]' Hearing these words of Krishna, [Arjuna] having touched water, sat on the earth with concentrated mind and

thought of the god [Shiva]. After he had thus sat with rapt mind at that hour called Brahma of auspicious indications [the period of approximately one and a half hours before sunrise, considered the best time for spiritual practice in Hinduism[162]], Arjuna saw himself journeying through the sky with [Krishna]. And [Arjuna], possessed of the speed of the mind, seemed to reach, with [Krishna], the sacred foot of Himavat and the Manimat mountain abounding in many brilliant gems and frequented by Siddhas and Charanas. And the lord [Krishna] seemed to have caught hold of his left arm. And he seemed to see many wonderful sights as he reached [that place]. And Arjuna of righteous soul then seemed to arrive at the White mountain on the north. And then he beheld, in the pleasure-gardens of Kuvera the beautiful lake decked with lotuses. [...] And then he arrived at the regions about the Mandara mountains. Those regions were covered with trees that always bore blossoms and fruits. And they abounded with stones lying scattered about, that were all transparent crystal. [...] And they were adorned with many beautiful retreats of ascetics, echoing with the sweet notes of delightful warblers. [...] And thus going through the sky and firmament and the earth, he reached the spot called Vishnupada. And wandering, with Krishna in his company, he came down with great velocity, like a shaft shot (from a bow). And soon [Arjuna] beheld a blazing mountain whose splendour equalled that of the planets, the constellations, or fire. And arrived at that mountain, he beheld on its top, the high-souled god [Shiva] having the bull for his mark, and ever engaged in ascetic penances, like a thousand suns collected together, and blazing with his own effulgence.

[Shiva] of cheerful soul, smilingly said unto them, 'Welcome are ye, ye foremost of men! [...] What, O heroes, is the desire in your heart? [...] I will grant everything ye may desire.' [...] And the god [...] granted him [...] the accomplishment of his vow. Then [...] Arjuna, with hair standing on end, regarded his business to be already achieved. Then Arjuna and Krishna filled with joy, paid their adorations unto the great god by bowing their heads. And permitted by [Shiva] both Arjuna and [Krishna], those two heroes, almost immediately came back to their own camp [...]."[163]

~ THE MAHABHARATA

By traveling to the abode of Shiva, it sounds like Krishna and Arjuna visited heaven in their OBE. In Hinduism, Shiva is believed to reside at the peak of Mount Kailash, which was identified as the earthly location of the mythical Mount Meru—the most sacred mountain of Hinduism which is said to extend into heaven. The incredibly beautiful gardens Krishna and Arjuna see, inhabited by ascetics or spiritually advanced people, is how heaven often appears to people in NDEs. And Shiva is described like the great light people are often greeted by in heaven, that shines like a thousand suns. Could the OBE of Krishna and Arjuna date back to the time of the Children of the Sun when they were able to pass easily from one sphere to another and travel from the earthly realm to heaven in OBEs?

The mantra Arjuna uses to leave his body is never given; we only know it was called Pratismriti, which is a type of spiritual knowledge that was never meant to be recited, but instead remembered and transmitted in secret.[164] This indicates that the knowledge of how to have OBEs was passed on secretly.

Giant statue of the god Shiva in India,
who is one of the major gods of Hinduism.

Interestingly, in this astral experience, Shiva grants Arjuna the "pasupata astra," one of the most powerful supernatural weapons said to exist—the word "astra" meaning supernatural weapon. In the stories preserved in Hindu texts there were said to be many different kinds of them. Strange that Arjuna received an *astra* in the astral! Not long after this, Arjuna rides through the sky (in the physical world) on a flying/celestial chariot, known as a vimana. The way these weapons and chariots are described sounds as though they were forms of technology viewed from the perspective of people who had either lost or never possessed it themselves. These weapons and flying vehicles are always bestowed by "the gods" (the Children of the Sun) to those virtuous or worthy enough; and while riding a vimana Arjuna sees these gods flying high up in the sky in thousands of vimanas.[165] It could be concluded from this that these tales were based on events that may have occurred long before they were written, originating from a time when a lost civilization that had advanced technology and/or contact with extraterrestrials existed—likely during the times of the Children of the Sun. The *astra* weapons may have utilized technology that involved the fifth dimension somehow, which we don't understand today. What this could all possibly indicate, is that the OBE of Arjuna, and the understanding of OBEs found in this text, may date back to the same time as the technology described alongside it.

Depiction of a flying vehicle (vimana) as described in Hindu texts. These seem to have been advanced aircraft remembered by people who neither possessed nor understood such technology—hence it's shown as flying by being carried by a giant bird.

Today there are still Hindus (and non-Hindus), who see Shiva (and other Hindu deities, like Yama) in OBEs and NDEs. For example, a woman saw the Trimurti of Vishnu, Shiva, and Brahma in her NDE—above whom was the light of Om.[166] Another man saw Shiva in a spontaneous OBE.[167]

A reference to what sounds like lucid dreaming appears in the Mandukya Upanishad, which has been variously dated to between the fifth century BC to second century AD.[168] It lists different states of consciousness, one of them being the state of dreaming while in the subtle body, called Taijasa, saying:

> "Those who know this, by mastering even their dreams, become established in wisdom."[169]
> ~ MANDUKYA UPANISHAD

Gaining mastery over one's dreams implies learning to control them, which would probably mean becoming lucid in them.

There also appear to be references to astral projection and to becoming lucid in dreams in the texts of one of the four major branches of Hinduism known as Shaivite Tantra or Kashmir Shaivism, whose followers venerate the god Shiva as the expression of the ultimate reality/godhead.

In the Shiva Sutras (the founding text of Shaivism), there are references to bringing "turya," which its practitioners believe is the ultimate state of consciousness comparable to Shiva, into dreams and deep sleep.

> "In the three states of wakeful, dream and deep sleep states, the bliss of the fourth state of turya should be dropped like oil. [...]
>
> He [the yogi] [...] keeps energizing the three states of consciousness (wakeful, dream and deep sleep) and the three states of activity (beginning, middle and end) with the first, the bliss of turya or the memory of it."[170]
>
> ~ SHIVA SUTRAS

This has been interpreted in Shaivism as being in a blissful state of consciousness at all times.[171] Although it sounds like attempting to do this could lead to having an OBE or lucid dream, this is not the goal of the practice and neither do modern Shaivite practitioners describe having OBEs as a result. Instead, they go into a state of meditative absorption said to result in a state of bliss they then attempt to integrate into the states of waking, dreaming, and deep sleep.[172] We are yet to find a clear description of this occurring in dreams or deep sleep by anyone who has experienced it. The meditation practices proscribed for reaching and maintaining this state for any length of time would necessitate withdrawal into a retreat/monastic life, which restricts life experiences and thus the ability to acquire self-knowledge and to go through most of life's tests. And while ordinary consciousness can experience states that feel blissful, the capacity it has to feel spiritual states is limited; it's by merging with the higher part of one's Being I call the Spiritual Son, on the path of the Spiritual Sun, that greater spiritual properties are imparted into consciousness. Being in a state of complete blissful consciousness at all times, including during sleep, in my view seems to have developed out of unrealistic ideals.

Then there is a description of what sounds like astral projection in the text Tantrasara,[173] which is a summary of the much larger text Tantraloka—a compendium of ancient Shaivite teachings and practices, and one of the major texts of Shaivism. Both were written by the Shaivite practitioner Abhinavagupta in the tenth century based on much older traditions.[174] He wrote the practices in a vague way, seemingly to make it difficult for those who weren't practitioners to fully interpret them.

In the Tantrasara, there is a meditation practice (which we give a variation of in chapter 23) said to cause "a newly born" "pure body to rise" that has "unlimited power," which sounds very much like projection in the astral body with its seemingly limitless abilities to fly, go through objects, etc., in the astral plane. The Tantrasara describes this practice in a cryptic and abbreviated way, and so the translator explains it more clearly as follows:

> "[...] the *acarya* [teacher] should remain steady in the state of pure consciousness. It is like a tranquil sea from where the creative consciousness (*samvit*) begins to break into waves. The first creative impulse of consciousness causes the pure body to rise. This newly born body is characterized by the unlimited power of Bhairava [a form of Shiva]. This body is really the supreme form (*para murti*) of the Lord [...]." [175]
>
> ~ H. N. CHAKRAVARTY, TANTRASARA, INTRODUCTION

The waves may be referring to the sensations of vibrations or an electrical current going through the body often felt during the astral split. However, projecting in one's astral body seems to have been misunderstood as creating a new nonphysical body each time, as it was in the Yoga Vasistha. A similar belief is held in Tibetan Buddhism and Bon, where the astral body is viewed as an illusory body created by the mind at each projection. We discuss Tibetan Buddhism and Bon shortly, and how they share many similarities with Shaivite Tantra, which they seem to have largely derived from.

Despite the seeming mentions of lucid dreaming and astral projection in Shaivite texts, we have not come across any mention of them in modern Shaivism.

YOGA NIDRA

There is no known ancient tradition of having OBEs that has survived till today in India. The only thing that comes close is the practice of yoga nidra.

Yoga nidra is loosely based on passages in ancient Hindu texts that refer to dreamless sleep. The oldest of these are the Brihadaranyaka and Mandukya Upanishads, which say that when the mind finally tires and settles it enters dreamless sleep, where it's said to rest in the divine Self. Rather than being a sort of "black out" in our existence, dreamless sleep is regarded as one of the highest states someone can experience while alive. This is based on the observation that during dreamless sleep there are no sensory impressions (or at least, no recollection of them). Nothing seems to exist—there is not the sense of any separate observer or object, not even one's own body or mind. Without these, it's believed there can be no sense of individuality, and thus no desires that arise from it, nor the suffering that desire gives rise to; all that can be said to exist (or so it's reasoned) is the Self. Essentially, the belief is that everything other than the Self is illusion, which includes the entire sensory world; only the Self really exists. Therefore, dreamless sleep is believed to be a blissful experience of complete union with the Self, where all is one.[176] The Brihadaranyaka explains it as follows:

> "As a man in the arms of his beloved is not aware of what is without and what is within, so a person in union with the Self is not aware of what is without and what is within, for in that unitive state [of dreamless sleep] all desires find their perfect fulfillment. [...] In that unitive state there is neither father nor mother, neither worlds nor gods nor even scriptures. [...] In that unitive state ones sees without seeing, for there is nothing separate from him."[177]
> ~ BRIHADARANYAKA UPANISHAD

However, this belief is contradicted in the Chandogya Upanishad, in which the ancient Vedic god Indra says:

> "[...] in the state of dreamless sleep one is not aware of oneself or of any other. The state of dreamless sleep is very close to extinction. In this knowledge I see no value."[178]
> ~ CHANDOGYA UPANISHAD

Indra then passes beyond the identification of the Self with dreamless sleep, to discover the Self's reality. It seems there were conflicting ideas about dreamless sleep being debated at the time the Upanishads were created, and today findings from studies on sleep are also contradicting some of these Hindu ideas about dreamless sleep, as does having OBEs, as I'll discuss in a moment.

Ancient Hindu texts refer to the state of consciousness in deep, dreamless sleep as prajna and yoga nidra, and say that it's possible to be conscious during it.

> "[In the third state of consciousness of deep sleep, Prajna,] one neither dreams nor desires. There is no mind in Prajna, there is no separateness; but the sleeper is not conscious of this. Let him become conscious in Prajna and it will open the door to the state of abiding joy."[179]
> ~ MANDUKYA UPANISHAD

> "[The ocean] becomes the bed of the lotus-naveled Vishnu when at the termination of every Yuga that deity of immeasurable power enjoys yoga-nidra, the deep sleep under the spell of spiritual meditation."[180]
> ~ THE MAHABHARATA

The god Vishnu while in yoga nidra.

Today, there is a practice called yoga nidra, which is used in an attempt to experience the state of the same name described in ancient texts, though was only created in the 1970s and is largely based on modern techniques of relaxation, as there are no surviving ancient descriptions of how to experience the state of yoga nidra (or prajna). However, the use of the term yoga nidra is quite misleading, as it doesn't lead to becoming conscious within dreamless sleep. Instead, it's directed at consciously experiencing the state between waking and sleeping, without actually falling asleep. It involves relaxing the body as much as possible, while remaining awake, typically by methodically relaxing each body part in a guided meditation.[181] One single-observation study of a yogi found he produced delta brain waves, which characterize deep sleep, while in a practice of yoga nidra, so perhaps some understanding of this was the basis behind the concept of yoga nidra. However, the yogi was not actually asleep.[182]

The famous Hindu ascetic Ramana Maharshi (1879 - 1950) advocated for consciously experiencing the state of dreamless sleep, which he called *jagrat-sushupti*, but stressed it could only be done while awake:

> "Effort is required and it is possible in the waking state only. There is the effort here: there is awareness also; the thoughts are stilled; so there is the peace of sleep gained. [...] It is neither sleep nor waking but intermediate between the two. There is the awareness of the waking state and the stillness of sleep. [...] It is the state of perfect awareness and of perfect stillness combined. It lies between sleep and waking [...]."[183]

This state between waking and sleep is described in the Mahabharata as a way to see how our thoughts turn into dreams as we fall asleep, and likewise how our dreams become our thoughts again as we wake up. This is possible to experience by remaining conscious during the transition stage of going into and returning from the astral plane.

> "The passage of our notions as they exist during wakefulness into those of dreams, and that of notions as they exist in dreams into those of wakefulness, become directly apprehensible in that state of consciousness which is called dreamless slumber. That is eternal, and that is desirable."[184]
> ~ THE MAHABHARATA

However, while this is happening, someone is still not fully asleep. So it's apparent that yoga nidra isn't a practice to experience dreamless sleep, but the transition between wakefulness and sleep in which someone is still awake. It's a method to remain conscious while the perception of bodily senses and external stimuli can start to diminish, as one is entering the state of sleep and so is beginning to detach from the physical body and world as they enter the astral plane. This is a very pleasant, relaxing, and spiritual experience for most, as it is to rest in a state of conscious awareness, but yoga nidra isn't a method for experiencing union with one's higher Self/Being, or with the Source. If this were truly a profound experience of being one with the Self, it would be a very mild one. It's possible to experience and attain far more on the path of the Spiritual Sun.

It's possible to have a temporary experience of unity with the Source while out of the body, but that's a different kind of OBE and takes place in a higher dimension, which I explain later in this chapter. To permanently reunite with one's Being requires a lengthy spiritual work, which I write about in other books.

Some of the more mystical experiences people have had during yoga nidra that we've read sound like they fell asleep and had an OBE, though it could also be their imagination—for example, they looked down upon their body sleeping, or traveled to a distant place.[185] [186] Because it's training oneself to remain aware while going into sleep, it can also increase the ability to lucid dream, as some have experienced.[187] The practice of yoga nidra may be quite an effective way to have OBEs if it were modified to allow sleep, and there are people who are doing this.[188]

We are out of the body in the astral plane during all stages of sleep—whether deep, light, "dreamless," or dream-filled. This is increasingly being borne out by scientific studies on sleep. Studies have shown that people can become conscious within and have a lucid dream during both the REM and NREM (which was previously believed to be dreamless) stages of sleep—specifically the first and second stages of NREM sleep, with no lucid dreams confirmed so far in the third and fourth stages of NREM, which are the stages of deepest sleep.[189] But studies have also shown that we do sometimes dream during deep NREM sleep,[190][191] as well as experience other states of consciousness in which one can hear sounds from their environment, or think without imagery for example,[192] and so scientists now realize that NREM and deep sleep are not always dreamless—they could just be more so than REM sleep, or we could simply be able to remember dreams better when they occur in REM sleep. Those who became lucid during NREM sleep had a typical OBE, and did not report anything unusually profound. Again, this is because we are in the astral plane at all stages of sleep, and so if we become conscious during any stage of sleep, including during deep (NREM) sleep, we will simply have an OBE in the astral plane.

It's not really possible to be conscious and remain in dreamless sleep, and so yoga nidra or prajna as it's defined in Hindu texts is paradoxical, which explains why there is no technique for truly experiencing it in Hinduism. Once someone is conscious out of their physical body, they become aware of sensory impressions, which are of the astral environment around them, whatever that happens to be at the time. If one is fully conscious out of the body, these impressions are not being generated by the subconscious, and are therefore not dreams, so it is dreamless. But that is not what ancient Hindu texts meant—they were referring to a state in which someone is conscious while asleep, but without receiving any sensory impressions.

The closest state to this that I know of is what I call "astral blindness," which is when someone out of their body cannot hear, smell, touch, or taste anything, and can only see blackness everywhere. This can happen when someone becomes lucid in a dream—immediately the dream can disappear and it's as though they're in a void of blackness. I believe this is due to an incomplete connection between the astral and physical bodies, causing the senses of the astral body to cut out. It can be possible to get out of this and see, but the blackness usually causes one to return to the physical body. This is the closest experience that would technically fit the description of yoga nidra, but of course it's not a blissful one, being instead confusing and disorienting.

Based on my experience and the evidence, I'm in agreement with Indra (as he is quoted in the Chandogya Upanishad) on this one. It seems being conscious during the state of deep sleep became synonymous with being united with one's highest Self in some Hindu philosophies, because basic consciousness was identified as the highest part of one's Being and dreamless sleep was seen as a state in which everything is absent except one's Self/consciousness. However, I explain in other books that the consciousness we ordinarily have is not the highest part of one's Being—there are other much higher parts of consciousness, which exist in higher realms than the astral plane. An experience of unity with the Self does not mean we have to lose all our perceptions—instead, as we reunite with the higher parts of our Being, our inner self becomes transformed so that we feel more of the spiritual in creation and have a greater perception of its infinite beauty and wisdom.

THE OLDEST UNDERSTANDING OF OBES IN HINDUISM

It seems there is an older understanding of OBEs that has been preserved in some Hindu texts. The out-of-body journey that Arjuna and Krishna undertake in the Mahabharata may date back to a very ancient time based on its descriptions of what sounds like advanced technology and given that they are described as having the ability to travel to heaven in an OBE. The Yoga Vasistha, which contains the OBE of Saraswati and Lila, is said to have been composed by one of the seven founding sages of Hinduism, who is likely to have been one of the wisdom bringers that founded the Religion of the Sun after the global flood of around 9,700 BC.[193] These two sources clearly describe having OBEs purposefully. Although their oldest surviving copies appear quite late, they are likely to have been taken from earlier copies of texts now lost, which were based on even older oral traditions. Then what seems to have happened, possibly thousands of years later, is that very different ideas about sleep were developed or at least first recorded around the time of the oldest Upanishads, and these influenced Shaivism, and gave rise to the practice of yoga nidra. These ideas became widely popular in the public, and eclipsed the older, secret tradition of having OBEs in Hinduism, so that today no tradition of having OBEs has survived in India.

ANCIENT SITES AND OTHER DIMENSIONS

Before moving on to other accounts of OBEs, in this section we'll focus on ancient sites. This is because sacred sites in the Religion of the Sun, although fulfilling several functions, could be used for having OBEs, as we've already seen in Egypt. So here we'll explore the beliefs that explain why. This background is useful to have, because in the remainder of the chapter, we look at sacred sites in different places, and the evidence that indicates they were also used for having OBEs.

THE PURPOSE AND USE OF SACRED SITES IN THE ANCIENT RELIGION OF THE SUN

After researching sacred sites for more than a decade, we've come to realize that many sites of the ancient Religion of the Sun were built to symbolize the path of the Spiritual Sun (aka the path to enlightenment) and had been originally intended to facilitate the journey upon it. Much of this journey actually occurs in, or is connected to other dimensions, and so ancient sites were built to represent these other realms and the path of the Spiritual Sun that leads through them.

As I explain in my book *Ancient Solstice*, the path of the Spiritual Sun leads one through hell and heaven within themselves, to ultimately return to their higher Being and the Source/the Spiritual Sun, just as the sun appears to journey through the darkness of winter to ascend back to greatest light at summer. Because of this, sites in the ancient Religion of the Sun were often designed to represent both the higher and lower realms, and the path leading through them to the Source/Spiritual Sun—usually being aligned to the celestial body or region where the Source was believed to be located, such as the northern circumpolar stars, or the sun.

This same essential pattern of traveling a path leading to heaven, sometimes into the presence of the Source, is one of the most common experiences in NDEs; instead of a path, it's a tunnel seen as leading up into and through the stars to heaven, where the light of the Source shines like the sun, though many times brighter. And so the path of the Spiritual Sun, and the journey to heaven in the afterlife, came to share much of the same symbolism as they are both based on the structure of nonphysical realms and an ascent to heaven. Both can be seen as symbolized by ancient sites of the Religion of the Sun.

By building ancient sites to replicate the structure and layout of other realms, as a kind of mini replica of them, they expressed the main cosmological beliefs of the builders. They could then serve as a form of religious teaching about these realms and about the path of the Spiritual Sun, their different areas could serve as places of initiation and instruction, and they could be used to facilitate OBEs to other realms.

These ancient sites were then often repurposed or copied by kings who sought to ensure their passage to heaven after death by being buried within them. Common people, who didn't have this privilege, were instead usually buried outside in their surrounds with the same aim. These sites could also be used by initiates who sought to travel to heaven during OBEs while alive. And so ancient sites in the Religion of the Sun could serve those who sought to ascend to heaven in their quest for enlightenment, those who sought to reach heaven after death, and those who sought to visit heaven and return during life. In all cases, they were seen as access points or portals to heaven, which is how they were often remembered in ancient texts and accounts, as we saw in Egypt and will see in many other parts of the world.

They are incredible representations of the structure of the different realms of creation and of the path to heaven and the Source, and were built to serve practical spiritual purposes, which in the case of the Great Pyramid, may have even involved some form of technology. We'll now explore how they symbolized other realms.

THE COSMIC AXIS AND WORLD MOUNTAIN

As we'll explain further in chapter 8, people in the many traditions that derived from the ancient Religion of the Sun saw the cosmos as divided into three main realms: our earthly realm, below which is a nonphysical underworld/hell (often associated with water), and above which is a nonphysical heavenly realm (associated with the sky, stars, and sun). These three realms were seen as being connected by what has been referred to as a cosmic axis, which came to be called an axis mundi in twentieth century comparative mythology.[194] Hell was commonly seen as having nine regions, and heaven likewise. Above them all, at the summit of heaven and atop the cosmic axis, was the Source of all creation (the Spiritual Sun), symbolized by the sun. Because the cosmic axis connected these realms together, it was seen as the place where one could travel to them.

Earth, heaven, and hell, were symbolized by a mound or mountain—with its foundation said to stretch down into the underworld, and its summit to reach up to heaven. At its summit was the Source/Spiritual Sun. This mound/mountain is generally referred to as the world/cosmic mountain, and in Egypt as the primordial mound. The cosmic axis was said to run through the center of it, standing at the very center or navel of the world and of creation itself.

This structure was seen as operating at a number of levels. At a planetary level, the primordial mound and mountain was synonymous with Earth itself, and the cosmic axis with the axis it rotates upon. This axis was seen as stretching into nonphysical realms—down into hell one way and up into heaven the other—through the portals and tunnels that lead to them from the astral plane, which people commonly travel through in NDEs.

On a microcosmic level the world mountain was synonymous with the human physical body and the cosmic axis with the spine. This was seen as an as expression of the ancient axiom "as above, so below"—the human body being a microcosm of the universe. Heaven and hell then were not just connected to our earthly realm, they were believed to be connected to the physical body.

In the ancient Religion of the Sun, sites typically included a representation of the world mountain and/or cosmic axis. The world mountain could be symbolized by a pyramid, mound, henge, or temple, and the cosmic axis by a staircase, tower, passageway, avenue, tree, obelisk, or pole (such as the European maypole). The cosmic axis ran through or into the center of a site—at one end in the depths of the earth/underworld/hell (often terminating in an inner chamber), and the other directed toward the heavens and Source (often being aligned to the northern circumpolar stars or the sun at a solstice or equinox).

These ancient sites were often said to be the center or navel of the world, where creation first emerged. Of course, this couldn't literally be true of every ancient site that was built to symbolize the cosmic axis; instead, they were intended to recreate the structure of the cosmos that emerged at the beginning of creation wherever or whenever they were made.

What these sites reveal is that their ancient designers understood how unique this physical world (along with its etheric component, the astral plane) is. It's only here that all three realms converge, and not just in time and space, but also within us.

Left: An illustration of the world tree from Norse tradition, which acts as the cosmic axis that connects the physical and eight nonphysical worlds of its cosmology together.
Right: European maypole, which is made from a tree, and is a symbol of the cosmic axis.

CREATION AND THE PRIMORDIAL MOUND

The beliefs that underlie the concept of the world mountain and cosmic axis can be found in perhaps the oldest and most prevalent creation myth of ancient Egypt, which says that at the beginning of creation the Spiritual Sun rose from within the inert primeval waters of the cosmos (called *nun*), and by its radiance caused a mound of earth (the primordial mound, called *benben*) to emerge from the watery abyss. This mound could be shaped like a pyramid or round-topped (which is important to remember when we come to the rounded mounds of Europe). However, one of the most common ways Lara has seen it portrayed is divided in half with the sun in the middle. These two halves are referred to as mountains, and likely represented the duality of creation. The Spiritual Sun (as the sun and supreme creator god Atum or Ra) was then said to have seated itself on a lotus throne at the center of this land, or to have emerged from within a lotus at its center.[195][196][197]

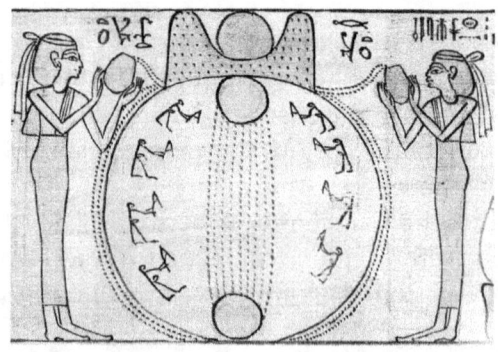

An Egyptian depiction of the mound arising from the waters at the beginning of creation. The waters are poured by two goddesses, linking them to the waters of the womb. The primordial mound is at the top center of the image, where it is portrayed as a lump of earth divided in two with the sun rising between its halves.

Left: Symbol of Aker containing the depiction of the primordial mound with the sun rising/setting upon it, which is held on the backs of two guardian lions. Center: Symbol of the primordial mound made by the two largest Great Pyramids as the sun sets on the summer solstice. Right: A temple design that was frequently used in ancient Egypt, which depicts the primordial mound as the two walls either side of the entrance, which has a symbol of the sun carved above it.

In traditions of the ancient Religion of the Sun, the vastness of the cosmos was sometimes likened to an endless ocean, and so the myths could be said to be describing the emergence of planet Earth from the dark void of space, like an island of dry land from the depths of the sea. However, it's likely that the primordial mound was symbolic of a principle underlying creation itself—representing matter taking shape out of the vast sea of cosmic energy, which occurs not only with the birth of a planet, but also a human being.

A similar creation story is found in Hinduism, in which the god Narayana/Vishnu (who encompasses all the Vedic sun gods[198]) lay asleep on the serpent Ananta (meaning "endless") on the infinite cosmic ocean. When he awoke, a lotus flower grew from his navel, and its petals opened to reveal the god Brahma who emerged to make creation.[199] And so while in Egypt there was a mound that had a lotus at its center, in India the lotus emerged from the navel of the supreme god; both the center of the mound and the navel of the body were symbols of the center of the world where the cosmic axis was located.

Left: The Spiritual Sun/Son in Egypt as Horus seated on a lotus. Right: Brahma seated on the lotus that has emered from Vishnu's navel, who is afloat on the cosmic ocean.

This very ancient understanding of creation underpins all the sites that were built to symbolize the world mountain and cosmic axis.

ANCIENT EGYPT

All Egyptian pyramids are thought to represent the primordial mound of ancient Egyptian religion,[200] which is synonymous with the world mountain and Earth—something the Great Pyramid expresses in its dimensions, as noted earlier, as it encodes the earth's weight, equatorial longitude, circumference, radius, and even rate of rotation. The Great Pyramid was built at the center of Earth's landmass, thereby expressing the principle of standing at the very center, or navel, of the world.

Additionally, the Great Pyramid incorporates measurements to do with the earth's relationship to the sun in its dimensions, which symbolically position the sun at its peak. The pyramidion/capstone at a pyramid's peak is said to represent where the rays of the sun first fell at the beginning of creation,[201] and the pyramid shape is believed to represent the rays of the sun descending from its apex.[202] In ancient Egyptian creation myth, the Spiritual Sun was said to sit upon his lotus throne at the center of the primordial mound, and so it's likely that the peak of the pyramid (where its pyramidion/capstone was placed) represented the throne of the Spiritual Sun.

Top left: Pyramidion with the Spiritual Sun illustrated on it; the bird represents the Ba (the spirit) of Ra (the sun god).[203] The Spiritual Sun was illustrated on pyramidions as this is what they were meant to represent. Notice the bird is perched on the symbol of the primordial mound. Top right: Obelisk from Egypt, which is yet another symbol of the cosmic axis. Similarly to pyramids, they were capped with a golden (specifically electrum) pyramidion that represented the *benben*/primordial mound. It was designed to reflect the sun's light, thus creating the appearance of the sun taking its seat upon the mound at dawn each day as at the beginning of creation; obelisks were usually carved with hieroglyphs dedicated to the Spiritual Sun.[204 205] Bottom: The sun at the peak of the Great Pyramid.

It seems the cosmic axis could extend vertically through the center of the site, through the peak of the pyramid for example, or this axis may have been seen as the site's central tunnel or avenue, or both. At the Great Pyramid for example, the descending passage runs directly down into a cave beneath the pyramid that appears to have symbolized hell, and at its other end points toward the northern celestial pole, the location of heaven. It inclines at just over 26 degrees, being the acute angle in a right triangle formed on the basis of the golden section, used prolifically in Egyptian art and architecture,[206] [207] but it's also close to the tilt of the earth's axis at 23.4 degrees. Egyptian kings were sometimes depicted in artwork as being titled at an angle while resurrecting/traveling to heaven—along the cosmic axis—with their feet said to be in hell within the earth, and their hands in heaven.[208]

Depictions of Osiris (or the king) resurrecting at an angle, as in this image, were seen in ancient Egypt as connected to the slope of the sun's rays reaching the earth, but may also have been seen as connected to the tilt of the earth's axis at some earlier time before the knowledge of this connection was lost. The slope of the triangle symbolically represented Horus, (its base Isis, and vertical side Osiris), and so Osiris here is becoming "Horus of the Horizon." The triangle beneath him is filled with sand, in an allusion to the sands around the Great Pyramid.[209] The angle is similar to that of the descending passage inside the Great Pyramid, and illustrates what it was believed to represent—ascension from hell to heaven, along the path of the sun.

Not only pyramids, but temples in Egypt were also often built to have the same symbolic structure as the cosmic axis. Some were positioned along the Nile River so that its water would enter them and recreate the scene of the primordial mound arising from the waters at first creation. Some also had shrines on their roofs and crypts beneath them, likely symbolizing heaven and hell respectively.[210]

The so-called "relieving chambers" above the King's Chamber resemble the ancient Egyptian symbol the *djed* pillar, which represented Osiris' spine. In the story of the life of Osiris, the *djed* was made of a tree that enclosed the body of Osiris, and became the pillar of a temple,[211] associating his body and spine with a tree, which was a common symbol of the cosmic axis. That Osiris became a pillar of a temple indicates his body acted as the support that held it up, and some believe the relieving chambers in the Great Pyramid act as an architectural support. In the Pyramid Texts, the pyramid itself is said to be Osiris, and so it seems the Great Pyramid symbolized the physical body on some level (particularly the body of Osiris), which secretly enclosed the symbol of the spine as its relieving chambers, and that these were symbols of the cosmic axis.

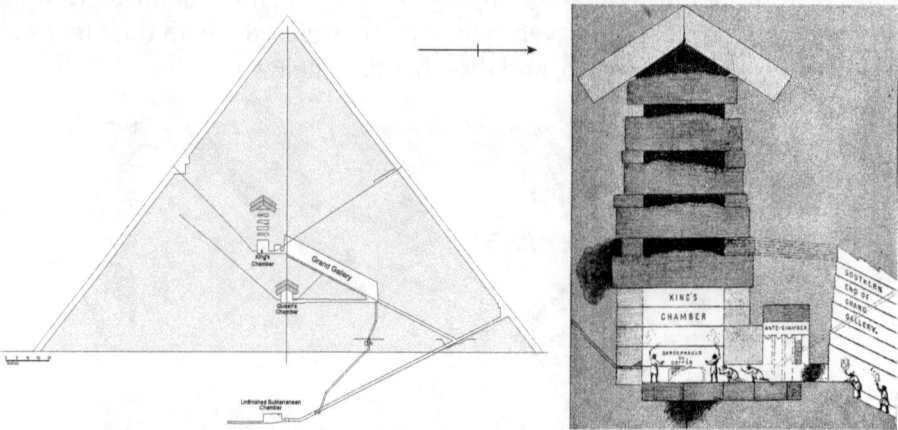

Left: Diagram showing the Great Pyramid's interior layout and the subterranean chamber beneath it, which possibly symbolized the entrance to hell. The passage from this chamber inclines at just over 26 degrees and exits the pyramid, pointing toward the north celestial pole, seen as the location of heaven. It may have represented the earth's axis and the cosmic axis, which was seen as connecting all the diferent realms to each other. Right: Cross section drawing of the King's Chamber of the Great Pyramid showing the relieving chambers above it.

Left: Osiris portrayed as the *djed* pillar, which represented his spine and resembles the design of the relieving chambers. Right: The king performing the raising of the *djed* ceremony, which symbolized the resurrection of Osiris. The angle it's held at (approximately 21.5 degrees) may have distantly been connected to the tilt of the earth's axis.

The ancient stela that still stands between the paws of the Great Sphinx describes the site of the Great Pyramids as "the Splendid Place of the First Time."[212] This first time was called Zep Tepi; it was when creation began with the arising of the primordial mound, and the gods (the Children of the Sun) first incarnated on Earth. Although this could be taken literally, it's more likely the Great Pyramids and Sphinx were built as a symbolic recreation of this event, and became one site of many that represented it across the world—though probably being the oldest surviving.

We believe that the Great Pyramids and Sphinx are the most ancient representation of the cosmos with its different portals and realms, and thus the oldest place the symbols of the world mountain and cosmic axis are found. These beliefs spread with the dissemination of the ancient Religion of the Sun, and became the template for ancient sites across the world—built as pyramids, mounds, stone circles, earthworks, henges, temples, etc. For example, pyramids can be found in Sicily, Sardinia, Russia, China, Cambodia, Indonesia, the Maldives, the Canary Islands, the Azores, Mauritius, Central America, South America, and some of the Pacific Islands. The fact that many of these sites developed so differently, yet according to the same principles, indicates the knowledge they were based on must have first spread among different peoples a very long time ago. We'll now take a look at some of these ancient sites to discover more about them and just how prevalent these ideas were.

Pyramids were not just built in Egypt—they were built in many parts of the world. They symbolize the primordial mound/world mountain.

SUMER

In Mesopotamia, a style of pyramid was built by the Sumerians called ziggurats. The oldest religious text in the world, the Kesh Temple Hymn, describes one of these ziggurats. The text was found in Iraq, is written in Sumerian, and has been dated to 2600 BC.[213] It states that the temple (ziggurat) reaches into heaven and also descends into the underworld, and was laid out according to the structure of heaven and earth. It's said to belong to the Anunnaki (Anuna gods), which is one of the names given to the ancient race that founded the Religion of the Sun that we refer to as the Children of the Sun.[214]

> "[...] house, rainbow reaching to the heavens! House whose platform extends into the midst of the heavens, whose foundations are fixed in the *abzu* [the primeval sea beneath the underworld that was the source of all creation[215]] [...] at its upper end rising like the sun, at its lower end spreading like the moonlight [...]. House of the Anuna gods possessing great power, which gives wisdom to the people [...] reposeful dwelling of the great gods! [...] which was planned together with the plans of heaven and earth, ... with the pure divine powers [...]."[216]
>
> ~ KESH TEMPLE HYMN

Model of a Sumerian ziggurat, which looks like a stepped pyramid and mountain.

Here we have the image of a great mountain that rises from the primeval watery abyss up through Earth into heaven, forming a connection between them, clearly representing the world mountain, and primordial mound, just as pyramids in Egypt did.

In the second oldest religious text in the world, the Epic of Gilgamesh, which is also Sumerian, the main character Gilgamesh travels through a pair of sacred mountains (the mountains of Mashu) to reach heaven. Just like the Kesh temple, the mountains of Mashu are described as reaching up into heaven and down into the netherworld.

> "To Mashu's twin mountains he came,
> which daily guard the rising sun,
> whose tops support the fabric of heaven,
> whose base reaches down to the Netherworld. [...]
> For twelve double-hours its interior extends,
> the darkness is dense, and light is there none. [...]
> Gilgamesh [...] took the path of the Sun God [through the gate of the mountains]."[217]
> ~ THE EPIC OF GILGAMESH

Lara realized that the twin mountains of Mashu that guard the rising sun sound like the two largest Great Pyramids of Egypt, which appear similar in size. They symbolically form the twin mountains in the Egyptian hieroglyph for horizon, and are where the Great Sphinx, which faces due east (and thus sunrise on the equinoxes), "guards" the daily rising of the sun.

As in Egyptian texts, Gilgamesh enters a gate to travel the path of the sun god to heaven, and his journey follows the same structure as that of the Egyptian sun god (and initiate). The "twelve double-hours" refer to a day of twenty-four hours divided into two equal twelve-hour parts, which occurs only at the equinoxes. In the Egyptian text Amduat, like Gilgamesh, the initiate as Ra travels through the Duat over the course of the twelve hours of the night (in darkness) to reach heaven and the realm of the gods. We believe the journey of Gilgamesh is likely an ancient reference to the Great Pyramids being a place that symbolized the path of the Spiritual Sun to heaven, and as having been used for OBEs to heaven. That would make the Epic of Gilgamesh one of the oldest references to the Great Pyramids in the world.

TIBET

The pre-Buddhist Bon religion of Tibet also describes a pyramid which is connected to the other realms. At the very center of their most ancient sacred land, Olmo Lungring (also known as Shambhala), there is a mountain in the form of a pyramid with nine levels (the "Pyramid of Nine Swastikas"). As in the Epic of Gilgamesh, we again see mountains and pyramids conflated. The nine levels of the pyramid represent the nine realms of heaven that ascend into the sky, and the nine regions of the netherworld that descend beneath the earth. This pyramid is said to be the place where the three planes of existence—the heavens, the earth, and the nether regions—meet. It's believed that "From the mountain the adept may travel freely, ascending upward or descending downward to other worlds and dimensions," as stated by a practitioner and one of the foremost Western scholars of Tibetan Buddhism and Bon, John Myrdhin Reynolds (aka Vajranatha).

While there is a physical region that corresponds to Olmo Lungring, it's also believed a metaphysical version of it exists in a more spiritual dimension as the celestial archetype of what appears in the physical world.[218] This is a similar idea to what the Egyptians believed about the Great Pyramids, in that they were meant to be a copy of what was in the celestial Duat,[219] and as we've read in the Kesh Temple Hymn, what the Sumerians believed about ziggurats, which were made according to "the plans of heaven and earth." What they all essentially state is that they were built to represent some of the layout and features of other dimensions.

Illustration of Olmo Lungring with the pyramid of nine levels as its center at the Yung Drung Kundrak Ling Bon Monastery in Sikkim, in northeast India.

In Bon tradition, Olmo Lungring is the most ancient, sacred place on Earth.

> "Olmo Lungring or Shambhala, this imperishable sacred land, which is the spiritual center of the world, existed on earth from the very beginning of the human race. It was the place where the celestial gods of the Clear Light (`od gsal lha) descended from heaven to earth in order to take up incarnation as human beings and ensoul the physical bodies which had been prepared for them. Since that time of the beginning, Olmo Lungring has been the sanctuary of wisdom and the receptacle of the highest mystical teachings being

brought down from above. All of the inhabitants of that land have entered upon the path to enlightenment, and for this reason it is said to be the land of the Vidyadharas beyond the Himalayas, spoken of in the Puranas and other ancient books of India."[220]

~ JOHN MYRDHIN REYNOLDS, OLMO LUNGRING: THE IMPERISHABLE SACRED LAND

This belief is very similar to what the ancient Egyptians believed about the Great Pyramids as being the first dwelling place of the gods during Zep Tepi, "the first time." Olmo Lungring is said to have been inhabited by an ancient race of celestial origin who eventually mated with humans and disappeared.[221] [222] We believe this is yet another reference to those we call the Children of the Sun—an ancient, giant, long-lived, more spiritually perceptive race of extraterrestrial origin that founded the Religion of the Sun on Earth untold ages ago, spoken of in numerous traditions, like in Sumer as the Anunnaki, and as the gods who took human form in the first age of time, Zep Tepi, in Egypt.[223] They are also likely the Vidyadharas mentioned in the previous quote, who were a group of demi-gods in ancient Hindu texts that had supernatural powers and whose name means "wisdom holder" in Sanskrit.[224] As is evident at other sites of the Religion of the Sun, the primary focus of the inhabitants of Olmo Lungring had been the path to enlightenment, and no doubt their pyramid had symbolized the ascent upon it.

In Buddhism, the sacred geography of Shambhala was interpreted as the literal layout of planet Earth. However, its layout was symbolic, and was likely to have been based on the accounts of a very ancient site of the Children of the Sun that represented the cosmos with the world mountain/pyramid at its center.

MOUNT KAILASH

The Pyramid of Nine Swastikas has been identified by many scholars as Mount Kailash in western Tibet. There are numerous connections between them; as one example, the pyramid of Bon tradition was called a crystal monolith,[225] and the name Kailash may derive from the Sanskrit word for crystal.[226] Stone with a high component of crystal was used in the King's Chamber of the Great Pyramid, and so the crystal some pyramids were associated with may have played a part in how they functioned.

Mount Kailash is considered sacred by about one-fifth of the world's population, as it's a holy site in Hinduism, Buddhism, Jainism, and Bon. It's considered a gateway to heaven. Hindus believe it's the abode of the god Shiva, known as the "Lord of Yoga," where he is attended by the Vidyadharas. Jains believe it's where Rishabhanatha, the first enlightened being, attained liberation.[227] (Lara writes how Rishabhanatha, Shiva, and the Norse god Odin, may have been based on the same person in *The Ancient Religion of the Sun*.[228])

In the Hindu epic the Ramayana, Mount Kailash is referred to as a pyramid, and in the Vedas as a cosmic axis[229]—a position it continued to hold later in the Hindu story of the Churning of the Milky Ocean where its equivalent Mount Meru was used as the axis to rotate the cosmos.[230]

The south face of Mount Kailash has a large fissure running down it that is stepped and filled with snow, making it appear just like a spine as many have noticed. In the practice of yoga, the spine is called *meru danda—meru* referring to Mount Meru as the axis of the world, and *danda* meaning staff.[231] As with the Great Pyramid, in India we find an association between the cosmic axis and spine.

The south face of Mount Kailash with a fissure running straight down from its peak that looks like a spine.

> "How long have people been coming to this sacred mountain [Mount Kailash]? The answers are lost in antiquity, before the dawn of Hinduism, Jainism or Buddhism. The cosmologies and origin myths of each of these religions speak of Kailash as the mythical Mt. Meru, the Axis Mundi, the center and birth place of the entire world. [...] Indeed, Kailash is so deeply embedded in the myths of ancient Asia that it was perhaps a sacred place of another era, another civilization, now long gone and forgotten."[232]
>
> ~ MARTIN GRAY, SACREDSITES.COM

It's possible that Mount Kailash was a sacred site of the Children of the Sun from a very distant time, or perhaps was identified as one due to its pyramidal shape and spine-like fissure.

HINDUISM AND MOUNT MERU

Mount Kailash has been identified by some as being the physical location of the legendary Mount Meru, the most important mountain in the Hindu, Buddhist, and Jain traditions. Mount Meru is yet another version of the world mountain, as it's said to be the axis of the world that stands at the center of the universe. It's said to reach down beneath the ground into the nether regions and extend into heaven,[233] just as the ziggurats of Mesopotamia.

It could be depicted as a pillar upon the back of a turtle, afloat in the cosmic ocean. As a number of researchers have noted, very similar ideas existed in the Americas, as Native North Americans saw Earth as an island carried upon the back of a turtle in the primeval waters (as discussed further on), and the Maya of Central America used the turtle to symbolize the earth afloat in the cosmos, from which the cosmic axis sprouted.[234] [235]

Hindu texts locate the heavenly end of Mount Meru at the north pole (where the devas/gods live), and its other at the south pole (where the asuras/demons live), identifying it as the earth's axis.[236] In the Hindu epic the Mahabharata, Draupadi and the Pandavas set off on their final journey together to reach heaven by attempting to climb Mount Meru.[237] The orientation of Mount Meru reveals that heaven was believed to be located in the northern circumpolar stars, and that it pointed toward it, just as the passageways of pyramids in Egypt did.

The accounts of Mount Kailash/Meru and of pyramids in Eastern traditions identify them as being places that represented the path to enlightenment where one ascended to heaven, just as pyramids in Egypt were.

Many Hindu and Buddhist temples were built to replicate Mount Meru, and thus were based on the same essential symbolism as pyramids and ziggurats. The Hindu temple Angkor Wat in Cambodia was even designed so that at the equinox the sun appears to rest momentarily at its peak that was built to symbolize Mount Meru; thus, just as in Egypt, the sun appears to take his throne atop the primordial mound. Mount Meru has even been depicted with a lotus at its peak,[238] the very throne of the sun in ancient Egypt.

The steep stairs leading up the four smaller temple peaks of Angkor Wat, surrounding its largest central peak, are said to represent the path to enlightenment—the steepness reflecting the difficulty of ascending the path to heaven.[239]

Left: Mount Meru being used as the axis to churn the cosmic ocean. Notice the sun god Vishnu seated upon a lotus as its peak. Center: Alignment of the rising sun at the equinox with the peak of Angkor Wat, which symbolized Mount Meru. It has four outer towers and a larger central tower, a quincunx motif that recurs at ancient sites as we'll see in a moment. Right: Illustration of Mount Meru upon a stepped-pyramidal platform with a lotus at its peak.

BUDDHISM

Buddhist stupas are said to represent the body of Buddha, the path to enlightenment, the sacred world mountain (Mount Meru), and the universe all at the same time.[240] Their mound is also said to symbolize the womb,[241] and some are pyramidal in shape. They were used as burial places for Buddhist saints, but in pre-Buddhist times had been used for rulers and other elites.[242] A common element of them is a wooden pole placed in their central channel, representing the tree of life.[243] Their central channel and spire also represent the cosmic axis and spine.[244] This same fusion of meanings is found at the Great Pyramid as it is within other symbols of the cosmic axis/mountain, and reveals how these things were seen as interconnected in the ancient Religion of the Sun. However, stupas developed much of their own unique symbolism specific to Buddhism. The pagodas of Buddhism and Taoism derived from stupas,[245] and are yet another version of the cosmic axis.

Left: A Buddhist stupa, which depicts the body of Buddha (his eyes are on each side, which look in the four directions). It incorporates a stepped pyramid, and round-topped mound—both symbols used to illustrate the primordial mound and cosmic axis in ancient Egypt. It's incredible how pyramids in Egypt could be considered the body of Osiris, and that stupas are considered the body of Buddha, revealing how these ancient beliefs were preserved and adapted.

Right: Pagoda in China built in 652 AD. This one has a tiered design, similar to ancient stepped pyramids.

CHINA

The legendary Mount Kunlun from the Taoist tradition of China is yet another version of the world mountain. It's said to extend from the subterranean Yellow Spring up to heaven in the northern circumpolar stars. It's the central pole of the earth, called the Pillar of Heaven, and its peak culminates at the northern pole star where the throne of the supreme deity (Taidi) is located. Mount Kunlun's center is said to be equivalent to the navel, and its peak the head of the body, clearly associating it with the human body. It's encircled by water, upon which it's believed not even a feather can float, and so only winged (flying) beings can reach it. It functioned as a ladder one could travel to heaven upon and become immortal.[246] [247]

In China as in Egypt, pyramids were built or later reused as tombs for some of its emperors, who believed they would become immortal gods in the afterlife.[248] They saw the northern circumpolar region of the stars as the celestial location of the imperial palace where they would continue to rule after death, and oriented their pyramids toward the cardinal points (as the Great Pyramids are) to direct themselves toward the circumpolar stars just like the king in the Egyptian Pyramid Texts.[249]

CENTRAL AMERICA

The concept of the cosmic axis was central to the beliefs of the ancient Maya of Mesoamerica. Scholars have identified a number of their sites as having been built as replicas of the Maya cosmos, which had the cosmic axis at its center. Like the Egyptians, the Maya built pyramids that represented the mountain said to have emerged from the primeval ocean at the beginning of creation (called the First-True-Mountain). These pyramid mountains were the location of the central cosmic axis, and were thus believed to be portals through which one could communicate with nonphysical realms. The temples at their summits were accessed by single steep stairways up the face of the pyramids, likely representing the difficult ascent upon the path to reach heaven at their symbolic peaks.

These beliefs managed to survive the Spanish conquest among the descendants of the ancient Maya, particularly those in rural areas. Today, modern Maya people lay out their ritual altars based on the same principles. They create a replica of the structure of the cosmos by marking out a square to represent the four cardinal directions of creation, and then establish the center or navel of creation in the middle. This pattern is known as a quincunx. At the center, they place a symbol of the Maya world/cosmic tree (as explained in the next section), which represents the cosmic axis. For the ritual this becomes the actual center of the cosmos, which is then said to open a portal that allows communication with the otherworld and the beings that inhabit it. Whatever the scale, whether an ancient pyramid city, or a small altar, the basic principles have been found to be the same, showing how these Maya beliefs have been passed down for thousands of years until today.[250]

Evidence for these beliefs is found among what is considered the oldest civilization of Central America, the Olmec, which preceded the Maya. At their city of La Venta in Mexico they built a pyramid, which scholars believe represented a sacred mountain that was considered a portal to the otherworld. Adjacent to it was a sunken court that acted as the primeval ocean, and nearby were carvings depicting the world tree along with rulers communicating with beings of the otherworld. These beliefs are again later evident at one of the earliest Maya sites, Waxaktun in Guatemala, where the "First-True-Mountain" of the world was built as a pyramid rising out of the primeval waters of creation, represented by its adjacent sunken plaza decorated with carvings of fish. Similar pyramidal mountains of creation that embodied the cosmic axis were built at some of the most well-known Maya sites—at Palenque, Copan, and Chichen Itza.[251]

These Maya beliefs reveal one of the reasons why pyramids were chosen to represent the structure of creation—it's because they create a quincunx. Their four sides form a square, which represents the physical world delineated by its four directions, and at their center is a peak, which is the location of the cosmic axis, rising into heaven.

Like the pyramid of Tibetan Bon tradition, some of the most important Maya pyramids in Central America were built with nine levels to symbolize the nine regions of the underworld.[252] The Temple of Inscriptions in Palenque, Mexico is one of them. It has nine terraces, as well as thirteen interior chambers which represented the thirteen levels of heaven in Maya tradition.[253] King Pakal was interred within it, just like the kings of Egypt and China were in their pyramids. In his tomb he is shown being reborn as a god to eternal life (after becoming one with the Maize God, the equivalent of Osiris) before being transported along the sacred world tree (symbol of the cosmic axis and Milky Way[254]) to the realm of the gods in the sky.[255] It's clear that the kings of Mexico, like those of China and Egypt, believed the structure of a pyramid would help facilitate their journey to the heavenly sky world.

The ancient pyramid of Kukulcán at Chichen Itza in Mexico, which is stepped, just like some pyramids in Egypt, and has nine levels said to symbolize the nine regions of the underworld. The heads of two feathered serpents are carved at the base either side of one of the staircases—the open mouths of snakes were used to represent the entrances to heaven and the underworld (as explained in chapter 5). At the top of the pyramid are three doorways, which may symbolize the entrance to the astral in the center, with the door to the left leading to the underworld and the door to the right to heaven. Scholars believe the pyramid was built to symbolize the First-True-Mountain (world mountain).[256] A similar temple design can be found in Asia.

Some Maya pyramids, as well as similarly designed stepped pyramids in Asia, have further features that indicate their intended connection to the otherworlds, and appear to be based on the same symbolism as Aker of Egypt. Sometimes Maya pyramids were topped by a building with three doors, which we believe represented the gateways to the different dimensions, with the central door symbolically leading to the astral plane; the door to the right, to heaven; and the door to the left, to the underworld/hell. At the base of the pyramid, either side of the staircase, there were sometimes a set of serpents guarding access to these gateways, corresponding to the guardian lions depicted in the symbol of Aker.[257] In Mexico, jaguars were also used as the equivalent of lions, and so the Maya made a version of "Aker" using jaguars, sculpting a double-fore-bodied jaguar throne,[258] which presumably the king would sit on as the risen/resurrected Son/sun.

Left: Double jaguar throne at the ancient Maya site of Uxmal. Right: Maya king seated on a double jaguar throne in place of the Spiritual Son/Sun, making the Aker symbol of ancient Egypt.

The Maya also used a symbol similar to the horizon hieroglyph found in Egypt, called "Split/Cleft-Mountain." As in Egypt, it depicts a mountain split in two equal halves, and from its cleft the Maize God, who represented the sun, rises as he resurrects. Among the Maya, it too was a symbol of the primordial mountain/mound (First-True-Mountain) that first emerged from the primeval ocean at the beginning of creation.[259]

An ancient city in Mexico with pyramids, Teotihuacan, encodes Maya cosmological beliefs and shares numerous similarities with the Great Pyramids of Egypt. For example, its three main pyramids likewise appear to be aligned to the belt stars of Orion, and its Pyramid of the Sun shares almost exactly the same base area as the Great Pyramid.[260] Beneath the Pyramid of the Sun is a cave-like chamber that was believed to be an entrance to the underworld; similarly, there is a cave-like chamber beneath the Great Pyramid, and it too was likely symbolic of the entrance to the underworld. Archaeologists working with the National Institute of Anthropology and History in Mexico City believe that Teotihuacan was designed as a landscape that symbolized the cosmos according to ancient local beliefs, intended to act as a replica of the universe and its three levels—the earth, heavens, and underworld. One of its pyramids, known as the Temple of the Feathered Serpent, is thought to symbolize the sacred mountain of creation that had emerged from the cosmic ocean at the beginning of time, and was the center of the world. The open space in front of the temple was even designed so that it flooded to represent these waters. This echoes the rising of the central primordial mound from the cosmic waters in Egypt's story of creation, and indicates that these pyramids in Mexico were also representations of the world mountain and primordial mound. It's thought that the ancient builders believed that from the Temple of the Feathered Serpent one could communicate with the different levels of the cosmos.[261]

THE WORLD TREE

In addition to a mountain, the cosmic axis could be symbolized by a tree. Many cultures, including the Maya, Germanic/Norse people, and ancient Egyptians symbolized it in this way.

The sacred world tree of the Maya, Wakah-Chan, was central to their beliefs. It was said to symbolize the universe—its roots reached down into the underworld, its trunk was the middle world of Earth, and its branches stretched up into heaven at the north celestial pole. The tree itself formed a route of communication between these realms.[262] It was the central axis of the earth and cosmos, though was also synonymous with the Milky Way when it appeared to arch through the sky in a north-south direction. It was illustrated with a bird in its branches known as Seven Macaw/Itzam-Yeh, which scholars have identified as represented by the Big Dipper in the northern circumpolar stars. The Maya world tree was also associated with the human body and spine. Because the world tree could be symbolized by the Milky Way, so too then the Milky Way was seen to represent the spine (as it did also in Egypt), with the head positioned in the north. The Maya Maize God was synonymous with the world tree and his body was often portrayed as one with it. The Maya world tree was usually depicted as having a cruciform cross shape, which was based on the Milky Way aligning north-south and crossed by the sun's path on the ecliptic (traveling east to west). After the Spanish conquest, the Maya identified the Christian cross with their world tree, their shape and some of the beliefs surrounding them already being similar.[263] [264]

The sacred world tree of the Norse, Yggdrasil, likewise stood at the center of creation, with its roots and branches stretching into the underworld and heavens, connecting all the nine worlds of Norse cosmology together—including the physical world—to the numerous nonphysical worlds or dimensions. It was a symbol of the cosmic axis,[265] as was the related sacred Irminsul pillar, made out a tree trunk and used by the ancient Germanic people. Both the Irminsul and Yggdrasil were associated with Odin, and the Irminsul was seen as the body of a Germanic god, likely that of Wodan/Odin.[266]

The sacred trees of the Maya and Germanic peoples were depicted in similar ways. They could both be illustrated with forked branches; at this fork a bird could be shown, perched atop the tree (just as a bird was said to perch atop the primordial mound in Egypt). The Yggdrasil could also symbolize the Milky Way (as did the world tree of the Maya), but with the constellation Cygnus as the bird in its branches.[267]

The symbol of the world tree and cosmic mountain can also be found in Northern and Central Asian traditions, where the world mountain is described as a four-sided pyramid, sometimes with numerous levels. At its center, which is also the center of the cosmos, stands the world tree with its branches reaching up into heaven to the North Star. It's said to connect the heavens, the earth, and underworld together.[268]

The cosmic tree could also symbolize the human body, with feet together and arms outstretched in the shape of a cross; one of the reasons a tree was used to symbolize the human body is because the nervous system looks like the roots and branches of a tree. As we've seen, the bodies of Osiris, possibly Odin, Buddha, and the Maya Maize God, were all synonymous with the world tree and cosmic axis.

Left: King Pakal being reborn to heaven at the base of the cosmic tree, which is cruciform in shape and has a bird perched at the top of it. Right: Illustration of the Maya cosmic tree with a bird perched at the fork in its branches.

The Yggdrasil (left) and Irminsul (center) trees of Germanic religion were portrayed/described in a very similar way to the Maya cosmic tree—with forked branches that a bird or the sun could be perched upon, just as in ancient Egypt. They symbolize the human body, with its nervous system (right) that looks like the branches and roots of a tree, with the spirit perched/enthroned in the head/brain.

The bird can symbolize the Spiritual Son/Sun (one's higher Being) or the soul/consciousness, perched in the head/brain. For instance, the Pyramid Texts describe the soul of the king as a falcon perched in his skull atop his body, which is likened to a tree that his soul takes flight from at death. This is likely the meaning behind the winged/feathered headdresses of numerous ancient traditions, which represents the bird of the Being and/or the soul/consciousness perched at the top of the body and spine. As the translator Susan Brind Morrow has pointed out, a falcon was chosen because of its circling flight pattern, representing the circling rotation of the stars around the north celestial pole where the projected axis of the earth was seen as terminating. So again we see the symbol of the cosmic axis was related to the human body.

The ancient Zoroastrian symbol of the Faravahar, which is thought to represent the *fravashi*—each one's spirit/higher Being that resides in the spiritual world. It's very similar to the winged sun disk of ancient Egypt, being derived from the same ancient symbol. It shows that the Being or soul of a person could be symbolized with the wings of a bird. This was then represented as being "perched" within the head in the symbol of the winged/feathered headdress below.

Left: The ancient Egyptian god Osiris wearing a headdress flanked by two large feathers, which he was often depicted as wearing. Center: Winged headdress of the Greek god Hermes/Mercury, who holds the winged caduceus in his right hand, which is another symbol of the spine and cosmic axis surmounted by wings. Right: Native American chief wearing a traditional feather headdress. The winged/feathered headdress was a symbol used in the ancient Religion of the Sun. It was likely worn by some of the wisdom bringers who spread the Religion of the Sun to different parts of the world, which could be why they were often remembered as "bird men."

EUROPE

We believe some of the ancient mounds of Europe were also symbols of the primordial mound—though round-topped rather than pyramidal. Glastonbury Tor in England is the most striking example; just as described in Egypt, the Tor/hill appears to rise from out of what was once a great floodplain representing the primeval waters, and at the winter solstice, the sun rises to crown its summit. Evidence indicates that some European stone circles and circular earthworks (henges) also represented the primordial mound, including Stonehenge. Their avenues and passages aligned to the sun appear to symbolize the cosmic axis and path of the Spiritual Sun. We discuss these sites in more detail further in the chapter.

Glastonbury Tor rising like the primordial mound from out of a sea of mist. The Tor used to be surrounded by water as the area around it had been a wetland, though the mist creates a similar visual effect.

NORTH AMERICA

Thousands of mounds and circular earthworks in North America were also built to symbolize the primordial mound/cosmic axis, as explored later in the chapter in the section on North America.

SUMMARY

These comparisons could go on, as the symbol of the cosmic axis can be found in numerous traditions. Each became a replica of the structure of the cosmos (and on a microcosmic level, the human body), which emerged at the beginning of creation, as well as the central point that connected its different realms together, and which could be used to access them. While local people may have believed some of these sites, like the Great Pyramids, were the first of their kind in the world, it's more likely they were based upon the first sacred site established by the Children of the Sun on Earth long ages ago, built time and again. How far back these kinds of ancient sites were first created, we will probably never know.

Over time, some appear to have been misunderstood as being for the dead only—believed to be a gateway they could use to transport their soul into heaven—which is why they were built as tombs for kings, or in some cases later used by kings as tombs. This occurred at least in Egypt, China, Europe, and North and Central America.

Model of a Chinese pyramid in one of its museums, which was used by a Chinese emperor as his tomb.

In Taoism it's said that immortals of the highest degree ascend with their physical bodies into the sky to join the sun, moon, and stars in the High Pure Realm at death, while those of secondary degree leave their bodies behind, and only their spirit ascends.[269] Like the ancient Egyptians, Taoists saw the northern circumpolar stars as the location of this spiritual realm, which they aimed to get to, and had OBEs within life as practice for entering it permanently at death, as we explain further on in this chapter.

A similar belief is also held in Tibetan Buddhism and Bon, where it's based on the abilities said to have been possessed by an ancient race of celestial origin. In Bon tradition, this ancient race is called the *dmu-gshen* and they were said to be the original inhabitants of Olmo Lungring. They are known by other names across different traditions; we refer to them as the Children of the Sun. The *dmu-gshen* were said to have once been connected at all times by a cord of light that extended from the crown of their heads to their celestial home in the stars.

One explanation for this is that the *dmu-gshen*/Children of the Sun believed their celestial home was not literally in the stars, but in heaven, which they located in a higher nonphysical realm amid the stars. As we've seen, heaven was repeatedly located beyond the body in the northern circumpolar region of the stars in traditions of the Religion of the Sun, and this appears to derive from the beliefs of the Children of the Sun.

At death, the bodies of the *dmu-gshen* were said to dissolve into light, and their consciousnesses return along the cord of light to the celestial origin of their race (heaven). However, this cord was eventually severed, so that their bodies stayed on the earth and required tombs.[270]

We believe that ancient pyramids are those tombs, those "places of ascension" as they were called in Egypt, used by the descendants of the Children of the Sun to induce for those in life and in death the ability to "pass from one sphere to another" once naturally possessed by their ancestors.

To sum up, sacred sites around the world, such as pyramids, mounds, circular earthworks, stone circles, stupas, pagodas, sacred trees, and poles (such as the maypole of Europe), symbolized the world mountain and/or cosmic axis that connected the three levels of hell, earth, and heaven together. They were based on the concept of the primordial mound that arose at the beginning of creation, which was synonymous with the physical body, and its central axis particularly with the spine. These sites were believed to be places where one could communicate with other-dimensional realms, and a number were actually used for having OBEs.

These sites represented the world mountain and cosmic axis because the path to enlightenment traverses them, and this path was originally their focus. It was envisaged as the steep and difficult climb upon a mountain, specifically the world mountain, to reach the Source/Spiritual Sun at its peak; it's a very long and difficult process of transformation, testing, and initiation that leads to heaven and the reunification with one's higher Being. It was seen as leading up through the spine in the body to the crown of the head, up through the earth from the underworld and into the heavens, and up out of the world of matter into that of the spirit, all of which were symbolized by ascent upon the world mountain and cosmic axis, and thus the sites that were built to symbolize them.

This is why the Buddhist stupa is still today said to represent the path to enlightenment. As we've seen, the inclining inner passage of the Great Pyramid of Egypt was seen as the path leading from hell to heaven, specifically along the rays of the sun, i.e. the path of the Spiritual Sun, and so it too encoded the path to enlightenment. This path was also represented by the stairs leading to the apex of Sumerian ziggurats and Central American pyramids.

Another possible example is found at the ancient site known as Gunung Padang located in Indonesia, built at the summit of an extinct volcano. In 2023, a research team led by the Indonesian geologist Danny Hilman Natawidjaja published a paper proposing that the site, which has been considered sacred by the local people throughout history, is actually an ancient pyramid enclosing inner chambers that was built upon over thousands of years, starting somewhere between twenty-five and fourteen thousand years ago. The findings are controversial. Yet no matter whether it's a very ancient pyramid, or a much later sacred site built atop a mountain, it's still evidence for the belief that a mountain could symbolize the path to enlightenment—as the name of the site in the local language means "mountain of enlightenment."[271]

I will discuss the connection between the world mountain and the path of the Spiritual Sun (to enlightenment) in more detail in another book specifically about the path.

What we have here is an amazing convergence of beliefs about religious structures that were similarly designed, used, and astronomically aligned (as explained in *Ancient Solstice*)—despite being found as far afield as Egypt, Mesopotamia, Tibet, India, China, Europe, and the Americas. Given the similarities between them, there was clearly a transmission of knowledge about other dimensions across parts of the world with the spread of the Religion of the Sun. And that spread was vast—affecting a very large number of the ancient sites on Earth.

NORSE/GERMANIC

OBEs and dreams feature prominently in old texts that preserved religious myths, teachings, and histories of the Norse of Northern Europe. Norse religion was itself based on a more ancient Germanic religion stretching back thousands of years that derives from an even older Indo-European tradition, which was centered upon the sun. Like Hinduism, which is also in the Indo-European family of religions, it has its roots in the ancient Religion of the Sun.[272]

The chief god of the ancient Germanic pantheon was Odin, who was said to have been a real person that became revered as a sage and knower of great mystical knowledge. One of the abilities he is described as having is the ability to astral travel.

> "Odin could transform his shape: his body would lie as if dead, or asleep; but then he would be in the shape of a fish, or worm, or bird,

or beast, and be off in a twinkling to distant lands upon his own or other people's business."[273]

~ ODIN'S FEATS, THE YNGLINGA SAGA

Odin flying on his horse Sleipnir that he was said to be able to ride to nonphysical realms. In Norse tradition, Sleipnir was synonymous with the world tree Yggdrasil that Odin hangs on during his initiation, and is likely to be the same "horse" said to bear someone to heaven in the Kolbrin (as quoted earlier).

Taking the shape of a fish, worm, beast, or bird likely refers to the different laws of the astral plane that allow one to travel underwater, through the earth, across the ground, and fly through the air, just like these animals, while traveling to distant lands in an instant describes the ability to travel extremely fast and be in distant places instantaneously in the astral plane. However, the description may have also been influenced by ideas about shapeshifting derived from Shamanism.

Norse texts describe different nonphysical parts that each person has, and nonphysical realms where people go when they die. What they called the *hug* is generally thought to correspond to the psyche, which could separate from the body. It could appear in the form of the person, but was also said to be able to take the shape of an animal. When it did, it was referred to as the *ham*.[274] It's speculated that the *ham* may have referred to the astral body, as it was said to be able to journey out of the body and return.[275] However, ideas about the *ham* appear to have been heavily influenced by or derived from Shamanism, in which shapeshifting into animals to travel beyond one's body is a central practice. It's found, for example, among Siberian shamans and Native Central Americans, as explained later in this chapter.

An account published in 1531 says that there were many in Norway and Lapland (a region of northernmost Europe) at the time who could leave their bodies for three whole days, and upon waking recount things from long distances away.[276] This indicates they were traveling in the astral plane, which is like an etheric "copy" of the physical world, where everything in the physical world exists and can be seen in its etheric component. The experiences cited were from among the Sami people, whose religion was heavily influenced by that of the Norse, and vice versa. Three days is a very long time to be asleep; usually someone can't sleep that long and not naturally wake up without drugs, so it's likely they ingested something.

An important practice in Norse religion was Utiseta, meaning "to sit outside." This practice could involve meditation combined with sleep (which is the method for having OBEs) with the purpose of obtaining spiritual guidance. Expert in Norse mythology, Maria Kvilhaug, who has studied the deeper meaning of the stories found in the Old Norse texts known as the Eddas, explains it as follows:

> "Sleeping by a river or on the top of a sacred mountain, dozing off within sacred groves, or sitting in silence upon a burial mound are all practices that are described in the Edda as Vision Quests, allowing us to conclude that deep, all-night meditation in power spots, that is, in a sacred space thought to be particularly powerful in a magical, mysterious and religious way, was a known practice during the Viking Age. These practices all lead to the Vision usually in a land sometimes known as Svavaland [the Land of Sleep] [...]."[277]
> ~ MARIA KVILHAUG, THE SEED OF YGGDRASIL

Depiction of a practice of Utiseta.

Kvilhaug realized that sleeping to go on a vision quest was used particularly as part of an initiatory path in which the initiate, under the direction of their guide, would travel to other dimensions that belonged to death and the afterlife, to seek out spiritual beings.²⁷⁸ She says this is most clearly illustrated in the poems about King Helgi from the Poetic Edda. They begin with the king and his earl Atli (whose name means magician/sage/priest) going on a spiritual quest to the otherworld (Svavaland) by going to sleep. Kvilhaug says this is really the poetic retelling of the initiation of a king, and that Norse texts strongly suggest that Germanic kings had to go through a great initiation before they were accepted to their position, as they were expected to be semi-divine and possess esoteric knowledge.²⁷⁹ This was part of an ancient tradition in Europe (as explored further in the next section):

> "[...] it makes sense that Atli and the king always fall asleep before they travel to Svavaland, which is in fact the land of going to sleep. This element is about dreams. Everything in the story happens in the realm of dreams [...] what appears to be a fairy tale may be broken down into the elements of the structure of initiation, and each element actually describes what would happen during a ritual."²⁸⁰
> ~ MARIA KVILHAUG, THE SEED OF YGGDRASIL

In one poem, Helgi even has a near-death experience in which he is visited by a valkyrie (a female spiritual being) who urges him to change his life, and undergo the trials of initiation.²⁸¹ These practices reveal that the followers of Germanic religion knew about the astral plane as the place where we go when we sleep, where the deceased go, and where gods reside, and that having OBEs (and meaningful dreams) was an important part of their religion. It also reveals that having an OBE was central to an initiation that kings (and many others in Germanic society) underwent. Elements of these practices became symbolically interwoven throughout ancient Norse myths and legends.

Valkyries visit a man who was sleeping.

The initiation ritual appears to be a version of the ritual of the Twice Born of Egypt, but which was conducted within some of the ancient passage mounds of Europe (as explored in more detail in the next section). It was the most important rite in the Norse initiations of Odin. Many stories in the Eddas encode this initiation, describing how the initiate entered the underworld realm of the goddess, symbolized by the mound, where they endured a series of trials (having to overcome things like hatred, rage, and greed, and to prove their esoteric knowledge), went through a kind of death, and were served mead by a priestess referred to as "Sun Cauldron Woman." This mead was held in cauldrons representing the wells of knowledge and regeneration found in the underworld, and the name of the largest among them Odrerir (translated as "Spirit/Poetry/Ecstasy Blend/Brew"), indicates the mead was a blend or brew of ingredients. It was associated with accessing the heavenly realm of the afterlife, the entrance to which was sought in the initiation. At the culmination of the ritual, the initiate was said to have resurrected and been spiritually reborn,[282] just as they were in ancient Egypt.

A picture stone from the Viking Age, which portrays a scene from the story of Odin and Gunnlǫð in the Prose Edda. It shows Odin in the form of an eagle after being served ritual mead in a drinking horn by its female guardian Gunnlǫð, which occurs within a secret chamber inside a mountain.[283] The mead was the property of giants, who were often guardians of ancient, esoteric knowledge in Norse tradition.[284] They would have been the surviving knowledge keepers from the Children of the Sun. It's interesting they had a secret chamber inside a mountain, as this seems to be yet another version of the secret chambers within pyramids, mounds, and beneath temples. It may also have been connected to the symbol of the world mountain, as pyramids and mounds were.

However, instead of being reunited with the sun as their Spiritual Father as in Egypt, in Norse texts the sun—which was the most important deity in Scandinavia during the Bronze Age (approximately 2000 – 500 BC)—was represented by a beautiful, golden maiden (often a valkyrie), who was seen as the long-lost beloved wife of the initiate that they reunited with as a symbol of their own spiritual self.[285]

As mentioned, Germanic tradition is connected to the Vedic tradition of India, as both derived from an earlier, common Indo-European source. Still today, Vedic Brahmins (priests) undergo an initiation that is considered their second, spiritual birth, after which they become known as Dvija, meaning "twice-born" in Sanskrit. However, under the former caste system, it wasn't just Brahmins, but the men of all three upper/noble (Aryan) castes that became twice born before assuming their roles.[286] This is believed to have derived from an ancient Indo-European tradition that entered India with their migrations.[287] It seems to us that the same system of twice born initiation for men with important roles in society also entered Europe, where it became the basis of a rebirth ritual involving OBEs inside its ancient chambered passage mounds. So many men undergoing this initiation as a rite of passage before assuming a role in society may explain the vast numbers of ancient passage mounds across Europe, built to accommodate the men of each settlement. OBEs then would not just have been the secret practice of a small number, but a vital part of society.

Today in India, the twice born ritual does not involve OBEs, but centers around the initiate being given a sacred thread, which they are expected to wear from then on. It's possible, however, that it became far removed from the original rite which had involved OBEs. In support of this is what appears to be a version of the twice born ritual involving OBEs found recorded in Zoroastrian texts (as discussed further on in the chapter), and Zoroastrianism is known to be closely related to Vedic religion.

Another term the twice born may have been known by, we think, is "sons of the sun." The ancient Germanic people who entered Scandinavia and became the Norse were remembered as having called themselves sons of the sun. In ancient Egypt and in Ireland too, there is record of the kings calling themselves sons of the sun, and in numerous places across the world where the sons of the sun traveled and established kingdoms and the Religion of the Sun.[288] Becoming a son of the sun also implies a spiritual birth, as it indicates someone who has been reborn as a son of the Spiritual Sun as their Heavenly Father. As mentioned previously, this is a spiritual process that occurs when the part of one's higher Being known as the Spiritual Son is "born" within them. However, it's likely that very few who used this title were actually sons of the sun in a spiritual sense. Instead, they probably acquired the title through birth/genealogy (as described in a number of ancient sources). Another possibility, however, is that there may have been a time when it was acquired by undergoing some version of the twice born initiation (involving OBEs). For instance, the title "sons of Sun Cauldron Woman" appears in an Old Norse poem, which, as Kvilhaug has identified, alludes to the central rite of Norse initiation. The title indicates the initiation was conducted by a priestess of the sun within a burial mound. As we'll see next in the Celtic section, a stone basin carved with a symbol of the sun, believed to represent a cauldron, making it a "sun cauldron," was found inside an ancient chambered mound in Ireland where it was likely used in some form of the twice born ritual:

"Son! As your father, I have counselled you, as have the sons of Sun Cauldron Woman, toward the Horn of the Heart that he brought from the death-mound [...]."[289]
~ SONG OF THE SUN

In Egypt it was Osiris who was believed to have first gone through the death and resurrection that the Twice Born ritual emulated. In Germanic tradition it was Odin. In the most central event of all Norse tradition, Odin hangs on the world tree Yggdrasil for nine days and nights as an act of self-sacrifice—even piercing himself with a spear. As explained earlier, this tree was believed to stand at the center of the cosmos as the cosmic axis, where it connected the physical world to the numerous nonphysical worlds of Norse cosmology. Thus, it was believed to be the place where one could travel to them. And so while on the tree, Odin has a kind of near-death experience and travels out of his body to visit some of these nonphysical realms (including Hel) where he obtains secret, mystical knowledge by drinking from their wells/cauldrons, after which he then resurrects and brings this knowledge back to share with humanity. Kvilhaug believes this event portrays in symbolic form the initiation that many men in Norse society underwent.[290]

The three wells at the roots of the world tree that Odin drinks from, which were associated with the mead that was drunk during rituals.

The hanging of Odin shares some striking similarities with that of Jesus. Jesus hangs on a cross until the ninth hour, Odin hangs on a tree for nine nights; both are pierced with a spear; both have a drink (Jesus has vinegar, Odin has mead); both undergo death or near-death as an act of self-sacrifice; both then have an OBE to hell; and both later resurrect. In another similarity, Jesus is placed in a rock-hewn tomb for three days before resurrecting and ascending to heaven, while in the Norse story of Odin and Gunnlǫð, Odin enters a mountain where he stays for a period of three nights seeking wisdom and knowledge, before escaping the cave as an eagle and flying home to the seat of the gods in the heavenly realm Asgard. Many believe that either the Christian or Norse sources copied from the other, but we offer a different explanation, which is that both were based on the same initiation that was central to the path of the Spiritual Sun, and which the initiation of the Twice Born was based on. We'll discuss how Jesus was connected to the Twice Born further on in this chapter.

Left: Odin hanging on a tree and pierced with a spear as an act of self-sacrifice.
Right: Jesus nailed to the cross, being pierced by a spear, as an act of self-sacrifice.

It's possible the Twice Born ritual was conducted at the Externsteine in Germany, which is a very large natural rock formation that has a number of ancient manmade sites carved into it. One is a small stone altar that has alignments to the summer solstice sunrise and sunset. Another is a cave with resonant properties and a mysterious bowl shape carved into the floor at the rear of the cave. There is also a sarcophagus, and a large natural feature that looks like a crucified man, complete with a hole in its side.

This ritual may have also been conducted at the ancient mound site of Uppsala in Sweden; however, the largest of these mounds were used as burial places for kings and were likely to have acted as pyramids did, to send the king to the heavenly realm of the afterlife (called Valhalla).

There are also numerous ancient sites known as "stone ships," which are standing stones arranged in the shape of a ship, mostly found in Scandinavia, but also Northern Germany and the Baltic states. These stone ships are sometimes found as standalone monuments, but also occur en masse in "gravfält" (grave fields). Smaller ship settings were often used for burials,[291] but the larger, more monumental ship settings generally have a lack of grave finds.[292] Many stone ships have solar alignments, like Ale's Stones (Ales Stenar) in Sweden, for instance, which has its prow aligned to summer solstice sunset. Petroglyphs in Sweden depict sun-related rituals occurring in ships, indicating stone ships may have been used for rituals. They are likely to have been based on the ancient Indo-European concept of the sun riding through the sky on a ship, found also in ancient Egypt, where the sun god Ra used a boat to travel through the sky world of the Duat/astral plane. The Egyptian king was believed to use a similar boat after death to journey through the afterlife[293]—sailing the starry stream of the Milky Way to heaven—and the Germanic elite are likely to have been buried within stone ships that were believed to function in the same way. Perhaps there were some, however, that were used for rituals to do with the journey to heaven for the living.

It's also possible that Goseck Circle in Germany, which dates to 5,000 BC and is aligned to the winter solstice, was used in a similar manner to Stonehenge, as explained next.

Left: Ancient petroglyph in Sweden of a man in a ship worshiping and perhaps riding with the sun. Center: The stone ship Ales Stenar, which is aligned to summer solstice sunset. Right: The sun god in Egypt riding on his ship across the sky and through the Duat/astral plane.

The ancient Norse/Germanic religion has undergone a revival, and there are many practitioners of it that have had dreams, OBEs, and even NDEs with Norse gods—particularly Odin.[294]

CELTIC

Although there are no records we've come across that clearly describe OBEs in historical Celtic texts, they contain allusions to them in their stories about journeys people made to the "otherworld."

One of the clearer examples of an out-of-body journey is found in the story of Rhonabwy's Dream from the Mabinogion—a collection of Welsh prose compiled in the twelfth to thirteenth centuries from older oral traditions. In the story, the medieval warrior Rhonabwy falls asleep on a yellow ox skin, which was believed to bring good luck. He then has a very vivid dream in which he travels back in time to the days of King Arthur. He speaks with Arthur himself, and sees the various people and places of the time in great detail, and watches Arthur and one of his men play symbolic games of chess. Arthur laments that such scum as Rhonabwy now protect the island after such fine men had protected it in the past. Rhonabwy eventually awakes to find he had been asleep for three days and nights. It's possible this was based on a real lucid dream experience. It's interesting he slept for three days, as this is how long some of the Sami were said to sleep when they traveled out of the body.

There is evidence that journeying to the otherworld in OBEs formed a part of initiatory rites performed in some of the ancient mounds, temples, and stone circles of Europe and Britain, and that these rituals and sites were fundamentally the same as those in Egypt.

Illustration of an ancient Celtic journey in the otherworld.

Traveling to the otherworld was a rite of passage for Celtic kings,[295] just as it was for Norse kings,[296] and Egyptian kings (who were expected to undergo the ritual of the Twice Born),[297] as they were all based on the same ancient tradition. For example, legend has it that Cormac, the High King of Ireland who ruled from the ancient site of Tara, was led by the god Manannan Mac Lir into the heavenly otherworld called the Land of Promise, where he bathed in the fountain of knowledge, and then awoke back in Tara having gained the knowledge of life and death—this tale has been interpreted as a symbolic and poetic retelling of the initiation of an Irish king.[298] Europe is estimated to have had thousands of ancient chambered mounds and dolmens, only hundreds of which remain today. Great ancient passage mounds, like those of Knowth and Newgrange in Ireland, contain inner stone chambers, as do the pyramids of Egypt, where these initiations were surely held, as explained shortly.

Newgrange in Ireland. Its inner stone chamber was likely used for having OBEs.

In one of the Celtic books of the Kolbrin, a similar ritual to that of the Twice Born is described. It may have been conducted in one of the passage mounds of Europe:

> "I was a Sleeper in the Great Stone Chambers of Initiation [...]. I prepared myself by the Dread Rites and became worthy to be called an Inheritor of the Ancient Wisdom. [...] When a man enters the Great Stone Chambers of Initiation he receives an infusion of the Divine Essence. His soulspirit is awakened to conscious awareness and passes out, to leave the mortal body still and silent within its tomb. He comes into the presence of Beings who know the will of The Supreme Spirit, he learns awful secrets, he knows whence he came and whither he goes. He is one reborn and awakens to rediscover himself."[299]
> ~ THE KOLBRIN

This clearly describes an OBE that occurs as the result of being "infused" with something. Notice he says he was "a Sleeper" in the stone chamber, indicating the initiate would have a conscious OBE while they slept there overnight. Also notice how he refers to the awakening of his "soulspirit" while his body slept, which is similarly described in the Pyramid Texts in which the king is made to "wake, for he sleeps."

Even though the pyramids of Egypt and the mounds of Europe look very different, there are some key similarities in their design that indicate they were built to perform the same function based on the same beliefs.

They were both symbols of the womb of the Spiritual Mother. The womb of the Mother was symbolized by the pyramid in Egypt and the earthen womb-shaped mound in Europe. The chamber used by the Twice Born in Egypt was called the Womb of Rebirth, though particularly the stone sarcophagi in the chambers of the pyramids were seen as the Mother's womb where those who "died and resurrected" lay. Similarly, Newgrange was known as the womb of the goddess (which was associated with the Milky Way, as was the womb of the goddess of the pyramid in Egypt),[300] [301] and the chamber of Knowth contains a stone cauldron associated with the cauldron of rebirth in Irish mythology, in which the dead could be placed and drawn out alive again.[302] It seems the cauldron of Europe performed the same role as the sarcophagus of Egypt. In the Kolbrin, a cauldron of rebirth, just as found in Irish and Norse myth, is named as part of the ritual of the Twice Born in Egypt. The initiate inhales from a brew prepared in it before sleeping within the Womb of Rebirth:

> "The Aspiring One is of Earth, he is earthbound. He sits within the cavern before the Cauldron of Rebirth and Regeneration, and inhales

the smoke from the brew of release. He rises above himself, flying on wings [...]."[303]
~ THE KOLBRIN

Also in the Kolbrin, a cauldron that symbolized the womb was part of the ritual used to initiate druids, which sounds similar to the ritual of the Twice Born.

> "Of the druids it is said that Pair Keridwen, the Cauldron of Higher Love, represented to them the womb [...]. To become a druid required immersion in a bath with a decoction from the cauldron. After immersion for a prescribed time, the residue of the bath, infused with the man's evil, was poured into a pit. His spirit was thus cleansed and renewed, but henceforth any wrongdoing would have a twofold effect."[304]
> ~ THE KOLBRIN

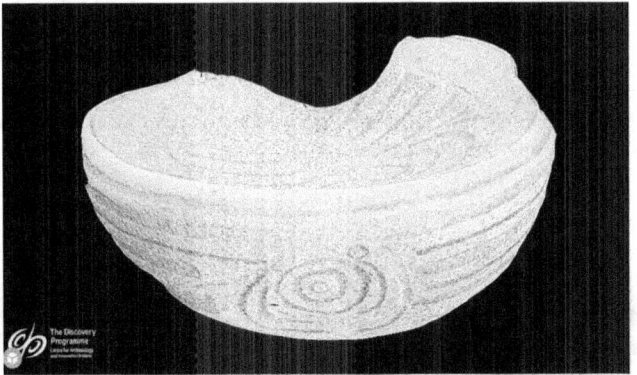

3D model of the stone basin inside the chamber of Knowth, which is carved with a symbol of the sun.

The chambers of the pyramids of Egypt and most mounds of Europe were situated at their approximate center, and were accessed by one long, narrow stone passageway or corridor—in both, this passage was the symbolic birth canal of the Mother Goddess. However, rather than the exit passageway aligning to the northern circumpolar stars as in Egyptian pyramids, the passages of European mounds were usually aligned to the sun at the solstice or equinox. The initiate of the British Isles was directed in their spiritual rebirth toward their Father Sun,[305] as the pharaohs were toward the sun as their Father Atum along the east facing corridor within the pyramids of Saqqara, before they turned north.

While working on this book it suddenly struck Lara that the effect of looking out the narrow stone passage from within the chamber of a European mound toward the rising sun on a solstice or equinox created the same visual effect as traveling through the dark tunnel into the light of heaven commonly experienced in NDEs. The increase of the sun's light as it rose would have enhanced this effect even more, making it appear as though the light was getting closer and brighter as it does in NDEs as one travels toward it through the tunnel. She realized the passages and avenues of numerous ancient European sites had been designed to emulate the tunnel/portal to heaven. This realization was key to unlocking their meaning and purpose.

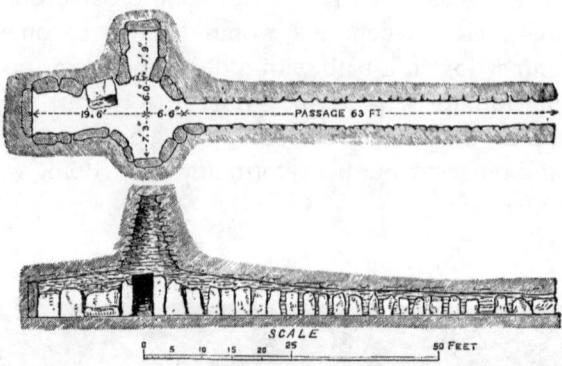

Aerial view above, and cross section below, of the chamber and passage inside Newgrange, which was aligned to winter solstice sunrise. Notice its cruciform shape which was used in symbols of the cosmic axis.

Left: Looking out from inside an ancient chambered mound (this photo is from Taversöe Tuick in Scotland). Right: Recreation of traveling through the tunnel into the light of heaven commonly described in NDE accounts.

It's also another correlation between Egypt and Europe. Both had built structures that emulated crossing the portal into heaven, and that even sought to send someone through it in an OBE from within their stone chambers. In both Egypt and Europe, pyramids and mounds were also used as tombs for the elite. In Egypt these pyramidal tombs were said to send the deceased through the portal to heaven, and it seems likely that the burial mounds of Europe were built to serve the same purpose.

A good friend of ours who has visited numerous chambered mounds in Britain and mainland Europe found that some felt quite like sensory deprivation chambers, being very quiet, dark, and temperate on the inside due to their thick walls and other architectural features that shielded them from noise and the elements outside, making them well suited to having OBEs and/ or incubating dreams.

It also looks like the standing stone circles of Europe, particularly those in the British Isles, that had an avenue aligned to the sun at a solstice or equinox, like Stonehenge in England, Callanish I in Scotland, and the Grange Stone Circle at Lough Gur in Ireland (the largest stone circle in Ireland), are based on the same belief and design. At Stonehenge at sunrise on the summer solstice, the sunlight shines down an avenue that would have once been flanked by upright stones, into the center of the stone circle, and the same thing happens at Callanish,[306] and Grange circle. These avenues are likely to have been the equivalent of the passages in European mounds, again representing the tunnel leading to heaven; looking toward the sun from within the circle along the avenue would have created a similar effect, though lacking the darkness created by a roof.

Left: Illustration of the rising sun shining along the avenue into the center of Stonehenge on the summer solstice. Right: The standing stones of Callanish, which are laid out in the shape of a Celtic cross—the sun shines along its axis, which is the avenue that leads to the circle, on the summer solstice. Both likely represent the tunnel/portal to heaven.

The mounds and circles these passages/avenues lead out from to the sun appear to have represented the earth, which someone departs from to ascend to heaven. For instance, Stonehenge's inner circle of bluestones encode the diameter of the earth, and the outer stones (the Sarsens) the radius of the moon as though orbiting around it,[307] and so like the Great Pyramid which encodes the dimensions of the earth, including its radius, it too was likely intended to be a representation of Earth. Many of the mounds of Europe are also clearly Earth-like, being constructed as giant roundish mounds of earth, and were likely built to represent the earth, like the round bluestone circle of Stonehenge, and it's likely that other stone circles and circular henges in Europe were too.[308]

Like the pyramids of Egypt, they appear to have been built to symbolize the primordial mound that arose at the beginning of creation, which represented the earth like an island afloat in the cosmos (and was synonymous with the womb of the Spiritual Mother Goddess). In Egypt this mound could be pyramidal, but also round-topped, just as European mounds are. In Europe, the primordial mound could also be symbolized by henges, which are essentially large circular earthworks made by digging a ditch around their perimeter. Sometimes these ditches are on the inside of the circle, meaning they could not have served a defensive purpose and were more likely to have been symbolic. These kinds of earthworks are also found in the Americas—particularly in the United States, where their symbolic meaning has been better preserved, as discussed further on in this chapter. These circular henge earthworks appear to have been intended to recreate the sense of an island. The largest stone circles in Britain were built within henges, potentially indicating that stone circles and henges had the same purpose and meaning. Though their design was often simpler, they were based on the same beliefs as those held by pyramid builders.[309]

 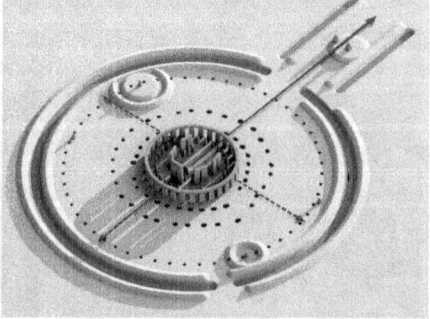

Left: Aerial of Avebury showing its earthen ditch on the inside of the exterior bank. Right: Recreation of Stonehenge as seen from above; it too has an earthen ditch and bank surrounding its inner standing stone circle. Goseck Circle in Germany was likewise built inside an earthen ditch and bank.

The Druids believed the entrance (portal) to heaven (Gywnva) was located in the northern sky at the point where the sun reached its height at the summer solstice,[310] and this ties in with the design of Stonehenge, which aligned to summer solstice sunrise, as a symbolic gateway leading from the earth to heaven.

Those ancient Britons gathered at Stonehenge to celebrate the summer solstice likely saw it as the time of ascension into heaven, just as it was in the Pyramid Texts. No wonder it became one of the largest burial sites in Britain,[311] as people must have buried their dead there in the hope they would be transported to heaven in the afterlife. The surrounds of the Great Pyramids also became a massive burial site, being known as "the Necropolis" (burial place).

Perhaps rather than Stonehenge being used for OBEs for a select few, there may have been large public ceremonies conducted there at the solstices (when it's known a large number of people from around Britain would gather there) based on the belief that it was a gateway to heaven—both allowing the deceased through in one direction as they departed from Earth, and the light of the Spiritual Sun shining from heaven in the other toward the living.

But even though it's far more exposed and allows many more people inside than pyramids or mounds, it's still possible Stonehenge may have sometimes been used for initiations as a kind of portal to heaven for the living, as pyramids and mounds were. Its inner stones have been found to have acoustic properties—they amplify the noise within the circle, but only for those inside it. There's also evidence that suggests a privacy hedge was grown around its perimeter, which would have prevented people from looking in. Based on these findings, researchers have speculated that Stonehenge may have also been used as a secretive, ritual site for a small, elite group.[312] [313]

In Celtic religion, just as in Norse religion, mounds were seen as gateways to the otherworld,[314] which seems to be a distant memory of how they'd been used for having OBEs during an initiation in which the initiate traveled to the otherworld.

A reference to this initiation is found in the writings of the Druidic bard Taliesin; his writings preserve some of the few surviving references to Druid beliefs. Taliesin recalls how he was swallowed by the goddess Ceridwen and entered her womb and underworld realm where he underwent a mystical death, and drank from her cauldron, before being reborn;[315] [316] this shares many similarities with the Norse and Egyptian initiations (where Ra is swallowed by the goddess Nut and is then reborn from her womb) and is based on the same tradition of initiation. A priestess likely played the part of Ceridwen in the ritual, who was known as the guardian of the cauldron,[317] just as there were priestesses who guarded the cauldron in Norse initiation. These priestesses are part of an ancient tradition that spread across the world as part of the Religion of the Sun; the Celtic priestesses were known as "the daughters of fire," and were recorded as singing, "may the fiery bright sun take us to the lasting kingdom,"[318] which is a reference to the Spiritual Sun (which would have been present as the sun aligned to the passage mound) taking them to the heaven of Annwn/Annwfn.[319]

The initiation of Taliesin also correlates to the structure of European mounds, which were built as representations of the womb of the great mother goddess.

In one of the poems of Taliesin there is a reference to a portal to the otherworld of Annwfn opening up before a cauldron. The cauldron belongs to the king of the otherworld and is surrounded by nine virgins who are likely the priestesses that guarded it. The portal is entered in darkness as lamps were needed for light, the darkness likely due to it being within a dark chamber. In the poem, it's King Arthur and his men who travel through it, as it was part of a long tradition in which kings had to undergo this initiation.

> "The first song I sang was concerning the cauldron
> That's warmed at the fire by the breath of nine virgins.
> The cauldron of Annwfn's king [...]
> It was never designed to boil food for a coward [...]
> And before Annwfn's portals, the lamps were burning."[320]
> ~ THE BOOK OF TALIESIN

It surely took courage to enter upon the journey to the otherworld. Annwfn is described in Welsh lore just as heaven in other traditions and in near-death experiences is—as a beautiful, abundant place of eternal youth, free of suffering and disease. And so here we have the same theme of traveling through a portal to heaven. However, in Welsh mythology the otherworld could also be home to hellish creatures that tortured countless souls according to their sins, and these were clearly demons that had come through the portal from hell.[321]

Detail from an ancient Celtic cauldron showing a cauldron being used to bring dead warriors back to life who then ride away on horses to fight anew. In Welsh tradition the Cauldron of Rebirth was called Pair Dadeni[322] and corresponds to the Womb of Rebirth in Egypt.

The Celtic king of the otherworld was Gwyn ap Nudd—he shares similarities with both Osiris of Egypt and Odin of Germanic tradition, and we suspect all three may be the same ancient teacher of the Religion of the Sun whose memory was preserved in different cultures. All were the lead male figure in this initiation of rebirth, and all were identified with the constellation of Orion, which plays a key cosmological role in the path taken by the initiate and the deceased to heaven as it was visualized in the stars—specifically as the one who stood at the entrance to the portal to heaven. Gwyn ap Nudd and Osiris were both the rulers of the otherworld, while Odin and Gwyn ap Nudd both had the role of guiding the souls of the dead through the otherworld.[323]

After writing this section, Lara happened to be drawn back to a comment on YouTube made two years ago in response to a video she had made about Odin.

> "I had a dream of Odin when I was pregnant. He looked a lot like the image in 2:45 but his hair was much longer and he was a giant. He was hovering over a tunnel that served as a portal. When I went through the portal day became night and then back to day and the road twisted upside down (though it felt right side up). My dream is bits and pieces now but there was a valley filled with every flower."[324]

Image of Odin from 2:45 mentioned in the comment.

Remarkably, this woman describes Odin standing by a portal which leads through a dark tunnel to a place full of flowers, which heaven is so often described as being in NDEs, yet we're not aware of anyone making the connection between Odin and the portal to heaven until now.

The Celtic otherworld Annwn was referred to by several names, including "Mound Fortress," "Four-Peaked Fortress," and "Glass Fortress."[325] The use of the word fortress seems a strange choice to describe the otherworld, until you realize that ancient mound sites look like hills, and hills in Britain were often used as forts. And so the term fortress could easily be replaced by the word hill or mound. Thus the term mound fortress is really a way of saying that ancient mounds were places connected to the otherworld. The term four-peaked fortress remains a mystery, but the term glass fortress surely refers to

Glastonbury Tor, which was known to the Celts as the Island of Glass. It's an artificially shaped hill aligned to the rising winter solstice sun that was seen as a portal to the otherworld of Annwn, and was associated with Annwn's king (Gwyn ap Nudd) and King Arthur.[326] Glastonbury Tor seems equivalent to an Egyptian pyramid, Gwyn ap Nudd to Osiris, and King Arthur to the pharaoh. Given that it's known as a portal to the otherworld, we wondered whether there is an ancient initiatory chamber still undiscovered within Glastonbury Tor or that was perhaps part of a now vanished temple that used to stand upon it.

As it turns out, legend has it that inside Glastonbury Tor there is a hidden cave in which the king of Annwn resides with the Cauldron of Rebirth, and through this cave one can pass into Annwn.[327] And so there probably really was once a chamber of the Twice Born (or related British equivalent) beneath Glastonbury Tor used for inducing OBEs. Glastonbury Tor became a place for the dead, as they were brought here in ancient times for their final journey to the otherworld.[328] What is likely to have happened at Glastonbury Tor, as at so many of these ancient portal sites, is that it was used as both a portal for the living and the dead, with the portal for the living having been first.

I had an OBE in which I floated above Glastonbury Tor, observing its terraces; I was then able to look into the mound to see inside it, and saw a treasure. This was part of an initiation I went through out of the body on the path of the Spiritual Sun at a stage of resurrection—the treasure represented something spiritual I acquired as a result of it. This experience came not long after the OBE I had in which I had lain inside the sarcophagus of the Great Pyramid with Anubis present (which had been preceded by another experience inside it involving a star shaft), as mentioned earlier. These experiences showed me that the Tor and Great Pyramids are connected to the path of the Spiritual Sun and even to each other.

Glastonbury Tor is a striking depiction of the primordial mound that arose from the waters of the cosmos and which the Spiritual Sun was seated upon at its summit/center. It was known anciently as an island, as the low-lying plain around it used to be inundated with water. Yet today, even though the water is gone, it can still appear as an island, though surrounded by a lake of mist.[329] At the winter solstice, the sun appears to rise up its terraces before clipping the top of the tower that stands at its peak.[330]

Sun rising over Glastonbury Tor—a striking symbol of the Spiritual Sun rising to take its place at the summit of the primordial mound at the beginning of creation.

Silbury Hill in England also appears to have been built as a symbol of the primordial mound. It's the tallest manmade mound in Europe, comparable in volume to the pyramids built in Egypt around the same time. An enormous ditch, one hundred meters in diameter, was dug around it, which was filled with water[331] (likely continuously from underground springs), creating the appearance of an island. It was once covered in the white chalk limestone found in the area,[332] which would have given it a similar appearance to the Great Pyramid when it had been covered in white limestone. At the equinox, the sun can be viewed rising up along the side of the mound to its summit. It may have been used for rituals involving OBEs, but no chambers have yet been discovered within it. In 2000 Silbury Hill suffered a massive internal collapse caused by modern exploratory tunnels; if there was an inner chamber, it may be damaged beyond recognition.

The idea of a portal opening up within an ancient mound may sound too far out, but recent experiments within one of them support the idea. In 2015 the sound engineer Steve Marshall published the results of a series of acoustic experiments he conducted at a number of mounds and barrows—particularly West Kennet Long Barrow of the Avebury complex in South West England. The results reveal that ancient portal sites in Europe may have been built to harness resonance and sound to induce OBEs.

West Kennet Long Barrow consists of an open forecourt leading into a central passageway inside an earthen manmade mound. Within the mound, five inner stone chambers are nested off the central passageway, which is aligned almost due east to sunrise on the equinox.

At the entrance of West Kennet Long Barrow looking into its inner chambers.

Marshall discovered the barrow has a number of acoustic design features and properties. Its central passage was found to resonate at 9 Hz, which is a low frequency of sound that's inaudible, but can have psychological effects (as mentioned, the King's Chamber of the Great Pyramid was also found to resonate at low frequencies). He found that any sound made in the forecourt caused the passage to resonate (speculating that low chanting was used) and that the forecourt's shape helped to funnel sound into the passage (toward its innermost western chamber). Marshall proposes that the resonance of the passage could have been used to sympathetically induce brainwaves of the same frequency in people within in its western chamber during rituals.[333]

Theta brainwaves oscillate between 4-8 Hz; we produce these in the stage between waking and sleeping, and also when awake but in a deeply relaxed state of mind.[334] Alpha brainwaves oscillate between 8-12 Hz; these waves are produced when we're in a state of wakeful relaxation with our eyes closed.[335] This conscious but deeply relaxed state with eyes closed while transitioning into sleep is precisely the state that is most conducive to OBEs, indicating the barrow's resonance of 9 Hz could have been designed to induce OBEs. Marshall says, "the lowest resonances of the tomb have the power to induce sleep or trance—that mysterious region between waking and sleeping, between life and death, where the material world and the spirit world meet."[336]

Marshall suggests it's likely that other ancient passage mounds have the potential to influence brainwaves, and says that Newgrange and Fourknocks in Ireland, Barclodiad-y-Gawres in Anglesey, and the three dolmens of Antequera in southern Spain, also show signs of low frequency sound resonance in their chambers.[337]

Marshall experimented by having someone sit in West Kennet Long Barrow's western chamber while the passage was made to resonate. The subject was a fourteen-year-old boy, who sat in the chamber on a late summer evening in near darkness while a drummer in the forecourt played a slow but constant drumbeat. Marshall says:

> "The boy later reported that with eyes open, he could just make out the end stones of the W chamber, which at first appeared to be moving slightly. On one stone of the back wall a small black circle appeared, which grew in size; it took on the appearance of a passage leading to another chamber, which he thought he could see into. He then continued to listen with eyes closed and was convinced that on two occasions someone had joined him [in] the chamber, but he had been entirely alone."[338]

It's amazing the boy said he saw what sounds like a portal open up and then felt the presence of nonphysical beings; he may have perceived something of the astral/otherworld with the help of the barrow's resonance.

An earlier study published in 1996 on ancient chambered mounds in the British Isles also confirmed some have acoustic properties. It was done by Robert G. Jahn and Michael Ibison of Princeton University, and Paul Devereux of Penzance. They studied the sites Wayland's Smithy and Chun Quoit in the UK, as well as Cairn L, Cairn I (both of Loughcrew), and Newgrange in Ireland. In summary, they found each "sustained a strong resonance at a frequency between 95 – 120 Hz," with most at 110 - 112 Hz, and speculated that since these frequencies are well within the adult male voice range that the resonance may have been a design feature used to enhance chanting within the chambers during rituals. In some cases they even found rock art within and on the exterior of the sites that resembled the chamber's acoustic patterns.[339]

Marshall similarly found that four of West Kennet Long Barrow's five chambers resonated at close to a perfect fourth interval (two at 84 Hz and another two at 110 Hz), which are within the male voice range.

A 2008 study was then conducted on the effect these frequencies have on brain activity by Ian A. Cook and Andrew F. Leuchter, Professors of Psychiatry and Biobehavioral Sciences at the University of California, together with Sarah K. Pajot, an undergraduate in neuroscience and psychology. Thirty healthy adults listened to tones of 90, 100, 110, 120, and 130 Hz while their brain activity was monitored with EEG. The study found that at 110 Hz the activity in the left temporal lobe of the brain was significantly lower than at the other frequencies, and prefrontal cortex activity shifted from a state of higher activity on the left at most frequencies to right-sided dominance at 110 Hz. The left temporal region is implicated in the cognitive processing of spoken language, and so the authors suggest a decrease in its activity may "allow other mental processes to become more prominent." A shift from left to right brain activity is generally associated with meditative and other altered states of consciousness, and the authors suggest it may indicate a change of emotional state. They summarize their findings, saying "These intriguing pilot findings suggest that the acoustic properties of ancient structures may influence human brain function."[340]

And so it seems that frequencies close to 110 Hz, which we've nicknamed "the megalithic frequency," may have been targeted specifically by the builders of ancient megalithic sites in the British Isles because they help someone shift from an intellectually driven state of mind, to one more receptive to mystical experiences—and we would say, particularly OBEs. The findings on the acoustic properties of these ancient sites, and the effects they have on the living, particularly in having mystical experiences, indicate that they were not originally built primarily as tombs.

Moving on to another component of the Celtic ritual of traveling to the otherworld, we take a look at the central Druid concept known as awen. In Celtic tradition, the substance Taliesin drinks from the cauldron is called awen.

> "The Lord God will give me the sweet awen
> As from the Cauldron of Ceridwen."[341]
> ~ TWELFTH CENTURY BARD PRYDYDD Y MOCH

This awen is the equivalent of the mead served from the cauldron during the Norse version of the initiation, as there are references to mead being served from a cauldron in the old Welsh poems of the Taliesin, where it's called "the gift of the Druids."[342] Both the mead and awen are also likely the same as the "infusion of the Divine Essence" the initiate receives in the excerpt from the Kolbrin quoted earlier in this section, being the same or similar brew used by the Twice Born of Egypt called Koriladwen,[343] which contains the name adwen and clearly seems connected to awen. And so we see that the brew used in Egypt was also used in Europe as part of the same ritual, conducted within structures that had the same symbolic meaning.

However, in Celtic lore, awen was typically understood as a kind of divine poetic inspiration deriving from the outflowing power/spirit of the Source/God that has been called "the breath of God," as the word awen is derived from the root word meaning "to blow."[344] This outflowing is likely to have been based on the spiritual radiance of the sun and stars that manifests in the physical world as electromagnetic energy, which appears to have been harnessed in the Great Pyramid and perhaps also in ancient European sites in some way by aligning them to the sun and building them at places high in natural energy.

The symbol for awen is thought to have been invented by the Welsh bard Iolo Morganwg, though he claimed it was an ancient Druidic sign. It symbolizes the rays emanating from the rising sun at the solstices and equinoxes; it was later enclosed in three circles representing the circles of creation in Druid belief.[345] This clearly indicates that awen was believed to radiate outward from the Spiritual Sun, and that this outflowing was of particular interest to the ancient Celtic Druids at sunrise on the solstices and equinoxes—which so many ancient European initiatory chambers were aligned to. It seems no coincidence that one of the symbols said to have once existed at the entrance to the initiatory chambers of the Twice Born in Egypt (possibly beneath the Precinct of Amun-Ra at Karnak, which was aligned to sunrise on the winter solstice) is described as very similar. It was "the symbol of the sun and from it extended seven hands. This represented the sun of life dispensing the vitalizing forces of life from their fount within the circle of creative consciousness."[346]

Left: Druid symbol for awen. The three black dots represent the sun at the solstices and equinoxes, with three rays extending from them. Right: Ancient Egyptian depiction of the sun with its rays extending like arms with hands at their ends.

However, awen was also the name of the brew that caused the initiate to have an OBE, and was cryptically alluded to by Celtic bards whose predecessors had once been initiated. Since awen was both the outflowing spirit and a brew, the bards at times credited their divine inspiration to both God and the cauldron. In ancient times it's likely that the wisdom bards were said to have gained by drinking from the cauldron was a reference to the mystical knowledge they'd acquired out of the body during their initiation, though could have referred to any mystical knowledge believed to come to them from the Source/God. This could be one of the reasons why awen is defined as "a state of altered consciousness in which the poet receives knowledge of matters beyond what can be routinely learned [...] that claims its origins in ecstasy (the transported state of being beside or outside of oneself) and supernatural visitation."[347]

The dual use of the word awen gives us a big clue that the awen originally harnessed as electromagnetic energy to induce OBEs in ancient sites may have been anciently replaced by the awen that was brewed in the cauldron, and probably thought to be infused with the divine essence of the Spiritual Sun.

The references to rebirth in Celtic tradition seem both to refer to being brought back from the realm of the afterlife, which someone was believed to have visited in their initiation, and to the completely new perspective on life their OBE gave them. Certainly, emerging from the dark womb-like mound into the light of day after possibly spending a day or days having mystical experiences, would have felt quite like being reborn. The ritual of rebirth mimicked and used the same symbols as the spiritual rebirth that occurs on the path of the Spiritual Sun, which is the result of an inward spiritual death and rebirth, not a physical one, and we say is what the initiation was originally based on.[348]

That many of the ancient sites of Europe were used for having OBEs, particularly during initiations that attempted to send someone out of their bodies to heaven, we call our Ancient Europe OBE Theory.

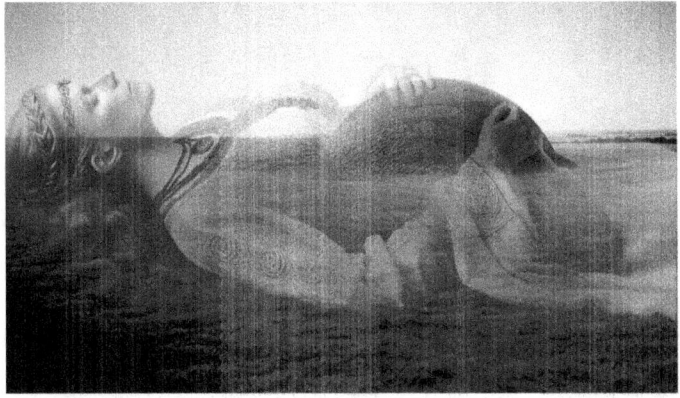

This image begins a series of illustrations depicting how we believe ancient European mounds may have been used, as described in our Ancient Europe OBE Theory.

MALTESE

The ancient stone temples of Malta—at least some of which were likely roofed in their original state—seem to be yet another version of the mound and pyramid, which were also likely used for rituals involving OBEs. Mother Goddess figurines have been found at Malta's temples. The layout of many Maltese temples emulates these figurines, as their design follows the curves of their bodies. Thus, like the pyramid and mound, their inner chambers symbolically created the interior of the Mother goddess.

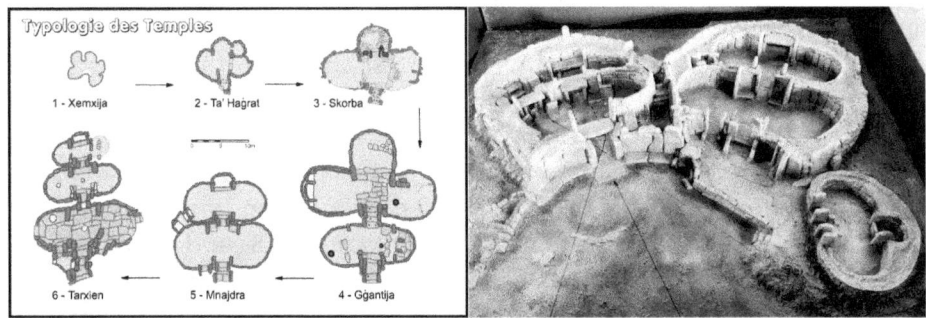

Left: Layout of some of the temples in Malta. The bottom right layout in particular is strikingly similar to West Kennet Long Barrow's. Right: Model of the Mnajdra temple complex; the lines indicate its alignment to the solstices and equinoxes.

Also like pyramids and mounds, many of Malta's temples were aligned to the sun at the solstices and equinoxes,[349][350][351] and to the stars. All those with mapped ground plans have been found to align to the star Sirius (the star of the Egyptian goddess Isis, and brightest in the sky).[352] In some of the temples the light of the sun and/or the star Sirius shines down their central passageway (or through a hole in the temple wall) into an inner chamber where there would have only been room for a small number of people to conduct a ritual, just as in the passage mounds of Europe. And as in the mounds of Europe, some of the temples featured giant stone bowls that seem to be the equivalent of the cauldrons used by the Norse and Celts. They also feature stone trilithon doorways that look very similar to the trilithons of Stonehenge and those of chambered mounds throughout Europe. All these features, and many others too numerous to detail here, shared in common among ancient European sites, reveal their interconnectedness.

Trilithon doorway (left) and stone bowl (right) found within the Tarxien Temples in Malta.

In Malta there is also an ancient labyrinthine underground temple complex with many ornately carved and decorated chambers known as the Hal Saflieni Hypogeum. This was one of at least two such hypogeum complexes in the Maltese archipelago. A small study was completed at the Hypogeum by Rudi Toffetti who found that its innermost chamber—referred to as the "Holy of Holies"—into which the winter solstice sunrise would have originally shone, had a high level of natural energy[353] (as the King's Chamber of the Great Pyramid seems to). Also like the King's Chamber and European mounds, the Hypogeum has special acoustic properties. It has an "oracle room" that has features which indicate its purpose was acoustic. Sound travels from it throughout the complex. It has been found to resonate particularly at the frequencies of 70 Hz and 114 Hz. These frequencies are within the male voice range (though the lowest an average male voice can reach is 80 Hz), and tests found the resonance was produced most in response to a male voice while chanting and singing in the oracle room. These frequencies may have been used because of the effect they had on human brain activity by, for example, inducing hypnogogic states[354] that would have been conducive to OBEs. Toffetti speculates that the Hypogeum was "a portal [...] toward otherworldly [...] dimensions," and that its central chamber could have been used by initiates "who worked with the astral forces."

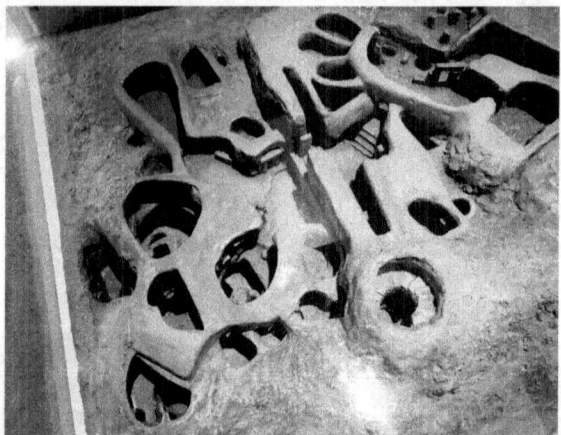

Model of the Hypogeum showing its many small chambers that may have been used for dream incubation and OBEs.

Some goddess figurines found at the Hypogeum were depicted sleeping or lying on couches, possibly alluding to the sleeping practices that could have gone on there. Toffetti also postulates that the dark and quiet lower levels of the Hypogeum were likely used for dream incubations and astral travel.[355] This could explain the multiple, small inner chambers built into many of the Maltese temples—they may have enabled people to incubate dreams or to have OBEs in separate chambers at the same time.

Thousands of human remains were found to have been deposited in some of the rooms of the Hypogeum's upper level.[356] As at other ancient portal sites, it's likely the site was seen as a portal to the otherworld for both the living and the dead.

Sleeping goddess statue found within the Hypogeum on Malta.

GÖBEKLI TEPE

Göbekli Tepe is a huge cluster of around thirty megalithic standing stone rings/enclosures located in modern day Turkey. According to mainstream archaeology, it's among the oldest megalithic sites in the world. Remarkably, there's evidence that indicates its enclosures may have been built to serve as portals to heaven and were possibly used for having OBEs.

Nine of its enclosures have been investigated so far, with approximately another twenty-one still buried (as per ground-penetrating radar).[357] The site was used and added to over a fifteen-hundred-year period, with the first stone ring erected at around 9,600 BC. Many of the stone pillars are carved with symbolic arrangements of animals.[358] Four of the excavated enclosures were aligned to the brightest star (Deneb) of the Cygnus constellation, with one, known as the Lion Pillars Building, aligned to equinox sunrise, and another Enclosure F, oriented toward summer solstice sunrise.[359]

Some of the stone enclosures excavated at Göbekli Tepe.

While nearing completion of this book, Lara recalled seeing part of a presentation the author Andrew Collins gave years ago in which he had mentioned something about one of the pillars at Göbekli Tepe representing a kind of portal to the afterlife. She wondered if it could be connected to the ancient portal sites we'd written about to this point—as it turns out, it is, and like us, Collins has identified numerous ancient sites as having been used as portals to the otherworld, including Göbekli Tepe.

Andrew Collins has spent years studying Göbekli Tepe. Together with his colleague, engineer Rodney Hale, he identified its alignments to Cygnus and used them to date the enclosures; what they found shows that due to the shift in the position of Cygnus over time, new enclosures were built to accurately align to it again.[360]

In particular Collins has attempted to reconstruct the beliefs of Göbekli Tepe's builders, and to track these same beliefs in other ancient traditions across the world. The most detailed carving at the site is known as pillar 43 or the Vulture Stone, which is part of the oldest stone ring uncovered so far, known as Enclosure D, dated to around 9580 BC.[361] Collins believes it's the key that unlocks the central belief Göbekli Tepe was built around.

Pillar 43 is covered in reliefs of numerous animals, abstract objects, and a human figure. According to Collins, pillar 43 is a map of the sky and the animals covering it depict constellations. Of particular note is a scorpion near the bottom of the pillar, above which is a vulture that has a disk almost as though balanced on its outstretched wing. The scorpion is identified as the constellation Scorpius, and the vulture as Cygnus, while the disk is identified as the soul of the recently deceased in the form of its head. As Collins points out, the soul was believed to reside in the head and the people of the region symbolized it using a solid circle during the era of Göbekli Tepe's construction. A headless man appears at the very bottom of the pillar, who is believed to be the deceased and owner of the soul (and head). However, to any observer, the disk clearly looks like the sun, and we suspect that at Göbekli Tepe the soul was not only identified with the head but also the sun, and that the soul's journey in the afterlife was associated with the apparent journey of the sun across the sky, just as it was in ancient Egypt. That's why we would add to the interpretation by saying that the disk may represent both the soul (symbolized by the head) and the sun.

Pillar 43.

What the pillar depicts, Collins says, is "the path of souls"—the way the dead travel to reach heaven in the afterlife; this way was identified with the dark rift of the Milky Way. Although the Milky Way itself is not illustrated on the pillar, in the sky its dark rift is flanked on either end by Scorpius and Cygnus, and so it's indicated by the depiction of these two constellations on the pillar. Particularly, Collins says, it portrays them as how they would have been viewed at night at the time of the pillar's construction with Cygnus at the top (in the region of the northern circumpolar stars) and Scorpius at the bottom (just after it had set beneath the western horizon). Scorpius was seen as guarding the portal of entry to the dark rift likely because it's only one of two places in the sky where the sun crosses the Milky Way (the other being in the vicinity of Taurus, Gemini, and Orion on the opposite side of the sky).[362] Scorpius was thus seen as the entry point of the sun and soul to the dark rift. In other traditions, like in Egypt, North America, and Britain, the focus was on Orion as the entry point to the Milky Way, which is likely why guides of the dead and lords of the afterlife like the Celtic Gwyn Ap Nudd, Norse Odin, and Egyptian Osiris, were identified with Orion as he who stood by the portal to heaven.

It's the very celestial configuration Collins has identified on pillar 43 that Enclosure D, and a number of later enclosures, were aligned to, which of course strongly indicates that this is what pillar 43 was intended to portray.

In short, pillar 43 may be the oldest depiction of an OBE in the world (though one occurring after death). The oldest written descriptions of OBEs appear in the Sumerian Epic of Gilgamesh, and Egyptian Pyramid Texts, and all three share key elements in common.

Reading Collins' interpretation, Lara realized immediately what it meant. If Collins is correct (which we believe he is), then Göbekli Tepe's builders had depicted the portal to heaven. This portal leads from the astral plane, through the dark tunnel that traverses vast regions of the stars before opening out into heaven, where the deceased are greeted by the Spiritual Sun as the light at the end of the tunnel, which they often feel at one with, as described in so many NDEs. The sun's crossing of the Milky Way at Scorpius must have signified the soul entering the portal, before traveling through the darkness of the Milky Way's dark rift and then emerging into the heavenly region of the northern circumpolar stars where the soul and sun are shown as united on pillar 43.

Additionally, Collins has found numerous correspondences between the beliefs that appear to be depicted at Göbekli Tepe and those of other cultures, including ancient Egypt, lending support to his interpretation.

In Egypt, the Mother Goddess was depicted with her body arching across the sky and painted with stars. Her body was the Milky Way, which appears to arch over the sky in a path of starlight. The dark rift was her womb and birth canal; she was shown swallowing the sun that traveled through the darkness of her body, and into her womb, from where it would be reborn. The passage of the sun through her body was used to represent both the path that the soul of the dead took to reach heaven[363] and, secretly, the path of the initiate. Collins interprets the vulture on pillar 43 as the guide of the soul, which he says may have been another symbol of the Mother Goddess, based on the afterlife beliefs in the surrounding region, and the fact that in ancient Egypt the Mother Goddess was often depicted with outstretched vulture wings.[364]

Left: The Egyptian goddess Nut with outstretched wings. Right: The Cygnus constellation.

The path of souls as depicted on pillar 43 also shares similarities with the king's out-of-body journey into the afterlife as narrated in the Pyramid Texts. As discussed earlier, the king was identified as a bird of light whose wings allowed him to fly into the heavenly region of the northern circumpolar stars. In Egypt, the soul was depicted as the Ba, which had the body of a bird. This is illustrated by the bird Cygnus on pillar 43, which may have been seen as a falcon in ancient Egypt, and would depict the soul of the king which was described as a falcon of light. In the Pyramid Texts, the king travels together with his Heavenly Father the sun to rise with him into the northern circumpolar stars, illustrated by the disk of the sun on the wing of Cygnus in the northern stars on pillar 43. In the Pyramid Texts, the king must travel along the Milky Way to get to the northern circumpolar stars, which is indicated between the scorpion and vulture on pillar 43.

The placement of Scorpius at the entrance to the portal to the dark tunnel leading to heaven makes sense of a strange set of characters in the Epic of Gilgamesh. As mentioned earlier in the chapter, Gilgamesh travels through a long dark tunnel to reach heaven; his journey shares similarities with the journey of the sun god Ra in Egypt. But what Lara couldn't understand is why, in the Epic of Gilgamesh, the gate to enter the tunnel is guarded by a pair of scorpion men. It just sounded so bizarre, but now it makes sense given that Scorpius guards the portal to heaven on pillar 43, and the sun's entrance to the dark rift in the sky!

> "There were scorpion-men guarding its gate [...]
> at sunrise and sunset they guarded the sun."[365]
> ~ THE EPIC OF GILGAMESH

Collins has also found traces of these afterlife beliefs in the vicinity of Göbekli Tepe, among the later Bronze Age peoples of Anatolia, revealing they survived in the region over thousands of years.

> "[...] this same concept of a second birth in the afterlife was present among the Bronze Age peoples of Anatolia circa 3500–1200 BCE. They called it 'the day of (one's) mother,' the transformation process being achieved through the intercession, not of a biological mother, but of a primeval mother, whose chthonic womb enabled rebirth in the next world."[366]
>
> ~ ANDREW COLLINS, THE CYGNUS KEY

This next world was called the "Meadow of the Blessed," where the soul lived out a second life,[367] and is fundamentally the same as the Egyptian concept of Aaru, and Greek Elysium.

We had already identified this belief as being used as the basis of ancient sites in Egypt and Europe—that is, the souls of the dead and of living initiates were seen as being born into a heavenly afterlife by way of a Great Mother goddess whose womb was symbolized by pyramids, mounds, temples, and stone circles aligned to the sun and stars.

Could Göbekli Tepe's circular stone enclosures have also represented the womb of the Mother Goddess in some way? Could they too, like pyramids and mounds, have served as portal sites for the living and dead?

Two enclosures at Göbekli Tepe (C and D) feature porthole stones, which are stones that had holes carved out of them; these are too small for an adult to fit through, but could be used to sight celestial objects. The remains of stone rings were also found scattered around the site, which the site's lead excavator, Dr. Klaus Schmidt, called "soul holes." Collins proposes both the portholes and soul holes served as portals for the site's priestly class, and possibly also for the dead, to pass into the spirit world.[368] Specifically the porthole stones were orientated to the setting of the brightest star in Cygnus, Deneb, which as is illustrated on pillar 43, was seen as located in heaven. Thus, the portholes and soul holes may have functioned in the same way as the northern shaft in the King's Chamber of the Great Pyramid, to direct someone out of the body to the portal to heaven, meaning Göbekli Tepe could have served the same function as the pyramids, mounds, and stone circles we have explored to this point.

> "[...] during rites and ceremonies, a person entering the site's enclosures approached between the twin central monoliths and focused their eyes on the porthole stone. The stone would form a bridge or portal between the liminal realm created by the enclosure's circular interiors and the otherwordly environments thought to exist beyond the physical plane."[369]
>
> ~ ANDREW COLLINS, THE CYGNUS KEY

Left is an ancient site in England called Mên-an-Tol that may have either once been part of a standing stone circle or a nearby "portal tomb."[370] It's believed the hole stone may have been used for passing the dead through in a ritual of rebirth.[371] It's possible, like the porthole stones of Göbekli Tepe, that those of the British Isles may also have functioned as a kind of portal to heaven in some way. Right: A modern sculpture on a private estate in England called "Heaven's Gate."

Additionally, the carving of a pair of crouched felines facing in opposite directions appeared above a doorway in one Göbekli Tepe's enclosures; this is just like the symbol of Aker in Egypt, which represented the entrances to the portals to heaven and hell.[372]

Collins and Hale also discovered that a number of enclosures at Göbekli Tepe appear to have been designed to have certain acoustic properties—they theorize the ratios they were constructed with may have been intended to optimize the acoustics produced within the enclosures (in the form of ritual chanting or talking by a priest/priestess to an audience inside), particularly to optimize sounds made at a fourth musical interval.[373] If true, it would mean that somehow these acoustics were used to help induce the mystical experiences these enclosures were built to facilitate.

ZOROASTRIAN

Zoroastrianism became the state religion of Persia (what is today Iran) from the sixth or seventh century BC. It was founded by Zoroaster/Zarathustra, who is generally believed to have lived during the second millennium BC, and existed over thousands of years to this day—although it's estimated there are only 110,000 to 120,000 adherents remaining. It was derived from the earlier Indo-European religion in the region (and thus from the ancient Religion of the Sun), which Zoroaster reformed; among other reforms, he opposed cruel animal sacrifice and the excessive use of the ritual drink haoma it had fallen into.[374] Zoroastrian texts contain accounts of OBEs, though no tradition or practice of having OBEs has survived today in Zoroastrianism. It has suffered numerous periods of intense persecution in its history, during which nearly all of its texts were destroyed.[375]

Zoroastrians believe in a nonphysical realm called *menog/mainyu*, where people go when they die. Everything in the physical world has its *menog/* etheric counterpart that exists in *menog*, but in addition it's also where heaven and hell exist, and nonphysical beings reside, both those that are divine and evil, as well as each one's higher Being.[376][377]

Zoroastrians believe that everything consists of both physical and nonphysical parts. All living beings have an eternal soul, called an *urvan*.[378] Humans also have *baodh*, which is said to be the receptacle of knowledge and wisdom, and the source of reason, intellect, and memory (and sounds like the human mind). All beings and inanimate objects also have an invisible etheric body/aspect, *kehrp*. The *kehrp* is said to be the counterpart of the physical body, reflecting its state of health, being the receptacle of energy (and sounds like it may be the equivalent of the Ka of ancient Egypt, and pranic sheath of Hinduism, which I refer to as the personality). Zoroastrians also believe in a *tevishi*, which is a nonphysical body that's created and shaped by our tendencies, desires, values, and beliefs (which sounds like it may correspond to an emotional or mental body). Then there is the *ushtan*, which is an energy connected to one's breath, comparable to prana in Hinduism and qi in Taoism. The *kehrp, tevishi*, and *ushtan* are believed to be the perishable nonphysical parts of us, as they are said to disintegrate after death. The *urvan* and *baodh*, however, are those parts that continue to exist after death. Though spiritual, it's said that in themselves they don't make one divine; it's their proper use that does. Highest of all is the *fravashi*,[379] one's own higher Being which guides them throughout their life. Through living in accordance with divine law, *asha*, it's said one could be united with their *fravashi* after death, becoming a "united fravashi"—a divine being that can work to help others from the spiritual realm. The *fravashi* was symbolized by the person inside a winged sun disk in the sky.[380][381]

A number of stories in Zoroastrian texts also reveal that it's possible to travel to the otherworld (*menog*) in OBEs. Following are four accounts of OBEs from Zoroastrian texts.

The first is from the Book of Arda Viraf, and narrates how a man called Viraf is chosen as the most righteous among men to undertake a journey to the afterlife to prove Zoroastrian beliefs are true. It's unknown when it was originally written, only that it reached its final form between the ninth and tenth centuries AD.

Viraf is given a drink of wine in three golden cups containing an unspecified drug (referred to as *mang*) and has what sounds like an OBE or NDE; his wives express concern that he may die, but they are assured Viraf will return unharmed after seven days. These three cups are likely connected to an ancient ritual drinking vessel consisting of three cups specially joined together found in the Eastern Mediterranean and Europe, and to the three wells/cauldrons that Odin drinks from in Norse tradition as part of his OBE.[382]

After finishing the drink, Viraf says grace, lies down and sleeps for seven days, after which he awakes and recounts what he experienced:

> "And the soul of Viraf went, from the body, to the Chinvat bridge of Chakat-i-Daitik, and came back the seventh day, and went into the body. Viraf rose up, as if he arose from a pleasant sleep, thinking of Vohuman and joyful. And those sisters, with the Dasturs of the religion and the Mazdayasnians, when they saw Viraf, became pleased and joyful; and they said: 'Be thou welcome, Viraf, the messenger of us Mazdayasnians, who has come from the realm of the dead to this realm of the living.'" [383]

In his account Viraf was first met by two divine figures who guide him:

> "In that first night, Srosh the pious and Ataru the angel came to meet me, and they bowed to me, and said: 'Be thou welcome, Arda Viraf, although you have come when it is not your time.'" [384]

Meeting a divine figure and being told it's not the deceased's time to be there are two things that happen quite often in NDEs. Then he says:

> "I came up to the Chinvat bridge, the very wide and strong and created by Auharmazd."[385]

A bridge or barrier is often seen in NDEs as a place where they choose to cross into the land of the dead or turn back to return to their physical body. He then sees his own religion and deeds in the graceful form of a young woman, which is reminiscent of the life review many go through in NDEs.

After Viraf crosses the bridge, he is shown heaven and hell by his guides:

> "Afterward, Srosh the pious, and Ataru the angel, took hold of my hand, and said: 'Come on, so that we may show you heaven and hell; and the splendour and glory and ease and comfort and pleasure and joy and delight and gladness and fragrance which are the reward of the pious in heaven. We shall show you the darkness and confinement and ingloriousness and misfortune and distress and evil and pain and sickness and dreadfulness and fearfulness and hurtfulness and stench in the punishments of hell [...].'" [386]

The account of Viraf is very similar to that of Zoroaster himself in the text Zand-i Vohuman Yasht, the oldest surviving copy of which is dated to around AD 1400, though its contents are known to be much older.

In it, God (Ahura Mazda) gives Zoroaster a drink that causes him to go on a dream journey to the realm of the afterlife lasting seven days, just as Viraf does. In it he sees a very wealthy person as having a foul soul, residing in "the wicked existence" (which sounds like hell), and a poor man in "Best Existence" (which sounds like heaven). This account contains elements often found in NDEs, and may have resulted from someone putting their body in a near-death state.

Modern illustration of Zoroaster.

"He took hold of Zoroaster's hand; He, Ahura Mazda, is the beneficent spirit, Creator of the material existence, and holy; He laid the wisdom of all knowledge, in the form of water, on the hand of Zoroaster; and He said: 'Drink forth.' And forth Zoroaster drank it; thereupon, the wisdom of all-knowledge intermingled into Zoroaster.

For seven days and nights, Zoroaster was in the wisdom of Ahura Mazda. Thereupon, Zoroaster beheld men and animals in the seven regions of the earth [...]. On the seventh day and night, He took away the wisdom of all-knowledge from Zoroaster. [...]

[Zoroaster thought]: 'I have slept a long time [...].'

Ahura Mazda asked [...]: 'What didst thou see in the merry dream produced by Ahura Mazda?'

He, Zoroaster, replied: 'O spiritual and beneficent Ahura Mazda! Creator of the material existence! I saw a prosperous person having immense wealth, who was infamous in the material life, of a foul and feeble soul, and he was in the wicked existence; he did not seem welcome to me. I saw a helpless poor man having no possession, his soul thriving in the Best Existence; he seemed welcome to me.'"[387]

I doubt the drink that caused Zoroaster to go on his seven-day-long journey was water, as here again we find the same experience of traveling out of the body to the realm of the afterlife for seven days, as we saw with the Twice Born in Egypt earlier in the chapter, and so it looks like the journeys of Zoroaster and Viraf are very likely to have been based on the same procedure. The drink that both Viraf and Zoroaster consumed has been identified as the ancient ritual drink of Zoroastrian religion called haoma,[388] the ingredients of which have been lost to history.

A third similar account is that of King Wishtasp/Vishtasp, who converts to Zoroastrianism after having an OBE in what is considered the most important event in the history of Zoroastrianism, as he went on to become instrumental in the diffusion of the religion. In the account, Ahura Mazda sends a spirit messenger to the king, who gives him a drink of *hom* and *mang*, described as "the illuminating nourishment which would give his soul eye vision over the spiritual (*menog*) existence." Afterward, "When [Wishtasp] drank, he became stard [spread out, sprawled] immediately, and they led his soul to paradise and showed him the value of accepting the Religion. When he emerged from stard-ness he called for Zoroaster..."[389] Another version of the story says that Zoroaster healed the king's horse, and then gave the king a drink of consecrated wine, after which the king left his body and ascended to heaven, returned, and converted to Zoroastrianism.[390]

Then there is the experience of the very powerful and influential third century Zoroastrian priest Kartir. He authored a set of inscriptions at a site called Naqsh-e Rajab, near the ancient city of Persepolis in Iran, and was the only non-king granted the right to have an inscription.[391] His inscriptions describe an OBE he had in which he is led by divine guides through the realm of the afterlife. He had asked the gods to be shown the reality of heaven and hell so that he and others could be sure they existed, and in his ensuing OBE is shown both. There is no mention of Kartir ingesting anything to have his experience.[392]

Kartir holding an inscription describing his OBE.

It appears haoma played a part in initiation rites in which it was used to give Zoroastrian priests an OBE,[393] as was similarly done in Egypt and Europe as we've already seen. However, it's possible there had once also been meditative and substance-free techniques for having OBEs, as there were in other Indo-European traditions, but that these were lost during the many persecutions of Zoroastrianism.

GNOSTIC AND CHRISTIAN

Jesus has a number of OBEs in the ancient Gnostic texts that were excluded from the Bible, while his disciples have dreams, which I include in the section on dreams further on.

In the ancient Gnostic text Pistis Sophia, Jesus describes an OBE he has in which he journeys through the realms of heaven and returns. These realms are clearly linked to the spiritual light of the sun, as Jesus taught the knowledge of the ancient Religion of the Sun,[394] but this became lost and veiled with the creation of Christianity. Insertions in parentheses below are mine.

> "Jesus said: 'It came to pass then, when the sun had risen in the east, that a great light-power came down, in which was my Vesture, which I had left behind in the four-and-twentieth mystery (there are twenty-four hours in a day, so it is at the completion of the path of the sun), as I have said unto you. [...]
>
> It came to pass then, when I saw the mystery of all these words in the vesture which was sent me, that straightway I clothed myself therewith, and I shone most exceedingly and soared into the height. [...]
>
> I came before the [first] gate of the firmament, shining most exceedingly, and there was no measure for the light which was about me, and the gates of the firmament were shaken one over against another and all opened at once.
>
> And I left that region behind me and ascended to the great *æons* of the rulers and came before their veils and their gates, shining most exceedingly, and there was no measure for the light which was about me. It came to pass then, when I arrived at the twelve *æons*, that their veils and their gates were shaken one over against the other. Their veils drew themselves apart of their own accord, and their gates opened one over against the other. And I entered into the *æons*, shining most exceedingly [...].'
>
> When then he had said this to his disciples, he said unto them: 'Who hath ears to hear, let him hear.' [...]

> Now when Mary (Magdalene) had heard the Saviour speak these words, she exulted greatly, and she came before Jesus, fell down before him, adored his feet and said unto him: 'My Lord, hearken unto me, that I may question thee on this word, before that thou discoursest with us about the regions whither thou didst go.'"[395]
> ~ PISTIS SOPHIA

The Pistis Sophia details teachings on very high mysteries Jesus is said to have given the disciples after his resurrection. It was discovered in 1773 and is believed to have been written between the third and fourth centuries AD.[396] Today, it's classed among the texts that are referred to by scholars as "Gnostic," a word which means "having knowledge," in reference to a particular kind of knowledge that is gained from inner, transcendental experience. They espouse the teachings of Jesus, but share a worldview rejected by the early Church, as Gnostics sought their own personal spiritual knowledge (gnosis), which they gave greater authority than the conventional doctrines and traditions of the church.[397] This is probably one of the reasons Gnostic texts were excluded from the Bible and banned. And this is why they were lost for over a thousand years and have only come to light relatively recently.

Jesus has a number of OBEs in ancient Gnostic texts in which he visits heavenly realms and returns.

In a much more recently discovered ancient Gnostic text, Jesus has another OBE. It appears in the Gospel of Judas, which is thought to have been discovered in Egypt sometime between 1950-1980. It then surfaced in the antiquities market in Geneva in 1983, and was published in English in 2006. It's believed to have been written in the second century AD,[398] and contains a dialogue between Jesus and Judas that reveals Jesus had prearranged his betrayal with Judas, whom he considered one of his most advanced disciples. In the following excerpt, Jesus leaves his disciples after speaking with them, then reappears the next morning and tells them he visited other holy realms that night.

> "Judas said to him, 'When will you tell me these things, and [when] will the great day of light dawn for the generation?'

But when he said this, Jesus left him.

The next morning, after this happened, Jesus [appeared] to his disciples again.

They said to him, 'Master, where did you go and what did you do when you left us?'

Jesus said to them, 'I went to another great and holy generation.'

His disciples said to him, 'Lord, what is the great generation that is superior to us and holier than us, that is not now in these realms?'"[399]

~ THE GOSPEL OF JUDAS

In the Gnostic text Dialogue of the Savior, what sounds like an out-of-body experience is recorded in which Jesus takes some of the disciples (Judas, Matthew, and Mary Magdalene) to the edge of heaven and hell (the abyss) to show them what he (the Word) represents. Words in parentheses are mine.

"Then he (Jesus, took) [...] Judas and Matthew and Mary (to) [...] the edge of heaven and earth. And when he placed his hand upon them, they hoped that they might (see?) [...] it. Judas raised his eyes and saw an exceedingly high place, and he saw the place of the abyss below.

Judas said to Matthew, 'Brother, who will be able to climb up to such a height or down to the bottom of the abyss? For there is a tremendous fire there, and something very fearful!' At that moment, a Word came forth from it.

As it stood there, he saw how it had come down. Then he said to it, 'Why have you come down?'

And the Son of Man greeted them and said to them, 'A seed from a power was deficient, and it went down to the abyss of the earth. And the Greatness remembered it, and he sent the Word to it. It brought it up into his presence, so that the First Word might not fail.'"[400]

~ THE DIALOGUE OF THE SAVIOR

Jesus is also attributed as teaching about OBEs in a little-known text called the Essene Gospel of Peace. The Hungarian philologist/linguist, philosopher, and psychologist Edmond Bordeaux Szekely claimed to have come across the Essene Gospel of Peace (among other ancient manuscripts about Jesus) while studying at the Vatican in 1923, and published its translation, though the Vatican denies it ever existed.[401]

Here Jesus says that with sleep we enter another eternal realm, which he associates with the stars, just as the astral is associated with the sky and stars in Hinduism and ancient Egyptian religion.

> "[Jesus said] close your eyes, Sons of Light, and in sleep contemplate the oneness of all life everywhere. For I tell you truly, in the daylight hours are our feet on the ground and we have no wings with which to fly. But our spirits are not tied to the earth, and with the coming of night we overcome our attachment to the earth and join with that which is eternal. For the Son of Man is not all that he seems, and only with the eyes of the spirit can we see those golden threads which link us with all life everywhere."[402]
> ~ THE ESSENE GOSPEL OF PEACE

He then goes on to describe a practice to have an OBE, by concentrating on the stars.

> "[Jesus said] And when darkness gently closes the eyes of the angels of the Earthly Mother, then shall you also sleep, that your spirit may join the unknown angels of the Heavenly Father. And in the moments before you sleep, then shall you think of the bright and glorious stars, the white, shining, far-seen and far-piercing stars. For your thoughts before sleep are as the bow of the skillful archer, that sends the arrow where he wills. Let your thoughts before sleep be with the stars; for the stars are Light, and the Heavenly Father is Light, even that Light which is a thousand times brighter than the brightness of a thousand suns. Enter the Holy Stream of Light, that the shackles of death may lose their hold forever, and breaking free from the bonds of earth, ascend the Holy Stream of Light through the blazing radiance of the stars, into the endless kingdom of the Heavenly Father. Unfold your wings of light, and in the eye of your thought, soar with the stars into the farthest reaches of heaven, where untold suns blaze with light. For at the beginning of the times, the Holy Law said, let there be Light, and there was Light. And you shall be one with it, and the power of the Holy Light Stream will fill your whole body, and you will tremble before its might. Say the word "Light," as you breathe deeply of the angel of air, and you will become the Light itself; and the Holy Stream will carry you to the endless kingdom of the Heavenly Father, there losing itself in the eternal Sea of Light which gives birth to all creation."[403]
> ~ THE ESSENE GOSPEL OF PEACE

What caught our attention is how similar this description is to the afterlife experience of the king in the Egyptian Pyramid Texts. The king too leaves his physical body behind, breaking free from the confines of Earth, to soar in his light body like a bird into the heavenly realm of his father in the stars as he becomes one with the light. Consider how similar some of this wording is:

> "The energy forces of Unis are all around him.
> His female angels are under his feet.
> His spirit powers are above his head [...]
> His heart throbs as he lives in the form of every star[404]
>
> moving outside the bonds, he is free[405]
>
> Say the words: O light, bird [...] As you become a bird of light[406]
>
> O winding stream of the glittering sky, open the path for Unis, that Unis take the path.[407]
>
> Unis goes around, carried in the realm of stars,
> Pure, alive on the numinous horizon,
> His light body among them, washed white,
> Among them in the hand of his father,
> In the hand of the universe.[408]
>
> You flow with your father the universe [...] made of starlight you are free."[409]
>
> ~ THE PYRAMID TEXTS

What this may well mean is that the stream of light that Jesus refers to is the same as the winding stream of stars in the Pyramid Texts, which is a reference to the Milky Way that as we've seen, was the tunnel, birth canal, and path that led from the portal in the astral plane to heaven. And Jesus actually tells us this is where it leads—to the kingdom of the Heavenly Father. Not only that, but he says this stream of light leads back to its source, the eternal Sea of Light, which sounds like the Source that people see in NDEs as the light shining in heaven.

If this description really originated from Jesus, it tells us he had the ability to travel through the portal to heaven in OBEs. This is not an OBE that most people can have, as I'll explain further on, and shows that Jesus was spiritually advanced (if that wasn't clear already).

But how is it that Jesus is recorded as describing the most central OBE in Egypt (and the ancient Religion of the Sun), in such a similar way? It would indicate that there were other people who knew how to have this OBE naturally too, and that the knowledge of how to do it may have been passed down over thousands of years. Could it be that Jesus was describing an OBE that the initiates of Egypt (the Twice Born) had not after death, but in life? As Lara writes in *The Ancient Religion of the Sun*, she believes there is evidence that Jesus learned the Religion of the Sun during his "lost years," and that he had connections to Egypt. He too taught about becoming Twice Born or "born again."

The most well-known OBE (or NDE) Jesus is said to have had (in Christian tradition, not explicitly in the Gospels) occurred after his crucifixion, while he lay dead in the tomb before resurrecting. During this time, he's said to have descended to the realm of the dead in the underworld; this experience is known as "the harrowing of hell." Different reasons were later put forward as to why Jesus went to hell—to conquer the devil, to defeat death, to complete his humiliation, and/or to raise the just who'd died before receiving his redemption.[410]

Jesus entering hell out of the body after his crucifixion.

But what if there is a different explanation for what happened to Jesus during that time? The events of Jesus' death bear some resemblance to the ritual of the Twice Born, who also had an OBE in the realm of the afterlife, and there is evidence to suggest that Jesus was also given a special drink before his OBE with the help of secretive initiates.

There is already evidence that Jesus arranged events in his life leading up to his crucifixion. For instance, in ancient Mandaean texts it says that Jesus and John the Baptist became priests of an ancient religion together prior to Jesus' Baptism, and thus already knew each other,[411] while the ancient Gospel of Judas reveals that Jesus prearranged his betrayal with Judas.[412] So it's not a stretch to consider that Jesus could have arranged more, including the most important events in his life—his crucifixion and resurrection.

In the Gospels of Matthew and Mark, before Jesus is crucified, he is offered wine mixed with gall or myrrh, which he refuses.[413] Hours later while on the cross, in Matthew and Mark, Jesus is again offered a drink, this time of wine vinegar, which he again refuses (as also narrated in the Gospel of the Kailedy, a text we introduce in a moment). In the Gospel of Luke there is no record of any drink at all. But curiously in the Gospel of John, Jesus asks for a drink once he declares his task finished, and after he drinks, almost immediately leaves his body:

> "Later, knowing that everything had now been finished, and so that Scripture would be fulfilled, Jesus said, 'I am thirsty.' A jar of wine vinegar was there, so they soaked a sponge in it, put the sponge on a stalk of the hyssop plant, and lifted it to Jesus' lips. When he had received the drink, Jesus said, 'It is finished.' With that, he bowed his head and gave up his spirit."[414]
> ~ JOHN 19:28-30

Was this drink really vinegar, or was his request for a drink at the appropriate moment really a cue to be given the bitter drink used by the Twice Born for releasing the spirit and making the body appear dead?

> "This concerns the mystery of the Twice Born. It relates to those born again, to those who have endured the awfulness of the false death which many do not survive; who have drunk deeply from Koriladwen, the smooth bitter brew which releases the spirit; who have entered Ogofnaum through the thundering doors."[415]
> ~ THE KOLBRIN

Jesus being offered a drink while on the cross.

Before moving on, we need to introduce another text we'll be referring to along with the canonical Gospels. It's The Gospel of the Kailedy, which is a text that contains a more detailed retelling of Jesus' life. It's said to be an ancient collection of accounts about Jesus that were preserved alongside the Kolbrin, and published for the first time in 1998. The term Kailedy is said to mean "wise strangers" in reference to Joseph of Arimathea and a group of Jesus' followers who are recounted as fleeing to Britain to escape persecution, and are named as the source of the majority of the Kailedy's narrative, which was subsequently preserved in Britain for nearly two thousand years.[416] [417]

Returning to the events of the crucifixion, in the Gospel of John, Jesus is declared dead after his side is pierced with a spear by a Roman centurion, sparing him from having his legs broken.[418] In the other canonical Gospels and the Gospel of the Kailedy, however, neither are his legs broken or his side pierced—in Mark and the Kailedy the centurion merely declares he is dead.[419] It's possible the centurion was also in on things in some way, as in the Gospels, there were centurions who followed Jesus.[420]

These events give us a clue as to why Jesus could have asked to be given a drink that knocked him unconscious. The purpose of the drink may have been to put him in a near-death state, meaning that he would appear dead to all those around him without actually dying. This could have saved him from having his legs broken (and possibly from being gouged by a spear), so that although horribly tortured, his injuries may have been survivable. Taking a drink that caused someone to appear as if dead for days, as we have seen, was used by the Twice Born of Egypt. And we'll soon see that some mysterious white-robed men even make an appearance in the events of Jesus' resurrection.

Jesus' body is taken away by Joseph of Arimathea, who was a wealthy member of the supreme Jewish council in Jerusalem, the Sanhedrin, but secretly a follower of Jesus.[421] He's likely to have been a relative of Jesus, which is why Pilate allows him to take Jesus (in accordance with the law as his next of kin) and the other members of the Sanhedrin are unable to stop him.[422] Joseph has a stone tomb of his own (stone chambers were used by the Twice Born, symbolizing the womb) that had already been prepared, and takes Jesus there the evening before the Sabbath.[423]

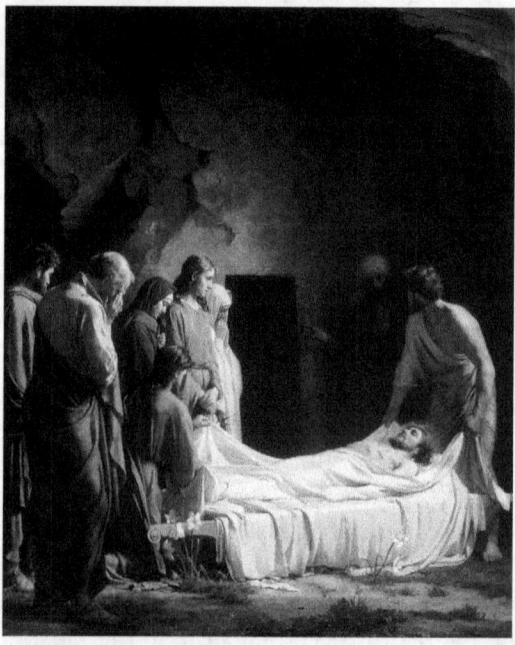

Jesus placed in the tomb belonging to Joseph of Arimathea.

The betrayal seems to have been timed so that Jesus would be left in the tomb on the Sabbath (our Saturday), as on this day, under Jewish law, Jews had to rest.[424] The Kailedy mysteriously says that things happened on the Sabbath that were not to be written.[425] It appears the Sabbath allowed secretive people around Jesus to take him away, likely to be healed, unseen, undisturbed, and unrecorded.

The Kailedy does mention that there were disciples of Jesus who took Jesus' body away on the Sabbath—they had got around the guards stationed at the tomb by telling them that Jesus had been hurriedly placed in a tomb that wasn't his due to the approaching Sabbath, and that they were taking him to his proper tomb. This had apparently satisfied the guards,[426] who are only mentioned in Matthew's Gospel but not the other canonical Gospels. Of course if this really happened, it was a ruse, as in the canonical Gospels there is nothing of Jesus being moved to another tomb.

According to the Gospels, those who took him on the Sabbath weren't his Jewish disciples, as the disciples didn't visit the tomb on the Sabbath, but only Peter and one other disciple did the following day on Sunday.[427] Mary Magdalene, and other female followers of Jesus, went first on Sunday morning at dawn. They found Jesus was gone but there were one or two men waiting inside—in Mark's Gospel it's one young man dressed in a white robe, in Luke's it's two men in gleaming clothes. He/they tell the women that Jesus is risen, and give them instructions to tell the disciples where to meet Jesus.[428]

The men who greet the women at the empty tomb are often portrayed as angels, but in two of the Gospels they are simply described as men in white robes. Who were these "men in white"?

"[...] when they looked up, they saw that the stone, which was very large, had been rolled away. As they entered the tomb, they saw a young man dressed in a white robe sitting on the right side, and they were alarmed. 'Don't be alarmed,' he said. 'You are looking for Jesus the Nazarene, who was crucified. He has risen! He is not here. See the place where they laid him. But go, tell his disciples and Peter, "He is going ahead of you into Galilee. There you will see him, just as he told you."' Trembling and bewildered, the women went out and fled from the tomb."[429]

~ MARK 16:4-8

These men may have been from among the Twice Born, who helped arrange everything, and provided enough time for Jesus to recover (and likely to be tended and healed) for his first short appearance to the disciples that night (his next appearance was a week later).[430]

In the Gospel of John, in addition to "two angels in white" sitting in the tomb, there is also a nearby "gardener" who Mary Magdalene sees and talks to before she recognizes he's Jesus.[431] In the Kailedy however, this gardener is not Jesus, but another plant, possibly from among the Twice Born, who instructs Mary on what to do next,[432] and was probably made into Jesus by the Gospel writer who never explains how Mary didn't recognize Jesus immediately.

The resurrected Jesus appearing to Mary Magdalene outside his tomb as "the gardener." Why did Mary not initially recognize him? Was it because the writer of John was trying to reconcile contradictory accounts of who Mary met outside the tomb?

There are numerous contradictions and elaborations in the four Gospels; for example, in Matthew's account the man in the white robe appears to have been embellished into an angel that descended from heaven, rolled away the stone, and caused the guards to collapse with fear as if dead—likely to explain how Jesus got past the large stone and guards, having no other explanation at hand.[433]

Who were these men in white—were they from the order of the Twice Born still active in Egypt, or by that time had it moved elsewhere? This is a question we are yet to answer, but it's almost certain Jesus spent time with other spiritual groups during his "lost years," and one of these looks likely to have been the Twice Born. We call this our Jesus Twice Born Theory.

Having said this, it seems obvious that Jesus didn't take a drink that put him in a near-death state to have an OBE to heaven, as the Twice Born had done. As we've outlined already, Jesus is recorded as having OBEs to heaven before his crucifixion, and if these accounts are true, then he certainly had no need to go through the crucifixion and risk his life for such an OBE! Rather, the events of Jesus' life were arranged to symbolically portray the initiations on the path of the Spiritual Sun, in which betrayal, crucifixion/death, and resurrection are central. These events are what the ritual of the Twice Born was originally based on, which is why the events of Jesus' death and resurrection share similarities to the Twice Born ritual.

However, it's possible Jesus had no drink at all, as narrated in most Gospel accounts, and really did die and revive, and miraculously heal, as has happened to so many who've had NDEs. The difference is that Jesus foretold his resurrection, knowing for some time it would occur. It seems, regardless of whether he drank anything or not, that many of the people involved in the events of his death and resurrection were prearranged, likely including some from among an ancient, secret spiritual order.

One more very interesting correlation—as we saw at Göbekli Tepe, Scorpius was seen as guarding the entrance to the tunnel leading to heaven. Scorpions are associated with betrayal, and it can be no coincidence that betrayal preceded Jesus' death, and that Jesus is recorded as arranging it with Judas. In Greek mythology Scorpius (as a scorpion) was the opponent of the Orion constellation (as a hunter).[434]

It seems Jesus intended the events of his life to be carried forward as part of a new teaching/religion for the world, and for that certain events had to be fulfilled and people around him had to play their part. We don't wish to diminish what Jesus did at all, and we don't think this does—it only reveals how much more human involvement there was, and thus difficult and dangerous what he did was. Things could have easily gone wrong at any moment, and facing that takes a lot more courage than simply thinking it's all going to be supernaturally taken care of by angels materializing and rolling away stones, etc. Our aim is to shed further light on why Jesus did the incredible things he did with the hope that people will come to understand more of his message.

There is much more to say about all this—more than can be covered here. Lara writes about it in a chapter on Jesus in her book *The Ancient Religion of the Sun*.

There is also an often-cited reference to an OBE in mainstream Christianity, which could instead be an NDE (as we explain in chapter 5). It appears in the New Testament, where Paul said:

> "I know a man in Christ who fourteen years ago was caught up to the third heaven. Whether it was in the body or out of the body I do not know—God knows."[435]
> ~ 2 CORINTHIANS 12:2

Also in the New Testament, the disciple John receives the vision recorded in Revelation while "in the Spirit." It begins:

> "On the Lord's Day I was in the Spirit, and I heard behind me a loud voice like a trumpet, which said: 'Write on a scroll what you see and send it to the seven churches [...].'"[436]
> ~ REVELATION 1:10-11

John pictured sleeping while receiving the vision recorded in Revelation.

Is it any wonder that Gnostic texts, so named because of their emphasis on personal, mystical experience, contain references to Jesus having OBEs? They also contain references to the disciples having OBEs and symbolic dreams, often involving Jesus in some way. Thus, these texts reveal that OBEs and dreams were an important part of the transcendental experiences of Jesus, the disciples, and the ancient Gnostics.

No tradition of Gnostic Christians survived, as they were obliterated by the Church. Yet today there are numerous Christians who've been given OBEs through divine intervention, in which they are shown important messages, often by Jesus, even though they may not know what OBEs are. One example is of Bill Wiese who had an OBE that lasted twenty-three minutes in which he was pulled out of his body at 3 a.m. and taken to hell by Jesus, so that he could come back and tell people what he saw.

> "You might ask, 'Bill, how do you know this wasn't just a bad dream?' Well [...] on the way back from this experience I had viewed my body lying on the floor. This was not a near-death experience. This was an out-of-body experience that comes under the classification of a vision in the Bible. You remember in 2nd Corinthians 12:1 and 2 when Paul was caught up into heaven in a vision? He said whether in the body or out of the body, he didn't know. Well the Lord just happened to show me that I left my body, so that's how I know it wasn't just a bad dream. [...] I got up at three o-clock in the morning, and suddenly I was pulled out of my body and I found myself falling through the air and I landed in a prison cell in hell. [...] I was fully awake and cognizant, just like I'm standing here now. It was just as real."[437]
> ~ BILL WIESE

TAOIST

Taoism is an ancient religion that developed in China, the roots of which go back to the Religion of the Sun. It has shaped Chinese culture for more than two thousand years, and for a time was China's state religion. Travel in the astral plane was part of the secretive practices of Taoism, and its texts preserve what appear to be some of the oldest recorded astral projection exercises in the world.

Taoist immortal flying through the air.

Taoist texts describe mystical flights to supernatural realms, and the ability of one's subtle spirit to travel while one is physically sitting in one's room, the spirit said to be able to traverse ten thousand miles in a single day. These flights were undertaken particularly to receive teachings from spiritual beings.[438]

> "It is the subtle spirit which darts beyond and knowledge which stretches within . . . That is why Lao-tzu [the founder of Taoism] says there is no need to cross one's threshold to know the world, nor to look out of a window to see the celestial order."[439]
> ~ HUAI-NAN-TZU

References to astral travel can be found in a seventeenth century Chinese novel about one of the legendary Eight Immortals of Chinese mythology called Han Xiangzi. It follows his journey to achieve immortality and then convert his Confucian uncle Han Yu (Tuizhi), who was a real historical figure that lived from 768-824 AD, to Taoism.

In this first excerpt, Han Xiangzi performs a "sleeping prayer" and his "yang spirit" travels to heaven.

> "Everyone was laughing secretly, unaware that Xiangzi did not intend to sleep, but was performing a sleeping prayer. While he was asleep on the mat, snoring loudly, his sweat pouring like rain, his yang spirit went straight to the gate of Southern Heaven. The celestial general guarding the gate [...] led Xiangzi straight up to the Precious Palace of the Numinous Empyrean for an audience with the Jade Emperor."[440]
> ~ THE STORY OF HAN XIANGZI

In a subsequent OBE, the yang spirit of Han Xiangzi travels to the underworld.

> "Earlier on, when Xiangzi had drunk three cups of wine and lay sleeping on the floor, everyone around thought he was drunk, while in fact he had sent out his yang spirit to go directly to purgatory. [...] Xiangzi [...] left the underworld, and returned to the world of humans. There he feigned to awaken from his drunken slumber, without letting ordinary mortals realize what had really been going on. [...] 'I didn't fall down drunk, but instead went before King Yama in the underworld [...]' Xiangzi explained. 'That's why I went to sleep. [...] While I was lying here, my spirit traveled to the underworld.'"[441]
> ~ THE STORY OF HAN XIANGZI

There is an often-quoted account of astral travel from this same story, in which Xiangzi is witnessed lying asleep, while at the same time appearing in another room:

> "Using his divine powers, Xiangzi shook his sleeves, fell to the ground, and with his drum as his pillow fell fast asleep, snoring and motionless. His primordial spirit, however, went straight into the banquet room

and said, 'My lords, here I am again.' [...] When Tuizhi walked out the gate with the officials to take a look, there really was a Taoist sleeping on the ground and snoring like thunder. And yet inside, in the side room, there was another Taoist beating a fisher drum and singing Taoist songs. The officials all said, 'Although there are two different people, their faces and clothes are exactly alike. Clearly he is a divine immortal who can divide his body and appear in several places at once.' [...] Thereupon Tuizhi said to the Taoist, 'Leaving the body is nothing but a fraudulent trick. How dare you come here and cheat me? I will burn this body of yours—let's see what abode your primordial spirit will go to then.' At that moment, the Taoist in the side room came walking out, and the Taoist sleeping on the ground woke up. The two merged into one."[442]

~ THE STORY OF HAN XIANGZI

Although this sounds like an OBE, it's also quite different, as when someone has an OBE, other people in the physical world don't see them, just as they don't see people out of their bodies dreaming. I suspect this account may have been based on knowledge about OBEs, but was embellished.

Han Xiangzi uses his ability to astral project to try and convince his uncle to devote himself to his own cultivation so as to escape hell and the cycle of rebirth. Yet he seems to have wished to hide his OBEs from profane onlookers by pretending he was drunk or sleeping heavily.

The astral projection exercises that Xiangzi may have used, or ones like them, appear in ancient Taoist texts of the Shangqing School (also known as Mao-Shan), a name meaning "Highest Clarity/Supreme Purity." This particular branch of Taoism is dated to around AD 300, though the teachings it preserves may be older. It's one of the main sources of sun worship in China, and may be a continuation of the ancient sun worship of the Shang dynasty[443]—which is China's oldest historically verified ruling dynasty, dating to 1600 BC. Lara writes how the Shang and earlier legendary dynasties that preceded it in China are connected to the ancient Religion of the Sun and to ancient Egypt, and this may explain how ancient practices of sun worship, and of astral projection sharing some similarities with ancient Egyptian OBEs (as explained shortly), came to be preserved in Shangqing Taoism.

These texts describe what could be forms of astral projection, which are said to have been passed down orally from ancient times before being written down:

> "Now, the practice of 'High Transcendence of the Sun and Moon' represents the profound teachings of the ancestral masters of the Supreme Oneness. In ancient times, these teachings were passed down orally, without relying on written texts. Today, they are

recorded in writing so that future generations who have affinity may easily explore them."[444]

~ THE INCOMPARABLE MYSTERIOUS, ORIGINAL GREAT METHODS OF THE JADE HALL OF THE THREE CELESTIAL REALMS

However, even though they were written, they were not intended to be shared publicly, but were kept within the order of the school:

"This knowledge is highly secretive and must be approached with great care."[445]

~ THE INCOMPARABLE MYSTERIOUS, ORIGINAL GREAT METHODS OF THE JADE HALL OF THE THREE CELESTIAL REALMS

To begin with, students had to follow a series of precepts such as purifying the mind from anger and resentment, speaking without falsehood, remaining undisturbed by desire, not getting drunk, avoiding promiscuity and arrogance, refraining from killing and harming life, and much more.[446]

Students then had to be assessed and make a serious pledge; their priority had to be their own self-cultivation:

"[...] students of the sect should possess a nature as pure as jade, flawless and unblemished. The foremost priority for those who aspire to learn the truth is to cultivate oneself. The essence of self-cultivation lies in eliminating selfish desires, refining the spirit, and nourishing the essence to replenish insufficient vitality. When vitality is sufficient, one may then seek the path of immortality and receive the teachings. The teachings are not passed on without verifying the recipient's sincerity and commitment, nor without solemnly pledging to heaven and declaring to the earth."[447]

~ THE INCOMPARABLE MYSTERIOUS, ORIGINAL GREAT METHODS OF THE JADE HALL OF THE THREE CELESTIAL REALMS

Only then could they receive these practices, "the profundities [of which], cannot be known by those who are not advanced."[448]

These OBE practices were for those who had reached a certain level of spiritual development, and their primary purpose was not for having OBEs, but for obtaining immortality.

They were used to prepare one for leaving the body at death (called "shedding the shell") and returning to the celestial realms. There are two stages—both involve the "immortal spirit" (which is said to be developed in the Taoist practice of internal alchemy) leaving the body and traveling into the cosmos. As a first stage, the Taoist practitioner seeks to journey to the sky, which is called *fei-t'ien*, or rising to the sky. This is to leave one's body, rise up, and be received by the guardian deities of the stars, sun, and moon, and absorb their celestial energy under their protection before returning to Earth. Then at the second stage, which is said to be far more difficult and takes one much farther away from their body, they journey from constellation to constellation, which is called *fei-hsing*, or flying in the sky, in which they are said to walk the patterns of the stars.

The methods for this could involve purification rites, offerings and petitions to celestial deities, talismans, incantations, dances, and visualizations. These OBE practices were especially carried out on the solstices and equinoxes, and at key transitions of the moon. The practitioner drew protective talismans on the ground around their body to make sure it remained unharmed while their spirit was away traveling (I give methods for this in chapter 27).[449]

It's very interesting that these practices sought to harness the qi (known also as chi) of the sun, moon, and stars for traveling out of the body, and that certain days of the sun and moon were seen as particularly conducive. Qi is a term used in Chinese culture that essentially means energy, or more specifically vital energy; we see references to this energy in the Pyramid Texts of Egypt, where it is called "life force," and in Hinduism, where it is known as prana; it may also be the same as the Celtic awen. Thus, these practices sought to use celestial energy for inducing what sound like OBEs.

Here are some examples where these practices are described from the Taoist text The Incomparable Mysterious, Original Great Methods of the Jade Hall of the Three Celestial Realms, which uses a series of visualizations and recitations for harnessing and directing celestial energy. The practices are described in a cryptic way, as they were intended only for those who could understand their symbolic language.

> "[...] I visualize the Sun rising in golden radiance, illuminating my true form. I set out to the Palace of the Sun.
>
> [...] Blazing sunlight rushes and soars, spreading essence over thousands of miles. Demonic power dissipates in flames, the mundane and impure is cleared away. Ascend to heaven with a fast pace, harnessing qi and rising to the heights. [...]
>
> Then ride the fiery dragon towards the palace of the sun. [...]
>
> In your mind, enter the palace of the sun, merging with it as one. After a while, forget about your physical body, in joy and harmony like spring. [...]
>
> The qi energy increases, light is exuberant. Mastering control, you soar through the air. [...]
>
> The celestial source flows throughout, light penetrates the majestic towers. The sky reflects in all directions [...]. Ascending with the

speed of the sun, the true body flies up. In oneness reaching to the celestial palace. [...]

Those who know it, when they practice it diligently, then their body is filled with bright light, and they are a friend of every truth. They attain Tao and turn into a real person. They will take their place among the flying immortals of the Sun and Moon [...] freely soaring through the skies."[450]

~ THE INCOMPARABLE MYSTERIOUS, ORIGINAL GREAT METHODS OF THE JADE HALL OF THE THREE CELESTIAL REALMS

Apart from harnessing the energy of the sun, and its reflected energy on the moon, the practitioner also sought to harness the energy of the stars emanating from the group of stars known as the Big Dipper, which is part of the northern constellation Ursa Major. This group of stars is central to Taoism, as it's seen as the gateway to heaven that rotates around the northern pole star,[451] which as mentioned earlier, was viewed as the location of the highest heaven and the abode of the Supreme Deity at the peak of Mount Kunlun.

A Taoist leaving their body by visualizing the Dipper.

"[...] on the third and seventh day of the month, at midnight, enter the room, connect with the stable qi energy. Close your eyes and inwardly see how your entire body rises gently and flies up, ascending toward the center of the Big Dipper [...]. Continue for some time until you feel that your body is within the Big Dipper. Strive to achieve this and you will feel heat in your body, this indicates the union of the real qi with virtue [which in Taoist philosophy can be described as a state of living in the world while being connected to the heavens through one's actions]. Visualize the purple light of the Dipper descending upon your body, illuminating your internal and external being. As you arrive in the Dipper [...] Then go from star to star paying your respects [...]."[452]

~ THE INCOMPARABLE MYSTERIOUS, ORIGINAL GREAT METHODS OF THE JADE HALL OF THE THREE CELESTIAL REALMS

The practitioner is then meant to travel to each star of the Dipper, offering prayers to their respective deities, such as:

> "[...] may I ascend as an immortal and ride the clouds [...] may I ascend as an immortal and travel through the hidden realms [...] may I ascend as an immortal and enter the sacred hall of the Great Sage."[453]
> ~ THE INCOMPARABLE MYSTERIOUS, ORIGINAL GREAT METHODS OF THE JADE HALL OF THE THREE CELESTIAL REALMS

Perhaps a prayer like this was what Xiangzi used as his sleeping prayer to astral project, mentioned earlier in this section.

After these prayers, the practitioner imagines the qi/energy of the stars entering their spirit body.

> "After the prayer, close your eyes, cease thoughts, forget your form, and go into sleep. After this, visualize that you are at the bowl of the Big Dipper, with rays of black, yellow, red, and purple qi entering your body."[454]
> ~ THE INCOMPARABLE MYSTERIOUS, ORIGINAL GREAT METHODS OF THE JADE HALL OF THE THREE CELESTIAL REALMS

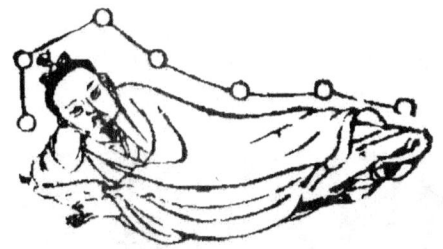

A Taoist going to sleep while visualizing the Dipper.

In the practice, these energies are gathered and utilized in the body in order to purify, strengthen, and harmonize one's own energies for the purpose of attaining immortality.

Shangqing Taoist texts also describe what sounds like an OBE to heaven. To reach it, the practitioner had to firstly pass through the three gates of the nine heavens. Each gate would only open if the practitioner could present certain knowledge (in the form of a tablet) to their respective guards. Once through these gates, the practitioner floated in the void before finally arriving at the Golden Gate of paradise that led to the Celestial Capital at the very center of creation. Once through the gate, again after showing a tablet, they enjoyed themselves in paradise. The experience ended when the practitioner returned to their physical body. The main method used to reach heaven was concentrating on the stars by visualizing oneself walking upon them—specifically those of the Big Dipper (of which Taoists believe there are two invisible stars in addition to the visible seven, making nine in total, corresponding to the nine heavens). This was likened to climbing a ladder of stars that would take one up through the various heavens, flying within the void, until reaching the last star corresponding to the highest heaven.[455]

The gates sound like they could be referring to portals to heavens, and the void sounds like the space between stars or perhaps even the dark tunnel that leads to heaven, which people commonly see as traveling through the darkness of outer space and the stars in NDEs. The entrance to heaven is also sometimes seen as a golden gate in NDEs.

It's remarkable that these Taoist OBEs are similar to those had by the Twice Born in Egypt and Jesus, who were said to travel out of the body to heaven in the stars. What's most striking is how Taoists seek to harness star energy for traveling to the stars out of the body, just as in the Egyptian Pyramid Texts where it says that the king "sets out with the light, He embraces the constellations, [he] harnesses their energies."[456] This reveals that in the ancient Religion of the Sun, celestial energy was not just harnessed in its physical manifestation as electromagnetic energy for inducing OBEs, but also in its astral/spiritual manifestation. This would provide another reason why ancient peoples aligned the sites they used for having OBEs to the sun, moon, and stars—to harness their qi, or spiritual energy.

In Egypt, as in Taoism, these OBEs were part of the preparation for the final return to the spiritual region of the stars at death—and in Egypt and Taoism, it was specifically the northern circumpolar stars.

An artifact from the ancient Sanxingdui culture in China, described as a sun wheel, however, Lara realized that it's just like the symbol of the Duat/astral in Egypt.

Similarly to Taoists, Tibetan Buddhists and Bons prepare for death by practicing dream and sleep yoga (as explored next), and so it seems in the Religion of the Sun, having OBEs could serve a very serious purpose in preparing someone for their transition to the afterlife.

The evidence indicates that having OBEs was part of an ancient wisdom tradition in China that derived from the ancient Religion of the Sun.

TIBETAN BUDDHIST AND BON DREAM YOGA

The oldest surviving unbroken tradition of lucid dreaming is found in Tibet, which is why Lara felt it was important to research it and has written much of this section.

To research dream yoga, Lara read through numerous old and modern books available in English written by Tibetan practitioners of it, and also sought out the oldest surviving sources of the practice, as she always likes to go to the earliest primary source documents on any subject and work her way forward in time from there.

In Tibetan Buddhism, the nonphysical realm where dreams take place, and where the deceased go, is called *bardo*—though *bardo* is not a place; rather, it's seen as a state of consciousness that occurs between or in the transition to other states. It's described in detail in the Tibetan Book of the Dead (Bardo Thodol), which according to Tibetan tradition, was composed in the eighth century, then hidden in Tibet, and later rediscovered in the fourteenth century. It explains what the deceased can do in *bardo*—these are the same abilities one has in the astral plane—namely being able to do anything without dying or being injured, being able to see even if one is physically blind and so on, to travel through any object, and travel anywhere one wishes instantaneously.

> "[...] the body which now you possess being a mental-body of [karmic] propensities, though slain and chopped [to bits], cannot die. [...] O nobly-born, again listen. 'Endowed with all sense-faculties and power of unimpeded motion' implies [that although] you may have been, when living, blind of the eye, or deaf, or lame, yet on this After-Death Plane your eyes will see forms, and your ears will hear sounds, and all other sense organs of yours will be unimpaired and very keen and complete. [...] O nobly-born, 'unimpeded motion' implies that your present body being a desire-body—your intellect having been separated from its seat—is not a body of gross matter, so that now you have the power to go right through any rock-masses, hills, boulders, earth, houses, and Mount Meru itself without being impeded. [...] That, too, is an indication that you are wandering in the Sidpa Bardo. [...] O nobly-born, you are actually endowed with the power of miraculous action, which is not, however, the fruit of any samādhi, but a power come to you naturally; and, therefore, it is of the nature of karmic power. You are able in a moment to traverse the four continents round about Mount Meru. Or you can instantaneously arrive in whatever place you wish; you have the power of reaching there within the time which a man takes to bend, or to stretch forth his hand."[457]
>
> ~ THE TIBETAN BOOK OF THE DEAD

A painting of the "peaceful" and "wrathful"
deities said to inhabit the nonphysical realm of *bardo*.

What sounds like a description of astral projection is contained in one of the most well-known sections of the text: The Six Root Verses of the Six Bardos. Here the term *bardo* is used to describe the different states of consciousness, one of them being dreaming. It says that when the state of dreaming begins, one should keep their consciousness undistracted and in its natural state of awareness, blending sleep with wakefulness.

> "O now, when the Dream Bardo upon me is dawning!
>
> Abandoning the inordinate corpse-like sleeping of the sleep of stupidity,
>
> May the consciousness undistractedly be kept in its natural state;
>
> Grasping the [true nature of] dreams, [may I] train [myself] in the Clear Light of Miraculous Transformation:
>
> Acting not like the brutes in slothfulness,
>
> May the blending of the practicing of the sleep [state] and actual [or waking] experience be highly valued [by me]."[458]
>
> ~ THE TIBETAN BOOK OF THE DEAD

However, the practice of astral projection as it's commonly understood is not taught in Buddhism. What comes closest is a discipline called "dream yoga" found in Tibetan Buddhism and Bon, which is dedicated to having lucid dreams, and also "clear light sleep," which I explain further on. Bon is a religion that began in Tibet before the arrival of Buddhism, but accepts the teachings of Buddha and shares much in common with Tibetan Buddhism, including dream yoga. Tibetan Buddhism and Bon appear to be derived from a mixture of influences—from Buddhism, Hinduism, Shamanism, and very distantly the ancient Religion of the Sun.

Dream yoga is part of teachings in Buddhism that are collectively known as Tantra, which is a class of texts that are generally considered more esoteric in nature. The exact origins of Buddhist Tantra have not been historically verified, but they date to at least the fifth century AD in northern India.[459][460] In Tibetan legend, dream yoga is traced back to a region called Oddiyana that existed in medieval north India, which is seen as the place where Buddhist tantric teachings flourished and from where they were disseminated to Tibet.[461][462] Buddhist Tantra is particularly similar to Hindu Shaivite Tantra.[463][464] It seems to us that Tibetan dream yoga has its roots in the practice of mastering one's dreams mentioned in the Hindu text the Mandukya Upanishad. And Tibetan clear light sleep is based on the same practice of bringing consciousness to dreams and deep sleep as found in Shaivite Tantra.

Tantra is only practiced by some Buddhist sects—primarily in Tibet and Japan.[465] These sects believe it was an esoteric teaching Buddha gave to a select few disciples.[466] The Dalai Lama states that there were ancient Buddhists who outwardly followed the exoteric teachings of Buddha, but practiced Tantra in secret. According to this tradition, Tantric teachings were kept so secret they were not written down for over seven hundred years.[467] This gives some indication as to the secrecy with which the knowledge of having OBEs was treated, as it seems to have similarly been treated in ancient Egyptian religion, within Hinduism, and Taoism.

A Buddhist practitioner of yoga and tantra who has obtained powers (known as a mahasiddha) flying through the sky. However, rather than referring to astral projection, this may actually be a depiction of someone who has been granted powers by demons to levitate (of which I knew a case, as I explain in chapter 27).

There are a number of texts that contain the philosophy and practices of dream yoga. These date to as far back as one thousand years ago (though earlier copies are said to have existed), and have been accompanied by an oral tradition in which their interpretation is said to be preserved.

Dreams, *bardo* (the astral plane), and the body one travels with in *bardo* (the astral body) are viewed in Buddhist and Bon cosmology as all being illusory, just as everything else is, and so in dream yoga (as it's taught to lay people) lucid dreaming is used to further realize the illusory nature of things. This is accomplished by doing things while lucid dreaming that are meant to prove its illusory nature, such as changing or multiplying objects; deliberately doing things that would ordinarily get one killed, like jumping off cliffs; and meditating with the purpose of realizing that all states of dream consciousness are from one's own mind.[468] The Dalai Lama explains the goal of dream yoga by saying, "in Buddhist context the practice [of lucid dreaming] is aimed at the realization of emptiness."[469] This goal is very different to that of the Religion of the Sun, where in lucid dreams and OBEs we explore life in other realms and learn for a spiritual purpose. The nonphysical properties of the astral plane and the ways it can be influenced by our psyche seem to have been interpreted as reinforcing the Buddhist world view.

One of the major and oldest sources of dream yoga practice is a text called the Mahamaya Tantra,[470] which first surfaced in the late ninth to early tenth centuries.[471] However, this text mainly describes dark tantric sexual practices, saying that one of the results of this is the acquisition of powers, some of which are exercised while consciously out of the body. (I will explain the difference between light and dark tantrism in another book.) These are generally not discussed publicly.

For example, the yogi is instructed to abduct and "enjoy sublime celestial girls"[472] while out of the body. The text also describes some practices to aid dream yoga that are said to give great virility and power, divine sight, magical abilities, long life, an alluring form, the ability to conjure miracles, to transform one's appearance at will, etc.,[473] and is clearly black magic. And while the goal of dream yoga is generally explained to the public as realizing emptiness, in this text the goals described are very different—almost all of them involve acquiring mundane powers.[474] In this excerpt for example, it describes a list of things that the practitioner of dream yoga can do while out of the body:

> "The yogi has knowledge, masters yoga, and weaves Indra's Web.
>
> He beguiles and paralyzes, slays, dissuades, and more.
>
> He tames, magnetizes, and so forth; he flies through the sky.
>
> He enters the citadel of another [which means to possess the body of another], is invisible, and so on.
>
> He causes hostility, renders mute and moves under the earth [...]."[475]
>
> ~ MAHAMAYA TANTRA

Anyone who has spent time traveling in the astral plane, as I have, will have encountered other people and entities who attack them while out of the body in some of these ways: by attempting to deceive them, paralyzing them (making them unable to move), and making them mute. This is done to lead the sincere astral traveler away from the knowledge of the light, and to stop them from being able to defend themselves using incantations (as these require being able to speak). In the Mahamaya Tantra, wisdom is said to be kept secret so that other beings don't realize it and liberate themselves, as they are needed to continue manifesting the world.[476] This would provide a motive for keeping others who travel in the astral plane away from knowledge.

The Mahamaya Tantra also describes taking possession of someone else's body from the astral plane. Entities enter the body of another from the astral plane during channeling, demonic possession, to some degree in schizophrenics, and in a few other circumstances, but only those who have taken the way of darkness take possession of another's body.

In the Mahamaya Tantra, these yogis are described as attaining powers quickly through pleasure, and without discipline, austerities, or hardship,[477] which is the opposite of the discipline and difficulties those who take the path of the Spiritual Sun face.

It's of note that so many of the deities described in this tantra and in other Tibetan Buddhist and Bon texts look like demons—with fangs and claws, wearing human skin, and holding skullcaps and weapons, and are described as "wrathful."

Some seriously "wrathful" looking beings, which are totally black and look like monsters, in this nineteenth century depiction of the protectors of the Gelug tradition of Tibetan Buddhism (which the Dalai Lama belongs to).

Another of the oldest and most major sources of dream yoga is Mother Tantra: The Tantric Cycle of the Sun of Compassion, which is from the secret portion of a larger set of works simply referred to as the Mother Tantra (Ma Gyud), which is the highest tantra in the Bon tradition.[478] Lara has not been able to find an English translation of it (it's published in Tibetan), so she can't read what's in it, though it's said to contain the horrific practice called *chöd* (in which one goes to a frightening place and visualizes offering one's body as a human sacrifice for demons and gods to feast upon, using human bones as instruments, etc.[479]),[480] and this text would likely be where the practice originates in the Bon tradition.[481]

There are dream yoga texts that don't contain dark practices as far as Lara can see.[482] However, Buddhist (and Hindu) Tantra generally contains many practices that are awful as well as those that would be considered dark in the Religion of the Sun (including some which also contain dream and sleep yoga teachings), such as casting spells over people to make them do things; eating foul bodily substances; and directing followers to commit immoral acts.[483]

As it turns out, there are many practices in dream yoga that overlap with practices I give in this book, such as developing concentration as a foundational practice for developing the ability to lucid dream, developing and maintaining the ability to concentrate by concentrating on an object (starting with short, frequent sessions and increasing them gradually), being aware throughout the day in order to be lucid in dreams (with increased awareness in daily life bringing greater awareness in dreams), questioning whether one is in a dream during the day to provoke questioning in dreams, waking up multiple times in the night to practice (in dream yoga there are three wake-ups in the night that are approximately two hours apart), remembering dreams, reciting mantras, concentrating on one's heart, and using visualization.[484] That's because there are basic practices that are fundamental for anyone to do who wants to be able to have OBEs, and they will essentially be the same whether now or hundreds of years ago. I have only learned about dream yoga while researching for this book, so have only now discovered these similarities.

Despite these similarities, because there are dark practices within dream yoga texts and within Buddhist Tantra generally, I recommend against using specific practices of dream yoga. There are indications that some of the cosmology of Buddhism partially derived from the ancient Religion of the Sun, but its aims, view of creation, and practices are very different, and so it's long removed from it now. The origin of Bon is different to that of Buddhism—Bonpos believe their religion derived eighteen thousand years ago from the teachings of an enlightened being who took incarnation as an incredibly long-lived prince. He resided in a now long-lost kingdom to the west of Tibet known as Olmo Lungring (discussed earlier in this chapter). Tibetan Buddhism and Bon seem to contain elements of what outside observers of the inhabitants of this kingdom might try to create so as to imitate their religion, but interpreted through the lenses of Buddhist and Shamanic theology. They also seem to have long incorporated dark practices.

In Tibetan Buddhism and Bon, a more advanced practice than dream yoga is called sleep yoga, and the highest goal of sleep yoga, and indeed all sleep practice, is a kind of dreamless sleep, which is called "clear light sleep." In this state, one is said to be conscious while asleep, but without dreams or sensory impressions—instead abiding in empty awareness, or clear light. This is meant to be a kind of preliminary experience of the clear light (*sunyata*, "emptiness") that accomplished yogis believe they can be liberated into at death, which is the ultimate aim of Buddhists and Bons.[485]

From my own experiences I can tell that what's happening in the experience of clear light sleep is that the successful practitioner is having an OBE, so they are conscious while asleep, and if they can maintain concentration, are without dreams, and because they have separated from their bodies, they are also without the sensations of their physical body and surrounds. Yet the clear light they see is likely a product of visualization. To go into the clear light, the practitioner visualizes an image of light, such as that of the sun or moon, or shining within their heart. They then widen the image to spread over their mind, so that they lie down "with the mind brightened. Thus the mind is never covered with darkness even during sleep."[486] [487] What's happening is that as the person falls asleep this visualization becomes all-immersing and real in the astral plane, as imaginative visualizations do, so that they seem to be clear light, but what they are seeing is probably no more real than any other dream image they were to project either consciously or subconsciously. During clear light sleep it's said that dream images do arise, but one is able to resist being distracted by them.[488] This demonstrates that the practitioner is in the astral plane, and not a higher realm of light, and is simply holding a projection of a scene of light through concentration. It's likely that the practitioner then even dreams of being in clear light.

Experiences of light do happen in OBEs and NDEs, but their context is different. There is also a realm of pure light that one can go to out of the body via going into the heart, but it's experienced by having a different kind of OBE than we have when we project into the astral. I explain more about this further on.

It seems that Hindu ideas about yoga nidra and bringing the state of Turya into sleep were the basis of the ideas that developed into sleep yoga in Tibetan Buddhism and Bon, though in accordance with Buddhist philosophy, the idea of experiencing any kind of individual or higher consciousness or Self through it was removed.

GREEK

References to OBEs, the astral, and astral body can be found in ancient Greece. The famous Greek philosophers Plato and Aristotle wrote about the concept of aether, which was associated with air and located in the celestial regions. Aristotle added it as a new first element to the four existing earthly elements, making five in total, though he said it was unlike the other four—being invisible and comprising the celestial spheres that held the stars and planets in their motion.[489] The Greeks appear to have derived this concept from ancient sources, as *akasa*/ether is also considered the first of the five elements in Hinduism where it likewise corresponds with the sky and atmosphere. Ether being identified as a fifth element corresponds to the astral plane being part of the fifth dimension.

Left: Statue of Plato. Right: Statue of Aristotle.

A Greek Neoplatonic philosopher Proclus, who wrote commentaries on Plato, developed these ideas further and spoke of the existence of subtle planes, as well as of two subtle bodies (called *okhema*, meaning "carrier"): the "luminous vehicle," which was the immortal vehicle of the soul, and the "pneumatic vehicle" of vital breath (*pneuma*), which was mortal.[490] [491]

> "Man is a little world [microcosm]. For, just like the Whole, he possesses both mind and reason, both a divine and a mortal body."[492]
> ~ PROCLUS

These bodies seem to correspond to the Ba and Ka of ancient Egypt, and to the subtle body and pranic sheath of Hinduism, indicating again these were already ancient concepts. The ideas of *okhema* went on to influence ideas of the "body of light" in the occult circles of the Renaissance, and those of the later "astral body" in the nineteenth century.

Then there is the interesting case of the ancient Greek philosopher Hermotimus of Claxomenae, who was a Pythagorean.

> "[...] the soul of Hermotimus of Claxomenae was in the habit of leaving his body, and wandering into distant countries, whence it

brought back numerous accounts of various things, which could not have been obtained by any one but a person who was present. The body in the meantime was left apparently lifeless."[493]

These journeys were said to have lasted several days and nights at a time, while his body lay motionless as a corpse. Hermotimus' vulnerable state was tragically taken advantage of, as his enemies found out and killed him while he was away on one of his journeys.[494] These journeys clearly sound like they were conscious travels in the fifth dimension, since Hermotimus saw things of the physical world that could be verified on his return. Yet these OBEs were not entirely normal, as in a natural OBE the body only sleeps—it does not appear dead, and could not have slept for days on end without interruption, nor without waking to the noise of intruders, etc. What was Hermotimus up to? Was he putting his body into a semi-comatose state using substances to have OBEs? Or did he develop an ability like that possessed by the priests of Atlantis, being able to leave and return to his body at will, though eventually being caught off guard?

Another case is that of Timarchus of Chaeroneia as recorded by Plutarch. Timarchus had an OBE while sleeping in the crypt of Trophonius—a cave where people would go who sought a visionary experience or healing. Timarchus spent two nights and a day in complete darkness and isolation, and upon emerging told of his experience:

The crypt of Trophonius in Greece where Timarchus had his OBE.

"He said that on descending into the oracular crypt his first experience was of profound darkness; next, after a prayer, he lay a long time not clearly aware whether he was awake or dreaming. It did seem to him, however, that at the same moment he heard a crash and was struck

on the head, and that the sutures parted and released his soul. As it withdrew and mingled joyfully with air that was translucent and pure, it felt in the first place that now, after long being cramped, it had again found relief, and was growing larger than before, spreading out like a sail; and next that it faintly caught the whir of something revolving overhead with a pleasant sound. When he lifted his eyes the earth was nowhere to be seen [...]."[495]
~ PLUTARCH, MORALIA

Many who've astral projected have experienced some of the sensations described, particularly hearing a kind of whirring, buzzing, or whistling sound, while often feeling light bodily vibrations in the moments they were leaving their body.

Timarchus is then guided through the experience by the voice of a being he cannot see, which is another common element in OBEs.

"After an interval someone he did not see addressed him: 'Timarchus what would you have me explain?'

'Everything,' he answered [...]."[496]
~ PLUTARCH, MORALIA

While Timarchus is not told everything, he is shown Hades (hell), and how each soul is connected to a star, and that each also has a daemon (which is not a demon, but a Greek concept that I interpret in this experience as one's higher Being) that guides them through their lives, and how those souls who are led by their passions and contend with their Being suffer in lower realms, while those who are responsive to the influence and training of their Being go on to higher realms.

Interestingly, the voice explains the OBEs of Hermotimus of Claxomenae, saying:

"The story as thus told is indeed not true: his soul did not leave his body, but gave its daemon free play by always yielding to it and slackening the tie, permitting it to move about and roam at will, so that the daemon could see and hear much that passed in the world outside and return with the report."[497]
~ PLUTARCH, MORALIA

I suspect the Greeks may have thought the soul leaving the body indicated death, and the voice talking to Timarchus was therefore explaining that Hermotimus was not dead (it says he was asleep) in a way that a Greek of the day could understand and thus help Timarchus understand his own experience (as he also had not died). The tie that connected Hermotimus to his daemon sounds like the cord that connects our astral body to our physical one, and so according to this it does seem like Hermotimus was astral traveling.

After this, Timarchus' experience ends abruptly:

> "When the voice ceased Timarchus desired to turn (he said) and see who the speaker was. But once more he felt a sharp pain in his head, as though it had been violently compressed, and he lost all recognition and awareness of what was going on about him; but he presently recovered and saw that he was lying in the crypt of Trophonius near the entrance, at the very spot where he had first laid himself down."[498]
>
> ~ PLUTARCH, MORALIA

Many who've had OBEs will know how it feels to return rapidly to their physical body like this (though without any pain).

SHAMANISM

It's often said that Shamans are able to leave their bodies and travel in a spirit world. Shamanism is a different tradition to the Religion of the Sun, so it's not something I discuss in great detail, but I will say something about it here as so many people who look into OBEs wonder if Shamanism is related.

Shamanism is a term that's often loosely used to describe ancient beliefs, and the term shaman often broadly used as the name for a figure of authority in pagan religions, sometimes interchangeably with priest/priestess, sage, or mystic. However, this is incorrect, as shamanism has a limited and well-defined set of beliefs and practices, and is its own specific ancient tradition.[499] Looking back into the past it seems that Shamanistic religions and the ancient Religion of the Sun (which survived in the many traditions that had stemmed from it) were the two largest types of religion in the world prior to the onset of Christianity (the practice of the dark occult under many guises I'd say would have been the third). Some of the edges between Shamanism and the Religion of the Sun blurred where they came into contact with one another, but they were two distinct religious practices.

Siberian shaman with a drum, which they use to put themselves into a trance.

What's interesting is that the fundamental cosmology found in Shamanism resembles that in the ancient Religion of the Sun. For instance, Siberian shamans see reality as being divided into three worlds. The physical world we inhabit lies between two nonphysical worlds—an upper world in the sky inhabited by gods, and lower world beneath the earth inhabited by demons—and these worlds are said to be connected by the cosmic axis that extends through the center of the world (as a mountain and/or tree) and terminates in heaven in the northern circumpolar stars, as in the Religion of the Sun. Shamans are believed to be able to travel in these nonphysical realms, and sometimes attempt to ascend the cosmic axis to reach the upper world/ heaven, as those in the Religion of the Sun did also.[500][501]

We'd say these beliefs became commonly held because of the vast influence the Children of the Sun had on religion across the world. Shamanism likely adopted certain beliefs from them in the distant past, but it's also possible that practitioners of Shamanism experienced the reality of this cosmology themselves through OBEs and NDEs, further reinforcing these beliefs.

Despite these few similarities, however, the practice of Shamanism is fundamentally different to that of the Religion of the Sun.

The primary role of a religious authority in the Religion of the Sun was to teach people how to attain the reunion with divinity, while the shaman's role is to resolve and prevent crisis in their community by communicating with spirits.[502]

Rather than using meditative exercises to have OBEs as in the Religion of the Sun, shamans use trance, which is usually self-induced while drumming, though can additionally involve consuming various intoxicants, such as the *amanita muscaria* (fly agaric) mushroom, and strong tobacco and alcohol.[503]

As we've seen, those who wished to advance in the Religion of the Sun had to have a level of moral purity, and commit to their own self-cultivation, which involved gradually ridding themselves of their egos. The initiatory process tested one's goodness and its ultimate goal was the reunion with divinity.

Shamans, however, usually come to their position because they are forced by spirits, often based on anomalous physical characteristics.[504] This forcing is the basis of the so-called "shaman's disease," said to precede becoming

A shaman in Alaska attempting to exorcise evil spirits from a sick boy.

a shaman in the majority of cases. A typical example of it was narrated by the wife of shaman, who said, "That was how he became a shaman, after the sickness, after the torture. He had been ill for seven years. While he was ailing, he had dreams: he was beaten up several times, sometimes he was taken to strange places."[505]

Anna-Leena Siikala was a professor emeritus at the University of Helsinki who specialized in shamanism, folk-belief, mythology, oral storytelling, and traditionality. She described shaman's disease by saying:

> "The symptoms are both mental and physical; there are frequent mentions of pains in the head and the limbs, states of torment, with visions and voices, fits reminiscent of manifestations of hysteria, and so on. The patient turns to shamanizing in order to be healed, and this means is often mentioned as being the last and the only way of attaining equilibrium. [...] Often the shaman's account mentions that neglect of shamanizing causes a return of the sickness."[506]

Unlike in the Religion of the Sun, in which someone would become an authority generally through developing wisdom and purity, in shamanism there is essentially one main qualification. As Siikala wrote:

> "The basic qualification for becoming a shaman is control of the technique of ecstasy and the formal study of this technique. People with a certain nervous susceptibility are, however, best suited for this, and people easily roused to hysteria have the best potential. Thus it is often exceptional individuals who seek to become or are sought out as shamans. The long initiatory stage is then preparation for the control of ecstatic behaviour. [...] Study centres round ways of using mechanical means of stimulating the nervous system—rhythmical music, singing, dancing and drugs—as best suits each individual, and practice in the psychic mechanism of the technique of ecstasy."[507]

Shamans follow a completely different path of initiation than those in the Religion of the Sun. Siberian Shamans go through a very distinctive initiation before beginning their role, which is described as their "birth" as a shaman.[508] During it they lie in a trance state as if asleep for days, while their body is said to be cut into pieces by spirits to determine whether they have an "extra bone," which indicates their inherent ability to be a shaman.[509] As part of this they acquire their "spirit-helpers" who are said to help them in their trances.[510] This practice of being cut into pieces is quite similar to that of *chöd* in Tibetan Bon and Buddhism, as these traditions incorporate elements of Shamanism. Spiritual birth (being born again, or becoming twice born) in the Religion of the Sun is completely different; it's when the part of one's Being I refer to as the Spiritual Son incarnates within someone at a certain stage on the path of the Spiritual Sun.

During shamanic trances, which are conducted as séances, the lights are extinguished and the shaman invokes their spirit-helpers often by imitating their animal calls (by growling and whistling, etc.). The séance climaxes as the shaman reaches the height of their frenzy and meets with their spirit-helpers either by becoming possessed by one or more of them, or relaying messages from them to the audience, or sometimes "traveling" to other worlds with their spirit-helpers (which can sometimes occur during periods in which they lose consciousness, in which case they have what sounds like an OBE), later retelling what they experienced. As part of this the shaman often takes on some of the postures and movements of animals like clawing their hands, or assumes other grotesque bodily postures, such as rolling their eyes back in their head, curling out their tongue, and expanding their belly.[511]

A shaman of the Native American people in westernmost Canada, after having spent several days in the woods being initiated and possessed by the "cannibal spirit."[512]

Shamanic experiences can also involve "shapeshifting" into an animal. This was part of shamanic practices among pre-Columbian peoples like the Aztecs, and is still practiced among indigenous peoples in Mexico where shapeshifting shamans are called nagual—a word that derives from the Aztec language.[513] This apparent ability to shapeshift may be based on a kind of OBE shamans induce, as found in the next excerpt.

Left: A stela from the pre-Columbian Zapotec culture in Mexico possibly showing a shaman shapeshifting into a jaguar. Right: A pre-Columbian mask that apparently symbolizes the soul's out-of-body journey into the underworld where it transforms into a jaguar. The human half of the head is spotted, resembling the *amanita muscaria* mushroom, which indicates that's probably what was ingested to induce the experience.[514]

Following are some excerpts from the experience of a shaman during a trance, which they induced in themselves as part of a study:

> "It was a very light trance, because I was asked not to move a lot. My nose began to tremble as it used to do in the beginning of each trance (now I am able not to move at all). Then my hands and my arms started shaking lightly. An inner vision of a wolf face, very close to my face, came soon after. Then an owl (two close representations are joined). I have to add that these visions were not seen as precisely as they are with our eyes. It may happen that the visions are quite similar to how we see with our eyes, but sometimes it's more like the feeling of a presence than the image of it. But despite the fact that I don't really see it, I "know" what or who it is. [...]
>
> I find myself in a completely dark place (I don't know if it is the reason why the shamans call it "black world"). The first impression is the loss of time perception, like being in a timeless space. My strength is increased a lot (I can hold and beat the drum, which weighs 8 kg, for hours without any difficulties). My perception of pain is considerably reduced. For instance, at the beginning of my practice, my body hurt a lot because I had to manipulate the drum made of thick wood. But amazingly each trance was painless, while when I was back to my normal state, I felt a lot of pain in every part of my body. [...]
>
> My eyes (closed during every trance) have visions like geometrical patterns, places or entities called spirits by the shamans. They can appear to me as men, or women, or animal patterns, that I can suddenly speak with. I feel like I can also detect discords in my environment. When discord is present, my nose can "smell" it. Or, I guess, it is not the odor but the information at the root of the odor. My hands act like they are responding to these discords by performing gestures that I have absolutely no control over. I also can feel forms (more often like balls) in the air. My hands can turn around, try to soften them or to move them gently. [...]
>
> My sense of self seems to be receding because I don't feel like I am myself anymore; I lose the perception of who I am, or who I used to be. I suddenly feel like the animal or the entity I am supposed to be possessed by. As I am a wolf, for example, I can feel paws in place of my hands and a muzzle in place of my nose. I don't speak anymore but howl like a wolf."[515]

As you may see, this is a very different experience to the OBEs that have been discussed so far; none of the exercises for astral projection in ancient texts of the Religion of the Sun that we've found involve trance. That's why we don't include trance experiences among the three types of OBEs that were practiced in the Religion of the Sun at the beginning of the chapter.

For one, the trance experience occurred while the shaman was physically awake and active (while drumming), rather than asleep as in an OBE. Their movements are described as getting more frantic the further into the trance they go. The shaman described entering complete darkness, whereas in an OBE someone sees the astral plane. The shaman shook and trembled at the onset of their trance; bodily shakes are not part of the sensations experienced during astral projection. The shaman moved out of their body in ways they have no control over; in an OBE we retain a normal sense of control over our movements. The trance experience involved the loss of the shaman's sense of identify and they perceived themselves transforming into and being possessed by an animal, whereas in an OBE someone continues to feel and appear as they do in life, and retains their normal sense of self. OBEs in the Religion of the Sun never involve being possessed by another entity.

There are said to be two types of trance shamans go into. One is called a "wandering trance," which is when they journey away from their body. Those in which they lose consciousness are likely to be the only type that could involve astral projection. The other is called a "trance of possession," which is when their body becomes possessed by another entity.[516] In the West, this kind of possession is commonly known as channeling and mediumship. I don't know of anything other than demons entering other people's bodies (this is something I have witnessed happening to a channeler myself), and I've heard former Satanists say that it's demons in disguise who appear to mediums often as dead relatives or figures from the past.

In Shamanism it's believed that by vibrating the cosmic axis, one can access the other realms it connects to. Rhythmic drumming, dancing, singing, etc., are believed to induce these vibrations.[517] However, rather than vibrating some external axis, we believe the real meaning of these practices is to vibrate the axis within the body of the participant. The shaking and trembling experienced at the onset of trances seems to be the result of this "vibrating," which likely has to do with stimulation of the nervous system that does indeed run through the central axis of the body, the spine.

Vibrations can be part of the sensations of astral projection too, yet in this case it's not the physical body that vibrates, but the astral body. These vibrations usually come as a natural result of doing an OBE practice, as we've not found any explicit mention in texts of the ancient Religion of the Sun in which someone seeks to induce physical vibrations in themselves, though it's possible that the use of electromagnetic energy in their OBE practices may have helped induce astral vibrations in some way.

There have been studies done on the brain changes produced in shamans during trance. One found there was a decrease in connectivity in the pathway of the brain that processes sound, accompanied by an increase in activity in the areas of the brain involved in internally directed thought. This indicates that because the sound of the drum is so repetitive, sound altogether becomes blocked out by the mind, allowing the shaman to extend their internally directed state.[518]

Another study measured the brain activity of a shaman during a trance and compared it to the brain activity of control groups of normal, schizophrenic, manic, and depressed people. The shaman was extensively trained in Mongolian Shamanism, and is the first Westerner to have achieved the designation of *udgan* (a Mongolian female shaman). The experience the shaman had while being measured in trance is the one quoted above. The study found that her brain activity during trance shared some similarities with those that occur during other altered states of consciousness, such as meditation and psychedelic experiences—notably a shift from left to right brain activity. However, what's troubling is that it also found her brain activity shared similarities with those who are depressed, manic, and schizophrenic, i.e. those who have dissociative disorders. The study says the difference between the shaman and those with the disorders is that the shaman was able to induce and terminate the pathological brain state at will.[519]

Trance sounds as though it's putting someone into a state that's different to an OBE. An OBE, as is commonly described, is when someone's body falls asleep while they remain conscious and travel in their astral body in the astral plane. Instead, the shaman is still physically awake and moving during a trance, but has the sense of being separated from their body (and even their identity), so I wonder if it's more akin to a liminal state between waking and sleeping. Other common liminal states are sleep paralysis, sleepwalking, and psychedelic experiences, which I discuss in part 5. Her experience sounds particularly similar to psychedelic experiences, as while on psychedelics people also generally still move around physically and yet feel separate from their bodies. Some of the visuals the shaman described in her trance sound similar to those commonly seen in psychedelic experiences, such as the "visions like geometrical patterns," and the appearance of a multitude of entities that she "can suddenly speak with."

As I discuss in part 5, sleep paralysis and psychedelic experience are both states that are more open to the influence of demons; I also discuss how these liminal states are related to schizophrenia, a condition that seems to involve demonic influence—so it's interesting the study found similarities between the brain activity of a shaman in trance with that of

Ancient depiction of a shaman from the pre-Columbian Jama-Coaque culture of Ecuador.

schizophrenics. All this, coupled with the fact that shamans are usually chosen by spirits who force and later possess them, indicates that trance is more open to the influence of demons, and so I don't recommend it. I've seen a Shamanic ceremony in an OBE and it was of the dark side, so I would think there would be a high risk of a demonic influence.

I wonder if the initiation shamans go through in which they experience being cut into pieces while out of the body is actually part of a process in which "the spirits" (demons) attempt to disassociate parts of their psyche, rather than, or in addition to, looking for an extra bone. Disassociating parts of someone's psyche could make it easier for that person to enter a trance, and also make possessing them easier, and this may be why it's an essential part of becoming a shaman. That a shaman in trance could induce brain activity found in those with dissociative disorders indicates that the ability to willfully disassociate parts of their psyche is something shamans develop. Given all of this, it seems too much of a coincidence that their initiation involves a kind of fracturing of themselves into pieces.

Even though the journeys shamans have while in a trance are often thought of as OBEs, they seem to be their own type that is mostly different to astral projection, and use different methods than those used in the Religion of the Sun.

NORTH AMERICAN

As in other parts of the world we've explored so far, there's evidence that ancient sites were also used in North America as access points to the other realms/dimensions, particularly to heaven, possibly having been used for OBEs at some distant time in the past.

Among the mound building cultures of North America there was a belief that we each have two souls—one they called the "life-soul" and the other the "free-soul." The life-soul is said to be a mindless force that animates and is attached to the body, and could be dangerous after death, while the free-soul is what's more commonly understood as the soul—being that part of us that leaves the body at death, retaining its sense of identity and memory. It often stayed in the vicinity of its physical body for a time after death before starting its journey into the afterlife.[520] The life-soul sounds very much like the Ka of ancient Egypt, and pranic sheath of Hinduism, which I refer to as the personality, and which becomes a mindless ghost at death—being an energetic form that gradually disintegrates along with the physical body; while the free-soul sounds very much like the Ba of ancient Egypt, which today is often equated with the soul or consciousness, and which is that essential part of a person that lives on after death as recounted in NDEs.

Both the life-soul and free-soul were symbolized by skulls, though the skull representing the free-soul was shown with fire coming out of its mouth to illustrate how it leaves the body and lives on after death.[521] The otherworld which the soul entered was believed to be a mirror image of the physical world,[522] which the astral plane indeed appears to be, often being likened to a copy of it, as it's the etheric component of all that exists here—therefore appearing like a mirror image of it.

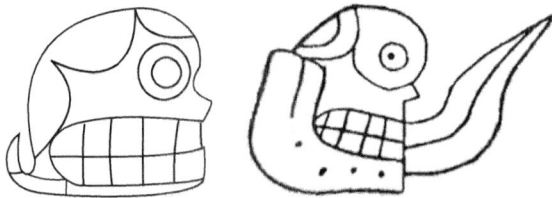

Left: Skull representing the life-soul with a vacant stare to show its mindless nature. Right: Skull representing the free-soul with a flame coming out of its mouth, symbolizing the soul leaving the body at death.

It was from this point that the free-soul began its journey on what many Native Americans called the "path of souls." As Andrew Collins has demonstrated, this afterlife journey is essentially the same as the one undertaken by the ancient Egyptians and by people in numerous ancient cultures around the world.

The free-soul of the deceased was believed to first travel west, to the edge of the earth's disk, where it would take a great leap, aiming to enter a portal in the sky, which was a slit in the fabric of space itself. This portal was located within what appears to be a fuzzy looking star, but is really a nebula called Messier-42 or Orion's Nebula, found in the "sword" of the Orion constellation. If the soul entered the portal successfully, from there it entered the Milky Way, and would begin its journey on the path of souls by traveling along its dark rift.[523]

At the point where the dark rift appears to split into two paths, the soul would be judged as to whether it had been sinful or not. If sinless, it continued along one path to the heavenly sky world in the region of the northern circumpolar stars, where it encountered the celestial beings and power animals that inhabited it, and was reunited with its ancestors. If sinful, it took the other path leading to annihilation or sometimes reincarnation.[524]

The symbol of this portal was an open eye on the palm of a hand. The three belt stars of Orion form the severed wrist, and the eye represents the portal, called *ogee*.[525]

Native American eye-in-hand symbol, representing the constellation Orion (hand) and the portal to heaven believed to be located within it called *ogee* (the eye).

It's remarkable how similar this death journey is to what people experience in

NDEs today, and to the king's afterlife journey in the ancient Egyptian Pyramid Texts. For example, the king too is said to leap up into the stars as he rises toward heaven.[526] In his journey, he too directs himself toward Orion, travels the Milky Way, and enters the heavenly realm in the northern circumpolar stars—the difference being that the king wasn't judged as other ancient Egyptians were. This "leap" sounds as though it was an attempt to imitate what those who have NDEs often experience. That is, once out of their bodies, those in NDEs often fly (by being drawn by some invisible force) from where they died on Earth, up into the sky and into the tunnel that leads to heaven. The leap sounds like a kind of "do it yourself" attempt to achieve the same thing.

The similarities with Egypt don't stop there, as in North America they also built pyramids, though made of earth. Countless numbers of ancient earthen mounds were built across vast regions of eastern North America—in the areas of the Great Lakes, Ohio River Valley, and Mississippi River Valley. They were often built as flat-topped pyramids.[527] The earliest evidence for them has currently been dated to approximately 5,500 BC (however, as most have been destroyed, there were possibly older sites).[528] Many of these earthworks also align to the solstices and equinoxes.[529]

Map of mound sites in North America.

Mound building in North America followed a sequence, with various sites being built then abandoned (and sometimes later refurbished), and then other mound sites built elsewhere and likewise abandoned, etc., down through thousands of years by different cultures, but all based upon the same ancient religion, indicating they were all connected, as Graham Hancock writes:

"[...] all shared the same mound-building obsession and continued to express it in the same ways. [...] Despite the fact that different cultures were involved at different periods, every resurgence of mound-building was linked to the reiteration and reimagination of the same geometrical and astronomical memes. This was not 'chance' or 'coincidence.' [...] It's not unreasonable, therefore, to suppose that some kind of cosmic 'sky-ground' religion lay behind the alignments to the solstices and the equinoxes at Watson Brake and at the other early sites—a religion sufficiently robust to ensure the continuous successful transmission of a system of geometry, astronomy, and architecture over thousands of years."[530]

Among the numerous mound and earthwork sites of the Americas are those that are circular and geometrical, often consisting of an earthen ditch and bank, which is astronomically aligned. Researchers have noted many similarities, and sometimes identical features shared in common with ancient sites in Britain like Avebury and Stonehenge, which are enclosed within a circular earthen ditch and bank, and some in North America even date to the same time periods.[531]

Circular earthworks aligned to the solstices have a long history in Europe. The first ancient circular earthwork sites in Central and Eastern Europe date to between 4,800-4,600 BC.[532] [533]

Similar ancient circular earthworks in the Americas and Europe.

The largest of these anywhere in the world is part of the Newark Earthworks complex located in Ohio in the United States. It was built by the Hopewell culture between 100 BC – AD 400,[534] who may have built as many as 50,000 mounds and earthworks.[535]

William Romain is among those who've studied Newark Earthworks the most. Romain is an American archaeologist and archaeoastronomer who's written books about the site and been awarded for his contributions to Ohio archaeology. He's demonstrated that Newark's earthworks correspond to Native American beliefs, and has done much to decode their meaning and purpose.

Native Americans believed the cosmos was essentially composed of three realms—our earthly realm, which was positioned above the watery realm of the underworld, and suspended beneath the celestial vault of the sky-world. The four cardinal directions were defined by the spatial relationship between Earth and the sun. At the intersection of these directions was the center of the world, where the world navel or tree was located, which connected Earth with the realms both above and below it.[536] As discussed earlier in the chapter, this was the fundamental belief held about the structure of the cosmos and its other dimensions in the ancient Religion of the Sun, as found in the many traditions derived from it, and shared in common with Shamanism.

Artifact found at a Mississippian mound site with a symbol showing the spatial relationship between the earth and the sun, with their cyclical movement defining the four directions.

The Native Americans also held a similar belief to the ancient Egyptians about first creation, which is told in what is perhaps their most widely held belief, called the Earth Diver myth. This says that in the beginning, a water creature (variously a beetle, duck, toad, otter, etc.) dove down to the bottom of the primal waters and brought up a little piece of mud, which spread out in four directions (sometimes on the back of a turtle), becoming the earth, which was visualized as a great, circular flat island afloat in the primal waters of the cosmos.[537]

Romain believes that ancient North American sites were based around this myth. He demonstrates that the circle symbolized the earth in Native American lore, and thus the circular earthworks were intended to represent the primordial circular island of Earth, with everything beyond it visualized as the primal waters. Some were even surrounded by moats to symbolize these waters. Romain also proposes that mounds were often built in the shape of local mountains to symbolically represent the world mountain, or cosmic axis, which linked the three realms of the cosmos together. These mounds could be built at the center of circular earthworks, revealing they were intended to represent the cosmic axis of Earth, and were also a symbol of the primordial mound of Native American tradition.[538]

A painted shell found at a Mississippian mound site showing the cosmic axis (the striped pole in the center) being vibrated by two dancers holding what look like rattles and drums. Maypoles in Europe were also often striped.

What this means is that ancient mounds and circular enclosures in North America are very likely to have had the same meaning as pyramids in Egypt.

Solving the meaning of these ancient sites in North America helps to unlock the meaning of similar sites in Europe. Given all the similarities we've covered between ancient sites in Europe and those in Egypt, it seems obvious now that the circular earthworks (known as henges) in Europe, such as at Stonehenge, Avebury, and Goseck Circle, were likewise intended to symbolize the earth as the primordial mound like an island afloat in the ocean of the cosmos, and this would explain why such efforts were made to dig enormous ditches around them—to create the visual of a great round island.

As we've seen, ancient sites in Egypt and Europe were used as portals to another dimension, particularly to heaven. Remarkably, Romain concludes that this was the purpose of the Newark Earthworks of the Hopewell too, saying:

> "In fact [...] it may even be that the Hopewell considered the geometric enclosures to be actual gateways, or doorways, to the otherworld. Certainly, the idea of architectural structures being used to create entrances to the otherworld was known throughout North America. The circular hole in the top of the Ojibway shaking tent, for example, was specifically meant to allow for 'soulflight travel . . . to the Hole

in the Sky and [a]cross the barrier to the spirit realm' (Conway 1992:253). Likewise, the circular hole in the top of the Pawnees' earth lodge was meant as a symbolic link between the heavens and earth (Nabokov and Easton 1989:139). And, too, the wooden pole located in the center of the Plains Indian Sun Dance lodge was meant to connect the earth and sky (Nabokov and Easton 1989:168). [...] The point here is that the idea of architectural elements, like the Hopewell enclosures, being used as gateways to the otherworld is an idea that was well known throughout Native America. Indeed, one gets the impression that the geometric enclosures were in many ways analogous to the oversized community houses known as karigi that are used for ceremonies by the Inuit, Yupik, and other native peoples of Alaska and Canada: On ceremonial occasions the community gathers at the karigi. It is a nexus between the secular, and sacred worlds; passage by celebrants through the house entrance tunnels, doorways, and smoke holes symbolizes the passage between worlds and between different states of being. The karigi smoke hole serves as a passage permitting movement and communication between the world of the hunter and the hunted, between the world of the living and the dead (Hirschfelder and Molin 1992:144). In the same way, to step inside the boundary of a Hopewell geometric earthwork was perhaps to step into a threshold or doorway—a doorway somewhere between this world and the next, a doorway between life and death."[539]

~ WILLIAM ROMAIN, MYSTERIES OF THE HOPEWELL

Given the similarities between the ancient mound and earthwork sites of North America, we believe it would have been the purpose of all those built for religious use from their very inception, going back to at least 5,500 BC.

Romain and other researchers in the field have described Newark Earthworks as a kind of spiritual machine, just as researchers in Egypt have used the word machine to describe Egyptian pyramids. Romain has proposed that the Newark Earthworks were "ritualistic machines used to assist souls to journey to the sky world." Archaeologist Bradley Lepper wrote that they "were likely to be conceived to be more like machines. The giant enclosures were enormous engines of ceremony and ritual intended to do something." And researcher Gregory Little has described them as "magic machines of earth [...] utilized in rituals that involved complex ceremonies where groups of people moved from one area of the mounds and earthworks to another."[540]

Given that burials were found within many of the mounds and earthworks,[541] particularly of the elite, it's clear these "machines" were used just as pyramids were—to facilitate the passage of the soul of the deceased through the portal to heaven.

Depiction of an ancient North American mound site. These mounds could be shaped like flat-topped pyramids, though made entirely of earth.

For example, the Great Circle earthwork at Newark was designed to create a bridge from Earth into the Milky Way leading to the heavenly sky realm, to assist the soul in entering the *ogee*, or portal to heaven, as Andrew Collins describes:

> "At Great Circle in Newark, Ohio, for instance, a bird effigy mound at the center of an enormous circular plateau, nearly 1,200 feet (366 meters) in diameter, is directed east-northeast toward the earthen structure's only entrance. A person standing on the mound, known locally as Eagle Mound, in the hours of darkness immediately before the summer solstice around 2,000 years ago would have witnessed a spectacular sight. Rising vertically into the sky, framed perfectly within the entrance to Great Circle, would have been the Milky Way, looking as if it formed a natural extension of an imagined path that started at the bird mound. Following the course of the Milky Way would have taken the eye to where the starry stream splits in two at the start of the Great Rift, almost as if the whole visual spectacle symbolized a cosmic tree, or a forked sky-pole, linking Earth to heaven. And between the 'branches' or fork would have been the stars of Cygnus, the celestial bird, located almost directly above its terrestrial counterpart on the ground. Shortly afterward, as the first rays of dawn consumed the glittering light of the stars, the midsummer sun would have appeared exactly where the Milky Way (the Path of Souls) had risen into the sky just a few hours earlier."[542]
> ~ ANDREW COLLINS, FOREWORD, PATH OF SOULS

Eagle Mound appears to be the equivalent of the falcon that the king of ancient Egypt was said to be transformed into out of his body at the summer solstice, before then ascending the stream of the Milky Way until reaching the northern stars where the Cygnus constellation may have represented him in heaven as a bird of starlight in flight.

Collins has recognized these similarities, saying:

> "Clearly, Great Circle with its bird effigy mound acted like the sarcophagus, coffin, tomb, and pyramid in ancient Egypt, as a means of enabling the rebirth of the soul in the next world."[543]
> ~ ANDREW COLLINS, FOREWORD, PATH OF SOULS

But there is evidence they were also used by and for the living as access points to the otherworld too.

Based on archaeological finds within the earthworks, Romain suggests they were used for large Shamanistic rituals in which people dressed as animals, used rhythmic drumming and dancing, ingested the hallucinogenic mushroom *amanita muscaria*, and smoked strong tobacco to induce altered states of consciousness and make contact with the otherworld.[544] As discussed in the previous section, these kinds of practices are part of shamanic religion, and would have been brought by the Native Americans in their migrations from Siberia to the Americas. The evidence showing that the earthworks were used in this way further indicates they were built for accessing other dimensions by both the living and the dead, as ancient portal sites were in other parts of the world.

Depiction of a shaman found at a Mississippian mound site; he is dancing while vomiting "black drink," which was a Native American drink that was very high in caffeine.

Yet what seems to have occurred in numerous cultures in the Americas is a comingling of the beliefs and practices of Shamanism with those of the ancient Religion of the Sun, and we wonder if at some earlier time these kinds of sites were used for having OBEs as they were in other places where the Religion of the Sun was practiced before the practices of Shamanism prevailed.

OTHER

In Japanese tradition, people who can "fly anywhere in their dreams" are called *tobi-damashi*, meaning flying soul.[545]

In Europe, ideas about the out-of-body realm continued into the Renaissance where they emerged in what is known as the Western Esoteric Tradition, particularly with the Rosicrucians, Paracelsians, and Alchemists. By the nineteenth century, Theosophists began using the term *astral* to refer to aspects of the out-of-body experience. The word derives from the Late Latin *astralis*, from the Latin *astrum*, or from the Greek *astron*, which means related to, or coming from, the stars.[546] And so today we have the terms astral projection, astral travel, astral plane, and astral body.

OBES TO HEAVEN

As we've seen, the order of the Twice Born in ancient Egypt were able to induce OBEs not just to the astral plane, as normally occurs with sleep and astral projection, but to a region higher than it, which is commonly called heaven. Today, heaven is usually only accessed by people who've died (and later revive in an NDE), in which they travel through the portal from the astral plane to heaven in the commonly described tunnel going into the light, which opens out into heaven.

However, it was said that there were people in the past who had once been able to pass from one sphere to another easily—meaning from one dimension or realm to another (i.e. from the physical to the astral and to heaven)—but this ability was lost, and then people had to pass through a grim portal, which is the tunnel seen in NDEs.

Those who were able to access heaven easily, we believe, were the Children of the Sun. As mentioned, in the ancient traditions of Tibet, the Children of the Sun (the *dmu-gshen*) were said to be connected by a cord of light stretching from the crown of their heads to the stars, the realm of heaven. It seems this cord of light was the connection that once enabled them to travel out of the body during life to heaven. So rather than just having OBEs in the astral plane, they also had them in heaven.

As far as I know, most do not have this connection to heaven that the Children of the Sun once possessed. However, we do have this kind of connection to the astral plane, which is what allows us to travel to it in OBEs and dreams and be influenced by things in it during waking life. Additionally, almost all people also have a connection to hell, which is what allows them to pass into it during nightmares. I explain more about this connection where I discuss nightmares in chapter 26. So what people have today may be the inverse of what the Children of the Sun once possessed.

The connection to hell can be cut off and the connection to heaven re-established on the path of the Spiritual Sun, and I will discuss this in other books.

I once had an OBE in which I traveled to heaven; I was at an intermediate stage on the path of the Spiritual Sun. I arrived there with spiritual help and without going through any portal. I saw an incredibly beautiful natural landscape, where I could perceive divine beauty in everything. I saw people who I knew were the deceased, happily living and working in the fields. What I saw matches closely the heavenly paradise the ancient Egyptians called Aaru. They believed that those who had died and then successfully passed their afterlife judgement, in which their good deeds had outweighed their bad, moved on to a beautiful, bountiful, and peaceful land, without suffering or pain, where they were greeted by their deceased loved ones and even pets, and could live off the land among the gods in eternal spring.[547] [548]

Ancient Egyptian depiction of Aaru, which is a more heavenly version of Earth in the afterlife.

Today, there are many people who visit heaven in NDEs and describe it just as the ancient Egyptians did, and as I saw in my OBE. I'll give just two examples from a very large number of NDEs:

"Suddenly, I was in a place that was very calm. I can't even describe the calmness because I've never felt anything like that on Earth. I was in a field. There were hills. There was a gentle breeze. Every color was more vibrant than any colors I have seen before. The sky was bright blue and clear. The grass was a vibrant green. There were trees in the distance that were the deepest green I have ever seen. It was warm there. It wasn't like a sweltering summer day [...]. It was a wonderful, comfortable warm that filled my entire body.

There were people next to me laughing and running around. I recognized them as friends of mine who had previously passed on. My childhood dogs were there too. Soon, I was joining them. I remember feeling happier and more at peace than I have ever felt. It was like taking the happiest day in your life, hold onto that feeling, then multiply it by ten. It was a sense that nothing mattered, not time or deadlines, nothing hurt anymore. It was absolute peace. I wanted to stay there forever."[549]

"[...] [the angel] and I were teleported to the center of a vast golden field. I could hear the most beautiful music and I could feel it moving through me. The breeze blew against the tall golden wheat stalks, and as it did, I could feel the spirit of all things living around me: animals, plants, the elements. I was one with them. I looked up and saw a huge ball of light that cast the purest, warm light all around me and felt God touch my skin. He knew me, he loved me no matter how imperfect my Earthly life had been. I was perfect and whole. I felt no pain. The angel took me up higher, and I felt like I was soaring endlessly. I could see a huge waterfall with no beginning and no end. Love and peace reigned here. I sensed the presence of loved ones that had passed on, but I didn't see them."[550]

Experiences in heavens after death must be temporary as it's clear from NDEs that people are reborn time and again to live new physical lives.

There are numerous references to the connection to heaven in traditions of the ancient Religion of the Sun.

For example, in ancient Hindu texts, the term yoga was often used to describe the practice by which one traveled out of the body after death along a path of sunlight extending from the crown of one's head to heaven and the sun.[551] This "path of sunlight" seems to be just another way of describing the cord of light possessed by the Children of the Sun. The word yoga is derived from root words that mean "to attach, join, harness, yoke." Yoga had the aim of "yoking" or joining one's consciousness to the supreme divinity,[552] which was seen as the Spiritual Sun. Establishing a connection to heaven in life, which one then traveled along at death, seems to have been the underpinning goal of yoga.

The first Vedic king of the solar dynasty ascending to heaven along the path of sunlight stretching from the crown of his head.

Taoists did OBE exercises with the aim of traveling to the celestial realms of the sun and stars as practice for their final journey to heaven there at death.

Researcher Bibhu Dev Misra realized that in ancient Egypt, perhaps its most prolific symbol, the ankh or "key to eternal life," was a knot in a cord that tied someone to the Spiritual Sun, allowing them to return to its heavenly realm after death, and that its equivalent in Hinduism is called the *pasha*. It was also known in Vedic philosophy as the Sutratman, meaning "Self-thread" or "Soul-cord" (sutra means "thread/cord" and Atman "the self/soul"). This cord was believed to transmit the energy (prana) of the Spiritual Sun and supreme creator (known as Brahman) to every living thing via their breath. At death, the knot in one's cord was untied, the breath ceased, and the soul was believed to return upward along the cord to the Sun/Brahman.[553] This "breath cord" was said to be possessed by all living beings, whereas the "cord of light" extending from the crown of one's head and/or third eye was said to have only been possessed by those more spiritually developed. This seems to indicate that there is more than one type of cord of light, and that the Children of the Sun had developed the "crown/third eye cord" in addition to the "breath cord."

We think the concept of these cords of light connecting one to the Spiritual Sun and stars must have at least partly derived from ancient NDEs. A common experience in modern NDEs is having the sense of being pulled by some invisible force up into the sky, through a tunnel toward a light like the sun, into heaven. It's easy to imagine how this could be described as being pulled up into heaven by a cord extending from the sun to each individual, and no doubt ancient people experienced the same thing after death that people do today, and that some of them too returned to share their NDE. It then makes sense that ancient Egyptian gods might hold the symbol of this cord (the ankh) to show their connection to heaven and the Spiritual Sun/Source.

Left: The ancient Egyptian god Horus holding the ankh in his right hand.
Right: The Hindu god of death Yama holding the *pasha* (rope) in his left hand.

Ancient Egyptian gods were often portrayed holding the ankh. We suspect this may have been to show they had a connection to heaven, which had once been possessed by the Children of the Sun.

As we've explored, many pyramids that were constructed as tombs were built as devices thought to help propel the king to his heavenly destination after death. However, the order of the Twice Born in Egypt used the Great Pyramid of Egypt, not as a tomb, but rather, it looks likely as a kind of device to send someone through the portal to heaven in life. This is likely to have begun as a substance and near-death-free experience, in which electromagnetic energy and perhaps sound were harnessed to enable this special kind of OBE. However, eventually the experience became dependent on a blend of substances that induced a near-death state, and then even this became lost.

As described in the Pyramid Texts, the ability to travel to heaven also required a level of spiritual development. The king had to raise his serpent of light (called the kundalini in Hinduism), and open his inner eye (the third eye in Hinduism), which are both part of re-establishing a connection to heaven, and which I describe further in chapter 28.

Left: A king in Egypt with a serpent on his forehead, symbolizing the risen kundalini. Right: An image from the shrine of the boy king Tutankhamun showing the king connected to a star by what look like rays of light extending to or from his forehead (the region of the third eye). This may have been based on the cord of light that was said to have connected the Children of the Sun to heaven.

Much later, Jesus emerges after his "lost years" teaching about becoming born again, i.e. "twice born," and possessing the remarkable ability to travel out of his body into heavenly realms. It seems that Jesus was either born with a connection to heaven or developed it.

OBES TO THE SOURCE

There is another kind of ancient OBE which I've had myself, though it is much, much rarer, and takes someone beyond the fifth dimension and even heaven, to the Source. I refer to it as a Source experience. It can occur in part of the practice of alchemy, which is how I experienced it, and which I'll explain in another book. According to ancient Hindu texts, it can also occur when one silences their mind during meditation, rather than concentrates it. As I've experienced it, the sensations of this type of OBE are very different to astral projection.

When it happened to me, instead of feeling like I was coming out of my body, I collapsed in upon myself, into my heart, as though being swallowed by a black hole that was not black, but a pure and total light. I erupted into an existence where there is only light that has no shadows, and I as a thinking and feeling person was reduced to nothing apart from consciousness, and expanded into consciousness, into its pure light, which was boundless and profoundly alive with the consciousnesses of other beings. The experience was overwhelming and is unlike anything experienced during an OBE in the astral.

It was however a very short, momentary experience. This is because basic consciousness is just a fragment of the Being that is still under the laws of creation, and so it cannot stay there. The laws and duality draw it back and it gets expelled rapidly. It has to be united with its Being, and fulfill certain conditions such as eliminating the darkness that surrounds it and overcoming the laws keeping it in creation, for it to go permanently into the Source.

This experience is a central theme of the ancient Vedic/Hindu texts the Upanishads (particularly those that are considered the principal and oldest among them) where it's described numerous times. It's said to be a very ancient practice, which gave someone with a pure heart the highest mystical experience, called samadhi (though the term samadhi has been used to refer to numerous different spiritual experiences and states).

Once Lara and I realized it was this kind of OBE the composers of the Upanishads were referring to, it was like having a key that unlocked much of their meaning. Knowing what they were describing, we realized that the composers of the Upanishads were being quite literal and specific about how to do this ancient practice, and what someone sees and experiences as a result of it. It seems much of the discipline of ancient Vedic yoga was aimed at somehow permanently recapturing this Source experience.

Illustration of a Vedic yogi reciting the mantra of the Spiritual Sun (Gayatri).

Without having had this experience or at least knowing about it accurately, the passages describing it can easily be interpreted in a more mundane way, as being a realization that someone can have while meditating without having any kind of OBE.

Here are some examples of passages from the Upanishads where this higher Source OBE is described.

> "When the five senses are stilled
> when the mind is stilled,

when the intellect is stilled,
that is called the highest state by the wise.
They say yoga is this complete stillness
In which one enters this unitive state,
Never to become separate again."[554]
~ KATHA UPANISHAD

"In the depths of meditation, sages saw within themselves the Lord of Love, who dwells in the heart of every creature.

[...] He is the inner Self of all, Hidden like a little flame in the heart. Only by the stilled mind can he be known.

[...] Know him to be the primal source of life whose glory permeates the universe, who is beyond time and space, yet can be seen within the heart in meditation."[555]
~ SHVETASHVATARA UPANISHAD

"Let us meditate on the shining Self, changeless, underlying the world of change, and realized in the heart in samadhi."[556]
~ TEJOBINDU UPANISHAD

"Sage Shvetashvatara realized the Lord in meditation through infinite grace and imparted this highest wisdom to devoted disciples. This highest mystical experience, revealed at the dawn of time, must be shared only with one whose heart is pure [...]."[557]
~ SHVETASHVATARA UPANISHAD

The evidence for people having had this Source experience traces back to the oldest Hindu text, the Rig Veda, which contains passages that describe it. This experience clearly informed the understanding and cosmology of its composers, and is very ancient. The following excerpt addresses Agni, the god of fire, who is one of the most worshiped gods of the Vedas, and was used as a symbol of consciousness.

"Holding in his hand all soul powers, he [Agni] places the Gods in hiding and sits in secrecy. The sages who control their intelligence find him there, when they praise the mantras formed by the heart. [...] Agni enters with secrecy into the secret place, the universal life. Those who perceive him dwelling in the secret cave [of the heart] [...] then Agni declares the vastnesses to them.

The entire universe dwells within your nature, in the ocean, in the heart, in the power of life.

> Inspired wise poets, they of deep meditation, obtain the words and the highest state. [...] Seeking to find they have seen the ocean and for these humans the sun revealed itself."558
>
> ~ RIG VEDA

In this Source experience, through controlling one's intelligence (higher mind, consciousness) with the aid of mantras, consciousness (Agni) enters the heart out of the body (in secrecy), and discovers the vastness of the entire universe and the ocean of universal life contained within it. Then, "the sun revealed itself," meaning through this Source experience the true nature of the sun was revealed. This experience is likely one of the reasons why the Spiritual Sun was seen as the ultimate physical form of the Source in the Vedas.

This Source experience is encoded into one of the most prolific symbols of the ancient Religion of the Sun, which is the symbol of the sun god seated on a lotus flower as his throne. In the Upanishads, the heart, in which they say the Self is hidden, is compared to a lotus flower. In Hinduism, as well as in other branches of the ancient Religion of the Sun, the lotus was the seat or throne of the sun god.559 The sun god was symbolic of the Source and one's higher Being, which is why the Self/Brahman in the Vedas, Upanishads, and other Yogic texts was identified with the sun.

> "The Sun, the Self of the world, is the prana placed in the heart."560
>
> ~ YOGA YAJNAVALKYA

A closed lotus bud resembles a heart, and when looking at an open lotus from above, its beautiful yellow center looks just like the sun, so it's as though the sun is hidden within its closed petals and seated upon it once open. Thus, the symbol of the sun god on his lotus throne has a deeper meaning—it alludes to the Being and Source being hidden in the heart, and found within it during this higher Source OBE where the all-encompassing light of consciousness shines in the heart like the light of the sun.

> "In the city of Brahman is a secret dwelling, the lotus of the heart. Within this dwelling is a space [...]. As great as the infinite space beyond is the space within the lotus of the heart. [...] everything is contained in that inner space."561
>
> ~ CHANDOGYA UPANISHAD

This is another literal description of what is experienced beyond the body when one enters the spiritual region in their heart—they go into an infinite expanse of light where everything exists in its purest form.

Left: A lotus bud turned upside down resembles a heart. Center: A lotus flower from above; its golden yellow center looks like the sun enclosed within its petals. Right: The sun god Vishnu within a lotus.

This kind of OBE was an important spiritual practice in the ancient Religion of the Sun, which is not widely understood, as it's so difficult to do and so few people reach its goal.

It seems it was this practice that allowed the writers of the Upanishads to experience many profound truths about the Source (they called Brahman) and the Being (they called the Self/Atman). Yet the experience of this higher OBE also seems to have sometimes misdirected them or have been misinterpreted, as it seems to have led to the idea that someone can attain a permanent unification with the Source through meditation, which even then became through realization. However, as I mentioned earlier in this section, in meditation it is a very short experience, while in the ancient Religion of the Sun there is a long-term process of inner purification and transformation one needs to undergo to attain a permanent unification with their higher Being and return to the Source.

This experience is also likely to be the basis of the Buddhist belief in the "clear light of the void/emptiness" called *sunyata* we referred to previously, which they believe is the underlying reality behind all things and is the ultimate state they aim to attain. Their early teachings appear to be based on Hinduism, particularly those found in the Upanishads (as some scholars have noted[562]), and they likewise practiced techniques for stilling the mind in meditation, and so it's possible there were Buddhists who also experienced this higher OBE at some time. However, the Source and Self/Being are absent in their doctrine and so without it, Buddhists pursue "emptiness" as their goal instead. They also speak of the "clear light" of the void as a state of mind that can be experienced while asleep (instead of dreaming) and entered immediately after death. This again seems to be a kind of later misinterpretation of the experience of having an OBE into a higher plane of light than the astral plane.

Buddha is often portrayed as seated upon a lotus, partly preserving the symbolism of the sun god seated upon his lotus throne.

The Source experience may have also been described in the Hindu epic the Mahabharata, where it's attained by someone who firstly purifies their heart of sins like anger, pride, vanity, and illusion—though it's a little bit different, as the practitioner is said merely to behold the light in their heart, rather than be immersed into it.

> "A pure-minded person, by purification of his heart, is able to destroy the good and evil effect of his actions and attains eternal beatitude by the enlightenment of his inward spirit. That state of peace and purification of heart is likened to the state of a person who in a cheerful state of mind sleeps soundly, or the brilliance of a lamp trimmed by a skillful hand. Such a pure-minded person living on spare diet perceives the Supreme Spirit reflected in his own, and by practicing concentration of mind in the evening and small hours of the night, he beholds the Supreme Spirit which has no attributes, in the light of his heart, shining like a dazzling lamp, and thus he attains salvation."563
> ~ THE MAHABHARATA

Something that also sounds similar was described by a wandering sadhu called Tota Puri around 1864 while he was instructing Ramakrishna. He was a follower of Advaita Vedanta, a Hindu sect which seeks the ultimate knowledge of the Vedas, believed to be most fully expressed in the Upanishads.

> "Brahman, the one substance which alone is eternally pure, eternally awakened, unlimited by time, space and causation, is absolutely real. Through Maya, which makes the impossible possible, It causes, by virtue of its influence, to seem that It is divided into names and forms. Brahman is never really so divided. For, at the time of

Samadhi, not even a drop, so to say, of time and space, and name and form produced by Maya is perceived. Whatever, therefore, is within the bounds of name and form can never be absolutely real. Shun it by a good distance. Break the firm cage of name and form with the overpowering strength of a lion and come out of it. Dive deep into the reality of the Self existing in yourself. Be one with It with the help of Samadhi. You will then see the universe consisting of name and form, vanish, as it were, into the void; you will see the consciousness of the little I merge in that of the immense I, where it ceases to function; and you will have the immediate knowledge of the indivisible Existence-Knowledge-Bliss as yourself."[564]

What the description lacks importantly is light that is alive with consciousnesses, mentioning only void, and so it's possible that while some belief in the experience was passed down over thousands of years, it may have been understood as referring to other types of meditative states. The experiences Ramakrishna is described as having for example, seem very different and more trance-like, and I have yet to see an accurate description of this Source OBE in more modern Hinduism or Buddhism, meaning the secret knowledge of it may eventually have become lost.

OBES IN THE COSMOLOGY OF THE ANCIENT RELIGION OF THE SUN

To summarize, what we find in so many of these ancient sites and texts related to OBEs is evidence for one of the most fundamental beliefs in the ancient Religion of the Sun. Understanding it allows us to begin to see ancient sites through the eyes of their builders.

It's something our research on the ancient Religion of the Sun has been leading to, but we've been more fully able to comprehend while writing this book, as OBEs were such a large part of it.

The belief essentially seems to be this:

We are born here in a limited sense of the word—in that we come into it to be restricted to material form, as we are really spiritual beings inhabiting physical bodies. The lower realms of matter, including the physical realm and its astral component, as well as hell, are those of our Earth Mother, and are like a great womb. We call it "womb world," where we gradually learn through countless lives/reincarnations. We are like a little spiritual seed planted in it. Even though there is light here, it's really very dim compared to the light of heaven, as it's mixed with so much darkness, making this quite a dark realm, like the inside of a womb. Hell within the earth, the place of greatest darkness, also forms part of this realm of learning within the Mother, and was seen as her womb especially.

Yet we have the potential to become born spiritually—to become twice born, or born again. This is a spiritual birth in which we leave the womb of our Spiritual Earth Mother (portrayed as the ancient Egyptian Neith/Nut and symbolized by Jesus' human mother Mary) to enter the realm of our Heavenly Father (the Egyptian Atum and Jesus' Heavenly Father).

The force that enables one to do this is the Spiritual Son/Sun symbolized by Osiris (and his son Horus) and Jesus—son of the Spiritual Earth Mother and Heavenly Father. The Spiritual Son is a higher part of us, and incarnates within those who fulfill the inner requirements; this was symbolized as the birth of a divine son at the winter solstice, as it's when the sun seems to re-emerge out of the time of greatest darkness as though it is born—representing the Spiritual Son germinating in the darkness of the material world and body.

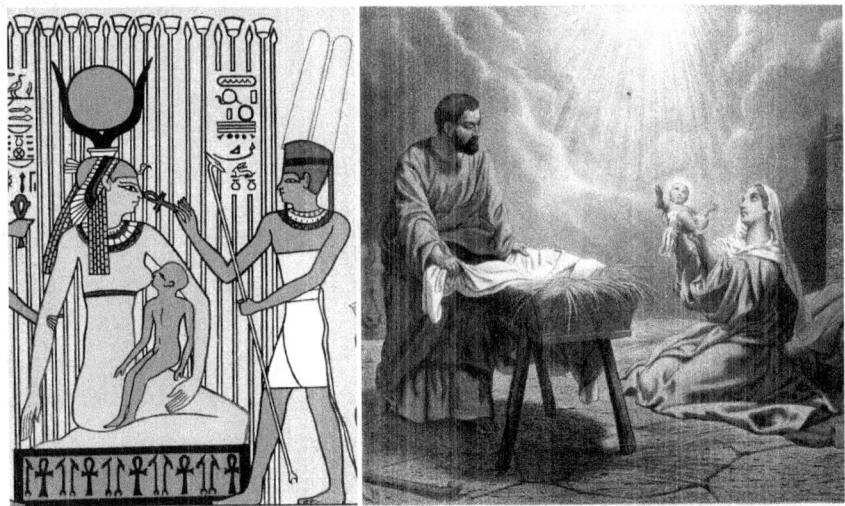

Left: Isis having just given birth to the Spiritual Son Horus.
Right: Mary having just given birth to the Spiritual Son Jesus.

This spiritual rebirth eventually takes one through the portal leading from the astral plane to heaven, commonly seen in NDEs as the tunnel leading into the light of the Source that appears thousands of times brighter than the sun. However, for those who are twice born, this is not a temporary stay between lives on Earth, but a permanent rebirth out of womb world due to a transformation of consciousness, and happens not just as part of death, but is an inner level achieved in life (and fully experienced at death). As it says in the Kolbrin, "the immortality of the common folk and the immortality of the Twice Born were not alike."[565]

This is why pyramids, mounds, stone circles, and temples were often built to symbolize the earth (sometimes replicating its dimensions) and at the same time the Spiritual Mother (often replicating her shape)—they were symbols of "womb world." This was further emphasized through the inclusion of stone coffins or cauldrons representing the womb of the Mother Goddess. In Egypt, pyramids were built to not only represent the four-dimensional physical world, but also the fifth dimension, as this constitutes the entirety of womb world.

The womb of the Spiritual Mother could be variously symbolized as the earth, the sky beneath the horizon, and the dark rift of the Milky Way. These might seem contradictory symbols until you realize what they all represent. Each are fitting symbols of a Spiritual Mother's womb, which is a cosmic place of darkness, concealed from view, as well as a place that the sun (representing the Spiritual Son) can be said or perceived to travel through (during the hours of darkness, the night).

Stone sarcophagus and bowls that may have all been seen as the "womb of rebirth."

The next striking design feature some of these sites share is a long tunnel or avenue, leading from out of their usually dark inner stone chamber to the outside world. In the case of Göbekli Tepe, instead of an avenue, "soul holes" and porthole stones were used to recreate a kind of tunnel effect. Specifically, this tunnel or avenue was aligned either to the sun at a solstice or equinox, or to the stars—particularly to those that never set in the Northern Hemisphere, the northern circumpolar stars (as in Egypt), or to the brightest in the sky, Sirius (as on Malta), or to the brightest star of Cygnus, which is in the northern region of the sky (as at Göbekli Tepe). What this means is that when the sun or stars were aligned, someone who emerged from the inside of the pyramid, mound, circle, or temple, appeared to travel from the darkness of the earth into the light of the celestial realms. They were treated to a similar visual effect as those who travel out of their body in an NDE through the tunnel/portal into the light, from the astral plane to heaven. The tunnel/avenue/portal was seen as the birth canal of the Mother leading to the sun and stars, which were viewed as the heavenly realm of the Father.

Left: Photo looking out from inside a chambered cairn (mound of stones) in Scotland. Center: Recreation of traveling through the tunnel into the light in an NDE. Right: The dark rift of the Milky Way appearing to stretch from Earth into the northern circumpolar stars, like the tunnel that leads to heaven.

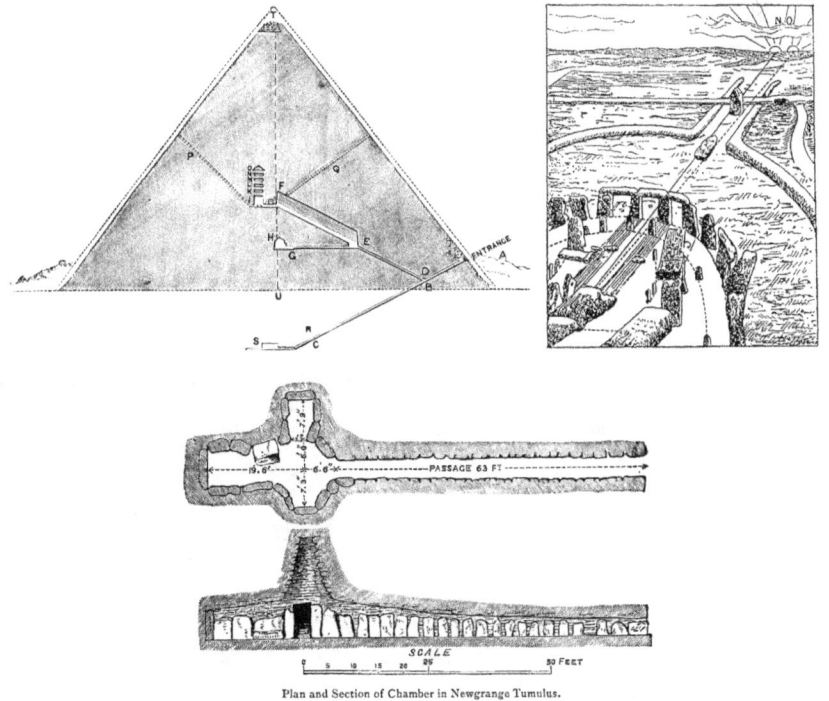

Ancient sites that had a long tunnel or avenue aligned to the stars or sunrise at a solstice, symbolizing the birth canal of the Spiritual Mother leading to rebirth in heaven. Top left: The Great Pyramid. Top right: Stonehenge. Bottom: Newgrange.

This birth canal could be symbolized as the dark rift of the Milky Way, which is a perfect symbol for it if you think about it. The tunnel people go through to reach heaven in NDEs is accessed through a portal in the sky. The tunnel is often described as dark and huge, sometimes as winding, and as passing through the stars. This could well be likened to traveling through the huge dark rift that appears to wind its way through the Milky Way's stream of stars. This is why the ancient Egyptians referred to the Milky Way as the winding waterway, and symbolized the sun god and soul as traveling along it on a boat. This sun ship became one of the major symbols of the ancient Religion of the Sun, and was associated with the journey of the soul (as the sun) through the other-dimensional realms of the afterlife—specifically to reach heaven.

The body of the Egyptian goddess Nut was portrayed as painted with stars and arching across the sky like the Milky Way, which the sun god Ra was shown as traversing in a boat. Her body could also be portrayed as a river, as she and the Milky Way were also associated with the Nile River. No doubt there would have been rituals in which the solar boat (barque) of the pharaoh would have sailed the Nile next to the Great Pyramids to symbolize his journey to heaven. Similarly, the avenue from Stonehenge leads to the River Avon, which is believed to have been sailed in religious processions, in which it too could have symbolized the Milky Way and the journey through the tunnel to heaven. This same symbolic template also appears to have been used at Newgrange in Ireland, which was built along the River Boyne, named after the goddess Boann. She and the river were associated with the Milky Way, which was known as "the way of the white cow"—the cow being a symbol of the goddess,[566] as it was in Egypt. It's been suggested that Newgrange represented the womb of Boann, which was impregnated at the winter solstice by the god Dagda as the light of the sun that penetrates into Newgrange's inner chamber, conceiving the divine son Aengus.[567] So as in the pyramids of Egypt, we have a divine triad of Father, Mother, and Son symbolized at a British mound.

Left: The ancient Egyptian Mother goddess Nut with her body arched across the night sky and painted with stars; the sun travels inside her body before being reborn. Right: The Milky Way, which appears to arch across the sky, just like the body of Nut.

The earth and womb world were also synonymous with the mound that arose from the primeval waters at the beginning of creation, and so these sites were also symbols of the primordial mound. The mound symbolized matter itself, which manifests from out of the sea of cosmic energy. In the duality of creation, material substance was seen as belonging to the feminine half, as matter was associated with darkness and earth. It is this substance that our body is made of, and so the primordial mound was at the same time a symbol of matter, the earth, the human body, and the body and womb of the Spiritual Mother.

Ancient sites that were likely to have been symbols of the womb of the Spiritual Mother, the earth, matter, the human body, and primordial mound.

The earth was viewed as an island afloat in the vast cosmic ocean from which it had taken shape. Our bodies too take shape and float in the dark waters of our mother's womb.

At the center of this mound was the cosmic axis that connected the three realms of the cosmos together—the underworld (hell), physical and astral planes, and heaven. The axis led through the body of the Spiritual Mother—her mouth the tunnel and axis that led straight down into hell, and her birth canal the axis tunnel that led up into heaven. Native Americans portrayed the entrances/portals of these tunnels (either to heaven or hell) as a slit in the sky, which is how I have seen the portal to hell. This slit could well be likened to a mouth and vulva, which is how they were often portrayed in ancient art.

Native American *ogee* symbol inside a circle, which looks like an open mouth. It represents the portal in the sky leading either to heaven or hell.

Ancient sites not only represented the primordial mound, but also its axis (the cosmic axis), often as a passageway, stairway, or avenue. However, this axis could be symbolized on its own as a pole or tree. These sites were then seen and used as places where one could access other realms.

The axis within the body is the spine, which is the center along which the higher and lower dimensional parts of us are connected, and so these sites sometimes incorporated symbols of the spine as they were also symbols of the human body.

The axis of our body extends to our head, and it was through there that one developed their connection to heaven. The head was equated with the region of the northern circumpolar stars, where Earth's axis extends. It was there that consciousness (the soul), joined together with the Spiritual Son/Sun, was believed to reach heaven.

At the beginning of creation, the Spiritual Sun was said to be enthroned upon this central axis, and so ancient sites were often built so that the sun was positioned at their peak either symbolically (as at the Great Pyramid) or astronomically (aligned at either an equinox or solstice). Or they were aligned so that the sun shone down their central axis at a solstice or equinox, along the avenue or tunnel that led into them. The secret meaning of this is that creation doesn't just happen within the universe, it can happen within us. The Spiritual Son/Sun taking up his throne upon our body, at the top of our axis, as the golden halo so many ancient deities were depicted with, is the fulfillment of creation within us; it is when we are truly born. These ancient sites and their secret mysteries were originally directed toward this goal.

A composite of ancient sites and their alignments to the sun. From top to bottom: Temple of Kukulcán at Chichen Itza (Mexico), Stonehenge (England), The Great Pyramids and Sphinx (Egypt), and Angkor Wat (Cambodia).

ANCIENT OUT-OF-BODY EXPERIENCES

Deities in the Religion of the Sun were often shown with halos to indicate their divinity. From left to right: Horus (Egypt), Jesus, Vishnu (India).

The portal to heaven was called Akhet in Egypt, and the symbol for it was visually recreated in the silhouette of the Great Pyramids and Sphinx against the setting summer solstice sun, as the summer solstice is when the ascension to heaven was often celebrated in the ancient Religion of the Sun. As the sun set into the symbolic Akhet, it appears to crown the Great Sphinx, forming a halo around its head. The Great Sphinx used to be surrounded by a small lake, appearing as an island—as another symbol of the primordial mound.[568] Once likely carved in the image of Anubis, the Great Sphinx acted as the guardian to the site of the Great Pyramids and the portal to heaven. But when crowned by the sun, the Great Sphinx symbolizes a twice born.

Illustration of the Great Sphinx with the sun forming a halo around its head, which occurs at sunset on the summer solstice. It's possibly the oldest portrayal of a halo in the world.

We believe the Great Pyramids likely date to around forty thousand years ago and are where this belief largely originated; it then spread to other parts of the world, like Europe, the Americas, and China, possibly in very ancient times, and then certainly again with the much later diffusion of the Lost Civilization of the Sun.

The inner chambers of these pyramids, mounds, and temples, are small—usually only allowing enough room for a few people to be present for an alignment that may have occurred just once or twice a year. This indicates they may have been used for ceremonies and initiations that were rarely conducted, as it's likely only few initiates met the required grade to do them. Records indicate these initiations involved OBEs in which the initiate would travel through the portal to heaven and return. However, it's possible that OBEs just to the astral plane also formed part of other initiatory rites conducted there, or were the only type where the means to send someone through the portal didn't exist.

Photo taken inside the King's Chamber looking toward the sarcophagus. The chamber is not much bigger than what can be seen in the photo; it's only large enough for a small gathering of people.

At some later time initiations were likely given to those who didn't meet the grade, but that still gave them an OBE of heaven, or perhaps just an OBE; upon their return they were considered to have been reborn to a new life in which they now possessed the knowledge of the mysteries of life and death, and had complete faith in the existence of the spirit beyond the body and death. In ancient times, kings had to undergo it. This initiatory tradition seems to have become the basis of a mystery school that branched into many streams across the ancient world that spread with the Religion and Lost Civilization of the Sun. The initiation of the Twice Born appears to have been the basis of the central initiation that so many ancient mystery schools concealed, such as in the Eleusinian Mysteries of Greece, mysteries of the Maya in Central America,[569] the mysteries of Odin and of the Celts in Europe, and others.

In the Eleusinian Mysteries it was adapted to cater for huge numbers of people being initiated together. In this case, OBEs could not practically be involved, but rather an "experience" of the realms of the afterlife was created through dramatic plays performed before initiates who had unknowingly ingested a psychoactive drink.[570]

Ancient depiction of the Eleusinian Mysteries.

The initiation of the Twice Born was based on events that occur on the path of the Spiritual Sun, particularly at the stage of spiritual resurrection.[571] Yet few people ever reach this stage, and so over time this basic symbolic initiatory formula must have been adapted to be used for people at different standards and in different circumstances. It conveyed important knowledge about the afterlife and the structure of creation, while veiling within it the knowledge of the path of the Spiritual Sun. What this means is that even within this secret initiation, symbolic knowledge of an even more secret initiation was concealed.

Related beliefs about the afterlife also developed among the mass of believers, which essentially seems to have been that heaven was the afterlife destination for all those who had faith and lived righteously (in Egypt, this was according to the divine laws of Maat). This appears to be why ancient sites, like the Great Pyramids and Stonehenge, became some of the largest burial grounds in the ancient world—people were buried there in the hope of reaching heaven in the afterlife. Huge seasonal ceremonies for the dead were conducted at some of these sites at the solstices or equinoxes (like Stonehenge), as these were the times of year when the portal to heaven was believed to be open, and the sun was seen as taking the soul along with it to heaven (on board its ship).

Having OBEs wasn't restricted to initiations though; they seem to have been used by those in ancient esoteric orders particularly for learning about the afterlife and preparing for it, and for receiving guidance from spiritual beings. As we'll see in the next section, dreams, like OBEs, were seen as taking place in the realm of the afterlife, allowing the living to have contact with the spiritual beings that resided there, and so divine guidance was also sought through dreams, particularly through the practice of dream incubation.

Before finishing, there's an important distinction to be made between the beliefs of the ruling elite, the mass of lay followers, and of those within schools of initiation. The Kolbrin states that there were three forms of religion in Egypt. Two were visible—that of the highborn (the elites, including the king), and that of the people. The third form was not made public—it was the knowledge of the Sacred Mysteries kept hidden by the Enlightened Ones and Twice Born, which was behind and veiled within the other two.[572] There's evidence to suggest that these three forms were maintained in other places where the Religion of the Sun spread.

And so the journey to heaven had a different meaning for all three groups. Yet these journeys were portrayed using much of the same symbolism. For lay people, heaven was the place where they could sojourn between lives (reincarnations) if they lived righteously enough. For kings, their passage to heaven was seen as more assured because they traced their lineage back to the Children of the Sun (who were known to have had a connection to heaven). For aspirants of the path of the Spiritual Sun, they sought to use "womb world" for its purpose, to develop their greater spiritual potential and reach spiritual rebirth permanently into higher realms.

All sought to make a journey through darkness to reach heaven—for lay people this was a transition through the dark tunnel after death, but for those seeking enlightenment, it meant making a journey through the dark depths of their own psyche and the initiations of the path during life.

So much makes sense now. These ancient beliefs were based on the structure of the other dimensions and the progress of consciousness through them. The countless NDEs of people today have now vindicated these ancient beliefs, revealing they were based on what really exists beyond the body. The ancient sites and rituals of the Religion of the Sun were used to cater for people at all levels, to help them move through this process toward the light.

Knowledge of the out-of-body realm was a large part of the ancient Religion of the Sun, and OBEs were used in what appears to have been its most central initiation ritual, which was conducted at some of the greatest ancient sites in the world. These OBEs gave its followers an experience of the different regions of the afterlife, knowledge of the purpose of life, and an unshakable faith in their existence after death. What this book provides is some of the ancient methods for having OBEs that can potentially provide profound experiences too, but naturally at home.

ANCIENT SITES USED FOR OBES

There's enough evidence to indicate that there were sacred sites used for having OBEs in ancient times. We've gone through that evidence in this chapter, but will summarize it briefly here.

In ancient Egypt, pyramids could be built and used for the OBE kings had after death. Yet ancient texts together with the special features of the Great Pyramid in particular, such as the acoustic properties of the King's Chamber, suggests it was used for having OBEs in life. Secret chambers within Egyptian temples may also have been used for OBEs, like those beneath the Precinct of Amun-Ra at Karnak Temple Complex, and those possibly existing beneath the Sphinx Temple.

In Europe, there are references in old Celtic and Norse sources that allude to OBEs occurring in ancient chambered mounds. Some of these chambers have been discovered to have acoustic properties that may help induce mystical states. We'd say that Newgrange in Ireland, West Kennet Long Barrow in England, and the Hypogeum in Malta are sites that display some of the strongest evidence for having been used for OBEs, though many others could have—particularly those with inner chambers. Glastonbury Tor and Silbury Hill in England are not known to have inner chambers, but if they did, we'd say they'd also be strong candidates for having been used for OBEs. Even open sites like Stonehenge are speculated to have been used for rituals for a small elite group, and these may have involved OBEs given the design of the site and its meaning.

Pyramids in China and Central America were used by kings as they were in Egypt, to facilitate the OBE the king had after death. Though perhaps there were some that had been used by the living for OBEs too.

There's evidence to indicate that many other sites around the world, which we call "ancient portal sites," may have also been used for having OBEs in life—such as ziggurats in Mesopotamia, mounds in North America, pyramids across the world, and one of the most ancient megalithic sites in the world, Göbekli Tepe in Turkey—but as far as we're aware, there aren't enough surviving records in these cases to show whether they really were or not.

As explained in the next chapter, there are also many sacred sites that are known to have been used for the ancient practice of dream incubation. Although not specifically intended for having OBEs, the practice of incubating dreams would almost surely have sometimes resulted in them, meaning that OBEs could have occurred in any of the sacred sites around the world used for dream incubation.

ANCIENT PORTAL SITES

It's evident to us now that the idea of ancient portals, stargates, and resurrection machines is not in the realm of fantasy, but is based on the fact that it's possible to travel out of the body to other dimensions, and to build sites that facilitate these and other mystical experiences.

What's also incredible is just how many ancient sites were believed to be places where one could access other realms, and were possibly used for OBEs.

In fact, it seems the majority of ancient sites in the Religion of the Sun had this as one of their purposes, to the point that one of the main purposes of building an ancient site in this religion appears to have been to open a gateway to heaven. How far back in the past the tradition of building these sites first began, nobody knows. As mentioned earlier, Tibetan legend states it traces back to the very beginnings of humanoid life on Earth.

We call these sites "ancient portal sites." Here is a list of the ones we know of so far.

- The pyramids of Egypt.

- Pyramids in Central and South America.

- Pyramids in China.

- Ziggurats in Mesopotamia.

- Göbekli Tepe in Turkey (identified by Andrew Collins).

- The temples of Malta (including the Hypogeum, identified by Rudi Toffetti).

- Many of the chambered mounds, barrows, and dolmens in Europe.

- A number of stone circles in Europe (possibly all?), including Stonehenge in England.

- Glastonbury Tor in England.

- The Externsteine in Germany.

- Likely at least some of the woodhenges and circular earthworks in Europe, such as Goseck Circle in Germany.

- The earthly location of Mount Meru (wherever that may be, possibly Mount Kailash?). Clearly people didn't build Mount Kailash, but we wonder whether there was a site either on a mountain or that looked like a mountain, that was an ancient portal site in the very distant past, that became the basis of this legendary place.

- The Pyramid of Nine Swastikas (location unknown, though somewhere in Central Asia, possibly just another name for Mount Meru).

- Most of the mound sites of North America, as well as many of its earthworks (the largest of these, Newark, has been identified by Gregory Little, Andrew Collins, and William Romain).

The basic elements of these sites and what they symbolize are as follows:

- The pyramid, mound, stone/wood/earthen circle/enclosure, and rounded temple: variously the primordial mound, world mountain, human body, the earth, the body and womb of the Spiritual Mother, and the physical and astral realms (which were all seen as connected).

- Inner stone chamber: womb of the Spiritual Mother.

- Sarcophagus, stone cauldron, stone bowl: her womb even more specifically.

- A passage, opening, or avenue leading in and out of the site, or porthole stone: the birth canal of the Spiritual Mother, synonymous with the portal/tunnel to heaven, and the cosmic axis. These may have also served to direct someone to the entrance to heaven out of the body. Staircases up pyramids also represented the cosmic axis.

- Alignment to the northern circumpolar stars: the direction along the cosmic axis through the tunnel toward where heaven was believed to be located.

- Alignment to the solstice or equinox or to a star: the Spiritual Sun shining from heaven, and enthroned upon the body at the head/peak of the axis.

Left: Opening of the shaft in the north wall of the King's Chamber in the Great Pyramid. Right: Hole stone at the ancient site of Mên-an-Tol in England. These and similar features at other ancient sites may have been intended to direct someone out of the body either in life (during an OBE) or after death, through the portal to heaven.

Ancient portal sites were based on the structure of what really exists in other dimensions, particularly the portal that leads from the astral plane to heaven, and we call this our Ancient Portal Site Theory.

These sites served as gateways to the astral plane, to heaven, and beyond to the Spiritual Sun. As we've seen, these gateways were used for the dead, as they were believed to be access points they could use to get to heaven.

But they also served purposes for the living—some appear to have been used for having OBEs, and all of them would have been viewed as places of communion with spiritual beings, with the energies of heaven, and with the Spiritual Sun (which is another reason why they were aligned to the sun and stars). A gate allows movement in both directions, and so it's likely these sites were not only seen as enabling people to pass through to heaven, but also, for things of heaven to come down to Earth.

Even though it isn't possible to use many of these portal sites for having OBEs as they were in the past (they are too dilapidated, aren't open to the public, can't be slept in, etc.), they (and perhaps modern replicas of them if they were created) can still be used for connecting with heaven, spiritual beings, and the Spiritual Sun and Source during ceremonies and practices, and we hope that by bringing back this lost knowledge, many more people will use these ancient sites again for the purposes they were made for.

CHAPTER FOUR

Ancient Dreams

The most common type of visit to the otherworld recorded in ancient sources are dreams, which is understandable since they are how we experience the fifth dimension / astral plane on a daily basis.

References to dreams can be found in most ancient cultures, in which they were commonly recognized as an out-of-body source of communication with spiritual beings. Dr. J. Donald Hughes in his article "Dream Interpretation in Ancient Civilizations" says:

> "Although early human beings had several different ideas concerning what dreams are, they seem always to have invested dreams with great significance. That the soul left the body during sleep and actually experienced the dream events elsewhere, possibly in a supernatural world, was a widespread belief. In virtually every primal society investigated by anthropologists, the people treated dreams as an especially important way of receiving messages from the world of power and spirit, from the gods and other powerful beings."[1]

SUMERIAN

The earliest surviving written account of a dream is found in the ancient Sumerian text the Epic of Gilgamesh, which is the oldest notable surviving work of literature and the second oldest religious text in the world, dated to around 2100 BC.[2] This is not surprising given the greater numbers of texts that survived in Mesopotamia in contrast with cultures that used oral traditions as a means of preserving knowledge.

The religions of ancient Mesopotamia were derived from the Religion of the Sun, and clear records of sun worship survive there.³ Dreams were very important in these religions, as they served as a means of receiving divine guidance, particularly about the future.

Their use and importance is revealed in the Epic of Gilgamesh, which follows the story of an ancient Sumerian king called Gilgamesh, who throughout his adventures has dreams that are given by the gods to foretell his future, which are always symbolic and need interpretation.⁴ At one stage in the story, Gilgamesh and his companion Enkidu conduct a ritual a few nights in a row in order to invoke these prophetic dreams, which they direct toward the sun god. It is the oldest recorded ritual of dream incubation.

"Facing the sun they dug a well,
they put fresh water in ...

Gilgamesh climbed to the top of
the mountain, to the hill he poured
out an offering of flour:

'O mountain, bring me a dream, so
I see a good sign!'

Enkidu made for Gilgamesh a
House of the Dream God, he fixed
a door in its doorway to keep out
the weather.

In the circle he had drawn he made
him lie down, and falling flat like a
net lay himself in the doorway.

Gilgamesh rested his chin on his
knees, sleep fell upon him, that
spills over people.

In the middle of the night he
reached his sleep's end, he rose and
spoke to his friend:

[...] My friend, I have had the first dream!

[...] Enkidu spoke to his friend, [gave his dream meaning:]

'My friend, your dream is a good omen, the dream is precious and bodes us well.
[...] And next morning we shall see a good sign from the Sun God.'"⁵

~ EPIC OF GILGAMESH

The Gilgamesh Dream Tablet, which dates to 1600 BC and preserves a section of the Epic of Gilgamesh in which Gilgamesh describes his dreams to his mother, giving the tablet its name.⁶

In another ancient Sumerian text dated to 2100 BC, the father of Gilgamesh, the Sumerian priest-king Lugalbanda,[7] prays to the sun god when he is near-death with illness, and is healed by him, and then goes to sleep with the purpose of incubating a dream.

> "The king lay down not to sleep, he lay down to dream — not turning back at the door of the dream, not turning back at the door-pivot. To the liar it talks in lies, to the truthful it speaks truth. It can make one man happy, it can make another man sing, but it is the closed tablet-basket of the gods."[8]
> ~ LUGALBANDA IN THE MOUNTAIN CAVE

Lugalbanda then receives guidance from a god in his dream, revealing that dreams were seen as a means of interacting with them. It also sounds like dreams gave one access to the secret store of the knowledge of the gods.

EGYPTIAN

The first record of a dream in ancient Egypt is dated to between 2150-2055 BC, and appears in the literature called Letters to the Dead, as these were letters people wrote addressed to the deceased and left in their tombs. For example, one is written by a man to his recently deceased wife, asking if he could see her again in his dreams; another is addressed to a man's deceased father, asking if he could stop another deceased person from harassing him in his dreams. They reveal that people in ancient Egypt believed the deceased inhabited the realm of dreams and could interact with those who were alive and dreaming there.

Another record of dreams in ancient Egypt appears in writings about the lives of three pharaohs who were each visited by a god in their dreams. For example, Pharaoh Amenhotep II (who ruled between 1427-1401/1397 BC) is recorded as seeing the god Amun in a dream, giving him confidence in an upcoming battle. This reveals that the ancient Egyptians also believed it was possible to communicate with divine beings in dreams.[9]

One of the most famous ancient dreams is inscribed on the so-called Dream Stele at the base of the Great Sphinx. It describes how the young prince Thutmose IV (reign 1401-1391 BC) fell asleep in the Sphinx's shadow and had a dream when the sun was at its zenith that the Sphinx (who was also the sun god) told him that if he cleared the sand and uncovered the Sphinx, he would make him king of Egypt.[10] Although it could be true, it's also possible it never happened and the king wanted to show he had a divine mandate to rule, but in either case, it shows just how seriously the ancient Egyptians believed in dreams as a source of divine guidance.

Joseph interpreting the dream of the Egyptian king.

The Dream Stele is still there today, between the paws of the Sphinx, where it retells the ancient dream of Pharaoh Thutmose IV who cleared it of sand.

Other ancient Egyptian texts and artifacts indicate that dreams were seen as sometimes being illusory and ephemeral, or in the case of bad dreams, as involving negative or hostile beings of the netherworld.[11]

As the Duat was the place where the deceased went, and where gods and negative beings resided or could act, it's apparent the ancient Egyptians believed that dreams took place in the Duat, the astral plane.

Dreams are likely to have played a very important role in the ancient, initiatory schools of Egypt. This is illustrated in perhaps the only clear, firsthand account of someone who was initiated into a surviving Egyptian mystery school. This account was incorporated by Apuleius, who lived in the Roman Empire during the second century AD, into his fictional novel *Metamorphoses* (a.k.a. *The Golden Ass*), which is widely believed to be derived from real initiatory experiences—likely his own.[12] The entire initiatory experience is guided by dreams, as both initiates and priests have dreams given to them by divine beings that reveal who is to be initiated and when.

This starts toward the end of the story, after the main character of the novel Lucius, who has suffered a series of terrible misadventures, falls asleep exhausted after begging the goddess Isis for deliverance. Isis then appears to him in a dream:

> "When I had poured out my prayers, ending them in pitiful lamentation, my fainting spirit sank back, once more engulfed in sleep. I had scarcely closed my eyes when a divine apparition appeared, rising from the depths of the sea, her face worthy to be adored by the gods themselves."[13]

Isis instructs Lucius to seek a religious procession dedicated to her rites that will be out the next day, and to approach its high priest whom she will send a dream to also:

> "[...] have faith in my power to oversee the execution of my orders, for at this very moment when I am here with you I am with my priest too telling him, in dream, what he must do."[14]

Upon meeting, both Lucius and the priest recognize one another from their dreams, and Lucius is taken back to join the school to prepare for his initiation into it. Lucius receives nightly dream guidance from Isis, and has a prophetic dream that later comes true, giving him continuing faith on his spiritual journey.

A Roman statue of the goddess Isis.

Painting of a religious procession of the goddess Isis.

> "No moment of rest, not a night, passed without some admonishing visitation from her. She urged me again and again to become an initiate to her rites for which I had long been destined [...]."[15]

Lucius becomes eager for his initiation, but the high priest tells him it can only be conducted upon a sign given by Isis.

> "I entreated the high-priest to hasten my initiation into the mysteries [...]. But he [...] restrained my insistence gently and kindly [...]. He told me the proper day for a person's initiation is always marked by a sign from the Goddess, that the officiated priest was likewise indicated by her [...]. None of his order had been so wrong-minded, so determined on their own destruction, as to dare to take office rashly or sacrilegiously, and without the Goddess' direct command, and thereby commit a deadly sin."[16]

There is evidence that corroborates this was really practiced in the Isis mysteries, as the Greek writer Pausanias, who was writing around the same time as Apuleius, recorded that no one was allowed to take part in the festivals of Isis held at her shrine in Tithorea in Greece, without having first been invited by her in a dream. There are also inscriptions in which priests of Isis state they had been called by Isis herself to become her servants, just as Lucius had been.[17]

Finally, both Lucius and the high priest are given the sign they were waiting for in their dreams the same night:

> "One dark night, in commands as clear as day, she proclaimed that the hoped-for time had arrived, when she would grant me my dearest

wish. [...] before the light of day shone I shook off sleep and hastening to the high-priest's rooms I met and greeted him at the entrance [...] but the instant he saw me he pre-empted my plea, saying "[...] Why do you linger here in idleness when the day has come which you've longed and prayed for endlessly [...]."[18]

Lucius is initiated into the mysteries of Isis. Then a year later, has another dream, this time instructing him to enter the mysteries of Osiris.

"[...] the ever-vigilant Goddess who kindly watched over me, once more troubled my sleep and spoke again of rites and initiation. [...] I suddenly realized that I had not yet been introduced to the mysteries of invincible Osiris [...]. The issue was not long in doubt, for the following night I had a vision [...]."[19]

In this vision, Lucius sees a priest who has a limp in his left leg carrying garlands. He awakes and begins searching for the priest. He finds him, and discovers this priest had a dream about him too:

"[...] after the morning prayers for the Goddess were complete, I at once began to ask about me, with utmost zeal, as to whether any there exactly resembled him of my dream. Confirmation came immediately, when I caught sight of one of the *pastophori* who not only limped like the man in my vision, but also was alike in his dress and appearance. [...] Without pausing for an instant I approached him, and indeed he was not surprised by our ensuing conversation since he himself had been ordered in a similar manner to preside over my initiation. In his dream, the previous night, he had been arranging garlands for Osiris when he heard from the great god's own oracular mouth [...] that a man [...] was being sent to him [and] the priest must perform his rites of initiation [...]."[20]

Ancient Egyptian priests.

Lucius is initiated into the mysteries of Osiris, but soon afterward, has yet another dream—this time urging him to be initiated for a third time.

Lucius wonders how he could possibly need a third, but while "anxious in the extreme, a kindly apparition, in a midnight visitation" explains it all to him. He then tells the priest of his vision, and so undergoes his third initiation ceremony.

At last, at the very end of the story, Osiris himself appears to Lucius in a dream urging him to become a priest, and to win fame for the mysteries through his work:

> "Finally, a few days later, Osiris, greatest of the gods [...] appeared to me in dream, and not in some semblance other than his own, but greeting me face to face, in sacred utterance [...]."[21]

It's possible that this sequence of events and the dreams that guided them are based on a true story. If so, it shows how schools of the Religion of the Sun functioned in the past, in which they were guided by the divine through dreams, so that the physical running of the school had a connection to the order of divine beings in the higher dimensions. Further evidence for the importance of dreams in the mystery schools and temples of the ancient Religion of the Sun is found in the use of dream books, and the practice of dream incubation, explored in the following sections. As we'll see, Osiris and Isis had been appearing to people in their dreams, stretching back to the times of ancient Egypt when they may have guided its esoteric schools, and were specifically sought out through dream incubation.

ANCIENT DREAM BOOKS

A major source of ancient literature about dreams comes from ancient dream books, which listed the meanings of events, beings, places, and objects that could be seen in dreams. They indicate that people saw dreams as a way divine guidance could be given to them about every aspect of their lives in the form of symbols. (These were not bound books, but sheets, scrolls, or tablets—the term "book" is used for simplicity to refer to a single written work.)

Dream books containing interpretations of dreams survive from ancient Egypt, Mesopotamia, and China, giving testimony to the value people put on dreams for their spiritual guidance, for predicting the future, and for practical daily advice. Books of a similar kind are immensely popular today, fulfilling a simple human desire for guidance from a divine, otherworldly source.

In ancient Egypt priests would interpret the dreams of worshipers, presumably using dream books as their guide. The earliest Egyptian dream book, which is dated to 1300 BC, was divided into sections that defined who could access certain interpretations based upon the characteristics of the dreamer. One section of dreams is only for the followers of Horus (the description of whom is lost) and another section has different dreams for the followers of Seth (who are described as being red-haired men with an immoral character). All later dream books were ordered into chapters by the type of dream, presumably to make them more accessible to the general public.[22] [23] Given how the followers of Seth are described, it's likely that the followers of Horus were considered to have a more religious and moral character, and may have had specific physical characteristics too. This is interesting, because it indicates that the character of the dreamer was seen as the determining factor in the kinds of dreams they had. This may have been based on an earlier division between esoteric and public knowledge, in which initiates had different dreams to those living an irreligious life. It's possible that an earlier, more esoteric approach gave way to one for the public and that the knowledge became watered down, or perhaps the selective esoteric orders continued, but hid their knowledge away. The fact that (to my knowledge) there are no more dream books of this divided kind means they were rarer and simply none survived.

The largest collection of ancient dream books was found among the ruins of the Library of Ashurbanipal, built in the seventh century BC in the capital of Assyria, now in present day Mosul in Iraq, where over thirty thousand texts were held mostly on clay tablets, including the Epic of Gilgamesh.[24] The name Ashurbanipal is derived from the sun god Ashur.[25] The Assyriologist Adolf Leo Oppenheim studied Assyrian dream books and discovered that the dreams listed were mainly of four kinds: messages from spiritual beings, human centered or created ones with an origin in the mind, premonitions, and lastly those having an evil source or bad omens.[26]

Clay tablets preserved from the Library of Ashurbanipal.

Depiction of the Ashurbanipal Library.

I recognize these four kinds from my own experiences, but I would add that many scenes and events are created in our dreams by spiritual beings and we may not directly see them as such, but may believe they arise from our minds. There are also lots of bad dreams that have their origin in the mind and may not arise from evil entities outside ourselves, while some dreams are nightmares that arise from being in a real place, which is hell. There are also lucid dreams where we are consciously in the fifth dimension, dreams arising from extraterrestrials, and dreams of real places and of meeting real people.

Although dreams are personal and in certain ways unique to each of us, a dream guide can probably influence what a person dreams. For example, a dream guide from Mesopotamia dating from around 1500 BC says, "If a man in his dream [treads in?] his urine with his foot: his eldest son will die."[27] Since this was probably commonly understood to be its meaning (as it seems to be a widely used guide), perhaps spiritual beings used the event in the dream to warn people when their eldest son was about to die and so several people may have had that dream and it may have come true, but it's unlikely this dream would have the same meaning today.

ANCIENT DREAM INCUBATION

Today, dream incubation is basically defined as going to sleep while holding a thought and/or an image of something we want help with, in the hope of receiving a solution in a dream.[28] In ancient times it was more complex than this, and often involved praying to a particular deity, performing rituals of purification, sleeping within a temple sanctuary, and fulfilling other conditions that may have required days to years to perform.[29] It was a very popular ancient dream practice—evidence for it can be found in Mesopotamia, Egypt, China, and Europe (particularly Rome and Greece).

People who wanted advice often went to a temple where they participated in a ritual and slept in the temple for the night in the hope they would be advised by spiritual beings in their dreams. These temples were managed by priests who often helped interpret the dreams received.

Ancient dream incubation has been classed into two types: those of a "therapeutic" nature in which the sick and injured sought healing or medical advice from a deity at a temple while they slept, and those which were "divinatory" in which a person sought dreams while sleeping at a temple from a deity about all other matters.[30] Ancient accounts tell of people being miraculously cured and guided by deities during and as a result of their dream incubations.[31]

There's evidence that a number of temples across Egypt were likely used for dream incubation. This evidence shows that dream incubation was practiced but doesn't directly state at what site. The most evidence for its practice is found particularly near the Serapeum of Saqqara (known as the "House of Osiris-Apis" to the ancient Egyptians)—a series of underground chambers, well-known in ancient mysteries circles for its megalithic granite sarcophagi—suggesting it was used for incubating god-sent dreams.[32] Ancient accounts show that the deities Sarapis (who is a Greek version of the Egyptian Osiris) and his wife Isis, were believed to communicate regularly with people through dreams, and evidence, though inconclusive, indicates incubation was commonly practiced at their sanctuaries.[33] A much later serapeum was built by the Greeks in Egypt as part of the Library of Alexandria and used for dream incubation directed toward Sarapis; it was one of the largest and most prestigious temples at the time.[34]

Left: Looking into the chambers of the Serapeum of Saqqara. Right: Greek statue of Sarapis.

Dream incubation centers began appearing in Greece by about 500 BC, and by the second century AD there were more than three hundred across Greece and the Roman Empire.[35]

Many of them in Greece were called asclepieia, as they were dedicated to their god of healing Asclepius whose healing power was sought in dreams. Large marble boards dated to 350 BC found at one of the most important asclepieia located at the site of Epidaurus were inscribed with the names, case histories, complaints, and cures of about seventy people who were successfully healed there.[36]

What remains of the ancient asclepieion in Epidaurus.
Photo on the right is the Abaton where people slept.

Scale model of the asclepieion of Epidaurus showing how large the site was.

Ancient murals depicting people being healed by the god of healing Asclepius at asclepieia in Greece, based on actual cases. Notice in the image on the right a snake (symbol of Asclepius) has its head on the shoulder of the young man lying down; in the foreground, the god Asclepius is healing the young man's shoulder while he is out of the body.

Records of dream incubation rituals used in Egypt and Greece survive in a number of different ancient papyri that surfaced in the antiquities trade from the seventeen hundreds onward, and were brought together in the collection known as the Greek Magical Papyri. The texts date from the second century BC to the fifth century AD. The editor of their English translation, Hans Dieter Betz, believes they are merely a fraction of the "magical books" that would have existed in ancient times and survived early Christian book-burning campaigns.[37] One of the oldest examples of dream incubation is a ritual written on a papyrus from Egypt dated to between 1991-1786 BC; similar rituals appear over a thousand years later in the Greek Magical Papyri. It says:

> "Make a drawing of Besa on your left hand and enveloping your hand in a strip of black cloth that has been consecrated to Isis (and) lie down to sleep without speaking a word, even in answer to a question. [...] [and say] come in this very night."[38]

Depiction of people practicing dream incubation in ancient Greece.

Prayers calling for divine guidance through dream incubation have been recovered in Anatolia, which belonged to the ancient civilization of the Hittites that existed in the second millennium BC.

> "May my god speak to me in a dream. May my god open his heart to me."[39]
> ~ THE PRAYER OF KANTUZZULI

> "What a great Old Man will not be able to say to me, oh God, explain it to me through a dream."[40]
> ~ THE PRAYER OF MUWATALLI

> "Either let me see it in a dream, or let it be discovered by divination, or let a 'divinely inspired man' [or 'priestess'] declare it, or let all the priests find out by incubation whatever I demand of them."[41]
> ~ SECOND PLAGUE PRAYER OF MURSILI II

In China, one temple in particular became renowned for dream incubation, and people would flock there on the winter solstice, even sleeping outside in the freezing cold when there was not enough room, bringing candles, incense, and blankets. It's speculated they chose that night, as it is the longest in the year, affording the most time for having dreams.[42]

I explain a ritual that can be used for dream incubation in chapter 13, based upon ancient records of how it was practiced in Egypt and Greece.

Going to sacred places for the night to have an OBE is also productive—even more so when you consciously project and are there with spiritual beings. I give an exercise for this in chapter 22.

HINDU

Hinduism has a long tradition about dreams, going back to its earliest texts, which reveal the many sources and functions of dreams.

Dreams are mentioned in the oldest Hindu text, the Rig Veda. The content of this text reveals that its religious practitioners were focused on right conduct, self-purification, and the removal of sins. It's within this context that dreams are mentioned in a few of its hymns—of concern are evil dreams, which were considered the evil deeds of the dreamer made manifest. Because of their relation to sin and impurity, it was considered very important to be rid of them. A number of passages call upon the sun god (the Spiritual Sun), and his daughter, goddess of the dawn, to remove evil dreams.

> "Drive you [Savitar, the sun god] the evil dream away. [...] Now we have conquered and obtained, and from our trespasses are free. Shine away the evil dream, O Dawn. [...] O Surya [the sun god], with the light whereby you scatter gloom, [...] drive away [...] every evil dream."[43]
> ~ RIG VEDA

More detailed information on how dreams were viewed is given in a later text, the Brihadaranyaka Upanishad, believed to have been composed in the sixth to seventh century BC, and also part of the Vedas.

It describes the realm of the afterlife as being the same realm in which dreams take place. In this realm, one's Self wanders freely apart from the physical body during sleep. Dreams here are described as a creation of one's own psyche.

"[...] it is written: While one is in the state of dream, the golden, self-luminous being, the Self within, makes the body to sleep, though he himself remains forever awake and watches by his own light the impression of deeds that have been left upon the mind. Thereafter, associating himself again with the consciousness of the organs of sense, the Self causes the body to awake.

While one is in the state of dream, the golden, self-luminous being, the Self within, the Immortal One, keeps alive the house of flesh with the help of the vital force, but at the same time walks out of this house. The Eternal goes wherever he desires."[44]

~ BRIHADARANYAKA UPANISHAD

In the Mahabharata, dreams are described as being a result of the mind's fascination with the external world, and as a continued manifestation of one's inner states—whether they be of goodness, passion, or darkness.

"When in consequence of the organs being fatigued, they cease to perform their respective functions, the owner of those organs, because of their suspension, is said to sleep. If, when the functions of these organs are suspended, the functions of the mind do not cease, but on the other hand the mind continues to concern itself with its objects, the condition of consciousness is called Dream. During wakefulness there are three states of the mind, viz., that connected with Goodness, that with Passion, and that with Darkness. In dream also the mind becomes concerned with the same three states. [...] Whatever states (of Goodness, Passion, or Darkness) are experienced by living creatures, as exhibited in acts, during their hours of Wakefulness, reappear in memory during their hours of sleep when they dream."[45]

~ THE MAHABHARATA

However, dreams were also seen as sometimes containing real events and messages.

In the Mahabharata, one of the main characters, King Yudhishthira, has a dream after he falls asleep in the woods. In his dream he is approached by a small group of deer who live there and are shaking with fear. They beg Yudhishthira to spare them, explaining that the deer of the woods have been hunted for food almost to extinction by Yudhishthira's men who are encamped in the area, and ask he please move his men to another forest so their numbers can increase again. Yudhishthira is overcome with grief, and agrees to their request; upon waking he explains his dream to his men and all of them agree to move at once.[46]

In another famous epic, the Ramayana, a demoness has a prophetic and symbolic dream in which she sees the hero Rama victoriously ascending into the sky with his wife dressed in white, and flying toward the north (the region of light and the sun in Hinduism), while she sees the villain Ravana pulled in a chariot by asses south into mud and dragged by a seductive woman dressed in red to the region of death. This dream clearly points out the paths to heaven and hell respectively and is full of symbolism as dreams sometimes can be.[47]

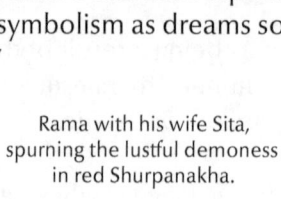

Rama with his wife Sita, spurning the lustful demoness in red Shurpanakha.

JAIN

In the Jain religion, dreams can contain prophetic revelations from the divine, such as the coming of great teachers, which are called Tirthankaras. The birth of the last Tirthankara in 599 BC is believed to have been announced through fourteen (or sixteen) dreams to his mother the night before he was born.[48]

CHINESE

The interpretation and meaning of dreams have been an important part of Chinese civilization from its inception right up until today. References to dreams can be found in the religious tradition of Taoism, which is a major religion in China that has connections to the ancient Religion of the Sun.[49] In ancient Chinese texts, dreams could contain real interactions and messages from the spirit world, or be a creation of one's own psyche.

The legendary first emperor of China, Yellow Emperor Huang-Di, was said to have had two dreams that he took so seriously that he chose his prime minister and general based on them, and then wrote a book on dream interpretation. A number of emperors who followed also had prophetic dreams about their leadership.[50] The earliest written records of China, known as oracle bones, which date back to the Shang dynasty (1600–1046 BC), contain dream interpretations.[51] The book *Duke of Zhou* Interprets Dreams, attributed to Ji Dan who reigned from 1042–1035 BC, is still used as the most popular dream guide in China today.[52]

In the Taoist text the Secret of the Golden Flower, which is believed to have been first written between AD 1113 and 1170, but based on a much older oral tradition,[53] dreams are said to take place in nonphysical, parallel realms.

> "Dreams are the wanderings of the spirit through all nine heavens and all nine earths."[54]
> ~ SECRET OF THE GOLDEN FLOWER

There's also a famous dream known as the *Butterfly Dream* written by a Taoist philosopher Zhuangzi who ponders upon the reality of life:

> "Once upon a time, I, Zhuangzi, dreamt I was a butterfly, fluttering hither and thither, to all intents and purposes a butterfly. I was conscious only of my happiness as a butterfly, unaware that I was Zhuangzi. Soon I awaked, and there I was, veritably myself again. Now I do not know whether I was then a man dreaming I was a butterfly, or whether I am now a butterfly, dreaming I am a man. Between a man and a butterfly there is necessarily a distinction. The transition is called the transformation of material things."[55]
> ~ THE ZHUANGZI

Zhuangzi dreaming of a butterfly (or a butterfly dreaming of Zhuangzi).

There is something to be said about Zhuangzi's pondering, as the place where dreams occur is a real place, where we spend much of our lives and return to at the end of our stay here.

By medieval times in China however, the highest form of sleep was seen as a dreamless one and dreams were incorrectly thought to be for those who had not reached immortality, as we see in the *Yün-chi ch'i-ch'ien*, which has extensive information about dreams.[56] I believe this is because by then the more ancient Religion of the Sun influence had waned and ideas about enlightenment being formlessness, nothingness, or emptiness then prevailed, probably deriving from the influence of Buddhism.

NATIVE NORTH AMERICAN

The use of dreams for guidance is also preserved in oral traditions such as those of many Native American peoples. For example, to the Iroquois of the Great Lakes region of North America, dreams were the most important source of both practical and spiritual guidance. Their dreaming practices were recorded by Jesuit missionaries in the seventeenth century, who wrote that the first thing the people of a village would do together each morning was share their dreams from the previous night. These were seen as containing guidance from the spirits and one's deeper self that could be important not only to the individual, but also to the community. Like many Native Americans, they believed that in dreams people traveled apart from their bodies, beyond the limitations of time and space, being able to see the future and the past, to visit the realm of the deceased and of spiritual teachers.[57]

Dream quests were practiced by the Ojibwe as a rite of passage—it was customary for boys who reached a certain age to go into the forest to incubate a dream.[58]

MAYA

Dreams were important in the ancient Maya religion of Central America, and still are in contemporary Maya religion. Ancient glyphs show that people were believed to each have a spirit/co-essence called a *way*, which was active when they dreamed and finally departed the body at death. There are indications that certain ancient Maya buildings were used especially as "sleeping places," and may have been used for dream incubation. Similar concepts survive in modern Maya religion, as it's believed that during sleep, consciousness leaves one's physical body and travels—the part that travels is called the *adiosich*, and it's said that when it enters or leaves the body one can experience a sensation like a gust of wind or buzzing in the ear, which has similarly been described by people who've had OBEs. To those who practice Maya religion today, dreams are a very important source of spiritual guidance.[59]

INCA

Dreams were an important source of spiritual guidance in the civilization of the Inca of South America, which flourished from the early fourteen hundreds AD until it was conquered by the Spanish in the 1530s.

They were seen as a means of receiving information about the future, which is indicated in the similarities between the Quechua words *muskuy*, meaning "to dream," and *musyay* "to divine." The Inca had special dream interpreters known as *mosoc* or "dreamers," whom they called upon to interpret their dreams and make forecasts of the future. As with the kings of ancient China, Egypt, and Sumer, there are records of the dreams that were received by Inca kings, revealing their importance.[60]

The last Inca king was said to have had prophetic dreams about the coming of the Spanish and their destruction of the Inca civilization, saying that he saw "enemies, iron people, came to our land, became involved in our houses, and carried off my royal being." The king then asked the high priest who was known as "the one who sleeps" to go and have dreams of his own so that he could interpret the king's dream. This indicates that dreaming, dream interpretation, and perhaps even having OBEs, was a very important part of the role of the high priest. The high priest returned and sadly confirmed the king's dream, saying that he himself saw, "red people, all beard, came from the other side of the sea, in boats of iron."[61]

Painting of the Spanish capturing the last Inca king, an event said to have been foretold by the king and his high priest in their dreams.

The wisdom bringer Viracocha, who is said to have brought the Religion of the Sun to South America and to have founded the ancient roots of the Inca civilization,[62] was recorded as appearing in dreams to a few of the Inca kings, sometimes in response to their prayers—in one shining so brightly he could not be looked upon, and in another as a shining child.[63]

Dreams have still been found to be important among indigenous rural peoples of the Andes of Peru, who live in the old stronghold of the Inca Empire. They divide dreams into those that come from "inside," which are those that are generated by one's own psyche, and those that come from "outside," being given by gods or spirits. They believe that one's vital principle, the *animu-anima*, travels outside the body in dreams.[64]

CELTIC

Dreams were commonly used as a form of communication with divinity in probably all Indo-European cultures, which all carried the Religion of the Sun in some form, including the Celtic. The Celts had an oral tradition that was eventually destroyed, but a little of it survived in later writings, particularly in Ireland, which avoided Roman occupation and is where some of its legends were recorded by Christian monks.

In Irish mythology, the king of the Firbolg named Eochaid went to the Druids for the interpretation of a dream and was told it meant a strong enemy was coming to confront him. These turned out to be the Tuatha Dé Danann, who conquered his people and settled in Ireland.[65] Note the role of the Druids as interpreters of dreams.

The Druids were known to have incubated and interpreted dreams.

The solar god Lugh of the Tuatha Dé Danann was said to have visited Dechtine (daughter of a Druid) in a dream while she slept at the ancient mound of Newgrange, to announce that she would give birth to his son, who went on to become the legendary hero Cúchulainn.[66] This supports our Ancient Europe OBE Theory, indicating that the ancient mounds of Europe were used for having OBEs, and for incubating dreams.

For the Celts, dreams were important not only for individuals, but also in the affairs of state where they influenced politics, warfare, and the welfare and appointment of kings; they were also sought for the purposes of healing, divine guidance, and prophecy.[67]

An ancient inscription at a temple of the Celtic sun god Grannus in eastern Gaul (now France) reads *somno iussus*, and refers to the ritual of dream incubation which people practiced there in sacred chambers in order to receive messages and healing from Grannus.[68]

The remains of the ancient temple of Grannus in France where people went to incubate dreams.

NORSE/GERMANIC

The Norse valued their dreams, especially for premonitions, spiritual messages, and contact with supernatural beings, although they were aware that many dreams were nonsensical and called these *draumskrok*, meaning "dream nonsense."[69] They also practiced a kind of dream incubation to try to get messages from the otherworld.

They attributed bad dreams and nightmares to dark elves, entities who lived beneath the earth because they couldn't stand light.[70] These sound very much like demons, which I discuss further on.

The most famous dream in Old Norse mythology is the dream of Odin's son Baldur, who foresees his own death.[71]

GREEK

The ancient Greeks recognized that the soul is contained within the body, and is subject to it while awake, but with sleep is set free to perceive more of creation. The famous Greek physician Hippocrates (ca. 460 BC – ca. 370 BC) wrote:

"He who has learnt aright about the signs that come in sleep will find that they have an important influence upon all things. For when the body is awake the soul is its servant, and is never her own mistress, but divides her attention among many things, assigning a part of it to each faculty of the body—to hearing, to sight, to touch, to walking, and to acts of the whole body; but the mind never enjoys independence. But when the body is at rest, the soul, being set in motion and awake, administers her own household, and of herself performs all the acts of the body. For the body when asleep has no perception; but the soul when awake has cognizance of all things."[72]
~ HIPPOCRATES

ROMAN

A scene from Virgil's *Aeneid* in which the god Mercury appears to Aeneas in a dream.

The epic poem *Aeneid*, written by Virgil between 30 and 19 BC on the founding of Rome, reveals the beliefs Romans held about dreams at the time. The main character Aeneas has a number of dreams in which gods appear to him, revealing factual information or providing guidance that helps him in his journey.[73]

GNOSTIC

In ancient Gnostic texts the disciples of Jesus have what could either be said to be meaningful dreams or OBEs, sometimes with Jesus in them guiding them, and at other times interpreted by Jesus after waking. They reveal that dreams and OBEs were an important way through which Jesus taught them, as many Christians still find today.

Gnostic texts contain accounts of Jesus appearing
to the disciples and Mary Magdalene in their dreams.

In the Gospel of Judas, the disciples have a dream:

> "Another day Jesus came up to [them]. They [the disciples] said to [him], 'Master, we have seen you in a [vision], for we have had great [dreams ...] night [...].'" [74]
> ~ THE GOSPEL OF JUDAS

They proceed to tell Jesus their dream, and Jesus interprets its symbolic meaning.

Then Judas Iscariot speaks up to say he also has seen a vision (in a dream).

> "Judas said, 'Master, as you have listened to all of them, now also listen to me. For I have seen a great vision.'" [75]
> ~ THE GOSPEL OF JUDAS

Judas proceeds to tell Jesus his vision, and again, Jesus interprets its symbolic, spiritual meaning.

A similar encounter is recorded in the Gospel of Mary (Magdalene). In it, Mary Magdalene tells Jesus that she had seen him in a vision.

> "And she began to speak to them [the disciples] these words: 'I,' she said, 'I saw the Lord in a vision and I said to him, "Lord, I saw you

today in a vision." He [Jesus] answered and said to me, "Blessed are you, that you did not waver at the sight of me. For where the mind is, there is the treasure.""" [76]

~ THE GOSPEL OF MARY

Likewise, in the Acts of Thomas, the disciple Thomas who has been sent on a mission to India by Jesus, sees Jesus in a dream who guides him on his mission.

"And when night fell and he slept, the Lord [Jesus] came and stood at his head, saying: Thomas, rise early, and having blessed them all, after the prayer and the ministry go by the eastern road two miles and there will I show thee my glory: for by thy going shall many take refuge with me, and thou shalt bring to light the nature and power of the enemy. And he [Thomas] rose up from sleep and said unto the brethren that were with him: Children, the Lord would accomplish somewhat by me to-day, but let us pray, and entreat of him [Jesus] that we may have no impediment toward him, but that as at all times, now also it may be done according to his desire and will by us."[77]

~ THE ACTS OF THOMAS

CHRISTIAN

There are a few pivotal dreams that occur in the four Gospels of the New Testament. Joseph (the "father" of Jesus) has four dreams in which he is given crucial guidance by the divine, firstly about Jesus' birth, and the rest about where to go to keep the child Jesus safe.

Painting of an angel appearing to Joseph in a dream, foretelling the birth of Jesus.

"[...] an angel of the Lord appeared to him in a dream and said, 'Joseph son of David, do not be afraid to take Mary home as your wife,

because what is conceived in her is from the Holy Spirit. She will
give birth to a son, and you are to give him the name Jesus, because
he will save his people from their sins.'"[78]
~ MATTHEW 1:20-21

The wife of the Roman governor Pontius Pilate also has a dream about Jesus' innocence just before Jesus is sentenced to be executed. She warns her husband, saying:

"Don't have anything to do with that innocent man, for I have suffered
a great deal today in a dream because of him."[79]
~ MATTHEW 27:19

Illustration of the dream Pilate's wife had about Jesus.

CONCLUSION

In ancient times people saw dreams as a connection to other realms, and used them as a source of guidance, including the Mesopotamians, Egyptians, Hindus, Chinese, Celts, Germanic peoples, Greeks, Romans, Jesus and the disciples, Native Americans, Mesoamericans, and others. This traditional view of dreams has persisted for thousands of years, as the practices of remembering and interpreting dreams and using dream books are still common today.

Many of the ancients knew that the psyche left the body with sleep, that dreams were a connection with the otherworld and its beings, and sought messages about their daily lives and even the governance of kingdoms. They also knew that many dreams were a reflection of the mind, and recognized that people dedicated to a more spiritual life had different dreams and were able to cater for their needs. We can only wonder what incredible experiences and teachings initiates may have had in the earlier esoteric schools that existed before these cultures, where the knowledge was still pure and less altered by time.

Despite the overarching view that people have taken of dreams throughout time, our modern civilization has developed a very different view of them. Today, they are disregarded by most as solely products of the subconscious mind—bizarre psychological ramblings—that have nothing to tell us. This stands largely in contradiction to thousands of years of religious and cultural knowledge all over the world, and to the writings of the most dedicated spiritual explorers of the human psyche, like the priests of ancient Egypt and the Vedic sages of India. In this book, I propose a return to the ancient way of viewing dreams.

CHAPTER FIVE

Ancient Near-Death Experiences

There are surviving accounts of near-death experiences in the records of ancient civilizations. What they allow us to see is that ancient people who died and returned had the same essential experience as people who have NDEs today. They attest to the fact that not only do these experiences share commonalities across different people and cultures, but also across time—stretching back thousands of years.

The earliest surviving reports are from the civilizations of Egypt, India, Mesopotamia, China, and Greece, where the oldest written records are found. Yet they are found worldwide, in European, African, Pacific, East Asian, and Native American cultures, as documented by NDE researcher Bruce Greyson, Professor of Psychiatry at the University of Virginia.[1]

Another researcher, Gregory Shushan, PhD, of the University of Wales, has studied ancient NDEs comprehensively and written a book *Conceptions of the Afterlife in Early Civilizations*.[2] He looked at NDEs in ancient civilizations, and says that some of the earliest are found in Sumer at around 2100 BC, in China in the eighteenth century BC, and in India from around 1500 BC.

Shushan has come to some startling conclusions. He observed that ancient NDEs not only share consistent occurrences, but also a common metaphysical meaning, and point to a "single experiential 'reality.'" He observed how there are similar core elements in the descriptions of ancient NDEs, even though there are cultural differences between them, and found they were too many to be a coincidence. This led him to believe that mystical experiences are the basis of religion and account for the similarities between religions.

Shushan also found that when cultural symbols were put aside, ancient NDEs resemble modern NDEs in many significant ways. He points out the most frequently recurring themes in the ancient accounts he studied correspond directly to some of the most typical elements in NDEs today, listing them as follows:

1. Ascending from one's body in an OBE. Even where the account doesn't mention whether it was an OBE, it's implied by people continuing to experience things after their body has died.

2. Seeing one's own corpse. Often the individual realizes they must be dead, but is paradoxically still alive. An example of this is in the Mesopotamian myth where the god Danu discovers beer is being made from the blood of his corpse, which makes him realize he is dead. And in Mesoamerica where Quetzalcoatl realizes he is dead when he sees his own corpse in a mirror.

3. Descending to underworlds in caves, passageways, tunnels, and into darkness in general.

4. Meeting deceased relatives or ancestors.

5. Being in the presence of a being of light, or a sun god. All the traditions studied by Shushan see realms of light.

6. Going through a:

a. Judgement, such as the weighing of the soul as described in experiences from India and China; and for those who committed bad deeds, being sent to places of punishment or recompense. Judgements are often administered or assisted by a deity or judges.

b. Life review, found in Egypt, Mesopotamia, and India, such as the Egyptian account of King Merikare whose life history unfolded in an hour.

7. Reaching obstacles or limits such as impassable water. In each civilization Shushan studied, the deceased are also stopped on the way to a higher or lower realm and face interrogation by a being of some kind, sometimes asking who they are, what the nature of divinity is, or what their true self is. Those unable to answer aren't allowed to pass.

8. Journeys to other realms or a return to a spiritual home.

9. A sense of oneness or union with the divine.[3]

The people who had NDEs in ancient times were often given a new sense of meaning in their lives from it, which is what many who've had an NDE say today.

Shushan believes that the ancient NDEs he studied were influenced by the culture of the experiencer, and that in turn, these NDEs also influenced the surrounding culture and caused them to adopt beliefs about the afterlife based on them. Shushan worked on the premise that all the cultures he studied, such as Vedic India and ancient Egypt, had little to no cross-cultural contact. However, I disagree with this premise, as there is evidence these cultures did have direct contact, at least for a time, and were each influenced by the Religion of the Sun in some way.[4] So I don't think the similarities between these ancient cultures can all be put down to NDEs.

But I agree that NDEs are tailored to the individual and are often influenced by the culture or religion of the experiencer—that is, divine beings explain and show truths in NDEs using the symbols and language that the deceased can understand, usually (though not always) from their own religion or culture.

In the following ancient NDE accounts, it will begin to become apparent that people who had NDEs then as they do today, experience the same core truths just with differing cultural and religious overlay.

GREEK

There are two detailed accounts of NDEs from ancient Greece. One is told by Plato in his book *The Republic*, which he authored around 375 BC, in a story called the Myth of Er (myth in this case meaning "word, speech, account").[5] It narrates the NDE of a soldier named Er who was killed in battle and then revived twelve days later on his funeral pyre, and who then told of what he had seen in the afterlife. Er said that after his soul left his body he traveled to a place where he saw two openings in the sky near each other—one in which souls traveled to, and the other from, heaven. Likewise, he saw two openings in the earth for those entering and returning from hell. Remarkably, these sound like the portals to heaven and hell described in so many ancient accounts and still seen in NDEs today. Between these openings were judges who directed those who had lived justly into heaven, and those who had been sinners into hell. Er witnessed how souls descended from heaven and ascended from hell after either being rewarded or punished tenfold for what they had done while alive, and were then prepared to reincarnate into another life on Earth to continue the process of their soul's learning. Before being reborn, each drank from the "river of forgetfulness" (described as the "cup of forgetfulness" in an ancient Gnostic text, and as a "stream of last forgetting" in a Roman account discussed shortly), which erased their memory just before they returned to a new body. It's interesting how these events also occur in NDEs today.

Another ancient NDE is retold by Plutarch, who tells the story of a man called Aridaeus who died after falling, but revived three days later, and subsequently completely changed his behavior for the better, as those who have NDEs commonly do. Plutarch recounts what Aridaeus told his close friends about his NDE, writing:

> "When his body became unconscious, the feeling at first was such as a pilot would have if he were hurled from his ship into the sea.

> Then, being somewhat recovered, he seemed to breathe with entire freedom, and to look round in every direction, as if his soul had been a single open eye. He saw nothing that he had ever seen before [...]."[6]
> ~ PLUTARCH, ON THE DELAY OF DIVINE JUSTICE

Aridaeus is taken through realms of the afterlife by a guide who shows him the souls of the deceased and how their appearance and destination differ. Some emit light and reside in a paradise of nature, while others are horrifically disfigured by their vices and are punished for the crimes they had committed in life accordingly. Those who had cleansed themselves of vice became clear of the marks on their soul. Some responded to the punishments and corrected themselves, while those who didn't were stripped of what it was to be human, in preparation to be reborn into the bodies of beasts. Aridaeus was also told about reincarnation.[7]

Finally, after being reduced to a state of utter terror, his experience ends:

> "Then he, as if suddenly forced through a tube by an intensely strong and powerful wind, alighted on his own body, and awoke hard by his own tomb."[8]
> ~ PLUTARCH, ON THE DELAY OF DIVINE JUSTICE

Scenes from the *Divine Comedy* by Dante, illustrated by Gustave Dore. Left: Dante being guided by Virgil through hell. Right: Dante shown heaven by his guide Beatrice. It seems likely that Dante's classic fourteenth century poem was based on accounts of NDEs and OBEs of the afterlife that were known at the time, perhaps including that of Er and Aridaeus.

EGYPTIAN

There is evidence for NDEs in ancient Egypt. Though there are no direct accounts of them, Egyptian funerary texts describe in great detail what they believed happened to someone after they died, and these descriptions share similarities with the accounts of NDEs and OBEs in other ancient cultures as well as with those had by people today.

These texts were used for funerals, and could be inscribed on the walls of tombs, on funerary objects, or written on papyrus and buried with the deceased. They were designed to ensure the successful passage of the deceased through the regions of the afterlife. Over the more than two thousand years of Egyptian history this funerary literature developed. What were at first exclusively texts for the tombs of pharaohs, as in the Pyramid Texts, became adapted for the burials of those of high rank, and then eventually for common people. This adaptation was necessary, as only the pharaoh was ensured transformation into an Akh (being of light) in the afterlife.

The Egyptian Book of the Dead describes the afterlife passage of the common person. For them, their fate hung in the balance on the scales of divine judgment. Instead of being read as hymns, these texts were now instructions left in the tomb to guide the deceased through the perilous journey of the afterlife to hopefully reach heaven. They include common elements often found in NDEs, such as a judgment based on one's good or bad actions in life, punishment for those who were found bad, and a heaven for those who were good. This indicates that it's very likely these texts were based on real NDEs and OBEs.

The most central scene from the Egyptian Book of the Dead, which shows the recently deceased person being judged before the god Osiris by having their heart weighed on scales against the feather of cosmic order. A kind of divine judgment in the afterlife based on one's good and bad deeds in life is one of the most common elements present in NDEs, both modern and ancient.

SUMERIAN

Also among the world's oldest surviving religious texts, though later than the Pyramid Texts of Egypt, is the Sumerian Epic of Gilgamesh (dated to around 2100 BC). It tells the story of King Gilgamesh who goes on a meandering journey to find eternal life. He is unsuccessful, but manages to travel to the afterlife and come back. He gets there by journeying through a long, dark passageway through a pair of sacred mountains that emerges into the heavenly paradise of the sun god, which is a beautiful garden made of jewels:

> "Gilgamesh [...] took the path of the Sun God [through the gate of the mountains] ...
>
> At one double-hour ...,
> the darkness was dense, and light was there none:
> it did not allow him to see behind him.
>
> At two double-hours ...,
> the darkness was dense, and light was there none:
> it did not allow him to see behind him.
>
> [This repeats until the twelfth double-hour.]
>
> [...] at twelve double-hours Gilgamesh came out in advance of the Sun.
>
> ... there was brilliance:
> he went straight [...] to ... the trees of the gods. [...]
>
> A lapis lazuli tree bore foliage,
> in full fruit and gorgeous to gaze on."[9]
>
> ~ THE EPIC OF GILGAMESH

Gilgamesh's journey to the afterlife essentially describes one of the most common NDEs. Many people who have NDEs, after leaving their bodies, find themselves traveling through a long dark tunnel that eventually opens out into a heavenly garden or natural landscape where they see a light like the sun (though many times brighter), which they perceive as the Source or God. As in these NDEs, Gilgamesh travels a long dark way (as if through a dark tunnel) into a heavenly garden where everything is made of jewels—likely to try and convey the way things look in heaven, which people who have NDEs describe as more colorful, luminescent, and alive. In the Epic of Gilgamesh, this garden is said to belong to the sun god, just as people in NDEs are greeted by a brilliant light they recognize as the Source.

Given the similarities Gilgamesh's journey shares with the mysteries of initiation in Egypt, as discussed in chapter 3, it's likely it was based on the ritual of the Twice Born.

INCA

Although there are no references to NDEs from the Inca civilization of South America, we believe there is evidence that they had information about the afterlife that is commonly experienced in NDEs.

The Coricancha, also known as the Temple of the Sun, was the most important temple in the Inca Empire. It was dedicated to the sun god Inti, and early Spanish eyewitness accounts describe it as "fabulous beyond belief." The entire temple was bedecked in gold and precious stones. Its walls were covered in sheets of gold, studded with emeralds and turquoise, and it contained a garden made entirely from gold, silver, and jewels.[10] It was used for observing the solstices and stars. It was aligned so that on the months surrounding the winter solstice, the rays of the rising sun would enter the temple and illuminate a gold effigy of the sun, which was designed so that it shone with such radiance one couldn't see the effigy itself.[11] On the winter solstice, the Inca king would enter the temple to light the sacred fire and seat himself with the mummies of past Inca kings.[12]

Illustration of the Inca king worshiping before
the gold effigy of the sun inside the Coricancha.

What struck Lara was how similar the interior of the Coricancha was to the description of the garden of the sun god in the Epic of Gilgamesh, as there too, the garden was made of precious jewels. And then she realized the Coricancha likely had a deeper meaning as a replica of heaven, commonly seen in NDEs today. The sun god Inti is the light of the Source/Spiritual Sun seen at the end of the tunnel, often described as far brighter than the physical sun, which in the Coricancha was made to shine with blinding brilliance. And the Coricancha's sacred garden of the sun god was likely made to represent the beautiful natural landscape of heaven, which is often described as the most perfect garden where everything appears more colorful, vivid, and alive. A garden of precious metal and jewels illuminated by the sun's light reflected by walls of gold was clearly an attempt to recreate it in the physical world.

No wonder the mummies of Inca kings were seated inside on a special gold bench—it was to represent them being in heaven (which the Inca called Hanan Pacha), where they were believed to have lived on after death. The Inca king would symbolically join them at the winter solstice—a time of spiritual rebirth in the Religion of the Sun.

Hanan Pacha was home to the sun god Inti, and moon goddess Mama Killa, as well as thunder, lightning, the planets, and stars. This would account for the various other temple areas of the Coricancha that were dedicated to the moon goddess, Venus, the thunder god, and rainbow god.[13]

Lara details how the Inca were part of the spread of the Religion of the Sun in *The Ancient Religion of the Sun*.[14]

Some of what remains of the Coricancha's stone walls, which were stripped of gold; a church was later built over it. Both the Coricancha and church were built with the purpose of directing people toward heaven.

MAYA

There were afterlife beliefs held by the ancient Maya that are likely to have been based on NDEs. Among the Maya, the Milky Way was believed to be the way the deceased traveled to either heaven or hell, as was similarly believed by Native North Americans and ancient Egyptians. It was seen as being divided by the ecliptic—the sun's annual path across the sky. The southern portion beneath the ecliptic and descending below the horizon (considered as being to the left of the sun) was the "black road" one took to the underworld hell called Xibalba. The northern portion (to the right of the sun) was the "white road" that led to heaven in the northern sky. Both roads could be symbolized by snakes.[15] Remarkably, this symbolism illustrates what those who've had NDEs often report, which is either traveling down a dark tunnel to hell or up a long, dark, sometimes winding tunnel into heaven, which could be likened to passing through the inside of a giant snake either going into the earth or up into the sky.

The Maya repeatedly portrayed beings from the otherworld appearing to those in the physical world as emerging from the mouth of a snake, in a symbol known as the Vision Serpent.[16] This likely illustrated how nonphysical beings were understood as traveling through these portals/tunnels to communicate with the living.

ROMAN

In the *Aeneid* (ca. 20 BC), written by the Roman poet Virgil, the main character Aeneas, accompanied by a priestess of Apollo (the sun god) as a guide, travels to the afterlife by entering a cave after doing a ritual, where he visits the hellish regions of the underworld called Tartarus:

> "This is the place where the path splits itself in two:
> there on the right is our road to Elysium, that runs beneath
> the walls of mighty Dis: but the left works punishment
> on the wicked, and sends them on to godless Tartarus. [...]
> Groans came from there, and the cruel sound of the lash,
> then the clank of iron, and dragging chains."[17]

Painting of Aeneas with his priestess guide, through the mouth of Tartarus (hell).

This is followed by a visit to a heavenly region called Elysium:

> "[...] they came to the pleasant places, the delightful grassy turf
> of the Fortunate Groves, and the homes of the blessed.
> Here freer air and radiant light clothe the plain,
> and these have their own sun, and their own stars."[18]

Painting of Aeneas in Elysium (heaven).

And then Aeneas is shown people being prepared to reincarnate into another human body by drinking waters of forgetfulness—another common scene in NDEs—by his deceased father:

> "Aeneas [...] asked [...] who the men are crowding the
> banks in such numbers.
>
> Then his father Anchises answered: 'They are spirits,
> owed a second body by destiny, and they drink
> the happy waters, and a last forgetting, at Lethe's stream.'"[19]

Aeneas returns to the world through one of the "gates of Sleep," which has led people to interpret Aeneas' otherworldly journey as a dream. But perhaps Virgil intended to imply that the realm of the afterlife and the place we go when we sleep are connected, and that what Aeneas really had was an OBE (or induced NDE).

Aeneas' journey follows a pattern of initiation from the ancient world that is very familiar to us now—an initiate undergoes a ritual conducted by a priestess of the Religion of the Sun inside a small, dark chamber of the earth (in this case a cave), in which they travel to the afterlife in an OBE, often involving a visit to both hell and heaven. Aeneas' journey appears to be distantly based on the ritual conducted by the Twice Born of Egypt, and it seems Virgil was basing the account on knowledge of the ancient mysteries.

CHRISTIAN

In Christianity, the most likely reference to an NDE is made by Paul (although as mentioned before, it's often cited as possibly referring to an OBE), who refers to the account as though it was from someone he knew. However, most scholars believe that Paul was referring to his own experience in third person, and it's speculated it may have been an NDE he had when he was stoned and left for dead on his first missionary journey.[20]

> "[...] I will go on to the visions and revelations from the Lord: I know a man in Christ who fourteen years ago was caught up to the third heaven. Whether it was in the body or out of the body I do not know—God knows. And I know that this man—whether in the body or apart from the body I do not know, but God knows—was caught up to paradise and heard inexpressible things, things that no one is permitted to tell."[21]
> ~ 2 CORINTHIANS 12:1-5

Then there is another text that claims to be the account of Paul's journey "up to the third heaven," which is part of the class of texts called the New Testament apocrypha. The text has an introduction that claims Paul's account was found buried in a box beneath his house, though scholars believe it was composed in Egypt in the fourth century.[22] In the account, Paul is shown what happens to both just and sinful people after death—either their rewards in heaven or punishments in hell. It contains many elements that can be found in NDEs both ancient and modern, including a divine judgment, a book that records all the deeds of the person's life that is used at their judgment, and a life review. For example, this following excerpt clearly describes a life review.

> "[Paul said] I wished to see the souls of the just and of sinners, and to see in what manner they go out of the body [...] and I looked carefully and saw a certain man about to die [...] and saw all his works, whatever he had done for the sake of God's name, and all his desires, both what he remembered, and what he did not remember; they all stood in his sight in the hour of need [...]. And the angel [...] said unto me: Hast thou believed and known, that whatever each man of you has done, he sees in the hour of need? And I said, yes sir."[23]
> ~ THE VISION OF PAUL THE APOSTLE

Painting of Paul having an OBE.

There's nothing that's clearly said to be an NDE in the teachings of Christianity, but lots of Christians are having them today. The earliest account of NDEs by Christians comes from hermits and ascetics living mostly in the Egyptian desert from around the third century AD. They told stories that were preserved through oral tradition until being written down by Christian monks in around the fifth century. They were later compiled into a volume that became known as the *Sayings of the Desert Fathers*.[24] In one of these stories called *The Evergetinos* there's a clear account of an NDE of an ascetic monk:

> "In the midst of his illness, he lost consciousness and his soul left his body and was taken off to be judged. There among the damned he found his mother. On seeing him, she said with astonishment, 'My child, are you, too, condemned to this place of the damned? For what reason are you, who said to me, "I wish to save my soul," here?' The brother, shamed by all that he had heard, was struck with gloom, unable to answer anything his mother had said. Afterwards, he heard a voice that said: 'At once, out of here.' He immediately woke from this ecstasy and unconsciousness and related with fear to those around him all that he had seen and heard, glorifying God."[25]

HINDU

There are NDEs described in the Hindu texts of India, where they were woven into stories and hymns. The first appear in the oldest texts—the Rig Veda, Atharva Veda, and Upanishads, and then later in the Mahabharata and Puranas.

These NDEs describe elements of the afterlife commonly found in Hindu texts, as well as the NDEs of other cultures—namely a judgment after death based on one's deeds, a hell for those who have done badly, a heavenly realm for the upright, reincarnation in which the consequences of one's good or bad actions determine the circumstances of their next life, and meeting deceased relatives who were believed to reside in a realm of the ancestors.[26] Given that so many people in NDEs today are met by their deceased relatives, it's no wonder ancient cultures believed in a realm where their ancestors continued to live.

One NDE in the Mahabharata even describes a realistic shared death experience or SDE,[27] which still occurs quite frequently today, and which I discuss in chapter 6.

The god of the dead Yama appearing to Satyavan who has just died, and his wife Savitri. Their story describes what is today called a "shared death experience."

But a feature found specifically across ancient Hindu NDEs is an encounter either with Yama, his messengers, or a visit to his realm. Yama is the Hindu Lord of the Dead, who is said to be the supreme judge of the deceased in the afterlife.[28]

A passage in the Hindu text the Garuda Purana describes how the sinful are dragged before Yama after they die;[29] its level of detail indicates it's likely to have been based on NDEs. The text is difficult to date—speculated to have been composed in the first millennium BC, but edited over a long period of time. It's largely to do with death and the afterlife, and is still used by Hindus for funeral rites.[30]

> "Those men who are intent upon wisdom go to the highest goal; the sinfully-inclined go miserably to the torments of Yama. Listen how the misery of this world accrues to the sinful, then how they, having passed through death, meet with torments. Having experienced the good or the bad actions, in accordance with his former earning, then, as the result of his actions, some disease arises. [...] In the last moment [...] a divine vision arises, all the worlds appear as one [...]. Then, at the destruction of the decayed senses and the numbing of the intelligence, the messengers of Yama come near and life departs. [...] The vital breaths of the sinful depart by the lower gateway. Then, two terrifying messengers of Yama are come, of fierce aspect, bearing nooses and rods [...]. As black as crows, [...] with ugly faces, [...]. The man of the size of a thumb [...] is dragged from the body by the servants of Yama, looking the while at his own body [...] they forcibly lead him a long way [...]. Here and there falling exhausted and insensible, and rising again, in this way, very miserably led through the darkness to the abode of Yama, the man is brought there in a short time and the messengers show him the terrible torments of hell."[31]
>
> ~ THE GARUDA PURANA

Of the modern Hindu NDEs that have been studied, many adhere to this essential narrative. Consider the following NDE of Chhajju Bania which occurred around 1980:

> "Four black messengers came and held me. [...] They took me and seated me near the god. My body had become small. There was an old lady sitting there. She had a pen in her hand, and the clerks had a heap of books in front of them. I was summoned .... One of the clerks said, 'We don't need Chhajju Banian (trader). We had asked for Chhajju Kumhar (potter). Push him back and bring the other man.' [...] Yama was there sitting on a high chair with a white beard and wearing yellow clothes. [...] Then I was pushed down [and revived]."[32]

Chhajju said that he later learned a person called Chhajju Kumhar had died about the same time he'd revived.

Lara also happened to stumble across a very clear NDE in the text Bhagavata Purana. It tells the story of Ajamila, who one day as he was walking through the forest came upon a drunk and lustful woman. Unable to control himself, he left his wife for the woman, had ten children by her, and lived a life of crime to support them. Lying on his deathbed, at eighty-eight years old, he saw three messengers of Yama, who are described as demonic in appearance and carrying nooses, who had come to take his soul to hell. Terrified, he called out the name of his youngest and favorite son, who happened to be called Narayana—the name of the supreme being/creator/God, also known as Vishnu. Hearing the name of their Lord invoked, three angels of Vishnu (spiritual beings) appeared, and forcibly stopped the demons from taking Ajamila. They then proceeded to explain that despite the sins Ajamila had committed, the mere utterance of the name of Vishnu (in any context, even in a song) is enough to atone for them and save someone from hell. Ajamila repents and is brought back to life. He then dedicates his life to the service of Vishnu, later dying again, but this time ascending to heaven, the abode of Vishnu.[33][34]

Spiritual beings rescuing the soul of Ajamila from demons and hell during his NDE.

What's so remarkable about this story is that there are numerous NDEs today in which people who have gone to hell have been saved simply by calling on the name of Jesus, even by singing a song with the name of Jesus in it (we've seen an account of someone who sang "Away in a Manger"[35]). They also often repent, are brought back to life, and go on to correct their ways and follow Jesus' teaching. What this Hindu NDE shows is that the exact same thing must have happened to people in India, though by calling on the name of Vishnu.

CHINESE

In ancient China a probable NDE was recorded around 498 BC. A man called Kien Tsze was ill for three days and after he recovered said:

> "I went to the residence of the emperor [of Heaven], where I much enjoyed myself. With the host of Shen, I wandered about in the all-ruling Heaven."[36]

China is also the source of the oldest medically recorded NDEs, which are found in the writings of a medical practitioner called Bian Que dated to ca. 90 BC, who noted two earlier accounts of NDEs from around 500 BC.[37]

By medieval times there were NDEs recorded in both China and Japan. Further research into the ancient past of these two cultures would probably lead to more NDEs being brought to light.

TIBETAN

Finally, I should mention the text Bardo Thodol, commonly referred to as the Tibetan Book of the Dead, which according to Buddhist tradition was written in the eighth century in Tibet. It was designed to be read to someone as they were dying if possible, and to their body after they had died for forty-nine days, until it was believed their afterlife fate had been decided.[38] Similarly to the Egyptian Book of the Dead, it instructed them on what they were seeing in the afterlife realm, and what they should do to reach heaven and liberation, and avoid hell and rebirth (or if they could not avoid rebirth, to be born into a good, religious human life). It contains many elements commonly seen in NDEs, such as having to realize one is dead, seeing one's own funeral, angelic and demonic beings, heaven, hell, a kind of limbo, a judgment based on one's good and bad deeds in life, punishment for sins/egos such as anger, and reincarnation. Even though these themes are portrayed through the lens of Buddhist theology, the existence of these elements means it has to have been based on real knowledge of the afterlife, likely gained through NDEs or OBEs.

It also describes the brilliant light people are often greeted by, which they identify as the creator/God/the Source. In the Tibetan Book of the Dead this light is described as shining forth from the heart of the deity Vairocana on the first day.

"[...] from the Central Realm, called the Spreading Forth of Seed, the Bhagavan Vairochana [...] will manifest himself to you. [...] The Wisdom of the *Dharma-Dhatu*, blue in colour, shining, transparent, glorious, dazzling, from the heart of Vairochana as the Father-Mother, will shoot forth and strike against you with a light so radiant that you will scarcely be able to look at it."[39]
~ TIBETAN BOOK OF THE DEAD

A 153 meter tall statue of Vairocana in China—the first deity said to be seen after death in the Tibetan Book of the Dead, whose heart radiates the light of the Source

Vairocana is the chief deity of Esoteric Buddhism and is known as the "Great one who comes from the sun;"[40] this is likely an ancient surviving reference to the sun being seen as the Source, which was carried forward from the times of the ancient Religion of the Sun. In Esoteric Buddhism, the brilliant light seen after death was identified with the sun, as it was in the many traditions that derived from the ancient Religion of the Sun.

PART 2
AN OVERVIEW OF OUT-OF-BODY EXPERIENCES

CHAPTER SIX

Evidence for Out-of-Body Experiences Being Real

I'll now take a look at the evidence showing that out-of-body experiences are real and that we do separate from our physical body. Although many academics support this stance, overall, mainstream science still takes the materialistic view that everything can be explained as being the result of physical processes.

This is mainly because events and data have to be measurable and repeatable in defined ways to be considered proof of something. The problem with this approach is that OBEs are of a multidimensional nature and no technology exists that can effectively study them, and so mainstream science hasn't been able to definitively prove or disprove what happens in them.

There have been many materialistic theories put forward to explain the phenomenon, but none of them actually explain what OBEs are. Yet there is a lot of evidence from people's OBEs and NDEs that show they are real, and that we can be conscious while out of our body, and that there is an afterlife.

NDEs in particular offer compelling evidence for the existence of consciousness outside the physical body. Because NDEs have been studied far more than OBEs, and the clarity and objectivity of NDEs tends to be greater overall than in OBEs (in most cases), I've mostly looked at NDEs here, yet some of the evidence of NDEs being real also applies to OBEs. They are both out-of-body experiences and share many of the same characteristics.

I know personally that we can consciously be in another dimension and that there is an afterlife—as I've had an NDE and many OBEs—and so studies aren't what convinces me, but I do find them interesting and valuable, and people's testimonies of their NDEs especially so.

TWELVE POINTS THAT INDICATE OBES AND NDES ARE REAL

A lot of research, studies, and anecdotal accounts of OBEs and NDEs support the notion that consciousness can exist outside the physical body. These are some I find especially compelling, though there are many more:

1. Verifiable Events. Many in OBEs and NDEs have provided accounts of verifiable events in the physical world that could have only been seen by someone if they were out of their body.

The largest attempt to verify whether NDEs contain real events was a study conducted between 2008 and 2012, led by Dr. Sam Parnia, who is one of the foremost researchers of NDEs. It studied 2,060 patients who'd suffered a heart attack across fifteen hospitals in the UK, U.S., and Austria. Of the 140 patients who'd survived their attack, 101 completed interviews. Nine percent of these had an NDE and of these, 2 percent had "described awareness with explicit recall of 'seeing' and 'hearing' actual events related to their resuscitation." Of these, one man's account of events while he was dead were verified as accurate. The patient was a fifty-seven-year-old man who described floating up to a corner of the room, seeing medical staff work on him, which he gave accurate descriptions of, and watching himself be defibrillated—his description of which was also accurate.

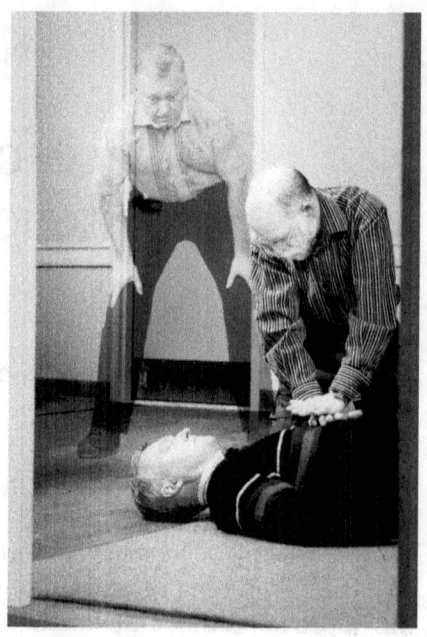

People in NDEs can see verifiable events while their body is dead, such as what those around them do while trying to revive them.

Referring to this patient, the study authors said, "one had a verifiable period of conscious awareness during which time cerebral [brain] function was not expected." They think the patient may have seen things that happened for as long as three minutes after his heart stopped, which is amazing, given the brain typically shuts down within twenty to thirty seconds of the heart stopping.[1][2] To me, it's incredible that a verifiable experience happened as part of a study—in this case the patient had an NDE while their heart and brain had stopped and survived to tell the tale, the NDE happened within a hospital partaking in a study, and involved events that could be verified with hospital staff physically. I think it reveals how inadequate so many studies of OBEs are, in which just one or a handful of people are often studied.

I've also seen things in some of my own OBEs that I was able to verify when back in the physical world, and people I know have experienced this in OBEs too. I once spoke to a woman on BBC radio who had been seriously ill in hospital and was virtually dead. She had an OBE and described how she left her body, hovered slightly above the ground, looked around the room, could see medical staff around her, was able to read her medical notes, and recalled how a doctor came into the room wearing a red turban. When later revived, she accurately described what had taken place in the room while she was unconscious. The notes she described turned out to be accurate, and staff were perplexed about her account of the doctor in the red turban as he was not the usual doctor and had only visited that day to fill in for an absent staff member—she was completely unconscious during the whole time of that doctor's visit and had no prior knowledge of it.

2. Out-of-Body Meetings. People sometimes meet and share an experience together in an OBE, as I did in my first OBE, and I've been told of it happening by several people who recalled their experiences to me. In NDEs there have been cases of a number of people who each died, met together in the afterlife, were revived and recalled their meeting.[3] In an amazing example, a team of firefighters in the United States died together in a forest fire and saw each other hovering above their dead bodies. They miraculously revived without injury, got to a safe place where they all knelt in a prayer of thanks, and verified their accounts with one other. They had similar experiences despite being an ethnically and religiously diverse group.[4]

3. Premonitions. People have had premonitions in OBEs, NDEs, and in dreams that later came true.[5][6]

4. Blind People Seeing. Several blind people (even some from birth) have said they could see in their OBE or NDE.[7][8][9]

5. Experiences While Brain Dead. NDEs cannot be due to brain activity, as many happen when the brain is clinically dead and not responding at all.[10][11]

6. Similarities Between Experiences. The NDEs of unrelated people in different cultures around the world, some far back in time, share similarities.[12]

7. Evidence for Reincarnation. Evidence for reincarnation also supports the idea that we exist beyond our bodies, as in reincarnation the body is a vehicle for something that continues from the life of one body to the next. There are cases of children who have recalled aspects of their past life and some among them have provided verifiably accurate descriptions of the past, while others carry birthmarks where wounds were alleged to have been on their previous body.[13][14]

8. Terminal Lucidity. Some mentally disabled people become normal just before death, even if parts of their brains had been destroyed by illness.[15] [16] [17] And lifelong deaf and mute people have been able to speak clearly just before death.[18] This indicates that consciousness was able to function normally once it started separating from a physically-impaired body/vehicle, as it would have been using its fifth-dimensional body that didn't suffer the physical body's handicap, which would have overridden the physical body due to the weakening of the interdimensional barrier allowing the influence of the fifth dimension to come through.

9. Miraculous Healings. Several people who had an NDE had miraculous healing resulting from them,[19] such as Anita Moorjani who died of cancer, but accepted the choice to return and was told she would be cured. Her cancer miraculously disappeared four days after she revived.[20] Another example is a man who after his NDE was able to open his hand which had been frozen in a claw position since birth.[21]

10. Shared Death Experiences. Apart from NDEs, there are also shared death experiences (SDEs). These occur when another person or people around someone who dies have a transcendental experience in which they share in the dying person's entry into the afterlife, sometimes even seeing or traveling some way with them into the afterlife. SDEs can happen to people close to the dying, or even remotely to those who are unaware that the person is dying. Since SDEs are experienced by those who are not dying themselves, and who are usually wide awake, they cannot be explained by any processes in the brain that occur at death, which are often invoked by scientists in an attempt to explain NDEs.[22] Dr. Raymond Moody has documented numerous SDEs in his book *Glimpses of Eternity: An Investigation into Shared Death Experiences*.[23] Moody had an SDE himself—his entire family experienced one at the bedside of his mother in hospital as she died, and the family members corroborated each other's experience.[24]

11. Extrasensory Perceptions around the Dying. Those in proximity to the dying have experienced hearing music, sensing presences, aromas, and seeing lights or vapor arising at the time of death,[25] and many of these experiences could be classified as SDEs.

People around those dying or who have recently died sometimes sense the presence of the deceased or other beings.

12. Deathbed Dreams and Visions. The dying often have dreams and visions related to the afterlife, including seeing spiritual beings and deceased relatives.[26] These are known as "end-of-life dreams and visions" (ELDVs). There are also numerous accounts of those alive having a dream in which the recently deceased appear to them, sometimes giving them the news that they have died.[27][28] Although not in itself evidence for dreams being more than creations of the brain, in the context of the other evidence presented, this nevertheless supports the observation that dreams occur in the same place that the deceased go and are OBEs in themselves.

In deathbed visions the dying indicate they see beings that aren't physically there. They usually claim to see deceased friends or relatives, and to a lesser extent, spiritual beings. One of the things that indicates they are more than just imagination is that some have seen relatives who appear as deceased when the dying person didn't know they were dead. What's also significant is that occasionally other people present will see the same vision as it's happening to the dying person.

Deathbed visions are quite common and they happen worldwide. There are also consistencies in the accounts as indicated in research.[29]

Many while dying are very conscious of their surroundings and are mentally lucid, in which case their visions may not be due to mental hallucinations. I believe they are partly seeing into the fifth dimension as the influence of their physical brain lessens, and many likely see actual beings or people from higher dimensions.

Near-death researcher Kevin Williams has a good article on the website near-death.com that gives fifty-two points he claims indicate how science has evidence supporting the validity of NDEs and the afterlife.[30] A wealth of supporting evidence can also be found on the IANDS (International Association for Near-Death Studies) website (iands.org) and in their journal,[31] as well as the NDERF (Near-Death Experience Research Foundation) website (nderf.org).[32]

THE LIMITS OF MATERIAL SCIENCE

Near-death experiences provide compelling evidence of consciousness existing outside the body and brain, as many occur when the brain is not functioning—that's when actually dead rather than in pre-death shutdown or revival. Under these circumstances, there is simply no way that an OBE can be caused by any bodily function. An example of this is of a woman who, after being brain and bodily dead and then revived by medical staff on an operating table, said she had been out of her body, went to the roof of the hospital, and saw a specific kind of shoe there. Medical staff then went to the roof and recovered the shoe, which was not visible from the ground, only from the air.[33] Cases like this cannot be convincingly explained by science.

Even of the few scientists who believe that NDEs show that consciousness exists independently of the body, most believe that ordinary OBEs are subjective experiences created by the brain. Yet although many are subjective, there are OBEs that have been verified by events and objects in the physical world.

It's worth defining when an NDE becomes an OBE, as many NDEs credited with being accurate descriptions of real events are technically OBEs as the person hasn't fully died. Logically, if you accept these kinds of OBEs as showing the existence of consciousness beyond the body, then clearly conventional OBEs could show the same thing.

No reasonable scientific theory explaining what OBEs are has been or can be provided because the kind of evidence I've outlined here, found in research and widespread accounts, has been disregarded. Yet academics and scientists haven't provided proof that OBEs aren't real either.

Their argument is based on the assumption that there's nothing nonphysical in existence to survive death, but to assume that because the body dies, "we" die, is not a provable basis from which to start.

Since we cannot measure interdimensionally, we have to look at evidence of interdimensional experience in the ways described in the previous section, as well as other evidence for interdimensional phenomena such as that found in quantum physics. For example, several theories in quantum physics support the existence of other dimensions and consciousness having an existence outside the physical body, particularly in the actions of tiny particles that don't follow the laws of our dimension. While none prove that consciousness exists outside the body and are purely theories, they nevertheless indicate these phenomena are theoretically possible.[34] [35] [36] [37]

I was interviewed on BBC radio with a woman who had just had an NDE, and Dr. Peter Fenwick, a leading NDE researcher who is also a senior lecturer in psychiatry at a prominent London college, and we disagreed about the objectivity of OBEs. The woman present in the interview was the one I mentioned earlier in the chapter, who had been unconscious with an illness in hospital and while in that state saw a doctor in a red turban. Although her case was presented as an NDE, Dr. Fenwick agreed with me that she technically had an OBE and not an NDE. Yet I was dismayed at the professor's suggestion that it would be appropriate having had such an experience for her to seek psychiatric care and take medication. It's pitiful that science can provide so little to a person who wants to understand their NDE/OBE. Can it not do better than offering them medication and a consultation with someone who has little or no out-of-body or near-death experience?

Yet the same professor later speaking at the IANDS annual conference said, "Neuroscience has come up against a block. The problem is that neuroscientists do not know what consciousness is and have no theories to explain its nature. That is because our science is the science of the external world, a hangover from the time of the Renaissance, and it does not deal with subjective experience, or with consciousness. This is the main problem facing neuroscience at the moment, and it may well be that NDE research will be one way of filling the 'consciousness gap' in neuroscience."[38]

Years later as I recall, the professor said he believed NDEs were related to mystical experiences. It's a pity he hadn't thought that at the time I spoke to him—we could have had a more productive discussion. But it's admirable he was later open-minded enough to change his position. Perhaps he'd done this in the face of undeniable and scientifically inexplicable evidence.

However, the facts I've described above aren't enough to constitute proof of the existence of consciousness outside the body for much of the scientific community, as that kind of proof requires that experiences can be replicated and subjected to strict controls. The issue I have with this view is that it requires verifiable proof for something that happens in another dimension, which is, by its nature, unverifiable from this dimension based on current scientific methods.

There's usually no actual physical evidence people in OBEs have traveled anywhere, apart from their accounts. But accounts of seeing distant objects, places, and events that really exist, show that the simplest explanation—that consciousness leaves the body and travels independently—must be true.

Even if scientific experiments on NDEs and OBEs were to succeed according to their own criteria, many theories could be put forward to try to explain the results that don't include the person's consciousness being separate from their physical body. Theories such as the effects of hormones, hallucinations, or the stimulation of various parts of the brain continue to be put forward to explain what people are experiencing when their body was technically dead and their brain was unable to function.

Given the evidence found in NDEs and OBEs that we as consciousness can exist outside and beyond our body, it's clear the brain acts like a receiver and is not the generator of the mind or consciousness, and that the body is a vehicle which we need to be able to live in the physical world. This is supported by several academics, one of which is Dr. Melvin Morse who has written a book on the subject called *Transformed by the Light*.[39] It's also supported by cases of people with damaged brains or with essential parts of their brains missing who nevertheless have been able to function normally.[40] [41] [42]

OBE and NDE studies essentially look at the behavior of consciousness. However, the nature of consciousness and the way it interacts with the physical body is unclear to science. The current status of our scientific knowledge of consciousness has been summed up by Alva Noë, Professor of Philosophy at Berkeley University:

> "After decades of concerted effort on the part of neuroscientists, psychologists, and philosophers, only one proposition about how the brain makes us conscious—how it gives rise to sensation, feeling, subjectivity—has emerged unchallenged: we don't have a clue."[43]

HAVING OBES AS PROOF FOR ONESELF

While studies are being made for OBEs and NDEs that have repeatable tests, it remains to be seen how much they will contribute to the mainstream acceptance of OBEs as real. The most practical way to really know is to have a personal experience of being in another dimension by having a conscious OBE for oneself.

One thing I've noticed is that some of the older academics I saw referenced years ago, who spent decades of their careers researching consciousness and OBEs, have died or are close to the end of their lives. Despite their research, many, if not all of them, had little to no experience of being out of their body themselves, and so they leave this world for the afterlife with as much real knowledge about it as anyone else. That is, without having seen much if anything of the otherworld while they were still in this life.

We can look at the experiences of those who've had OBEs and NDEs for evidence of the existence of other dimensions. However, for many it's more convincing to experience them personally. So the practical option for anyone wanting to know whether other dimensions and OBEs are real is to travel in other dimensions by having an OBE themselves. I give some suggestions of how to test whether one's own OBE is real in chapter 21.

While outside of our bodies we can be conscious in the fifth dimension and see something of it. No one can do this from the physical dimension, and that's why scientific studies have reached an impassable barrier.

Science has its limits, and so ancient religion, mysticism, and personal experience go where science is still unable to. OBEs allow us to go deeper into certain aspects of human life than conventional science allows us, since science is limited by its methods in an area of study that by its nature is non-physical and thus is based on inner personal experience.

CHAPTER SEVEN

An Outline of Out-of-Body Experiences

Every night when we fall asleep, we leave our body and travel to another dimension, but we're not usually aware of it; we normally just have dreams. Yet it's possible to be conscious of leaving our physical body, and to be in that dimension and be conscious of where we are. When this happens, we are having an out-of-body experience.

Having an OBE is simply being in another dimension consciously (knowing that we are out of our physical body), and there are several techniques to have them.

THE DIFFERENT KINDS OF OBES

Out-of-body experiences usually happen in one of three ways:

Firstly, from dreaming—this is called lucid dreaming. When this happens, we realize that we are in a dream and that we are out of our body, just as we are aware of being here in the physical world.

Secondly, they can occur from consciously leaving the body, usually while it falls asleep—this is commonly known as astral projection. In a typical experience someone feels themselves separate from their physical body, and float up out of it. Sometimes these experiences happen spontaneously, but they can also be learned so that someone can have them intentionally with the appropriate techniques.

Thirdly, they happen in near-death experiences. These are out-of-body experiences that take place with the death of the body.

As discussed in chapter 3, there is a much, much rarer kind of OBE, which generally occurs as a result of silencing the mind. In this kind of OBE, rather than feeling like one is coming out of their body, they feel as though they collapse into their heart, and erupt into the pure light of the Source or a plane very close to it, which is much higher than the astral plane.

Techniques for having OBEs intentionally are in no way done by inducing death or near-death experiences, but by using the natural connection we have to the fifth dimension through the normal process of sleep. It should be practiced without stressing, harming, or altering the natural state of the physical body in any way. Attempts to have out-of-body experiences should never be made by attempting to have near-death experiences, as this could prove fatal. The exercises are most effective the healthier and more psychologically sound a person is.

WHERE WE GO IN OBES

The most common place we go to when out of the body is the astral plane of the fifth dimension. Although astral plane is not a scientific term, it's the name that's most widely used. In an OBE we are out of our body and can know it, in the same way that we know we are in the physical world.

Dreams occur in the same dimension that most OBEs occur in, and when we dream we are actually out of our body. We can verify this by "waking up" in our dreams and having a lucid dream or by astral projecting and seeing unconscious or partly conscious dreamers, and by seeing things in the fifth dimension that exist in the physical world, and things that have already happened, or will happen, in the physical world that we hadn't known about, but can verify after waking.

To consciously project and have an OBE we normally need sleep, because with it our fifth-dimensional body separates from our physical one. Our fifth-dimensional body (the astral body) is connected to our physical one so that it's impossible not to come back to it, which occurs as soon as we wake from sleep. Messages are sent through this connection between one body and the other while we sleep, which allows a person in the fifth dimension to unconsciously influence their physical body while dreaming. For example, a person who dreams they are running can unconsciously move their physical arms and legs and an onlooker can see they are trying to run in their dreams. Likewise, the physical body can influence dreams while asleep. So if you stroke someone's hand while they are asleep, they may dream that someone is stroking their hand, etc.

When we consciously project, we leave behind everything that is not of the fifth dimension and above, including our physical body. Then what we see when we're in the fifth dimension is fifth-dimensional matter, including the fifth-dimensional counterpart of everything in the physical four-dimensional world, because everything that exists here also exists there. We can move fifth-dimensional objects there, but I've never found that doing this has moved the corresponding physical objects back here. The fifth dimension has its own matter, just as the physical world does.

Illustration of an out-of-body experience.

Just as there are laws governing and enabling life here, so too is the fifth dimension governed by its own laws. We can do things there we can't do here, like flying—we can jump into the air and stay airborne, we can fly upward, and then as many people have done, we can fly somewhere we wish to go. Life can look different there or it can look as normal as it does here, though it's possible to go through walls and objects, meet people and other beings, travel to distant places in the world and beyond.

SOME OF THE BENEFITS OF HAVING OBES

Being outside the body can be a profound experience, even life-changing. Many people after having an out-of-body experience for the first time relate how they were changed in their perception of who they are and what life was after feeling what it was to realize they were more than their body and life was more than just the material world.

Although it's possible to just travel and have random experiences, it's a huge waste of an opportunity to treat it superficially or like a hobby; it's far better to have the aim to do something fundamentally worthwhile. After all, in the span of a human life, time spent consciously in that dimension is very limited compared to the amount of time spent in the physical world, and so it makes sense to make good use of it.

Experiences in higher realms were part of ancient religious teachings, yet we today can leave our body and get our own experience of these other realities. Visions, divine visitations, spiritual beings of all kinds, and apparitions in religions and mythology all have their roots in higher dimensions. Beings both spiritual and malevolent exist in the fifth dimension, and if someone travels enough, they will meet both kinds, whether they have a belief about them or not.

OBEs can allow us to see the normally hidden influence that nonphysical beings have upon us.

There are other beings, and other parts of our psyche, that exist in the fifth dimension, which have their influence upon us here completely unknown to most. By having OBEs we can discover many of the unseen influences that act upon us from the fifth dimension.

Many paranormal phenomena such as hauntings and ghosts manifest into the physical world from the fifth dimension. It's possible to discover the source of these kinds of phenomena and more about them by consciously projecting into the fifth dimension. Paranormal researchers would do well to include astral projection as part of their tool kit.

We can get an understanding of death and near-death experiences, as in an OBE we travel to the same place the deceased usually go when initially leaving their body before moving on to other regions or dimensions.

In an OBE we can meet and receive teachings and guidance from spiritual beings, even some of those that are referred to in sacred texts. We can also be shown things and taught by our own higher Being (our Spiritual Father and Mother), which is what usually happens.

Spiritual being appearing to Joseph ("father" of Jesus) as he slept.

Apart from knowledge that is relevant to everyone, we can be shown things of a personal nature. We can learn about ourselves and be shown the things we need to change within ourselves to progress in the development of our consciousness/soul, by seeing what our spiritual obstacles and personal defects are. We can learn about the process of attaining liberation, and for those who take the path of the Spiritual Sun, they can be shown a higher level of knowledge.

By traveling out of the body we can see something of what is going on beyond the physical world, some of which applies to our life here. I'll illustrate this with something that happened to me.

When I moved into a new rented place I quickly set up the phone and internet, but a couple of weeks later they stopped working properly. The phone sounded scratchy and was cutting out intermittently, so I called the phone provider to get it repaired.

A few days later a man showed up in a green van. He wasn't very talkative. He went around the side of the house and a while later emerged and said it was fixed. He asked me to try the line; it worked fine, so I thanked him and he drove away.

A week later I had an OBE. I went outside the house, but something drew me to look closer at it. I went underneath the house to the phone line and saw a device on it, which I knew to be a phone tap. I then went from around the house and woke up back in my physical body. From then on, I knew to be mindful while I used the phone and internet.

About a year later there was trouble again with the line, but it was a bit different this time—it didn't have the same kind of interference as the first time. So I phoned the provider again, but this time a man arrived in a white van. He was friendly and talkative and went to fix it. I didn't mention the listening device and wondered whether he would find anything.

When he finished working under the house he said, "The line's fixed, but you had a device on your line. Someone was listening in to your connection. I've removed it now." I thanked him and he drove off. I had no problems with the line again.

MY FIRST OBES

The first out-of-body experience I had was with a small group of people doing a practice together. It was nighttime, and we did an experimental exercise. The aim was to astral project into the next room to discover a mystery object that had been placed in it. To prepare, we spent some time in the room beforehand and observed it as clearly as we could so that we could recreate it in our minds during our practice of astral projection.

I went into the room and looked at everything in it very intensively and in great detail: the ceiling, the walls, and all the objects. We were in silence and I tried to look as clearly as possible without thoughts clouding my perception. My awareness was particularly strong that evening, as I had been training myself regularly; it just "beamed." It felt so strong that as I faced the wall I could "see" who was coming in behind me. Without turning around I quietly said hello along with the name of the person; he was astonished.

I maintained this awareness as I carefully went to the room where we were doing our astral projection exercise, got into my sleeping bag, visualized the room and then became aware of my heartbeats and briefly concentrated on them.

Within seconds a powerful tingling sensation came over me and I lifted up into the air about two feet above my body. It was terrifying, like nothing I had experienced before. I involuntarily shouted, "Help! Help!" repeatedly, and looked around the room, but no one could hear me in the physical world because I was in the fifth dimension.

I looked around and saw that the person who had placed the mystery object in the room had also projected. He was sitting in the room, and beside him sat a spiritual figure; he had been drawn to the room by the power of the exercise. My fear unfortunately brought me back to my body. I looked around and realized that no one had heard me shouting.

Later on I spoke to the person I'd seen and he confirmed that the spiritual figure who we both knew of had been there. Although it was brief, it was an amazing experience; I had discovered that it was possible to leave my physical body and even meet people there. I also told him that nothing had been placed in the room and he said that was correct.

With that success I began to try astral projection at home. I had more success initially in the afternoons where I had an opportunity to lie down and practice without being so tired that I fell straight to sleep, like I often did at night.

My next experience occurred at home after I lay down on my bed on my back, relaxed my body, and began to concentrate on my heartbeat (which has been the most successful technique for me). As I concentrated on it, I felt as though I began to move with the beats of my heart. I was amazed to find that it kept getting stronger and stronger and I lifted out more and more with each beat. A tingling sensation went through my body along with a high-pitched noise until finally I was completely raised out of my body.

I wasn't afraid this time and calmly looked around the room—it was exactly as it appeared in the physical world, with the only difference being the colors and everything looked more intense, and that I was hovering above my body. A thought came to me that people have said it's possible to create your own reality when in the fifth dimension. I wondered how this worked and how real it would be, so I imagined a pink toothbrush—to my surprise, it appeared there in the room like a real object. I moved around a bit, looked around to see if it would be gone, but it was still there, as bright and real as everything else. I wondered what else I could imagine and I started thinking, but began to move downward and merge back into my body, until I woke up back into the physical world.

A day or two later I lay down to try to project by again concentrating on my heartbeat, only this time as soon as I tried to relax the tingling sensations began and I lifted up out of my body; this time it seemed almost involuntary. It was the same process of lifting out as before, but as I looked around, to my great surprise I was in my room, but the room was exactly as it had been when I was a child in the 1960s. I was a bit dumbfounded by this; then I heard the sound of the front door of the house opening and my parents coming in. My mother called my name and started to come up the stairs—her voice sounded younger. I was startled and merged back into my body. When I opened my eyes in the physical world, my parents had not yet come into the house. I believe I either projected into a recording of the past, or that it was a scene my Being had created for me.

A few days later during the afternoon, I had another OBE. This time I was feeling down about an inner state that I was trying to understand and overcome but couldn't. I lay down feeling a sense of defeat, even desperation, and almost as soon as my head hit the pillow I was lifted up into the air accompanied by the OBE sensations. This time I got up and sat on the edge of the bed. The fifth dimension was luminous and clear, and I looked at myself in the mirror—the reflection that came back was me, but with changes due to the inner state I was trying to understand. It showed in symbolism how that state affected me, but showed it in a profound way, a way that I could never have grasped here.

I had many other OBEs that helped confirm to me they were real experiences and that there were other, superior intelligences out there that were not human as we know them.

I continued my exercises with varying degrees of success. For example, I projected into a room where I was meditating with other people. I saw the others there, who were mostly asleep and had not consciously projected into the astral plane, but I could also see the thoughts and feelings of one person in particular; it was important for me to see, and I'm sure it was only shown to me because it was something that could help me.

I had heard about people who met up while out of their bodies and traveled together in the astral world. That was fine, but most of all I wanted information from which I could change myself, as that was my main concern. I wanted to stop being fearful, proud, angry, and all those horrible things that I was beginning to see that I was; I really wanted to change myself.

SUBJECTIVITY AND THE INFLUENCE OF THE MIND

Even though it's possible to have objective OBEs, it's often the case that what is seen in OBEs is influenced by our minds. This has made testing the validity of OBEs difficult—more difficult than testing that of NDEs. I've noticed that people in NDEs have much clearer and seemingly more objective experiences than those in ordinary OBEs do. I believe this is due to a mechanism of the brain, which is active during OBEs but not during NDEs, as in an NDE the brain is almost always dead. Brain activity must therefore contribute to the subjectivity of many OBEs.

This mechanism of the brain operates during waking life. So if you are to think now of your mother, you can "see" her in your "mind's eye" while also still being partially aware of your current surroundings. These mind's eye visuals can become very immersive when we daydream, so that the awareness of our surroundings may diminish to very little. This ability to visualize allows us to remember, plan, invent, etc.

While awake, these visuals are clearly separate to the perception of our physical surrounds—we generally know they are different and unreal. However, while out of our bodies this separation doesn't exist in the same way, as thoughts and feelings are themselves fifth dimensional; they are a type of energy that condenses into form in the fifth dimension. As we are in the fifth dimension in an OBE, when we have these kinds of mind's eye thoughts, they become laid over reality so that it's very difficult, or even impossible, to tell the difference between them. Rather than visuals in our mind's eye, they are now projections, a bit like holograms.

Our daydreams and thoughts can become very
immersive and block out our perception of reality.

So for example, if someone imagines being in a concert hall while in an OBE, it will become real for them and they will seem to be in one, even though it's not really there. Should they start thinking about eating ice cream, then they can suddenly be eating it, but it doesn't actually exist.

This mechanism of the brain is likely to be what's behind the creation of our subconscious dreams, as ordinary dreams consist mostly, if not entirely, of these projections.

Given that someone is rarely able to remain aware without getting lost in compulsive thoughts and daydreams while awake, in an OBE a person usually sees projections from their mind rather than what's really in the fifth dimension. Or they may partially see what's in the fifth dimension, mixed in with their own projections. Just because someone realizes they're in a dream it doesn't mean these projections from their mind automatically stop, neither are they automatically absent if they've consciously astral projected—very often they continue even though someone knows they're in the fifth dimension, and unless they're discerning they can believe they are real. Any fascination or absorption with these projections usually quickly brings an OBE to an end, as we lose conscious awareness of our surrounds and the experience turns into an unconscious dream.

It's possible for someone to project things from their mind about spiritual beings and places just as they can about anything else. This person may then see what they want to believe, maybe a deity telling them something about themselves they want to hear, convinced they are having a real spiritual experience when the whole thing is imaginary.

The effect of this brain mechanism is likely what the Twice Born of Egypt were trying to cancel out in their elaborate procedure to put themselves in a near-death-like state (something I recommend against), so that they could have as objective an experience as possible while out of the body.

This brain mechanism seems to be very active when on psychedelics, and I discuss this further in chapter 28.

It's important to take into account the possible influence of the mind and its projections upon whatever is seen in OBEs and dreams, and to look at experiences discerningly—being able to distinguish things in them that are real from those that are not.

This is why the study of self-knowledge is important for OBEs—we must be able to clear our psyche of its own projections as much as possible to see what's real while out of the body. It's also why a large part of preparing to have OBEs is training oneself to concentrate on and be aware of what we are doing and where we are while in waking life, reducing our thinking in visuals where we can. The only other way to have a clear experience is to be given one by spiritual beings who temporarily clear our psyche for us, and in my experience, this is mainly how objective experiences happen.

Subjects in experiments are unlikely to have this kind of self-knowledge, or much experience of the fifth dimension, and so their experiences are more likely to be subjective, adding yet another obstacle to scientifically proving OBEs are real.

Even though OBEs are more subjective than NDEs overall, there are still real and even verifiably real experiences in them. And even though dreams tend to be the most subjective type of OBE, people have nevertheless had dreams and lucid dreams that provide evidence of the afterlife and of consciousness being separate from the body. One such case is that of Claire Sylvia from Boston in the U.S. who had dreams in which she identified her anonymous organ donor whose heart and lungs she had received.[1] The fact that some OBEs can be subjective doesn't mean they all are—OBEs can be clear and allow someone to experience something they only could if consciousness was separated from the body.

CHAPTER EIGHT

Different Realms and Dimensions

So where do OBEs occur? Do they happen in another dimension, plane, world, or a parallel universe? How many dimensions/realms are there? And how are they structured?

In this chapter, I'll briefly cover what some in traditions of the ancient Religion of the Sun believed about other realms, and what science theorizes about them. I'll then give my own thoughts based on what I've experienced and have tried to work out.

OTHER REALMS IN ANCIENT RELIGION

Among ancient religions there was a widespread knowledge of and belief in other realms. Their texts describe numerous nonphysical realms, worlds, or planes of existence that are parallel to our own, both above and below, and usually inhabited by the deceased and supernatural beings. Their beliefs share similarities with one another, and also correlate with what people have seen in NDEs and OBEs both today and in the past.

In traditions of the Religion of the Sun, there was not just one realm, but a number of them. These followed the same essential structure—having an ultimate divine source, upper nonphysical regions of light or heavens, a middle physical world, and lower nonphysical regions of darkness or hells.

For example, Hindu texts detail multiple planes of existence. These include realms called *lokas*, with both upper ones of light, and lower *lokas* of darkness—in some texts it's said that seven upper *lokas* exist above the earth, and seven lower *lokas* beneath its surface. Other texts detail twenty-eight regions of hell.[1]

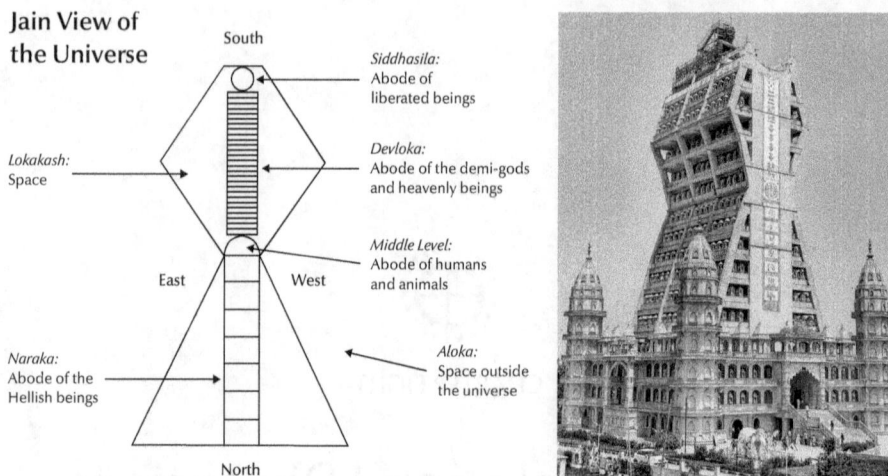

Left: Diagram showing the various heavens above, and hells below, the middle world of humans in Jain cosmology. Right: A Jain temple in India modeled on the structure of these realms.

The Inca believed in three worlds. Kay Pacha, literally meaning "this world" was the middle world in which we currently live; Hanan Pacha was the upper world, which was the home of the gods and where those who led a good life would ascend after death; and Uku Pacha was the lower world inhabited by demons and the wicked.[2][3]

Similarly, the Gauls (who were a Celtic people) believed in a heavenly world above, called Albios; the world of the living, Bitu, which we inhabit; and a dark world below, Dubnos. Gaulish druids believed in an otherworld that the souls of the deceased went to before being reincarnated.[4]

Likewise in ancient Chinese tradition there are three realms: the middle realm occupied by humanity; heaven in the sky above called Tian; and below the earth hell or Diyu, meaning "earth prison," where demons reside and the wicked suffer after death.[5][6]

Left: The entrance to the ten courts of hell in Buddhist and Chinese tradition at the theme park Haw Par Villa in Singapore, guarded by two of its most infamous demons. Right: Inside, visitors can walk through life-like recreations of the various torments suffered after death in the different regions of hell.

Taoist texts mention nine heavens and nine "earths" (referring to regions within the earth). Ancient Chinese tradition lists sometimes three, four, ten, and eighteen regions of hell.[7] In Norse tradition there are nine worlds, eight of which are nonphysical, including the dwelling place of the gods in the sky, and an underworld called Hel beneath the earth.[8] In Maya cosmology there are thirteen regions of heaven in the sky, and nine regions of the underworld beneath the earth.[9] In the Eleusinian Mysteries of Greece, there is record of a belief in nine higher spheres.[10]

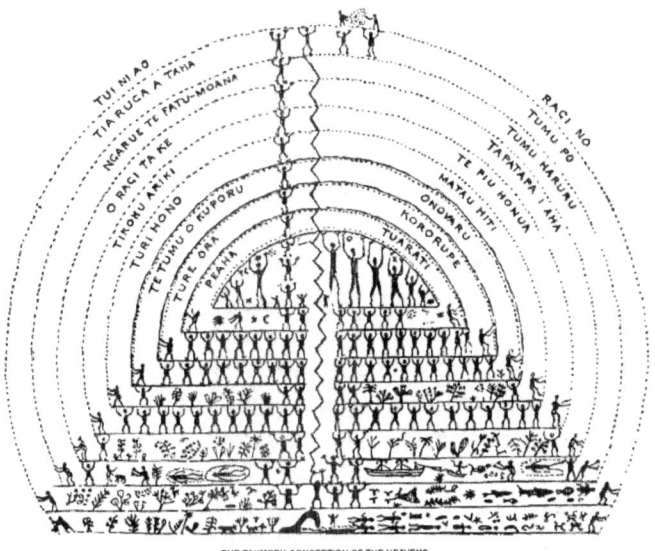

THE PAUMOTU CONCEPTION OF THE HEAVENS

Drawing made by a man of the Paumotu Polynesians in 1869, illustrating the nine heavens of their cosmology.

In an ancient Gnostic text with teachings attributed to Jesus, he speaks of thirteen "aeons" or nonphysical regions, as well as a Treasury of Light above, and the chaos of darkness below.[11] In the New Testament Paul mentions a third heaven, and in noncanonical texts, Paul is said to have visited seven heavens in one account and ten in another, while also seeing hell.[12]

Nine, seven, and thirteen seem to be common numbers when it comes to defining how many nonphysical regions there are. Four was also commonly used to delineate the physical world, usually through the four cardinal directions. These numbers appear in what I describe about the different realms.

IS IT ANOTHER DIMENSION?

The word dimension is commonly used to describe the out-of-body realm. What exactly a dimension is, and whether that realm really is another dimension is up for debate. However, there doesn't seem to be a better term. It's the simplest word that best describes the property of the OBE realm being real, nonphysical, and separate from this world yet accessible from it, that people can understand today. So when someone says, "the beings came from another dimension" or "he entered another dimension" or "she heard a voice from another dimension," we all know more or less what they mean.

This meaning has developed out of a fusion of ways it has been used in science, science fiction, and spirituality. To get more of an understanding about what it means, it's helpful to know how it developed.

The idea of another dimension (specifically the fourth) being connected to an unseen realm of matter was first briefly mentioned in the book *The Unseen Universe* by the Scottish mathematical physicists Balfour Stewart and Peter Guthrie Tait (who was a lifelong friend of the great physicist James Clerk Maxwell) in 1875. Then, in 1879 the idea was expanded upon greatly by German physicist Johann Zöllner, who equated the fourth dimension with a spiritual plane of existence, proposing it was the source of supernatural phenomena experienced in the three-dimensional world. Although not gaining scientific acceptance, the idea was picked up by Theosophists who equated the fourth dimension with the astral plane,[13][14] and so parallel spiritual dimensions firmly entered the realm of spirituality.

The idea was also used by the English writer H.G. Wells. In his 1895 science fiction novella *The Time Machine*, the protagonist travels back and forth in time, which is a fourth dimension.[15] A year later his short science fiction story "The Plattner Story" in *The Plattner Story and Others* recounted the experience of a schoolteacher who spends nine days in a parallel world located in the fourth dimension after a chemistry experiment goes wrong.[16] Thus the idea of parallel dimensions firmly entered the realm of science fiction.

But the idea of a fourth dimension also eventually firmly entered the realm of science. In 1907 the Russian-German mathematician Hermann Minkowski (who had been one of Einstein's professors) declared that space and time, which were thought to be independent, were in fact coupled together in a four-dimensional space-time continuum, simply called "spacetime."[17] This gained acceptance and our worldview changed to see the universe as four-dimensional instead of three. With time now occupying the fourth dimension, the association in spirituality between the astral plane and other dimensions got bumped up a rung, to the fifth dimension.

Yet science delved into the existence of a fifth dimension too. In 1921 the Swedish physicist Oskar Klein and German mathematician Theodor Kaluza proposed the existence of a fifth dimension in an attempt to unify gravity with electromagnetic force. This fifth dimension was not a parallel realm, but a tiny extra physical dimension rolled up within every point in spacetime, so small it was way beyond human perception (twenty times smaller than a hydrogen atom). While their approach later turned out to be partially inaccurate, their ideas formed the basis for further five-dimensional and beyond models. In 1938 Einstein and the German-American physicist Peter Bergmann attempted to extend four-dimensional spacetime to five physical dimensions to incorporate electromagnetism, but were unsuccessful.[18]

In the late 1960s, theories about other dimensions really got going again with the emergence of String Theory, which postulates the existence of no less than ten dimensions. String Theory gave rise to the fascinating idea that our universe might be a kind of three-dimensional island, or "brane" (short for membrane), afloat in ten-dimensional spacetime.[19]

Then, in 1999 a fifth-dimensional model was reasserted by the American theoretical physicist Lisa Randall and the Indian-American particle theorist Raman Sundrum. According to their theory, our four-dimensional universe may be a brane embedded within a vastly larger five-dimensional space, where other four-dimensional realms like ours may also be "afloat."[20] In 2021, a group of physicists from Johannes Gutenberg University in Mainz, Germany, proposed that the extra gravity currently attributed to dark matter may be the gravity belonging to unknown particles, which exist in a hidden fifth dimension, manifesting into our four-dimensional realm.[21]

I don't claim to know anything about physics, but I can say that the latest theories on branes and the fifth dimension appear close to what I was shown in a lucid dream. A few days before writing this, Lara and I were chatting as she was questioning our use of the word dimension to describe the astral plane and beyond (as we'd done so far), trying to understand what a dimension really was. I then related a clear dream I'd had just a couple of days prior, in which I was shown what our physical world looked like from the perspective of those who are dead.

A female spiritual being showed me a clipboard floating in space. It held a single sheet of what looked like a semi-transparent fabric veil. Between the veil and the wooden board was a layer of clay that was pressed out onto a smallish part of the board. The clay was matter in the physical world and the thin veil was between it and the surrounding expanse of the afterlife/OBE realm. The surrounding space was the place where I (being out of my body) and the dead were, not including those in hell, and perhaps those in higher realms.

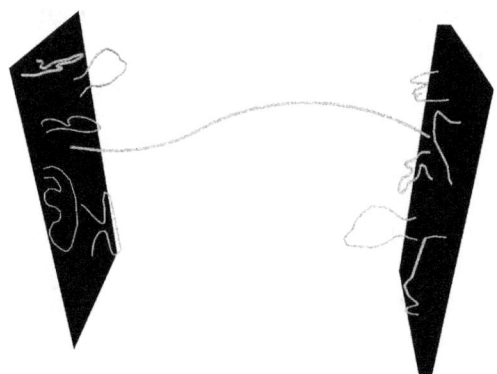

A pair of branes known as D-branes. A single brane is portrayed like the clipboard I saw.

Although we could make a few things out from the dream, it didn't seem to make enough sense to conclude much about the dimensions from it. For one, a clipboard seemed a strange choice, and so Lara went off to research to try to find some answers.

It didn't take long before she came to the latest theories about dimensions, and noticed the resemblance between the clipboard floating in the afterlife, and the "brane" floating in the fifth dimension. A brane can be portrayed as having the same shape as a clipboard, and essentially represents the same thing, which is our four-dimensional world, while the afterlife realm (including the astral plane) seems to correlate to the fifth dimension.

How remarkable that the story of creation in ancient Egypt describes physical matter as an island afloat in a kind of cosmic ocean.

We found it very interesting too that in science the fifth dimension has been used to explain electromagnetic force, because as I explained in chapter 3, there seems to be an association between electromagnetic energy and the fifth dimension, which ancient peoples appear to have harnessed to help induce OBEs. It looks like science could well be correct in associating a fifth dimension with electromagnetism, and that this energy is involved in OBEs in some way. It also seems to correlate with the ancient Egyptians' use of the five-pointed star to symbolize the Duat, in that the five points may indicate it is a fifth dimension, and the star may indicate this fifth dimension is to do with electromagnetic energy (the stars being the primary source of this energy). It's possible that a civilization in the past had advanced enough to discover this, and the knowledge of it survived in Egypt.

The veil I saw has also been referred to in ancient texts, and has been seen by some in NDEs as separating our physical world from the out-of-body one, like that of Donna Redabow who felt herself pass through a veil as she left her body, which she described as "this Saran wrap [plastic wrap] kind of veil; it was very thin, but it was something there."[22]

Although many of the ideas about dimensions are still theories, what I can say from my experience, which is also clear from the NDEs and OBEs of others both recently and throughout history, is that another nonphysical realm exists. Given its existence, it's very likely other dimensions exist too. And so lacking any better term, we've decided to refer to it as the fifth dimension.

OTHER DIMENSIONS IN SCIENCE

Science accepts the possibility that parallel dimensions and universes exist, which may be inhabited by other beings or versions of ourselves. Quantum Theory, Many-Worlds Theory, String Theory, and Many Interacting Worlds Theory all posit that there are multiple, parallel universes/dimensions, based on the observation that subatomic particles don't conform to the standard laws of physics that explain our four-dimensional physical world (of length, width, height, and time). This has led many physicists to believe there are other dimensions where different versions of ourselves exist and other possibilities are taking place simultaneously, and that these dimensions could even interact or come in contact with our own.

While physicists certainly don't describe other realms in the way ancient peoples did, their theories at least provide some scientific rationale for their existence.

There may also be other scientific clues to the existence of other dimensions, which are indicated by the spectrums of invisible light and the presence of "dark matter."

Our eyes see by perceiving light, but the human eye is only able to perceive a tiny fraction of the light spectrum in the range of approximately 380 to 750 nanometers (one billionths of a meter).[23] This lies somewhere in the range of the thickness of a soap bubble membrane,[24] in an electromagnetic spectrum of wavelengths that could potentially range infinitely.[25] For example, special equipment such as infrared cameras can detect infrared light, which is a lower frequency light emitted as heat that our eyes can't see, allowing images to be produced in the dark even when visible light is not present.

THE ELECTROMAGNETIC SPECTRUM

Diagram of the electromagnetic spectrum, showing the tiny band that is visible light.

There have also been many cases of the images of apparitions, UFOs, auras, demons, and ghosts being caught on special cameras; I don't know how many of these cases are real, but it's possible these cameras work by detecting wavelengths of light that are invisible to the naked eye.

But it's not only a large spectrum of light that we can't see; we also can't see most of the matter that exists. "Ordinary matter," which is the kind we see, is estimated to make up only 5 percent of all matter and energy in the universe—the rest science has dubbed "dark energy" and "dark matter," because we can't see it.[26]

And if that isn't small enough, even the estimated 5 percent of matter that we can see is made of atoms that are 99.9999999 percent "space." So for example, if the empty space was taken out of each of our bodies, we would be reduced to the size of a grain of dust, and putting these grains together, humanity would amount to the size of a sugar cube.[27] However, this space is not truly empty, but is full of quantum fields, which means the electrons inside atoms may occupy any point within it at any time.[28] And this goes back to the inexplicable behavior of subatomic particles, which some physicists have tried to explain using the existence of other dimensions.

What this may essentially mean is that there is an inconceivably massive amount of room and potential for other realms of reality to exist in our universe, right here and now, interpenetrating our physical world, teeming with other forms of life operating in higher and lower frequencies of light and energy beyond our perception.

WHAT REALMS EXIST?

It's very difficult if not impossible to know what other dimensions exist while alive in this dimension; I've never seen any signposts or neatly numbered dimensions. I base my view of what dimensions exist on the OBEs I've had and what's written in the ancient texts of the Religion of the Sun I've read. Many times I've found that what I've experienced out of the body has tied in with ancient sources, and I draw my understanding of the dimensions especially from these experiences. Putting this together, I'll summarize here what I've understood about the dimensions; there could be more than I mention here, but I have no knowledge of any others.

When we have an OBE, we, as consciousness and the psyche, pass from this dimension into another since we are multidimensional. The higher up, or closer to the Source the dimension is, the more refined its energy—becoming more spiritual and less material. All the dimensions seem to exist in the here and now and interpenetrate each other without mixing up.

There are four dimensions that are widely accepted in science. They constitute the physical world. The first three are length, width, and height. The fourth dimension is time. We often think of our world as three-dimensional, but if there were only three, everything would be completely static. Yet it has movement, as all life and the elements are constantly moving. Even stationary objects are in a continual state of change and thus movement, either growing or decaying. This movement happens because of and in time, which is the fourth dimension. Thus, our physical world is really four-dimensional.

However, the numbering of these dimensions in a linear sequence like this, starting at one, may already be misleading; it might be more accurate to think of frequencies of light and energy in which our physical world occupies a particular band—maybe somewhere in the middle as ancient peoples believed.

However, for the sake of having some kind of orientation, I've referred to dimensions beyond our four-dimensional world based on the same numerical sequence used by science.

The dimension that is directly next to ours I call the fifth dimension. It's the etheric component of all that exists in the four-dimensional realm we inhabit, but also includes places and beings that are nonphysical. It's the place we go when we dream, have OBEs and NDEs, and enter when we die.

These five dimensions make up the realm we ordinarily inhabit while waking and sleeping. This is likely why the ancient Hindus and Greeks included ether as a fifth element, as it's so connected to the physical world. It's probably also why the ancient Egyptian symbol of the Duat, or astral plane, was a five-pointed star within a circle—as mentioned, the five points may have represented the five dimensions and/or five elements, and the circle the enclosed space or realm they are part of—the world we primarily inhabit. Importantly it's a star pointed upward; I explain the reason for this in chapter 27.

In my experience I've noticed that there are two levels or planes in the fifth dimension—the ordinary astral and the higher astral, which is more spiritual. The ordinary astral plane is the easiest to get to and it's where we normally go to in dreams and OBEs. The ordinary astral plane has been referred to as the emotional plane,[29] and the higher astral as the mental plane.[30]

The fifth dimension is where the heavens and hells meet, as it's from the fifth dimension that one enters through the gate/portal either into heaven or hell, there being a separate portal for each.

As mentioned in chapter 3, Osiris describes this very simply and accurately. He calls the fifth dimension the "Land of the Horizon" from which there are two great gates—one leading to "the place of light" and the other to "the place of darkness."

The tunnel that many travel through in an NDE to go into the light and heaven is the crossing through this gate/portal to the place of light. This place was given many names in ancient traditions; today it's most commonly referred to as heaven and so that's the term I use for it. People who've gone there describe it as being more beautiful, vivid, real,

Hindu painting of the two paths leading from this world—one to heaven and the sun and Source above, and the other to hell and darkness below.

alive, and full of light and color than anywhere they have ever seen.

I don't know whether this first heaven beyond the portal is still part of the fifth dimension, but a higher aspect of it, possibly being another plane, or is another dimension entirely (making it the sixth). I've never seen anything definitive that would indicate it's another dimension. Whatever the case, I suspect that above it there are other more heavenly dimensions as ancient accounts indicate, but I can only speculate. Based on the initiations on the path of the Spiritual Sun though, I gather there are likely to be seven dimensions in total.

The soul/consciousness and the higher parts of our Being reside in heaven, which is why the deceased often feel they have come home when they enter heaven in an NDE. They also find themselves completely free of negative thoughts and emotions, as our egos (which I explain later in this chapter) remain in the astral plane when someone enters heaven; they cannot cross the portal with us to heaven and heaven certainly wouldn't be heavenly if they did. As I mentioned in chapter 3, I've also seen NDE accounts where people had to go through a kind of purification in light before they could cross the threshold into heaven, again indicating that lower energies and aspects of us have to be shed and left behind. That our consciousness and its higher parts reside in heaven also accounts for how these parts of us are able to perceive and feel heavenly things while we are in the physical world—it's because that's where these higher parts of us are dimensionally, even though they are nested within our physical bodies. The more the lower parts of us are shed, the more we can feel the perceptions of consciousness.

The heavenly dimensions seem to be comprised of nine heavenly planes, and a further three supra-heavenly planes—making twelve heavenly planes. When the Source above them is included, there would be thirteen heavenly regions in total.

The way to hell, like heaven, is accessed through a gate/portal in space in the fifth dimension, which is known in mythology as "the mouth of hell." I've been to hell many times while out of my body. Hell is where people go when having nightmares. Like heaven, it may be another dimension, but I've seen nothing to indicate clearly that it is. Demons, egos, the deceased, and those having nightmares all appear to pass seamlessly in and out of hell.

It seems hell is fifth dimensional also, but at a much lower frequency of energy, perhaps being a lower plane. It has different regions, and as ancient accounts indicate, may have nine regions just as heaven does. People who've been there in NDEs often report they were unable to feel positive emotions, and instead became totally immersed in their own negative feelings and energies. This may be due to something in the dimensional structure of hell that doesn't allow the emanations of consciousness and of heaven into it. Those in hell still have their consciousness, but it seems they are more cut off or removed from its spiritual feelings and perceptions.

The higher the heavenly plane or realm, the less darkness infuses it until at the highest they become like radiant light.

Every realm has beings inhabiting it that are of a like nature and who share in its vibration. The higher the heaven, the higher the vibration and current, likewise the lower the region of hell, the lower the vibration and current. In hell dwell demons with diabolical inner states. On Earth are people, a mixture of good and bad, and in the heavens are divine beings inhabiting the realms according to their light.

We can through earthly lives raise our inner level and move toward the heavenly regions, or succumb to inner darkness and gravitate toward hellish ones. Both light and darkness, heaven and hell, have their own purposes as the positive and negative are essential for creation to exist.

Beyond the dimensions is the Source, from which the dimensions/different realms arise.

The terms fifth dimension, astral plane, astral world, and astral are used somewhat interchangeably throughout this book, but they don't mean exactly the same thing. To be clear, the astral plane/world, or "astral" for short, is the nonphysical realm where most dreams and OBEs take place, and where people first go after death. The astral plane is part of the fifth dimension, but it seems there is more to the fifth dimension than the astral plane. The main difference between the way I use the terms astral plane and fifth dimension is that the astral plane does not extend beyond the portals to heaven and hell, whereas it seems as though the fifth dimension does.

It's hard to understand what a nonphysical "plane" really is. The dictionary definition is "a level of [...] existence or development,"[31] and I think that's a good way to describe it. Different planes seem to have different properties, and higher planes seem only accessible to people at a certain level of spiritual development or through spiritual help.

The astral/fifth dimension has often been referred to as eternity, and as being beyond time. But it seems logical to me that time must surely exist in some form across all of creation in all of its dimensions, as movement continues even in the heavens and so it's never truly beyond time. The dimensions beyond the fourth cannot therefore be a true eternity.

However, it's probable that time is different in the higher dimensions. For example, in the fifth dimension we can travel at the speed of thought, have premonitions, and visit the past, or at least a kind of reconstruction of it. In NDEs people often describe having a different experience of time, usually feeling as though they had been away from their bodies for much longer than they really were, sometimes seeing their whole life unfold in a life review in what was just a few minutes of actual physical death. In heaven, which people have visited in NDEs, they've also seen nature and people as though the effects of time are taken away, and as though there is no aging, death, or decay. Nevertheless, there is still a continuous movement of life. If there wasn't, all things would have to appear at every different place they could possibly be all at the same time, due to every possible movement being in the present. If this were to happen any meaningful existence would collapse, and the experience of heaven as it's been described would be impossible. It looks as though only the Source can truly be eternal and beyond time; when we go into it in an OBE, everything seems to collapse, including our body and everything that's not consciousness.

OUR BODIES IN OTHER REALMS

The accounts of near-death experiences demonstrate that there is more to us than our physical body, and that we are multidimensional beings. In an NDE, a person's physical body is clinically dead yet they remain lucid and psychologically intact. Our psyche is therefore comprised of components which we can't see here, but which exist in other dimensions/realms.

The very common sensation of astral projection (and of NDEs) is feeling oneself start to detach from one's physical body in another nonphysical body. This is often called the "astral split" because one feels the two bodies split and separate from one another. It's common to then feel oneself rise or float up away from the physical body in this nonphysical body. During an OBE, people find themselves traveling in this nonphysical body that looks just like their physical one, though sometimes semi-transparent. They also find it has different properties—it can fly, go through solid objects, do anything without getting injured, etc. A fairly common sight is of a "silver cord" connecting the two bodies together. The sensations of this nonphysical body returning to the physical one can be just as clear, with the two sometimes gradually merging back together until locking into place.

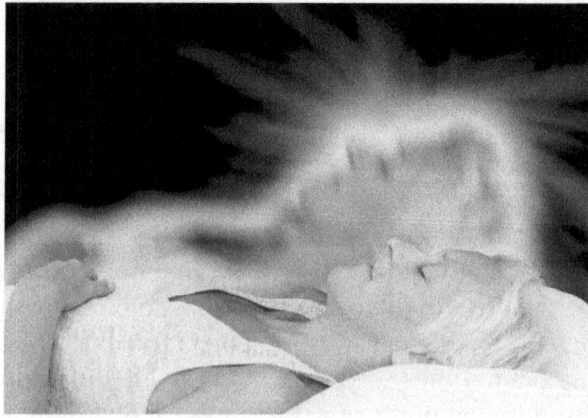

Depiction of the astral body separating from the physical body.

This nonphysical body is popularly referred to as the astral body. There were ancient peoples who referred to it and to other nonphysical bodies as well, though using different terms. Ancient texts say quite a lot about the nonphysical bodies we each have, sometimes describing the different types and even the different planes they are for. They are referred to in ancient Egyptian, Hermetic, Hindu, Zoroastrian, Greek, and Taoist texts (a number of these references have been covered in chapter 3).

Some people say they've seen their physical body left behind when they've had an OBE, although I haven't personally. In this case it would appear we have two astral parts. Being in the fifth dimension, it's not possible to see physical matter—instead what we see there is the fifth-dimensional aspect of everything that exists in the physical world. So when someone has an OBE and sees what appears to be their physical body lying in bed, they can't be seeing their physical body; instead, it must be its fifth-dimensional aspect. This would necessarily mean that the astral body is not the fifth-dimensional aspect of the physical body, but exists in addition to it. Inanimate objects, like the bed, have a fifth-dimensional aspect that we see once we're in the fifth dimension, but they don't have an astral body. Having an astral body is unique to humans and other living beings, like dogs, though I don't know about every form of life. Do insects dream for example? I don't know.

Bodies are vehicles for the psyche to exist and operate within the different dimensions. Our physical body is the vehicle that allows us to live within this four-dimensional realm; it enables the nonphysical parts of our psyche to experience and respond to the physical world. In Hinduism the physical body was part of the "gross body" (gross indicating its materiality), along with its vital sheath, which may correspond to the personality as I discuss shortly.

Each person also has an astral body and a higher astral body for the two planes of the fifth dimension (ordinary and higher). These would correspond to the "mental sheath" and "knowledge/wisdom sheath" that together comprise the subtle body in Hinduism, and also the astral/emotional body and mental body in Western Esotericism.

It's very rare to come across accounts of people seeing or experiencing these different bodies, but I found this NDE account where one man did:

> "I noticed right away that there's different bodies to us. So we're not just a physical body; we're obviously an energetic body. So I'm the energetic body which is the real me [...] the physical body is just like a vessel that I experience this reality in. [...] And then we have an emotional body, and that body [is] like a blanket. It either carries a lot of weight or not. It's very electrical as well. And then we have a mental body too, where all our beliefs, our definitions of things, our thought processes, everything that's mentally going on, our traumas, live in the mind, and that to me has a separate energetic form. So it was very clear that we're not just one body, we're multiple bodies that all come together at once. [...] we need to be able to work on those bodies in order to lighten the load." [32]

In Hinduism each person also has a causal body, which seems like it would be for heaven or some higher part of it (which may be a sixth dimension). If heaven is another dimension, this would make sense as people would need to have some kind of a body to be able to go into the heavenly regions in OBEs and NDEs.

Since I can't be sure of whether there are other dimensions than these, I don't know whether there are further bodies—only that there are indications in ancient teachings that there are more nonphysical bodies, and that generally they symbolized seven bodies in the ancient Religion of the Sun, and these would correlate to the number of initiations of the path of the Spiritual Sun.

THE NONPHYSICAL PARTS OF OUR PSYCHE

Many of us have had the sense of being stared at from behind, or have experienced thinking about someone just before they called on the phone. Some, like Dr. Rupert Sheldrake, believe this is due to undiscovered waves akin to something like radio waves existing in the physical world.[33] Whether there is a physical element to them I wouldn't know, but I've seen how other people's thoughts and feelings travel in waves in the fifth dimension, reaching the recipient at their solar plexus.

The reason we can experience metaphysical phenomena like this is because our psyche exists in other dimensions. Being multidimensional, we are affected by things from other dimensions not only when we're out of our bodies, but also while we're here. This can produce scientifically unexplained phenomena.

In the physical world we can only see the physical manifestations of the psyche—how they affect one's facial expressions, one's tone of voice, movements, and behavior, etc.—but we can't see someone else's thoughts or emotions. That's because thoughts and most emotions originate and exist within the parts of our psyche in other dimensions. Because the dimensions interpenetrate each other, our fifth-dimensional thoughts and feelings have an effect on our physical brain and body.

I'll now outline the different nonphysical components of the psyche, which I've based on what I've seen in my own OBEs, and that correlate with a number of ancient beliefs.

MIND

The mind is the part of our psyche that acts as the intermediary between that which perceives and what is perceived. It works as a kind of translator or processor between consciousness and form, which is really between consciousness and the information it receives from the senses. It's the instrument that enables consciousness to interact in form, become aware of its own existence, and develop itself whether positively or negatively. NDEs and OBEs show that we can think in any of the dimensions up to and including at least the first of the heavenly regions, and so we have a mind in all these dimensions.

The conscious mind is our conscious cognitive faculties—it's our intellect, and our ability to reason, remember, plan, concentrate, visualize, and daydream. The subconscious mind is the part of the mind that's not being used, or that we're unaware of using, at any given moment.

The nature of the human mind is what differentiates us from animals. It allows us to think about ourselves, and to reflect upon our thoughts, feelings, and behaviors, making it possible for us to separate ourselves from them, therefore enabling us to change; whereas animals can't separate themselves from their thoughts and feelings, and so are locked in their inner states and controlled by them more than we are.

Perhaps the most central term in Hermeticism, nous, is often translated as mind, though it's also translated more specifically as the pure faculty of spiritual apprehension.[34] Nous was described as a divine part of the psyche, and was the instrument by which one gained knowledge. A different kind of mind was said to be possessed by animals.[35] In Hinduism, the mind is called manas—it is the faculty of perception that receives the information gathered by the senses, and is what distinguishes humans from animals.[36] It was meant to be directed by what in Hinduism is believed to be a higher aspect of the mind, buddhi,[37] which is usually translated as intellect, intelligence, or reason,[38] and seems to correspond to nous. I don't quite see a higher, spiritual aspect of the mind directing the human mind however, as from what I've seen, we have consciousness which uses a single human mind, merged with an animal mind, while animals have a single, more limited mind. The extra mental capacity we have over animals gives us the ability to separate ourselves from our animalistic nature, to self-reflect, and it allows consciousness and its spiritual qualities to function. It may be that nous and buddhi actually refer to consciousness as that spiritual part of us that can direct our mind.

PERSONALITY

As we develop, particularly in the first few years of childhood, we create characteristics in response to our environment, and these coagulate into a fifth-dimensional form that I call the personality. It becomes our means of expression, and is formed by the age of seven. It's with us for just one lifetime. It separates sometime after death, after which it's discarded, and looks like the deceased person. It can sometimes be seen or sensed by the living, which is when it's often called a ghost. It's likely to have been what the ancient Egyptians called the Ka,[39] what is known as the "pranic sheath" in Hinduism,[40] and what's known as the "la" or "energy body" in Tibetan Buddhism.[41]

Painting called *Apparition*, depicting a ghost.

CONSCIOUSNESS/THE SOUL

As a modern term, consciousness is often used to refer to the cognizance and awareness of the mind or brain, but I use it in the more spiritual sense to refer to one's spiritual essence—as that eternal, core part of us. It's that which experiences, is what's "awake," and contains our spiritual qualities, such as love.

In ancient texts it was often referred to as the soul, psyche, or spirit. In Gnostic texts it was given the name Sophia, and is compared to a drop of light that comes from the Source,[42] while in Hindu texts it's compared to a spark of light that comes from the Source,[43] and is called *chit*,[44] but was also known as the individual soul or jiva.[45] Hindu texts say that we possess a higher, spiritual intelligence that is meant to govern our mind, called *dhi*[46] and buddhi, which may also correspond to consciousness, but could have referred to the Being. In ancient Egypt, it was most likely the immortal part of the person they called the Ba. Consciousness is the small part of a greater spiritual Being that resides in the heavenly regions, and it can be rejoined with that Being on the path to the Spiritual Father.

Christian painting of a soul being carried to heaven.

EGOS

In modern psychoanalytic theory, the term ego is used to describe one's sense of self. However, I use the term very differently to refer to a specific kind of nonphysical entity that exists in great numbers within our psyche. This idea that we have many selves was taught by G.I. Gurdjieff, who claimed to have derived his knowledge from ancient sources. It was later expanded upon by his student Maurice Nicoll, who sometimes used the term egos to describe them.

There were lots of different names given to the egos in ancient Egyptian, Gnostic, Christian, Hermetic, Hindu, Taoist, and Buddhist texts, including tormentors, robbers, desires, passions, bodily demons, kleshas, poisons, afflictions, and sins. Asking the divine for their removal was one of the most common and important spiritual practices in the ancient Religion of the Sun, as they were seen as the primary obstacles to liberation/salvation.[47]

The Hindu goddess Kali symbolizes the Spiritual Mother who eliminates the egos. She is shown with the heads of the egos (as the many heads of the demon Raktabīja) she has eliminated strung around her neck, and holding one in her hand.

They are separate fifth-dimensional entities that have been created as part of the process of evolution, in which they were necessary for survival in the animalistic realm of nature. Each of us has created our own egos in past lives. We carry them as part of our psyche from life to life, and can strengthen and create new ones. Having a more complex mind as a human, people have created egos that are in many cases more twisted and perverse than those in animals. They are created and sustained from our own psychic energy.

They enter our psyche one at a time where they affect our feelings and thoughts. Examples of emotions aggravated by egos include pride, greed, fear, laziness, and anger. The egos are not part of the mind, they are separate from the mind itself.

They first enter us one at a time over some years as our personality develops when we're children. We can't see them directly here as they work beneath our conscious awareness, but we experience their repercussions as they go into our emotions, movements, instincts, and sexual feelings, and affect our thoughts.

The egos are strange things which profoundly affect our inner states, and yet they are quite invisible unless we are in a conscious OBE, or remember something about them from our dreams. In the astral they can appear as entities separate to us, in which case we may see something like a person or a creature doing an action of the inner state, such as being aggressive or stealing, or we can be aware of something incorporating into a person or creature as though they are possessed, or quite commonly, the egos may appear symbolically as animals. In the higher astral plane, which is much rarer to visit, we can clearly see the egos separately from ourselves and can discover a lot about how they work.

Sometimes, if we're conscious in the state between wakefulness and sleep, even just for a couple of moments (which can happen especially if we're trying to consciously project), it's possible to hear them as we enter the fifth dimension. The noise the egos make can consist of moans, screams, shouts, babble, and so on, which are heard as though they are real physical voices.

The egos exist within our subconscious in the fifth dimension, which is located within the earth in hell. They are necessary for us to acquire self-knowledge and can be eliminated from our psyche with divine help.

I say much more about the multidimensional nature of our psychology in my book on self-knowledge.

CHAPTER NINE

Near-Death Experiences

Near-death experiences are experiences outside the body in the fifth dimension and possibly beyond. In chapter 6, I presented some of the evidence that supports this, as well as for the existence of an afterlife, and for consciousness existing independently of the body. I'll give a more personal view in this chapter with an emphasis on their spiritual nature.

In an NDE, a person's body dies and their mind and consciousness continue to exist outside it. Strictly speaking, it takes place when the body is actually dead, and that usually means the brain is dead; in practice though, in many cases they do occur before actual physical death, often in the preceding unconsciousness.

These kinds of experiences differ to out-of-body experiences in some ways, notably in that there is usually no two-way body to consciousness process taking place anymore, meaning that consciousness is no longer sending information to the physical body, and vice versa, the brain is no longer affecting consciousness. This must account for the greater objectivity in NDEs generally in comparison to OBEs, which can be very subjective at times.

In an NDE, life in the physical world has (temporarily) ended, and the NDE is part of a wider process of death and moving on, whereas OBEs tend to contain more specific teachings related to a life that's in a continuing process of learning.

In an NDE, the deceased is beginning a journey that takes them to a future existence, determined by what they have done in life. They initially come out of their bodies into the astral plane, which normally appears just like the physical world.

NDEs are quite common; they exist in all cultures and happen to people of all ages. There are even accounts given from children as young as three. I've had one myself and it surprised me how easy it was to die.

Painting *Ascent of the Blessed* by Hieronymus Bosch, circa 1500-1504, showing the deceased going through the portal to heaven as the tunnel into the light—a common feature in modern NDEs. It reveals people must have had the same experience hundreds of years ago.

EXPERIENCES IN NDES

The term near-death experience is said to have been coined by the psychiatrist Dr. Raymond Moody in 1975. Although, I think "after-death experience" could be a more accurate term since people's bodies really die in them and so they are not "near-death" but actually dead, while a person's consciousness/soul never really dies and can never be near death. It's for this reason that Dr. Sam Parnia, one of the leading researchers of NDEs in the world, thinks they are better called "actual death experiences."[1] "Temporary death experience" is yet another option.

We can get a lot from watching or reading people's accounts of their NDEs. One of the things I find is that every person's NDE is unique, although there are strikingly similar elements in them. In his book *Life After Life*, Dr. Moody identified eleven elements common to most NDEs: separation from the physical body, declarations of death, a sense of the indescribable, an overwhelming sense of peace, a buzzing or ringing noise, moving through a dark void or tunnel, meeting others, an encounter with a being of light, a life review, an approach to a border or limit, and a return to the physical body.[2] While other researchers have arrived at different results, and some have not found a particular order to the experiences,[3] Moody's list still contains some commonly repeating elements found in most NDE studies.

The tunnel or corridor that many see is a passageway from the astral plane to a different realm or dimension; there is one that goes into a higher, heavenly region, and the other is the corridor that the deceased go down on their way to hell and devolution.

Many who remember going through a review of their lives say it gave them a greater understanding of how their actions affect others. Some were also aware of a decision being made to return to their lives. In a significant number of cases however, the experience is an unpleasant one, even hellish.

Most of the experiences are clearly personalized for the individual. This is most apparent when there are direct contradictions between people's experiences. For example, some are told hell doesn't exist, whereas for others their NDE is of being in hell. The host of the *Next Level Soul Podcast*, Alex Ferrari, has come to a similar conclusion after interviewing lots of people who've had NDEs on his show, saying, "from my experience of talking to so many near-death experiencers [is] that each one is tailored for the person, and at the stage of where they are."[4]

Some of those who die are shown things in their experience by spiritual beings using the forms of their religion and culture, probably as these are what the person will most readily comprehend, and some religious forms do contain truths. There is a tendency to see spiritual beings in NDEs in the way a person expects they will look.

Most commonly in the West people see Jesus. Dr. Janice Holden, who is current president of the International Association for Near-Death Studies (IANDS), has studied NDEs for over thirty years. She found that after comparing descriptions of Jesus from different NDEs, no two were identical, as for example, he could have a different eye color and voice. She also noted two accounts in which the deceased had been greeted by a spiritual entity who told them they were about to meet Jesus and were asked how they would like him to appear, as the entity told them that Jesus is happy to appear in whatever way is easiest for them to perceive. This raises the question of whether people are really seeing Jesus—another possibility is that they're seeing a spiritual being or their own Being taking the form of Jesus.

Holden says that people also interpret what they see differently. For example, many are greeted by a being of light; she says some identified it as God, while others say they don't know what it was and simply call it "the light" or "a being of light." This, she says, indicates that "it is very much the possibility that we influence how things appear in NDEs based on what we are prepared to perceive."[5]

Much of what people are given in NDEs is, I believe, due not to their ability to intellectually comprehend religious ideas, as the abilities of the mind can be hugely expanded in an NDE, but to comprehend in a deeper, more profound sense. This comprehension is a result of their spiritual development, which is how developed their consciousness/soul is.

OBEs and NDEs have long contributed to religious beliefs, as some were incorporated into religious teachings. On one hand, people's religious beliefs have often been confirmed by having an OBE or an NDE, but on the other, these experiences can also change beliefs and make people look for answers outside their formerly-held belief whether it was religious or atheistic.

If the experiencer is an atheist, they can have an experience that results in them adopting a religion, or if they have enough religious freedom where they live, they can be shown things that cause them to convert to a different religion. Many have converted to Christianity after their NDE, as Christianity contains the teachings of Jesus, a real being at an advanced level of spiritual development, who taught profound and important truths. As limited and as flawed as the religion that developed around Jesus' message is, it still contains some of his actual teaching—enough to provide most people with a more moral and spiritual way to live that is easily understood and followed. And so spiritual beings can direct people to it who are at a certain level of spiritual understanding and that they see will benefit from it.

Drawing from 1912 that depicts Jesus appearing to a man who has just died.

However, not all NDEs are Christian. Many people have NDEs where they are shown truths without the use of any specific religious or cultural forms, which some might call "New Age," while some are shown forms from a number of different religions. One example is the NDE of Robin Landsong, who was raised in an irreligious and abusive household in the United States, and then smuggled to Zimbabwe at the age of eight, where she was abandoned in a remote village in 1977 during the Rhodesian Bush War. She had two NDEs within days of each other. In the first, she was greeted and taught by someone she only later realized was Jesus. In the second, she found herself in the presence of another being who taught her, and only later recognized was Shiva. And yet she says, "I wasn't raised Christian and I certainly wasn't exposed to anything Hindu."[6] I've also seen the NDE account of a Christian woman who saw things from ancient Greek religion in her experience. The psychiatrist Carl Jung saw things from both Hinduism and ancient Greece in his NDE.[7]

It can be easy to draw absolute conclusions from any one near-death or out-of-body experience. For example, someone may have an NDE in which they are shown that truth is what matters, not a particular religion, while someone who is saved by Jesus in their NDE can conclude that Christianity is the only way. If you look at these experiences with the understanding that each person's NDE is given according to what that individual needs to understand and put into practice in their lives, then I think they can be seen in a broader context.

Personally, I like to study the actual content of NDEs themselves, as I find that people can interpret their NDE based on their existing beliefs, or those they later develop, without realizing it. These interpretations can be quite subjective and limited to their understanding of spirituality, and to their experience of other dimensions, which is usually based on just one NDE, rather than decades of exploring the psyche and fifth dimension through regular OBEs, remembering dreams, and repeated contact with and teachings from spiritual beings in them.

Today we find ourselves in a unique situation. Advances in medical science are enabling more people to be brought back from death, and have therefore increased the number of NDEs. At the same time, advances in technology have allowed people to share their NDEs directly with a global audience using platforms like YouTube. We can now watch and read hundreds (if not thousands) of personal NDE accounts of people from different countries, cultures, and walks of life. What I think these NDEs provide us with are real accounts of the afterlife, and these accounts often contradict the long-held doctrines of many religions. I think this provides humanity with a special opportunity to see what religious beliefs hold up in the face of what people are consistently experiencing after death.

It's common for people to have difficulty explaining their experience to others, and a high proportion return from the experience with a belief in a loving creator/Source/God, supernatural beings, the importance of becoming more loving, reincarnation, heaven, and hell. From the NDEs I've looked at, those who've had hellish NDEs almost always return with a sense of urgency about using their lives wisely and wanting to be close to divinity, even if they were atheists before it happened.

OBES AS A WAY TO LEARN ABOUT THE AFTERLIFE

Studying people's near-death experiences can bring us a great deal of understanding of what they are and why they happen, but it's possible to understand more by seeing things related to death during OBEs. These kinds of experiences are usually given by spiritual beings to help us understand things that are important to us. In OBEs, I've seen things about death I had no prior knowledge of, like a tunnel, the toll collectors, ghosts of the deceased, hell, and heavens. After the experiences I would sometimes find similar accounts in ancient sacred texts.

In OBEs it's possible to see ghosts, as we're in the dimension they exist. Here we might get some manifestations such as fleeting shadows, eerie feelings, and the like—but there you can see exactly what's causing it. Ghosts are discarded mental forms, personalities that are unable to comprehend anything new—they are trapped in the past. As an example, many years ago I'd heard that an old school friend of mine had died in a motorbike accident; he had been dead for three days. That night I saw him while out of my body. I went closer to him but stopped, as I was surprised to see an atmosphere of violence surrounding him. You can feel these kinds of energies as a substance over there—it irradiated from him and became the element in which he existed. He turned toward me and I could see the violence in him, so I left his ghost to his world.

When back in my body I wondered about that atmosphere surrounding him, as I had not thought of him as a violent person, but looking back I began to see it. Thinking about how he became a biker after leaving school, I realized he'd lived with strong, violent emotions, and this was his overriding psychological trait, which is why his ghost lived in that element after his death. I could have found out more about his character if I had observed his ghost longer or asked it questions, but I felt in that case I'd seen enough.

Japanese illustration of a ghost
by Utagawa Toyokuni I, 1812.

I realize that an account like this doesn't prove the existence of life after death to anyone else—most experiences out of the body don't—but it's typical of what someone may find when they encounter the figure of a deceased person, although the experience would of course vary according to the deceased, their personality, and their situation. It's less common to see the actual person who has died though, as it seems they are quickly moved on either to heaven or hell, and so it's more common to just see their ghost in the fifth dimension.

In an OBE, spiritual beings may teach us what we need, but not necessarily what we think we want to be taught. We can't expect to be given a guided tour of the process of death. It's more likely that over time, through a series of lucid dreams and OBEs, someone will have experiences from which they'll be able to piece together a few parts of the afterlife. But then again you never know, they may be taught a lot in a single OBE.

They would have to be prepared to learn uncomfortable things too, particularly as some people enter hell, as many who've had NDEs will testify.[8][9] Experiencing hell in an OBE is mostly the result of intervention by one's own higher Being who takes us there safely.

CHAPTER TEN

Looking at the Evidence Presented by Materialist Science That OBEs Aren't Real

If you've done any searching on the Internet for information about OBEs, you've probably come across news articles that claim it's now proven that OBEs aren't real—and that they're merely illusions generated by the brain. I'm going to address this claim here, and look at the main evidence used to support it.

I'm not a scientist, but I do have lots of experience of having OBEs (and have had an NDE). I feel it's important to address claims like these, as they can be used to demean those of us who use OBEs for spiritual purposes, and instill the idea that the debate on whether OBEs are real or not is over.

I may not have summarized the studies as well as they could be, but you can find them all in the references if you'd like to get a better understanding of them yourself. Although I often disagree with the conclusions, I still value the work of their authors, whose studies have helped many people and even saved lives. I'm only giving my views on what the results of these studies show for our understanding of OBEs.

I'll firstly cover a few short topics put forward as showing OBEs are unreal—namely the failure of accurately reading numbers and words while out of the body in experiments, the common phenomenon of seeing tunnels, and parallels between psychedelic experiences and OBEs. I'll then look at the main scientific argument presented as proving OBEs are illusory and some of the studies used to support it.

DEFINING OBES

To begin with, I think it's important to define what an OBE is, to ensure we're working from something neutral and objective, as the belief they are illusory can be there from the outset by being written into the definition.

I would define an OBE as "a person perceives they are out of their body," as I feel it leaves us open to question whether someone's perceptions are real or not, whatever they believe about them.

The prevailing materialist view favors the definition "a person seems to see the world from a location outside their body," which already implies OBEs are unreal because of the word "seems." Apply it to another activity in life and you'll see what I mean—you "seemed" to have breakfast, for example. I think if it's uncertain as to whether you really had breakfast, it's better to say, "you perceived having breakfast," and then to question whether what you perceived was a real event or not.

The difficulty with using a single definition for OBEs is that there appear to be different types of OBEs—or at least those that happen under very different circumstances.

There are those OBEs I consider real, and there are those that may be due to sensory illusions, and those definitely due to sensory illusion as with the case of virtual reality. In the case of real OBEs, I argue that someone's consciousness is really outside their physical body. In those due to sensory illusions, someone's consciousness remains within their body, but they have the sense of being out of their body. Materialist science puts these in the same category, and by doing so, I think conflates illusory OBEs with real ones. Yet there is no reason why both can't exist.

To give you an idea of just how different the circumstances under which OBEs can happen are, there was a questionnaire conducted on 339 people who said they'd had an OBE.[1] The circumstances of their OBE ranged from things like while on some kind of drug (anything from pharmaceuticals, to vitamins, to psychedelics), driving, in an accident, in extreme pain, under anesthesia, emotionally stressed, extremely fatigued, running a high fever, and having a heart attack, etc. These are cases in which they can happen involuntarily, and there are many others, such as while falling asleep, during sleep (dreams are a form of OBE), during episodes of sleep paralysis, from death or bodily trauma, during seizures, due to brain damage or disorder, during intense anxiety and/or abuse, and from psychological disorders. There are also those that occur voluntarily from taking psychedelics and using virtual reality.

Interestingly, the top four conditions under which the overwhelming majority of people in that questionnaire had an OBE were while "feeling physically relaxed" (78% of people), "feeling mentally calm" (77%), while "dreaming" (35%), and during "meditation" (26%) (note that people could select all answers that applied). Thus, there seemed to be two broad categories that emerged—those who'd had their OBE while in a relaxed state, and those who'd had it during a time of psychological and/or physical stress. It's likely they were due to different mechanisms being triggered in the body and brain.

In my own work on OBEs, the type I advocate for are those had intentionally through using spiritual techniques (in a relaxed state and free of substances), which includes both willed projection and lucid dreaming.

Again, from the questionnaire above, 93 percent felt their OBE was more real than a dream, 83 percent felt positive emotions during it (specifically peacefulness), 78 percent became interested in psychic phenomena after it, and 84 percent wanted to do it again! To believe this is all due to some kind of disorder seems counterintuitive at the least.

Those who've had NDEs commonly recall that being out of the physical body feels like their innate state—some felt or were told that when they were out of the body (in a heavenly place), they were "home." I also argue that not only do we come into this life from nonphysical dimensions and return to them at death, but spend a large part of our lives out of the body, as we leave our bodies while we sleep and dream. It's no wonder then that there are so many reasons why people can have OBEs, and that they happen so often, given that being out-of-body is consciousness's default condition.

I think it's important to take this perspective into account as we look at what materialist science says about OBEs.

EXPERIMENTS ON READING WHILE OUT OF THE BODY

It's often said that if someone could project out of the body to a location where numbers and words had been placed beforehand in the physical world, and could read and then accurately recall them upon returning, it could prove OBEs are real. But so far most experiments like this, as far as I've heard scientists say generally, have failed.

One successful study was done by the professor of psychology Dr. Charles Tart on a woman who'd claimed she'd been able to have OBEs since childhood. She was hooked up to an EEG machine while she slept each night and attempted to leave her body and accurately see a five-digit number that had been placed in the room beyond her physical sight. She made a few unsuccessful attempts, as although she said she could leave her body, she found it difficult to navigate to the number to be able to read it clearly, but during the fourth night, after a period of anomalous EEG activity, she woke and called out the five-digit number accurately: 25132. The chance of guessing it was 1 in 100,000.[2] Critics have stated that the woman could have stealthily brought in a mirror and flashlight to look at the number while Tart wasn't observing her as she was sleeping;[3] although Tart couldn't disprove this, he had no reason to suspect she had, and said it wasn't possible for her to get up to the shelf to look at the number while hooked up to the EEG.[4]

Tart conducted similar experiments with the famous OBE'er Robert Monroe, but although Monroe said he was able to have a few OBEs during the experiments, he'd been unable to successfully navigate to the number while out of the body, nor see anything else that could be verified physically.[5]

Tom Campbell, who cofounded the Monroe Institute together with Robert Monroe, said they found it much more difficult to accurately see numbers and letters that were in the physical world while out of the body than they did images.[6] I also read about the personal experiments of someone who claims to have had a lot of OBEs. He said he could see places and objects that he later verified in the physical world, but could never correctly read the random playing card he'd pulled from a deck and placed face up on a shelf out of sight, or other words or numbers, such as house numbers, as they often became blurred.[7]

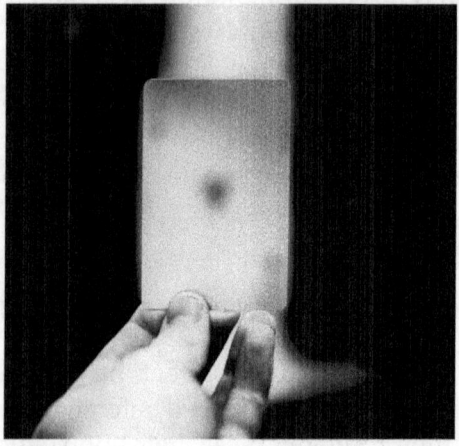

Reading words and numbers while out of the body can be difficult as they often appear jumbled or blurred.

I think the reason for the failure of many of these kinds of experiments (though clearly not all) is not to do with the reality of OBEs themselves, but more so with the difficulty of firstly having OBEs, then navigating to a specific location while remaining conscious and unhindered by subconscious imagery, and then reading something. Myself and others I know have sometimes been able to read text clearly while in an OBE (I've also successfully remote viewed numbers, which is an experience had while conscious in the physical world). But there've been other times in OBEs in which I've found it difficult to read or view numbers and hard to read words, as they've jumbled up and I couldn't see them properly.

I'd say the reason for this is that in the fifth dimension matter is more fluid and malleable (which is why we can move through solid objects, travel under water and fly, etc.), and what we experience there is also far more affected by our minds, which can project visuals onto it and distort what we see. The difficulty we can have in reading in the fifth dimension may indicate just how active our minds are in interpreting words and numbers generally.

I've had success with seeing objects while out of the body accurately, maybe because our mind is less engaged in what we see than read, so I'd say that's what future experiments would be better focused on. There are already many other things that show OBEs are real though, which I outlined in chapter 6.

SEEING TUNNELS

Tunnels are sometimes seen in OBEs, when falling asleep, and most impressively in NDEs, where they're often part of an elaborate experience in which people go through many things before and after traveling through one.

Some materialists have latched onto tunnel experiences as indicating OBEs are illusions created by the brain, as the brain can create tunnel-like visuals under certain circumstances. The theory goes like this: shock or psychedelics can induce inhibition in the neurons of the brain's cerebral cortex, and this produces circles on the cortex, which creates visual lattices, spirals, cobwebs, and the illusion of going down a tunnel. These visuals are referred to as form constants.[8] I've seen them when I was gassed at the dentist; speaking to people, I've found it's fairly common for them to have seen these form constants at some time in their lives.

Heinrich Klüver's form constants: tunnels, spirals, honeycombs/gratings, and cobwebs.

It seems clear the brain creates these patterns and that they can overlay what we see to create a false reality, and this theory seems like it could explain at least some of the vortex and tunnel-like visuals seen during psychedelic trips. It's possible it may also explain some OBE tunnel experiences, though I'd say usually only in certain circumstances where things like substances, trauma, or extreme tiredness are involved, but I don't think it can account for all tunnels.

Tunnels are commonly seen in NDEs where the person and their brain are usually dead, with no measurable brain activity. No brain activity means no active neurons, and no active neurons means no form constants. Form constants therefore cannot create NDEs, nor do they explain the very clear, coherent, and meaningful experiences people have while out of the body before, after, and often while going through a tunnel.

I've traveled through a tunnel in an OBE—it was the portal to hell described in numerous ancient sources, and I explain the experience in chapter 26. It was a slit in space that led to a long dark corridor that I and other people walked along, leading down into hell. It looked similar to a tunnel you might see in the physical world and nothing like a form constant. It was just one part of a detailed experience where it was relevant to the context, just as tunnels often are in NDEs, and was not just a random visual.

We know that not all tunnels are form constants, and neither are all cobwebs or honeycombs. These things really do exist in the physical world, and there's no reason to discount their existence in other dimensions too. Just because some tunnels are form constants, doesn't mean they all are. Remember the last time you drove through a tunnel—ask yourself, did it really happen, or was it one of Klüver's form constants?

COMPARISONS TO PSYCHEDELICS

The perceptions people can have of being out-of-body while on psychedelics are sometimes offered as evidence that OBEs are hallucinations. As materialist scientists generally assume what's experienced on psychedelics is a hallucination, it's inferred that the sense of being out of the body would be an illusion too.

Yet just because what's experienced on psychedelics can be illusory, perhaps including the sense of being out-of-body, doesn't mean that all OBEs are therefore illusory, as most are experienced without being under the influence of psychedelics or any other consciousness-altering substance. This would be a bit like saying that because some people see illusory spiders when taking psychedelics, all spiders are hallucinations even when not taking psychedelics.

As I'll explain in chapter 28, as part of my Psychedelic Brain Barrier Theory, I think there's a process that's activated in some psychedelic experiences which forces people's perception open to experiencing something of the fifth dimension while awake, which can include experiences of consciousness beyond the body, but which is heavily overlaid by projections from the mind and possibly affected by visual illusions caused by the brain's response to certain chemicals. Although in some ways related, I discuss how psychedelic experiences are not the same as intentional, substance-free OBEs.

THE CENTRAL SCIENTIFIC EXPLANATION FOR WHAT OBES ARE

There is now a central argument made by materialist science to explain what OBEs are, which is based on a number of studies I'll go through shortly.

The argument is that there is a part of our brain (called the temporoparietal junction or TPJ) which is believed to be where our sense of who and where we are is constructed, and when this is disturbed, we can have an OBE. The TPJ is where information that's collected about the outside environment is integrated along with information gathered from within the body.[9] It's constantly processing information about our body posture and its position in relation to the environment. It's argued that when the TPJ is disturbed, it causes a failure or disruption in that process, leading us to experience distortions in our body position and sense of location, meaning we can then feel as though we are out of our bodies, i.e. are having an OBE. The psychologist Susan Blackmore summarizes it by saying:

> "The TPJ is deeply involved in our sense of embodiment – the feeling that 'I' live inside my body and control it. Other brain areas close to the junction of the parietal and temporal lobes are ideally placed to bring together sensory information, emotions and memory to construct a body-schema and body-image (Decety & Lamm 2007).
>
> [...] body schema refers to the continuously updated model of your body with its posture, actions, and position in space. This body schema is combined, at the TPJ, not only with hearing, sight, taste, and smell, but with the vestibular system that keeps our balance, and with thoughts, imagination and memories that are sustained in other parts of the temporal and parietal lobes, and with intentions and control functions handled in the frontal lobes to create a rich sense of self that goes beyond just the body.
>
> If the TPJ is disturbed, some of the functions needed to create an accurate body schema fail [...] and the result is an OBE."[10]
> ~ SUSAN BLACKMORE

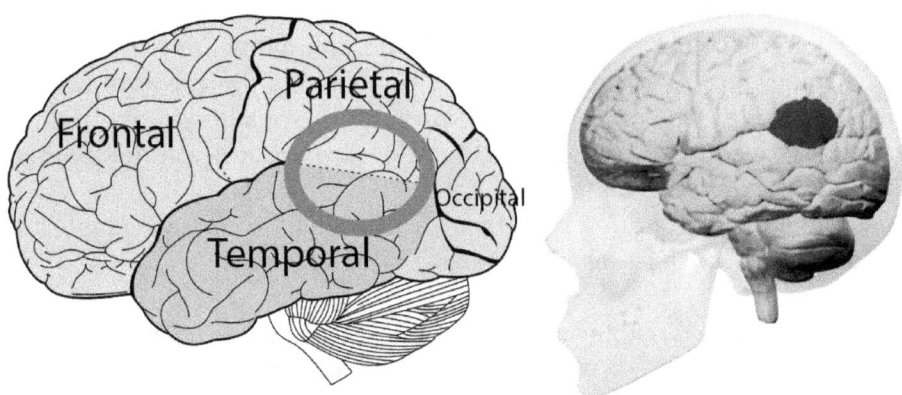

The location of the TPJ in the brain, circled (on the left) and marked (on the right). It's found on both sides of the brain in the same spot.

From what I understand, the studies that have led to this argument have either disturbed or studied disturbances to the TPJ in some way. Some have disturbed the TPJ through electrical stimulation and have induced OBEs. In others they have studied people whose TPJ is already disturbed (as in the case of brain damage and seizures) and who've had OBEs sometimes as a direct result. In others, those who had OBEs were studied for indicators of disturbed body schema and correlations were found. And in others studies they have disturbed people's sense of body schema using virtual reality to produce sensations of being out-of-body. I'll look at each of these types of studies in more detail in a following section.

ANOTHER EXPLANATION – THE BRAIN LIMITER THEORY

But what if this argument was turned on its head—so that rather than the brain being the constructor of consciousness in the body, it is a limiter of consciousness to it? What the studies on the TPJ could then show is that this part of the brain is responsible for continuously limiting the perceptions of consciousness to a perspective from within one's physical body, causing someone to identify themselves with it. Then, when the TPJ is disturbed, some of those limitations may be interrupted, causing us to experience a state where consciousness is not limited to the body.

There are those who've described this in many of the NDE testimonies I've seen. Having been without a functioning brain, and then being revived and having their brain work again, they have a unique perspective of experiencing the brain from different ends. They've often said how they could perceive much more while out of their bodies—they could see colors we don't have here, had 360-degree vision, could experience things from the perspective of multiple people at the same time, could experience or see different events occurring in separate locations simultaneously, could understand far more than they could here, communicate telepathically, sense things, etc. On returning to their bodies, their impression was that the brain serves to limit the perception of consciousness, rather than as materialist science sees it, which is the other way around, as the very thing that creates consciousness.

Consider this description by a man who died on the operating table and had an NDE in which he felt himself leave and return to his body:

> "[...] our brain is nothing but a biological, I call it a spirit trap because our brain is wired to allow us to perceive what I call this illusion we live in [...] with our five senses and it's only as good as our senses. When you come out of this body, there's so many more senses that we have; it's not just these five senses. There's frequencies and everything's vibrating; everything in the universe vibrates, everything. Even though it looks solid in this life, it could be liquid in another dimension which is vibrating at just a slightly different frequency for example. [...] our five senses perceive what our brain is programmed to perceive. [...] But once you come out [...] you have so many more

> senses. For example, there's colors I saw we don't even have here, so how can I tell you what color it is and it's nothing like the colors we have here in our spectrum."[11]
>
> ~ MARK HODGES

In this scenario, the brain's function is to limit the perception of consciousness to specific frequencies, which only a certain band of energy and color resonates within. This is an incredibly important task if you think about the level of accuracy in body schema needed to chop food with a sharp knife, or drive a car. Our brain is what allows consciousness to operate and keep its body alive in the physical world.

This would mean that the brain, and possibly the TPJ particularly, does have a role in constructing our sense of self in relation to our body and environment—its role seems to be to constrain consciousness to its particular physical body, constantly causing it to identify with it by forcing it to perceive from the perspective of it spatially through its limited five senses. I call this theory my Brain Limiter Theory.

Soon after coming to this conclusion, I found that Dr. Bruce Greyson—Professor Emeritus of Psychiatry and Neurobehavioral Sciences at the University of Virginia and cofounder of the International Association for Near-Death Studies (IANDS)—had come to one very similar. In his book *After* he describes how NDEs indicate that the mind is independent of the brain, and that rather than the brain being the producer of the mind, the brain instead acts as a filtering mechanism for the mind.

Greyson calls this the Transmission or Filter Theory, and says that variations of it have existed for more than two thousand years going all the way back to Hippocrates.[12]

He explains his variation of it, saying "the brain works like a filter to block out information the body doesn't need for survival, and selects from the thoughts and memories stored in the mind only the information that the body needs."[13]

I would say that it works differently to this though. Rather than selecting thoughts, I think the brain limits our perception, causing us to generate thoughts based around whatever we perceive. If we could perceive more, we would naturally think differently.

He explains further by saying that "the mind 'out there' has this incredible array of consciousness, and it's too much for us, it would overpower us to be able to perceive all these things, so the brain evolved to filter out all the quote 'irrelevant stuff' and just let in a small fraction of our consciousness that'll help us survive in the physical world."[14]

However, I don't think this is the fundamental reason why the brain limits consciousness. The only reason that information from "out there" (other dimensions) would overwhelm us is because our brain can only process a limited amount of information at any one time.

Many of those who've had NDEs say that they comprehended or perceived things in their experience in ways that were far more profound than they could have done while in life. Their mind and consciousness did not have any trouble processing or understanding what they perceived during their NDE. It's only once they returned to the body and had a physical brain again that they often found they were unable to process and access that information again. This shows how the brain is limiting consciousness and the psyche while we're in the physical world. It would explain why those who've had NDEs sometimes say they received huge amounts of information during it and felt like they knew everything in their experience, but are unable to remember specifics upon reviving.

Greyson makes the same point, and narrates someone's NDE as an example:

> "She told me that once she woke up back in her physical body, she could no longer understand things that were obvious during her NDE [...]. [She said] '[...] as long as I am on earth, I will never be able to comprehend it [...] because I only have a human brain. Here we can really think about only one thing at a time, and there you know—really know—everything. You can't compare it to earth things. [...] I'll never be able to feel what I felt there, while I'm here, because I'm back in this human body again. It is way beyond, superior, bigger than anything a human brain can comprehend, and more wonderful, too.'"[15]

There were people in the past whose brains were larger. For example, Cro-Magnons, who lived in Europe twenty to thirty thousand years ago, are said to have had the biggest brain of any human species. Today our brains are about 10 percent smaller than those of Cro-Magnons (though could be as much as 20 percent[16]), which is smaller by about the size of a tennis ball (or two). Our brains have been shrinking ever since that time and continue on a downward trajectory.[17]

It's possible that people with larger brains had areas of it that were more able to receive and process spiritual/nonphysical information—meaning their brains were less limited. Theoretically, our brains could be like this too, with areas suited to receiving and processing extra information of a spiritual nature. This would allow us to better comprehend overall reality and our relationship to it, enabling us to live better and more meaningful lives. In many cases, this could improve our ability to survive in the physical world, for example, by not becoming so self-destructive, intuitively being able to sense danger, being happier and healthier, etc.

However, there is a limit to how many spiritual perceptions the brain can let in, and how little it confines our consciousness spatially to our bodies, before we would cease to identify with our physical bodies enough to have the will to participate and survive here. I don't think the brain needs to filter out everything irrelevant to physical survival, just enough, and this is the reason why the brain acts as a limiter, rather than to prevent us from being overwhelmed by other-dimensional information.

Yet the scales can tip in the other direction too, so that the brain limits the perceptions of our consciousness to such a degree that we become engrossed in the material world as if that's all that exists, and this starts to run counter to the purpose of life even to the point where we can become completely destructive toward it. I think the human brain is too limited and animalistic, and this has had a negative impact on our ability to perceive and understand more of reality, causing us to identify with the material world so much that we have largely lost the ability to fulfill the spiritual purpose of human life.

Often when people think of spiritual perceptions, they think of psychic abilities, like seeing beings from other dimensions, or having premonitions of the future, however, there's so much more to it than this. It includes being able to feel for other beings, i.e. empathy, to sense one's connection to other beings, i.e. love, and being able to perceive the life and divinity in nature, and these are the kinds of perceptions that make up so much of NDEs. When the brain is so limiting as to cause these senses to diminish to a point where they are hardly there, human life becomes very brutal—often even more so than in animals. When these severely diminished senses are combined with a high intellect and/or oppressive ideology, you have a recipe for disaster.

With an understanding of the brain as a limiter, we can begin to understand the mechanism behind altered states of consciousness. For instance, during practices like meditation and concentration, people often experience things like a sense of expansiveness, timelessness, a feeling of oneness with all life, divine love, inner peace, perceptions of spiritual dimensions, sensing nonphysical presences—all feelings, if you notice, that are frequent features of NDEs in which the brain is often dead. What practices of meditation and concentration do is to quiet and still the mind. A still mind equals a still brain. Although our brain never totally shuts off while alive, its activity can be reduced, getting us closer to an inactive brain as in NDEs. By reducing brain activity, we reduce the influence it has on consciousness, thus allowing consciousness to escape its grip and experience something of its true nature.

How remarkable that many ancient peoples understood this in some way by developing methods of spiritual practice that control, direct, and overcome the brain.

As you'll read in subsequent chapters, ancient practices for having OBEs usually involved two important ingredients: quieting the mind using concentration, and using visualizations and affirmations to overcome the identification with one's physical body. These are precisely some of the things needed to overcome our brain's limitations. They still the brain's activity, which is constantly confining us to our body. And they help us to separate ourselves from our brain's program. Combined with sleep, they allow consciousness to consciously separate from the physical body (temporarily).

Divine intervention was yet another factor in ancient OBEs, as spiritual beings are likely to have a way to affect the brain by temporarily turning it down, thus allowing people to perceive beyond their five senses—as in visions, shared-death experiences, premonitions, etc.

It's possible the compounds in psychedelics disturb the brain's functioning too (perhaps including or specifically that of the TPJ), but in far more incoherent ways, so that people partially experience consciousness beyond the bounds of the brain's limits. This means that the sense of limbs elongating, a distorted sense of body shape, and dissolution of body perception and self often experienced on psychedelic trips may be a kind of garbled busting out of consciousness from the brain box.

Those in a more intellectual state of mind are said to find it more difficult to have willed OBEs.[18] Both Lara and I have found that when we've been engaged in demanding intellectual work, it's been much harder to have OBEs and they happen far less spontaneously. There seems to be a thread here. There may be a connection to the mechanism of the TPJ or to some other part of the brain, as intellectual/mental activity may strengthen the brain's limiting mechanism either permanently (in people who have a more intellectual persona) or temporarily (when doing intellectual work), so that consciousness is more solidly locked into the physical body and material world.

Though I don't yet know how this would work, I thought it worth mentioning, especially for those interested in having intentional OBEs. Of course, I don't think this means people need to abandon intellectual activity if they want to have OBEs. Instead, I think it means there needs to be an understanding that there is a time and place for intellectual activity, and that if someone wants to have OBEs, they may need to work around it by factoring in breaks from it. For those who want to have OBEs and are more intellectually inclined, this may sound like an unfair disadvantage, but there may be disadvantages to having a less intellectual approach too. Ideally, we'd all be intuitive and perceptive, while at the same time objective and grounded in reality. But this all goes back to the limitations of the human brain; all of us can get around and even alter some of these by doing spiritual practices and gaining self-knowledge.

It's not just the brain that's limiting the perceptions of consciousness though. The dimension we're in also constrains it. Because dimensions consist of matter/energy at various levels of frequency, we can usually only perceive spiritual things according to the density of where we are. It's like looking at light through a cloth—the denser or heavier the weave, the less light we see. This density increases in hell and decreases in heaven toward the Source. This is why people who go to hell in NDEs, even though they are there as consciousness without the limitations of their physical brain (which is often dead), don't perceive in the expansive way those who go to heaven do. The density of hell prevents it, and they are in a different region with its own events and energetic environment, so what they perceive is different too. The astral plane is probably between heaven and hell in its density, and so the perceptions of consciousness there are not as constrained as they are in hell or in the physical world, but neither are they as unconstrained as in heaven. This is why dreams are fairly similar in terms of our level of perception to here, as the astral plane is likely closer to the frequency of the physical world than heaven or hell are.

For many, the studies of the connection between disturbances in the TPJ and resulting illusory OBEs seemed conclusive. However, I think the Brain Limiter Theory provides another reasonable explanation for the same evidence. There are probably many materialist scientists who'd say there is no proof for it, yet I don't think it can be disproven either. I would argue some of the points I listed in the chapter Evidence for Out-of-Body Experiences Being Real can be taken as evidence—particularly the NDEs of those blind from birth in which they could see (point 4), those NDEs had while braindead (point 5), and the cases where people with brain damage have become normal shortly before death (point 8). This means there are at least two theories that may explain the OBEs induced in the following studies (except those in the virtual reality study, as I'll explain).

CURRENT SCIENTIFIC STUDIES ON OBES

OBES INDUCED BY ELECTRICAL STIMULATION

During some medical procedures involving the brain, neurosurgeons have inadvertently induced what are described as OBEs in their patients when trying to treat them for medical conditions.

One that's often referred to as showing OBEs are not real is a groundbreaking study by neurosurgeon Olaf Blanke published in 2002.[19] He accidentally discovered that stimulating the part of a patient's brain called the TPJ (discussed in the previous section) induced an OBE. Initially the patient reported she was "sinking into the bed" or "falling from a height." Increasing the electric current led to her to say, "I see myself lying in bed, from above, but I only see my legs and lower trunk." Two further stimulations induced a feeling of "lightness" and "floating" about two meters above the bed, close to the ceiling. In further stimulations she reported alterations in the size and motion of her limbs, and when she closed her eyes, she felt her upper body moving toward her legs.

I don't see that there is enough information in the study to know whether this OBE was real or an illusion—I think the experience was incoherent as large parts of the patient's perception of their surroundings are missing, whereas in intentional OBEs the experience is generally much more complete and coherent. Looking at it through the lens of the Brain Limiter Theory, it's possible the electrical disturbances to the TPJ caused glitches in the brain's sensory limitations so that the patient's consciousness did experience some kind of incoherent blips of being out of the body.

To me, Blanke seems to draw two conclusions from his study. Firstly, he says, "These observations indicate that OBEs and complex somatosensory illusions can be artificially induced by electrical stimulation of the cortex." I agree—OBEs whether real and/or illusory may be able to be induced through the use of electricity.

Blanke then concludes his study by saying, "Although we do not fully understand the neurological mechanism that causes OBEs, our results imply that vestibular processing may be important." It's possible that vestibular processing (our sense of balance), or a disruption to it, may play some role in OBEs.

Unfortunately, some members of the public interpret Blanke's study as proof that OBEs aren't real, but in my view all it indicates is what Blanke himself concluded—that OBEs may be able to be induced by electrically stimulating a part of the brain, and vestibular processing may play an important role in them.

The stimulations did not induce anything close to the complex and often profound experiences people can have in OBEs (including those in NDEs), and so I don't think what this one patient experienced can be taken as being representative of all OBEs; from what I can tell, it was also not repeated in other patients in the study who were subjected to the same stimulation.

Some have used this study to infer that all OBEs are merely illusory alterations in bodily perceptions generated by the brain. But I don't think what the patient experienced is provably an illusion, and if it were, I don't think it can be inferred that because it was, all other OBEs are illusions too. I think the study only shows that this area of the brain is involved in experiencing a certain kind of OBE that may or may not be real. In my opinion, if what the patient experienced was real, it shows OBEs can be induced electrically; if it wasn't, it shows electrical stimulation can alter someone's perception of their body.

I don't think it proves OBEs are generated by the brain because people have reported having OBEs while totally dead during NDEs. For instance, if the TPJ was stimulated in a clinically braindead corpse, it would not affect the sense of being out of the body if that deceased person was having an NDE, as the TPJ is no longer working, meaning that the brain cannot be the generator of all OBEs.

Several years later in 2007 another patient had roughly the same area (right TPJ) electrically stimulated by neurosurgeon Dirk De Ridder. "An out-of-body experience was repeatedly elicited during stimulation," he says in his study and that, "[the patient's] perception of disembodiment always involved a location about fifty centimeters behind his body and off to the left. There was no autoscopy and no voluntary control of movements of the disembodied perception. The environment was visually perceived from his real-person perspective, not from the disembodied perspective." The patient's sense of being just fifty centimeters away from but still seeing from his real location is not what I would call a real OBE, as in an actual OBE we as a whole—with our movements, perception, and sense of location—leave our bodies. I think this study mostly shows that the part of the brain that was stimulated is involved in the body-environment relationship.[20]

OBES IN RELATION TO BRAIN DAMAGE

In another report by Blanke published in 2011 he describes how a boy with a lesion in his right angular gyrus (in the TPJ region) had his brain measured while having a partial epileptic seizure.[21] The boy is said to have had a partial bodily illusion, then became unconscious and had an OBE, which is referred to as a "full own-body illusion." However, it's possible that neither were illusions and that his seizure caused disruptions to the mechanism of his brain limiting his consciousness to his body. Even if his partial bodily illusion was an illusion, I don't think it means his OBE while unconscious was an illusion too. It could have been, but it may have been a real one due to his loss of bodily consciousness. I think what this shows again is that certain parts of the brain may be involved in OBEs, not that all OBEs are illusions.

There's more evidence for the TPJ being involved in OBEs. This comes from a study published in 2004 of six patients with brain damage—five with damage to their TPJ. They all had some form of OBE or autoscopy experience (seeing their body from outside of it). Some of these experiences had occurred during seizures, another while waking from sleep, and one patient when her brain was stimulated electrically[22]—this is the same patient from Blanke's study discussed earlier.

These experiences were quite different: some were like OBEs, though seemed to contain unreal events projected by the mind, and others more typical autoscopy experiences.

OBEs are often presented as a type of autoscopy experience, as they are in this study, and because autoscopy is believed to be illusory, it's argued that OBEs are just a form of autoscopy illusion.

Autoscopy is a rare experience in which people perceive their surrounds from outside their physical body, or see a second version of themselves (a doppelgänger). There are cases of people who've experienced autoscopy during times of intense stress,[23] while being abused,[24] when suffering from a psychological disorder,[25] and due to brain damage,[26] [27] all while physically awake. These experiences tend to be limited in that the person sees a double of themselves, or looks at their physical body from a short distance away, for a short time.

Although someone can look back and see their sleeping body as separate from them during an OBE (though this is uncommon in my experience), actual OBEs are often very different to autoscopy. OBEs are different in that they usually occur when someone is asleep, they can involve the entire series of sensations of leaving one's physical body (and later returning), and can involve far more complex experiences—the person usually moves away from their body to another location entirely, can have a supernatural encounter with nonphysical beings and places often depicted in ancient religion, and can even see things that can be later verified as occurring in the physical world, which they would have otherwise had no knowledge of.

From my reading of the 2004 study, the authors say they provide neurological evidence that autoscopy (AS) and OBEs share important central mechanisms, and suggest they represent certain disorders of body perception and cognition (or body schema). Specifically, to me they seem to suggest both are due to the simultaneous breakdown of two processes. The first is "related to a failure to integrate [...] information with respect to one's own body" which they say is a disintegration that occurs to one's personal space. The second is a vestibular dysfunction, which they say leads to a disintegration between one's personal and extrapersonal (external visual) space. In my view they appear to argue that these disintegrations are caused by a dysfunction of the TPJ while someone is in a state of partially and briefly impaired consciousness.[28]

Remember that the TPJ is the area of the brain where information from the brain is integrated with that from within the body, and so from what I understand this study suggests that both OBEs and AS are a result of a failure in this integration due to a sudden dysfunction of the TPJ. My interpretation is that it seems the authors have concluded that OBEs and AS are based on the same mechanism because the subjects' experiences involved the same area of the brain; and it's inferred that because AS is due to errors in bodily perceptions this must be the cause of all OBEs too.

In the case of brain damage and seizures, I would say that the brain is impaired and dysfunctional, thus altering the perceptions of consciousness, though not necessarily making them unreal in all cases. As in any OBE, these experiences can be overlaid with unreal images from the mind. Again, this could be a case where the brain's limitations are forcibly interfered with due to a malfunction in the brain's working, allowing consciousness to experience from perspectives outside the body. But I certainly wouldn't say "impairment," "disorder," and "dysfunction" is occurring within those who have intentional OBEs naturally. The same part of the brain (the TPJ) may (or may not) be involved, but the mechanism that gives rise to intentional, natural OBEs is clearly different, and like I said earlier, I think is to do with a willed reduction in brain activity through the use of spiritual practices.

SENSORY DISORDERS IN PEOPLE WHO'VE HAD OBES

A study by Braithwaite et al at the University of Birmingham published in 2010 conducted a survey and test on sixty-three undergraduate students, seventeen of whom reported having had an OBE.[29] From what I can tell, these seventeen only answered differently to the others on two parts of the survey, which were those taken as indicating instabilities in the brain's temporal lobe and distortions in the processing of body-based information. For example, they'd said yes to questions such as, "Do you ever sense the presence of another being, despite being unable to see any evidence?" and "Do you ever have the sensation that your body, or part of it, is changing or has changed shape?"

The students were also asked to imagine themselves in the place of a figure on a computer screen, and then identify its body parts. For example, the figure was shown wearing one glove, and the student was asked to identify what hand they (as the figure) were wearing the glove on, i.e. their right or left hand. Those who'd had OBEs responded more slowly and incorrectly.

In my understanding, based on these findings, the study authors suggested that OBEs are a result of things going wrong in the brain's temporal lobe.[30]

It's hard to comment on the study without knowing what the actual OBEs of the seventeen were like. It also makes it more difficult to conclude much when questions about sensing supernatural presences are included, as these may also indicate at least some that had OBEs were more psychically sensitive, perhaps due to a weaker brain limiting mechanism, allowing them to experience OBEs more easily. Or, they may have had a kind of involuntary and spontaneous OBE more common among those with certain sensory issues.

Another study published in 2017 by Lopez et al I think suggests something similar. It looked at 210 people who'd experienced dizziness, compared to another 210 who hadn't. Dizziness can be an indicator of a vestibular disorder, which occurs in the inner ear and affects someone's sense of balance. They found that 14 percent of people with dizziness had said they experienced an OBE at some time, compared to 5 percent of those with no dizziness. Those with dizziness said they only had an OBE after they began experiencing dizziness for the first time. The number of OBEs in the dizziness group was even higher among those who experienced depersonalization-derealization, depression, and anxiety.[31]

Again, it's hard to comment without knowing what the OBEs people had consisted of—whether they were full-blown or just feelings of falling, flying, or floating, etc. Nevertheless, I think there's enough here to make an argument for there being different types of OBEs among the 420 people studied, as the fact that the OBEs in the dizziness group only began occurring after they first experienced dizziness (though I couldn't see the data on how long ago that was) in my view shows that their OBEs were probably caused by the disorder, which seemed to be further exacerbated by other conditions. So I think we can say there may be a type of OBE (floating, falling, forms of autoscopy probably mostly while awake) that occurs in people with vestibular disturbance. However, I think we can also say that there is a less frequent type or types (perhaps full-blown while asleep or going to sleep) that occur in individuals with no vestibular disorder. As far as I'm aware, scientists do not generally make any distinction between different types, and therefore I believe may use those that occur during times of brain and bodily disorder to draw conclusions about those that do not, which in my view is wrong.

Although it's certainly true that people with sensory disorders can involuntarily have OBEs caused by the disorder, it's also true that perfectly healthy people with no history of medical problems can have OBEs too. I've seen how anybody who applies the right techniques with enough discipline can have an intentional OBE—we don't need to have a sensory disorder!

As you will have read in chapter 3, there are accounts of Jesus, Krishna, Hermes Trismegistus, and Odin all having OBEs. What is it that they all have in common? Is it a vestibular disorder, or was it their dedication to experiencing spiritual dimensions?

It's simply not possible to conclude that everyone who has OBEs has sensory problems—in fact most probably don't when you consider the sheer number of people who've had an OBE and/or NDE as I mentioned in chapter 1. It's a large proportion of the population, and I think it would be safe to say that not all of them have sensory issues, and that not everyone who hasn't had an OBE is free of sensory issues.

VIRTUAL REALITY

Some claim that virtual reality experiments have shown that OBEs are illusions similar to virtual reality itself. In an experiment by Dr. Henrik Ehrsson, subjects were filmed from behind and their image was projected in front of them using virtual reality. In the resulting study, Ehrsson says: "I report an illusion in which individuals experience that they are located outside their physical body and looking at their body from this perspective. This demonstrates that the experience of being localized within the physical body can be determined by the visual perspective in conjunction with correlated multisensory information from the body."[32]

In the supplemental material many of the participants made spontaneous remarks like, "Wow! I felt as though I was outside my body and looking at myself from the back!" and "It was weird, almost as if I was looking at someone else or some kind of dummy!"[33]

Statements like "I felt as though" and "almost as if I was" indicate to me that the participants realized they were seeing an illusion. In an actual OBE it feels completely real and not like an illusion at all. The study abstract starts by saying, "I report an illusion..." In my view however, it does not follow that because an illusion of being out of the body was created in this experiment that all OBEs are illusions.

This is the one study where I feel confident that these were not real OBEs, but were illusions generated by tricking the brain. There have been other fairly similar studies using virtual reality to induce a sense of being out-of-body,[34] [35] but I think fundamentally they're all working the same way, which is by tricking the brain into thinking the body is in a position it isn't.

Dr. Ehrsson states, "There has been no way of inducing an OBE in healthy people before [this study] apart from unsubstantiated reports in occult literature."[36] Clearly I have a difference of opinion here.

CONCLUDING THOUGHTS

So we see that parts of the brain probably play a role in OBEs, that virtual reality can create the illusion of an OBE, and that psychedelics are somewhat related to OBEs but subject to other influences because of the action of chemicals in the brain. Yet in my view none of this is proof that all or most OBEs are illusions. Additionally, the number of OBEs studied are very small, and I think can't possibly represent all OBEs.

It seems to me that most of the studies on OBEs usually assume that OBEs are the result of illusions generated by the brain or are distortions in body schema, and that evidence is then presented to suggest that the OBEs that were investigated in the studies are the result of one or both of these things. To begin with the belief that OBEs are illusions is, in my view, philosophical speculation and could be seen as a kind of religious belief. To truly study OBEs neutrally, I think, means to at least be open to the possibility that other dimensions and other-dimensional parts of us exist.

Charles Tart, the American psychologist and parapsychologist, who was a professor emeritus of psychology of UC Davis, I think sums this up well—making an important differentiation between *science* and *scientism*:

> "Scientism, a dogmatic materialism masquerading as science, dismisses the NDE from the outset as something that cannot be what it seems to be, namely, a mind or soul traveling outside the physical body, either in the physical world or in some nonphysical world. So the NDE is automatically dismissed as a hallucination or, more likely, as some kind of psychopathology. But what if we practice actual science and look, with a view as objective as possible, at experiences like the NDE without prejudging them as impossible? [...]
>
> Hundreds of experiments have shown that the human mind can sometimes do things that are paraconceptual to our understanding of physical reality; that is, they make no sense given our current understanding of physics and reasonable extensions of it, but they happen anyway. They are empirical realities. [...]
>
> So if in an NDE a person feels outside her or his body, or claims to have acquired information about distant events, for example, it may be an illusion in a particular case, but you cannot scientifically say it

must be illusion. You have to examine the actual experience, the data, not ignore it or prejudicially 'explain it away' without really paying attention or being logical. Thus psi phenomena give us a wider view of reality that calls for a careful look at NDEs, rather than dismissal out of hand."[37]

~ CHARLES TART

Certain brain activity noted during an OBE, or specific brain stimulation inducing an OBE, is not proof that all OBEs are entirely brain generated. The brain must be involved in OBEs as it is in all our lived experiences, whether waking or sleeping. It would be involved in the astral split process, and I think it's involved in the mind's projection of illusory images once we're in an OBE.

However, the brain is inactive during an NDE where the person is clinically dead, and yet they still experience being out of the body. As I've said, I think NDEs are much more objective for this reason, as the brain is unable to interfere in the experience and to create illusions. NDEs show that the brain is not an essential part of the experience of being out of the body, and therefore it cannot be the creator of all of them. We can have brain activity and have an OBE, and we can have no brain activity and still have an OBE (in an NDE).

Materialist science struggles with NDEs for this reason, and so the involvement of the brain in NDEs is seen as an unresolved issue by some in it. As Dirk De Ridder puts it, "Whether these regions [of the brain] are activated in patients who report disembodiment as part of a near-death experience—and if so, how—is a provocative but unresolved issue."[38]

Rather, the accounts of NDEs show that the brain is the limiter of consciousness, and I think this is a better fitting explanation. Once the brain and body are dead, consciousness then has nothing limiting it to the physical body, and so is freed from it.

The fact that people sometimes see things that aren't real during OBEs and occasionally in NDEs doesn't mean that we never see what's real in them. "Sometimes illusions" doesn't equal "always illusions;" just because we "sometimes" see unreal things in OBEs, doesn't mean OBEs themselves are unreal. I know the mind can overlay reality in OBEs, but I also know that we can and do see real things in them and frequently do in NDEs.

It's unfortunate that OBEs are usually investigated as the result of some form of psychological problem, physical brain disorder, or illusory brain activity, and a lot of other evidence that they aren't always the result of this is often ignored. If we put the shoe on the other foot for a moment, we could imagine conducting a study on materialist scientists to see if we can find correlations between their inability to perceive anything but the physical world with types of brain disorders. From the outset, we could take the position that other dimensions exist, and anyone who wasn't aware of this must therefore be experiencing some kind of disorder. The study could be conducted on just a handful of scientists based on the assumption that they can't perceive reality fully, and we could then draw conclusions about all scientists from it. Major news organizations might pick up on these studies with headlines about how those who have an interest in science have been found to be less able to perceive reality due to certain disorders, and scientists might feel quite uncomfortable in society talking to anyone, even friends and family, about their interest in science. What an awful situation that would be, and yet it seems to me that's the situation many people who have OBEs are in.

As I see it, the main issue is that OBEs happen in another dimension, which there's no way to measure, and so the default position for materialist science is that OBEs must be illusions. Some then study the parts of the physical body, like the brain, and its relation to our senses and psychology, in an attempt to understand OBEs, without taking into account the possible existence of anything apart from the physical world.

I looked at a sample number of studies to identify the kind of language used when drawing conclusions about OBEs from the evidence presented. They used the expressions: "look like," "suggests a," "have been claimed," "suggesting that," "are expected to," "might be," "may be associated with," "likely to be caused by." The authors hesitate in making definitive statements and yet the media and general public often make it seem as though the matter has been settled by these studies.

As I mentioned in chapter 3, I think that as well as the brain, electricity within the body is somehow involved in OBEs, so scientists are getting closer to understanding the physical mechanism by which OBEs happen by stimulating certain parts of the brain with electricity. I'd say what may work better is electromagnetic energy targeted at the body, perhaps specifically at the brain, at certain frequencies.

Although I find the role of the brain interesting, it's not psychological or sensory disorder that's the common factor in most OBEs—it's unconsciousness, as most occur when we are asleep or dead, or passing into these states, and so I believe we can sometimes be aware of the process of leaving the body in real time. This is what we actually experience, and I see no theory that makes a stronger case than we are simply aware of what's really happening to us when we have an OBE.

We take what we experience in daily life as being real, while understanding we sometimes get it wrong and see or imagine things that aren't real. In an OBE things aren't as clear as in daily life, as there is a considerable overlay of our mind's images on the experience. Yet we can still take the actual experience of being out of the body as real, while allowing for the greater tendency of seeing illusory things, bearing in mind we do sometimes see verifiable things in OBEs.

There are so many reports of accurate perception at a distance during OBEs, of premonitions, of more than one person meeting in an OBE, of people who have no brain activity during NDEs having an OBE, of the deceased appearing to loved ones in dreams who didn't know they had died, and much more, such as those I gave in the chapter Evidence for Out-of-Body Experiences Being Real. I see this as far more compelling evidence for OBEs being real experiences of being out of the body than anything I've found so far in studies or experiments. I've personally had such a huge number of experiences which have shown to me that OBEs are real, that I've long ago just got on with learning from them in ways I describe in this book, which is something I reckon the skeptics are missing out on.

I'll finish with a quote from scientist Nancy Rynes, who was an atheist before she was hit by an SUV while riding her bicycle, and had a long, profound, and elaborate NDE:

> "It was a big shift for me as a scientist all of a sudden to have my entire world flipped upside down. [...] I was really lucid. I want people to understand, I wasn't like hallucinating or anything. I know what a hallucination is like and this is not one of them."[39]

PART 3
DREAMS AND LUCID DREAMING

CHAPTER ELEVEN

Dreams

Every night when we sleep, we dream, whether we remember our dreams or not. In our dreams the process of thinking and daydreaming from the day continues, but without a physical body to bring us back to reality, the images from our subconscious become real for us, and we exist in a model of the world that has been projected from our subconscious. Not all dreams are subconscious projections however, as there can be things in them that really exist and take place in the fifth dimension, and as mentioned previously, sometimes verifiably so. Others may be a mix of actual events and subconscious projections, while others are clearly scenes or places that are put there by spiritual beings for the purpose of teaching us.

We are born into this world via the dimension we dream in and return to it with death. We also return to that dimension every night when we sleep, but we don't normally realize it. In a clear out-of-body or near-death experience we can see that dimension as it is.

When we sleep, we leave behind our physical body, which holds our psyche onto the physical world, and all that is nonphysical of us enters the fifth dimension. We still however have a connection to the physical body, which makes it impossible to not come back to it when we wake up. While we dream, messages are sent from the fifth dimension through this connection to our physical bodies and vice versa.

Dreams can tell us many important things about ourselves and are an indispensable tool for self-discovery. But if you're looking to conventional science to tell you about the function of dreams, you'll probably be disappointed as it doesn't have the means to study their origins and the actual events in them can't be seen by current scientific means, as they are beyond this dimension. But it's possible to understand them by having OBEs as part of a broader study of the psyche and consciousness.

Fifteenth century Chinese illustration of a dream.

DIFFERENT KINDS OF DREAMS

ORDINARY DREAMS

The most common type of dream is what I would call an ordinary dream, which is one that is generated by the subconscious. When we're dreaming we don't normally see what's really in the fifth dimension, or we only partially see it through the haze of subconscious images, which are projected onto it. Even if what we see there is real, we don't normally realize or question that we're there. To see what's really there, we must be clear of the images projected by our minds.

CLEAR DREAMS

Sometimes when we're dreaming we do see what really exists in the fifth dimension, because we can have periods of lucidity. In these times we can interact with other people and beings that are really there, partake in real events, and/or dream about a place that really exists in the physical world (even though we may never have seen it before).

SPIRITUAL AND SYMBOLIC DREAMS

As ancient people believed, it's possible to be sent a dream from the divine. Spiritual dreams can either be sent from spiritual beings, or one's own higher

Being (the feminine aspect of the Being I refer to as the Spiritual Mother, and the masculine aspect the Spiritual Father). These dreams contain information that helps us in some way. This is why some ancient peoples valued them so much as a guide.

It's possible to be taught and visited by spiritual beings in dreams.

Dreams and OBEs are a medium of communication between this dimension and the next, and between divinity and humanity. As we've seen, that's because when we dream, or have an OBE or NDE, we go to a dimension where spiritual beings exist and operate.

To give us dreams, spiritual beings or our own Being will clear the projections of our subconscious temporarily. These spiritual-sent dreams then have a different quality to them than ordinary dreams, as they are generally meaningful and clearer.

Spiritual beings will sometimes teach us directly in our dreams in ways that are easy for us to understand, yet more often they give us dreams that have a symbolic meaning. Messages can be communicated in the form of a symbol, a number, or words; events, situations, and people can also carry symbolic meanings, depending on what they represent to us. Even entire dreamscapes can be created for us to learn something in.

These dreams are usually given without us asking as part of the help from above, but dreams can also be given in response to prayers, as is the case with dream incubation.

The guidance and information we receive can apply to any avenue of life. For instance, we can be told about things that are happening far away and then wake up in the morning and discover they're true. We can be shown premonitions of the future which we would otherwise have no way of knowing about. We can be warned of things to avoid, get information about situations we're about to face and people we know, be shown what people are thinking about and planning for us, and how to deal with many kinds of situations.

We can also receive spiritual guidance and be given knowledge of things that are beyond this dimension. We can be shown what people face after death, and even what's ahead for us personally in the afterlife. We can be taught about what harmful behaviors we need to change to be able to develop spiritually, and be shown how our spiritual progress is going.

The possibilities are almost limitless, and the more someone learns to use them, the more they can begin to trust them because they are so accurate and precise, if they can interpret them that is.

The level of teachings we get in the fifth dimension is entirely due to our capacity to understand and receive them. Knowledge is given according to one's own merits, when someone is prepared for it and has earned it.

It's also important to realize when to keep silent about what we've seen in an OBE or dream. Some teachings or messages relate to us personally or are intended for us only; these are given in the trust we won't share them, and if we do, we may not receive any experiences like this again for some time, until they see we can be trusted. I don't think this applies to general experiences or ones that were given to be shared with others though. One's intuition and whatever relevant experience they may have help with assessing what can be shared of one's dreams and OBEs.

LUCID/WAKING DREAMS

Lucidity in a dream can be so great at times that we can realize we're dreaming and in the fifth dimension. By waking up in a dream like this, we can be conscious in the fifth dimension just as if we had projected there. This kind of experience is generally referred to as a lucid dream, but it's more accurate to say that we wake up out of a dream into a conscious experience of the fifth dimension. I discuss lucid dreaming further in chapter 14.

BAD DREAMS AND NIGHTMARES

Bad dreams, such as being chased, falling from heights, violence, and other unpleasant events, are usually the result of what's happening within the psyche during daily life. Many negative states and strong emotions often go unnoticed during the day, but they manifest at night into these scenes. Nightmares are different from the usual bad dreams; true nightmares are a trip to hell. I explain more about bad dreams and nightmares in chapter 26.

DREAMS FROM DEMONS

Apart from spiritual beings, demons are also present in the fifth dimension, and they too can make us have certain dreams, usually with the aim of taking someone off their spiritual track using lies and deceit. I discuss demons in dreams in chapter 26. I also discuss what demons are in chapter 25 and how to protect oneself against them in chapter 27.

Dreams from demons are not something that most people need to be concerned about. Almost all people mostly just have ordinary dreams, along with bad dreams and nightmares.

WHY WE DREAM

When we're sleeping, the process of daydreaming from the day continues, and I'm sure this is mostly how and why we dream. When we daydream, we're just partly aware of the reality of where we are in the present moment, and so when we sleep and go to the fifth dimension, we carry on daydreaming but without the stability of the physical world to bring us back to reality while in a place where the images produced by our minds become our reality.

Usually in dreams our psyche is locked into the images and model of the world it has unconsciously created, and we're without self-awareness and so don't question or realize where we are. As I mentioned in chapter 7, this seems to have something to do with the brain, as in NDEs people are completely lucid (they don't dream), and this is generally when their brain is dead, meaning it no longer has any influence over the psyche of the deceased person.

It also seems to have to do with the mind. The mind continuously processes information, and as part of this generates thoughts and images almost without ceasing. As we go to sleep, this process continues, but in the fifth dimension the images it generates become immersive. Because of this, and because of the influence of the brain, we dream continuously while in the fifth dimension, never realizing that we've left our bodies or that we are in another dimension, no matter how bizarre the events of our dreams may be.

It also has to do with our egos. They constantly seek to trap and control us by giving rise to and causing us to identify with their particular thoughts and feelings (whether they be of frustration, anxiety, arrogance, etc.), thereby allowing them to feed from our energy. They do this not only during the day, but also while we sleep. The images they usually generate in our mind's eye become immersive while we're in the fifth dimension, and so while we're there during sleep they're able to keep us slavishly locked within an unceasing stream of scenarios, causing us to remain fascinated and reacting to them. Dreams can be incoherent because of this, because we respond to one dream scenario or character after another, thereby generating the next one and so on, solely from our own minds and egos.

If you study your dreams, you might find a pattern in which you think of something in your dream, and then it happens, and then you think of what will occur next, and it does. For example, you might be hiding, and be afraid that a person will find you, and then they do. Then you think about running and getting away to a certain place, and you do, etc. In the dream, we believe these things are really happening to us, when they are usually just the result of our projected thoughts. These scenarios can involve things we've been involved in during daily life, or they may involve unknown people and places, but can all be derived from the impressions stored in our subconscious.

We can have periods of lucidity, though rarely, which allows us to separate ourselves from this process and to "wake up" in a dream; this is why so many people have experienced at least one lucid dream in their lives.

There are different reasons why we can become lucid in dreams. It can be the result of spiritual help. It can happen because an event is so bizarre it causes us to question the reality of it and where we are. It can be because the dream feels so real, bringing us to the level of consciousness we have in waking life. But it can also come as the result of resisting the hypnotic trance the egos keep us in, by making the effort to perceive consciously in the moment in daily life, free of their influence, thus having more conscious dreams. In fact, we can train our minds to question where we are, and to "wake up" in dreams to have a lucid dream.

What we do here, we do there; and what we are here, we are there. So if we bring more awareness into our lives here, we tend to have clearer dreams. Also, the freer we are of low inner states during the day, the less those states produce bizarre, dark, and bad dreams.

DREAMS AS AN INSIGHT INTO OUR PSYCHE

As we have no physical body or forms to bring us back to reality when we sleep, our mind is free to wander unhindered, and so a person often does things in dreams they wouldn't ordinarily do in daily life. Thus, dreams are an insight into our psychology—they are what we are when stripped of the conventions, norms, morals, and laws of society that exist in the physical world, and are in the place where the subconscious roams, living out its fantasies, pleasures, and fears. Appearances can be deceiving as even the most outwardly pious person may have dreams where they commit adultery for example. We can therefore learn a great deal about ourselves by studying our dreams—both those that are meaningful and those created by the images and false scenarios projected by our mind. In this latter type, even though a person may do ordinary things, they can also do bad or bizarre things, perhaps being violent, lustful, fighting, or stealing.

It's very useful to see these different egos not only in dreams but also during daily life, as then they can be understood and removed (I write about how to get rid of egos in my book on self-knowledge). As they reduce or go from our psyche in daily life, they are reduced or removed from our dreams as well.

SYMBOLS IN DREAMS AND OBES

Spiritual beings or our own Being often communicate messages to us in dreams and OBEs in a symbolic way. What usually happens, especially in dreams, is that we find ourselves doing something in a situation often involving other people that may seem fairly ordinary or even strange on the surface, but that we intuitively feel has a symbolic meaning containing an important or useful message. Sometimes these dreams can be much clearer than our usual dreams, and even have a spiritual feel to them.

Symbols are sometimes a clearer and more direct means of communication in the higher dimensions than ordinary language is. It's possible to convey a lot of meaning through symbols in a way that is easier to remember than written text or spoken words. Sometimes symbols can appear in the dream or OBE, or the entire experience itself could have symbolic meaning. Each symbol can potentially have many different meanings, and we can often grasp the correct meaning intuitively, especially since they are given to us personally by spiritual beings who have taken into account what these symbols mean to us.

John while "in the Spirit" being shown the visions of Revelation using symbols.

Events and circumstances can be symbolic. For example, someone could dream of themselves needing to do an important job, but being unable to walk because an old pair of trousers they're wearing have become too tight on them. Intuitively, they may feel those trousers are old ideologies which they have outgrown and need to let go of to be able to move ahead. We could see graffiti sprayed over the walls of our home, representing harmful slander than is being spread about us personally, or a fire on the horizon symbolizing an impending event that could be devastating to us, and that we need to escape. Someone could see themselves driving a big truck, which can only travel very slowly, representing the heavy load of many responsibilities that person is carrying.

People we know can also appear in our dreams symbolically, as they can represent something to us—whether we think of them as working hard, being easily led astray, faithful, lustful, etc. For example, an old friend, perhaps someone we used to spend time a lot of time partying with may appear recurringly in dreams, representing the dreamer's own hedonistic and degenerate egos that they haven't broken free of.

I often saw people in my dreams from different times of my life like this. They usually represented figures I had associated with due to my ego-driven affinity with them. The next day I would reflect on the egos that created the affinity, to understand them better. I knew by getting free of the ego-based affinity I had, it would bring about new people and circumstances in my life.

A lot of what I learned in my dreams and in some of my OBEs was in relation to my own inner states, to my egos. I would apply the information I had received in them to my daily life. If for example, I remembered acting with an ego in a dream, or saw an ego in a dream, I would look for that ego within myself the next day, as I knew that whatever I saw in my dreams was the very thing that I needed to urgently change.

Spiritual beings may also use an object that's meaningful to us, but may mean little or nothing to someone else—a cup we use as part of our personal routine, perhaps given to us at a certain time in our lives, may carry an additional meaning to us than other cups do. We could also be shown symbols that have a meaning in our culture. In one OBE for example, a poor woman in a desperate situation gave me a wooden spoon. In my culture a wooden spoon is an old symbol of love, and so using intuition together with the knowledge of the symbol's meaning I understood that no matter how poor a person was, or where they were, they still could send an altruistic love not only to me, but to humanity.

For someone who wants to understand a symbol or a meaning in a dream, they should go with the meaning that's most obvious to them, because it's their dream and is meant for them. They should try to capture its meaning intuitively too. We can have greater intuition in an OBE or relatively clear dream than we do in daily life, so it's worth paying attention to what we felt a dream, or an event or symbol within a dream, meant when we first responded to it during our experience and also as soon as we woke up after it.

There are also many symbols that have common meanings: the ancient solar cross for example, or the serpent devouring its tail. It may be useful to get a basic understanding of these kinds of symbols from the Religion of the Sun to refer to in case you see a common symbol like these. Many spiritual symbols found in ancient places and texts around the world have their origin in the fifth dimension.

The meaning of a dream or OBE may be vague in the beginning, but if someone persists and understands how to interpret their symbolism, they'll find their dreams can become their own daily guide to their life, which they learn to greatly value.

DREAM GUIDES

Ancient people often used dream guides, which give the meanings of different dreams. I haven't included a dream guide in this book as I believe it's more important to learn how to interpret our own dreams. This is because a dream guide will have a fixed explanation as to what a particular dream means, but it may not be the meaning of our dream.

If for example I have a dream about flying in an airplane, I could look at a guide and it may say something like "an airplane shows how your overall spiritual development is going." But my dream may not be related to that at all. A plane could mean my overall spiritual development, but what if the context is different? I had a dream in which I was in a plane, but it was related to escaping a disaster that would befall many people; it had nothing to do with spirituality. On the other hand, I've had dreams in which I was in a plane and they were clearly in relation to my overall spiritual development. Yet if I had relied upon a dream guide telling me a plane in every dream was related to spiritual development, I wouldn't have understood the warning.

So, there are two important things to consider: what a scene or object symbolizes and what context it's in.

Think about a plane for example—what does it do? It's able to travel the longest distance in the shortest time, taking us to a completely different and faraway place, which can signal a sudden, big change or transition in one's circumstances. Is the dreamer flying it or does it have a pilot? What size is the plane? Does it take passengers or is it a single seater, or a double? Were there any passengers? If so, who were they? A plane full of strangers will have a different meaning to an empty one, or one that's shared with a spouse for example.

Consider what was happening to it. Where was it going? Was it flying properly? Was it about to crash?

An airplane can be a common dream symbol, but its meaning depends on the context it's in and what's happening to it.

It's good to look at as many angles as we can, keeping in mind that we do have the sense of intuition that can allow us to understand the meaning of a dream immediately. Sometimes it works and sometimes we need to analyze elements of the dream to figure out what it means.

A single explanation or two in a dream guide isn't going to give us a consistently accurate interpretation to go by, as our dreams are tailored to what we understand.

Additionally, meanings are different between individual people and between cultures, and so a wooden spoon would mean something different to me than it would to most other people whose culture doesn't give it the meaning mine does. Likewise, dreams about weaving mammoths' hair are unlikely to have the same meaning today as they did before the end of the last ice age. Spiritual beings will use what the individual understands in order to teach them.

There are common things we all share, such as cars, houses, and fire, and these will have a similar meaning for all of us, which is why dream guides generally work. But it doesn't take much to work out what these things mean in our dreams by basing it on what they mean to us, because our dreams have been tailored to us and to what we understand.

I would therefore recommend someone learn to interpret the symbols they see in their dreams themselves. There aren't that many timeless symbols we're going to come across. If someone does for example see a pentagram, or a solar cross, and doesn't know what it represents, they can look it up and find its standard meaning—it'll probably be the intended meaning of the symbol that was shown to them.

There are (relatively) timeless symbols that don't change, and these are found on the path of the Spiritual Sun. I'll say more about those individual symbols in a book specifically about the path. Those who embark upon it will potentially have greater knowledge and teachings given to them and have some dreams that are different, which was why in ancient Egypt there were two different dream guides, one for irreligious people and another for those of religious and upright conduct.

PREMONITIONS IN DREAMS AND OBES

It's quite common to have premonitions in dreams and OBEs, which is to see or be told something of the future before it happens. Especially common seem to be premonitions about the death of people we know.

I've had so many premonitions in dreams and OBEs, including about the deaths of both my parents.

In 1993 I had an OBE in which I visited my parents' house. In it I saw a symbol indicating that something had gone seriously wrong with my mother; I looked at her eyes, and they looked back strangely. The next day I came home to find a message on the phone from my father saying that my mother had died. I called him back and he said she was still alive but dying, so my wife and I packed our bags, got in the car and drove through the night to my parents' house.

When we arrived, my father looked distraught. We went to the intensive care ward of the hospital and I was shocked to see my mother—she looked appalling, like a corpse that had been dead for a long time. She didn't know where she was, but she just about recognized me. Her eyes were exactly as I had seen them in my OBE. They disturbed her nurse, who kept backing away from her exclaiming over and over, "She's looking at me, she's looking at me." My mother had died and had an NDE, but a being over on the other side told her it wasn't her time to be there yet, and so she was sent back to her body.

Yet she was still in a desperate struggle for life. She'd had pneumonia without knowing it and her lungs collapsed; the doctor took us aside and told us that she was likely to die. Weeks passed as she struggled to live. Then one night in the astral plane I saw her in her wheelchair coming out of the hospital. The next day my father asked whether I thought she'd live. I told him, "Yes, she'll be coming out." From that day onward she very slowly began to improve. After about eight weeks she was well enough to leave the hospital, but was still very weak and ill.

Staff at the hospital in the intensive care ward dealt with the most serious cases and said she was the sickest they'd ever seen a person who'd still lived; they referred to her as the woman who died.

Then toward the end of 1995 I had a very clear dream in which I was told my father's heart was no good and that he would die. I really believed this, so I called him and spoke to him on the phone and he said he'd just had a pain in his chest. I tried to get him to go to hospital to get his heart checked with an ECG, but he said he'd already gone to the local doctor about his chest pain, and that the doctor checked him with a stethoscope and said his heart was fine. I insisted this was bad advice and that he should go to the emergency section of the hospital instead straightaway, but he wouldn't listen to me.

A couple of weeks later in an OBE I saw my father acting like he was very confused and frustrated, and was being carried out of his house on a stretcher. I knew this meant he was about to die. I told my parents I was coming to see them, but they insisted I didn't go.

Three days later I got a call from my parents' next-door neighbor to say that my father had died of a heart attack. I immediately organized a flight there.

USING COMMON SENSE

Although dreams can sometimes be a source of guidance, it's important to always use common sense. Primarily we need to respond to life based on what's happening in the physical world. Dreams can provide extra information that builds upon information we already have in our waking life, but they're not a replacement for it.

Sometimes it can be very difficult to determine the source of a dream, what it means, or whether it has any meaning at all. The egos and subconscious have such a huge influence on our dreams, creating situations that seem real and can easily mislead us if we attach meaning to them.

For example, we might have a fear that our house will be destroyed in a natural disaster, as perhaps these disasters are being reported in the news; then at night we can dream our house is destroyed by that disaster. This is because what we've thought about during the day and any underlying emotion we felt, say a slight anxiety, even if it was for a passing moment and seemed completely insignificant, can manifest into realistic scenarios. If we aren't really watching this process, it would be easy to think that the dream is a warning.

If in doubt, I suggest using common sense and basing one's decisions on what one knows to be true in the physical world.

CHAPTER TWELVE

How to Remember Dreams

There's so much to learn from dreams and OBEs that it's worth trying to remember them better by practicing dream recall.

It's easy to miss dreams when we wake up, but by learning simple techniques we can remember them better, and our ability to remember usually increases with practice. Following are the techniques I've found to be most effective.

BEDTIME AND MORNING EXERCISES

These exercises can be done before bed, and every morning upon waking.

1. PLAN AHEAD

Just before going to sleep, have the intention to remember your dreams in the morning when you wake up, because if you do this enough times, as soon as you wake up, it will be as though a little program starts in your head that reminds you to remember what you've been dreaming about. Normally a thought comes in and says "get up, shower, work" or whatever it is. If you've thought about that beforehand, it's become a routine. So what you need to do is to kind of re-educate yourself to think about remembering dreams first when you wake up rather than other things.

2. LIE STILL UPON WAKING

When you wake up don't move even a finger. Simply open your eyes and close them again and begin to remember your dreams from the first one you can remember. Try to see it in as much detail as you can, then you may find more dreams appear. Carry on remembering the ones from earlier in the night if you can. It may take a bit of training not to move when you wake up, but if you try time and again, you'll train your body.

It's important not to move when we wake up because by moving, the physical and fifth-dimensional bodies become merged, so we become locked into our physical body, whereas when we just wake up, they often have a looser connection, which makes remembering dreams easier.

3. PRONOUNCE A MANTRA

If you still can't remember any dreams, continue to lie still for a little while with your eyes closed to see if any appear. If they don't, then pronounce a mantra. A mantra is a series of sounds, a word, or words that have psychic effects, just as music and other sounds do. Mantras have these effects depending upon their words or sounds, which are often based upon the vowels A, E, I, O, and U. The sound of each of these vowels has a vibration, which affects the vibration of the psyche due to the law of vibratory affinity. Each vowel has a different tone and therefore has a different effect. Chanting mantras lightens one's inner state and can increase psychic faculties.

Any simple mantra will help with remembering dreams. This is because of how the vibration of pronouncing a mantra works on the psyche, and also because it helps to focus the mind and relax the body. Here are a few mantras which I've put together. I've combined the names of the Spiritual Sun from different ancient cultures, which is very appropriate for remembering dreams, as it's usually done in the morning around sunrise.

Ra Om
The first is Ra Om, which pairs the ancient Egyptian name for the Spiritual Sun, with the mantra of the Spiritual Sun in India. It's pronounced by elongating the sound of each letter like this: Rrraaaaaa Oooooommmm, and repeating.

Utu Om
Another is Utu Om, which starts instead with the ancient Sumerian name for the Spiritual Sun. It's pronounced by elongating the sounds of each letter except t, as in: Uuuuutuuuuu Oooooommmm, and repeating.

Inti Om
Another is Inti Om, this time starting with the name of the Spiritual Sun used by the Inca of South America. It's pronounced: Iiiinnntiiii Oooooommmm, and repeating.

Take a breath between each word if you say it aloud. I prefer to pronounce it mentally (silently) as I find vocalizing it makes me more awake, but see what works best for you.

If you pronounce one of these or any other mantra, repeating it over and over again for a while, you'll notice dreams beginning to appear. As they do, stop the mantra and concentrate upon each dream. Then if you need to, pronounce the mantra again several times and try to remember more.

If you still don't have much success, pronounce the mantra verbally for a while, and afterward pronounce it mentally.

4. GO OVER YOUR DREAMS

When you remember your dreams, see what kinds of dreams they are, and whether you can find any meanings or messages in them. It's useful to look for anything in relation to self-knowledge, or spiritual knowledge, or anything you can learn from. Some useful things to watch out for include any egos such as anger or fear, whether you've been to any real places, whether you've been flying or have been lucid, whether there are any symbols you can recognize and intuitively capture the meaning of, whether you had any mystical experiences, or whether the same dream recurs.

If we're in doubt about what we see and don't understand it, we can try using our intuition to work it out. Later, if we get more knowledge, we may understand those dreams better.

5. SLEEP WELL

Having regular patterns of sleep and getting enough sleep also helps.

DAYTIME EXERCISES

There are also things we can do during the day to help with dream recall:

1. KEEP A DREAM JOURNAL

Some people find it useful to keep a journal where they record their dreams. The advantages are that otherwise it's so easy to forget a dream and there may be things we don't understand now that we may later. We can also build an overall picture of our dream life, finding things that are repetitive, prominent, or important, as patterns emerge over time.

The main disadvantage is that other people could find it and may discover things that are personal. If you decide to keep a dream journal you may want to leave out things that are too personal, or put them in a code of some sort.

2. TRAIN DREAM RECALL BY REMEMBERING EVENTS OF THE DAY

There's another exercise that's similar to dream recall, but it's like a dream recall of the day. At the end of the day, we just briefly go back over what happened during it. This helps to crystallize in our mind the things that have happened, which helps to train the memory in this type of recall, and gets us to reflect upon what we did.

When we look at what's happened in the day, we look not just at the things we did, but also at the emotional states we had, and if we can, see if we can spot them in our dreams later when we wake up. I have more information on a daily practice to remember and reflect on inner states in my book on self-knowledge.

3. BE MORE AWARE AND IN SELF-OBSERVATION

The more aware we are in daily life, the more likely we are to remember our dreams. By perceiving where we are and what we're doing and by practicing self-observation, we momentarily come out of thoughts and daydreams and are aware of the physical world. This helps us to have a clearer general level of awareness, which tends to result in clearer dreams that are easier to remember. Likewise, the less we're in low inner states during daily life, the less those states influence our dreams, allowing us to have more meaningful dreams. I explain how to practice self-observation and awareness in my book on self-knowledge.

CHAPTER THIRTEEN

Dream Incubation

It's possible to increase the chances of receiving spiritual teachings in dreams by doing the ancient practice of dream incubation. As explained in chapter 4, many ancient peoples sought guidance from the divine in their dreams, often through prayer, ritual, and/or sleeping at a sacred place—these practices are called dream incubation.

People still have success with forms of dream incubation today, and even studies have shown its effectiveness.[1][2] In one conducted at Harvard University, after just one week of dream incubation half the subjects had dreams related to the problem they wanted to solve and the majority of these believed their dreams offered a solution.[3] In another longer, four-week study, two-thirds of the participants had dreams related to the problem they were trying to solve.[4] And so this exercise is just as useful now as it was in ancient times.

As one modern example, in her twenties Dr. Kathy J. Forti had asked to be shown in a dream why she had broken out in blemishes on her face that wouldn't go away. That night she had a symbolic dream showing that the real blemish she needed to deal with was her vanity. In the physical world, when she decided to address her vanity, her facial blemishes went away.[5]

Knowing that spiritual beings and each one's own higher Being exist, and seeing the ways in which they work, I'd say that most successful dream incubation is due to divine intervention. Most studies, however, tend to rule out divine assistance as a factor and instead attribute the phenomenon to the workings of the subconscious, without explaining how the mind is able to acquire information in a dream that it had not previously received.

Dream incubation was an important and widespread practice in the ancient Religion of the Sun, as evidenced by its use in the many traditions that derive from it.

Lara and I have put together an outline of how to do it based on surviving records in ancient Egypt and Greece (particularly based on the Greek Magical Papyri and Demotic Magical Papyri), and these contain rituals that were formulated to be practiced by individuals at home. It's likely the Greek practice derived from ancient Egypt, and that the ancient Egyptian practice is very old, having its origins in the ancient Religion of the Sun.

These rituals, while each slightly different, contain elements in common, and it's these elements we've used to create the ritual.

Like any exercise, it works best by being consistent and practicing it every night for a period of time. Participants in studies who completed four weeks had better results than those who spent less time.

Bear in mind that not everything we see in a dream is certain to be true. Some could be wrong due to the subconscious mind, while demons can also appear in disguise and give misleading information. So we need to be discriminating and intelligent in our assessment of our dreams.

Overall though, according to studies, most people when practicing for more than two weeks get information related to what they were asking for, and so for most people this looks to be a useful exercise with a reasonable chance of success that connects us to guidance from spiritual beings.

Depiction of dream incubation being practiced at the asclepieion at Epidaurus in ancient Greece. Snakes were allowed to roam freely as they were symbols of the god Asclepius, whose healing was sought in dreams. The snake is still used in medical emblems today.

I'll explain the elements involved in ancient dream incubation first, and then outline the steps of the actual practice.

THE ELEMENTS OF ANCIENT DREAM INCUBATION

PURITY

Perhaps the first and foremost ingredient of ancient dream incubation was purity.

The entrance to one of the most important temples of dream incubation in Greece was inscribed with the words:

"Pure must be he who enters the fragrant temple; Purity means to think nothing but holy thoughts."[6]

In the Greek Magical Papyri many of its dream incubation rituals require purity, saying things like:

"Go to sleep, pure," "Being pure in every respect," "Go to sleep after having kept yourself pure for three days," "Sleep pure. You must have [the place] where you perform absolutely pure," "Purify yourself before your everyday lamp," and do this "in a [hidden] place which is clean."[7]

The ancient requirements of purity and devotion often set as a prerequisite for a successful dream incubation are likely to have been based on the fact that experiences and knowledge in the fifth dimension are given to us by spiritual beings according to whether we're fit to receive them, and this can be based on our level of behavior and whether we've taken steps in our lives toward positive spiritual development. The ability for someone to adhere to requirements of purity (perhaps abstaining from harmful foods and activities) and undertaking acts of devotion (perhaps praying to a deity each day for a certain time period), as set by a temple priest/priestess, would help demonstrate someone's willingness and readiness to receive knowledge from the divine.

Depiction of a dream incubation temple in ancient Greece.

It was also important to maintain purity within the temple itself. Thoughts are energetic and alter the energetic atmosphere of a place, which is why people had to keep their thoughts holy to enter, as well as their behavior. This is a key principle of creating and maintaining a sacred space, as it becomes charged with the energies of what happens within it, and if done correctly, can be made more conducive to spiritual things. Most people will be practicing this at home, and so the same principle can be applied to one's room.

Purity will mean different things depending on what spiritual level someone is at. In ancient times, at minimum it usually involved bathing, and abstaining from meat, alcohol, and sex (specifically I would say of a mundane, not alchemical kind, for reasons I'll explain in another book) for a period of time.[8] Those aspiring to a higher spiritual level may look to set themselves further requirements.

It's worth reflecting on whether there are any changes we need to make to be fit/ready to receive the knowledge or experience we're asking for.

FORMULATING A PETITION

Ancient dream incubation rituals usually included a pre-written petition, with a spot to insert one's own personal request, leaving it up to the individual to work out what they wished to ask for.

Although people have successfully used dream incubation to solve a problem or to resolve an issue, for those who want spiritual knowledge, it's generally better to ask for issues that are spiritually important, because spiritual beings and/or our own Being tend to help us if we are really sincere and want spiritual help more than superficial material things. There could be really important material issues that affect you though, so I would ask for help with those if they are important enough.

Besides asking for general spiritual guidance, other suggestions could be asking about a personal matter related to one's own spiritual development, understanding a symbol previously seen in a dream or an OBE, asking to be being taught by a particular deity or one's own Being (either one's Spiritual Father or Mother), or asking to be taken to a spiritual place.

A very simple example of a petition could be something like, "I ask you Spiritual Mother, please show/teach me X in my dreams tonight."

>Ancient petitions could be more complex. They could include:
>
>>Calling the being by a number of the names it is known by
>>
>>Describing its appearance and role
>>
>>Specifying why it was being called upon
>>
>>Giving a timeframe to receive an answer by, usually that night

Here are a few examples:

> "SACHMOUNE [the Egyptian goddess Sekhmet] PAEMALIGOTEREENCH, the one who shakes, who thunders, who has swallowed the serpent, surrounds the moon, and hour by hour raises the disk of the sun, 'CHTHETHONI' is your name. I ask you [...] reveal to me concerning the things I wish."[9]
> ~ THE GREEK MAGICAL PAPYRI

"Come to me, Thoth [the Egyptian god], Eldest one, Eldest one of Re, who went forth from Atum, who was born from the limb of Atum! Come to me, Thoth, heart of Re, tongue of Tatenen, throat of the one whose name is hidden! Come to me, HEFKAE HEPKA HEBIKE NEKHE-P-KAI! Come to me, Lord of Truth, who loves Truth, who reckons [lifetimes?], who judges Truth, who does Truth! Come to me in your beautiful face in this good night and make answer to me concerning everything about which I am entreating here today, truly without falsehood therein!"[10]

~ THE GREEK DEMOTIC PAPYRI

"O Isis, O Nephthys, O noble soul of Osiris Wenefer, come to me! I am your beloved son, Horus. [...] come to me tonight! Teach me about such and such a thing about which I am asking; quickly, quickly; hurry, hurry."[11]

~ THE GREEK DEMOTIC PAPYRI

"Hermes [the Greek God], lord of the world, who're in the heart, O circle of Selene, spherical and square, the founder of the words of speech, pleader of Justice's cause, garbed in a mantle, with golden sandals, turning airy course beneath earth's depths, who hold the spirit's reins, the sun's and who with lamps of gods immortal, give joy to those beneath earth's depths, to mortals who've finished life. The Moirai's fatal thread and dream divine you're said to be, who send forth oracles by day and night; you cure pains of all mortals with your healing cares. Hither, O blessed one, O mighty son of the goddess who brings all mental powers, by your own form and gracious mind. And to an uncorrupted youth reveal a sign and send him your true skill of prophecy. [Add the matter you wish to be shown]."[12]

~ THE GREEK MAGICAL PAPYRI

WRITING OUT THE PETITION

In ancient rituals, petitions could be written out on a strip of linen cloth, papyrus, tinfoil, or the leaves of laurel or rush. Most of these aren't practical today, and things have changed with the availability of paper. But you could still do it the ancient way if you like.

"Write these things [on leaves] of laurel and place them by your head."[13]

We suggest writing the petition out while under the light of the sun or stars (and then speaking it). In ancient times the sun and stars were thought to imbue things with their energies, and they are also the manifestation of the divine light. Dream incubation petitions could be written out before the setting sun, but could also be spoken to the sunrise, full moon, or moonrise.

> "With this write. Prayer to him, toward the setting sun."[14]

> "Recite this both at sunrise and moonrise."[15]

> "[...] the invocation itself is spoken when [the moon] is full. But you will accomplish a better encounter at sunrise [...] when the god is on the [increase] [...]. Say, therefore, to the rising sun [the following] prayer."[16]

Yet, many dream incubation petitions were written down and spoken to a lamp in one's room before going to bed, and so we're putting the option to do both.

> "Take a clean strip of cloth and write down all the names. Say the same things to the lamp seven times. Let the lamp be facing east and let it be next to a censer on which you will make an offering of lumps of frankincense."[17]

NOT SPEAKING

Most of the rituals specify not speaking to anyone once the ritual has started, saying things like:

> "Say it [the petition] seven times and go to sleep without speaking."[18]

> "[...] lie down to sleep without speaking a word, even in answer to a question."[19]

This is likely because speaking to others easily disrupts one's focus, which needs to be kept on the petition in the important moments of transitioning into sleep. If someone's distracted, they can easily become scattered and daydream, leading to scattered dreams.

RECITING THE PETITION

A common element of dream incubation ritual was reciting one's petition aloud to a lit lamp seven times:

> "Go to the lamp, say seven times the following formula, extinguish the light and go to sleep."[20]

This is likely to be because in the ancient Religion of the Sun fire was seen as a manifestation of the light of the divine—particularly that of the Spiritual Sun[21]—and so by addressing it, one was addressing themselves to the divine.

Beside the lamp was often a censer where frankincense was burned while this was done, and in some rituals, the petition itself was circled about in its smoke. This was likely to have been to purify and spiritually energize it.

> "[...] set up the censer. Then make a burnt offering of frankincense and carry the [petition] around the vapor while saying: "Lords, gods, reveal to me concerning the [X] matter tonight, in the coming hours. Emphatically I beg, I supplicate, I your servant and enthroned [initiated] by you."[22]

PLACEMENT OF PETITION AND IMAGE

Ancient peoples would attempt to get close to the being they were petitioning. This was done through sleeping in temples consecrated to them, where they were believed to dwell, and where large icons of them would have been on display.[23] But it was also done at home, where people would sleep with images of the being close to them—for example, they could be drawn on their hand, or placed in their pillow.[24] This is why in the ritual, representations of the being that is petitioned are set up in the dreamer's room and brought close to them.

Left: Engraving of Sarapis seated, with what looks like his magical name below, on a small stone from ancient Rome (possibly used for dream incubation).
Right: Engraving of Sarapis and Isis on a small stone from ancient Greece.

> "On a jasperlike agate engrave Sarapis seated [...] and on the back of the stone the [magical] name [of Sarapis], and keep it shut up. When need [arises] [...] going off [to bed] without speaking to anybody, go to sleep holding the stone to your left ear."[25]

The petition itself was also usually placed either beside one's head, or under their pillow:

> "Having written it [...] wrap the leaves in a new handkerchief and lay it under your head."[26]

Petitions could be held in the left[27] or right hand[28] in dream incubation rituals, though the left seems to have been more common, perhaps because it was seen as more receptive.

REMEMBERING DREAMS

For remembering dreams, the Greek Magical Papyri advises:

> "Have near you a small tablet so that you may write as much as [the spiritual being petitioned] says, lest after going to sleep you forget."[29]

SLEEPING DIFFERENTLY

Sometimes the dreamer is advised to sleep on the ground on a rush mat. This may be because it caused the dreamer to sleep lightly, thus having more dreams they better remembered. The effect of sleeping in an unfamiliar place, like within a temple or at a sacred site, may have had the same effect. In the Epic of Gilgamesh, Gilgamesh sleeps sitting up, with his chin rested on his knees, while Druids were recorded as sleeping with their hands on their cheeks while incubating dreams. And many Native Americans would sleep out on high places, like mountaintops.[30]

While these options may not be feasible or practical, there may be other ways of introducing something unfamiliar into one's sleep routine, perhaps by dressing differently for bed (in clothing kept aside especially for dream incubation), or by sleeping lying in a different direction in bed, or on cushions/a mat set up on the floor, or in a different place than one's usual bed.

WHAT'S NOT INCLUDED

Some dream incubation rituals could include awful things, which we haven't included for obvious reasons. Incubation rituals could also attempt to coerce gods, but I wouldn't think a divine being would respond favorably to force.

As I mentioned, we've included the most common elements in dream incubation rituals, and thankfully none of these are horrible.

DOING THIS RITUAL IN A TEMPLE OR AT A SACRED PLACE

In ancient times, dream incubation was often practiced at temples devoted to it, or at other sacred places.

The following ritual could easily be adapted to a temple setting with other people. Doing it at an outdoor location requires more flexibility—the candles, incense, and the image of the deity you're petitioning could be left out, and the petition could simply be repeated by starlight. Or, if you're doing it with a few people, a central outdoor altar could be set up.

AN ANCIENT DREAM INCUBATION RITUAL

STEP 1. FORMULATE YOUR PETITION

Decide what you wish to be shown as clearly as you can. Also decide who you are addressing the petition to—either a spiritual being of light in the Religion of the Sun, or your own higher Being. Try to choose a spiritual being that is known to be real—whether by ancient or modern accounts. If you're asking your own Being, the petition can be directed to your Spiritual Father or Spiritual Mother.

Work out the wording of your petition. Start by addressing the being you have chosen—you can simply name them, but in ancient petitions it could also include other names they were known by, and a description of them and what they were known for, and why they were being called on specifically.

Next, state what it is you want to be shown in a dream, asking that you be given an answer, including the timeframe you need to know by if there is one.

STEP 2. CLEANSING

Plan out a timeframe before your practice of dream incubation in which you will adhere to standards of goodness in your behavior—in ancient rituals this could be for a minimum of three days.

Also cleanse the room where you will practice dream incubation. Clean and tidy it. Take out any items that might be considered spiritually impure. You may like to decorate it so that it has a temple-like atmosphere as much as is reasonably possible.

STEP 3. CLOSENESS TO THE DIVINE

Set up at least one representation of the being you are petitioning in your room—either as a statue or picture. Place it above or on a table, and then place an unlit candle and an incense burner before it. Make sure the candle and incense can burn safely without there being any risk of starting a fire.

As an option, you can also choose to have another, perhaps smaller, representation of that being to keep as close to you as possible while you sleep. It could be a separate drawing, amulet, or statue, or could also be drawn onto your petition.

If you have chosen to petition your own Spiritual Father or Mother, choose the image of a god or goddess that best represents them to you.

As an optional addition, praying to the deity being petitioned could also form part of your dream incubation ritual. You could do this in whatever time you feel leading up to your incubation. Another option would be to spend time reciting a mantra related to them if there are any.

STEP 4. WRITE OUT THE PETITION

Material
You can simply write your petition on a piece of paper. Or if you'd like to do it the ancient way, you could write it on one of the following: a strip of linen cloth, laurel leaves, or rush leaves. The paper or linen can be any color except black (as this color is used in rituals of darkness).

Timing – Simple Option
For the simplest option, you can write your petition at any time leading up to your dream incubation.

Timing – Celestial Option
As a more involved option, on the day you will do your ritual, you can write out your petition in one of two ways.

>   **1. Sun** - Write it while facing the sun at or soon after sunrise, or not long before it sets, while outside in the sunlight (ideally when the sun is not covered by clouds, though it's ok to do if overcast).

>   **2. Stars** - Write it while under the light of the stars, after the first star has appeared. This option is more difficult, because you need to be able to see, so if you need more light, use a candle or fiery lamp. (But make sure it's in a fireproof holder and there is no risk of starting a fire. For a less mystical option, you can always just use a flashlight!) You can do it while the moon is out—either waxing or full is ideal, but not new (as new moons or "black moons" are used by the dark occult), and also if possible, as it rises. Again, it's ideal if the stars and moon are not covered by clouds.

Once you have written it, also then speak your petition while facing the sun or stars (depending on what you have chosen), repeating it seven times. If you can't say it aloud for any reason, then repeat it mentally.

STEP 5. PURE THOUGHTS
When you are ready to go to bed for the night, enter your room as consciously as you can, and remain concentrated on what you are doing, not letting "impure" (negative, harmful, distracting) thoughts enter your mind.

STEP 6. LIGHT THE CANDLE AND INCENSE

Light the candle and burn incense (frankincense was recommended in ancient times, but any kind should be fine). Make sure that they are in fireproof containers where they can burn safely and there is no risk of starting a fire.

STEP 7. INCANTATION AND CIRCLE OF PROTECTION

Recite an incantation to clear your room of any negative being, and then draw a circle of protection around it. See chapter 27 for this.

STEP 8. DON'T SPEAK TO ANYONE

Once you have done your circle of protection, don't speak to any other person, even in answer to a question, for the remainder of the ritual until you wake up from sleep (unless you need to).

STEP 9. RECITE PETITION

Say your petition aloud to the image/statue of the being you are petitioning and to the candle, which should be illuminating it. Repeat it seven times. On the last time, say it as you hold and circle the petition in the smoke of the incense in a clockwise direction (the petition is moved around in the smoke, while the incense remains still).

STEP 10. KEEP YOUR PETITION NEAR

Place your petition under your pillow, or if you are using a linen cloth, as another option you can wrap it around one of your hands. If using leaves, it's a good idea to wrap them in a natural fabric, e.g. cotton or linen, before putting them under your pillow as ancient people did (so they don't make a mess).

If you are using a smaller image of the being you are petitioning, place this as close to you as you safely can, maybe under your pillow, on your bedside table, hanging from your bedhead, or on the wall above your bed.

STEP 11. EXTINGUISH THE CANDLE AND INCENSE

Extinguish the candle and incense so they are not left burning unattended.

STEP 12. GO TO BED

You can go to bed and simply hold your petition in your mind as you go to sleep, asking and praying that it's answered. As another option, you could visualize traveling to the being you are petitioning, to the holy place they reside, and delivering your petition to them, or visualize a divine being or nature spirit taking your petition for you. Or you could do an OBE practice of your choice related to the being you are petitioning.

STEP 13. REMEMBER YOUR DREAMS

Try to remember your dreams—you could do this by going through the steps for remembering dreams given in the previous chapter. One ancient ritual recommends keeping a book by your bed that you can easily write your dreams in if you wake in the night, or once you get up in the morning.

STEP 14. REPEAT

Now that your petition is already written out, you could repeat this ritual the following nights if you wish from step 5 onward. If the petition you have written down becomes unreadable in any way, replace it by doing step 4. This ritual can potentially be repeated for weeks if wanted, but if you sense you are not getting an answer within a reasonable timeframe, it's time to reassess—there may be some criteria in your life and behavior you need to fulfill first or there might be an issue with what you're asking.

DREAM INCUBATION AT SACRED PLACES

In the past, people often practiced dream incubation in a temple, perhaps somewhere a particular deity was thought to dwell; there is some truth in this because spiritual beings are present in the fifth dimension and may appear where we call them. They can still use and appear at ancient sites of the Religion of the Sun, which some of them may have even been involved with while alive. They also gather in places where people do spiritual practices, such as in meditation rooms or sacred places, particularly when the quality of the practices done there is high.

Ideally, temples could be built or buildings repurposed to recreate some of the atmosphere of the dream incubation temples of old, and to conduct successful dream incubation practices. If it's possible, you could try to practice dream incubation at a sacred place; it could be one dedicated to a particular deity that you're aiming to receive guidance from, or even a site that was used for dream incubation in the past. I've seen a proposal to revive dream incubation as a tourist activity in Egypt,[31] and dream incubation events have recently been initiated at ancient sites in Britain in cooperation with the British Pilgrimage Trust.[32] [33]

There are some things to take into account if you're practicing at an old site, however, which I discuss further in chapter 22 in the section Projecting to a Sacred Place. Many ancient sites may have been used for dark practices, and not everything encountered in dreams there can be benevolent.

To really recreate the dream incubation of the past though, it needs more than just a temple and an attempted simulation of ancient rituals. Dream incubation was part of an ancient religious system that maintained a contact with the higher worlds through adhering to spiritual principles. Ideally, the ancient Religion of the Sun and its order of initiates who have experience of the higher worlds and grades of wisdom and knowledge need to return also—to administer the temples, and to help guide people to and through their experiences, as they once did in the past.

CHAPTER FOURTEEN

Lucid Dreaming

We can become conscious in the astral plane by becoming aware that we're in a dream and are out of our body in another dimension. This is commonly known as lucid dreaming; in it we can do the same things in the fifth dimension as we would when we project from bed.

However, there's a difference between recognizing we're in a dream, yet still being in the projections of our mind, and knowing we're in a dream and seeing what's really there in the fifth dimension.

Exercises to have lucid dreams basically involve questioning to see whether we are in the fifth dimension or in the physical world. This is done during the day to record the question in the subconscious so that it's repeated while dreaming, which thereby prompts us to realize where we are.

The things we do during the day naturally become recorded in our subconscious. It then projects what it has recorded onto the astral plane, which combines with what's really there and becomes the scenes that form dreams. In most cases they seem real to us, but they are mostly just our own creation. Yet everything that exists here has its fifth-dimensional form because things are multidimensional, so if we're awake in that dimension, we could see our house, town, friends, etc., but in a dream what we see tends to be altered. So bear in mind that even when we do realize we are in a dream, we can still find the dream images continue to a certain extent.

The fifth dimension has different laws than here; for example, we can fly and move through objects. So if we question ourselves here using things that only occur in the fifth dimension, like flying, then we know what dimension we are in if they happen.

There are various things we can do to check where we are, but two that I've found have proven to be very successful are jumping and pulling one's finger.

THE ASTRAL JUMP

The first involves jumping slightly into the air with the serious intention of floating or flying. Obviously, we're not going to fly here, but if we do it in the astral plane then we will fly. If we do it enough here, then we begin to do it in dreams. Then when we jump and we float or fly, we can easily realize where we are and become conscious in the astral plane.

When practicing this we don't need to jump very high, just slightly, but we do need to seriously question where we are and whether we are in the physical world or in the astral. It's important to do this questioning sincerely, really asking ourselves the question. If we do it, but think we are really in the physical world, we will jump in our dreams thinking we're in the physical world and it won't work; we may just land straight back down or fly convinced we are in everyday life. We need to really do it with the feeling we're going to fly. When you have flown a few times in the fifth dimension you know how it feels.

PULLING A FINGER AND IT STRETCHES

Years ago, in 1991, I had seen how my body was flexible in the astral, and how I could stretch it, so I thought if I could pull my finger in the astral and it stretched, I could use pulling my finger as a more discreet way of checking whether I was in the physical world or the astral plane. So I tried it in the astral and it worked; my finger stretched. Using this technique and the questioning jump for a time, I was able to become aware that I was in the astral plane about every other night consistently.

To do this check, we question whether we are in the physical world or in the astral world and pull our finger at the same time. In the fifth dimension, matter is different, so if we pull our finger there it stretches—then we can realize we are in the astral.

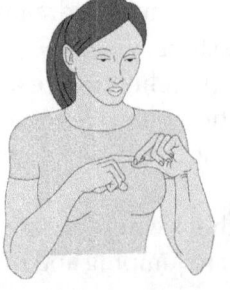 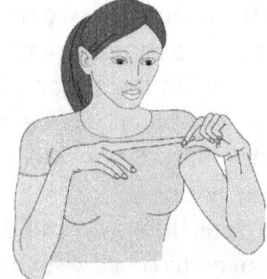

This is useful when it's inappropriate to jump in the air no matter how discreetly, and we want to check where we are (you don't want to look strange by bounding around the office for example).

QUESTIONING WHICH DIMENSION WE'RE IN

It's the question and the following check that will get recorded in the subconscious. The question should bring about that feeling of really wondering "Where am I?"

It's important to do it frequently, checking often during the day. Eventually this becomes recorded in our subconscious and we start doing it in our dreams.

The question itself can be anything that will bring about that feeling and get us to check. So for example, we can ask whether we are in the physical world or in the astral plane, or wonder how we got to the location we are right now, whether there is anything strange happening around us, when we last went to sleep, asking what place we are in, etc.

When questioning, it's best to do it with awareness, looking around carefully at the place we're in, the objects around, etc.

If we don't question where we are by sincerely doubting and wondering, when we question in the dream, we can be convinced that we're in the physical world even to the extent of jumping up into the air, floating, and wondering how we could float in the physical world, or thinking that we can float in our physical body. This has happened to me and to many others very often.

I also used certain things as triggers to prompt me to question whether I was in the astral plane such as the stars at night. For example, I would check where I was and pull my finger and jump every time I saw the stars, and then whenever I dreamed of stars I would remember to question where I was, and it worked! I'm sure it had more of an effect because if spiritual beings wanted me to be conscious, they could put me in a dream scene with stars. Whatever you use to check though, do it safely. Don't abandon safe behavior to check for the astral.

One time in a dream I saw a spiritual being in front of me and he jumped up in the air doing somersaults. I thought that couldn't happen and realized I was out of my body.

Seeing strange things happening in daily life can also be used to remind us to question where we are because strange things happen very often in dreams. We might be looking into the night sky and see something unusual flying around for example. Whenever we see something strange or unusual, we can use it to question whether we're in the physical world or in the astral world. Then we can either pull our finger or jump to check where we are.

Sometimes we might make checks in a dream and still not realize we're dreaming. As I've mentioned, that's happened to me and many others before. For example, one time I was dreaming that I was walking along a street in my hometown, and I decided to check whether I was in the physical world or the astral, and so I jumped to check. I floated and landed a little way ahead, and I said to myself "this is strange, I can float in the physical world." I took another jump, floated in the air, and made another landing softly farther ahead. I made many giant steps like this. I jumped again and somersaulted as I floated in the air; I was still bewildered as to how I could do all this in the physical world. As I came back to the ground I woke up in bed and realized how close I'd been to waking up in the astral plane, but not close enough. It showed me that the way I questioned in the physical world was done without believing I was in the fifth dimension, as I was convinced I was in the physical world every time I checked—so that was what I recorded in my subconscious and it appeared in my dreams.

Another time while practicing with a group of people I had a strange experience. I was lying down and saw that one man in the group wasn't in his sleeping bag or in the room, so I got up to take a look. Something felt strange, so I checked my body and it was solid; it was physical, nothing stretched, and I tried to jump to float but it didn't work. I thought I wasn't in the astral and I decided I would lie down to continue my exercise to perhaps have an out-of-body experience. As I lay down, I woke up without realizing that my body had been sleeping, and saw that the person was sleeping in the room—he hadn't gotten up after all. This illustrates how easy it is to be in the astral and believe it's the physical world.

I have found it most effective to do physical rather than mental checks, such as jumping or pulling my finger as I've already described. Anything safe that provides a physical check will work. I have tried slowly putting my hand through an object while in the astral. But on one occasion I couldn't get it to go through the object and I didn't know where I was. Had I made a second check using something else such as pulling my finger, I probably would have confirmed that I was in the fifth dimension.

REMINDERS

A large part in getting the questioning recorded in the subconscious is remembering to question where we are in the first place. To help with that, we can set reminders to trigger our questioning, like for example leaving notes around our house, setting an alarm clock to go off at regular intervals, or having a reminder on a computer appearing at intervals. After a while though, it's easy to start ignoring or not bothering to use these mechanical reminders.

Having an overall plan for OBEs and spiritual work provides a direction that will have someone doing and thinking about spiritual things more, thus increasing the likelihood of them remembering to question where they are. As part of a plan like this, someone could bring spiritual activities into their day with things like astral exercises, awareness walks, meditation/concentration, mantras, and meeting and practicing with like-minded people.

AWARENESS

The clearer our level of conscious awareness in daily life, the clearer our dreams will tend to be, ad the more likely we are to have a lucid dream. I say "tend to" because there can be other factors that make them less lucid and difficult to remember.

I've found it useful to practice being aware, which is a matter of getting out of the usual daydreaming, and "waking up" to the present moment by clearly perceiving where we are and what we're doing, while also being aware of our own internal state. If we catch ourselves daydreaming, we immediately go back to what we're doing in the present so that our perception wakes up. This waking up is momentary, but it has a good overall effect if it's practiced enough. I explain how to practice awareness in depth in my book on self-knowledge.

The more we can practice being aware of what our inner state is, and of where we are and what we're doing, the greater the effect it's going to have. By combining this with questioning which dimension we're in, we greatly increase our chances of being conscious in the astral plane.

To get started with practicing being aware in the present moment regularly, it's useful to use these three activities to help to remember to be aware and to train oneself in it. These are things someone is likely to be doing each day, but usually without being fully aware of doing them:

1. Washing hands
2. Putting shoes on and taking them off
3. Eating

To do this exercise, try to concentrate upon each of these activities, being aware of doing them and not allowing your mind to interfere and take you off into daydreams. If you do go into a daydream, go straight back to the activity you are doing. This helps with remembering to be more aware generally. I started doing this exercise back in 1990; I used it for a while and it helped me quite a lot. Someone can start with these three, but most daily activities can be used for this purpose.

Discovering how awareness works is a matter for experimentation. If you know about self-observation, then you could apply it too, because awareness should be done with self-observation and is really part of it.

You could also try awareness walks, where someone goes for a walk each day if they can with the intention of being aware, observing oneself, and at intervals, performing reality checks to question whether they are in the physical world or the astral world. A walk to work or anywhere on a daily basis can be used as an awareness walk and be incorporated into a daily framework of spiritual activities.

I've found going for walks in nature to be very good for practicing being aware of the present moment. This picture of me was taken in 1993.

After two years of practicing conscious projection, I was fortunate to live close to the countryside and some small mountains. At that time I could concentrate on my practices all weekend without interruption, and on any days or hours I had free during the week I would go out for walks for hours to just concentrate on what I was doing, trying to be aware all the time. Then I would go back home and practice concentration, meditation, or conscious projection.

This built up a strong level of concentration and I was often able to lie down, concentrate on my heart, and leave my body. As soon as I came back into it, I would concentrate on my heart and again leave my body, and would keep repeating this. At the time I also learned to go into the astral by concentrating on where I wanted to go, which proved pretty effective.

GOING BACK INTO A DREAM TO LEARN MORE ABOUT IT

If we remember a dream when we wake up, we can go back into it. This is useful if we want to understand more about it. This can also be done as an OBE or dream incubation practice. It's done by remembering the dream and placing ourselves back in it as we're falling asleep, as though we're still in the dream, using our memory and imagination.

If we really place ourselves in it and sleep arrives, we'll find ourselves back in that dream. It's possible to then remember how we got there, and to realize we're out of our bodies in the astral plane.

WATCHING DREAM IMAGES WHILE FALLING ASLEEP

As we're falling asleep, we can use the start of the dream images to astral project. To do this, we relax our body as we go into sleep, watching for the first dream images that come up, and then when we're aware of the dream images becoming real, we slowly get up from bed. If we catch it at the right moment, we'll get up in the astral.

It's a little hit and miss as it's so easy to just fall asleep instead, and so you really have to get the timing right; it takes a bit of practice.

These dream images are different from thoughts. They appear to be almost real—we get to know them as we experience them.

PART 4
TECHNIQUES FOR HAVING CONSCIOUS OUT-OF-BODY EXPERIENCES

CHAPTER FIFTEEN

Preparing for Conscious Projection

To be successful in consciously projecting, we need to have effective techniques and learn to use them skillfully. Building skills for conscious projection is similar to building skills for almost anything. It's like an athlete training to run a race.

Although out-of-body experiences can happen spontaneously and without any practice, preparation is usually required for most people; it makes it easier to project. If you want to have OBEs on a regular basis, you're likely to need regular practice.

One of the first things to do is to prepare your environment. As much as you can, try to have a quiet surrounding where you can be undisturbed. Have a reasonably harmonious environment that's not a mess, and have some quiet time before you begin. It will be more difficult if you go straight from the TV or computer to your exercise.

The first thing to learn is to relax, and then to concentrate and visualize.

A RELAXATION EXERCISE

It's important to relax the whole body. When we're tense it's more difficult to focus upon the exercise and for the physical and astral bodies to separate and fall asleep; we need sleep for conscious projection. So an exercise of relaxation prepares us for the projection exercises that will follow.

There are many relaxation exercises. I'll give a simple one I've used a lot; it's essentially the technique used in the practice of yoga nidra. It's a matter of relaxing all the muscles in the body as follows:

Lie down on your back with your legs straight and your arms by your side, or if you're sitting, remain in a position you can maintain with the minimum amount of tension.

Go through each muscle, relaxing them all one by one. You can start anywhere as long as you go through each muscle methodically, relaxing each one completely.

Pay particular attention to the face once you get to it. There can be little areas of tension that are easily overlooked—relax them all.

Once you have checked everywhere, repeat the procedure—just to make sure that there are no areas of tension you have missed or that have been reintroduced—and aim to be totally relaxed.

If you find it easier, you can say in your mind "right foot relax," "right calf relax," "right knee relax," etc., or just "right foot," "right calf," "right knee," (as in yoga nidra) as you go through and relax each body part, to help yourself stay focused.

In this state one is now ready to begin their exercise of projection.

This can be practiced every night before going to sleep and also before doing concentration exercises.

Spend whatever time on this exercise it takes to relax your muscles, which is normally about five minutes once you learn to do it properly.

There's a variation on this technique you could also try. Relax each muscle of the body by tensing each muscle slightly and then immediately letting it go loose. Go through the whole body this way, paying attention to parts of the body that could be tense.

Once someone feels confident they can relax their body, they are ready to learn to concentrate and visualize.

THE ANCIENT PRACTICE OF CONCENTRATION

Concentrating and quieting the mind are referred to in a number of ancient sources as being methods for astral projection (see chapter 17).

Concentration was also an important practice in the ancient Religion of the Sun generally, as the ability to focus the mind is necessary for carrying out any spiritual exercise successfully, including those to astral project. Practitioners of ancient Hindu yoga (which derives from the Religion of the Sun) trained in concentration, and this training became a fundamental discipline in Eastern religions, particularly Buddhism.

There are ancient references to training oneself to concentrate in the Hindu text the Yoga Sutras of Patanjali, which is considered the foundational text of yoga, though is based on much older yogic teachings.[1] It starts by saying:

> "Yoga is the process of ending the fluctuations of the mind. Then, the seer dwells in his true nature. At other times, when he is not in the state of yoga, man remains identified with the thought-waves in the mind."[2]
>
> ~ YOGA SUTRAS OF PATANJALI

In other words, yoga was the discipline of learning to control one's mind (rather than one's body, as commonly thought). This was based on a very ancient understanding of yoga, as the earliest mention of yoga appears in the oldest Hindu text of all, the Rig Veda, where it refers to yoga as a method of controlling one's mind:

> "Seers of the vast illumined Seer [the Spiritual Sun] yogically controlled their minds and their intellects."[3]
>
> ~ RIG VEDA

The Yoga Sutras outline some different types of concentration exercises, such as concentrating on an object, which I cover in this chapter.

However, it also goes on to list numerous extraordinary powers that can be gained through practicing a profound level of concentration, such as being able to reduce oneself to the size of an atom, gain the strength of an elephant,

Yogi meditating on the bank of the Ganges River in India. The earliest description of yoga indicates it was practiced in a seated pose before the sun, while stilling and concentrating one's mind.

and make oneself invisible. Although the ability to concentrate can increase our abilities in the physical world quite dramatically, it's nowhere near to this degree. Instead, these powers may have largely been based on experiences yogis had in the fifth dimension where the laws are different. They probably didn't make such a clear distinction between the physical and astral as we do today, and may have been engaged in long concentration practices where they experienced remarkable things while out of their bodies, perhaps without realizing they were in an OBE, as I and others have done. By practicing concentration, they certainly would have been having OBEs, and by concentrating on an object, they could have been going into the object while out of their bodies and getting knowledge about it (as I describe further on). By concentrating and having OBEs, we can have some of the abilities the Yoga Sutras describe, such as levitating, while out of our bodies.

There is another possible explanation. Some of these powers were said to have been possessed by the ancient Children of the Sun, who were remembered as being more psychic and as having less animalistic bodies than we do. Those who wished to emulate them may have thought it was possible to gain these powers by practicing some of their ancient spiritual knowledge, not realizing that human physical bodies are far more limited in what they can do, and so many of these powers became unattainable and only legendarily attributed to a tiny few in history.

WHY CONCENTRATION IS IMPORTANT FOR OBES

It's important to be able to concentrate on the exercise of projection we're doing without being distracted from it by other thoughts, as willed conscious projection usually occurs when the mind is concentrated at the exact moment sleep arrives.

For this reason, most techniques for conscious projection are variations of concentrating the mind and/or visualizing.

Being concentrated is having the mind and the whole of one's attention on one thing alone.

In ancient texts, the key to having OBEs was being able to remain conscious in the present moment while falling asleep, and this was often done through using exercises of concentration, as it keeps one firmly focused and aware in the present.

In the Tibetan Book of the Dead quoted in chapter 3, it says that sleep is entered consciously when consciousness is undistractedly kept in its natural state. In the Tantrasara, leaving the body occurs when one remains "steady in the state of pure consciousness [...] like a tranquil sea." Likewise in the Yoga Vasistha it says that astral projection occurs when thoughts stop, allowing consciousness, whose natural state is tranquil and silent, to shine.

The moment we lose awareness, which is maintained through concentration, can be the moment we fall asleep unconsciously. It's a bit like walking a tightrope, which is why it needs training. The same applies when we are consciously out of our bodies in the fifth dimension—the moment we lose awareness, the moment we often lose the conscious experience and go into a dream or wake up in our physical bodies.

This was shown to Lara over a decade ago in an OBE using a simple visual metaphor. She saw a teacup resting in a saucer. The tea inside the cup was fluctuating, as if it was being shaken, though the cup and saucer itself were still. Once the tea inside the cup became still, the cup floated up away from the saucer, and this was said to represent how OBEs happen. When our psyche (that which is in the cup) is stilled, we are able to naturally leave our bodies (the saucer) consciously.

So why does concentration allow us to have OBEs? There appear to be two main reasons.

One of the reasons seems to do with how the brain works. As I discussed in chapter 10, the brain works to limit the perceptions of consciousness to the perspective of its physical body and the physical world. This constant identification with the physical body needs to be overcome to be able to have an OBE. This is where concentration can help.

Concentration focuses and stills the mind. By stilling the mind, we reduce brain activity. The less brain activity, the less influence the brain has over the perceptions of consciousness. This allows consciousness to break free of some of the limitations the brain places over it. The result is that consciousness naturally experiences more of its true nature, which is not limited to a physical body. When the mind (and brain) is focused as we fall asleep, consciousness naturally separates from the physical body. Normally this separation only occurs during unconsciousness, so concentration brings about the conditions for separating consciously.

This is likely why Eastern traditions, like yoga, Taoism, Jainism, and Buddhism, say that by stilling the mind, one's true being naturally manifests: "Yoga [concentration] is the process of ending the fluctuations of the mind. Then, the seer dwells in his true nature."[4] Ancient concentration practices are methods that were developed and used to overcome some of the brain's limitations.

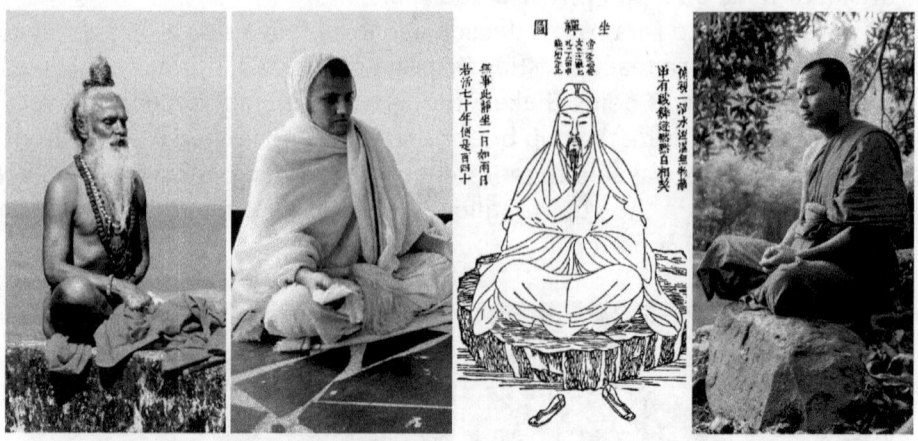

Concentration is a fundamental practice in the major Eastern religions (from left to right): Hinduism, Jainism, Taoism, and Buddhism.

In fact, as ancient texts like the Rig Veda and Upanishads describe, when the mind is completely silenced, which is to still it even more than when it's concentrated, consciousness is set free from all limitations placed upon it by the brain, and even by the mind itself, and returns to its most natural, original state. That is, it briefly returns to the Source and has a Source experience, as I described in chapter 3.

Another reason is likely to do with the way we transition into the astral plane as we fall asleep. As we start to separate from our physical body, it seems that at least some of our egos go with us, which is why we can sometimes hear them as separate voices in the moment of going to sleep or waking. Joined with them, our state of daydreaming in the physical world turns into dreams as we enter the astral. When we concentrate, we temporarily become aware and thus clear of egos, which likely allows us to enter the astral free of them, and thus consciously.

In Eastern traditions concentration was recognized as a state in which one was free of the egos. In daily life, it's often once we start thinking that we lose awareness of our surroundings and inner state, and the egos begin manifesting in our psyche. By concentrating or stilling the mind, we are able to stop this process for as long as we remain concentrated. This is the same state that enables conscious astral projection.

If someone practices concentration well, they can feel completely conscious and clear of egos, allowing the person to abide in their true nature, which is consciousness. No wonder concentration was pursued as a main method for attaining enlightenment. The problem is that unless the egos are eliminated, they will always return—and this is something I deal with in great detail in my book on self-knowledge.

However, all we need to be able to astral project is to concentrate and be clear of egos long enough to go into sleep.

For OBEs to occur, concentration needs to be combined with sleep, as it's with sleep that our astral body separates from our physical body. This differentiates concentration practices in which someone remains awake and can experience heightened perceptions while still in their physical body, from concentration that is combined with sleep in which someone can then leave their physical body consciously.

HOW TO TRAIN IN CONCENTRATION

To be able to concentrate for astral projection, it's best to train oneself to concentrate and visualize for a period of time before beginning astral exercises, and after learning to relax. This need not take long, and someone can always continue to develop their concentration after they have begun to try to consciously project. Someone won't lose anything by starting their projection exercises straightaway, but just bear in mind, they are less likely to succeed until they improve their ability to concentrate.

For those who wish to project, it's best to aim to make concentration exercises part of one's daily routine of exercises for conscious projection, to keep one's mind sharp, focused, and more ready for it.

In daily life, they can also try to concentrate upon whatever activity they do at any one time. Sitting exercises of concentration also train and develop the ability to concentrate upon any projection or spiritual exercise.

We can develop concentration by concentrating on whatever activity we're doing; it doesn't have to be a sit-down meditative exercise.

Being concentrated upon one thing is different from having the mind completely silenced. There are techniques for silencing the mind, but I'm not including them here because they are not specific to the subject of conscious projection.

I was painting a room once where the walls had patterned wallpaper. I painted over the pattern only to find that as the paint dried, the pattern showed through and I had to repaint the walls again. I had set out to treat this decorating as an exercise in concentration, so as I painted, I tried to concentrate upon every brush stroke. It felt almost painful to bring myself back to the awareness of what I was doing as my mind kept wandering, but whenever it did, I kept bringing myself back. The pattern showed through the second coat, so I applied a third, and it appeared through that too.

A friend suggested I paint it with gray to block out the pattern underneath, so I did. It looked better, but there was still some pattern showing, so I put another coat of gray on, followed by the actual color. Still some pattern showed through, but I didn't get despondent, I just kept concentrating on what I was doing. By the seventh coat, the walls were evenly covered and looked clear of the pattern. I managed to sustain a good level of concentration and remained unconcerned with either success or failure. At night I was conscious in the astral plane; it was very lucid and I was given a profound and meaningful teaching.

Unusual psychic phenomena can occur when concentrating. I've had quite a few experiences of them. During one concentration practice I sat on cushions in front of a candle and concentrated on it. I looked at it in great detail and with full awareness, but after some time I realized my eyelids were closed and yet I was still seeing, but in a different way. As soon as I realized, it became dark as my eyes were closed. My vision had returned to normal and I opened my eyes. Another time when I was concentrating on a candle, I focused just right and went out of my body straight into the flame, then in a millisecond I was back in my body; I felt no sensation of heat from the fire and hadn't even realized my physical body had fallen asleep.

Although it's rare, it's possible to project with our eyes open. For example, while concentrating upon an object and looking at it, the concentration can be so intense that with our eyes open we can go straight out of the body and into the object.

VISUALIZATION

We can astral project by using visualization and it can also be used as an exercise to prepare for projection. When we visualize something, we consciously imagine or remember it, and the more concentrated we are in the visualization, the better it will be.

If our mind is focused enough, it's possible to visualize and see something that's real which we know nothing about. This is demonstrated in some kinds of remote viewing. The more concentrated we are, the better we can visualize and pick up on fifth-dimensional information.

No matter how well we visualize something, the subconscious will have some kind of effect, but in well concentrated and successful visualizations the effect of the subconscious is minimized.

We can visualize something that's entirely from our imagination and project with it, as long as we're concentrated on it—although what we're imagining may have an effect upon what we experience in the fifth dimension.

I prefer to use real things so as to minimize the effect of my subconscious upon the fifth dimension, and because it's easier to stop the visualization of something real from becoming fantasy.

There's a difference between this kind of visualization and fantasy. Visualization has an order and a structure, unlike the randomness that some of the free-flowing fantasy imagination creates. With fantasy the mind goes where it wants without a continuous direction or sustained concentrated thought. Most of what exists in fantasy is a product of the subconscious, and its random scattered images make it less effective for projection.

PRACTICING SITTING CONCENTRATION AND VISUALIZATION

The more we practice concentration and visualization, the better we become at it. And with daily practice, our chances of projecting will dramatically increase. The practices are done sitting or lying down.

I've given some concentration and visualization exercises in this book as examples; they are ones that have worked for me, but they're obviously not the only ones that will work. The essential element in having successful projection exercises is concentration, and there are many variations of concentration and visualization. With the ability to concentrate, most exercises will work, which is why it's so important to develop these skills. Even using sound, mantras, and guided meditations requires a degree of concentration to be successful.

I've divided concentration and visualization exercises into two types: those done on an object or a place, and those using imagination. Each of them has a particular purpose.

It's important not to force one's mind. To help adjust to the exercises I recommend trying them for a very short period of time initially, such as five to ten minutes, and then gradually increasing the time depending upon what one feels they need and are comfortable with, for example, to twenty minutes.

Then when someone goes to do their exercise to project, their mind is already trained to concentrate and visualize and the projection is more likely to succeed.

I suggest practicing concentration/visualization exercises daily to prepare for projection and then maintaining them daily whenever one wants to consciously project.

THE PROBLEM OF CHATTERING THOUGHTS

One of the main obstacles is the continuously chattering, daydreaming mind.

> "Steadfast and continuous practice is needed to still the mind of [fluctuations]. [...]
>
> Disease, inertia, doubt, carelessness, laziness, sensuality, delusion, impotency and instability are the barriers that distract the mind.
>
> Sorrow, despair, unsteadiness of the body and irregular breathing are the symptoms of a distracted mind.
>
> To remove these meditate on one principal."[5]
> ~ YOGA SUTRAS OF PATANJALI

Attempts at conscious projection usually fail because the mind is unable to be concentrated on one thing. It chatters away all day, so when we try to do an exercise to project, the mind carries on chattering. Thoughts that were active during the day continue to be active and they interrupt the exercise, causing it to fail.

However, in daily life, when we're aware and concentrated upon whatever activity we're doing, we train and educate our mind to be focused upon one thing and cut down the chatter and interfering inner states (egos), so that when we do our exercise of projection, we have a more focused mind and are more able to concentrate upon the exercise, making it more likely to succeed.

During our daily lives it's necessary to be able to think and plan, remember things, solve problems, carry out tasks, etc., but the problem is that it's so compulsive—the mind just runs of its own accord. The mind is scattered, the thoughts go on and on, and it's difficult for it to be on one thing and be profoundly concentrated for any period of time.

To help focus the mind it can be useful to set aside a period of time, say a weekend or a week, in which we simplify our daily tasks so that we can concentrate on them one at a time, and incorporate concentration exercises for ten to twenty minutes at a time, or longer, into our day.

When we train our mind to concentrate, it's possible to direct it at will to a psychic task such as conscious projection or meditation and be successful in it.

The ability to focus the mind is not something that happens overnight, although it is possible to get it right occasionally in the beginning. It takes time to gradually educate the mind to be concentrated on just one thing, as it's not used to functioning like that. It requires a great deal of practice to train the mind to focus.

If we're not concentrated when trying to project, we either get taken into sleep by a thought, or become restless and unable to sleep. In both cases, practice is needed to address the lack of concentration and the issues with sleep, as long as there are no other factors such as illness interfering.

CONCENTRATION AND VISUALIZATION ON AN OBJECT

> "Meditation on an object can produce extraordinary sense perceptions, the mind gains confidence and this helps perseverance. [...] [Concentration] is fixing the mind to one point – the object being meditated upon."[6]
> ~ YOGA SUTRAS OF PATANJALI

I'll explain a technique I've used quite a lot, which is to visualize the details of an object and remember it. It's useful training for increasing the ability to concentrate and visualize when we go to do our exercises for conscious projection.

To practice it, first pick an object—it can be anything. A popular object for this is a lit candle, but if you use a candle, make sure you only use it if it is safe to do so and there's no risk of starting a fire. Sit down and place the object where you can see it clearly. Then concentrate upon it in great detail, observing how it looks, perceive its textures, shapes, colors, the material it's made of, the way light reflects on it, etc., observing whatever you can about it.

When you've clearly observed it, then close your eyes and recreate the object in your mind, exactly as you've seen it. If there are things you can't recreate because you didn't look at them properly, or if the image is fading away, open your eyes and look at it again. Study it, then close your eyes and recreate the image again in your mind. Keep doing this to visualize it as clearly as you can.

A variation of this exercise using a candle is a method in Jainism used to develop what they call one-pointedness, which is essentially concentration. In this variation, concentrate on the lit candle with your eyes open, observing it closely as mentioned above. Ideally this is done in a darkened room with the candle against a plain background at eye level. When you close your eyes, visualize the flame at the center of your brow. If you're having difficulty, open your eyes, observe the candle again, and then close them and visualize the flame again, repeating this for the minimum you need to. The candle is used as a symbol—the wax is the body and the flame represents consciousness (although we are consciousness and aren't separate from it). The exercise should be done remembering its deep meaning; it's meant to help one understand their spiritual center.[7]

We can also vary the object we use for the exercise, for example, we can use a glass of water, a plant, flowers, etc.

This exercise using an object gently trains the mind to concentrate and visualize. It's best to do it regularly (at least once a day for five to ten minutes) at a different time from projection exercises and whenever is convenient, but not for more than ten minutes initially. If you want to do it more times each day then do so, but increase it very gradually, because the mind needs to be educated and trained and shouldn't be forced.

Remember to close your eyes when you are recreating the object in your mind and to recreate it often. Don't try to stay there with your eyes open or force yourself to keep staring at the object for a long period of time.

Essentially this same exercise is used in Buddhism, where it's referred to as *kasina* meditation. It was widely known among the Buddhist schools of India, and may have been based on a technique that existed before Buddha's time. It's found in a commentary written in the fifth century AD that was intended to summarize Buddha's teachings, but differs in style to the main methods of Buddhist concentration.[8] The *kasina* method involves concentrating on an object with one's eyes open, before closing them and recreating the object in one's mind, and then repeating the process until, as a first stage, one is able to see the object with one's eyes closed exactly as it appears with them open.[9] There is a list of things given to concentrate on, and one of them is fire.[10] Today there are Buddhists who use a candle for the fire *kasina*, as I have used for visualization many times.

CONCENTRATION AND VISUALIZATION ON AN OBJECT WITH IMAGINATION

Here's another exercise which is an extension of the first technique.

To do it, take an object and sit down where you can see it clearly. Then concentrate upon it in great detail using the first technique, observing how it looks, seeing its textures, shapes, colors, the material it's made of, the way that light reflects on it, etc., discovering everything you can about it. When you've clearly seen it, then close your eyes and recreate the object in your mind exactly as you've seen it. If there are things you can't visualize because you didn't look at them properly, or if the image is fading away, open your eyes and look at it again. Study it, then close your eyes and visualize the image again in your mind. Keep doing this process so that you visualize it as clearly as you can.

When you have clearly visualized the object (while having your eyes still closed), imagine, perceive, and visualize the inside of the object. In the case of a candle for example, go inside the flame and visualize the inside of the flame. Go further exploring anything else you would like to explore about the object. As you are visualizing/concentrating on it, feel yourself being the object; if using a candle, what it feels like being a flame burning on the tip of a wick. At that point you could ask questions to explore the object, such as: What is fire made of? How does it work? What is it for? What is it to be the object? If we pursue the answers far enough, we can go beyond what the logical mind can find the answers to and momentarily have a silent mind, rather than just being concentrated. Or if we stay concentrated enough, we can have an OBE if the conditions are right.

We can learn to focus our mind very well through this simple, but powerful technique. On the surface it looks mundane, but it can be quite a spiritual exercise.

The composer(s) of the Yoga Sutras of Patanjali understood this, as it says that by concentrating in a profound way upon objects, someone can get knowledge about them that is beyond what the mind can ordinarily find out.

> "Dharana (concentration) is fixing the mind to one point—the object being meditated upon.

> Dhyan is the uninterrupted flow of the mind to the object.
>
> When the mind becomes one with the object this is Samadhi.
>
> The three together [are called samyama] [...].
>
> By mastering samyama the light of awareness and wisdom arises. [...]
>
> By practicing samyama on the sun, knowledge of the entire solar system is obtained.[11]
>
> [...] Gradually, one's mastery in concentration extends from the primal atom to the greatest magnitude."[12]
>
> ~ YOGA SUTRAS OF PATANJALI

This type of concentrated visualization can be done on any object, though I prefer to use those that are natural. It can be done with a flower in a vase at home, a glass of water, a plant or rock in the garden, and so on.

We can also do this exercise in a quiet and safe spot outdoors using a tree, a mountain, an ocean, a lake, or river, etc. We can also visualize a place by being there or by looking at an image of it.

To build up one's skills, I recommend varying the objects and continuing with at least ten minutes each day. It's best to gradually increase the time spent on this exercise, beginning with just a little.

As with the previous exercise, we open our eyes to see the object and then close our eyes when we're visualizing. You can keep repeating this several times if you wish, but don't try to stay there with your eyes open or force yourself to keep staring at the object for a long period of time while observing it.

IMAGINATIVE VISUALIZATION

> "Also, meditate on anything that appeals to you."[13]
>
> ~ YOGA SUTRAS OF PATANJALI

This technique is a visualization of something we can't physically see, but which really exists, and can be either an object or place.

To do this exercise, instead of looking at something physically present and trying to recreate it in your mind, close your eyes and visualize an object or a place that you know of which is not present, creating it solely from your memory and/or imagination, with the aim of seeing it in detail as though it were real, or creating the experience of being there. These memories can be based on having seen the object or visited the place, or it could be based on looking at photos and videos of it. Imagination is then used to fill in any missing gaps to create an immersive and lifelike visualization.

For example, you could visualize yourself as though you were sitting and quietly observing an ancient site, like watching the clouds roll over the ancient mountaintop city of Machu Picchu as the sun rises. Or you could visualize yourself traveling around by either walking or flying/floating—for example seeing and feeling yourself flying over the Great Pyramids of Egypt through the desert air, or exploring it at ground level, touching and feeling the stones.

Objects or places could be created from memories whereby you try to remember the past as clearly as you can, as you may have visited the place before, or watched documentaries about it. But where you can't remember, or haven't seen something, then you can imagine or even try to perceive what it looks, feels, smells, and/or sounds like—for example, what the grass looks like up close around Stonehenge, or what the bird songs at Delphi sound like.

Although almost all of what's seen using imagination is likely to be from the imagination, visualization can facilitate "remote viewing" in which we see something that's really there, and is a form of seeing or communicating beyond the five senses. Remote viewing has been thoroughly tested and it shows that our minds send and receive information beyond our physical brain. I'm sure this happens because our psyche is in the fifth dimension and so we can pick up on fifth-dimensional phenomena with it.

I used to do remote viewing quite often. When I was a child, I took part in an experiment in which we were to try and pick up on what a man at a different location was trying to communicate with his thoughts. To do this, I first visualized him and the place where he was, and was able to accurately see what he had communicated from a distance.

> "Knowledge of the subtle, the hidden and the distant is gained."[14]
> ~ YOGA SUTRAS OF PATANJALI

If you decide to try this type of visualization, keep to the same time as the other exercises.

SUMMARY

To recap, for those who would like to use these exercises to prepare for projection:

Learn to relax your body—it takes a short time to learn to relax—and then train yourself to visualize and concentrate to prepare yourself for projection.

Start with short daily exercises of concentration lasting five to ten minutes, and gradually increase the amount of time to twenty or thirty minutes as you feel comfortable with it.

Relax your body before doing a concentration exercise.

Begin your exercises of projection whenever you're ready, but I suggest maintaining daily concentration exercises whenever you're doing nightly projection ones.

If you want to use these exercises to project, firstly do your concentration/visualization exercise. Then lie down, relax, and begin to concentrate upon what you remember of the object or visualization, continuing to visualize it in your mind as you fall asleep.

You can also continue to look at the object, but ideally you would look at it from a position you can sleep in. If you decide to do the exercise this way, keep observing the object until you feel you have observed it thoroughly, then close your eyes and hold the image of it until it fades. Once it does, open your eyes, look at it in detail again, and when you have concentrated on it, close your eyes and recreate the image again. Keep doing this over and over. As you do this exercise you may drift in and out of sleep, and this can be a very good way to project.

CHAPTER SIXTEEN

The Process of Conscious Projection

Every time we go to sleep, we leave our physical body behind and go into the astral plane of the fifth dimension. This normally takes place unconsciously, but with astral/conscious projection we are aware of some or most of that process taking place.

If you've ever had a sensation of falling just as you're going to sleep, what you've been aware of is your astral body going back into the physical one. You'd fallen asleep unconsciously and weren't aware of splitting into the fifth dimension, just of the moment of going back into your body as you woke. The normal process of projecting and coming back to the body is usually not as alarming as this because we are not caught by such a surprise.

When we carry out a projection technique it causes us to go through the process of sleep consciously. We are then aware of all or some of the processes that take place within the transition period between wakefulness and sleep, until the two bodies separate.

We can project at any time—we just need to sleep. Many people have great success with an afternoon nap, particularly when they are not too tired when they try. The night has its own advantages though; the atmosphere is quieter and more conducive to mystical things.

It's possible to project many times in one night, going out into the fifth dimension, coming back, going back out again, and so on.

ASKING FOR SPIRITUAL ASSISTANCE

We often have OBEs because we are helped to by spiritual beings or our own Being, and what we experience there can often be due to a message or teaching they wish to impart to us. So for those who want to do something that has a spiritual purpose, it's important to ask for spiritual assistance from spiritual beings or one's own Spiritual Mother or Father before doing an exercise of projection, and even before going to sleep at night if one wishes to receive helpful messages in dreams. We can do very little of significance without the help of spiritual beings, and it is they who give us the important experiences we need to have.

We can also ask for help to be taken to different places or shown things, but for that someone needs to be open to what they see, and to be intuitive, without letting their emotions impede them.

THE PROCESS OF SPLITTING FROM THE BODY

With whatever exercises and programs we do use to project, the first thing we need to do is to get into a position in which we can sleep, lying down in bed for example. That's because we detach from the physical body with sleep. For most people, the most effective position for projection is to lie down on their back. Don't attempt astral projection by doing anything unsafe, harmful, or stressful—the exercises are for when we are comfortable and relaxed.

Then we need to be able to relax our body because tension will hold us into it. Next, without moving, we go straight from the relaxation to our technique for projection.

There are different phenomena, sensations, and so on that happen as we begin to fall asleep and leave the body. As someone practices projection they may feel all of them, some of them, or none of them, in which case, they may just find themselves in the fifth dimension without being aware of projecting there.

After relaxing and beginning an astral projection technique, one's body may feel very heavy, yet strangely at the same time someone may feel very light. Sometimes it can feel as though just one body part has separated or is in a different position. For example, a foot might feel as though it's pointing in a different direction, or a hand may feel as though it has lifted up. This can indicate that the split has already happened and we simply need to get up to be able to start moving and traveling in the fifth dimension, or sometimes just that the astral split is starting to happen but is not complete.

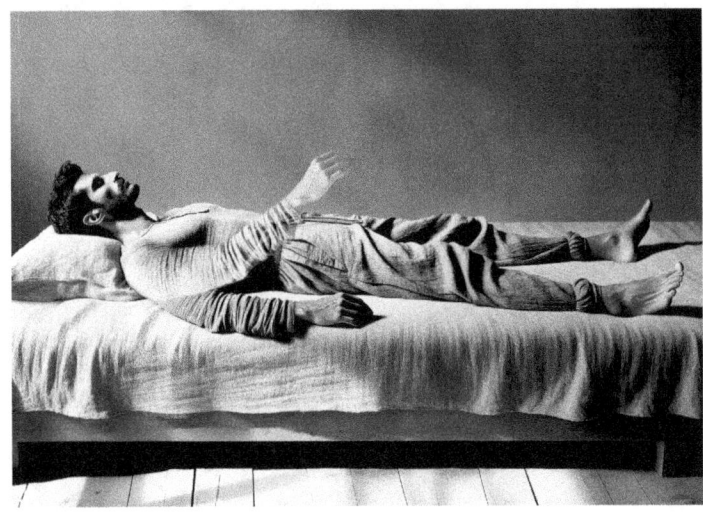

At other times we simply rise out. As someone practices a technique for projection they may hear a faint, very high-pitched noise whirring like a motor inside their head, feel unable to move, and then experience a kind of electric sensation passing through their body. As this happens, they may feel themselves rising and lifting up out of their body. As they lift, they have projected—they're in the fifth dimension.

The sensations of projecting can sometimes be different to the way I've just described. For example, when concentrating on a technique our heartbeats may seem to intensify, and as they get stronger, there is a feeling of moving with them. The sensation increases as we go higher and higher with each beat, until we rise up out of the body.

Sometimes during an exercise there may be a feeling of being unable to move, which is commonly known as sleep paralysis, and can happen both while falling asleep and waking. This is because the physical and astral bodies are separating (or in the case of waking, remerging together) and the movement of the physical body is being switched over for movement of the astral body, which happens as we go into the fifth dimension. If the exercise is continued successfully, the process will complete—the immobilization will pass and the astral split will occur.

STEPPING OUT INTO ANOTHER REALM

Once we project, we are then in a completely different dimension. If we've projected high up out of our body, then we know we're in the fifth dimension, but if our astral body has projected just a little way out, by lifting up just slightly into the air for example, we can be unsure as to whether the astral split has happened.

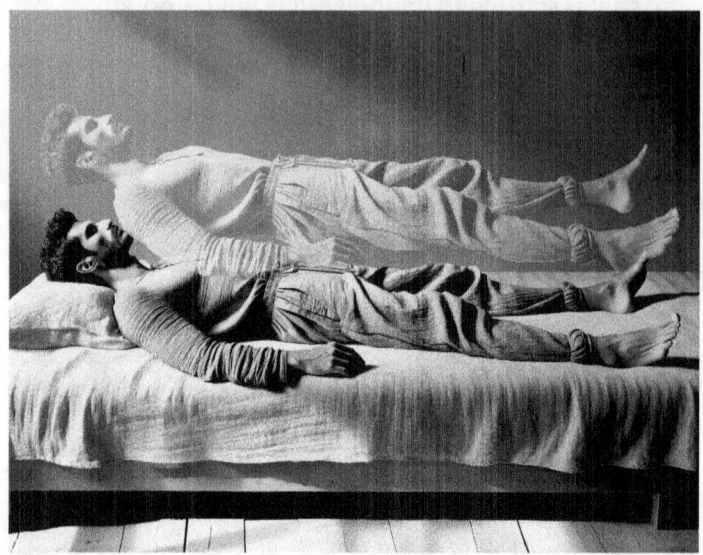

It's possible to check whether projection has occurred by getting up and examining the place we're in to see if anything there is different to how it would be in the physical world, whether the room is exactly like it is normally, or if there's anything strange.

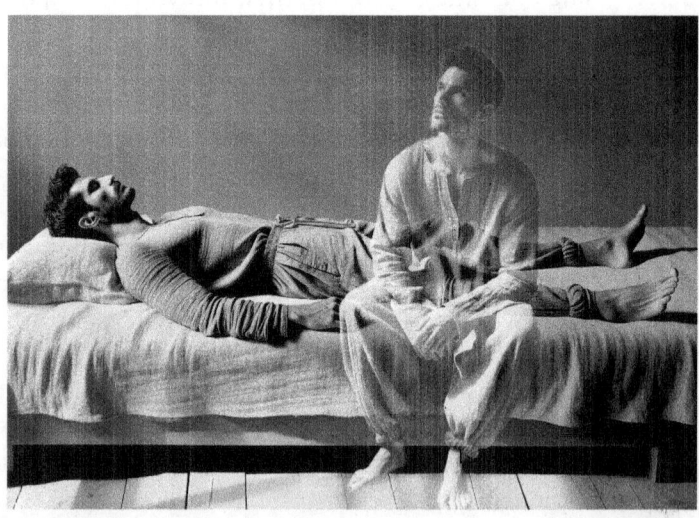

Another way of checking is to jump a little in the air and try to float. If it's the fifth dimension we can fly and a whole new dimension is open to us to explore—but don't try jumping out of the window or anywhere that's unsafe. Always use safe methods to check whether you are in the fifth dimension.

A way of checking without getting up is to try pushing our arm through the bed beneath us—if we're out of the body then we can feel our arm pass into and through the bed. This is useful for when we don't want to disturb someone sleeping next to us, or risk disrupting our practice.

If someone is in the fifth dimension there are many possibilities open to them, which I outline in subsequent chapters. They may wish to explore by walking outside their house and taking off from the ground and flying (but don't jump from a height), or by traveling to a place they want to go to.

As I explained earlier, I found my first experience a bit frightening, going into the unknown, not knowing if I would ever come back. But experience has taught me not to worry.

We dream every night in the fifth dimension and nothing bad ever happens to our physical body. We don't get stuck out there; we always come back because our astral body is attached to our physical one—we only have to move during sleep or wake up and we're back in our body. Neither can anyone else or another being enter our physical body while we're projecting; again, we leave our bodies every night and this doesn't happen. Other people or beings can't enter our bodies unless we open ourselves up to them and give them permission to, as is the case with channeling, which I completely recommend against.

NINE MAIN STEPS FOR CONSCIOUS PROJECTION

I'll enumerate the steps to take to project, to make it clearer for those who would like to try having OBEs themselves.

1. Believe it's possible – It's important to have the genuine intention of projecting, and at least being open to the possibility it's real. Going into it thinking it won't work can spoil it. Once someone has had an OBE, keeping a positive attitude, believing they can do it, and not being beset by failures remains important.

2. Ask for spiritual help – Virtually every meaningful experience will be due to spiritual assistance. We get protection against demons too.

3. Relax – Relaxing first makes it easier to project.

4. Remain still – Once someone's begun their relaxation, they should try not to move from that moment on. Remain still during exercises of projection.

5. Don't get sidetracked by the split sensations – Try not to get distracted by the sensations or noises that occur with the process of the split, as this can also bring the exercise to an end. Ignore the sensations and carry on with your exercise as though nothing is happening. If you get sidetracked with the process that's taking place, that's as far as you're likely to go.

6. Don't get distracted by noise – Concentrate on your exercise and don't get distracted by background sounds unless there's something important you should attend to.

7. Try not to scratch an itch – Unless there is a medical reason, learn not to scratch a minor itch in your body. If you scratch it, it will spoil your exercise. It's difficult to ignore it at first, but if you train yourself, you'll have far less exercises ruined. Many exercises come to an end in this way and it can be very hard to get back into the same stage of projecting once you've moved.

8. Continue through the sleep paralysis stage – When you notice that you've reached the sleep paralysis stage where you feel immobilized, don't worry, continue with your exercise and try not to move at all because you are very close to astral projecting. You'll learn when to get up in the astral plane through practice and experience.

9. Stay concentrated and allow the process to unfold – Conscious projection is a sensitive exercise; if we do anything out of place, or feel afraid or excited, it can be over immediately. Let the projection process happen without trying to speed it up. Be concentrated at all times. This is all you need to be concerned about and the rest will take place as a result of your mental focus.

CHAPTER SEVENTEEN

Summary of Ancient OBE Techniques

This chapter provides a short overview of the different types of OBE techniques that were used in the ancient Religion of the Sun; the following chapters then explain how to do them.

These findings are based entirely on our own research into ancient texts and sites that belong to traditions of the Religion of the Sun; from it we've been able to piece together the kinds of exercises ancient peoples used to have them naturally.

THE SEVEN KEY COMPONENTS OF ANCIENT OBE EXERCISES

We've identified what appear to be the seven most common components used in ancient exercises of astral projection.

1. Asking for divine assistance, i.e. prayer.
2. Lying down, remaining still, and sleeping.
3. Stilling/quieting/concentrating the mind (most often through the use of visualization and/or mantras).
4. Overcoming the mental attachment to one's physical body and the physical world (through relaxation and visualizations).
5. Harnessing sun and star energy in its nonphysical higher-dimensional aspect and/or in its physical form as electromagnetic energy.
6. Utilizing resonance from low frequency sounds and specific harmonic intervals.
7. Practicing in purpose-built portal sites, i.e. astronomically aligned pyramids, mounds, and stone circles/enclosures.

The exercises in the following chapters are essentially based on different combinations of these key elements, though always including sleep, as this is generally needed for the physical and astral bodies to separate.

Components one through four can easily be practiced at home without the use of anything external.

Five through seven become increasingly difficult to incorporate, as they rely on things external to us.

Five draws upon the sun and stars either spiritually or physically. It's possible to do exercises that attempt to harness the spiritual/astral aspect of sun and star energy using visualization alone, and this is something that can be done at home. Using their physical aspect however, as electromagnetic energy, may require an external aid to really be effective.

Using sound as in point six also requires external aid, and I discuss this in the following section.

This appears to be why some ancient sites were purpose-built with special electromagnetic and resonant properties. If it could be understood, used safely, and safeguarded from misuse, maybe something utilizing electromagnetic energy and sound to induce OBEs as these sites once did could be recreated.

Until then, as far as we know so far, the way to attempt to harness electromagnetic energy for having OBEs may be to practice during the hour and a half before sunrise (as Krishna and Arjuna did), which can be done at home, as the energies of dawn have a very special, spiritual quality to them. Other options would be to practice at ancient sites of the Religion of the Sun and power spots in nature.

THE USE OF SOUND AND BINAURAL BEATS

Since ancient people appear to have used sound to help with inducing OBEs, it's worth looking at whether there are any ways sound can be used today.

Some ancient sites appear to have been designed so that they resonate with low frequency tones in their chambers. To listen to low frequency tones as an aid to OBE practice in a similar way today is not as simple as it may seem, as special audio equipment (large subwoofers) is needed to play these low frequencies as they are not something that standard speakers or headphones can produce.

Binaural beats are seen as a way around this. They are created by sending two slightly different tones to each ear separated by less than 30 Hz, for example 250 Hz to one ear and 256 Hz to the other, which can be played on reasonable quality stereo headphones as long as they are capable of reproducing the frequencies. In response the brain produces a sensation of a third sound, called the binaural beat, which is the difference in frequency between them, in this case 6 Hz. The binaural beat isn't heard by the listener, but is an "auditory illusion" perceived by the brain. This allows for the brain to generate the illusion of low frequency tones that are inaudible without the use of special equipment.

It's thought that the binaural beat can entrain brainwaves to the same frequency. Binaural beats are often used at low frequencies to induce Theta and Alpha (low frequency) brainwaves that are present during meditation, relaxation, and sleep.

The scientific work on them is quite preliminary, and a lot of the findings are contradictory at the moment. Some studies indicate that listening to binaural beats can decrease anxiety, improve relaxation, and help with falling asleep for some.[1] Another has shown they produced no change in mood,[2] and another that people reported feeling more "bad tempered," "depressed," "confused," and "mixed up," after listening to them.[3]

Although binaural beats were first discovered in 1839 by the physicist Heinrich Wilhelm Dove, Tom Campbell, Dennis Mennerich, and Robert Monroe were the first to develop binaural beats as a means of helping to induce OBEs; their research went on to become the basis of the Monroe Institute, which uses binaural beats as a key part of its course programs. It also went on to spark the modern binaural beat phenomenon.

Today, binaural beats are commonly used as a method to induce OBEs; there are lots of videos on YouTube for instance, which claim to help induce lucid dreaming and OBEs by incorporating binaural beats.

However, Campbell says that low frequency binaural beats don't cause people to have OBEs, but can help someone enter a meditative state, which is the state conducive to having them. He qualifies this further by saying that "you have to cooperate with them," which I take to mean that the binaural beats in themselves don't create the meditative state, but that the listener needs to consciously embrace them as an aid in their meditation. This may explain why studies in which binaural beats are played to people who are not told what they are nor what their purpose is can feel no change, or even a negative change, in their mood, while those who are told they are to aid with helping to sleep, etc., are more likely receive their intended benefit.

Campbell says that while binaural beats may be like a shortcut to entering a meditative state, he likens them to training wheels on a bicycle, and says they are most suited to beginners who are not good at meditating, as they are unnecessary for those who are trained in meditation, and eventually hold someone back from properly developing their own skills and going further in their experiences. He says that not only can someone have OBEs without them, but that they should at some point.[4]

There are studies that show that developing one's own skills is more effective than listening to binaural beats, and that having these skills enables someone to use binaural beats more effectively than those who are unskilled.

For example, one study found that progressive muscle relaxation and sleep hygiene (i.e. good sleeping habits) were more effective than binaural beats for helping to fall asleep.[5] I outline simple techniques of muscle relaxation in this book, which are used in the practice of yoga nidra, and form one of the key components of an OBE exercise routine. The study indicates that doing relaxation techniques like this are actually more effective than listening to binaural beats.

Another study shows how powerful learning to meditate can be. It tested two different binaural beats—one that was intended to facilitate the meditative process and the other to hinder it. These were tested on a group of novice meditators (with an average of eight months of experience) and on a group of experienced meditators (with an average of eighteen years of experience) while meditating. The results showed that the facilitative beats produced positive brain changes in the experienced meditators, while producing no effect in the novices. Furthermore, the brain changes in the novices indicated they were negatively impacted by the hindering beats, while the experienced meditators were not. The results illustrate the benefits of developing meditation skills, as they indicate the experienced meditators were able to use external stimuli to enhance their practice, and also to overcome hindering external stimuli, while the novices could do neither.[6]

This would turn the predominant thinking about using binaural beats for meditation on its head, as rather than the binaural beats being a shortcut to reach meditative states for those who are unskilled at meditation, they may actually require someone have meditation skills to be able to really use and benefit from them. This would make sense, and I'd say is a principle that can be applied to using external aids for having OBEs generally. While everyone tends to look for some external quick fix, it requires skill to use external aids to enhance OBE practice, which is developed through practicing the right techniques.

With the right techniques and practice, it seems that most can reach at least a basic meditative state (or learn to decrease their anxiety, relax, etc.) without the need for binaural beats, and that developing these skills allows someone to use external aids like binaural beats more effectively than those who don't.

Monaural beats are an emerging alternative to binaural beats. The main difference is that they are processed through the inner ear (the natural way sound reaches us), whereas binaural beats are solely processed in parts of the brain which are stimulated. Exactly how binaural beats work is not yet fully understood,[7] and so they are generally recommended with caution.

I've never used binaural or monaural beats, so I can't comment on whether they are effective for having OBEs; I've preferred to learn how to enter meditative states without them. I'm also wary of using things that bypass the normal mechanisms of the brain and alter it more directly (e.g. through the use of binaural beats) because of how complex the brain is and any unintended consequences this might have. For that reason, if I were to use sound, I'd choose options in which the sound reaches and is processed through the ear itself (though not too loudly, as it can cause hearing damage).

To use sound for helping to have OBEs, it would be a matter of experimenting based on what ancient people were using.

As explained, using low frequency tones as ancient people did is difficult, as it requires special equipment or a megalithic chamber! For practical at home use, monaural beats may be an option—selecting beats within the Alpha and Theta range.

110 Hz (and those between 110 - 114 Hz), "the megalithic frequency" as we call it, is high enough to listen to with a good quality set of speakers or headset, and there are people who have incorporated this tone into music specially geared toward OBEs and meditation.

From the evidence that has come to light so far, fourth and fifth intervals appear to have been an important feature in some ancient places where OBEs were practiced, including those of the F# chord as found in the King's Chamber of the Great Pyramid (an F# chord contains both a fourth and fifth interval when played with four notes, with the F# root note, C#, A#, and the inclusion of F# at the next octave). These intervals could be used when intoning mantras among more than one person.

Monaural beats (at conducive frequencies), the megalithic frequency, fourth and fifth intervals, and an F# chord, or music which incorporates these could be played in the background during any OBE practice, or beforehand to help one enter a more conducive state for having OBEs.

A LIST OF ANCIENT OBE TECHNIQUES

Here are the elements we've found that were used as part of ancient exercises for having OBEs. They were used in different combinations, though sleep, lying down, and/or remaining still were always described or can be inferred. We covered the accounts of them in detail in chapter 3, where we provide their sources:

KEEPING THE BODY STILL

The Hindu text, the Yoga Vasistha, emphasizes how Saraswati and Lila kept their bodies still before leaving them; they are described as remaining calm, quiet, and motionless.

REALIZING WE ARE NOT THE BODY

To get oneself into a state of pure consciousness leading to astral projection, the Hindu Shaivite text Tantrasara says one needs to realize that the true self is not the physical body, and to let go of the attachment to their physical body.

The Yoga Vasistha implies something similar, saying that someone can leave their body once they understand the illusory nature of physical reality (although as I've explained, this is not really true—but it's helpful for astral projection to understand that the physical world is not all there is). Saraswati and Lila also have an OBE after they "lost the remembrance" of the physical world.

In Taoist OBE practice, one is said to immerse themselves in the visualization so that they forget about their physical body, joyfully and harmoniously; elsewhere the practitioner is instructed to "forget your form."

SLEEP

In Taoist practice one is told to close their eyes and go into sleep before beginning their practice.

In the Essene Gospel of Peace, Jesus is attributed as instructing someone to sleep after visualizing the stars to travel to them out of the body.

Hermes Trismegistus, Arjuna, Xiangzi, and Timarchus all go to sleep before having their OBEs.

QUIETING THE MIND

In the Yoga Vasistha, the goddess Saraswati instructs Lila on how to have an OBE. The technique essentially involves quieting the mind (so that "the hosts of thoughts perish"), therefore allowing consciousness to manifest. It's implied that this state naturally leads to an OBE (when combined with lying still).

In Taoist practice, one is instructed to "cease thoughts" before beginning their OBE exercise.

The Tantrasara contains a practice where a pure and tranquil state of consciousness is said to precede what sounds like astral projection.

CONCENTRATION

In the Corpus Hermeticum, Hermes Trismegistus describes what sounds like an OBE, which he has by concentrating (making his mind intent) on what sounds like divine reality (the things which are) while going to sleep. He also explains this as being receptive of Poimandres (the mind of God, the Spiritual Sun), while his eyes were closed and his body slept.

Saraswati and Lila have an OBE by shaking off all their thoughts and cares, and continuing in fixed attention, i.e. by being concentrated, so that they lose all remembrance of the external world.

Jesus says to think on the stars before traveling to them out of the body, likening it to an archer who skillfully shoots their bow at a target.

VISUALIZATION OF THE SUN AND STARS

Jesus explains how to leave one's body and enter the heavenly realm of the stars by visualizing them while falling asleep, which he describes as seeing them in "the eye of your thought."

In Taoism there are practices to visualize and travel to the sun and stars in one's "true body."

HARNESSING THE ENERGY OF THE SUN AND STARS

Taoist practices sought to harness the nonphysical energy (qi) of the sun, and the stars of the Big Dipper in the northern region of the sky, for traveling to them out of the body.

Similarly in the Pyramid Texts, the king harnesses the energies of the stars for having his OBE.

In the Hindu text the Mahabharata, Krishna and Arjuna travel in the astral by conducting a simple ritual—firstly touching water, then sitting on the earth facing east (toward the sun). They were said to do this during the one and a half hour period before sunrise, which is seen as especially conducive to spiritual practice in Hinduism.

MANTRAS

Arjuna repeats a mantra as he falls asleep, and then meets Krishna out of the body.

In the Egyptian Pyramid Texts, the king is said to repeat a kind of mantra as he is transformed into a "bird of light" while out of his body (I explain this further in chapter 20).

And as mentioned next, ritual chanting appears to have been utilized at ancient sites used for OBEs.

SOUND AND RESONANCE

There are ancient sites that were used and built for having OBEs, which were designed to have certain acoustic properties.

The King's Chamber of the Great Pyramid enhances sounds made within it, but even when it's quiet produces low frequency sounds. Many of these are said to roughly form an F# chord (which contains a fifth interval, as well as a fourth interval when the F# note from the next octave up is included). Chambers at West Kennet Long Barrow also resonate at low frequencies and at close to a fourth interval. And some of the enclosures at Göbekli Tepe may have been designed to optimize acoustics when used for activities that involved sound produced within them for an audience—in particular, their ratios indicate they may have been built to optimize sounds made at a fourth interval.

As mentioned above, West Kennet Long Barrow produces low frequency sound at 9 Hz. This frequency is within the Alpha range, which is produced by the brain during states of wakeful relaxation, and is conducive to astral projection. Other ancient European mounds may have similar properties.

A number of ancient megalithic mound sites in the British Isles have chambers that resonate between 95 – 120 Hz, with most at 110 – 112 Hz. The frequency of 110 Hz has been found to create changes in brain activity that could assist mystical experiences.

The inner stones of Stonehenge amplify noise made within the circle.

The Hypogeum of Malta was built so that sounds made from an "oracle room" are projected throughout the underground complex, which resonates particularly at 70 and 114 Hz (114 Hz being very close to the frequencies of 110 – 112 Hz found in British sites).

The Hypogeum, the chambers of some ancient mounds in the British Isles, and the sarcophagus of the King's Chamber[8] appear to have been designed to resonate particularly at frequencies within the male voice range, suggesting they were used for activities that involved vocals, likely ritual chanting.

Altogether, what this points toward is the incorporation of ritual chanting in the activities conducted within these sacred spaces to help induce mystical states and experiences. Given they appear to have largely been used for having OBEs, it's reasonable to infer that ritual chanting was used in OBE practices.

PRAYER

In the Taoist text The Story of Han Xiangzi, a Taoist sage has an OBE after performing "a sleeping prayer." Prayer was also used as part of Taoist practice to travel out of the body to the stars.

The ancient Greek Timarchus, who slept at a cave where people sought visionary experiences, had an OBE after saying a prayer.

TRAVELING TO A SPIRITUAL PLACE

Krishna instructs Arjuna while out of the body on how to travel to a place in the astral (in this case to the god Shiva). Krishna and Arjuna travel to Shiva by concentrating their minds on him and by "remembering," i.e. visualizing him.

Saraswati and Lila travel to a number of spiritual places while out of their bodies by willing where they wanted to go, described as being "led by the pure desire of their souls."

PRACTICING AT SACRED PLACES

In the Norse/Germanic texts of the Poetic Edda there are references to a practice called Utiseta, meaning "to sit outside." It involved some kind of all-night meditation at places considered sacred, both manmade and natural, with the goal of obtaining a spiritual vision in the land of sleep.[9] This could have been a way to have OBEs, or to incubate a dream.

However, people in the Religion of the Sun didn't just find sacred places where they could practice OBEs; they built their sites to have them—lots of them, all over the world. We call these ancient portal sites. The majority of ancient sites in the Religion of the Sun were built to serve as gateways between the physical world and heaven, which as we've explored, included the Great Pyramids as well as other pyramids around the world, various sites in Europe, Göbekli Tepe in Turkey, and earthworks and mounds across North America. Originally, one of their primary uses was likely to facilitate OBEs to heaven.

DREAM INCUBATION

Although dream incubation is not specifically a practice for having an OBE or lucid dream, it would have surely led to them. Ancient peoples would gather to sleep the night at sacred places, particularly at temples, to have a dream sent from the divine. With so many people concentrated on having dreams and reaching out to spiritual beings for guidance, they would no doubt have had many conscious experiences in the astral too.

ANCIENT TECHNIQUES USED IN THIS BOOK

In this book I've included variations and forms of all the ancient techniques listed here.

Although concentration is listed as just one, all exercises for having OBEs require being concentrated on them, including those to quiet or still the mind. They also all require keeping the body still, and sleeping.

In some cases, the exercise I describe is almost exactly the same as the ancient one. So in the case of Arjuna practicing a mantra while falling asleep, I explain this same exercise—the difference being the mantra used.

In other cases I describe a variation of an ancient exercise, using the same method. For example, while Jesus describes how to concentrate on and visualize the stars in order to project into them, Arjuna and Krishna concentrate on and visualize Shiva to go to him in the astral. I explain exercises that use concentration and visualization to project to a destination—either into one's own heart or to any other spiritual place in the astral of one's choosing, including the stars.

I also include visualization exercises from ancient traditions that are used to quiet the mind and bring someone to a state of consciousness, said in ancient texts to be conducive to astral projection.

Some ancient OBE exercises attempted to harness the energies of the sun and stars to help with astral projection, and I include practices that try to recreate how they may have been practiced.

Although I haven't included prayer as a technique on its own, asking for divine assistance is recommended before beginning any exercises of projection, and some of the techniques incorporate prayer within them just as in some ancient techniques.

As in the Eddas, I also recommend practicing at sacred places, though this is not practical to do except on special occasions, which could be on a retreat with a group of people. Ideally, new sacred places of the Religion of the Sun would be created that utilize the ancient principles that helped to enable OBEs.

I've only included exercises in this book that Lara or I have used, but there could be many others that work. Whatever exercises someone chooses though, they should make sure they are safe to do.

CHAPTER EIGHTEEN

Kayotsarga

This is a very simple exercise for astral projection and can be a good option for beginners, or for those who have trouble visualizing, but can also be an effective exercise for someone at any stage. We think it's also a good exercise to use to train for astral projection. One can learn to keep their body still, to remain aware while their body deeply relaxes, and to become comfortable with the sense of separating and being separate from the body—all key elements needed for astral projection.

Kayotsarga is the name of an ancient practice (and standing meditation pose) in the religion of Jainism. It's not used for astral projection, but as one of its most important meditation exercises. However, we realized that it's described as an exercise for astral projection in the yogic text Yoga Vasishtha (discussed in chapter 3 in the section Hinduism); as far as we know, we're the only ones to have identified it for this purpose in recent times.

Here is an abridged version of the excerpt from the Yoga Vasishtha describing it (a longer version appears in chapter 3):

> "[Saraswati and Lila] stood motionless on the spot, as if they were sculptures engraven on marble columns, or as pictures drawn upon the wall. They shook off all their thoughts and cares [...]. They remained still, calm and quiet and without any motion of their limbs [...]. They continued in fixed attention without any external sensation [...]. They lost the remembrance of the phantom of the phenomenal world [...]. They then began to move with their own bodies [subtle/astral bodies] [...]. With their new bodies they rose as high as one span above the ground [...]. Then they flew higher and higher by force of their intellect [...]. Here the pair in their etherial forms, looked about [...]."[1]
> ~ BRIHAT YOGA VASISHTHA

This excerpt depicts Saraswati and Lila as practicing kayotsarga, while standing and remaining completely still in the kayotsarga pose (though kayotsarga can also be practiced while sitting or lying down, as we'll explain shortly). This excerpt says they left their bodies while standing up, which as mentioned in chapter 3, seems unlikely, as usually we need to be in a position to sleep in order to have an OBE. Practicing kayotsarga while lying down, however, is conducive to having an OBE.

Jainism is one of the three most ancient surviving religions in India, along with Hinduism and Buddhism.

Jains believe their religion traces back to the great teacher (called a tīrthankara) Rishabhanatha, who is said to have first promulgated their spiritual knowledge and founded civilization in our current age of existence millions of years ago. The tīrthankaras of Jainism are often depicted standing in the kayotsarga pose.

In Jain texts, Rishabhanatha is the same person as Ikshvaku,[2] a very important king in Hinduism who was likewise the founder of its religion and civilization in this age, revealing these two religions share a common root. Both ultimately derive from the ancient Religion of the Sun, though Jains don't believe in a supreme creator/god (believing only in enlightened beings), whereas Hindus do, and in the earliest Hindu scriptures they identify the supreme creator with the sun—this is probably the main doctrinal difference that spurred the division between them.

Artifacts recovered from the ancient Indus Valley Civilization that existed in Pakistan and northern India between around 3,300 – 1,300 BC show people in seated yoga poses, as well as standing in the kayotsarga pose, revealing that both practices are very ancient.[3]

HOW TO PRACTICE KAYOTSARGA

In this section we explain how kayotsarga is practiced as a form of meditation at any time; in the next section we'll explain how it can be used specifically for astral projection.

The word kayotsarga literally means "body" (*kaya*) "give up" (*utsarga*)—indicating the aim of the practice.[4]

The practice is to keep one's body completely still and relaxed, so that the sense of one's body disappears. For the duration of the practice, one then tries to maintain a deep and complete sense of awareness and inner silence, experiencing their nature as a soul/consciousness—as different from the body, and as separate from it.[5]

The name kayotsarga is also given to the standing posture it's often practiced in, which is with body standing up straight (spine and neck in a straight line without stiffness), gaze directed straight ahead, feet parallel and slightly apart, arms hanging close to the body, palms open facing inward, with fingers straight and pointing down.[6]

It can also be done while seated (a cross-legged yoga pose is usually recommended with hands in *bhairava* mudra position) or lying down (straight on one's back).

This practice can help with training for all exercises of astral projection, and of course, especially for kayotsarga as an OBE exercise. Doing it also brings the spiritual benefits of the meditation exercise.

To use it for training to have OBEs or as a meditation exercise it can be done anywhere comfortable, at any time, though ideally outside at sunrise or sunset while facing the sun (being careful not to look at it directly).

Choose a posture, either standing (in the kayotsarga pose), seated, or lying down. In Jainism, it's typically recommended that someone face the direction of east or north. These directions are connected to the ascent of the sun in the northern hemisphere, and we believe, remain from a time when this practice was done in connection with the sun.

Remain as still as you can for the duration of the practice. Keep your eyes closed, half-closed, or open (blinking is fine), depending on what you prefer.

The founder of Jain religion Rishabhanatha in the kayotsarga pose.

Relax your body, mentally going through each part of the body and relaxing it. Try to relax so that you lose the sensation of your body as much as you can.

Then spend however much time you like in inner silence, perceiving all that is occurring in the present moment in complete awareness. Each time a thought arises, go back to that state of awareness.

The aim is to get the sense of your true nature—one that is spiritual, and exists independently of the body.

KAYOTSARGA OBE EXERCISE

An international Jain meditation organization describes the four stages of kayotsarga as follows:

> "Stability of body
> Relief from all kinds of tension
> Abandoning the gross body and coming closer to the subtle one
> Realizing the detachment of soul from the body."[7]

These stages are certainly conducive to having an OBE, which is probably why kayotsarga was used for having OBEs in the past.

To do this exercise:

Lie in a position you can hold completely still for the duration of your OBE exercise. Usually that is comfortably in bed on one's back, with arms and legs straight, much like the kayotsarga pose, but lying down. Close your eyes.

Take a few deep breaths and then allow your breathing to settle into a rhythm as you would have while sleeping.

Go through your body relaxing each part of it, as outlined in chapter 15. Aim to relax your body so much that you lose sense of it. Keep it as still as you reasonably can, while still breathing comfortably etc.

Keep as silent as you can in your mind, not thinking, but simply perceiving. Listen, for example, to the sounds of the night, and to the sound of the silence between sounds. Be aware, for example, of the atmosphere of the night, of the spaciousness behind your closed eyes, to all that is in the present moment. Whenever you drift off into thought, bring yourself back by perceiving the present, just being.

You may start to sense that you are different from your body—that your body is falling asleep, yet you are still awake. It may feel like the body is a separate object, like a container, which you feel like you can move around in, and even move out of and leave.

Continue with the practice for as long as you like, or until you feel like you can move out of your body and do so, or fall asleep into dreams.

THE FLAME OF CONSCIOUSNESS

This exercise is similar to the one above, but instead of perceiving the present moment, one visualizes a candle flame as representing one's consciousness, awake and aware in the moment.

Lara created it based on kayotsarga combined with another Jain meditation using a lit candle, which is described in chapter 15, in the "Concentration and Visualization of an Object" section. In the Jain meditation, one seats themselves before a lit candle and concentrates on it, then closes their eyes and visualizes the flame at the center of their brow where it represents one's consciousness.

To do this OBE exercise, spend some time before your astral exercise looking closely at the flame of a lit candle, observing as much as you can about it so that later you will be able to visualize it. Ideally you would do this just before your astral exercise, but I would extinguish the candle before starting your astral exercise, or make sure it's in a fireproof container, so that there is no risk of starting a fire.

Then lie down and close your eyes, ready to do your OBE exercise. Take deep breaths, relax, and remain still and silent as in the OBE exercise of kayotsarga described in the previous section.

Then visualize, trying to really "see," the flame of the candle burning on the wick a short distance in front of you. Feel that the flame represents you as consciousness, pure, shining, and made of light, and constantly existing. If you lose concentration, and lose sight of the flame, bring yourself back to it.

There is something very magical about a flame shining in the darkness. In the ancient Religion of the Sun, fire was seen as being of the same substance as the sun, which itself was seen as the physical manifestation of the divine light of the Source.[8] Each soul is like a small flame from that great spiritual fire.

CHAPTER NINETEEN

Concentrating on the Heart

One of the most effective exercises for conscious projection is concentration on the heart, and is the one I've used most. A variation of it is used in Tibetan Dream Yoga. In the Hindu Yoga Sutras of Patanjali, one of the objects given to concentrate on is the light within. Given that one's inner light (one's Being/Self) was believed to reside deep within the heart, no doubt this exercise involved concentrating on the light within one's heart.

> "Also meditate on the Inner Light which is serene and beyond sorrow."[1]
> ~ YOGA SUTRAS OF PATANJALI

Virtually anything that focuses the mind upon one thing can be used to project, but concentrating on the heart is a very simple and effective technique for having OBEs. However, like any exercise that uses concentration, it does require practice.

Concentration on the heart can be a very spiritual experience, as the heart is not only a vital organ of the physical body, but also has spiritual aspects, which is why it's referred to so much in spiritual art and literature.

CONCENTRATING ON HEARTBEATS

Conscious projection is more effective when we're relaxed and are lying on our backs where we can fall asleep, as we need sleep for the physical and astral bodies to separate.

This can also be done as an exercise in itself without using it to project, in which case it can be done sitting up at any time.

To project with it, lie on your back and relax, and begin by gently perceiving your heartbeats. If you can't perceive them, take three deep breaths and you should feel your heartbeats almost straightaway. If you still can't feel them, you can imagine your heart beating until hopefully you can begin to feel it beating.

Following are three different ways of concentrating on one's heartbeats. Just one of these methods is used per practice session.

METHOD ONE

Once you begin to notice the beats, concentrate on each of them. Keep focusing on your heartbeats.

METHOD TWO

Once you are aware of your heartbeats and have concentrated upon them for a short time, try to feel them throughout your body until your whole body is a heartbeat. One of the things that can happen with this method is that our astral body begins to move with the beats of the heart, independently of our physical body and subtly at first, but the movements increase until they lift someone out of their body.

METHOD THREE

Once you are concentrated on your heartbeats, you can direct the beats to various parts of your body. For example, you could direct them to the tip of your nose, the palms of your hands, the soles of your feet, and so on, until eventually you feel that your whole body is a heartbeat. A variation of this is to try to feel the pulse or beat of the heart in one part of your body, and keep feeling the beat in that part and stay on it. This can work very well.

When concentrating on the heart, I've found it's best to remain in the same position until projecting, rather than getting up when I feel the first signs of the split beginning to happen. I've found it's better to continue with the exercise until I've projected, usually by rising or floating up out of my body—and then at that stage getting up and moving around.

VISUALIZATION OF THE PHYSICAL HEART

For this technique, someone lies down on their back or sits down comfortably. Once they're relaxed, they direct their attention to their physical heart with the purpose of visualizing it within their own physical body.

To do this exercise, begin by gently concentrating on the heart and visualizing it in detail: imagining its shape, size, color, etc. Next, further explore in detail other areas of the heart like the texture of its muscle, its surfaces, the chambers, the arteries attached to it, and so on. As you explore the inner and outer parts of the heart, try to find out how it works, what it's made of, and what it's for. Carry on exploring the heart until you project.

This technique for projection can work more effectively if someone does a ten-minute exercise of visualizing their heart at some point during the day before their projection exercise. In this way they familiarize themselves with the technique and gain experience of how to do it before they try to project with it.

For this particular technique, it's better to remain in the same position until projecting, rather than getting up when we think we've projected into the astral plane.

VISUALIZING THE HEART IN STAGES

A variation of visualizing our physical heart is to visualize it in stages. To do this, someone in their first attempts could for example explore the outer part of their heart only, until they feel they've got it right. Their next exercise could be exploring inside the chambers of the heart. Later on, they may wish to explore the arteries attached to the heart, and so on. When using this progressive technique, you should always retrace all the stages you have already learned to visualize.

In other words, you keep progressing by visualizing more and more areas of the heart, but always retrace what you've learned to visualize before until you cover the whole heart. It's important to aim to explore your heart in depth.

VISUALIZING THE HEART AS A SPIRITUAL PLACE

Another variation of visualizing the heart is to visualize it as a spiritual place. This can bring benefits associated with the heart's spiritual aspects. I outline an ancient variation of this exercise in chapter 23, but you could also make your own.

Here are a couple of ideas for this exercise:

VISUALIZING THE HEART AS A TEMPLE

Direct your attention to your heart and visualize it being like a temple, a place with light and with the layout of a temple as you would imagine it to be, or visualize an actual temple if you've been to one, especially if it was in an OBE.

VISUALIZING A SPIRITUAL PLACE IN THE HEART

Direct your concentration to your heart, imagine it as a place of light or divine fire, go into it, and visualize any spiritual place or spiritual being there. Fall asleep visualizing all this.

WHEN TO KNOW WE'RE OUT OF THE BODY

When someone is concentrating on their heart and coming out of their body, they shouldn't let the sensations of the split distract them, but keep focusing on their heart. They'll know when to stop concentrating on it and know they're out of their body when they lift up out of it. At that point, if their eyes are still closed, they can open them.

However, sometimes the split isn't clear and we can be out of our body and not realize it. So, if you're trying to project, be aware of strange things happening to you, like feeling that your body is sideways even though you're lying on your back, or having parts of your astral body move separately from your physical body, like being able to move your arms or legs while your physical body is stationary. Or feel your bed shake in rhythm with your heartbeat. Or feel as though you are being tilted or are moving in a circular motion. If anything like this happens someone has either split or has partly left their body. If they're not rising up and seem static, they could try slowly getting up from the bed to see if they are in the fifth dimension, because they may just catch the moment after they have split and then can find themselves in the fifth dimension. But if they are not quite there, they'll move their physical body and be awake.

If you're trying to concentrate on your heart but find you're distracted by your breathing, be aware of your heart physically beating, then visualize and concentrate on it, forgetting about your breathing. If you think about breathing at any time, go straight back to concentrating on your heart. Eventually with some practice, being distracted by breathing will subside.

It's also possible to concentrate on breathing to astral project, and many people have had success with it, but I don't mix concentration on the breath and the heart in the same practice. If you're concentrating on your heart, forget about your breathing—let it go on normally and just stay with your heart. If you concentrate on breathing alone as an exercise, stick to it; don't switch between it and the heart or anything else, or you may spoil the exercise.

CHAPTER TWENTY

Mantras

Sound permeates the universe, and it has a profound effect upon the psyche, which is largely underrated. Every sound has its corresponding impact within us; you only have to think of the impact of music, or try having a pleasant day in the garden next door to someone using a pneumatic drill.

Mantras have been used for spiritual purposes since antiquity. They are constantly repeated vocalizations, words, or phrases. They can stimulate higher faculties, positively affect our psyche, elevate our inner state, and can help with increasing intuition, astral projection, remembering dreams, and much more. As mentioned, Arjuna used a mantra to astral project. However, using a mantra for astral projection still requires someone to be concentrated upon it for it to be effective.

The sounds of the mantras used here work according to vibratory affinity, where the note or sound made by one thing causes the same note or sound to be produced by another. This is how music produces a response in us—it hits notes of affinity within. The voice carries these vibrations in the same way as music, whether spoken or sung. Mantras not only help to focus the mind, but they can also create vibrations that help the astral split.

Following are some mantras that we've brought together to be used for astral projection. So far in ancient sources we've only found one mantra where there is evidence it may have been used specifically for astral projection (explained in the following section). That doesn't mean there weren't others, only that either the mantras that were used haven't survived, or that the mantras that were used survived but the knowledge of their use for astral projection didn't.

Knowing that mantras were used in ancient times for astral projection, and knowing from my own experience that mantras work as astral projection techniques, I've put together a list of mantras in the section Mantras of the Sun—which are either ones I've created, or existing mantras I've repurposed. These are not the only mantras that could work; there could be many others.

Brahmin students in India reciting the Vedas in the ancient Sanskrit language. The oldest known mantras in the world are derived from the literature of the Vedas, which was sung as part of a long oral tradition before being written down. In India, mantras have been used for many religious purposes, including having OBEs.

Each word is pronounced with the same tone so they are evenly repetitive. Some of them use ancient Egyptian words, however, no one really knows how ancient Egyptian was pronounced. There have been many attempts made by scholars, but a lot of it is speculation and guesswork, especially when it comes to vowels. So I've put my suggestions of how to pronounce them based on how I think they would have sounded, and also what works better for a mantra.

AN ANCIENT EGYPTIAN MANTRA

While reading the Pyramid Texts, Lara came across what sounds like a mantra used by the ancient Egyptians as part of an OBE. The passage, which is carved into the east wall of the antechamber of the pyramid built for King Unis, reads:

> "O light, bird,
> This is in your mouth
> Aeeee
> As you become
> A bird of light
> This is in your mouth

Aeeee
The praised gold
You rise burning,
Praised, this is your life force.
[...] Give praise to you, soul, shining white bird
[...] [the King] comes out, the shining falcon."[1]
~ THE PYRAMID TEXTS

It says the sound "aeeee" is pronounced by the king as he rises and is transformed into a bird of light. This passage's position within his pyramid indicates he was meant to repeat it while out of his body as he left his tomb, to ensure his transition through the portal (on the eastern horizon) that led from the Duat (astral plane) to the heavenly region in the sky.[2] Although the Pyramid Texts describe the OBE the king has after his death, and although this mantra appears to have been used for traveling through the portal that leads from the astral plane to heaven, it may have been based on a practice done by people in life to induce an OBE, perhaps even inside the Great Pyramids, and would still be effective as an exercise for projecting into the astral plane.

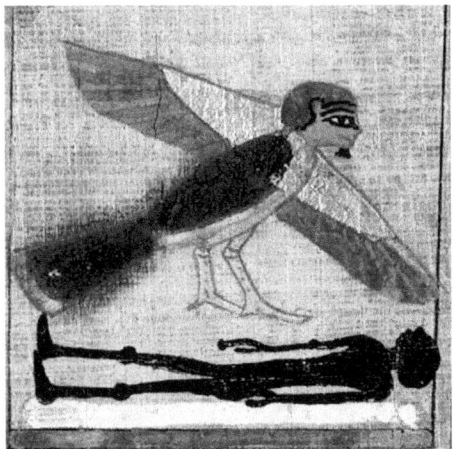

The soul leaving the body as a bird
from the Egyptian Book of the Dead.

But Lara had wondered how it was said. The next morning, she was woken very early by the loud call of a bird right outside our window, and listened to it as she gradually merged back into her body. It would trill some complex notes, and then repeat a few times what sounded like "aeeee"—a lower short note followed by a longer, higher pitched one. Then it dawned on her that the passage where the sound is mentioned was to do with becoming a bird, and that it was likely Aeeee was intended to imitate a bird call.

This can be used as a mantra for astral projection by simply repeating Aeeee over and over, starting by saying it aloud and gradually getting quieter until just pronouncing it mentally, or pronouncing it mentally from the beginning, as I explain further on in this chapter.

A is pronounced as in "ah" and e as in "be."

Although adding a sentence may be less effective, another option is to say:

"I take flight like a bird of light. Aeeee Aeeee Aeeee," repeating Aeeee as many times as one likes before starting again.

While saying the mantra, another option is to feel and imagine lifting up out of your physical body.

MANTRAS OF THE SUN

These are words and mantras from the ancient Religion of the Sun.

Amun-Ra

This is not an actual mantra, but was the most popular name of the Supreme Creator, Source, and Spiritual Sun for hundreds of years in ancient Egypt. The name Amun means "invisible" and "the hidden one."[3] Ra is the Egyptian name of the sun. Thus Amun-Ra refers to the invisible, spiritual source of all creation that emanates from the sun.

It's pronounced Aaaamuuuunnn Raaaaaaaaaa.

A – The vowel "a" is pronounced as in the word "far."

Mun – The "u" could be pronounced like "oo" in the word "foot" or in "moon," depending on one's preference.

Ra – Pronounced as in the word "mantra."

Atuma

This is the name of the supreme creator of the Children of the Sun (called the Children of God) in the Kolbrin, and is the root of many similar names for heaven, the Source, and the sun in ancient cultures that followed the Religion of the Sun, including ancient Egypt.[4] In Egypt, Atum was the creator and Spiritual Sun, who lifted the soul of the king from his pyramid to the celestial heaven,[5] making Atum an essential part of the king's OBE.

It's pronounced Aaaaatuuuuummmmaaaaa.

A – The "a" is pronounced as in the word "far."

Tum – The "u" could be pronounced like "oo" in the word "foot" or in "moon."

Om So Hum

This Hindu mantra begins with the most famous of all mantras, Om, which represents Brahman—the supreme source, who is identified with the sun. Chanting Om is generally used to connect one with the divine both within and without. It is written as Aum in Sanskrit, making it similar to the name above. "So Hum" means "I am That." It's a phrase that originates from an ancient Hindu text in which the author identifies their true self as being the same as Brahman, whose light shines through the sun.[6]

It's pronounced Oooooooooommm Sooooooooooo Huuuuuuuummm.

Om - The "o" is pronounced as in the word "or," with a subtle "au" intonation.[7]

So - The "o" is pronounced as in the word "home."

Hum - The "u" as in the word "hum" and "hungry."

Om Tat Sat

This is a Hindu mantra given by Krishna as meaning "the Supreme Absolute Truth," corresponding to the three words of the mantra. Om refers to the supreme source, Tat to "all that is," and Sat to truth. They are considered the three names of Brahman.[8]

It's pronounced Ooooooooommm Taaaaaaaaat Saaaaaaaaat.

Om - The "o" is pronounced as in the word "or," with a subtle "au" intonation.

Tat/Sat - The "a" is pronounced as in the word "that."

Hari Om

In the Vedas, Hari is used to mean "golden" or "delightful,"[9] and is coupled with Om as a form of praise to Brahman. Hari is also interpreted as meaning "the remover" or "the one who takes away," and is used to refer to the Source/Supreme Being who is said to remove the sorrow, sin, and suffering of its devotees.[10]

It's pronounced Haaaaariiii Oooooooomm.

Hari - The vowel "a" is pronounced as in the word "far." The "i" is pronounced like "ee" in the word "street."

Om - The "o" is pronounced as in the word "or," with a subtle "au" intonation.

When saying these mantras aloud, breathe in through the nose and out slowly through the mouth while pronouncing the word, using one breath for each. For example: (breath) Haaaaariiii (breath) Oooooooomm.

Although I've listed six mantras, they are by no means the only ones useful for astral projection and more could be included in this or other related works in future.

Words in Sanskrit work better for mantras than those in English and most other languages, as they were developed by a society for whom spirituality was very important, and so many of its words, though sometimes short, express profound concepts that encompass more than a sole English word often can. The Vedas, which were composed in Sanskrit, and are the oldest body of work in Sanskrit, were sung long before they were written down, and so many Sanskrit words and/or phrases can be mantric already.

PROJECTING WITH MANTRAS

When using mantras to project, I've found it best to be lying down ready to sleep as with other OBE exercises, although any position you can sleep in will work. There are then three steps to it:

1. Relax your body and remove any tension.

2. Pronounce the mantra aloud for a time, then get progressively quieter until you are only pronouncing it mentally. From then on breathe as normal, as you no longer need to take deep breaths to pronounce the mantra aloud. Then continue pronouncing it over and over in your mind until you astral project or fall asleep. If you cannot pronounce it aloud in the beginning for any reason, pronounce it mentally from the beginning.

3. Project out of your body. The process of going into the astral plane with mantras is the same as with concentration. However, parts of the astral body may more noticeably begin to detach from the physical one. So parts of your astral body may move by themselves—an arm or a leg may lift up, or a hand or fingers move, or your face may be in a different direction to the one you're lying in. When anything like this happens, you may not realize your astral body has detached. I've known someone who said they were spinning around, wondering what was happening, not realizing they were already in the astral plane.

So if any of these things happen, or you begin to float, and you think you might have projected, slowly get up from your bed (you need to do it gently or you can wake yourself up), or roll over out of bed gently, or try to push your hand through the bed, and check whether you're in the astral plane in the ways I've mentioned in previous chapters. If you're in the physical world, you could go back to bed and try again; once the signs appear again, you could try getting up again. If someone keeps doing this, they will eventually get up in the astral plane.

Someone can train themselves to get up from bed whenever the parts of their body begin to move. They don't do this by imagining they are moving, or pretending or imagining they're getting up; they have to actually get up from bed purposefully—though gently and not abruptly. I knew someone who used a mantra and was aware of this, and astral projected ten times in one night, by getting up whenever an astral body part moved.

If someone manages to astral project with a mantra and comes back to their physical body soon afterward, they can go back into the astral plane by pronouncing the same mantra again. The best thing is not to move once we come back to our physical body. We can stay in the same position, pronounce the mantra mentally again, and take off. If you try this, you'll notice that the more you do it, the more you know when to get up. You'll reach a point where you won't need to decide when to get up; when the time is right, you'll learn to do it almost automatically.

When you choose a mantra, stick with it for the duration of the exercise—don't change to another one or to a different type of exercise or it will weaken it. Try to stay focused on the mantra or you could lose track of it and get taken away by thoughts.

The mantras in this chapter are spiritually meaningful. Having a sense of their meaning as we say them can bring about spiritual feelings that help the practice.

Like everything with astral projection, it takes a lot of patience, and for some people it can take a long time.

CHAPTER TWENTY-ONE

Astral Travel

In this chapter I'll give some suggestions as to the kinds of things we can do and what to look out for while out of the body, but someone's OBE is their own personal experience and is relevant to them, so they should follow their intuition if they can.

It's natural to want profound experiences every time someone has an OBE, but it doesn't usually work like that—a lot of the time someone may not see much, and it's easy to get confused when you're there. Sometimes astral experiences are just disappointing—someone makes lots of efforts only to find the experience is short or vague, or dim with diminished colors, and many of them have nothing much happening. Lara and I have had lots of these kinds of experiences. I think it's best to accept that not every OBE is going to be profound, and that many are likely to be unsatisfactory in the ways I just mentioned. I see it as part of the learning process.

It's also easy to waste an opportunity to learn something important when in the astral world. Time spent flying around nowhere in particular, looking at details on walls, imagining things, etc., is not the best way to use an OBE. It's better to get spiritual experiences if someone can. Sometimes we'll be taught by spiritual beings whether we're expecting it or not. Sometimes we may wake up in the astral plane in a situation that's full of symbolic meanings. At other times, however, we may have to seek out the learning.

TRAVELING TO DIFFERENT PLACES IN THE ASTRAL PLANE

There are different ways to travel in the astral plane. We can always walk, but it's much faster to fly.

We can travel to a specific place by visualizing and concentrating upon it, and then we can find ourselves there almost instantly, or we can travel by navigating our way there as we would do normally here. If you want to go back to a place you've been to before, visualize it and you can return there. We can also follow our intuition to do something or go somewhere when it feels right.

Often what we project straight into is what we need to learn from, as the experience we have is already given to us by a spiritual source, usually one's own Being, and so we don't necessarily have to travel anywhere; we become engaged in whatever experience is happening. Sometimes though the experience can be mundane and someone may feel they need to move on from it to do something meaningful.

We can ask our Being (either the male or female aspects of the Being referred to as the Spiritual Father or Mother) to take us where we need to go. Then either of them can take us somewhere that's important for us to learn from.

Or you can try to go to a temple or spiritual place if you know of one. Travel there by concentrating upon it, or asking your higher Being to take you there to be taught. If when you arrive you're outside the temple and aren't allowed in, don't be surprised, because there may be certain standards required for entry, and some are difficult to fulfill.

In the same way we can travel to a spiritual being, as Arjuna and Krishna did when they traveled to Shiva, by concentrating upon them, or asking our Being to take us to them. Again, however, there may be certain standards and tests you need to pass before you can receive their teaching.

Sometimes you may seem to be in a nowhere place, as though nothing is happening, or perhaps you just don't know what to do. You could ask for spiritual help, but another suggestion is to travel somewhere you know exists—like this you can learn how to get around.

There's no need to worry about getting stuck in the astral plane and being unable to return to the physical body. We always come back to our body after astral traveling. It's just that we are aware of the fact that we're in another dimension, instead of how we're usually there, which is dreaming and not being aware of it. We always come back unless our physical body dies, and being in the astral plane in itself won't cause that. We usually wake up straightaway after the experience, or if the OBE has become a dream, we'll just wake up from sleep normally later.

The hard part is staying out there, as we usually get drawn back to our body after just a short time. When that happens, someone usually begins to fade away, or travel backward at a rapid pace until they fall back into their body, or they just feel themselves merging back into their physical body and wake up physically.

It helps to hold onto an object in the astral to anchor ourselves there, and to remain as calm and clear as we can. It's important to watch for large emotions such as fear or elation at being there, because they can be enough to pull someone back to their body straightaway. You also need to be as aware as possible and to maintain that awareness for as long as you can, because any daydreams you have there turn into dreams, and before you know it, you're in a dream and you don't realize that you had projected until you wake up from sleep. When I first learned to astral travel, I often found I couldn't sustain myself there—I would soon fly back to my body, and so I held onto objects there and often moved around by securing myself and holding on to whatever I could find of astral matter.

Many times when I came back to my body involuntarily I would merge into my physical body, firstly being aware of being slightly higher than it, then feeling myself going into it, merging with it and waking up. At other times I would be aware of flying backward at great speed; it was as though everything became a vortex and I was drawn backward into my body, where I then woke up.

WHEN WE CAN'T SEE CLEARLY IN THE ASTRAL PLANE

Sometimes when we go into the astral plane we can't see at all, or things look very dim. Some of the causes for this I can think of are as follows.

The first is that the level of awareness in daily life and hence the level of awareness while out of the body is low. If so, then it's a matter of practice to increase one's level of awareness.

The second reason could be that someone's ego states are interfering and so they need to deal with them.

Thirdly, it could be that an outside sinister force or demonic entity is trying to stop someone from seeing and traveling, in which case, this can be dealt with by using methods of protection and by asking one's Being for help.

A fourth factor could be that one's physical body isn't up to it for some reason due to illness, tiredness, stress, etc. Feeling ill and tired robs someone's ability to practice and feel finer perceptions. The lack of perception in the physical world can affect the quality of perception in the astral.

And finally, a fifth reason is what I call "astral blindness," which I explained in chapter 3. To recap, this occurs when someone can only perceive blackness everywhere while in the astral plane. It can happen immediately after someone becomes lucid in a dream. It's probably due to being neither fully in the astral or physical body, but somewhere in the transition between them where the senses of one body are switched over for the other, causing the senses of the astral body to cut out temporarily. It's possible to get out of this and see, but the blackness usually causes one to return to their physical body.

I've heard of people saying "clarity now" loudly and firmly when they haven't been able to see clearly while out of the body and having success with it.[1]

THE PROBLEM OF CREATING ONE'S OWN REALITY

Many who go into the astral plane are happy to be in the projections of their subconscious, often without knowing that what they are seeing is just a projection from within themselves; moreover, some want to create their own experience by imagining something and making it "real."

This can be done, but I wouldn't recommend it because they're missing out on what's really there. In effect it's a bit like taking drugs and hallucinating instead of seeing reality. It's far more beneficial to see what's actually there.

As I said in an earlier chapter, one time in the astral I imagined a pink toothbrush, and one appeared in the room right in front of me—it stayed there with a hologram-like quality to it. I wondered whether it would disappear if I thought of something else, but it didn't; it was fixed and wouldn't change, just like any object in physical world. I'm sure this was a creation that existed in my mind alone, because if we created objects just by thinking about them, the astral would be a chaotic clutter of people's mental creations, but it isn't. I realized then how powerful the subconscious was in creating a false reality out of the body, and how much I would need to take this into account if I was to be able to know and see what was real in the astral plane.

Lara has had fairly similar experiences, where things and people she has thought of during the day appeared while she was conscious out of the body, and remained interacting with her, even though she realized they were subconscious projections. In other experiences, she realized she had been consciously interacting with projections from her mind out of the body, only after she'd woken up.

To see what's there we need to keep the level of our awareness high, resisting any tendency to daydream. Being in mental images over there can mean losing awareness of the fifth dimension and falling into an ordinary dream. It's better to have real experiences; they mean so much more in the long run.

TIPS WHEN ASTRAL TRAVELING

1. When you are flying to a place and encounter an obstacle, you should try to get away from it very gently if possible. Avoid being confused by it, otherwise you're likely to be back in your physical body straightaway.

2. Unless your intuition tells you otherwise, you probably shouldn't get distracted with what you see while traveling, because you can get sidetracked and may not make it to your destination. Many astral traveling experiences come to an end in this way. You need to be focused when you're traveling so that you get to your destination.

3. If you're flying at a very high speed, don't be afraid of it—just go along with it. If you try to slow down or stop it, you'll probably be back in your physical body almost immediately.

4. Thoughts about your physical body or worries of how you are going to get back can end your OBE.

5. If you arrive at a place and you can't see anything, try to be aware and look around, and if you still can't see anything, ask your inner Being to clear it, or use an incantation (which is explained in a later chapter).

6. If you're in the astral plane and you can't see the place you want to get to, visualize the place and you'll get closer to it or land there.

CHECKING WHETHER YOUR OBE IS REAL

If you want to know whether what you're seeing in your out-of-body experiences is real or not, you could set yourself tests to check.

In chapter 6 I looked at evidence for OBEs being real events, and in chapter 7 how the mind, particularly the subconscious, can make them subjective, obscuring our perception of what's really there. So what we see in OBEs could be created totally from the mind, a mixture of the mind and reality, or what's actually there.

So how can we tell? Well, having an intuitive sense about the experience helps, but there are some other things we can do. I've made a list, though it's not exhaustive, and you could come up with some of your own tests, but these are ones that have worked for me:

1. Seeing objects, places, or other things in the OBE that you have no knowledge of and then checking them back here. You can carry out tests to check all kinds of objects.

2. Seeing events while you're out of the body and checking what you've seen when you're back in the physical world.

3. Receiving information about the future and then seeing it come true.

4. Receiving information about someone (perhaps who fell ill or died and you didn't know) and verifying it as true.

5. Being sure about the lucidity of the experience itself, which is something you would have to experience to make a judgment about.

6. Meeting with others over there that are also having OBEs and then verifying the meeting once back in the physical world with them.

7. Experiencing things you had no knowledge of and then reading about them later in ancient books, sacred texts, myths, legends, etc.

    Even if you've verified that an experience was real, don't expect others to believe you. Some might, but many probably won't—that's just the way many people are.
    For a time in my OBEs I wanted to check whether they were real, so I looked for objects I hadn't seen in the physical world, which I could verify the existence of when I was back in my body. In one, I was staying somewhere I'd never been before and had an OBE. I lifted straight up from my body still lying horizontally until I was very close to the ceiling. I could see small marks on it, which I hadn't seen before as they were too small to see from the ground or the bed. I decided to look at them closely to see if they would be visible when I got back to my body. When I woke up, I stood on the bed and checked—the marks were identical to what I'd seen out of my body.
    There have been other times when I met other people in OBEs and saw many other things that convinced me that real objects, places, and events can be seen over there. After a while I felt there was no need to keep checking and I looked more for the meaning in what I experienced.
    Sometimes we don't see what's really there in the astral though, and that's not always due to the subconscious. It can also be that our perception is being altered by spiritual beings to teach us something. So if two people had

an OBE and went to the same place that exists in the physical world, they could see the same things that are really there, or perhaps only one of them would, or they may each see different things that aren't there in the physical world. This could either be due to their subconscious or to the influence of spiritual beings.

Everything that exists in the physical world also exists in the astral world, so if for example you throw a shoe on the roof of your house in this world, you can potentially go and see where it landed in the astral plane and check it later in the physical world.

CHAPTER TWENTY-TWO

Projection to a Place in an OBE

By visualizing a place as we're falling asleep, we can consciously project and travel to it in the astral plane. And if we're already in the astral, we can travel to a place by visualizing it.

Sometimes by doing this practice, we can find that even if we didn't manage to consciously project to the place we visualized, we can later find ourselves there in a dream.

It's possible to travel to a real place that's not a figment of the imagination. You might even prove this by checking details of the fifth-dimensional place you've traveled to when you're back in the physical world. Someone needs to experience it to understand that the fifth dimension is real, and that whatever exists here in the physical world also exists there in its fifth-dimensional counterpart.

However, one of the main differences when traveling in an OBE is that we can see not only things that exist in the physical world, but also ones that exist in the fifth dimension only.

AN EXERCISE TO CONSCIOUSLY PROJECT TO A PLACE

To do this exercise, when going to sleep, lie in a comfortable position (on your back is the most effective position for most people), relax your body, and visualize a place—it helps if it's somewhere you're familiar with.

Picture it as realistically as you can. You could try visualizing yourself walking in it so that it becomes more concrete, as though you were really there. Imagine you can perceive the things in that environment in an intense and real way. Hear the sounds, smell the surroundings, feel the temperature, and see things in detail. If you do this well enough you can directly project to that place. You could be aware of the stages of projection and lift up out of your body, or directly project there without being aware of the process.

It's best to visualize a place that really exists, because if you try to visualize a fictitious one, you'll create a projection from your own mind. Although it can help you to get into the fifth dimension, you'll be more liable to be in a fantasy once you're there.

If you chose to visualize a real place it will help if you visit it beforehand in the physical world and observe it in great detail, or instead of visiting it, if for example it's a place that's far away, to look at pictures and videos of it. Whenever you haven't been able to see something beforehand that is part of your visualization, try to imagine how it would be as realistically as possible.

If you want to visualize a place in nature it will help if you walk in the actual place and observe nature closely. Look at the trees, flowers, and bushes, smell the aromas, listen to the birds singing, and try to remember it all. Observe the way clouds travel, the way birds fly, what happens when the wind blows, etc.

If you're already in the fifth dimension and you want to travel somewhere, visualize it and you'll quickly travel there by flying, or sometimes it will be immediate and you'll just appear at that place.

You can train yourself for the night exercise during the day by practicing the visualization you're going to use at night to project with. Start with ten minutes each day and increase the time when you feel ready to.

PROJECTING TO A ROOM IN YOUR HOUSE

Another variation of this exercise is to try to project into a room in the place where you live. As it's somewhere you're familiar with it can be easier to visualize.

To do this exercise, before you go to sleep, go into the room that you intend to project into and study it in great detail. Walk around and use all your senses to perceive it. Look at all the objects, the different colors, the size of the room, the walls, the floor, etc. Be as aware as you possibly can be when you do this, not letting thoughts interrupt you. Spend as long as you need to really take everything in and to feel present and aware in the room.

Go to sleep visualizing the room in great detail, perceiving it clearly, placing yourself back in it with your imagination, feeling as though you're really there, with the intention of projecting there. If you do this well enough, you can rise out of your body into the room or go to that room once the split from the physical body occurs. If you didn't manage to project, you could instead find yourself waking up in a dream while in the room or while going to it. If you are a bit less successful, you could still dream about being in the room.

Of course, you don't need to stay in the room for the whole time that you are in the astral plane; you can leave the room and travel.

DISCOVERING A MYSTERY OBJECT IN A ROOM

A variation of the exercise above is to project into a room in your house or apartment and discover an object placed there by somebody else. You shouldn't know what the object is beforehand.

If you know someone who knows about projection, ask them to choose and place an object in a room you're familiar with. Before they place it in the room though, go there and study the room in great detail, just as in the previous exercise. When you leave the room, without you seeing, they place an object in it. It's a good idea to have an agreed spot where they place the object, so you know where to look if you project into the room.

At any time later, go to sleep visualizing the room in great detail, placing yourself back in it with your imagination, but with the intention of projecting there and discovering what the object is.

If you're successful, the next morning you'll be able to tell them what the object was.

PROJECTING TO A SACRED PLACE

A very uplifting variation of this exercise is to travel out of the body to a sacred site, or to sleep at a sacred location and project into it, with the purpose of learning more about it or receiving a spiritual teaching there. The Great Pyramids of Egypt are a good example of an ancient site that we can project to, but there are many other sacred sites in the Religion of the Sun, like Stonehenge in England and Machu Picchu in Peru that can be used, and these are the kind I recommend, as for at least some time in their history they were used for practices of light. They were often aligned to the sun at the solstices and equinoxes, and I detail a large number of them in my book *Ancient Solstice*.

Ancient people used to go to places that were sacred to them like temples, where they practiced dream incubation, though I'm sure many of them had conscious OBEs while they were there too and met with spiritual beings. I've seen spiritual beings appear in practice rooms while out of the body in the fifth dimension.

Whoever projects in these places could have meaningful experiences and perhaps receive spiritual teachings. Places that have been used for ceremonies and practices of light can become known to spiritual beings and form a kind of meeting point with them in the fifth dimension.

However, what you find if you go to an ancient sacred site in the fifth dimension would depend on your spiritual level and what's there in the astral plane now. You could for example discover some hidden mystery, or learn about the site's origin or functions. It may be a place of spiritual teachings, or you might find it mundane or distorted by your subconscious, or even that it has become a place used by demons—especially if it was used for dark practices during its history, like human sacrifice.

I've seen sinister presences at an ancient site—it was an old Roman amphitheater where violent gladiatorial sports had been held. Much later it became known in local legend as a place that had been used for witchcraft, as practitioners of the dark occult must have been drawn there by the energies of violence and suffering for conducting their ceremonies. If you discover a spiritually dark place you would do well to avoid doing practices or trying to project there, particularly at night, as what's around in the fifth dimension is likely to be unfriendly.

It's also advisable to use an incantation to clear a site of evil beings before doing a nighttime practice in a sacred place, just as a precaution (which I cover in chapter 27).

You could also project from your own home and travel to a spiritual place in the astral plane by visualizing it as you're going to sleep or after you're already out of your body.

It's possible to be taught in spiritual places in OBEs, but entry is not guaranteed into the temples over there, and there are probably different standards for different ones. Decades ago, not long after I had first learned to have OBEs, I thought I would try to go to a temple to be taught. So the next time I had an OBE I asked my Spiritual Mother to take me to one. I felt myself moving through space—it was as though I traveled at high speed for just an instant and then arrived at the outside of a temple. I saw there were others inside, but I couldn't get in. I knew why—it was because I wasn't worthy to enter. I just didn't have a high enough inner spiritual level to be allowed in at the time. There was nothing I could do, I just drifted aimlessly, like I was suspended in midair with nowhere to go. Eventually this drifted into a dream in which I was in a scenario where my egos were rampant. When I woke up, I realized that the egos I had seen in my dream were the ones that were most preventing me from getting into the temple. I was grateful to see what it was I needed to change.

MEETING OTHER PROJECTORS AT A SACRED PLACE

It's possible to meet up with others who are projecting in the astral, and then verify the meeting later when everyone wakes up, and it's such an incredible way to verify that OBEs are real. I know of several occasions when people traveled in the astral plane and met others who verified the meeting when they were back in the physical world. Some of these occurred at sacred places.

There are two ways of doing this. The first is to set a time and place to meet other projectors in the fifth dimension. I wouldn't be too concerned about being within the exact timeframe to meet the others—close enough is usually fine in practice. For example, you could set the meeting time as 4am UTC. People may begin their practice at 3am and then sleep for some time afterward, depending on what time it is locally for them, and you can find that people can project or wake up within a dream within that range of time and meet. Sacred places of the Religion of the Sun can provide an excellent meeting point for this purpose. The projectors don't need to live anywhere near each other or near the sacred site, making it possible to arrange it all online.

The second way to do it is for a group of people to stay physically at a sacred site and to practice astral projection there together to try and project into it and meet one another there in the astral. There are ancient sites of the Religion of the Sun like Arkaim in Russia where it's possible to camp at or very close to the site itself, though with other sites the group may need to stay at accommodation nearby. Of course, the best way to do it would be for the group to visit the site during the day, and then use their impressions of it to visualize it during their OBE exercise at night to try and get there. A modern temple of the Religion of the Sun would be great for this purpose too.

CHAPTER TWENTY-THREE

Ancient Visualizations

Here we present six visualizations we've created for having OBEs based on ancient traditions. Some were used for astral projection, some we have modified and adapted to be used for astral projection, and one we believe appears to have been used for astral projection in the past, but whose purpose was lost.

They are taken from Jain, Taoist, and Hindu practices that involve fairly complex visualizations, some of which are used to bring one to a state of conscious awareness. They help break the mental identification one has with their physical body and the material world, while strengthening one's identity with their true self as consciousness.

A text describing one of the practices says:

> "[...] one gains the firm conviction that he is free from the body [...] the conviction that the Self is identical to the body has been loosened [...]."[1]
> ~ TANTRASARA

This is a very conducive state for astral projection, where we need to be able to let go of the attachment to our body and the physical world while remaining conscious. Immersive visualizations like these help to keep the mind occupied and focused through the stages of falling asleep, and also help to quieten it. These practices can bring us to the same state ancient texts describe as being a prerequisite for having conscious OBEs.

Most of them also seek to harness the spiritual energies of the sun and stars to help with astral projection, as was done in ancient times.

As well as being effective for astral projection, these are beneficial to do as spiritual exercises in themselves, so even if someone doesn't astral project, they have spent time doing an uplifting meditation that is very soothing to do while going to sleep.

The visualizations and mantras are also deeply symbolic, and full of profound meaning. These are not just ordinary visualizations of any place or imaginary scene.

Most of the Jain meditations used here have been developed quite recently, but are based on their ancient philosophy of meditation believed to stretch back to their founder, who according to their tradition lived millions of years ago.[2]

I have ordered them approximately by level of difficulty. That way, someone can work their way toward the more advanced visualizations as their ability to concentrate strengthens if they like. That's not to say the simplest of them may not be the most effective at any stage.

PREPARATION

Before doing these exercises, it helps to familiarize oneself with the objects, scenes, and sounds involved in the visualizations. For example, some involve visualizing a lotus, a mountain, a storm, the ocean, the stars, or fire. To prepare, I'd spend some time looking at the actual object if you can, or pictures and videos of it. For example, you could watch a video of a storm.

What can also help is doing these exercises at some time during the day, before using them as an exercise of projection, perhaps sitting up, to train in the visualization.

Other exercises that are going to help are those that strengthen awareness (being conscious in the moment) generally, such as going for walks in which one practices being aware. I give exercises like this in my book on self-knowledge.

It's important to learn and memorize the steps of each exercise well so that the visualizations flow smoothly, and to stick to the steps without wandering off into imagining other things. It can take a few practices to do this and to reach the end the visualization, but persistence can pay off. Once accustomed to them, we can get into the mode of having an OBE almost as soon as we begin a practice with one of these visualizations.

STARLIGHT ENERGY

This is the simplest of the visualizations in this chapter. It's a good practice to start with for those still learning to visualize, as well as a good option for those who find it hard to visualize, though it can be an effective exercise at any stage.

It would be nice to practice it beneath the stars (while sleeping outside, protected if needed) or where the stars can be viewed through a window, but is not necessary.

It's based on ancient Taoist and Egyptian OBE practices, and an OBE practice attributed to Jesus.

In Taoist practices, the energies of the stars are visualized as descending into one's body and illuminating it, as is done in this practice.

"Visualize the purple light of the Dipper descending upon your body, illuminating your internal and external being. As you arrive in the Dipper [...]. Then, greet the stars and offer this prayer [...] may I ascend as an immortal and travel through the hidden realms [...]."[3]
~ THE INCOMPARABLE MYSTERIOUS, ORIGINAL GREAT METHODS OF THE JADE HALL OF THE THREE CELESTIAL REALMS

In the Pyramid Texts of Egypt, the king harnesses the energies of the stars for having his OBE, as in this practice.

"Unis [the king] [...] embraces the constellations,
Unis harnesses their energies.
The energies [...] make him wake
For he sleeps."[4]
~ PYRAMID TEXTS

In a practice attributed to Jesus, he also describes the light of the stars filling one's body, and then ascending into the stars in an OBE.

"[Jesus said] in the moments before you sleep, then shall you think of the bright and glorious stars [...]. Enter the Holy Stream of Light [...] and breaking free from the bonds of earth, ascend the Holy Stream

of Light through the blazing radiance of the stars, into the endless kingdom of the Heavenly Father. [...] And you shall be one with it, and the power of the Holy Light Stream will fill your whole body, and you will tremble before its might."[5]
~ THE ESSENE GOSPEL OF PEACE

Preparation
Before doing this practice, spend some time looking at or concentrating on the stars. One way to do this is to look at their reflection in a bowl of water out under the stars, similarly to what I was shown to do in an OBE I had in the Great Pyramid (described in chapter 3). We've found this allows the eyes to look at the stars in a more relaxed way, as rather than looking at them as a distant object, the water brings their image closer. However, the water needs to be very still to be able to see the reflection clearly.

Visualize the stars
Lie down comfortably, relax, and then visualize the stars in the sky above you, as if you can see through the roof or as if there is no roof obstructing your view. You may notice that it's difficult to focus on many, or more than one star at a time, so I recommend focusing on a particular constellation like Orion, Cygnus, or the Big Dipper, as ancient people did (though any constellation is fine), or on one star only, like Sirius or Deneb (though any star is fine).

Absorb the energies of the stars
See and feel the light of the stars/star reaching you, entering your body at the region of your heart and spreading throughout it, energizing your astral body, and visualize your astral body glowing and radiating with starlight.

Prayer (optional)
As an option, you could ask the divine (shining through the stars) for help with your exercise. Or you could simply direct your intention without words, by feeling a connection with the divine light of the stars.

Mantra Aeeee (optional)
As an option, you could then begin to repeat the ancient Egyptian mantra Aeeee, as described in chapter 20.

Continue like this until you project or for as long as you like. If you feel you have split from your body, check by using one of the methods I described in chapter 16. If you aren't in the astral, continue the practice if you wish.

SUN HEART

This visualization is based on the Taoist practice called "high transcending the sun." It was used to absorb the energies of the sun and to travel to it (either while out of the body, or in one's imagination) and to pay respects to its ruler (the Source/Spiritual Sun). We've modified the visualization so that the energies of the sun are used to help with astral projection.

It may be most effective to practice in the hour and a half before sunrise (a time seen as most conducive to practice in Hinduism and used by Krishna and Arjuna to have an OBE).

Here are some excerpts taken from the description of the Taoist practice we've based this visualization on:

> "[...] I visualize the Sun rising in golden radiance, illuminating my true form. [...] Blazing sunlight rushes and soars, spreading essence over thousands of miles. Demonic power dissipates in flames, the mundane and impure is cleared away. Ascend to heaven with a fast pace, harnessing qi and rising to the heights. [...] Then ride the fiery dragon towards the palace of the sun.
>
> The fiery dragon leads the way, piercing through, flying with radiant light. The spirit enters the transcendental realm, offering worship to Yuyi [The Great Sun Lord]. In an instant, ascending to the divine, it merges with spiritual radiance. In oneness pursuing to the root, incinerating the corpse worms. [...]
>
> In your mind, enter the palace of the sun, merging with it as one. After a while, forget about your physical body, in joy and harmony like spring."[6]
> ~ THE INCOMPARABLE MYSTERIOUS, ORIGINAL GREAT METHODS OF THE JADE HALL OF THE THREE CELESTIAL REALMS

This description is cryptic and uses symbols, which is why it's difficult to understand.

One important thing to take into account is that Taoists saw the external world as intrinsically connected to the internal body.

> "[...] the marvelousness of the Jade Capital and Qiong Hall, the profundity of the Primordial Venerable, is far beyond the high and bright heavens, yet it is also within the heavenly realm of one's own body."[7]
> ~ THE INCOMPARABLE MYSTERIOUS, ORIGINAL GREAT METHODS OF THE JADE HALL OF THE THREE CELESTIAL REALMS

Thus, while the sun was in the sky, it was also within one's heart (as also described in Hindu texts, explained in the chapter 3 section OBEs to the Source). The fiery dragon is a symbol of the qi/energy within one's heart,[8] which was elevated in the practice by uniting it with the qi of the sun, and used to travel to the sun. It was also a symbol of one's Spirit and the energy of the sun (both expressions of yang energy), as in Chinese tradition the dragon was synonymous with yang energy (as opposed to yin), and so in this passage it likely also represents the "yang spirit" that leaves the body, just as described in the Taoist text The Story of Han Xiangzi discussed in chapter 3. In Taoism it's said there are three corpse worms that live in the body and cause great harm—the upper causes heaviness in the head, the middle makes one crave sensual pleasures, and the lower causes one to lust after others.[9] I would interpret these as major types of egos, and the reference to the sun burning them away as the practice used in the ancient Religion of the Sun to eliminate them. The reference to spring may relate not only to the season of spring, but to the spring equinox, which in Taoism was celebrated by "welcoming the rising sun," and is part of the yearly solar cycle that was seen as expressing the cycles of rebirth and the attainment of immortality,[10] as it was in other traditions derived from the ancient Religion of the Sun.

This is a kind of concentration on the heart exercise as explained in chapter 19, particularly the type "visualizing the heart as a spiritual place."

Visualize the rising sun

Lie down comfortably, relax, and visualize the sun as though it's rising above the horizon before you. See its golden, divine rays spreading light everywhere, illuminating everything, chasing away all evil. Feel it purifying everything.

Imagine a light in your heart

Visualize a golden light, like that of the sun, in your own heart, radiating and shining.

Merge the lights together
Feel and visualize the light of the sun connecting with the light in your heart, energizing and elevating its energy.

Prayer to the Spiritual Sun (optional)
If you wish, say a prayer to the Spiritual Sun, perhaps asking it to help you project.

Radiate light
Feel and visualize the light in your heart radiating outward so that you lose sense of your physical body as it dissolves in its warm radiance. Also keep feeling the light of the sun connecting with your light and continually energizing it.

Mantra (optional)
If you wish, while doing the above step, repeat one of the mantras from chapter 20 in the section Mantras of the Sun.

Continue like this until you project or for as long as you like. If you feel you have split from your body, check by using one of the methods I described in chapter 16. If you aren't in the astral, continue the practice if you wish.

STAR TRAVEL

This is based on a Jain meditation that's incidentally called "Out-of-Body Experience,"[11] though that's not what it's used for in Jainism. As with the other Jain meditations, it's used to help one to feel themselves free of the physical body as consciousness. We've modified it slightly to incorporate elements from Taoist astral travel practice, and the OBE the king has in the Pyramid Texts. It's also somewhat similar to the practice of concentrating on the stars for astral projection that Jesus describes in the Essene Gospel of Peace.

Preparation
Before doing this practice, spend some time looking at or concentrating on the stars.

Visualize leaving the body
Lie down comfortably, relax, and then visualize yourself floating up out of your physical body. Look down on your physical body from just above it, then visualize floating up through your ceiling (don't go out a window), lifting up out of your roof, floating upward, and looking down on the roof and building.

Travel into the stars
Visualize yourself traveling and flying higher and higher up into the sky, seeing your surrounds from above. They get more distant, until you see your region, your country, and then Earth. Leave Earth and travel into the stars.

Travel through space
Travel wherever you would like to go in space. You could travel beyond the solar system, into the vastness of the cosmos, seeing beautiful galaxies, stars, and nebulas.

Feel free
Feel free and eternal, as a child of light, a child of the stars, as your true self—feel completely at home and at peace in the light.

Absorb the energies of the stars
Feel yourself absorbing the energy of the stars, feel their beautiful soft light radiating toward you and entering you. The stars are helping you, energizing you, and propelling you as you travel in your astral body of light.

Continue like this until you project or for as long as you like. If you feel you have split from your body, check by using one of the methods I described in chapter 16. If you aren't in the astral, continue the practice if you wish.

MOUNTAIN PEAK ENERGY

This is based on a Jain meditation[12] with only two small changes—namely we have made the source of the light the sun, and added the mantra Om. The mountain in the Jain practice is said to be the sacred Mount Meru where some of the great teachers (Tirthankaras) of Jainism attained liberation, which we discussed in chapter 3.

It also shares similarities with an ancient Taoist visualization in which one imagines themselves seated on top of the world mountain. It was used as part of astral projection, in which one sought to absorb the energies of the sun.

> "Visualize your own Dantian [energy] as the great sea, and let the sun rise from the sea. Place yourself at the top of your head, with your body like a mountain stone [explained elsewhere in the same text as: 'visualize yourself as Kunlun Mountain, being situated at the very top, with the sea below']. [...] The yang energy gave birth to the primordial sea, ascending from below. May the surging yang essence disperse the gathered yin. Within [the sun], there is a great deity, the Master Yuyi [The Great Sun Lord]. Descend this true qi [energy] and cleanse my physical form."[13]
> ~ THE INCOMPARABLE MYSTERIOUS, ORIGINAL GREAT METHODS OF THE JADE HALL OF THE THREE CELESTIAL REALMS

In Taoism, placing oneself at the top of one's head with one's body like a mountain, means to remain as still as a mountain, with one's focus at the crown of their head. For this practice it means to keep the body completely still, and to remain conscious and concentrated.

This practice contains symbols from the creation myth of the ancient Religion of the Sun, involving the primeval waters (the cosmic ocean), the primordial mound (world mountain), and sun, as discussed in chapter 3 in the section Ancient Sites Used to Connect with Other Dimensions. This practice symbolizes how creation moves from darkness and chaos, to light and harmony, both in the universe and within us.

Seated at the peak of a mountain in a storm

Lie or sit down comfortably, relax, and then imagine you are seated alone at the peak of a mountain that is surrounded on all sides by the ocean. Clouds cover the sky; you are in the midst of a storm, with rain, wind, lightning, and thunder. The ocean is turbulent. The storm symbolizes your inner state with its chaos of thoughts and feelings.

With calmness, the storm clears

However, as you become calmer and calmer, the waves and storm calm with you. As your body relaxes, the waves subside until the ocean is completely still. As your mind clears, every last cloud disappears until there is a pure pre-dawn sky. Feel that your body is as still as the ocean. Your mind is as clear as the cloudless sky. Your concentration and will are as immovable as the mountain.

The sun rises, energizing your consciousness
Then the sun begins to rise in the distance over the ocean. Its rays reach you and penetrate into your true self, your consciousness, energizing you. At first the sun is weak, but as it rises, it gets stronger and stronger, and its rays energize you more and more.

Mantra Om
As this happens, mentally pronounce the mantra Om, making the m vibrate through you.

Continue like this until you project or for as long as you like. If you feel you have split from your body, check by using one of the methods I described in chapter 16. If you aren't in the astral, continue the practice if you wish.

FIRE IN THE LOTUS

This is based on a Jain meditation known as *pindāstha dhyāna*.[14] We simplified it, adapted it to astral projection, and introduced the sun and the mantra So Hum into it based on the early practice of yoga in Hinduism. After we did this, Lara came across a very similar practice in the Tantrasara (a Shaivite Hindu text we explain shortly in the exercise called "complete light"), where the sun and a similar mantra Om Hum are used, just as we had included them. It seems the Jain and Shaivite Hindu practice derive from a more ancient, common source.

In the Tantrasara, this practice is said to cause "a newly born" "pure body to rise" that has "unlimited power." This sounds very much like astral projection, and so as it turns out, this is what this ancient practice may have originally been used for. However, projecting in one's astral body seems to have been misunderstood as creating a new nonphysical body each time.

Here is the description of what sounds like the practice of astral projection in the Tantrasara, taken from the easier-to-understand explanation by the translator. It's very similar to the practice we give here:

> "[...] one should think of the unity of the three—namely, the self, the sun, and the Lord—as coalesced into one. It is followed by the ritual practice of burning of the physical and the subtle bodies [which is done symbolically, not actually], and by this relinquishing I-consciousness in the physical body. [...] Afterwards, whatever remain as ashes are regarded as nothing but the residual traces of the former bodies. They are blown away by means of varma = hum representing the wind. Then, the *acarya* [teacher] should remain steady in the state of pure consciousness. It is like a tranquil sea from where the creative consciousness (*samvit*) begins to break into waves. The first creative impulse of consciousness causes the pure body to rise. This newly born body is characterized by the unlimited power of Bhairava [a form of Shiva]. This body is really the supreme form (*para murti*) of the Lord and is characterized by the mantra '*om ham*' [pronounced om hum[15] as outlined in chapter 20]."[16]
>
> ~ H. N. CHAKRAVARTY, TANTRASARA, INTRODUCTION

This visualization centers on one of the most important symbols in the ancient Religion of the Sun, which is the sun god in the lotus. As explained in chapter 3, this could be used to represent one's Being within the lotus of the heart. The lotus that we imagine ourselves lying on is symbolic of our own heart. The sun shining in the sky is symbolic of the Spiritual Sun, our higher Being, and the Source. The five elements are present as physical body (earth), fire, wind (air), rain (water), and sky (ether).

Afloat in a lotus

Lie or sit down comfortably, relax, and then imagine you are lying (or sitting if you are seated) at the yellow center of a beautiful, giant lotus flower—its petals can be pink, red, blue, purple, or white; any lotus color you prefer. The petals are open, and you look up at a totally clear blue sky—no sun, stars, moon, or clouds. The lotus is afloat in the vast cosmos where you are alone.

Fire turns the body to ashes

Then a tiny spark ignites in your heart, that spark becomes a golden flame, and that flame grows to become a beautiful spiritual fire that spreads until it consumes your whole body. There is no need to be graphic with this; you can visualize it very simply. You feel no heat or pain. It burns your body until it's nothing but a pile of ashes, and the fire dies out. See and feel your consciousness shining amid the ashes as a pure light, freed from the heavy mantle of your body, though still inside the lotus.

The wind blows the ashes away

In the distance you can hear wind approaching. You see clouds come over and cover the sky. The wind comes and blows the ashes of your body away.

The rain washes the ashes away

Next you hear rain approaching; it comes and washes every last remaining trace of ashes away. Your consciousness shines radiantly, washed clean. Then the rain passes.

The sun's light merges with your light

The clouds start to dissipate, and through the breaks in the clouds you start to see the rays of the sun, beautiful rays, shining on you. The clouds completely clear and the sun gently shines on you from above. As the light of the sun reaches you, it merges with the light of your consciousness. You shine back at the sun with the same light as the sun. Feel the light of the sun connecting with you and energizing you.

Mantra So Hum

While visualizing yourself beneath the sun, mentally repeat the mantra "So Hum" (or "Om So Hum" or "Om Hum" as other options) meaning "I am That" over and over.

Continue like this until you project or for as long as you like. If you feel you have split from your body, check by using one of the methods I described in chapter 16. If you aren't in the astral, continue the practice if you wish.

COMPLETE LIGHT

This practice is based on two related meditations from the Hindu tradition of Shaivite Tantra. They're described in the Tantrasara,[17] which is a summary of the much larger text Tantraloka—a compendium of ancient Shaivite teachings and practices. Both texts were written by the Shaivite practitioner Abhinavagupta in the tenth century based on much older traditions.[18] Much of it he wrote cryptically so that it could be understood by practitioners but not lay people, which makes interpreting it today difficult.

The practices are said to cause one to enter the state of yoga nidra, and were used for bringing the state of Turiya—that is of consciousness—into the three other states of waking, dreaming, and deep sleep. They're very similar to visualizations used in the practice of "clear light sleep" in Tibetan Buddhism and Bon,[19] and may be where it originated from. However, we've simplified and modified them to create a more free-flowing visualization for projection.

Essentially, in the first meditation, one visualizes a fire in the heart, which symbolizes pure consciousness. This fire is then imagined as spreading to dissolve whatever objects one looks at, which are "merged into transcendence," which is into the light as it spreads to consume everything.

In a related practice that directly follows, one pronounces the seed mantras "sa" and "ha." "Sa" is said to be that of creation, and "ha" of dissolution. Together, in the Tantrasara they are used to purify one of distracting thoughts, and are said to help one attain a state of greater consciousness.[20] These seed syllables are found together in the mantra svaha/swaha, which is traditionally pronounced in Vedic fire rituals before making an offering into the flames, an act which is symbolically related to this practice. Svaha became the symbolic name of the wife of Agni (the sacred fire)—she being the only thing that the fire cannot extinguish nor exist without—that is consciousness.[21]

Here is an excerpt from the Tantrasara describing the meaning of the sacred fire ritual in connection to this practice. It essentially says that the fire is symbolic of the Source, and the offerings into it the beings returning to it, which when their physical forms are burnt away, are all revealed to be made of light:

> "Offerings into consecrated fire (*homa*) is dissolution of all entities into the fire of consciousness of the Lord, who takes delight in consuming all and making them remain as the flame of fire alone. *Homa* is for the purpose of attaining this steady determinate conviction: 'All entities are made of the light.'"[22]

Continuing in the practice, one is meant to then take rest in conscious awareness, understanding and experiencing oneself, the consciousness, as "different from the body." The practitioner then "gains the firm conviction that he is free from the body [...] because the conviction that the Self is identical to the body has been loosened," which is said to be "followed by the 'void of sleep' (nidra) as the tendency toward" the external world disappears. The yogin is then said to experience a sense of "great expansion."[23]

We realized these practices and the state they bring someone to are conducive to astral projection.

Here are some excerpts from the Tantrasara that partly describe this practice:

> "One should meditate in the blissful and luminous abode of one's heart as the self-manifest, integral unity of the Self [...].
>
> One should meditate on the Lord [as a fire in the heart], the all-pervading One, the Lord of the 'wheel' presiding over those twelve powers of its rays, who is emerging outwardly through the outlets [the eyes] [...], and is the agent of creation, and so on.
>
> The *yogin* should meditate on the totality of entities, both external and internal, which have been dissolved into the [fire of the] Self, and are going to take repose (*visranti*) therein. Thus, the light of the Self shines forth."[24]

Flame in the heart

Lie or sit down comfortably, relax, and bring your attention to your heart. See and feel a beautiful, small, golden, spiritual flame burning in your heart, like the single flame of a candle, representing the light and energy of your being, pure consciousness, which is of the same light, energy, and fire as the sun and Source. Spend whatever time you feel like doing this.

Fire dissolves the body
See this flame start to spread so that it becomes a fire that dissolves everything in its path. It spreads to dissolve your body, leaving only the golden light and energy of the fire—like a radiant golden sea of energy. Feel yourself floating, free of the body, in this sea of light.

Fire dissolves the room/surroundings
The fire continues to spread, dissolving the bed (or whatever) beneath you, the floor, the objects in the room, the walls, the ceiling.

Mantra svaha
As you start to see things dissolve into light, repeat the mantra "sva ha" mentally and continue with it for the duration of the practice.

The mantra is pronounced S as in snake, V as in very, A as in father, H as in hello, elongating the A, so it's said svaaa haaa.

Fire dissolves thoughts
Whatever thought comes up, whatever image arises in your mind, see the fire dissolve it into light and say "sva ha." You might start thinking about how you need to buy some shoes, and you start seeing the shoes. Burn and dissolve the image of them into light, and then go back to visualizing the fire spreading. When another thought arises, do the same thing, and then go back to seeing the fire spread.

Fire dissolves everything
The fire continues to spread, dissolving the house/building and everything and everyone in it, and then dissolves the surrounds, the garden, streets, other houses, spreading out across the earth. The earth is a sea of light and you feel yourself afloat in it.

The light of the sun/stars expands until everything is light
Above you see the sky. Choose either to see the sun or the stars shining in it. Their light grows brighter and brighter, gradually expanding and filling the whole sky until there is only light. Another option is to see more and more stars, as though your eyes adjust to see more, until every space is filled with a star and there is only light. Float and bask in the light, which is beautiful and full of energy.

Continue like this until you project or for as long as you like. If you feel you have split from your body, check by using one of the methods I described in chapter 16. If you aren't in the astral, continue the practice if you wish.

CHAPTER TWENTY-FOUR

Further Considerations for OBE Practice

To do projection exercises at a higher level and improve the chances of having successful OBEs there are several things that can be done.

Whatever someone's success rate is, it can usually be improved by increasing the amount of practice done, by refining the techniques, and assessing how one approaches the practices. I'll go through some of the things that may be useful; it could be helpful to assess what's relevant to one's own personal circumstances.

TECHNIQUE

Learn the proper techniques and practice them correctly. This may take some time, so be prepared to allow for it.

It's worth using a variety of techniques over time, as if you stick to a small number, they'll probably become stale. Just make sure they are safe to do.

You could try the technique you're going to use to project with for ten minutes some time before going to sleep and trying your actual exercise. You'll become more familiar with and trained in it, so you'll know exactly what you need to do for the exercise on that night and are less likely to be distracted by thoughts.

Be consistent with your exercises. If you keep going every night, even if you have no success for a while, it may suddenly work. If you don't, then you'll lose your daily momentum and you'll have to build it back up again. If you only try sporadically, you're just hoping for a lucky chance and you'll never develop the exercises.

Do other concentration/meditation exercises at other times too. There's more to spirituality than astral projection. Other exercises help to put your mind in the right state for astral projection, which should be seen in the context of a wider spiritual quest.

Practice enough. Basically, the more we practice for astral projection, the more likely we are to succeed. The less we practice, the less likely we are to project.

PREPARATION

Try to project when your body is in a suitable state for it, and not when you're overtired, ill, or in pain. Don't force yourself, listen to your body, and make sure you get enough sleep. Also get your body used to doing the extra exercises gradually, particularly lying down on your back if you're not used to it.

Have a clear aim, understanding what you hope to achieve by having OBEs and how you're going to do it. You'll have a much greater chance of reaching your goals if you work toward them methodically.

But be realistic about what it takes. It's likely to take time and commitment, and even if you have a successful OBE, be prepared for the dedication and practice that it takes to repeat and maintain it.

You're unlikely to consciously project as soon as you have the techniques, and even if you do, to repeat it usually takes a lot of practice. Likewise, if you're moving to a higher level of practice, it's important to get into a routine and build up, just like in sports. No one becomes good at sports overnight, and if someone has been away from training, they need to gradually get back into it until they reach the level they left at, and improve from there. If you're consistent and have a well worked out program, you'll become good at it. You'll also learn how it works and gradually understand how you behave psychologically and physically when you're trying the exercises.

Later in this chapter I'll explain how creating our own program of exercises can focus our attention on having OBEs, and greatly increase our chances of success. It involves planning a series of exercises to do over a fixed time period, which is based on whatever someone feels comfortable with.

Best of all though is to meet with others who share the same spiritual interests. It can really give you a boost, which is important because it's easy to lose momentum and enthusiasm when you're alone.

THE ABILITY TO CONCENTRATE

Having good concentration is what it takes to consistently project, and so to improve your projection rate you'll have to improve your ability to concentrate. If you don't, thoughts will easily take you off track and even the best techniques won't be effective.

You may have a series of OBEs for a while without having much concentration, but that's due to spiritual assistance; it may be more important for you to have OBEs than you realize.

It's easy to know whether you need extra concentration practice—it's when you do your exercises and your mind keeps powerfully thinking about other things. Yet being able to hold your concentration enough to astral project isn't easy, and making the sacrifices to do what it takes to consistently have OBEs won't be for everyone, particularly since life makes other demands upon us. So for some, rather than setting an intensive program, it may be more practical to set aside periods of time, like one day on the weekend, or a couple of weeks every now and then, to dedicate to practice.

Whoever wants to have intensive periods of practice would have to set aside time for it and create a program, or attend a spiritual retreat, but there's an important aspect of concentration practice that can be done during daily life, and that is to learn to concentrate during daily activities. This greatly improves our ability to concentrate. So if you're doing something, say washing your hands, just focus on it. You can apply this to any activity, like putting your shoes on, making dinner, fixing something, and so on, increasing the number of tasks you practice with until you train your mind to be focused on one thing. Then when you go to astral project, you're already used to being on one thing, your mind is more focused on the practice, and it works much better.

It helps too to have an order in daily activities to avoid being scattered by lots of things going on at once. So ideally, in your daily activities you would focus on doing one thing at a time, and if possible, finish what you need to do on it before moving on to the next thing. Even if you have a lot of tasks to do and are under pressure, deal with the most important one, giving it your full attention, even if it's just for a few moments, before you have to do another task. Give your full attention to whatever you're doing at that moment.

Being concentrated on activities goes hand-in-hand with observing inner states such as feeling angry, tense, or afraid. When we observe them and come out of them, we naturally become more aware of what we're doing. It does take a lot of willpower to be focused on what you're doing throughout the day though, so do what you can while being natural with it.

HAVING A SUITABLE INNER STATE

Another factor involved in having an OBE is our inner state at the time. It's much harder to get into the mystical feeling of the practice if we're agitated or our minds are consumed with work or other tasks. That's why it can help to get into a more conducive state leading up to the practice by doing activities that can make us feel more spiritually perceptive, like spending time being aware particularly in nature, listening to spiritual music, burning candles and incense (safely), chanting a mantra, practicing meditation, etc.

These activities can make someone feel more perceptive for a while, but you'll find if you go through a busy or difficult time, you quickly lose the psychic sensitivity you've built up. This is why prolonged periods where someone can practice more intensely, like on a retreat, or at home using an astral program, are going to give better results.

Ultimately, it's most effective to raise the level of one's energies more permanently by doing a work of self-knowledge and inner transformation, which I will explain in other books.

PRACTICAL CONSIDERATIONS

When we try to project, it's inevitable that we're going to encounter difficulties, and we'll have to make some sacrifices to overcome them.

When something's not working it's tempting to give it up, but with astral projection, that can be the point at which to assess whether it's going to need extra time and effort to succeed. Bear in mind that failures add to our experience, as we don't only learn from successes, but from failures too.

A lot of people are fearful of having OBEs, as the fifth dimension is largely unknown and we have an inbuilt fear of the unknown. But experience tends to overcome it—once someone goes there enough times they realize nothing bad ever happens to them physically, and I've found that's when most people tend to stop being so afraid.

Another common fear is that some sinister entity will stop someone from coming back or harm them in some way. But although demons exist, they don't harm us physically.

Reducing the overall level of fear we feel generally helps too and that's done with self-knowledge, which I explain in my book on the subject.

Sometimes someone may feel they just can't be bothered to practice and will do something else instead. That's fine, but if they want to have OBEs and keep doing this, they shouldn't expect to have many OBEs. This is laziness and is best fought by overcoming its feeling of resistance, and doing what we need to. But it's important to distinguish between laziness and not being up to doing an exercise, whether through illness, tiredness, emotional problems, stress, or any other issue. If in doubt, I've found it's best not to do it. It's better to be sure laziness is the problem before doing an exercise when we don't feel like it.

Pain can sometimes arise when someone has been overdoing the exercises, or simply when they're not used to them. If we push ourselves or force the body to go through pain we can become negative toward the exercises, so it's important to refrain from pushing oneself to the point of pain.

The body and mind should be trained to do the exercises gently and gradually, and the capacity of endurance varies from person to person. After an illness, the body is even more sensitive and vulnerable to pain and discomfort, and so greater care should be taken in those times. When we've been ill it doesn't take long to get tired or feel pain, so once someone is ready to get back into practice after illness, it's best to just try the exercises for very short periods of time, according to what the body can tolerate, that is, before it becomes painful or uncomfortable. Stop if you feel you are forcing something or if the body feels uncomfortable with it.

If someone is simply trying to go back into the exercises because they've drifted away from them and they feel pain when they do them, the approach is similar. However, it will take less time to get back into them since the body only has to be trained to remain still in a position for a while. At the same time, they'll need to go back to the discipline of focusing their mind on the exercises.

Those who decide to practice having OBEs should make sure they get enough sleep; it's not possible to maintain a routine where we don't get enough, and if someone pushes themselves too much, they can lose their capacity to function properly during waking hours—this can be dangerous and can even lead to illness. The way to do it is to factor in extra time to one's normal sleeping time to accommodate astral exercises and always make sure to have enough sleep. For example, if someone's going to try an exercise to astral project for around thirty minutes, they could go to bed at least thirty minutes earlier than they normally would.

When astral exercises are new, it's interesting, someone may feel keen to try them, and there may be some success. But after a time they may find the practices feel stale, their success rate declines, and they become despondent with it. Mundane life generally runs counter to spiritual practices like this and can quickly bring efforts down. That's why it's important to always look for ways to improve, and to inspire and propel our efforts, often by talking to and meeting with others who are trying too.

SPIRITUAL CONSIDERATIONS

There's another factor to take into account when trying to have OBEs. It generally doesn't take many OBEs before someone encounters one or more spiritual beings, as there are spiritual beings influencing OBEs in the other dimensions, and they have requirements for us to receive their knowledge.

If someone isn't having OBEs much, or if the experiences are not profound or meaningful, it may be that they need to change what they're doing in life and the way they are. We especially need to watch out for pride in spiritual activities; it can cause more harm than good for a proud person to have profound OBEs. Pride bars the door to advanced spiritual development, as humility is a requirement for being given knowledge in the higher dimensions.

For spiritually-orientated people, OBEs aren't for pleasure or fun or having experiences, but discovering reality, notably our own, realizing the wrongs we've done and maybe still do, and changing and being a source of love and goodness in the world.

Spiritual beings don't give advanced knowledge to evil people, but according to grades of goodness.

PROGRAMS FOR HAVING OUT-OF-BODY EXPERIENCES

For most people, the most effective way to have OBEs is to carry out a program of exercises practiced over a predetermined period of time. I recommend practicing to have OBEs within the Religion of the Sun, as they should have a spiritual purpose. The other dimensions are spiritual and there should be supporting knowledge of what's out there. I don't wish to contribute to people's curiosity or thrill seeking, when I know how serious life is.

If you're planning your own program, take into account what you aim to achieve with it, what exercises you're going to do, and how long the program will be for. Work out the timeframe based upon what you feel comfortable with and use the astral exercises you think will work best for you.

After starting your program it's usually best to stick to it. If you don't keep to it, you'll find that the practices and experiences easily fall away. It takes a lot of effort to build up a positive momentum and not much to lose it.

It's easier with a group of people, so consider how long you realistically expect to maintain your program for when you plan it. If you're doing it alone it will be more difficult to sustain than if you were participating in a group program.

Programs can be created to learn about the exercises, to become more proficient at them, to achieve a goal like conscious projection, or to do something specific while out of the body like traveling to a certain place.

In your program it's worth taking into account what you will do during the day as well as in the evenings and nighttime.

Here are some things that can be done during the day to prepare for projection exercises at night:

Questioning – Question yourself genuinely as much as you can as to whether you are in the physical or astral world, and take a little jump or pull your finger to check.

Awareness – Be aware and focused on the things you do and be in self-observation when you can.

Concentration – If you can, do at least one concentration exercise for ten or more minutes every day. This should be done at a different time from your actual astral projection exercise.

Mantras – If you are using a mantra as your OBE exercise, you can practice this mantra during the day for whatever time you choose. You don't need to be lying down ready to project, but can simply be seated somewhere comfortable.

At night, you may want to do your exercise as you first go to sleep, and then sleep through the rest of the night uninterrupted. Or you may want to set your alarm to wake up in the night to give yourself an extra opportunity to astral project. Or simply take advantage of the opportunity to practice again if you wake up naturally during the night.

Be aware that the fear of not being able to sleep can keep you awake. Aim to create the conditions you need for a conscious astral projection while making sure you get the full amount of sleep you need for the night.

Don't forget to ask for spiritual assistance and use an incantation and circle of protection (I'll explain about these in a later chapter) before you start your astral exercise. And try to remember your dreams in the morning when you wake up.

Some people find it useful to keep a journal to plan their daily exercises. It can be used to draw up a weekly schedule of exercises—when they will be done and for how long. It could be updated with a new schedule each week.

It's useful to have a journal like this anyway whether someone's doing a program or not. I find it helps me to do what I need to. I wouldn't be absolutely rigid with it though—use common sense. For example, when something more important arises than what's written in your journal, deal with it. Once it's done, go back to what you were working on from your journal. Bear in mind there's only so much you can do in a day. You may find though, that if you work through your journal, and do everything as orderly as you can, you have more time than if you hadn't planned your day. This can help you to get to your spiritual exercises in the evening instead of leaving them until the end of the day and finding you've run out of time to do them.

Any program can get stale and lose effectiveness over time. If that happens, make another program, but a better one this time, taking into account the successes and failures of the previous one. In any case, when you've completed a program, I suggest looking back at what you achieved, seeing what worked and what didn't. It's worth trying to understand why things turned out the way they did.

It's generally more effective to go through a program with others, as it creates a supportive and at times inspiring environment. The strong impetus of being part of a group where everyone is working toward the same goal makes the program work better. I first learned to astral project in a group, and it helped me a lot.

Retreats with others who practice the Religion of the Sun would be an excellent way to focus upon having OBEs, just like how they could be used to focus on other kinds of spiritual practices. There people can focus solely on practice in a conducive environment dedicated to the exercises.

Taking a break from the usual concerns of everyday life can allow the thought process to slow down and take in different spiritual impressions. This can not only be good for getting experiences, but it can also give a different perspective on the way someone normally lives, and cause them to reflect upon what really matters.

There are lots of different activities people could do as a group; one example is to meet fellow members in the astral plane at an arranged location. This is possible, although happens rarely. You could meet nearby or at a well-known location anywhere in the world.

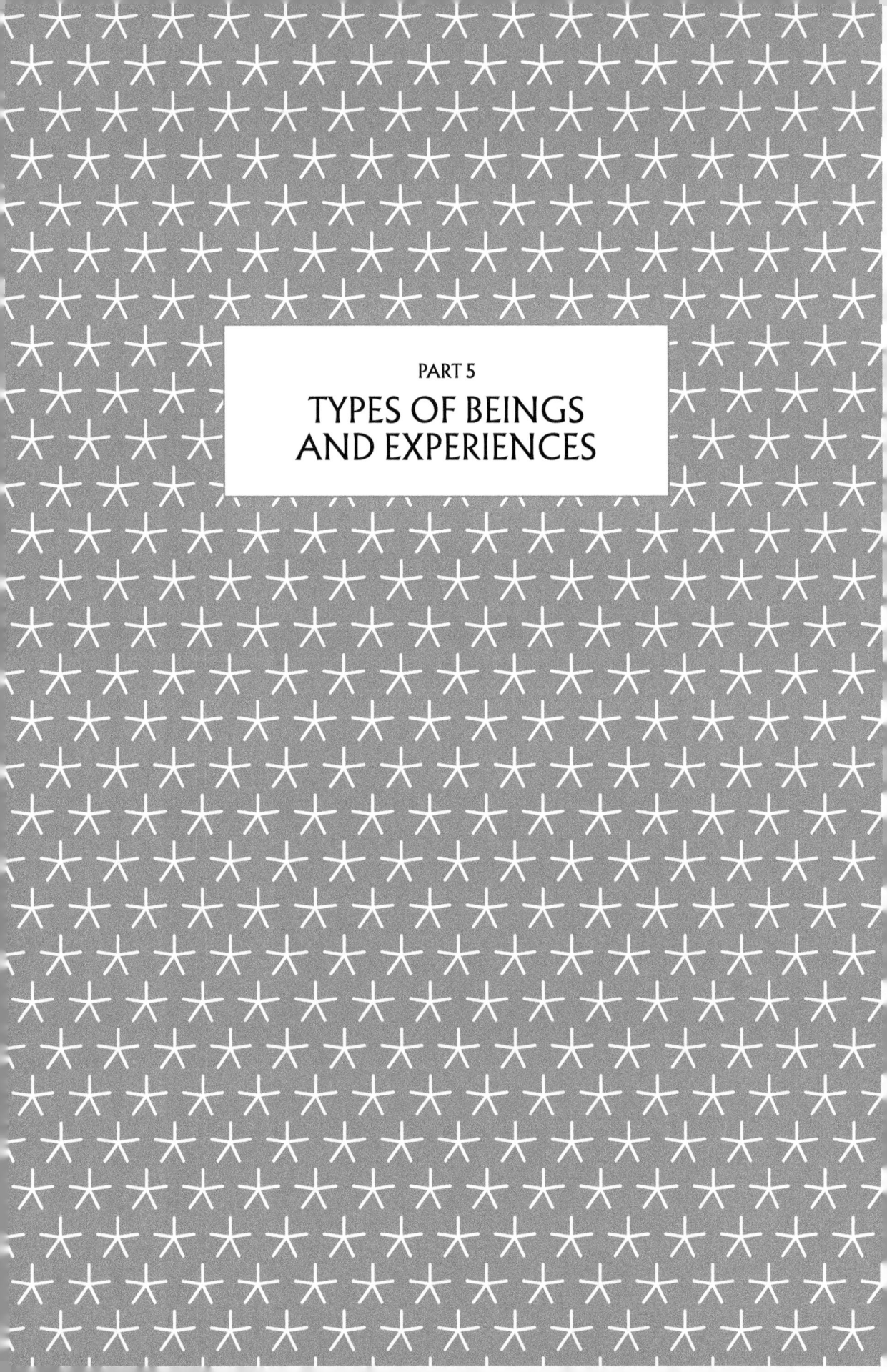

PART 5
TYPES OF BEINGS AND EXPERIENCES

CHAPTER TWENTY-FIVE

The Different Beings We Meet in OBEs

In this chapter I outline the different beings and entities we can encounter in the fifth dimension—in dreams, OBEs, and NDEs—that I know of. The beings I'll discuss here are real—they are not projections of the subconscious or archetypes—but have their own conscious and independent existence as we do. Many are described in folklore and ancient religions.

PEOPLE AWAKE IN THE PHYSICAL WORLD

It's possible to see people who are awake in the physical world from the astral plane—what is seen though is their astral part. If the person out of their body tries to interact with someone in the physical world, they don't respond as they can't perceive them, and that's because most people here are unable to perceive anything from other dimensions while in waking life. I know this because I've had several OBEs in which I've seen people walking, shopping, or doing spiritual activities, and in some cases I could verify they were real people who had physically been where I had seen them.

It's common for people in NDEs to see people in the physical world while they are out of their bodies, and to try to communicate with them. Often the people in the physical world can't sense the recently deceased, but sometimes they do. An example of this is the NDE of Ingrid Honkala, who drowned in a tank at the back of her home when she was three. She left her body and traveled to the maid who was inside listening to the radio; she hovered above her but found she was completely unaware. In an instant she then found herself above her mother who was on her way to work. She said her mother's name, and her mother immediately froze in her tracks, turned around, and started running back home, having sensed something was wrong. She ran straight to the back of the house, saw what had happened, and dove into the tank to rescue her daughter. Because of her intuition, she was able to get home in time to resuscitate Ingrid, who then lived to tell what happened.[1]

OTHER PEOPLE DREAMING OR CONSCIOUS IN THE FIFTH DIMENSION

As I've mentioned already, while in an OBE we can see and interact with other people who are out of their bodies—whether they are dreaming or consciously aware of being in the fifth dimension.

If we try to interact with someone who is dreaming, they usually look as though they are drunk and are unable to respond clearly due to being immersed in their own subconscious imagery.

One night while consciously out of my body I saw someone I knew. I could tell he was dreaming, so I asked him some questions to see if he could answer them, thinking that when I saw him again in the physical world I would see if he remembered anything of our conversation in the astral. However, his responses were unclear, even nonsensical, and he eventually became confused. I then thought of questioning him about a specific topic. The first thing that came to mind was fish—I don't know why I chose fish, but I wanted to see if he could remember anything about fish from his dreams when he woke up, but he became so agitated by the questioning I had to leave him alone. When I spoke to him about it later in the physical world, the most he could recall was something so vague it couldn't count as evidence that he'd seen me. He had been dreaming too heavily to be able to see and recall what was happening in the astral plane. It goes to show how strongly the subconscious states of the dreamer influences how much of the astral plane is really seen.

However, it's possible to meet up and interact with others who are consciously out of their bodies, which is something I and other people I know have done. For example, Lara bumped into a friend in a dream whom she often met to practice astral projection with. When the two met in the dream, they both realized they were dreaming at the same time and decided to hold hands and fly into the sky. After only a short time they both lost the experience, likely because of their excitement and not having a clear destination. But the next day they both remembered what had happened—and her friend challenged her to tell her which side she flew on (right or left), to which Lara answered correctly.

THE DECEASED

As discussed, it can be quite common to see the deceased while in the fifth dimension. We can either see their discarded personality (which is a kind of energetic shell, empty of consciousness) or the real person with their mind and consciousness intact. What we tend to call ghosts are the personalities and not the actual person who has died. Ghosts are usually seen or sensed in the physical world, but sometimes appear in a dream or an OBE.

While in an OBE, we can see those who have just died, with their consciousness intact, traveling to their afterlife destination, as the astral plane is the place where the deceased first arrive before crossing over to either the upper regions of heaven, or lower regions of hell. In chapter 26 I describe a conscious OBE I had where I saw a crowd of recently deceased people entering hell.

Painting of the deceased being moved on either to heaven or hell.

It can be shocking to see those who were once ordinary people living their lives, people who you may have known, being moved on through other realms, that perhaps they didn't even believe existed—especially into hell.

As mentioned, the presence of the deceased can also be sensed by those in the physical world. There are lots of accounts of sightings of ghosts worldwide, not only today, but in the past too, where some accounts have survived in folklore.

A 2023 poll conducted by Pew Research found that more than half of U.S. adults (53 percent) say they have been visited by a deceased family member, with most reporting they were visited in a dream.[2] An earlier 2009 Pew poll found that 18 percent felt they had been in the presence of a ghost.[3] A 2007 IPSOS poll conducted in the UK found that 44 percent of women and 31 percent of men believed in ghosts, and of these, 36 percent said they had seen one.[4] A study conducted in 1971 in the UK found that nearly 50 percent of people who'd lost a spouse said they had been in the presence of their deceased spouse, often on numerous occasions over many years.[5]

Hamlet in the Presence of His Father's Ghost by John Gilbert.

As well as taking visible forms, ghosts are also perceived as sounds, moving objects, lights, aromas, presences, and the feeling of being touched by someone, such as being kissed on the cheek.

Attempts have been made to scientifically explain the phenomenon of ghost sightings, yet I find none of them convincing. A common explanation is that they are a misrepresentation of visual/audio events, yet those who've seen a ghost claim to have been seeing clearly, and there have been cases where more than one person has observed the same event. Moreover, some ghosts have been captured in photos with no scientific explanation for their appearance.

Some believe that environmental factors, such as electromagnetic fields and infrasound (above normal background levels), reactions to toxic substances, or fungal hallucinations might be to blame for sightings. But these factors are quite rare and are unlikely to be present in the majority of cases.

Some believe that suggestion can explain many ghost encounters, so for example, if people are told a place is haunted they may be more likely to say they saw ghosts, but research doesn't support this. One study in Hampton Court in the UK, for example, found that suggestion had no effect on participants' claims of seeing ghosts.[6]

When a person dies (and their death is final), their personality splits apart from their mind and consciousness and becomes a ghost, discarded as an empty energetic shell. I became aware of this through encountering ghosts many times in OBEs. From what I've seen, a visible ghost usually has the appearance of the person who's just died, but because it lacks consciousness, isn't self-aware. I believe they are probably made of crystallized thoughts, feelings, and memories, which themselves are comprised of energy. This energy condenses into fifth-dimensional matter during the course of a person's life, and takes the shape of their body. There must be some way ghosts retain memories, but once they separate from consciousness, new memories stop being made, and so ghosts live in the past and are easily confused by new things. And since they have no new energy supply, they gradually dissolve over time.

I described in chapter 9 how I spoke to the personality of an old school friend who had just died, and that being without consciousness and some mental abilities, his personality was unable to comprehend anything new. While out of my body I told another ghost that he was dead and the result was the same—he was confused and became frustrated, as he couldn't work out his present situation. I'm sure this is because they cannot comprehend the new, as they are trapped in the past.

On another occasion, I decided to put a question to a ghost that he would need to have the ability to come up with something new to answer. He couldn't, and like the others, became confused. When seeing other ghosts later, I didn't mention this kind of thing to them again, as I didn't want to agitate or distress them.

It's a clue to their nature that the number of reported encounters with ghosts of ancient people seem relatively small. I assume this is due to them not having an energy source from which to sustain themselves. Over time their energy would inevitably dissipate and so they would all slowly evaporate into formlessness/nothing.

The egos of the deceased seem to manifest through ghosts, as I've seen ghosts acting with strong ego-driven emotions several times. These were ghosts of the newly deceased, and so perhaps their egos were using the ghosts before the consciousness of the deceased took a new physical body that they could incorporate into again, or perhaps ghosts have some residual "ego memory" which makes them feel emotions even though the actual egos aren't there. Perhaps I'll learn more about them in the future. I did notice once how a ghost felt happy seeing its former loved ones, so the emotions can be both "positive" and "negative."

A fairly common type of experience is sensing the presence of someone who has just died (particularly of those close to us), sometimes even before their death is known. I've experienced this myself. In this kind of encounter the "visitor" can be the actual person who is visiting their loved ones before passing on to the next stage of the afterlife.

Reports of ghosts indicate that many are associated with places they used to inhabit while they were alive. They tend to be around the people and places they were strongly attracted to in their lives, such as houses, place of work, etc., and are sometimes also sensed around their graves.[7]

The house I grew up in had a lot of poltergeist activity when I was a child. This sort of thing can be due to ghosts, but it can be due to other supernatural phenomena, which I think most of it was. There was one regular presence I considered a ghost though; it was of an old lady. I could sense her presence and sometimes heard her talking and laughing; a visitor heard her with me once too. I felt she had lived next door, and some years later my mother told me there had been an old lady called Mrs. Tims who had lived there from around 1910 and died there. I thought it must have been her.

Another different and quite strange ghostly encounter happened when I was about seven years old. As my friends and I were passing an old building from the Victorian era, I looked inside through a window and saw a man with a tall top hat and old-fashioned black clothes walking around. I saw him quite clearly, but he had a strange shadowiness to him. I called a friend to take a look and he saw him too. He turned to me and said, "It's a ghost!" The building had a single door, but it was locked with a padlock from the outside, so how did the man get in there? A startled shout went up from the lads, "Ghost!" and we ran away as fast as we could.

Although ghosts are often feared, I think much of this is due to fear of the unknown, as I found they are really nothing to be afraid of.

SPIRITUAL BEINGS

Spiritual beings are the most commonly encountered type of being in NDEs by far. They can also appear in dreams and OBEs, though mostly to those who are actively seeking their guidance. They are known by many different names across religions, such as devas, gods, heavenly immortals, angels, and ascended masters.

We find commonly held beliefs about them in ancient religions, especially those of the ancient Religion of the Sun. For example, they are seen as residing in heavenly regions in the sky, as serving different roles in service to the divine, are associated with light, have supernatural powers, are immortal, have nonphysical forms, and are benevolent. While some gods were the personification of divine forces beyond any individual, others were remembered as having once lived on Earth before ascending to heaven after having attained liberation. They served as the example of what one strove to attain and were the helpers one called upon to attain it.

Some of these are the spiritual beings we can meet out of the body today—they are those who've reached spiritual liberation, and go on to live as a conscious being of light in higher realms where they fulfill different roles in creation according to their level of spiritual development. One of these roles is to administer the process of death, which is why they appear in NDEs. They were extremely important in the ancient Religion of the Sun, as we can see from their countless depictions in ancient art, descriptions in ancient texts, and from all the petitions people directed to them. This is because they guide every aspect of our lives, and also the process of attaining liberation.

Spiritual beings portrayed by different cultures.

They often (but not always) appear in NDEs in a form that is comforting and recognizable to the deceased. However, in dreams and OBEs, they often appear more ordinary, perhaps as any other person—though radiating an extraordinary wisdom, peace, and love. In NDEs and OBEs people have witnessed their sense of humor too, seeing them laughing and joking.

Jesus commonly appears in OBEs and NDEs, though there are other beings from the Religion of the Sun who appear in them too. Lara had an OBE in which she invoked Odin (the greatest god of ancient Germanic/Norse religion), and he appeared. She posted her experience on YouTube and was amazed to see the response—more than seventy people replied in the comments that they too had met or been visited by Odin in a dream or OBE, and some even felt he had revived them in their NDE.[8] Anubis or Thoth from ancient Egypt can also appear in relation to one's karma.

Some spiritual beings appear in the astral plane when they are called, or because we are having an effective spiritual practice, or perhaps as a reward for something we've done, or positive changes we've made.

One of the main things we can do to learn while out of the body is to call a spiritual being in the hope they will arrive and teach us something. To do this, you can concentrate and humbly ask that a specific spiritual being please come to you. Be aware though you may get some kind of test first before they show themselves, like an event that could distract you, reveal whether your attempts are superficial or half-hearted, or make you angry. If you take the bait it's unlikely they'll appear; they may want to see whether you meet their standards to receive their teaching. Sometimes they won't appear at all though if we have other lessons to learn.

When I first began to call spiritual beings in OBEs, I soon realized that I had to be in the right state with the right attitude to be able to be taught by them. I knew I had to change a lot, so I never made demands for anyone to appear when I called, and I think this helped. So when no one appeared, I always looked for what I needed to change, and when they did, I was ready to be taught.

Following are two accounts of people meeting spiritual beings in NDEs:

> "Looking down I couldn't see any feet. I did see a silver cord attached to my body which had a luminescence to it. Looking around me, I

could see a room that appeared to be formed from pure white clouds, yet wasn't solid. In the room were three beings, made of shimmering crystal. Light shone through them like a glass prism, forming a rainbow. One was larger than the other two, but all of them spoke to me. I was afraid of them, and they seemed to realize this. Instantly, they transformed into what I recognized as angels. They didn't have bird wings, they had fibers like fiber optic cables that were shaped like wings and pure light shone through the fibers, forming colors in all shades. When they spoke, their messages were sent telepathically. They could read my thoughts.

Looking into their eyes, they were shades of intense colors that changed and shifted with electric sparks. Almost as if I were watching a DVD still spinning in a DVD player. And the love radiated from their eyes, as if I were the most precious creation God had ever placed into existence. It was as if they knew me intimately, yet I didn't feel uncomfortable feeling that they did."[9]

"I then became aware that there was a being to my left. I couldn't actually look at it because it was so bright. I didn't notice a face or anything like that. It seemed to be what I can only describe as a being of fire and it was tall and extremely bright. It wasn't hot though; I didn't feel any heat coming from it. It wasn't cold either. The color was also something I've never seen before or since. It was somewhere between white and gold. The closest thing to this color would be how the sun looks at midday.

It didn't say anything to me, but I understood immediately what it was there for. And it was emitting an intense feeling of love and compassion. It reached down and touched my body on the left side near the stomach area. [...] I felt a sensation of warmth where it touched me that spread throughout my whole body. Along with this came an immense feeling of what I can only describe as pure love and ecstasy. I've never ever felt a feeling as intense and good, before or since.

[...] I knew this being was going home and that is where I wanted to be. It refused my request without words. All of this was being communicated through thought, or more like just knowing."[10]

DEMONS

Many have seen demonic figures in nightmares or in dreams; some who consciously projected have met them or sensed their presence, regardless of whether they had any religious convictions or not.

Demons are frequently represented in religions throughout the world—called by many different names, such as asuras, *galla*, *tzitzimimeh*, the guardians of the netherworld, the lords of Xibalba, *daevas*, and *alu*—and they also frequently appear in NDEs. As with spiritual beings, there are commonly held beliefs about them across ancient religions. They are described as nonphysical malevolent entities that inhabit the underworld/netherworld/hell beneath the surface of the earth. They are associated with darkness, disease, possession, and nightmares, and are said to operate according to a structure, and to torture sinners in hell. They are the constant adversary of the gods and of good people on Earth.

Demons depicted in Japan (top left), Mexico (top center), Peru (top right), Sumer (bottom left), and India (bottom right).

Some may think these are just Christian concepts, but they are far more ancient and widespread. For example, in ancient Egypt, they believed in demons that inhabited the realm of the dead where they punished sinners, thousands of years before Jesus.[11] A similar belief is held in Hinduism, in which sinners are punished and tortured by demons in hell beneath the earth,[12] as was also the belief in ancient China.[13] This same belief is held in Zoroastrianism, from which much of the demonology found in Christianity derives. They also believed that people could become demons through certain practices. In ancient Mesopotamia, demons were believed to dwell in the underworld, which they could leave to terrorize people on Earth,[14] as was similarly believed by the Maya of ancient Mexico.[15]

Many have reported seeing demons in NDEs. A 1996 study looked at fifty reports of distressing NDEs and categorized them into three types; the third were of a hellish nature and included seeing demons.[16]

The following are a small selection of people encountering demons or negative beings in NDEs.

Matthew Botsford of Atlanta was shot and had an NDE in which he met demonic beings that knew everything about him and his past, and mocked and tormented him. He said how he felt their fingernails claw at his flesh.[17]

Howard Storm, a former Professor of Art at Northern Kentucky University, said how there were the worst imaginable people in his NDE, who were stripped of every impulse to do good. He said they were liars, and a mob of them taunted, screamed, and hit him and took pleasure in hurting him. They tore off pieces of his flesh and began eating him alive.[18]

An unnamed woman on the IANDS website said she encountered two creatures in her NDE and was attacked, saying:

> "The only way I think I can describe the horrific creatures is that they were demons. They are like nothing you could ever imagine or dream up and they were as real to me as anything is. They were small in size, the one that stayed was slightly bigger than the one that left, maybe 30cms in size. They were covered in thick dark spikey looking fur and had huge black eyes. I couldn't see any ears or a nose. It had a very large mouth, full of pointed sharp white gray teeth. It had arms and legs, which did not have fur. Its hands looked somewhat human in form, with sharp nails. They resonated pure evil."[19]

A depiction of demons eating people from fifteenth-century France.

Another person on the IANDS website:

> "An ethereal being with a no-nonsense countenance firmly grabbed my shoulder and proceeded to take me down a long rough-hewn vertical tunnel. It stunk, was hot, and the air was void of oxygen. The sounds of anguish and filthy dialogue are indescribable. We hit the bottom and were standing in wiggling worms up to my ankles; the stench and heat, oh the stench. Demons of every type were flying all around screaming obscenities and wailing."[20]

Former airline pilot Jim Woodford described seeing a demon in his NDE, which appeared from out of a hellish abyss:

> "It was on fire, its body was on fire. Its head was squat on its shoulders. [...] The look of hatred that I saw in its glowing eyes, not just for me, but for all of mankind will stay with me forever. [...] Now, for its size, it was large—it moved with an amazing nimbleness. [...] and it reared up out of the pit, and I was confronted by this creature, body on fire, dripping saliva, and the most horrendous face. But the other thing was there was screaming, and the screaming was coming not from its mouth, the screaming appeared to be coming from within the body. It was as though this creature [...] had consumed souls, and they were crying out for mercy. [...] And then, in addition to the screaming, I heard it speak my name. This creature knew me [...]. I wasn't that bad a person! [...] I concentrated on this beautiful light coming toward me. [...] when that light struck that creature, it screeched and screamed, and scrambled backwards like a rat running for cover."[21]

After hearing Jim's experience, Lara came across the description of a demon from Celtic tradition, said to be a beast "with a thousand souls, by their sins, tortured in the holds of its flesh."[22] This sounded similar to the demon Jim saw in his NDE, and we wonder whether it was the basis of the sacrificial burning wicker man of the ancient Celts. This was a giant body of a man made of wicker which the Celts are said to have filled with human criminals and then set alight so that they were burned alive within its body.[23] Their tortured screaming from within its body would have been just like the demon Jim saw, and it's possible the Celts knew of the same demon or type of demon, and viewed the criminals as the sinners who were punished within it.

The preceding accounts are just a small sample of the many accounts of demons in NDEs. It's clear that it's not uncommon for people to encounter them during one, and that people can have the same experiences of them despite differences of time and culture.

Angels and demons meet human beings in the common ground of the fifth dimension, which is why some of us who have OBEs or NDEs may see both spiritual beings and demons in the same experience.[24]

Demons are people, or once were, who have awakened in evil, or beings of light who have fallen, and they belong to a hierarchical structure that's organized according to the level of awakened evil consciousness they each have. They reside in hell and enter the emotional and mental planes, where they are often encountered by people having OBEs, usually because they attack them.

Demons operate in a hierarchy that's ordered by their level of awakened evil.

Sometimes in the astral world a being can appear in front of us, maybe telling us things. Through intuition we can tell if they are good or evil just by looking at them. By looking into their eyes we can often see what they are, because their eyes can reveal their evil, even if they want to hide it from us. However, if you are negative toward someone, your own subconscious can make them appear as an evil figure to you in a dream or an OBE. In that case your own negativity may persuade you that it was real. Or negative beings can use your dislike of the person to portray them as a sinister figure to fool you. This is another reason to work to get one's psyche as clear of egos and as objective as possible.

It's important to realize that not everything we encounter in the fifth dimension is benevolent; not everyone is benevolent here in daily life either, and we would be wrong to go around in day-to-day life with the illusion that everyone and everything is wonderful and loving all the time. Therefore, it's worth understanding what's in the fifth dimension, both good and bad, positive and negative, and in this way someone can be prepared for what they come across.

The struggle of opposites, of light and darkness, positive and negative, etc., is necessary for life to exist and also for our learning and spiritual growth. If we were to exist in light alone, we would have no knowledge even of our own existence. It's the struggle against the darkness that makes us strong and gives us knowledge.

People being tortured by demons in hell as depicted in Chinese tradition (top left), Christianity (top center), Hinduism (top right), Sumer (bottom left), and Buddhism (bottom right).

This duality exists in the fifth dimension, so we can experience positive and negative things while we're dreaming or in an OBE. Moreover, it's a dimension where the heavens and hells meet and is a portal to both, which is why it contains both angels and demons.

Demons inevitably come to try to stop anyone who takes the spiritual work seriously. But it's rare for them to have a physical body—virtually all of them now exist solely in the other dimensions—although I have met a couple of them who had, and they had extraordinary supernatural abilities.

For people starting out, it's important to learn to deal with fear when coming across a sinister entity or situation in the astral plane—it's worth remembering that they don't cause us harm physically so much as harm us through deceit or harm our spiritual development in some way. For example, when someone goes to the fifth dimension there may be a demon waiting to frighten them so that they fly back to their body, or to distract them so that they don't go somewhere more spiritual or discover what they need to.

They can stir up ego states, both in the astral plane and in daily life, inflaming passions and desires and leading one astray. They can cause the astral plane to look unclear or darkened. They can make an initiate of the path of the Spiritual Sun fall and do works on the astral body so that the kundalini, an essential aspect of the path, does not rise, rendering the body temporarily disabled for the path. One of those I met who had a physical body tried to do this to me, and I stopped him in the astral plane.

Demons often use deceit; they can say misleading things and can easily fool someone into taking their advice, which inevitably is harmful for the real spiritual work. They can even appear as one's idea of a spiritual being, preaching about love, etc., but their real purpose is to take people away from salvation and the path of the Spiritual Sun. In the astral plane people can call spiritual beings and get help and teachings from them, but sometimes when they call, a demon will arrive that looks exactly like the spiritual being they're calling, so use a protective incantation if you need to. If the being is evil it will go; if it is the real one, it will stay. As I've mentioned previously, you can also use your intuition, because sometimes you can tell an evil being just by looking at it, particularly if you look into its eyes, which can look dark and evil.

I've encountered so many demons while out of my body. They come time after time in many different guises. Sometimes they would be confusing such as when I saw a spiritual teacher, or what looked like him, and he started telling me something, but my intuition told me there was something wrong so I stared closely into his eyes. As I did, they appeared blackish and dark with an evil resonance about them. I immediately knew that it wasn't him but a negative entity, a demon in disguise. Deceit is a major weapon of the forces of evil.

Some demons are very complex. Early on in my spiritual journey in the early 1990s I had an OBE in which I went to a region of hell. Although it was dark there I could still see. I walked along a small track that extended far away until it became lost in a cloudy darkness. In the distance on the track there appeared a figure dressed in black with an entourage following him. They gradually came closer and I could see that the entourage was of a certain group of people who in the physical world are under the influence of the dark side and wear black as well. Eventually they were in front of me and approached me. I also walked toward them. The leading figure was a giant, while his followers were normal sized people. He had a somewhat distinguished appearance, like a late middle-aged person with great rank and responsibility. He left the others behind and walked toward me as I walked toward him. We stopped right in front of each other. I have a large astral body too (from a past life) and so I blocked him and asked him who he was—he replied "Bael." He looked closely at me and I looked at him. I looked straight into his eyes and to my astonishment I saw evil, but not the evil of the other grotesque beings I had previously encountered, but a great, deep, sublime evil intelligence.

It was an intelligence that was dark and yet was vast. His eyes were portals into a deep blackness, so deep they seemed to encompass all the darkness. And, as I looked in, the darkness looked back at me and he looked at me; he looked at me and through me, like he saw something more than physical eyes could see, like he knew who I was beyond my present life. I moved to one side and let him pass, as though we knew that to fight each other would have been in neither of our interests. He and his entourage kept walking along that road, disappearing into the foggy darkness.

In the Western world today many believe that the name of the leader of all demons is Satan, but this is not quite true. In OBEs I've learned that Satan is not the name of a certain individual, but is a title that's given to whoever the head demon is, as this leader can change. The actual esoteric title (used by spiritual beings) for the head demon is "Prince of Darkness"—prince in this case meaning "first among those of the same kind," which is the older definition of the word. Today the word prince is commonly used to refer to an heir to a throne, on the second tier in a hierarchy, but that's not what it refers to in the case of demons.

NATURE SPIRITS/FAIRIES

There is yet another type of being we can encounter in the fifth dimension, which is neither human, angelic, nor demonic—these are the spirits of nature, commonly known as fairies. It seems they are the consciousnesses of beings that are evolving through the higher dimensional realms of the earth and plants before taking bodies as evolving animals, and then again, much later as humans. They would be at an early stage in the journey of consciousness as it learns through the various forms of earthly life, which would mean they are not yet tainted by the egos (which are needed and developed by animals), and this must be why they appear as beautiful, happy, childlike beings of light. They have been depicted in the past in myths and legends as fairies, commonly in European folklore (including Celtic, English, Germanic, French, and Slavic),[25] but also in Indo-Iranian folklore as "exquisite, winged spirits renowned for their beauty," known as *peris*.[26] They were often seen by ancient peoples, but are rarely seen today. For example, in the Kolbrin it's said that the Druids "believed in a fairyland of Nature Spirits that manifest to mortals."[27] However, there are still sometimes children that claim to see them, as Lara did as a child, and even adults, such as the English artist and poet William Blake.[28]

It's possible to see them in OBEs and NDEs,[29] although the accounts of seeing them are rare; we don't normally come out of our bodies and see fairies around, even if we're outside in nature in the astral. I think this is because they ordinarily reside in the higher astral plane, or even heaven, but can travel to the ordinary astral and make themselves manifest to people while out of the body there and can also appear to spiritually sensitive people in the physical world.

EXTRATERRESTRIALS

It's possible to meet and interact with extraterrestrials while we and they are out of the body in the fifth dimension during OBEs and NDEs, or to contact them through the fifth dimension using telepathy while we and they are in the physical world.

Lara attended a group exercise to contact ETs with Dr. Steven Greer, founder of the Disclosure Project and the Center for the Study of Extraterrestrial Intelligence (CSETI), using his CE-5 protocol. It essentially involved doing a guided visualization outdoors at night in which everyone tried to reach out telepathically to ETs; it did not involve astral projection.

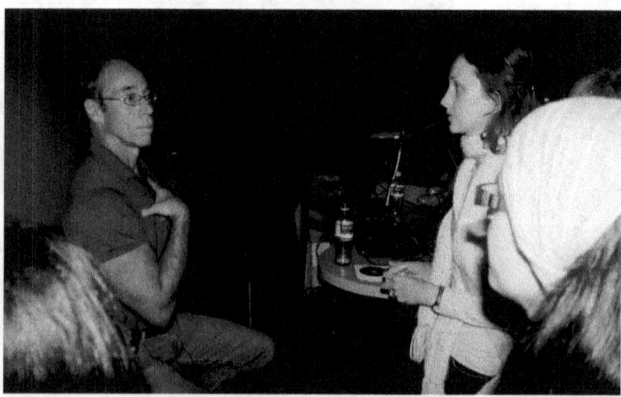

Lara speaking with Dr. Greer after his presentation.

One of the participants had a digital infrared camera, which they used to try to capture images of UFO craft. They randomly took pictures of the sky throughout the night, and although they couldn't be seen by the naked eye, many UFO craft of different types appeared in the infrared photos. Some attending saw craft with the naked eye on the horizon and also strange lights nearby. However, Lara remarked at the time that even though it was amazing that craft appeared, and so many, if felt as though the contact was still very limited, as there was no interaction with the extraterrestrials themselves.[30]

Spiritual practices with visualization work for contact because thought is fifth-dimensional, and so ETs may pick up on it when they are conscious in the fifth dimension or through telepathy. Telepathy involves being aware of receiving fifth-dimensional signals while conscious in the physical world, which works because our psyche consists of parts that exist in different dimensions simultaneously. This is likely how ETs became aware of Dr. Greer's gathering and came to observe it.

Trying to contact ETs telepathically, and using infrared cameras (or other forms of technology) to detect them, could be combined with OBE exercises afterward with the aim to meet them personally in the fifth dimension, to take contact further. The exercise could involve focusing one's mind on them while going to sleep.

I know ETs can establish contact with us through the fifth dimension as I've had several meetings with ETs in dreams and OBEs, and know others who have too. In a couple of instances this has been preceded by sightings of UFOs in the physical world the day before, revealing they may locate someone physically first. For example, one day while out in the garden I saw a UFO pass overhead, and then that night Lara was helped out of her body by an ET and shown different things about humanity and its interaction with ET civilization. She was later visited by the same ET again in the same way.[31]

I once met some beings in an OBE who identified themselves as extraterrestrials. They had very fit looking physiques, and it seems they took on the representation of the human form to convey something to me. They showed me certain exercises and how their abdomens were very toned—a bit like a bodybuilder's, but not as built up; more natural looking. I knew they were telling me I had to get myself into the same shape and use the exercises they showed me. They really seemed to think that keeping a human body in a healthy condition was very important and I've always tried to keep myself in reasonable shape since.

I've spoken to someone who had an OBE with extraterrestrials in which they saw a symbolic language on their craft; they later came across accounts of people who claimed to have physically encountered ET craft and drew the language they'd seen on it, which they believed was the same as the one seen in their OBE.

We're not the only beings capable of astral travel; ETs can have OBEs in the fifth dimension too, and would have far greater knowledge of the dimensions than we do as I suspect they use some kind of interdimensional mechanism to travel the huge distances they do through space.

There are NDEs in which people have seen and interacted with ETs. These experiences have included interacting with ETs and being shown extraterrestrial life on other planets, being shown Earth is just one planet we can incarnate on among an almost endless number of others for the same purpose of learning in physical life,[32] and that some who had formerly lived as an extraterrestrial on another planet have incarnated on this one in order to go through the accelerated learning Earth offers due to being engrossed in so much darkness.

There are many different types of ETs, but from those I have encountered and others' accounts of them, it seems the spiritual level of most of them tends to be higher than the average human being, but they too are in the process of learning from life and must also strive to attain salvation just as some of us do here. ETs would have their flaws and are not the same as the spiritual beings of the fifth dimension, though I'm sure that as long as their physical bodies have what's needed, they would be able to reach liberation and go on to become spiritual beings, just as we humans can.

ONE'S HIGHER BEING

In my experience, it's each one's higher Being that so often teaches and guides us in our dreams and OBEs, especially once someone begins working determinedly toward their own spiritual development, to help them use their experiences for that purpose.

We, and all living beings, each have our own higher Being. Numerous ancient texts in traditions of the Religion of the Sun describe this Being—in Hinduism it's called Atman and in Gnosticism the Monad. As we come into creation, our Being divides into different parts, with some parts staying in higher regions, while the soul/consciousness is the part that comes into the physical body to start the process of life. It's on the path of the Spiritual Sun that consciousness gradually merges back with its higher parts to become whole again, but with all the knowledge and experience it has gained from life.

The Monad/Atman, which is the whole androgynous Being that emerges from the Source, first divides into male and female—I call these parts the Spiritual Father and Spiritual Mother. They were often symbolized as a divine couple of god and goddess, who give birth to a Spiritual Son. According to ancient Gnostic texts, a spark of the Mother, which is consciousness, also descends into matter. The Father, Mother, and Son, remain in higher regions, from where they help consciousness.

These higher parts were symbolized in the ancient Religion of the Sun as a divine triad/trinity of Father, Mother, and Son. So in ancient Egypt for example, they were symbolized as Atum, Nut, and Osiris, and in another variation as Osiris, Isis, and Horus. In Celtic tradition they could be symbolized as Dagda, Boann, and Aengus. In the life of Jesus, they were symbolized as the Heavenly Father, Mary, and Jesus. I explain much more about this with many examples from ancient texts in my book *Ancient Solstice*.

Left: The Egyptian divine triad of Osiris, Horus, and Isis. Right: The Christian divine triad of Joseph, Jesus, and Mary. Both symbolize the higher aspects of one's Being.

Each of these higher parts has a role in helping consciousness in its development (though completely invisibly and unknown to most), and on the path.

The Spiritual Mother is the part that works most closely with us. Particularly, she works to eliminate one's egos and with one's energies during alchemy (as clearly described in Hinduism), and usually guides one in their OBEs, often showing them the egos they need to eliminate most urgently.

The Spiritual Son was symbolized as a savior, as it's this part that incarnates within someone at a stage on the path of the Spiritual Sun, at which time he helps someone in their development from within.

While the realm of the Spiritual Mother is that of "womb world" as explained in chapter 3, which includes the earth, hell, and astral plane, the realm of the Spiritual Father is the heavens. He is much more distant from us, as the one we return to when we graduate to his higher realms, though he guides us from afar on our journey back to him. The Spiritual Father can appear as a Supreme Being or force, but from what I understand, in OBEs he rarely shows himself to us unless there is a specific reason, such as at certain stages on the path of the Spiritual Sun. This would be why Jesus referred to him as "the Father who is in heaven," and "the Father who is in secret."

THE SOURCE

A common experience in NDEs is an interaction with what people identify as the Source or God, which they describe with different terms—I've also heard Om, infinite one, and the creator of the universe. There are some like Lara who say that in an OBE they have interacted with what they felt was the Source. I wouldn't know if it was the Source or some high Being or Beings. But it's possible to enter the Source in a particular kind of OBE as I explained in chapter 3 in the section "OBEs to the Source."

People most commonly see the Source as a beautiful light, like the sun, but many times brighter. They consistently describe it as the greatest source of love, peace, understanding, and goodness, which communicates with them telepathically during their experience.

Here are a few examples from NDEs.

> "The sun was this massive ball of white light that wasn't blinding at all as I looked right into it. It came flying through the apartment and engulfed me. I can't say that I knew I was no longer in my body but somehow I knew, as I was enveloped in this massive white light orb, that my body was below me.
>
> I experienced purity. I was basking in pure love, pure peace, true serenity. I felt no pain, only unconditional love. A kind of love I had never known before. Unconditional acceptance. The light was consciousness itself, intelligence beyond my wildest imagination or understanding, and I was one with it, like a parent cradling a sick child.
>
> I had returned home and finally felt whole. This was the creator, the source that I understood, to put a limited name on it, to be God.
>
> [...] I then felt a voice. The best way to describe it is a vibration emanated from the light into me and I instantly understood it as language. [...] Vibrationally, it felt like a lot of information was being sent into me."[33]
>
> ~ ANON

> "[...] God asked if I wanted to see his face, and I said sure [...] my attention was shifted around and I was facing a huge sun-like entity with millions and millions of souls mixed in with this entity. It looked like the sun except it was made up of millions of these little souls, and each soul had their own light that they generated and contributed to the overall effect of this very bright sun-like entity."[34]
>
> ~ AARON GREEN

"So the first thing I seem to notice was our sun. When I came out of my body I realized I was connected to the sun. That is where our spirits, our souls, get our energy from. I also realized there was a source behind this power, and I call it 'the infinite one' now. But you realize that you are just a piece of this source, and [...] we're all connected to this infinite one, and the sun is where we get the electricity from, and I believe all the stars are just transformers, for lack of a better word, that transfer this energy to us, into every living thing on our planet and everything in the universe."[35]

~ MARK HODGES

"[...] I could feel something coming up, and as it's coming up I'm going 'Oh my God, it's the creator of the universe. [...] This is so exciting.' And so 'boom,' face-to-face with the creator of the universe. And he doesn't have a face, he doesn't have a pronoun [...]. It's not a he, it's not a she, it's not an it. It is the creator of the universe and all I can describe what it seemed to be was like the aurora borealis. It was this wavy, different colors, electric being. [...] I started seeing the expanse of what this really means to be eternal, and people talk about multidimensional, and it was like [...] this is just so amazing. [...] I was getting information through this telepathy through my head—it felt like this way [motions in the video as coming through the top of her head]. Then all of a sudden love [...] was shooting through my body this way [motions to her upper body]."[36]

~ DONNA REBADOW

"And I just get this feeling right here [points to his heart] from the most dominant force you'll ever feel in your life. I knew it was God because you just know. It was that strong, I could compare it to being hit by lightning every time, just constantly [...]. And I had a bunch of questions in my head, and just in the order the questions were in my head they were answered. [...] I didn't see him at all, I just felt him—he gets on a knee and then gives me a hug. The hug was very tight and safe, and I did not want to let go. [...] I felt cared for, and I wasn't used to that. [...] I would say he's a male, right, because his dominance was just so manly, male, it was like the most macho male. But that hug, and his caring was [...] way more than a woman, so it's like kind of both, and all in one. So that's why I just kind of say Source, I don't really call him him, or her, I just say it."[37]

~ CHRIS BATTS

It's obviously beyond our capacity to understand the Source, and so people today and in the past have done the best they can to describe it, or whatever aspect of it they have experienced. Modern descriptions of the Source from NDEs are remarkably similar to those found in traditions of the ancient Religion of the Sun, revealing they are based on real experiences. For example, in Hinduism, Taoism, Gnosticism, and ancient Egyptian religion, the Source is described as beyond form, and as being both male and female at the same time. It's said to be supreme consciousness, power, peace, and love—the origin of the consciousness of all beings and creation, and the return destination of all those who achieve liberation. Just as in modern NDEs, in the ancient Religion of the Sun the Source is the ultimate light, and it's no wonder the symbol these ancient people used for it was the Spiritual Sun.

It's possible that people are in contact with the Source in NDEs and OBEs, but I would speculate it's also possible it could be a very advanced spiritual being, or their Spiritual Father, who may appear as the Source in order to teach them as part of their experience, as God and the Source are the concepts most people understand.

I tend to use the word Source instead of God, as God is typically associated with the figure of the Old Testament in the West. Recent translations of Old Testament texts by Mauro Biglino, who was an official Vatican translator of the Bible, and Paul Wallis, who was a theological educator and archdeacon for the Anglican Church in Australia, argue that key terms in them, particularly those that describe "God," have been purposefully mistranslated for theological reasons (starting from around 600 BC), and this has significantly altered the meaning of the texts. For instance, the term Elohim has been translated to mean a singular, nonphysical God, when this word actually refers to a plural set of beings who the texts reveal were a class of ancient, physical rulers.[38] This explains why "God" in the Old Testament is sometimes involved in physical events, demands human and animal sacrifices, war, and violence, and is so unlike the Heavenly Father of Jesus,[39] and the loving Source of NDEs, OBEs, and the ancient Religion of the Sun.

JUNGIAN ARCHETYPES

There are some that might argue that the beings I have just outlined don't really exist, but can be explained as "Jungian archetypes."

These are named after the psychiatrist Carl Jung who defined them. Jung was a colleague of Sigmund Freud, the father of modern psychiatry, though broke with him to develop some of his own very influential theories. One of these posits the existence of a "collective unconscious." This, Jung said, is the part of our unconscious mind that had evolved over millions of years which every human being had inherited as part of their brain. The collective unconscious is said to be composed of archetypes—which are universal primordial concepts that people expressed often as symbols and mythological beings.

The evidence generally put forward to support this theory is that common symbols and beliefs can be found across the world, in cultures that supposedly had no contact with one another. However, often these ancient cultures did have contact with one another, and many of their symbols and beliefs derive from the same source, which is the ancient Religion of the Sun that spread around the world. Lara has documented this extensively in her book *The Ancient Religion of the Sun*.

Another source of common symbols and beliefs is the other dimensions, and people's shared experience of them, as we documented extensively in chapters 3, 4, and 5 on ancient OBEs, dreams, and NDEs. OBEs can sometimes explain why distant cultures share the same or similar beliefs and symbols—because people within them experienced similar things while out of the body. That's why people still today can have the same essential religious experiences that people had hundreds and thousands of years ago.

The reason I bring up Jung is because people can argue that the beings people encounter out of the body are purely archetypal projections of the unconscious mind, which is why they appear so similar.

But they *would* appear similar if they really exist—far more so than if they were unconscious projections. For example, if you travel to Italy, and then a few months later I travel to Italy, we would share very similar stories about what we'd seen—the people, the cuisine, the buildings, etc. Thousands, millions of people could travel to Italy, and although their stories may all be a bit different, there would be recurring elements between them, since they had all been to the same place. It's the same when millions of people visit heaven, hell, or the astral plane.

CHAPTER TWENTY-SIX

Experiences of Dark Entities and Places

A significant number of people who've had an OBE have an interaction with a being that appears sinister or evil, or go to an unpleasant place. Another significant number who have NDEs report having a negative or even hellish experience. Dreams can also be full of unpleasant experiences and situations, while nightmares are simply terrifying.

Negative experiences can sometimes be caused by the subconscious, which is full of fear and aggression, but others are the result of encountering real dark places and beings. In this chapter, I'll look at the different kinds of negative experiences people can have while out of the body and their causes.

BAD DREAMS

A large percentage of the population suffers from having more unpleasant dreams than pleasant ones. Unpleasant dreams include those that involve violence, being chased, trapped, fighting, or falling, etc., and they go on a sliding scale from disturbing to terrifying. Bad dreams are different to true nightmares however, which I will discuss in the next section.

Bad dreams are usually a reflection of the state of one's psyche in the astral plane, where most dreams occur. It's not surprising that many dreams contain unpleasant, violent events if we take into account all of the negative states that people experience during daily life, like anger, stress, fears of all kinds, hatred, and violence.

These low states can also be voluntarily or subconsciously indulged in and even enjoyed. Think of how popular amusement park rides are for example, where the overriding emotion is fear. You only have to look at how many popular TV shows and movies contain violence, crime, and horror to see how much the emotions evoked by them are enjoyed and sought after—and it's not just through amusements, but through relationships and interactions with others as well. It's a self-perpetuating process, because the more that negative states are fed during the day, the stronger they become, and the more they turn into bad dreams at night. As an example, in a survey of two thousand people, 47 percent said they had a nightmare because of watching a scary movie.[1]

The psyche is just continuing its activity from day to night, from wakefulness to dreams. Negative states that are in the psyche during the day continue to exist at night in dreams, but there they emerge without the reality of the physical world to keep them in check. In dreams all those images and emotions that are part of the psyche become real events, projected from the subconscious. The psyche in the dream world can get reduced to its raw state where the most basic animalistic instincts and emotions are let loose, shaped by the model of the world created from the subconscious.

Even the most bizarre and bad dreams can reflect what exists in one's subconscious. It's only through a spiritual inner study that the root causes of bad dreams can be observed and eliminated.

NIGHTMARES

True nightmares have a different atmosphere than milder bad dreams; they are more horrific and feel more real. Medically they are classified as very bad dreams that someone wakes up from and can remember vividly.[2] There are lots of different studies on what causes nightmares. Eating a large meal before sleeping, or more usually having an upset stomach, is well-known to increase the likelihood of nightmares.

Generally, studies indicate that strong low emotions like depression, but especially intense feelings of stress and fear, also trigger nightmares.[3,4] Having frequent nightmares indicates that one's inner states are very low, and are based in the deep, subconscious regions of the psyche.

They occur when instead of going to the usual astral plane the dreamer goes into hell, and are a kind of experience of it. Almost all people (all those who haven't risen the kundalini) are connected to hell through a kind of energetic channel that descends from the coccyx bone (at the base of the spine) down into hell. Demons develop this connection, which is why they are traditionally depicted with tails. Raising the energy known as the kundalini up the spine and into the heavens is to do the opposite—it is to develop a connection to the heavens, which is normally an undeveloped potential.

The connection to hell has other consequences too, as through it the energies of one's egos in hell come up into the psyche, polluting it, and causing the psyche to vibrate at a lower level, dragging it down—making it very difficult for someone to come out of their low states, and smothering the spiritual feelings of consciousness.

It must be that certain triggers cause this connection to open and literally drag someone down so they go into hell while out of the body during sleep. These triggers seem to be both psychological, in the case of feeling intense fear, and also physical, in stimulating parts of the brain and body associated with lower emotions.

In ancient teachings, they describe a series of gates that separate the different regions of heaven and hell, and these gates are also said to exist within us—since we are psychologically connected to these realms.[5] There may be things that cause these gates to open. For example, an upset stomach may activate a connection in the abdomen. Another example is getting too hot while sleeping—this is known to cause nightmares as it makes the part of the brain most associated with negative emotions, such as terror and anger, more active.[6]

When I was a child, I went swimming in a pool with stale water in it and that night I had a nightmare in which I had to untangle a ball of fishing line that was much bigger than me. I felt terrible frustration as I labored at it, until I woke up feeling sick and vomited. It's notable that not every experience of hell involves fear.

With the right kind of spiritual change it's possible to stop having nightmares, but that requires a lot more explanation than I can give here, which I'll give in another book.

SLEEP PARALYSIS

There is a very common experience called sleep paralysis, which is when someone feels completely unable to move in the transition between waking and sleeping—it's only temporary, and can last from seconds to minutes. As many as half of all people have experienced sleep paralysis,[7] which is not surprising given, as I've mentioned, that it's a natural part of the process of falling asleep when the movement of our physical body is being changed over for that of our astral body or vice versa. For this reason, a sense of passing immobility is one of the sensations of astral projection.

Scientists explain it as waking before the natural physical immobility of sleep has ended.[8] However, in all the accounts of sleep paralysis I've heard, the person is not awake in the physical, but in the fifth dimension, which is why they can float out of their bodies, spin, and see nonphysical things. The experience ends when they actually physically wake up.

Most sleep paralysis experiences are negative. Up to 90 percent of sleep paralysis experiences are reported as being frightening (compared to 30 percent of dreams). In 75 percent of cases people can sense a demon during an episode, or feel partially out of their bodies.[9] Although people have seen different entities, demons are the most common.[10] Often someone will feel as though the demon is on their chest (or back, depending on which way they are sleeping), making it difficult for them to breathe. It can also often involve sexual feelings or sex with the demon, and I'll discuss this in more detail in the following section. It's worth noting that these kinds of negative sleep paralysis experiences rarely happen during astral projection exercises—at least those I know of, which are done using circles and incantations of protection.

Depiction of a typical experience of sleep paralysis.
Painting is *The Nightmare* by Henry Fuseli, 1781.

These kinds of experiences are not new—they have been recorded since ancient times across the world, and over one hundred terms have been identified as describing them.

For example, in Scandinavian folklore, sleep paralysis is said to be caused by a "mare," an evil, supernatural woman who sits on people's chests while they sleep. In Fiji it's described as being eaten by a demon, and is called *kana tevoro*. In Turkey it's called *karabasan*, meaning "the dark presser/assailer," and is caused by supernatural entities called jinn who hold the sleeper down and start to strangle them. In China it's called *gui ya shen*, meaning "ghost pressing on the body." In Mongolia it's called *kara darahu*, meaning "pressing by the Black," referring to the forces of darkness and shamans of the dark side. In Ethiopia it's referred to as *dukak*, meaning "depression," and is said to be caused by possession from an evil entity during sleep. In Sardinia, sleep paralysis is caused by a demonic creature called Ammuttadori, which sits on the sleeper's chest and suffocates them, sometimes ripping their skin. In Mexico it's called *subirse el muerto*, meaning "dead person on you." The examples go on and on.[11]

As you would expect, scientific literature says these experiences are merely hallucinations. Although fear and imagination can cause the subconscious to create a vision of a sinister entity, or perceive a physical person in the room as a demonic presence, I take essentially the same position as ancient peoples did, as I've had enough experience out of the body to know that demons are real, and that they really are appearing in these experiences—the energies and the presence of them are unmistakable.

Another common sensation reported during sleep paralysis is hearing humming, buzzing, hissing, zapping, and static noises[12]—which people also hear while splitting from the body during astral projection, indicating that sleep paralysis is occurring in the transition between dimensions.

It seems there is some mechanism in the transition phase, when we cross from one dimension to the other, which demons can take advantage of. I don't know exactly what mechanism they use; it may be as simple as that they seek out people to prey on, and seize on the moments of transitioning in and out of the fifth dimension when we're momentarily paralyzed. Or it may be that while consciousness is transitioning to the fifth dimension, there is kind of "barrier" that opens inside us, which allows consciousness passage out of and back into the body. Demons may be able to take advantage of this barrier being open. This does not ordinarily happen while we are fully awake or asleep, as during these times the barrier is sealed. I discuss this further in chapter 28, where I talk about psychedelics and other drugs, which affect this barrier while someone is awake, and can therefore open someone to demonic influence.

Clearly, demons understand sleep paralysis very well, and have been exploiting it for at least as long as we have records. The pressure people feel on them, making it difficult to breathe, may be part of the normal sleep process along with some technique demons use to make the person feel pinned in place so they cannot escape the demon and feel fear.

Even though demonic sleep paralysis can be terrifying, it's possible to deal with the demon and end the experience. Once someone gains some experience in expelling demons while out of the body, they realize that demons can't hurt them and that they have the ability to overcome them, and then are less afraid and better able to respond.

Lara had many of these typical sleep paralysis experiences over the years, which would inevitably seem to occur if she got up in the night and had been too tired to cast a circle of protection again properly before falling back to sleep. During these experiences she would sense a demonic presence enter the room in the dead of the night as she was in and out of sleep, and then feel the entity pull her out of her body and lay heavily on her back, often breathing menacingly down her neck. She would find herself completely frozen, just out of her body, lying in bed in the dark in the astral. At first she was terrified, but once she became more confident in expelling demons during OBEs, they became more of an annoyance, and dealing with them a protocol. She would simply focus her attention on moving her physical body in any way she could, maybe just lifting a finger, and that would be enough to bring her back to her physical body and end the experience. She would then make sure to really wake herself up so as not to fall asleep straight back into the experience, and then do incantations of protection to clear the room and cast a circle properly, and then continue sleeping undisturbed. Another way to do it though is to use incantations during the experience itself to expel the demon or disable it.

I myself don't have demonic sleep paralysis since demons won't get that close to me now.

Ancient peoples also used prayers, incantations, sacred texts, talismans, and spiritual symbols to deal with negative sleep paralysis. Even a medical article advises "praying or mentally reciting religious texts" as a method for ending an episode—probably because it has been found to work, along with what Lara did, which was to move any part of the body.[13]

INCUBI AND SUCCUBI

Incubi and succubi (incubus and succubus are the singular forms) are the names given to those demons that appear during sleep seeking sexual encounters with the sleeper, usually during an episode of sleep paralysis. Incubi are male demons, and succubi are female. Both are known to disguise themselves in the forms of young attractive people to seduce their victims, though could possibly be uncovered upon closer look by seeing their claws or serpentine tail. They have been named and described across ancient cultures—the earliest reference to a being having the characteristics of an incubus dates to 2400 BC in Sumer, where it was said to disturb and seduce women in their sleep.

It was often said that those who had sex with an incubus or succubus would be left feeling drained of energy, and eventually their health, mental state, and vitality would deteriorate, sometimes even leading to their death.[14][15]

It seems that demons can use sleep paralysis to obtain vital energy from people through sexual encounters, as a kind of energetic vampirism.

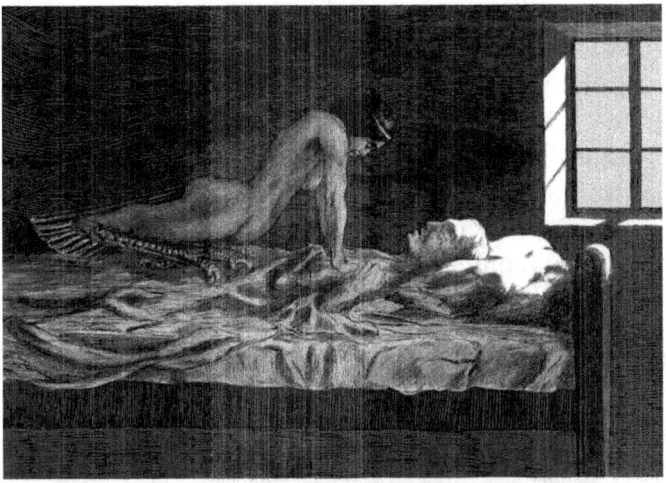

Illustration of a succubus.

Illustration of an incubus.

As with ending a negative sleep paralysis episode, when attacked by an incubus or succubus, it can be stopped by either saying protective incantations or moving any part of the physical body to wake up. Given that the demon will try to arouse and tempt their victim sexually, it's best to try and end the experience as quickly as possible.

ALIEN ABDUCTION (by Lara)

There is another common experience people have during sleep paralysis, and that is of being abducted by extraterrestrials. The most typical alien abduction experience occurs in the early hours of the morning, while someone is lying in bed sleeping, and starts with them feeling as though they have woken but are totally unable to move. The person then usually sees what appears to be one or more extraterrestrial entities—these entities can move through solid objects like walls. The abductee is sometimes lifted out of their bed into the air against their will, again, often through solid objects like the ceiling, and taken on board a craft where they undergo sometimes frightening and painful procedures, which can involve sexual acts and/or receiving implants. While some reportedly remember their entire experience, others remember fragments, and still others only recall it during hypnotherapy.[16][17]

Alien abductions are a highly complex phenomenon, and there appear to be many factors and forces involved in them, meaning there is no one explanation that can account for them all. Instead, it seems there are different reasons someone can have these experiences; it's only within the scope of this book to cover those related to OBEs.

The idea of alien abductions first appeared in movies in the 1950s—notably *Invaders from Mars*, in which the main character sees a UFO arrive from their bedroom window after being woken in the night. He and numerous other people are abducted by aliens and given "mind control" implants, but it all ends as though it had just been a bad dream.[18] The first reported "alien abductions" began shortly after this, and the first widely publicized case was that of Barney and Betty Hill in 1961, who only remembered it while under hypnotherapy. A film was made

Drive-in movie poster for *Invaders from Mars* from 1953.

about their story and aired in 1975. In the two years that followed, reports of alien abductions rose 2,500 percent.[19]

Although some think "abductees" must be crazy, studies have found they have no higher rate of mental illness than the average population. However, they have found there can be other psychological factors involved.[20]

There are studies that have identified sleep paralysis as a likely source of many abduction accounts. A study done at the University of the West of England on a group of people who claimed to have experienced "full-blown abduction" found that they were more prone to having sleep paralysis, sleep disturbances, OBEs, and nightmares than the control group. This was in line with other studies that had previously found a connection between sleep paralysis and alien abduction.[21]

The tendency to create false memories has also been found to possibly play a role in some cases. A Harvard study found that both abductees who could recall their experiences, and those who "recovered" them during hypnotherapy, had remembered or elaborated upon an episode of sleep paralysis. Both groups had a greater tendency to create false memories—about twice that of the control group who'd never had an alien encounter.[22] The researchers suggest that hypnotherapy puts someone into a state in which they are less able to tell the difference between actual memories and imagination, and that these abduction experiences are false memories derived from the abductee's attempt to explain things like waking up in strange positions, sleep disturbance, and panic attacks at seeing the image of an alien, based on existing cultural narratives.[23] [24]

Although scientists generally conclude that abductions are hallucinations experienced as part of sleep paralysis, I have a different view based on my experience of studying OBEs. I agree that they can occur during sleep paralysis, and that some of them could be created or elaborated through imagination, or could partially involve projections from the mind during the experience. However, I don't think this explains all abduction experiences, as what occurs in many of them sounds like an OBE, given that both the abductee and "aliens" are able to float, fly, and go through solid objects, which are all things we can do in the fifth dimension. It can also explain why abductees are convinced these things really happened to them, since they are not always just hallucinations.

John E. Mack, who was the head of psychiatry at Harvard Medical School, came to a similar conclusion. He became one of the leading researchers of alien abductions, investigating hundreds of cases. He concluded that these aliens shouldn't be considered physical entities, but other-dimensional, saying that the abduction experiences shared similarities with OBEs, and because of this, could be influenced by subjective psychological factors like the expectations and memory reliability of the abductee, and the influence of interviewer suggestions upon them. He found though that he could not fully discount them, and realized that materialist science was inadequate to wholly explain them.[25] I believe Mack was largely right in this, since most of these experiences seem to take place out of the body, where science cannot measure.

However, the rabbit hole goes even deeper, as the interdimensional aliens that abduct people during episodes of sleep paralysis may not be what they seem. Long-time UFO researcher Joe/Joseph Jordan has come forward with evidence that suggests the aliens in the cases he has studied are actually demons in disguise.

Jordan began researching UFOs in 1992, when he became a Mutual UFO Network (MUFON) Field Investigator. MUFON is the world's largest scientifically-based UFO investigation organization. As part of his work, Jordan started hearing alien abduction accounts and decided to investigate. He firstly made himself familiar with all the current major research on them. As he began investigating, he found a similar pattern in both the abduction accounts being reported to them locally as well as nationwide (in the U.S.). The experiences began with paralysis while sleeping in bed at night, were terrifying, and could not be stopped. That was until they came across the case of a man whose experience had stopped when he'd cried out to Jesus for help. Jordan approached other major abduction researchers to get their input on why this had happened. They agreed to talk, but only "off the record," admitting they had come across similar cases but had never made it public since they didn't know what to make of it, and because it could destroy their credibility. So, Jordan decided he'd find out himself and cofounded the CE4 Research Group to do it. What he uncovered shocked him—he found hundreds of similar cases, sometimes in which people had been abducted since childhood, but since calling on Jesus had their experiences stop for good:

> "Over the next ten years up till now I have worked with over four hundred abduction experience cases, all matching that first experience, that they've been able to stop the experience by calling out in the name and authority of Jesus Christ. [...] I did not ask for this piece of the puzzle; this happened to be the one I was dealt. I had no idea it would get this big. [...] I wasn't a Christian, I was a secular agnostic UFO researcher that had this dumped in my lap."[26]
> ~ JOE JORDAN

This led Jordan to identify these aliens as demons, and as interdimensional, not physical beings. Jordan has since converted to Christianity, and now helps people to end their demonic abduction encounters.[27] It's worth noting that CE4 Research Group also came across "a handful" of cases in which the encounter was stopped by calling upon other religious names—these names are not given, and are discounted by the now Christian group. It's also worth mentioning that there have been cases that Jordan and others have come across which have not been stopped by calling on Jesus. Jordan says this occurs in cases where people do not have a real relationship with Jesus,[28] but there may be another reason, which I'll come to in a moment.

The cultural narratives created in the 1940s and 50s would have given demons a great cover. By appearing as aliens, demons could disarm people, as most think these are physical encounters, and wouldn't suspect that calling on Jesus, or another spiritual power, would work. The illusion of being subjected to high alien technology gives people the impression of authority and that there is no sense in resisting. The alien's cruel behavior is explained as a necessary part of their supposed mission (which these aliens frame as being for a greater good), and as part of them being a different, less empathetic life form. Their black eyes are another cover—usually demons can be uncovered by looking into theirs, but black eyes might appear as a normal part of an alien. It's far easier for demons to disguise themselves as a "gray alien" than as a spiritual being and not be uncovered. Sex with them might serve the same purpose as it does for a succubus or incubus, though justified as part of a human-alien breeding program. Abductees are often implanted with devices that they believe are monitoring their health, or are probed and injected, but this is another cover for the implants and modifications that demons can make to someone's astral body that can block spiritual things working in us, and may even open up demonic channels. As Mark mentioned, he saw a demon trying to implant something into his kidneys while in an OBE that would have blocked the energy known as kundalini from rising. And they can play on people's wish to feel "chosen" as part of a special few. Even though their experiences were traumatic, abductees in the Harvard study said they were glad to have had them, which they are unlikely to have been if it had clearly been a demonic encounter.

Interestingly, alien abductions have also been reported while people have been on psychedelics, which essentially puts someone into a state close to sleep paralysis, and I discuss these in the chapter on them.

But the rabbit hole goes deeper still. Dr. Steven Greer, who has spent decades working with hundreds of high-level whistleblowers, says there are human operations that fake alien abductions, and that most of these are conducted by putting someone into a state of paralysis and extracting their astral body using directed electromagnetic energy (Greer says he experienced such an attack himself),[29] which is interesting, given the evidence that ancient Egyptians used some kind of electromagnetic energy to induce OBEs too. These man-made abductions may account for some of those experiences in which people call on Jesus for help, but find the experience doesn't end.

Greer says that all different types of abduction experiences get lumped into the same collection and mixed together, and so he says, "discernment is very important." He's found that 90 plus percent of information about ETs and UFOs in the public is disinformation, particularly intended to portray ETs as hostile.[30]

It's also important to distinguish alien abductions from other types of extraterrestrial experiences. There are many credible reports of people who've seen physical craft and extraterrestrial beings while completely awake, and alongside other witnesses. For example, the Disclosure Project, founded by Dr. Steven Greer in 1993, coordinated over eight hundred U.S. government officials, including those working at high levels in military and intelligence agencies, and high-level defense contractors, to testify about their knowledge, and in some cases eyewitness accounts, of extraterrestrials and extraterrestrial craft. In 2001, over twenty of these witnesses spoke at a press conference held at the National Press Club in Washington, DC.[31] Although including many government officials, this was not a project involving or sanctioned by the U.S. government. However, in 2017, the U.S. Department of Defense acknowledged that it has investigated UFOs as part of a secretive program. A Navy spokesperson also confirmed that there had been many unidentified and/or unauthorized aircraft that had entered military zones in recent years. Videos recorded by U.S. Navy pilots of three of these sightings were released to the public, and a Navy spokesperson stated that they represented just a fraction of the UFO incursions detected in Navy training ranges.[32] These videos were first released in 2017 and 2018 by a private company, but were later officially released in 2020 by the Pentagon in order to confirm the footage is real.[33] That is, the most powerful and

A UFO from the video "Gimbal" officially released by the U.S. Navy. Pilots exclaim they can see a whole fleet of these.

technologically-advanced military in human history has admitted that there are craft, which do not belong to them, and are using technologies unknown to them, here, among us.

As we've mentioned, it's possible to interact with and have a good experience with genuine ETs in OBEs, and I would call these experiences "out-of-body ET contact." Unfortunately, the legitimate existence of ETs is being hijacked by those with malevolent interests. We're also not ruling out that some real alien abduction may occur; it's simply beyond our field to explore it.

If someone is having what seems to be a demonic alien abduction experience, I would consider treating it like any other out-of-body demonic encounter.

DEMONS IN DREAMS

Just as spiritual beings can give us a dream, so can demons, and ancient practitioners of the Religion of the Sun knew this as we do today. In these dreams, rather than the demon appearing to frighten the dreamer, they instead disguise and hide themselves—maybe as someone we know or trust, or perhaps as ETs as I mentioned above. Their aim is to create a convincing dream that we'll follow as though it were from a spiritual or benevolent source.

For most, a scare from a demon or simply having their egos stirred up is enough to stop them from progressing further spiritually, but for those who press on, their methods become more sophisticated.

I know that demon-sent dreams are given directly to those who are attempting the path of the Spiritual Sun to throw them off track. I've also known demons to target them indirectly by sending a dream to someone around them, perhaps a close friend, who the demons know will tell them their dream out of care as a warning. I've also seen how demons have sent dreams to people around them who are hostile toward them or what they do, in order to motivate these hostile people to try and stop them from their spiritual work in some way.

For example, they may show someone (or someone close to them) that something they fear will come true even though it won't, to send them into low emotions. They may stir up strife between people by causing someone to feel negative toward another and take harmful actions against them. They may turn someone away from making the right decision, or cause them to make the wrong one.

Someone may for example have a dream in which a knowledgeable looking doctor is telling them that they don't have long to live. There may seem to be nothing evil about the dream on the surface, but spiritual beings tend not to tell us things that invoke strong fear in situations we can't do anything about. It's more likely they would warn someone of a health issue so that they get it checked and therefore help prevent it, or show it in a way that may reassure the person that it was meant to happen, or that in the end it will be alright, or bring some other understanding about it. To be able to distinguish between them, look at the outcome—was the dream helpful or did it just frighten you? I'd suggest using common sense and intuition so you aren't deceived by demonic influences.

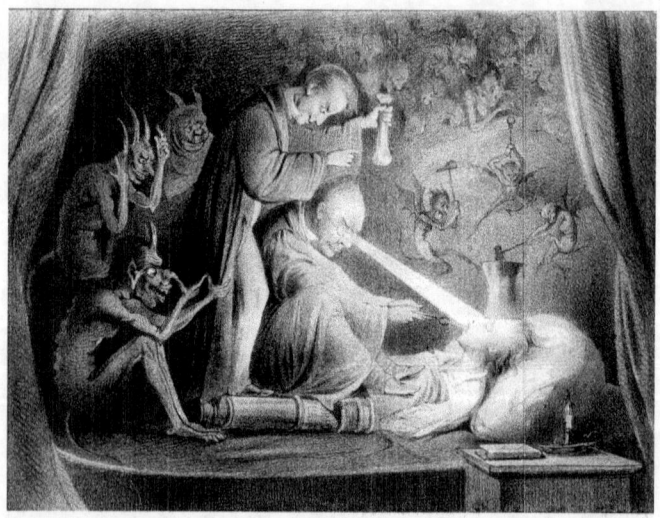

Demons tend to use our weaknesses against us and will often use things we're more prone to believing. Generally, if we're given a dream by a demon, it's because we've given in to the feelings they are trying to use against us in the dream. So if someone is already feeling fear around having health problems, they can give false premonitions about diagnoses. If someone already harbors a dislike or resentment against someone and believes they are doing the wrong thing, demons may show that person doing a bad thing or cast what the person is doing in a negative light and the dreamer may readily believe it, even though the person may be innocent. If someone has a tendency to think highly of themselves, they may create a situation that inflates the dreamer's pride. To the dreamer, the dream then justifies their fear, low state, or bad action. The way to combat demon-sent dreams is to get out of and be constantly on alert to one's egos. I explain about the egos in my book on self-knowledge.

It's possible to become so on guard against demonic influences that someone becomes aware of the sinister source within the dream itself. I've known people to do that, who've become skeptical of what they've been told in a dream, and have followed the person who was talking to them to discover they were a demon, or have pulled away the dreamscape to discover the negative source behind it.

EXPERIENCES IN HELLISH REGIONS

Light has its opposite in darkness, and the blend of these gives us the opportunity to experience creation. Just as heaven exists, so too does its opposite, hell, and it's vital for our learning that it does.

A hell beyond our physical world, located beneath the earth, has been called by many names in different ancient cultures, such as the Abyss, Hades, Tartarus, the Underworld, Uku Pacha, Naraka, Diyu, Xibalbá, Duzak, Hel, etc. It's portrayed as a place of suffering and cleansing, and as the abode of demons. Since ancient times, people have traveled there in OBEs and NDEs and have described what they saw.

It's estimated that between 1 – 15 percent of people who have an NDE have a distressing experience, and one of the main types is a visit to hell. The number may be higher, however, as those who have distressing experiences are less likely to share them. People from all walks of life, many having no religious beliefs, have given credible accounts of visiting hell in conscious out-of-body and near-death experiences.[34][35][36] In many cases during the experience the person feels a wish to change and calls on spiritual beings for help and forgiveness, after which they are given another opportunity and return to their bodies with the resolve to live a better life, with many understanding what it was that took them to hell. In some cases people have called for Jesus or a similar divinity even if they didn't believe in them, and are helped.

Sometimes a person who thought they were bad, or could be considered to be, has a heavenly NDE, while those who may have thought of themselves as good have a hellish NDE; in most cases it can't be foretold whether a person will have a hellish experience or a heavenly one.

I've had many experiences in which I have visited hell in an OBE, but it's not something you would do lightly or unprepared.

Traveling to hell while consciously out of the body is different to going there involuntarily during a nightmare. In nightmares the psyche is linked with hellish energies, but it isn't in a normal OBE. Demons can torment someone during a nightmare, and there is generally no escape from it unless someone physically wakes up, whereas in an OBE our psyche is normal and we know we're out of the body and have the possibility to defend ourselves against demons and be self-aware in the experience. There are many other people who have gone to hell in OBEs.

Rod Pickens says he was shown hell in an OBE after he'd watched other people's OBEs of hell online and had prayed for his own:

The Garden of Earthly Delights, inner right wing (hell), by Hieronymus Bosch, 1504.

> "I had a dream and my spirit left my body. It was like I was in my apartment and my spirit got pulled out of my body [...] on the right side of God [...] there was this big portal that opened up [...] and whoever that God has said 'depart from me' flew down this place [...] and all these different people would be sent to hell [for] adultery, fornication, so many different things [...] thousands upon thousands [of people] [...] anything we did in our life, our life testified against us, so you couldn't lie [...] I was more terrified than I can express. [...] [Then] on the left side of God, heaven would open up, so soft with brilliant lights, the colors were undescribable [...] I woke up, the dream scared me so bad [...] but I knew it was for a reason."[37]

Rod is a Christian, but interestingly he saw the two portals respectively leading to hell and heaven in the sky described by Osiris in the Kolbrin, and saw how one's life testified against them in their judgment, described in ancient Egyptian texts—though said to be done by one's heart.

Sometimes in the astral plane you can notice a kind of opening that looks like a mouth or a slit in the fabric of space itself. This is the entrance to or portal between the astral plane and hell.

Vision of hell, anonymous, 1594.

Whereas in positive NDEs the tunnel with the light at the end of it passes from the astral plane to a higher realm, in hellish NDEs the mouth of hell, the corridor, and the gates are a passageway to the lower regions. At the gates are the toll collectors (at the turnstiles) mentioned in early Christianity, and nearby are the waiting rooms, where some who recall NDEs say they were asked to go back to their lives on Earth as their time was not yet up.

I had a very jarring experience of going through this mouth/tunnel into hell many years ago, when I had just begun my spiritual path. I went through the mouth, then walked down a tunnel with deceased people who were going into hell through the turnstiles in a constant procession. I stopped at a waiting room and didn't pass through, then a spiritual being came in and told me I had to practice whether I wanted to or not. This experience showed me what my fate would be if I didn't change profoundly. This and two other similar OBEs, where I experienced the desperation of what it was like to be thrown into hell, drove me to change and to do my spiritual practices with sheer determination.

I've had many other OBEs in hell. In some cases, I went there to explore it of my own accord. On other occasions, I have been taken there by my Being to learn something, while at other times going there was part of something I went through on my spiritual path. I'll talk about these in another book where I can explain more about them.

I once spoke to a woman who had an NDE that was similar to what I saw in my OBE. She told me that she passed through the jaws of a crocodile and then found herself in a waiting room with other people. Someone came in and told her that she had to go back because it wasn't her time yet. This opening has been depicted as the open jaws of a monster in Christian art, as a female crocodile-headed deity Ammit who swallowed the hearts of the sinful dead in ancient Egypt, and as the open mouth of a snake or monster among the Maya;[38] it has been called "the mouth of hell."

Detail from the painting *The Second Coming* depicting the mouth of hell, by Georgios Klontzas, circa 1580-1608.

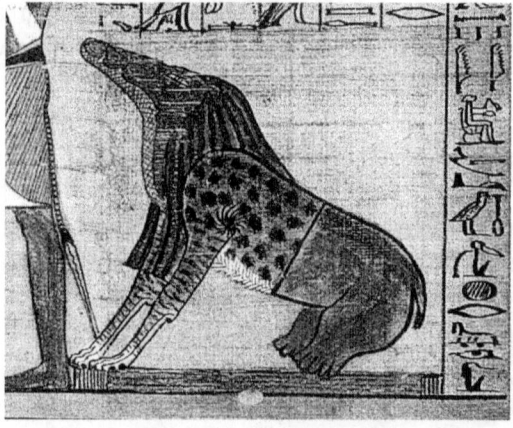

Egyptian depiction of Ammit, the being whose jaws open to devour the hearts of the dead who have led a sinful life.

Jesus in the Pistis Sophia describes people entering hell, which he calls the outer darkness, through the jaws of a great dragon, and a crocodile-faced being ruling over its first region.[39]

As far as I'm aware, there are two ways people go into hell in the afterlife. The first is by being put there for a time between lives and the second is by going into the hell of devolution. While the hell between lives is a short-term corrective learning measure, devolution is a much longer process that destroys the egos someone has developed, allowing their consciousness/soul to be cleansed; however, neither are permanent.

Just as the heaven between lives is temporary, so too the hell between lives must be. Its purpose is surely to "teach" people who would otherwise not change. Suffering in hell, although horrible, must be a way of learning or changing when someone's learning on Earth has fundamentally failed. After the time in hell between lives is over, the person would return to a human life, potentially with a resolve not to repeat the same mistakes. I would think that resolve would resound deeply in their soul from the suffering they had just endured.

There are other kinds of experiences of going into darkness that happen to someone on the path of the Spiritual Sun, particularly at the stages related to inner death, the descent into hell, and resurrection, which are themes that occur in many ancient sources that encode knowledge of the path. For example, Osiris, Jesus, and Odin each descend into hell after their deaths (in the case of Odin, after a death-like or near-death experience), which is symbolic of a stage on the path.

Hell and devolution and even demons exist for a reason. With evolving forces things are created, grow, mature, and reproduce, while devolving forces bring decay and degeneration; both these forces are necessary for life. The basis of good and evil lie in light and darkness operating in material form—two opposites whose gradients mixed give shadow, which gives the shades of gray that form everything.

While heavenly and hellish states exist within people, heavens and hells exist in other dimensions as opposite ends of the scale to each other. They and every scale of gray exist to give souls the experience of life, choice, and learning, so that they can acquire knowledge of their own existence and nature, and can return to their source as self-aware beings.

CHAPTER TWENTY-SEVEN

Protection against Demonic Entities

There are beings in the fifth dimension that have awakened and reached levels of aptitude in light, while others have acquired grades of awakening in darkness. Those that have awakened in darkness are referred to as demons, and descriptions of them can be found in numerous ancient religions, including those derived from the ancient Religion of the Sun.

Ancient statue of a demon from Assyria dated to ca. 800-700 BC.

Just as we have to protect ourselves, our belongings, our homes, etc., in daily life, we also have to protect ourselves in the fifth dimension against demonic entities.

In the ancient Religion of the Sun there were three ways to do this which can still be used:

1. Using incantations of protection, which are words, sometimes accompanied by gestures and/or visualization that call upon the divine to expel demons.
2. Drawing a protective circle around ourselves, or forming a threshold, which demons can't cross.
3. Using symbols of divinity to repel them.

I'll look at some examples of these forms of protection from the ancient Religion of the Sun, and then explain how they can be used today.

ANCIENT EXAMPLES OF PROTECTION

Various forms of spiritual protection can be found in texts, amulets, statues, paintings, and other works of art throughout history.

In ancient sources there are several accounts of evil beings being expelled, of divine beings offering protection, and of magical barriers that evil beings can't cross. Several religious figures were said to have expelled or defeated demons.

In Hinduism, Vishnu is seen as a protective deity, while Shashthi is the Hindu goddess of protection of newborn babies, and there are mantras that are recited to provide protection. There are many tales in Hindu texts of divine deities fighting demons.

The Hindu god Krishna killing the horse demon Keshi.

In Christianity, Jesus cast away demons and instructed his disciples to do so.

In Greece, the class of texts called the "technical" Hermetica (ca. 200 BC – AD 500) has instructions to call upon spiritual forces and beings for protection, and a medieval treatise *The Secret of Secrets* also contains instructions for protection against supernatural harm.

There are lots of references to demons in the Near East, in texts from Sumer, Babylon, Phoenicia, Assyria, and Canaan, and many protective practices and objects to deal with them.

Ancient Egypt had an arsenal of protective incantations, deities, symbols, paintings, texts, jewelry, and amulets.

PROTECTIVE OBJECTS

Ancient people used many kinds of objects as protection against supernatural evil forces—they could take the form of various natural or manmade items such as clothing, amulets, jewelry, symbols, certain items or statues stationed particularly at entrances to homes and temples, etc.

One of the best examples of an artifact offering divine protection is a small limestone amulet dated to the seventh century BC discovered in Syria, known as the Arslan Tash amulet.[1] It was likely designed to be hung over the door of someone's home to keep demons out. On one side it depicts what are likely to be demonic entities in the form of hybrid creatures—one swallowing a person—while on the other is an Assyrian warrior deity called Sasam holding a raised axe in a combative stance, presumably against the entities.

The Arslan Tash amulet.

It's inscribed with an incantation in Phoenician that essentially calls upon the sun god Assur and the warrior deity Sasam to stop demons from entering the house. Here is an excerpt:

> "Oh Flying one, from the dark room pass away!
>
> Now! Now, night demons!

From my house, O crushers, go away!

Oh Sasam, let it not be opened for him

And let him not come down to the door-posts

The sun is rising for Sasam.

Disappear, and fly away home." [2]

~ ARSLAN TASH AMULET

Equivalent warrior figures were depicted in other Mesopotamian cultures with lightning bolts to hurl at enemies and demons, sometimes with an axe, hammer, or club.[3] These and other characteristics are shared by the Norse god Thor and Hindu god Indra, and so it's possible they all derive from a more ancient common deity.

The tablet also mentions the ancient deity Baal whom I know to be an angel that fell and became a demon. He is not to be confused with Bael; I've met both of them in OBEs and so I know they are different beings.

There are two kinds of demons mentioned on the tablet, Fliers and Stranglers, and both are female. It's possible the Fliers are the precursors of actual witches, which are female demons that fly.

I knew a witch in the UK decades ago who was seen levitating over a church by a fairly large number of people; she showed me a clipping from a national newspaper describing it. I later discovered she was a demon. The reason it's female demons that fly as witches relates to special powers this type of demon has.

This was seen in a lucid dream Lara had. Soon after realizing she was in the astral plane, she was lifted into the air by a terrifying, flying witch who extracted electricity from the air and used it to electrify and inflict pain on her. I (my Being) appeared and stood

Etching by Goya made in 1796-1798 showing two witches levitating.

an open pair of steel scissors in the ground, and this made the witch disappear. Lara has kept a pair of steel scissors for protection ever since, and it's interesting that this was an old folk custom for disempowering and keeping witches away, though people no longer understand why it works.

Witches harness the electrical power in the air. Being female, their energies have a negative magnetic charge, and so they seem to use the resonance they have with this electricity, as for example, almost all lightning is negatively charged. They are neutralized by grounding the current they harness from the air to earth, thus depriving them of it.

The association between witches, flying, the night, thunderstorms, and lightning is found in ancient Germanic and Slavic folklore.[4] For example, in the Poetic Edda they are known as hags who are the workers of ill, and are referred to as "night riders."[5]

However, the term witch has been grossly misused in history to malign huge numbers of innocent women, some of whom may have simply been interested in herbal remedies—as women have been for time untold and still are today, as it was an important evolutionary skill needed for looking after the health of the family—or those who retained some practice of ancient folk and pagan traditions. It's also a popular self-designation among many women who work with herbs and nature rituals still today, and who hold Wiccan beliefs. There are also, however, those who self-designate as witches and can be part of the worldly hierarchy of the dark occult/Satanism; they often work with demons but haven't converted themselves into demons. When I talk about witches, I'm not talking about either of these kinds of women, I am talking about a very specific kind—someone who has become a female demon and has acquired certain powers. They are far fewer in number than the women who have been labeled or who today call themselves witches, and have probably always existed.

CIRCLES OF PROTECTION

There are records in the ancient Religion of the Sun of circles or barriers of protection being created to keep demons out; they are some of the most ancient practices ever written. I give a recommendation of how to draw and use them later in this chapter.

These first examples come from the great teacher of the Religion of the Sun called Osiris, who became the most famous god in ancient Egypt. They are found in the ancient Egyptian books preserved as part of the Kolbrin, where he is known as Yosira.

In this first instance, Osiris saves a man who was just about to be used as a human sacrifice. He sings an incantation and creates a ring to protect himself. He also draws fire out of the air to defend his life—this is a power that can be given to those who have the Spiritual Son within.

> "When Yosira came to Kambusis he found there a man of the Hestabwis bound and prepared for sacrifice, and he cried out against the deed but none gave ear to his word. So, standing off, Yosira placed a staff of power upright into the ground and danced around it, singing the song for drawing forth the spirit. When they saw this, the people were wroth against him and called upon their charmers to curse him so he departed from the Earth. Their curses were ineffective and when one charmer approached the dance ring of Yosira, Yosira called forth a tongue of flame which consumed the charmer. Then the people became afraid and fled. So Yosira released the man who was bound upon the place of sacrifice, but he was not yet whole. Yosira also cursed all those who offered the Hestabwis as a sacrifice to their gods; since that day no man of the Hestabwis was ever slain upon the altars." [6]
>
> ~ THE KOLBRIN

In this next instance, Osiris surrounds an entire land with a magical barrier that no negative entity could cross, and even had the power to bind and cast them back into the underworld/hell.

> "In those days men sought to appease the Formless Ones and the Spirits of the Night with offerings and worship. But Yosira forbade them this and he surrounded the whole land with a protective wall which no Dark Spirit could penetrate, while all those within were dissolved. Every Dark Spirit being neither male nor female and every Dark Spirit which clothed itself in the shape of a beast or bird was bound and cast back into the Place of Darkness." [7]
>
> ~ THE KOLBRIN

In ancient Egypt, circles of protection were an essential part of religious ritual and art. The circle was a symbol of the sun and its apparent encircling motion, which bestowed protection. The oldest evidence for the concept of circles of protection in Egypt is found in its earliest writings, the Pyramid Texts, where it addresses the king, saying, "For you are Horus [son of the sun god] encircled by the protection of his eye [the sun]." Pyramids, temples, and tombs were protected by encircling rituals,[8] and circles of protection were drawn (possibly using wands) around people, to keep out demons, ghosts, and sorcerers.[9] One of the major festivals in ancient Egypt was that of Sokar, which celebrated the resurrection of Osiris. As part of it, the boat of the god Sokar (who became associated with Osiris) was carried in a circle around the temple to symbolize the path of the sun and protect against evil forces.[10] Such an encircling ritual appears to derive from the oldest stories about the founding of the first sun temples in Egypt.

The concept of a protective circle forming a barrier against evil is found in the *shen* ring, which was one of the oldest and most prolific symbols in Egypt (and associated with the Spiritual Sun as explained further on). It was depicted as a circular loop of rope tied together that was believed to protect the king—wherever the king's name was written it always enclosed it, being stretched around it into an oval, and in that form is referred to today as a cartouche.[11]

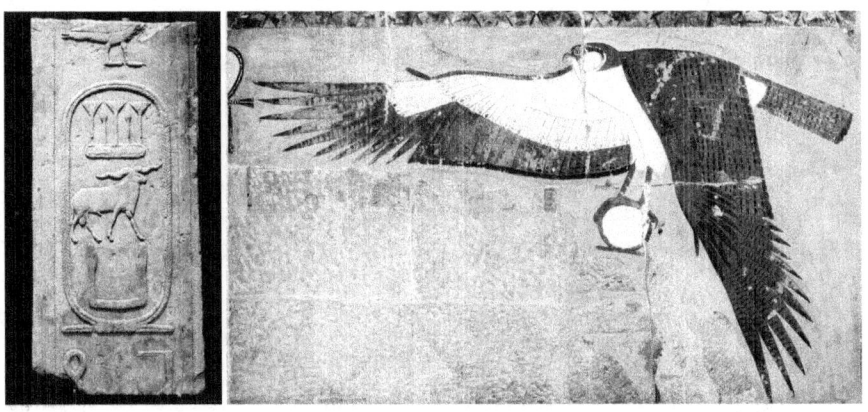

Left: A cartouche from Egypt, which is a loop of rope tied around the king's name, believed to protect him. Right: Horus holding the *shen* ring symbol.

Magic circles of protection were also used in Mesopotamia, where they were called *zisurrû*, meaning "magic circle drawn with flour." These were ritual circles drawn with flour around a person's bed while saying incantations to keep out demons, witches, sorcerers, and ghosts.[12] Enkidu draws such a circle around Gilgamesh when he goes to sleep to incubate a dream in the Sumerian Epic of Gilgamesh.[13]

There are also records of circles of protection in the surviving folklore of the Celts. They appear among some of the last few pagan traditions that were recorded in Scotland at the end of the eighteen hundreds in the collection of prayers, incantations, songs, lore, etc., called the *Carmina Gadelica*—some from men as old as ninety-nine. The pagan themes are still discernable under the layer of Christian influence. Included is the practice of drawing a circle of protection, called a "caim," which most likely originates from an ancient Celtic tradition. It involves saying an incantation while drawing a circle around oneself, described as follows:

> "In making the 'caim' the supplicant stretches out the right hand with the forefinger extended, and turns round sunwise as if on a pivot, describing a circle with the tip of the forefinger while invoking the desired protection. The circle encloses the supplicant and accompanies him as he walks onward, safeguarded from all evil without or within. Protestant or Catholic, educated or illiterate, may make the 'caim' in fear, danger, or distress, as when some untoward noise is heard or some untoward object seen during the night. [...] It is also called 'caim na corraig,' the encompassing of the forefinger, and 'caim na còrach,' the encompassing of righteousness." [14]
> ~ CARMINA GADELICA

The following words are said in one *caim*, which calls upon the Trinity. Though the Trinity is Christian, the three divine forces of the creator were also central to Celtic religion and thus pagan wording may have easily been adapted to Christian terms.

> "The compassing of God and His right hand
> Be upon my form and upon my frame;
> The compassing of the High King and the grace of the Trinity
> Be upon me abiding ever eternally,
> Be upon me abiding ever eternally.
> May the compassing of the Three shield me in my means,
> The compassing of the Three shield me this day,
> The compassing of the Three shield me this night
> From hate, from harm, from act, from ill.
> From hate, from harm, from act, from ill." [15]
> ~ CARMINA GADELICA

INCANTATIONS

Hymns, words, incantations, songs, and mantras of protection were also used in the ancient Religion of the Sun. They were often done in combination with drawing a circle of protection, as in the previous Egyptian, Mesopotamian, and Celtic examples.

I'll give the one I recommend most for use today, which is the incantation of the Spiritual Son/Sun, in a later section of this chapter. Following are some further examples of ancient incantations that were used as part of individual and community rituals.

This first example comes from the ancient text Songs of the Sage, which is believed to have been used by the community of Essenes who lived at the site of Qumran on the shores of the Dead Sea, where an ancient Judean form of sun worship survived. One of their religious buildings was orientated to allow the summer solstice sunrise in to alight the altar, and Jesus likely spent time with them.

The sage was the head priest of the community, and the songs he sung were to protect it from evil. An excerpt from one of these protective songs is as follows:

> "[...] before the might of his power all are terrified, they scatter and flee before the radiance of his dwelling of his glory and majesty. And I, the Sage, declare the grandeur of his radiance in order to frighten and terrify all the spirits of the ravaging angels and the bastard spirits, demons, Liliths, owls and jackals... and those who strike unexpectedly [...]." [16]
> ~ SONGS OF THE SAGE

Notice how the light and power of the divine is called upon to expel demonic entities. This is essentially what effective incantations do, whether calling upon the divine light of the Source/Absolute/Creator or a particular divine being, as it's the powers, presence, and light of the divine that evil can't stand and thus expels them. An incantation calls upon that higher power, and it's that power that acts.

Incantations were used against demons in Mesopotamia—the ancient Akkadian text Maqlû is the longest and most important record of them. It contains a series of incantations directed particularly at witches that accompanied the burning of effigies representing them, and the drawing of a circle of protection. The oldest incantations recorded in Maqlû are believed to be at least three thousand years old.[17] They were primarily addressed to the sun god Shamash, who was to judge the case (as the one from whom nothing can hide), and then send his rays of light as fire to vanquish the attacking demons.[18] In this incantation we again see the light and power of the divine invoked against evil.

> "You, Shamash, the judge, vanquisher of the wicked and the enemy, vanquish them so I not be wronged [...].
>
> You, O Girra [god of fire], it is you who are the burner of warlocks and witches,
>
> The annihilator of the wicked, seed of warlock and witch,
>
> The destroyer of the evildoers.
>
> I call upon you:
>
> Judge my case, render my verdict.
>
> Burn my warlock and my witch,
>
> Devour my enemies, consume the ones who would do evil to me!
>
> Let your raging (fire-)storm [or light rays] vanquish them." [19]
>
> ~ MAQLÛ

The incantation that follows then calls upon the god Nuska, who was said to protect the sleeping household from demons during the night, particularly from evil dreams.[20] Nuska was the divine personification of heavenly and earthly fire (becoming synonymous with Girra);[21] he was symbolized by a lamp, and illuminated the darkness, thus expelling the demons who lurked within it.[22] The series of incantations then continues addressing Shamash the sun god, as he rises in the morning and shines on the face of the reciter as their savior. The reciter also uses water in the ritual to symbolically cleanse themselves of all evil effects at dawn.[23]

An ancient winged sun disk from Mesopotamia, possibly representing Shamash.

Here is an incantation taken from the Greek Magical Papyri that is part of the "technical" Hermetica. Written in Greek, they contain material from Egypt dated from the second century BC to the fifth century AD,[24] and are likely based on ancient protective incantations used in Egypt. This incantation calls upon the Egyptian goddess Isis and god Thoth for protection, who were both major figures in the ancient Religion of the Sun.

> "Taking sulfur and seed of Nile rushes, burn them as incense to the moon and say,
>
> 'I call on you, Lady Isis, whom Osiris permitted to rule all of Egypt. Your name is LOU LOULOU BATHARTHAR THARESIBATH ATHER-NEKLESICH, ATHER-NEBOUNI EICHOMO CHOMOTHI Isis Sothis, SOUERI, Bubastis, EURELIBAT CHAMARI NEBOUTOS OUERI AIE EOA OAI. Protect me, great and marvelous names of the god; for I am the one established in the Temple of the Sun, SERPHOUTH MOUISRO, STROMMO MOLOTH MOLONTHER PHON Thoth. Protect me, great and marvelous names of the great god.
>
> ASAO EIO NISAOTH. Lady Isis, Nemesis, Adrasteia, many-named, many-formed, glorify me, as I have glorified the name of your son Horus.'" [25]
>
> ~ GREEK MAGICAL PAPYRI

The son of Isis, Horus, represented the Spiritual Son in Egypt, and thus this incantation would have been used by those who "glorified" and thus followed the Spiritual Son/Sun, and the Religion of the Sun in some form.

This next example is from the Atharva Veda, one of the most ancient Hindu texts (dated to between 1200 – 1000 BC), and is the Veda that deals with magical rituals, folk healing, and rites for daily activities. It contains numerous hymns for protection against demons, such as the one that follows, which is directed toward the god of fire and the Mother Goddess, and would have been chanted before a ritual fire (and possibly also the sun as the hymn indicates, as in the example from Mesopotamia). It's interesting to note how the reciter proclaims their own strength while diminishing that of the demons, as psychologically, it's very important not to fear them and to realize that with the help of the divine, they can be overcome.

> "May Agni Vaisvânara [the god of fire, all pervading], the bull of unfailing strength, burn up him that is evil-disposed, and desires to harm us, and him that plans hostile deeds against us!
>
> Between the two rows of teeth of Agni Vaisvânara do I place him that plans to injure us, when we are not planning to injure him; and him that plans to injure us, when we do plan to injure him.
>
> Those who hound us in our chambers, while shouting goes on in the night of the new moon, and the other flesh-devourers who plan to injure us, all of them do I overcome with might.
>
> With might I overcome the Pisâkas [demons], rob them of their property; all evil-disposed (demons) do I slay: may my device succeed!
>
> With the gods who vie with, and measure their swiftness with this sun, with those that are in the rivers, and in the mountains, do I, along with my cattle, consort.
>
> I plague the Pisâkas as the tiger the cattle-owners. As dogs who have seen a lion, these do not find a refuge.
>
> My strength does not lie with Pisâkas, nor with thieves, nor with prowlers in the forest. From the village which I enter the Pisâkas vanish away.
>
> From the village which my fierce power has entered the Pisâkas vanish away; they do not devise evil.
>
> They who irritate me with their jabber, as (buzzing) mosquitoes the elephant, them I regard as wretched (creatures), as small vermin upon people.
>
> May Nirriti (the goddess of destruction) take hold of this one, as a horse with the halter! The fool who is wroth with me is not freed from (her) snare."[26]

~ ATHARVA VEDA

It sounds like the writers of the Atharva Veda were also hounded by demons while sleeping at night in their chambers, as those who attempt to search for light can be today—particularly on the new moon, which I call a black moon, which is when the moon is totally dark. This is a time used and celebrated by demons as it is the time of least light, as it's at night without the sun, nor even any of its light reflected by the moon.

TALISMANS AND SYMBOLS

A talisman is an object that is ascribed with metaphysical power, which can include the ability to repel evil forces and protect someone from them. They generally incorporate religious symbols, as they can express the principles of divinity, which is what drives evil away. They were used particularly over entrances and worn on the body as amulets, but could also be placed in the home or in any space, or used in rituals, and were often incorporated into architecture.

The oldest symbols tend to be from the Religion of the Sun, many of which are still in use today. Many are based on or can be observed in astronomical cycles, like the annual path of the sun, or the transitions of Venus. Divine principles are found in nature and the cosmos, and so symbols that represent them then embody these principles.

These following ancient examples are the ones I would use, since they refer to forces, principles, and beings of light that really exist.

Two of the oldest and most widespread symbols that were used for protection in ancient times are the solar cross and the swastika. These are both symbols of the sun, with the four arms representing the sun's major annual stages at the solstices and equinoxes. The swastika adds lines at the end of the arms to show the sun's motion, and illustrates the sun's annual path, which also has a spiritual meaning as the path to salvation/liberation/enlightenment.

Solar cross.

The swastika is one of the most widely used symbols in Hinduism, where it is used to sanctify and protect temples, rituals, homes, and objects. One of the oldest depictions of a swastika connected to Hinduism was found in Pakistan on a seal dated to 3,000 BC that was used as a protective amulet.[27]

Swastika turning clockwise.

Ancient depictions of the swastika have been found across large parts of the world, including Europe, Asia, and the Americas; the oldest swastika was discovered in Ukraine carved onto the tusk of a wooly mamoth and dates to 10,000 BC.[28]

The ancient Germanic peoples also used it for sanctity and protection thousands of years ago in Europe. It was used interchangably with the solar cross, and was commonly known as Thor's hammer. Thor was an ancient Norse/Germanic deity who was the son of Odin and was seen as having the power to defeat evil. As mentioned earlier, he may be related to the axe-wielding deity on the Arslan Tash amulet. In Norse/Germanic mythology his hammer was used to defend the abode of the gods from the forces of destruction, chaos, and decay. Thus, the symbol of his hammer—and the solar cross and swastika—was used in Germanic rituals to sanctify anything that one wanted to protect from destructive forces, such as a marriage, a project, or plot of land.[29]

People have speculated about how the direction a swastika faces may affect whether it's a positive or negative symbol, as it has been portrayed with its arms pointing both clockwise and counterclockwise. The clockwise-facing arms (like in the image used in this section) represent the path of the sun's annual journey north of the Tropic of Cancer (which includes most of the Northern Hemisphere), while the counterclockwise arms represent it south of the Tropic of Capricorn (which includes most of the Southern Hemisphere). This is because the apparent motion of the sun's path throughout the sky over the course of a year is reversed depending on where you view it. If you observe it between the Tropics of Cancer and Capricorn you will see it sometimes clockwise and other times counterclockwise depending on the time of year. If you want to be precise, you would use a clockwise swastika if you live north of the Tropic of Cancer, and a counterclockwise one south of the Tropic of Capricorn, and either if you live in the tropics. I wouldn't be too concerned about it though, as either way, it's a symbol of the sun.

There's also evidence it was used in ancient times as a symbol of the annual rotation of the stars around the North Star—particularly the constellations Ursa Minor and the Big Dipper, which create the symbol of the swastika when their four different positions at spring, summer, autumn, and winter are illustrated. In this case, their motion is counterclockwise.[30] Again, the swastika is a symbol of the motions of the sun and stars, and for this reason is a spiritual symbol of light.

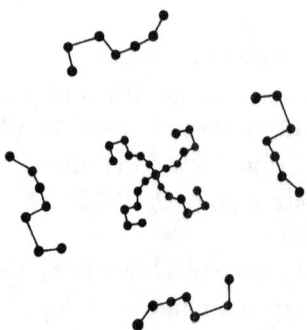

Diagram of Polaris the Pole/North Star (which is represented by the dot in the very center) as part of the Ursa Minor constellation, with the constellation of the Big Dipper around it. Both constellations are drawn four times, creating a swastika pattern.

The pentagram is another ancient symbol used for protection; the earliest representation of it was found in Sumer (in what is now Iraq) dating to 3,500 BC. There is evidence it was used to protect against evil in ancient Babylon and Hellenistic Greece.[31] It continued to be used that way in Europe, and it's commonly used for spiritual protection today. It also embodies astronomical principles, as Venus traces an approximate pentagram every eight years in its orbit around the sun.[32]

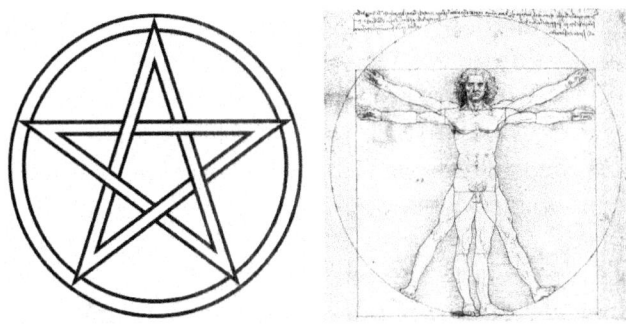

Left: Pentacle facing upright. Right: The sketch *Vitruvian Man* by Leonardo Da Vinci. You can see the correlation between the human form (with four limbs and head) and the pentagram (five-pointed star). In this five-dimensional realm we can either direct ourselves upward to higher/inner regions of light, or downward, to lower/outer regions of darkness.

If you're going to use a pentacle/pentagram, make sure it's the right way up, as this one is. Demons use this symbol inverted, which generally means upside down, with the single point downward. It's this use of pentacles by demons and their supporters that has associated it with evil, but it's the orientation of it that matters.

When the single point is downward, it symbolizes the dominance of matter (as the other four points represent the four material elements) over spirit, and attracts negative forces. When the single point is upward, it's the opposite, so that the spirit dominates matter, and it repels negative beings.

The five-pointed star essentially depicts a human the right way up (pointed toward heaven) and in alignment with divine forces. It illustrates the "head" (the upright point), the seat of consciousness, above and thus in control over the lower, animal zones within the body. But ideally it should also have a circle around it representing the sun, making it a pentacle, as then it symbolizes a divine being, a Son of the Sun, who is one with the divine.

A triangle or variation of it, such as the Celtic triquetra and triskele, and Norse *valknut*, with a point (or points in the case of the *valknut*) pointing upward represents the trinity of the Being and the three fundamental forces of creation, and so symbolizes divinity. It's likewise used by darkness when it's inverted with a point downward.

Triquetra.

Sometimes two triangles ascending and descending have been combined as a hexagram in what is known as the Seal of Solomon, but I wouldn't use them combined because of what descending forces can attract.

A simple cross symbolizes the material, as the four arms represent the four elements and four dimensions of the material world. It also represents the duality and union of male and female forces, and the solstices and equinoxes. Although the cross has an important meaning, it becomes a spiritual symbol when it's fully enclosed within a circle as in the solar cross, as the circle adds the symbol of the sun, bringing the spiritual to the material, which by encircling it is placed as its source and as greater than it.

A cross/crucifix with Jesus (as a Spiritual Son) on it represents the spiritual trapped and suffering within materiality, and Jesus dead on it is even worse as it represents the triumph of the material over the spiritual—neither are the positive symbols many believe them to be. Instead, an image of the resurrected Jesus or other Spiritual Son is a truly spiritual symbol, as is the resurrected Son over a cross—they symbolize the triumph of the spiritual over the material, and are thus protective.

An example of a Christianized symbol that is simple and illustrates the triumph of the Spiritual Son over the material is the Coptic Christian *crux ansata*, which is based on the ancient Egyptian symbol of the ankh. The oldest example of it ever found is in the ancient Gnostic text the Gospel of Judas,[33] which I discussed in chapter 3.

The *crux ansata* (with detail added inside the circle), on a cloth dated to the third to fourth centuries AD.

The ankh symbolized the eternal life of the spirit, just as the resurrected Spiritual Son does (whether as Jesus or Osiris), and has an ovoid-shaped loop atop a three-armed cross, which can illustrate the Spiritual Son/Sun risen/resurrected over the material. It was associated with the sun, and was one of the most commonly-used symbols in Egypt, often appearing on protective amulets in combination with other ancient Egyptian symbols.[34]

The Egyptian ankh symbol.

Another Egyptian symbol that was used for protection was the *shen* ring; during some of the earliest dynasties it was worn around the neck to protect the wearer. It's composed of a double strand of rope tied in an endless knot around the sun, which is said to signify the

The Egyptian *shen* ring symbol.

infinite nature of the sun and its eternal protection. Horus, an Egyptian god who represented the Spiritual Son, was often shown holding the *shen* ring above the king to illustrate him bestowing the sun's eternal protection.[35]

Other solar symbols in Egypt were also used for protection, such as the Eye of Ra, and the winged sun disk (the Behdety), which is associated with the Spiritual Son as Horus—famously known for his combat against the forces of darkness and evil.[36] There are also a host of other Egyptian sun symbols; another that could be used is the heiroglyph for Ra (the Spiritual Sun), which is a circle with a dot in the center.

Many other symbols used for protection today such as the Celtic triquetra and Norse *valknut* may not have been originally designed for a protective purpose, but were symbols in the Religion of the Sun representing spiritual principles and forces. Yet these spiritual principles have the power to oppose otherworldly forces of darkness and evil, and so symbols of them can be used for protection.

I'd say that out of the many symbols to choose from today, ones that are more protective would be those representing the Spiritual Sun; or those that embody divine light or a being of light such as the Spiritual Son, Spiritual Mother, or Spiritual Father (or the three of them together as a trinity); or a Being such as Odin or Jesus.

Even though symbols of the sun were commonly used for protection, these were not just representations of the physical sun, but of the Spiritual Sun, the divine source of the sun. This is why a symbol of the physical sun, like a mundane artistic drawing of the sun, is unlikely to have the same power as one that depicts the Spiritual Sun. Those who created ancient symbols of the Spiritual Sun imbued them with a spiritual meaning and they were used in a spiritual context.

There are more ancient symbols that could be used for protection—finding them is a matter of understanding the basic principles of light and creation and looking for a symbol that expresses those principles.

USING ANCIENT FORMS OF PROTECTION TODAY

I'll now talk about the practical use of the types of protection found in the ancient Religion of the Sun for people today, which is based on what I've found effective.

INVOCATIONS AND INCANTATIONS

We can call upon divinity to protect us from demons and expel them just as ancient practitioners of the Religion of the Sun did for thousands of years. Demons use the powers of darkness to assist them, but we can call upon the powers of light to assist us. This can involve calling one or more spiritual beings by name and imagining their presence, and then asking that they expel demons or protect us from them. Spiritual beings are the opposite of demons and can expel them.

Jesus healing a man who is demon-possessed by expelling it into the air.

It can also involve imagining divine light or the Spiritual Sun and asking for its protection or help to expel demons. This works because light drives out darkness, like when we turn on a light in a dark room; we fill it with light and darkness is no more. So too, when we ask the light to assist us and imagine its presence, the space we are in can get filled with divine light, which will clear away darkness and prevent it from entering.

There are incantations that have the power to return demons back to their hellish abode or to disable them, and lots of people have used them with great success. So it's worth experimenting with them—unless someone tries them, there's no way to know whether they're effective.

Incantations can be used in various circumstances, such as:

- Whenever someone sees a demon, or any sinister figure, or a being that they are unsure of in the fifth dimension, an incantation can be directed toward it, and if it's negative it will be disabled or expelled.

- If someone goes into the astral and it's dark, an incantation can clear the darkness away and allow them to see in the astral again.

- Before going to sleep, one can recite an incantation to stop demons attacking them while asleep (particularly in the transition stage between sleeping and waking). This needs to be done in conjunction with a circle of protection.

- Before doing any spiritual ritual or practice (including those to have an OBE), to clear the area so that no demons interfere. This is again best done in conjunction with a circle of protection to stop the demons from entering for the duration of the ritual/practice.

- To clear an area in the physical world. For example, someone may feel that there are negative influences present, or have an important task to do that they feel needs protecting.

Demon chasing ceremony in Japan.

There are various formulas that have been recommended for this purpose, and some things may work better than others. Whatever is used, I recommend repeating incantations three times. They work best when done strongly with a lot of conviction and when one's psychic energies are strong. However, becoming aggressive and angry is likely to ruin one's attempts, as someone will begin resonating more with the energies of the demons and will play into their hands. It's best to try and elevate one's inner state spiritually as much as someone can, as spiritual energies repel them.

THE INCANTATION OF THE SPIRITUAL SON/SUN

In the ancient Religion of the Sun, people called upon the Spiritual Sun for protection—usually symbolized as a sun god, as in Mesopotamia and Egypt—and used symbols of the sun for protection.

This is an incantation Lara and I put together. It's drawn from my spiritual experience and work, and is consistent with this same ancient solar principle and tradition, but is simple, easy to use, and we know to be effective.

It can be used either to call upon the Spiritual Son or the Spiritual Sun—choose one or the other. So say either the word Son or Sun; they sound the same, but it's the intention that's different.

> "I call on the light of the Son/Sun,
> The power of the Son/Sun,
> And the glory of the Son/Sun,
> To expel all/the demons."

Again, just say either Son or Sun, don't say both. If you wish, you could say "spiritual" before the word Son/Sun each time, if it helps you to focus on its spiritual aspect. You say either "all demons" or "the demons" depending on what you prefer.

This is repeated three times.

While saying the incantation, whether calling upon the Sun or Son, imagine a divine light emanating from the heavens, feeling its presence and energy, driving away the darkness and demons. This can help make the incantation more effective.

If it's appropriate, you could ask for a protective circle to be drawn around you afterward.

If you feel you need further protection against demonic attacks, while in the physical world or in the fifth dimension, you can use this longer incantation instead, which is done exactly the same except it has an additional line at the end:

> "I call on the light of the Son/Sun,
> The power of the Son/Sun,
> And the glory of the Son/Sun,
> To expel all/the demons,
> and repel all demonic attacks."

If you're in the fifth dimension and have used the shorter version and find that even though the demon appears to be gone, some attack from it continues, you can use this longer version.

The light of the sun and stars ultimately traces back to the divine Source of creation, and so calling upon it in an incantation is to call upon the divine itself.

The term "Spiritual Sun" (or Divine Sun) can refer to four different things.

The first is the Absolute, the divine Source, whose light shines through the sun and stars (stars being suns too).

The second is the sun in higher dimensions as an environment where spiritual beings dwell.

The third is the Father, who is a higher aspect of one's Being.

The fourth is a part of the Being known as the Son, which is what can merge with one's consciousness at a certain level on the path of the Spiritual Sun. The Spiritual Son was seen as a son of the Spiritual Sun, of the Source, and Heavenly Father, and was thus also associated with the sun and stars.

This incantation is short and to the point, which is very useful when in the astral particularly as we're often in situations where we have to act quickly and so need something that's easy to remember and repeat.

It also utilizes the formula of three times three, which can make an incantation more effective.

The more you practice this incantation, the more you'll remember to use it and remember the words to it in the fifth dimension. You can also start using it in your ordinary dreams if you practice it enough. It's important to memorize it fluently; it won't help if you're before a sinister entity in the astral plane and can't remember all the words.

I prefer to pronounce the incantation mentally, but I would think that most people would prefer to say it aloud if circumstances allow it, as saying it aloud can help the mind to stay focused on it. Another advantage is that the spoken word likely has greater spiritual power, and we're more likely to pronounce it aloud when we're in a dream or in the astral plane. It depends on the situation though, because there may be times when it's more practical to say it quietly, to whisper it, or say it mentally.

The incantation can be done by a group of people, and in that instance it's best if possible to all call upon either the Son or Sun, as it helps to make the petition even stronger.

As many people have experienced, demons and their followers absolutely hate Jesus. They hate anything about him: his words, images of him alive and resurrected, and words of praise about him, and seek to obliterate them entirely throughout the world. The existence of Spiritual Sons like Jesus threatens their very survival, as the Spiritual Son shines with immense light, and it's light that destroys darkness by its mere presence. These lines in the New Testament sum up this principle; demons hate the last line of it in particular, as it states the fact that they cannot overcome the light of the Spiritual Sun.

> "In the beginning was the Word, and the Word was with God, and the Word was God. He was with God in the beginning. Through him all things were made; without him nothing was made that has been made. In him was life, and that life was the light of all mankind. The light shines in darkness, and the darkness has not overcome it."[37]
> ~ JOHN 1:1-5

This is why people have found repeating things about Jesus effective for repelling demons; this incantation works on the same principle. All Spiritual Sons do this, and thus demons hate and are threatened by them, which is also why they work to stop any person from becoming one.

CASTING A CIRCLE OF PROTECTION

When the environment has been cleared of negative entities and forces with an incantation of protection, the area can then be protected and sealed so that they, or other negative entities, can't come back in straightaway. For this, a protective circle is needed.

A circle is used as it is a strong and stable shape, and is the shape of the sun, which embodies the perfection and wholeness of the divine. However, it can be drawn to fit any shape, such as a rectangular room or bed. The main thing is that it's completed and therefore sealed. I don't know how far it can be drawn—it wouldn't be very far though. I'd say around one's own immediate environment, such as one's room or house, or around a group of people proximate to each other. We can't encircle the earth and entrap every demon thereafter for example.

The Magic Circle by John William Waterhouse, 1886.

A circle of protection can form a barrier that stops any evil being from entering. It's drawn as a circle using one's imagination, while asking our Spiritual Father to work with the spirits of nature/fairies (which I discussed in chapter 25) to form the circle. It's made of light and held by the spirits of nature, who make the circle strong and sustain it. The Father is the male aspect of each one's own Being and has the power to do it.

Having expelled sinister entities using an incantation, you can then draw a circle to seal them out by saying the following words:

> "My Spiritual Father, please work with the spirits of nature to wrap a magic circle of protection around me [or the bed or the room or whatever you choose], so that no evil entity can harm me."

If you wish, you could simply begin with "Father" to make it shorter.

As you are saying this, imagine a circle formed by a beam of light being drawn around wherever you have chosen. It will help to extend your right arm and point with your index finger where you want the circle to be drawn as you are imagining it. You can do this with either your eyes open or closed. You can stand and turn around as you draw. Or if you are lying or sitting, you can lift your arm over and around your head, as you don't have to keep your arm straight as you draw. You could draw it in a sunwise direction, so for those north of the Tropic of Cancer, that is clockwise, and for those south of the Tropic of Capricorn, that is counterclockwise, and for those between the tropics it depends on the time of year. But as with the swastika, I wouldn't worry too much about it, as either way will work.

The statement is said each time we draw the circle, and this is repeated three times, making sure the circle is joined and complete. It's fine to say it mentally (that's how I prefer to do it), rather than aloud, especially in a group setting where it's difficult to say it together, though you may find it helps you to concentrate on it (at least until you get used to it) by saying it aloud.

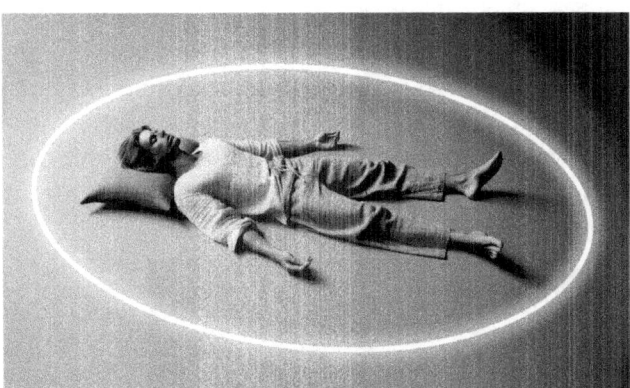

This can be done before going to bed at night, or at any time you feel you need to. Once it's done, no evil entity can get in. The circle stays throughout the night, even if we wake up a few times, until we move out of it physically, or another person or animal in the physical world crosses it. When we (or someone else or an animal) move out of or into the circle physically, it breaks. I don't know exactly what kinds of animals break the circle, only that an animal like a dog does, but an insect doesn't.

Moving out of the circle in our astral body as we fall asleep and go into the astral plane doesn't break it, as it was drawn from the physical world and is tied to the physical body. We can go in and out of our bodies and the circle will remain as long as it's not broken in the physical world.

I don't know how long an incantation lasts, but I wouldn't leave a gap between doing an incantation and drawing a circle. So once I've done the incantation, I do a circle straightaway.

Although we draw a two-dimensional circle, it encloses us in a kind of bubble of protection, as it stops evil entities from getting in not only around it, but also from above and beneath.

I'd say that the larger the area someone attempts to draw a circle around, the more difficult they may find it. So if they want to draw it around a whole house or building, as opposed to just the room they are in, they may find it harder to imagine light filling the whole space while saying the incantation, and more difficult to visualize the circle being drawn around it. This can affect whether it works, so it's worth bearing in mind what one's able to do.

It can be drawn on a moving vehicle such as a plane or a car as long as no person or animal enters or leaves it. It doesn't matter if people are moving around inside or outside the circle, as long as they don't cross it. This also applies to multilevel buildings such as apartments and multilevel houses. If someone draws a circle around their apartment or room, it's sealed, along with the people inside, but other apartments or other rooms (even those directly below, above, or beside) won't be. The seal is broken once someone goes into or out of the apartment or room.

If you're moving, like walking or running, and you want a circle of protection, draw it around your waist, touching you, and imagine the light of the circle expanding until it engulfs your whole body like in a cocoon that fills with light; this can last until someone else touches you.

I don't know how long an undisturbed circle can last, only that it must fade as energy dissipates in time.

Painting of a circle of protection held by the spirits of nature to protect against witches, by John Duncan, 1909.

We can draw it around others who are near us even if we're not in it. You say everything the same as when you draw it around yourself except that instead of asking for it to be drawn around yourself, you ask for it to be drawn around the other person or people. It's also possible to draw two circles—one around yourself, and then if you need to also around others (but one after the other, not at the same time). The circle can protect everyone inside it as long as no one goes in or out of it and breaks it.

Make sure you concentrate well while you do the incantation and circle of protection. If you lost concentration or were interrupted while doing the incantation, then start it over from the beginning. If you're unsure whether you've drawn the circle of protection well, start again.

I once taught this to someone who was a bit skeptical about it, but he nevertheless drew a circle around himself before he went to sleep. He woke up consciously in an OBE in the fifth dimension and found himself unable to move, with an evil-looking cat in front of him. He became frightened and started spitting at the cat, because that was all he thought he could do. Then he noticed that he had a circle of light around him and that the cat couldn't get in. He then woke up, back in his body. He should have used an incantation to make the cat disappear.

A depiction of a circle of protection from the book *The Astrologer of the Nineteenth Century*, 1825.

Lara had a similar experience where she fell asleep after drawing a circle of protection around the bedroom. She woke up in the astral in bed to the sound of angry grunting, and then saw its source, which was the dark figure of a demon angrily running around and around the circle of light, unable to get in.

In another she was practicing astral projection with a group of people who had drawn a circle of protection around the room they were in. She woke up in the astral in the room to hear and see a demon at the window who couldn't get in, but who was chanting an evil incantation to try and affect everyone's practice badly.

USING THE PROTECTIVE INCANTATION AND CIRCLE

If you go into the fifth dimension a few times consciously, you may be surprised how quickly you need to use these techniques. Once you use them, you'll see just how effective they are and realize that you're able to deal with evil beings and move around in the fifth dimension unhindered by them.

I now have a way of expelling demons that's different to anything I've written here, but I wasn't able to use it until recently; it's something that was given to me personally by my Spiritual Father. Before then I stuck to the same two incantations I knew, just because I found them to work and I didn't want to experiment with something else that may fail, knowing I had working incantations. I just wanted to expel the demon each time and get on with what I was doing. If you find something that works, you might want to stick with it, as it becomes automatic and you don't have to try to remember it when you encounter an evil entity.

One time, a horrible animal attacked me in the fifth dimension; as soon as I saw it, I used an incantation. It started running at me, then jumped and sank its teeth into my arm, even though I was in the process of expelling it. I continued my incantation but the animal stayed there. It only left when I had finished saying the incantation the three times I needed to complete it.

Many times I have been met by a demonic being who took the form of a spiritual guide to deceive me, but as I mentioned previously, you can learn to tell what they really are just by looking into their eyes. If you see that they are evil, expel them.

Years ago I met some people who appeared to be very spiritual and who impressed me with their ability to astral project at will every night. They had amazing psychic faculties, but I noticed they performed symbolic gestures the opposite way to the ones I did, that is, they performed them like those who are of darkness and use inverted symbols.

They gave me an object just before I drove home one evening and I put it in the back of the car. It became dark outside, and as I drove along a country lane, a strange looking animal jumped onto the road in front of me. I swerved the car, and the animal scampered to the side of the road and disappeared. I took the object out of the back of the car and threw it away.

One night in the fifth dimension I saw one of them doing a work on my spine, where the kundalini rises, and inserting things into my kidneys that blocked the flow of energy. After this, I asked the beings of light to undo what they had done to me. I performed a ritual to break their sinister influence and it worked (I will explain this ritual in another book).

I never saw them after that in the physical world, although some months later I met one of them again in the fifth dimension. This time however, I told him to show me what he really was. He lifted into the air, turned into a grotesque demon and disappeared into the darkness from where he came.

These were people who had awakened their consciousness for evil, or perhaps their bodies had been possessed by demons, but thanks to the protection of beings of light, they didn't harm me or anyone around me.

Démon d'assassinat by Louis Lebreton, 1863.

You can also use incantations of protection at night before you go to sleep, so that you clear away any dark beings or forces that might be there or might appear during the night.

If you come across something and you're not sure whether it's from the good or evil side, use an incantation to check. If it's good it will stay; if it's bad it will usually go or be disabled.

If someone thinks they're stronger than negative entities and has no need for incantations, they'll easily be deceived by them. Many people have been deceived by sinister entities, so if in doubt, use an incantation of protection.

If a sinister entity tries to frighten you as you're coming out of your body, right in the moment of projection or during sleep paralysis, it's possible not to give in to fear and to get past it by behaving as though you haven't heard or seen anything, and without worrying or moving, performing an incantation to get rid of it.

If you're expelling a sinister entity or figure and it begins to mock your incantation, it's trying to undermine your confidence, so be focused when you're saying it and continue until you complete it.

But I wouldn't try to use incantations with an underlying cruelty, even toward demons, as cruelty and conscious harm is an undesirable trait for anyone wishing to further themselves spiritually. Soon after I learned to use incantations in the astral world I experienced this cruelty, even though I never saw it within myself in everyday life. I was consciously out of my body in the apartment I was living in at the time. I walked down the hall and at the top of the stairs were two demons. I was sick and tired of them; they seemed to crop up all over the place in the astral with the intent of causing harm and ruining whatever good was being done. So I quickly surprised them by grabbing each one by the neck and holding them over the stairs so that their legs dangled in the air. Then I pronounced an incantation; they were going into fits trying to escape. As the incantation ended I released them and like a shot they went back to their diabolical abode. The fact that I was attacking demons was no justification for cruelty. That was taking pleasure in inflicting suffering, but when suffering needs to be inflicted to defend oneself, there should be no pleasure taken from it whatsoever. At the time, I still had lots of basic things to learn and much to change within myself.

USING SYMBOLS

Just as peoples in the ancient Religion of the Sun did, symbols can be used as a form of protection today. They can be worn as amulets in the form of jewelry or on clothing, or included as part of an altar, at the entrance to one's home or room, inscribed on objects, etc.

I recommend using those symbols I outlined earlier in the chapter, but I haven't used them all, and it's not an exhaustive list.

To use them for protection during sleep, dreams, and astral projection, they can be placed so they are visible in the room where someone sleeps or practices astral projection. They can be put above the bed, on an altar, above or on a door, etc.

Simple symbols are often the best to use (they can be easily drawn oneself), and can be very effective, but images of spiritual beings whether as paintings, amulets, or statues may also work. Those that are going to be effective are representations of the Spiritual Father, Spiritual Mother, Spiritual Son, and any person in history who became what is known in the Religion of the Sun as a Son of the Sun—that is someone who incarnated or had within them the part of their Being I call the Spiritual Son. Examples of people like this are Jesus, Odin, Anubis, and Thoth, but there are many others.

You could choose to use symbols and images from your own traditional culture, but bear in mind that many cultures degenerated and even incorporated things of darkness. Baal was widely worshiped for example, but he then became a demon. So you need to be sure that what you are using really represents the divine and is of the light. It's often possible to tell just by looking at it—if a deity looks monstrous, lustful, violent, frightening, or animalistic, then I would definitely steer clear of it.

Another thing to bear in mind is that some ancient spiritual symbols have developed negative connotations for people in certain cultures today, and so you may find that you're not able to openly display certain symbols, depending on where you live. It's sad that there is such ignorance of ancient history and religion—until there is more understanding, you could try wearing your symbols under your clothing or privately in your home if you feel it's ok to do so, and they will still be effective.

CHAPTER TWENTY-EIGHT

Psychedelics

People may wonder whether there is a connection between OBEs and the experiences people have on psychedelics, and whether psychedelics offer a way to have OBEs or similar mystical experiences.

I'll explain what I think the similarities and differences are, why I don't think psychedelics are a replacement for having OBEs naturally, and why I recommend against using them—particularly for those who are interested in pursuing the Religion of the Sun.

Psychedelics can have a synthetic or natural origin, although most synthetic ones are based on natural compounds, with exceptions that don't exist in nature and are instead lab created such as MDMA and 2CB. Naturally sourced psychedelics are compounds found in some plants and animals (such as certain fungi, cacti, vines, and toads) that induce changes in one's perceptions—people can see, hear, and feel things they wouldn't ordinarily. Psychedelics do this by creating chemical changes in the brain, and they have been used since ancient times. The psychedelic substance DMT exists naturally in the body, and may have a role in mediating our perceptions, as I discuss further on.

OUR PERCEPTION OF THE DIMENSIONS

Normally, there is a separation between our perceptions of the physical world and those of the fifth dimension. This is because our brain doesn't allow the perception of external things in the fifth dimension while we're awake (though is still connected to and affected by the parts of our psyche that are fifth dimensional, such as our egos). This separation is maintained by what I call "the natural interdimensional barrier of the brain." So even though the fifth dimension interpenetrates physical reality, we don't usually perceive things from it in our waking life, which is why we don't see or hear the deceased, people dreaming, demons, and deities around us even though they may be there. Likewise, we don't perceive physical things from the fifth dimension—only their fifth-dimensional component.

It's normally only once we've gone through the astral split as our body goes to sleep (or during NDEs or at death) that we then perceive the fifth dimension, which is when the perceptions of our physical body are switched over for those of our astral body.

However, as we fall asleep, we go into a transition stage between the two dimensions, and during the transition, before our body is completely asleep, we can sometimes hear and even see fifth-dimensional things. In the same way, we go through that transition as we wake up, and can continue to perceive things from the fifth dimension for a short time while merging back into our physical body. These perceptions overlay or appear coexistent to physical reality, as hallucinations induced by psychedelics do.

So for example, as I've mentioned previously, sometimes we can hear the voices of our egos as we drift off to sleep as though they were in the physical world. During the astral transition, though rarely, someone can see things from the fifth dimension as though made of brightly-colored light, looking almost cartoon-like, overlaid on the physical surrounds, similar to the visuals of psychedelic hallucinations, though not as chaotic, bizarre, or unstable. Sometimes what's seen can appear as real as the physical world. For example, Lara once woke in the night and saw me standing by the bed looking at her lovingly, as though I was physically there. She couldn't believe her eyes (as I was far away at the time) and so blinked a few times to see me still there until gradually fading away.

It's also possible to perceive things from other dimensions when people are more psychically sensitive, during spiritual practices, and/or in circumstances where supernatural phenomena are manifesting. For most though, this happens very rarely or never at all.

The natural interdimensional barrier of the brain probably develops as the brain does during childhood. This would explain why children can be more psychic and see things from other dimensions until a certain age.

BREACHING THE INTERDIMENSIONAL BARRIER

It seems that psychedelics work by forcing open the natural interdimensional barrier of the brain, partially disrupting it, causing someone to perceive physical and fifth-dimensional things at the same time, just as occurs during the transition stage of sleep. It's important to note that the fifth-dimensional things seen are almost always projections of one's subconscious in that dimension, which become as though they are real over there, just like dream images do. I'll return to this shortly.

In my view, the results of some studies done on psychedelics indicate this is what's happening.

For instance, those who've taken psychedelics were found to perceive the physical world and psychedelic-induced perceptions at the same time, with the psychedelic perceptions being overlaid on their surrounding physical environment. These psychedelic perceptions have been found to be linked to the state of dreaming. To me, this indicates that the interdimensional brain barrier has been artificially forced open without having gone through the natural process of sleep, so that someone is seeing both at the same time.

Psychiatrist Dr. Rick Strassman conducted a study on the effects of the psychedelic DMT from 1990 to 1995 at the University of New Mexico in the United States on sixty volunteers. Participants were provided with eye covers, and would close their eyes while "tripping," as otherwise physical reality would interfere with what they were seeing. Strassman wrote:

> "Visual images were the predominant sensory effects of a full dose of DMT. Usually there was little difference between what volunteers 'saw' with their eyes opened or closed. However, opening the eyes often caused the visions to overlay what was in the room. This had a disorienting effect, and it was less confusing to keep their eyes closed. That's one of the reasons we decided to place black silk eyeshades on all the volunteers before we gave any DMT."[1]

A subject who has taken psilocybin, and is wearing eye covers, being monitored by two guides as part of a clinical study at John Hopkins University in the U.S.

One of the volunteers said, "It was so real I had to open my eyes. When I did the scene was overlaid on top of the room. I closed my eyes, and that removed the interference with what I had been seeing."[2]

Research is now being conducted by administering psychedelics, including DMT, to volunteers at the Centre for Psychedelic Research at Imperial College London, which opened in 2019 as the first formal center for psychedelic research in the world. One of its first studies looked at the effects of DMT on brainwaves; Christopher Timmerman who led the study compared the experience of being on DMT to "dreaming while awake," saying, "It's clear these people are completely immersed in their experiences—it's like daydreaming only far more vivid and immersive, it's like dreaming but with your eyes open."[3]

During the time under DMT, the study found there was a drop in Alpha waves, which are those that dominate the brain while we're in a relaxed state, and an increase in Theta waves, which are associated with dreaming—and that the waves were generally more chaotic. To me, this indicates that psychedelics are interfering with the barrier that separates our perceptions of the physical world from the fifth dimension where we dream, so that someone can see their own dream images while awake; the chaotic state of brainwaves reflects the generally chaotic and subconscious nature of psychedelic experiences.

Another study in Brazil published in 2011 measured the effects of ayahuasca (which contains DMT) on the visual cortex of the brain. Normally the visual cortex is active when someone's eyes are open and inactive when they are closed. However, when participants were under the influence of ayahuasca, the visual cortex remained active whether their eyes were open or closed, indicating the psychedelic affected the visual cortex, forcing it to remain active.[4]

In Strassman's study, the subjects usually described hearing a buzzing, humming, whooshing, or whirring noise as their experience began, which is very interesting, as people commonly hear those sounds as they go through the astral split. Nearly all of the volunteers also felt "vibrations," which is another common sensation of the astral split.[5] It indicates the psychedelic is forcing the brain through the transition to fifth-dimensional perception that normally occurs as we fall asleep.

Strassman has come to a similar conclusion, proposing that DMT is naturally produced in our brains (specifically in the pineal gland), and may be what mediates our perceptions of the physical world and parallel dimensions, using the analogy of a television, saying:

> "Perhaps just the right amount of DMT is involved in the brain's maintenance of the correct receiving properties. [...] Too little, and our view of the world dims and flattens. [...] Too much and all manner of unusual and unexpected programs appear on the mind's screen. [...] The other planes of existence are always there. In fact, they are right here, transmitting all the time! But we cannot perceive them because we are not designed to do so; our hard-wiring keeps

us tuned in to Channel Normal. It takes only a second or two—the few heartbeats the spirit molecule [DMT] requires to make its way to the brain—to change the channel, to open our mind to these other planes of existence."[6]

It could well be that natural DMT has this function, but it's important to take into account the difference between chemically-induced experiences and natural ones, and the overwhelming effect the subconscious has on what is seen, as I discuss in the next section.

Strassman talks about the "psychedelic threshold" of DMT, which is crossed when "there is a separation of consciousness from the body and psychedelic effects completely replace the mind's normal contents."[7]

However, taking a psychedelic drug doesn't result in a true OBE, although it's possible it could happen sometimes, particularly at high doses, if the person goes into sleep. For a true OBE to occur, the body needs to go through the process of falling asleep, as that is when the bodies split. Usually on psychedelics the person doesn't fall asleep and there is not the same clear experience of leaving one's body as there is in an OBE; people don't feel their astral and physical bodies separating, or themselves rising up out of their physical body. They mostly involve altered perceptions while someone remains in the body and is often still partially aware of it, being able to open and close their eyes as in the studies mentioned, and can still talk and move, though sometimes with great difficulty. That's why hallucinating people can sustain injuries, which they don't remember getting, or end up in places they don't remember going to.

Illustration of a visual seen during a psychedelic trip. These often consist of complex geometric patterns and fantastical, morphing scenes, something rarely seen during natural OBEs. Visuals seen in natural OBEs are much more stable and truer to the type of perception we have in normal life.

It's a bit like the condition of sleepwalking, as in that case there is also a blurring or break in the brain's dimensional barrier, combined with a non-functioning of the sleep paralysis mechanism that normally stops the physical body from continuing to move around during sleep. This causes a person to move their physical body along with their astral one, while they are seeing in the astral (and not the physical). I used to sleepwalk a lot when I was a child.

It's interesting to note that there is a kind of barrier that surrounds the pineal gland that is activated during times of stress, which Strassman theorizes would stop it from making DMT when it shouldn't, and there is evidence this barrier is somehow broken in psychotic individuals[8] (something I'll discuss further in this chapter). While this may not be related to the dimensional barrier I'm proposing, it nevertheless indicates that such mechanisms exist.

There may be different mechanisms in the brain that are affected, depending on the psychedelic. For instance, in chapter 10 I discussed the part of the brain called the temporoparietal junction (TPJ), and how disturbing it in studies has been followed by OBEs. I argue that the TPJ, rather than constructing consciousness as materialist scientists believe, appears to play a role in limiting the perceptions of consciousness to the physical world, acting as a kind of barrier. Psychedelics may disturb the TPJ and/or other areas of the brain so that their functioning is disrupted, allowing consciousness to experience something outside of what the brain ordinarily limits it to perceiving.

Whatever the mechanism, I believe psychedelics overcome barriers in the brain, forcing it into the transition state between wakefulness and sleep, where a partial seeing into the fifth dimension occurs, although overlaid with subconscious images (I call this the Psychedelic Brain Barrier Theory).

THE INFLUENCE OF THE SUBCONSCIOUS

This breaching of the brain's dimensional barrier may sometimes allow people to see something of the fifth dimension, but it's usually heavily if not totally influenced and created by the person's psyche, so that they are immersed in images from their subconscious as though they are real. So far, I've yet to see any clear evidence that anyone on psychedelics has seen something objectively real from the fifth dimension.

Our minds create things that appear real in the fifth dimension, and so if we're having an OBE we can imagine something, say a flying elephant, and we'll probably see it. No matter how much we try to make it disappear or tell ourselves it doesn't exist, it can stay and seem totally real, and we may be unable to break the illusion. This is the same mechanism that can happen to a person who's taken psychedelic drugs, in that the illusory creations of the mind become unbreakable forms that can't easily be shaken off. We are also in these kinds of mental creations in many of our dreams.

As discussed in chapter 6, there are accounts of people in NDEs and OBEs seeing things which they had no way of knowing, and were then corroborated as being true once they returned to the physical world. To my knowledge, there are no such verifiable accounts from experiences on psychedelics. For example, no one in Strassman's study saw anything while on psychedelics that occurred in the hospital where they were, or its surrounds, which they could only have seen while out of their bodies, as has happened many times in NDEs.

Many claim to have encountered real nonphysical entities while on psychedelics. However, James Kent, author of a book on psychedelics, who has taken psychedelics many times, says that at some point he began to take an investigative approach to his psychedelic experiences, and discovered that the "elves" he saw (and are often seen in psychedelic experiences) were subconscious projections and not real entities:

> "I initially found it very surprising to be confronted by elves in my DMT experiences, and on psilocybe mushrooms as well, and did indeed perceive them as externalized, morphing, disincarnate beings. I even managed to carry on rudimentary conversations of sorts. However, the more I experimented with DMT the more I found that the 'elves' were merely machinations of my own mind. While under the influence I found I could think them into existence, and then think them right out of existence simply by willing it so. Sometimes I could not produce elves, and my mind would wander through all sorts of magnificent and amazing creations, but the times that I did see elves I tried very hard to press them into giving up some non-transient feature that would confirm at least a rudimentary 'autonomous existence' beyond my own imagination. Of course, I could not. Whenever I tried to pull any information out of the entities regarding themselves, the data that was given up was always relevant only to me. The elves could not give me any piece of data I did not already know, nor could their existence be sustained under any kind of prolonged scrutiny. Like a dream, once you realize you are dreaming you are actually slipping into wakefulness and the dream fades. So it is with the elves as well. When you try to shine a light of reason on them they dissolve like shadows."[9]

Kent puts the appearance of entities in psychedelic experiences down to the tendency we have to see faces in random shapes and patterns based on our evolutionary need to spot other humans and animals in our environment. Given the intense and complex imagery people see on psychedelics, he says it's inevitable people will see faces in the shapes and patterns that emerge and then "dream" entities into being as their mind latches onto them.

Photo of a sandwich (left), which has been transformed using Google software DeepDream (right), so that it resembles visuals seen on psychedelics. The software "uses a convolutional neural network to find and enhance patterns in images via algorithmic pareidolia," which basically means it seeks to create meaningful shapes and faces out of things that resemble them, but are not. So for instance, bits of bread that resemble a face, a mouth, or an eye, have been transformed into one. There is scientific evidence that DeepDream may be replicating what happens during a psychedelic trip.[10]

I would also say that during a psychedelic experience the mind is constantly unconsciously trying to interpret its surrounds, as it does while we're awake. For example, in waking life, for a split moment a rope on the ground may appear as a snake, and we freeze in fright until we look closer. I'd say this process is happening while on psychedelics, but with the ability to create projections there is no end to the snake and what it might morph into. One example of this was a volunteer in the Strassman study who heard a high-pitched sound which she said were the voices of impersonal angels.[11] I doubt they were; I'd say it's more likely that the woman's mind was trying to interpret the high-pitched whirring sound that occurs as we separate from our bodies based on preconceived ideas of what she might encounter while on psychedelics, and that her mind then distorted it.

However, it's also very likely that at least some of the entities people encounter while on psychedelics are their own egos, as these too can appear as separate entities that can interact with us while out of the body. In my experience, our own egos know us very well; in many ways they are like AI (artificial intelligence), but each one is limited to its program—they are unable to process new information since their intelligence would be derived from the cumulative data of one's own thoughts, emotions, and memories specific to that particular ego and its field of activity.

There have been anecdotal accounts of people taking psychedelics together and seeing the same thing. It's possible they are seeing the same thing in the fifth dimension. However, another possibility is that telepathy is involved in some way, as it's through the fifth dimension that our thoughts and emotions travel and can affect others.

In Strassman's study, participants commonly stated they didn't feel like they were dreaming or asleep, but were completely awake, aware, and able to observe and interact with their supernormal surrounds.[12] Although this can be taken as indicating that what they experienced was real, to me it's the result of the psychedelic forcing them open to the perceptions of the fifth dimension while in an awake state of consciousness, allowing them to view their own fifth-dimensional subconscious projections with the level of awareness they have while awake. This creates the sense that whatever they see is real.

As the Brazilian study noted, "By boosting the intensity of recalled images to the same level of natural image, Ayahuasca lends a status of reality to inner experiences."[13]

People have commented that there is no way that what they saw on psychedelics could have come from their own mind. Yet people often see and do things in dreams they feel they never would in real life. This is because there is so much in the subconscious that is unknown to each person, and just as in dreams, these unknown parts of the psyche can manifest while on psychedelics.

As a psychiatrist, Strassman often commented on the relationship between what his volunteers experienced during their psychedelic sessions, and their psychology as well as their psychological response to their surrounds, as there seemed to be a correlation. Repressed fears, their views of the world, their wishes and expectations, and parts of their psyche that they didn't wish to acknowledge, as well as any ill ease with their environment, often seemed to manifest in their experiences, with Strassman saying:

> "Psychedelics show you what's in and on your mind, those subconscious thoughts and feelings that are hidden, covered up, forgotten, out of sight, maybe even completely unexpected, but nevertheless imminently present."[14]

Even the seemingly most meaningful experiences subjects had during the Strassman study could have been a result of the subject's psychology, as they were from volunteers who had spiritual interests (already being involved in Wicca, Shamanism, or the New Age). Ideas and beliefs about spirituality also form part of the subconscious, and so they too can form unreal scenes and beings, even though they are on spiritual themes.

It's even possible that someone's own egos or demons could deceive them into thinking they're having a spiritual experience on psychedelics to convince them to keep taking them, diverting them away from more meaningful activities.

Psychedelic experiences can lead to confusion, as people expect and try to read meaning into what can largely, if not entirely, be something that is subconsciously generated. Spiritual practices and disciplines in the Religion of the Sun have been developed so that someone can progress objectively into inner and spiritual realms, without falling into the many pitfalls of the subconscious and its subjectivity. On psychedelics, the perceptions of the brain are artificially altered, which means the experiencer cannot maintain psychological objectivity in them.

NEGATIVE EXPERIENCES

Not all psychedelic experiences are benign; many are negative. In Strassman's study, twenty-five of the sixty volunteers had bad experiences. The high incidence of negative experiences, together with the physical risks posed to some of the volunteers, and the lack of meaningfulness and lasting benefit they reportedly derived from their experiences, led him to start questioning whether to continue.

Just as the subconscious can be filled with pleasures and high ideals, so is it filled with fears and all other negative emotions, and these too can manifest in psychedelic experiences, though without any way to escape them until the chemical wears off, like being trapped in a nightmare or bad dream—in some cases leaving people with lasting, disturbing, and even traumatic psychological impressions.

Besides the obvious problems with taking psychedelics, the wish to bypass the divine and forcibly extract experiences that one is not ready or fit to receive is a problem, and has its repercussions. When we have natural experiences as part of a spiritual faith, they are usually given to us by our higher Being, which guides and protects us during them. But by breaking their laws, and forcing oneself open to other dimensions, it's unlikely someone will be under that same protection and guidance.

DEMONIC CONTACT (by Lara)

It's common for people to see entities during psychedelic experiences—those most commonly encountered are said to be elves, aliens, clowns, and large insects, although other people and strange nonhuman beings also appear, including demons and spiritual-seeming figures, some of which are described as spirits and angels.[15] Beings that are clearly divine appear prolifically in NDEs, and often in meaningful OBEs, but large insects, clowns, and elves do not. Perhaps divine beings don't appear at all or so often in psychedelic experiences because they don't wish to reward and thus encourage something that is harmful.

However, demons look for any opportunity to manifest in people's psyche and thus affect the physical world, and psychedelics offer them an opening. During a psychedelic experience, someone is unable to end or wake up from the experience as they would from a dream or an OBE—leaving them open to influences from the fifth dimension for a period of time. They are often too out of control to use any kind of spiritual protection, and are thus vulnerable to whatever is waiting.

As one subject of a 1950s study on DMT exclaimed, "It is frightening because I cannot terminate it [by opening my eyes] .... How unpleasant! Oh, how bad. [...] Give me something so that I shall die quickly, it would be better to die."[16]

Interestingly, a common experience in Strassman's study was a kind of "alien abduction" where people found themselves being manipulated and monitored by nonhuman entities. It's possible this was their subconscious responding to the setting they were in, as they were being monitored while on DMT lying on a bed in a hospital. However, it's also possible these were demons disguising themselves as aliens, just as they have done during "alien abductions" that have occurred during episodes of sleep paralysis—something discussed in detail in chapter 26. The similarities between the alien encounters volunteers reported while on DMT to reports of alien abductions forced Strassman to consider a possible relationship between them; he makes the point that the accounts are so similar no one would be able to tell them apart.[17]

This opens up the alarming possibility that by partially putting someone into the transition stage between the physical and fifth dimension, psychedelics are affecting the same mechanisms that occur in sleep paralysis, a state which seems particularly open to demons as explained in chapter 26.

One of the experiences in Strassman's study shares similarities with an incubus sleep paralysis experience:

> "There were two crocodiles. On my chest. Crushing me, raping me [...]. I didn't know if I would survive. At first I thought I was dreaming, having a nightmare. Then I realized it was really happening. [...] It was awful. It's the most scared I've ever been in my life. I wanted to ask to hold your hands, but I was pinned so firmly I couldn't move, and I couldn't speak."[18]

Notice the feeling the volunteer had of being pinned and paralyzed, with a heavy weight on their chest, and being forced into a sexual encounter, all of which is typical of an incubus experience, but without any way to end it.

Sleep paralysis and psychedelics appear to share mechanisms in common: in both, it seems someone's dimensional barrier is partially opened, and in the case of psychedelics, a person is only partially in control of their brain, while during sleep paralysis someone is normally mentally lucid, but is only partially connected to and in control of their body.

Psychedelics alter the connection consciousness has with the brain. They cause artificial changes to the brain, and so they affect someone's perception, beyond the person's conscious control. This can mean that a person is only partially in control of their brain (and thus their body). During sleep paralysis, someone is only partially connected to their body—though not because of artificial changes to their brain, but because they are naturally transitioning into another dimension.

It's not just psychedelics that affect the ability of a person to control their brain—any substance that alters one's state of consciousness, like mind-altering drugs and alcohol, affects it.

Once someone ingests a mind-altering substance, the psyche loses control over parts of the brain, which may provide more opportunity for the person's egos to take control. This is probably why people can experience heightened and irrational ego states, like paranoia and aggression, while affected by mind-altering drugs and alcohol. But it may also provide an opening for demons to at least partially influence one's brain and thus body too, and in some cases, take possession for a time. Demons may actually use a similar mechanism to the egos to take control of someone.

I came across an example of a temporary drug-induced demonic possession on Reddit. The user ingested psychedelic mushrooms while alone in their apartment, and had called out asking to speak with anyone or anything that was willing, naively expecting an ancestor, spirit animal, or nature spirit. They describe in detail how they felt an evil entity enter them, saying:

> "As my pupils began to dilate [...] I felt this intrusive inhabitation suddenly, like an invasion inside my mind. Abruptly there was something else inside of me [...]. I experienced a divergence of consciousness and emotion. It felt like I was experiencing the world both as myself as I always have, and as something else! This other consciousness felt a nefarious excitement at its present circumstance [...]. At the same time, I felt my own consciousness get pushed aside, locked away, restrained. This thing in my head took control of my body! [...] the real me was still very much experiencing everything, but powerless to change it, like being the unwilling passenger to a reckless and belligerent driver. But I was utterly imprisoned in my own mind, and in this prison my jailer was torturing me [...]. Thankfully, after a few hours of enduring this torment, I started to slowly regain control of my faculties. [...] I was left spiritually torn to shreds and emotionally raw as an open wound. I had been sent tumbling down a metaphorical slope of anxiety and shame that afterward became a constant obstacle [...]."[19]

There are numerous accounts of people who felt possessed and were suddenly able to see and interact with demons while on mind-altering drugs, and even continued to do so once the drugs wore off.[20] I also remember watching the account of an NDE in which a man had seen demons taking possession of the bodies of those who were completely drunk.

All of this may explain why demonic influences seem to be more prevalent on psychedelics, and on mind-altering substances generally, and why demons seem to encourage their use. It's difficult to know exactly what mechanisms are at work though; it would take a lot more study to potentially figure that out, so for now this is the best we can speculate.

Demons have an incentive to appear as aliens during psychedelic experiences so as not to put people off taking them, as they offer them a valuable portal of influence into this world, and have done since ancient times. Having a study running according to a timeline would allow them to know when a person would become psychically open, which is perhaps why the volunteers in the Strassman study reported more alien abduction experiences than recreational DMT users. The use of psychedelics by regular users, and on scheduled retreats, would also likely allow demons to better predict when people would become psychically open.

Psychedelic inspired art.

Toward the conclusion of his DMT study, Strassman had an appointment with a therapist he saw regularly, whom he describes as "highly intuitive." Upon seeing him, she said, "I see evil spirits hovering around you. They want to come through this plane, using you and the drugs. I'm worried. This does not look good to me."[21]

One of the study volunteers seemed to have picked up on this, commenting to Strassman, saying:

> "There is a sinister backdrop [...] not-quite-pleasant side of this, isn't there? [...] During the experience there is a sense of someone, or something else, there taking control. It's like you have to defend yourself against them, whoever they are, but they certainly are there. I'm aware of them and they're aware of me. It's like they have an agenda."[22]

Both demons as well as someone's own egos would certainly fit this description—both are types of entities in the fifth dimension who could be waiting there to take control of someone against their wishes and best interests.

Many natural psychedelics have been used in shamanist ceremonies worldwide for thousands of years. Shamanism was often practiced by hunter-gatherers in places that were outside of the influence of the Religion of the Sun.

One time in an OBE Mark witnessed a shamanistic ceremony and saw it was from the dark side—it was typical of the shamanist ceremonies carried out today. Psychedelics are often used to open communication up to otherworldly entities; these entities are demons, though some shamans may be deceived into thinking they are spirits or gods. Other shamans knowingly work with demons, and intentionally deceive and use naïve people in search of spirituality for their malevolent purposes. Beings of light work in a very different way than this. Although people often report having what they believe to be spiritual experiences, we've read accounts of people who've taken ayahuasca with shamans and have either experienced demonic contact at the time or felt like they were semi-possessed by a demonic entity afterward that was driving them toward suicide.

People argue that only some experiences are bad. Yet if all of them were, there would not be such a belief that psychedelics offer some kind of spiritual experience, and demons would not have the portals open to them that psychedelics provide. It's the seemingly "good" experiences that keep the whole enterprise going.

I thought the account of one young Christian man summed it up quite well. He had taken many drugs in his youth, including psychedelics, but had given them up after his conversion. However, after speaking to a lot of people who'd done psychedelics while he was preaching on the streets, he became curious to take them again in order to investigate the truth about them. Not long after ingesting mushrooms, he felt demons start to surround him, and became unable to breathe (which is typical of a sleep paralysis experience). This led him to have either an OBE or NDE, in which Jesus lovingly admonished him for taking them, and showed him why he shouldn't. He partly summed up what he learned from his experiences using Christian terms as follows (I'd replace "the devil" with "demons" and "Jesus" with the "Spiritual Son," which includes but is not limited to Jesus):

> "You are just kicking the door open to the spirit realm saying 'hey, what's up guys, I'm here.' And the thing is, is that your spirit isn't even built up to understand what's even happening around you, and so the devil, he just dances around as a being of light. It's like [...] I had encounters with spirit beings [on psychedelics] before [...] I've had other dimension beings come to me, I had experienced all that, and they would teach me things that sounded good, and that goes back to what I was saying

is that what you're experiencing on these psychedelics is just enough truth to keep you bound. It's just enough lies to keep you bound. So it's like you're getting stuff that's like, 'this is good, this is good,' but boom at the end of it there's a hook that's gonna keep you bound to something. [...] As long as you're bound to something, the devil doesn't really care, as long as you're not with Jesus, the devil doesn't really care where you go. You know, it doesn't matter if your chain is ten feet or a hundred feet, you're still on a chain."[23]

Some of those into the dark occult, including Satanists, consume certain bodily fluids (which I won't describe) that likely overwhelm and override the pineal gland's barrier, forcing it to produce DMT—thus also breaching the dimensional barrier. This is based on an ancient lineage of knowledge stretching back thousands of years, long before DMT was chemically isolated and now smoked or injected. It's connected to human sacrifice, which is one of the reasons its practice was so prevalent among the dark occult then as it is now. Just as people on the light side seek spiritual experiences with other dimensions and beings, so do those of the dark side with their own kinds of beings. They use DMT to have OBEs and to see and interact with demons directly, but in a way that's not so affected by hallucinations. They obviously don't wish to spend time on self-development, self-purification, and disciplined practice to get experiences, and so they take substances, no matter what the cost of them may be.

SCHIZOPHRENIA

The symptoms of the psychological condition schizophrenia have been compared to the effects of psychedelics,[24] and to LSD-induced psychosis,[25] due to their similarities. Schizophrenics mostly hear voices, although they can also see separate entities and have other altered perceptions, and they cannot distinguish between their hallucinations and reality. In 2022 there were twenty-four million (or one in three hundred) people diagnosed with schizophrenia worldwide.[26]

Drawing of a face made by someone who was on LSD. Dr. Oscar Janiger, who studied LSD and its relationship to creativity, noticed the art produced by those while on LSD resembled art produced by schizophrenics.[27]

Many schizophrenics claim their voices belong to demons, and there is convincing evidence that supports this. After working with psychotic and criminally-insane patients for thirty-five years in some of the most volatile psychiatric institutions in the United States, and questioning scores of schizophrenics about their voices, Jerry Marzinsky, who is a retired psychotherapist, has come to the conclusion that schizophrenics are really hearing demons.[28] [29] [30] [31] Likewise, Dr. Kemal Irmak of the High Council of Science at Gulhane Military Medical Academy in Turkey, came to the same conclusion after witnessing faith healers in Turkey curing schizophrenics in as little as three months.[32] The voices schizophrenics hear are reportedly always negative and destructive, and are extremely averse to Jesus,[33] [34] [35] as you would expect from demons, saying things like, "You're going down there. You wait until you see what I'm going to do to you,"[36] and "Die in hell you insignificant little piece of [expletive]." Schizophrenics also often report seeing demons as though really in the physical world.[37] [38]

This condition often begins after drug or alcohol use, or even after getting involved in Satanism or Ouija boards, but there are other causes too.[39] [40] This indicates that for at least some people, their hallucinations begin after they have opened themselves up to demonic other-dimensional forces, as with Satanism and Ouija. Or, as with drug and alcohol use, have taken substances in which they voluntarily give up bodily and psychological control of themselves, and thus provide an opening for demons to come in.

I had always thought schizophrenia was due to hallucinations, but I realized for some cases at least, it was likely due to the way the mind interacts with the fifth dimension. I also realized how consciousness-altering drugs were using this same mechanism.

Schizophrenics are more likely to have much higher levels of naturally occurring DMT in their blood,[41] and the enzymes that produce DMT are more active in them,[42] and so it's likely that elevated levels of DMT are at least partly what's responsible for breaching their dimensional barrier, or are a result of it. Their barrier could be partly broken and they could be hearing demons taking advantage of the broken connection, which is mixing the physical and fifth dimensions.

I know that demons can also stir up emotions which then affect thoughts, but this is not the same as hearing voices in one's head.

I'm also aware that the egos feed from the energy of a person and have their root in hell, and so the energy taken by the egos provides energy for hell. Demons therefore have an interest in this energy-taking, and many schizophrenics say they feel exhausted after their voices have finished talking to them.[43]

I suspect that Jesus casting out demons is a related phenomenon. Perhaps he healed the bodies and brains of demon-possessed people and restored their barrier so they couldn't be influenced by demons anymore.

The causes and mechanism of schizophrenia, I think, illustrates how dangerous taking psychedelics can be, as it can lead to an imbalance in the brain causing hallucinations to reoccur even after the drug has worn off. A study found that 25 percent of those who'd been diagnosed with substance-induced psychosis later went on to develop schizophrenia (the rate being highest for those who'd used cannabis and hallucinogens).[44]

AFTER EFFECTS

Consciousness-altering drugs force the mind to be partly in the transition stage between the dimensions and this forcing can have a lasting effect on the mind, affecting not only the physical brain, but probably the fifth-dimensional brain too.

With long-term use they can cause persistent psychosis and flashbacks where hallucinations happen without taking the drugs. However, this can also happen in the short-term, as there are accounts of people who've taken psychedelics, even just once, that have continued to see hallucinations weeks to decades later, even leading people to commit suicide to try to escape.[45]

Forcing the brain with drugs can alter a finely balanced mechanism, leaving parts of it altered, impaired, or broken. Over a long time, the changes may become ingrained and may weaken the dimensional barrier. This can make the brain less sensitive to normal, non-drug related perceptions, which we use for actual spiritual experience and development, affecting one's finer spiritual perceptions and ability to perceive reality.

It can also cause mental and emotional instability, making the mind more scattered and the emotions stronger, which in turn affects inner states, dreams, OBEs, and spiritual development, and intensifies the effect of the egos.

It also makes one more susceptible to other-dimensional influences, as appears to be the case with schizophrenics. Some consciousness-altering drugs have clearly dragged people's psyche down into hells and opened it to the influence of demons and dark forces. Some cultures use them to have "mystical" experiences, but don't seem to understand the dark side, which they can fall prey to.

MYSTICAL VS. PSYCHEDELIC EXPERIENCES

People sometimes take psychedelics to have otherworldly or mystical experiences. Some feel their experiences have given them a new perspective on life—commonly they stop being an atheist, they are less afraid of death, and have gained the knowledge that there are other planes of reality. Although these are positive outcomes, psychedelics come with problems that make them harmful to anyone wanting to make long-term positive spiritual changes, and in my view, these are so severe as to rule out their use altogether.

The psychedelic experiences that Lara and I have read have largely been chaotic, confused, and vague compared to the symbolic, coherent, and meaningful

OBEs and dream experiences we and others have had, and that people have during NDEs. As one study volunteer put it, "The psychic channels may have been opened, but the trips were mostly without content or insights."[46]

That is, psychedelics may force someone's perception of the fifth dimension open, but the depth and meaning that can be found in spiritual experiences requires more than that—it requires a connection to the divine.

After years of experimentation, Strassman concluded something similar, stating that DMT was not inherently therapeutic, and that the broader context of what was going on in someone's life was more important to their self-development,[47] saying, "I expected psychotherapeutic, near-death, and mystical experiences during our work. However, the lack of substantial change induced by them made me wonder about their validity."[48]

While having a psychedelic trip is merely the result of taking a substance, having a naturally-induced experience of other dimensions is often the result of long practice, which derives from a yearning and serious commitment to experience something transcendental. This itself is usually the result of a shift in one's priorities toward the spiritual. This also then affects the content of the experience, as to truly be transcendental it needs to connect us with and invoke a response from the divine; and the divine wishes for us to take steady and self-initiated steps on the path of self-development.

Having said that, there are many disciplines that developed in the past which involved forcing or even harming the body through things like contortion and deprivation to activate things in the body that enable mystical experiences. This is a bit like taking psychedelics in that it's forcing an experience that one has not brought about through inner, spiritual development and having a connection to the divine. I completely recommend against it. Although useful and helpful, having mystical experiences are not worth harming the body for. Neither do I think extreme or painful disciplines of the body are worth spending time on in place of increasing and transforming consciousness, which can be done without it, and brings about changes that far outlast the body. What's most important in life is changing one's inner self for the better—a message received over and over in NDEs.

Ancient yogis strapping their bodies to hold poses.

It seems some people in the past resorted to taking substances because their psychic faculties and ability to consciously travel in the astral plane was inadequate and they were unable to have actual mystical experiences naturally, or had very infrequent ones, as these require much more effort. This is still the case today, as people use psychedelics as a way to easily have what seems to be a spiritual experience.

The volunteers in the Strassman study were already users of psychedelics, and Strassman noted a tendency among them not to pursue methods of self-development that required work, saying, "It was easier to talk about the transformative value of the psychedelic experience than it was to put into practice some of its contents. My colleagues may have had inspiring experiences, but they were not committed to goals that required work and sacrifice."[49]

This may be generally indicative of a difference in mindset between those who pursue psychedelics and those who pursue some kind of spiritual discipline.

Psychedelic users are often quick to point out the evidence for psychedelic use in ancient religions. Yet there were many people in ancient times using completely natural (substance-free) methods for having OBEs (and other mystical experiences). These are the only methods I have used for having OBEs, as I believe psychedelics can lead to long-term or permanent changes in the chemistry of the brain that unbalance it, and ultimately make it harder to have objective OBEs and dreams, to receive real divine guidance in them, and to do a spiritual work generally. Natural methods for having OBEs require being able to focus and still the mind and emotions, but the use of substances, like psychedelics, makes it harder to do this, and so these two paths lead in different directions.

To me, doing a spiritual work is the most important thing in life, and so I don't want to risk it in any way. This spiritual work is the basis of the Religion of the Sun, and thus why a movement toward using consciousness-altering substances is an alteration of its message.

For example, the Egyptian Pyramid Texts describe inner spiritual transformation as the means to see into and travel in other dimensions. They detail how the king raised his serpent of light up his spine (known as the kundalini in Hinduism) to awaken his other-dimensional abilities. This serpent was portrayed on the forehead of the king, and was said to be united with his soul as a bird (called the Ba), creating the symbol of the feathered serpent, commonly depicted in Egypt, allowing him to travel to the heavenly region of the stars in his light body. Raising this serpent is also what created his inner eye, which was portrayed as a third eye in both Egypt and Hinduism, and often depicted as the sun (and the eye of the sun god). This eye enabled him to perceive in the dimension of the afterlife and see "the holy aspects" of physical things.

> "The light body rises. It is a serpent.[50]
>
> Upon the seat of the older falcon, his eye with its power is his protection

It is created for him from the fire of his serpentine light body.
Over these is the image of the rising cobra at his head.
Give to Unis his terrible one. Its essence is an eye thrust out.
With it we see the holy aspects revealed.[51]

For the primordial sleeping serpent
Loves you.
She rises she rises
In the great embrace of the opener of the paths
As you in your light body rise on the numinous horizon[52]

Ah to the great serpent at the top of the spine [...] give Unis your love,
With the love that causes the spirit to rise [wall broken] with the light bodies[53]

His serpent rises on his crown
His guiding serpent is on his brow.[54]

Receive praise for you, soul, shining white bird,
That you rise from him, for you are a serpent.[55]

Unis does not see
That he has an eye within
It is not your eye
That is fully opened."[56]

~ THE PYRAMID TEXTS

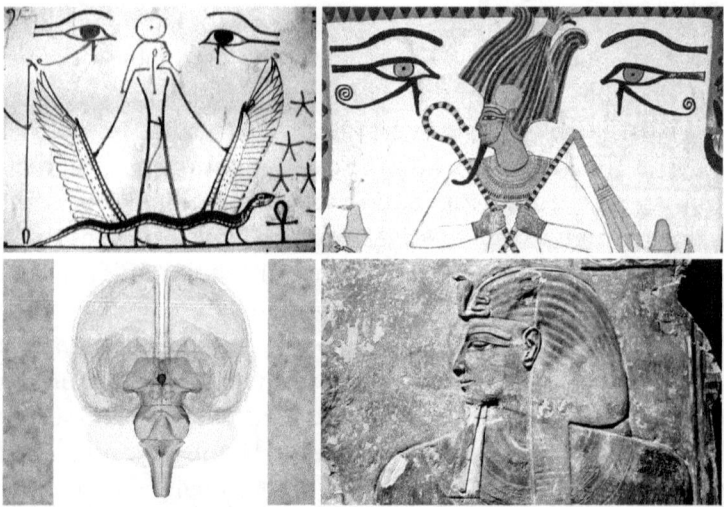

Top left: An ancient Egyptian figure spreads the wings of a serpent. Atop the figure's head is the symbol of the Spiritual Sun (the circle with a dot at the center), which is between two eyes, indicating its location at the mid-brow and region of the third eye. Top right: Osiris with the sun disk at the top of his head, which again is located between two eyes. Bottom left: Diagram of the brain from behind showing the pineal gland (the small dot in the center) within the brain stem at the top of the spine, which looks like the head of a risen cobra serpent. Bottom right: Egyptian king with a cobra raised upon his brow.

This inner eye had once been open in the Children of the Sun and had allowed them to perceive things from the other dimensions while in the physical world,[57] and perhaps allowed them easier access to these other realms through OBEs. Yet in the ancient Religion of the Sun there was a way to "reopen" this eye. As the Pyramid Texts indicate, the creation of the eye came as a result of raising the serpent of light (of purified sexual energy) up the spine, which rose through love and overcoming evil. Psychedelics don't have anything to do with this inner, spiritual transformation, and cannot produce these kinds of spiritual changes, which I will explain in another book.

A Buddhist stupa painted with the face of Buddha, with a sun disk between his eyes at the location of the third eye.

Strassman proposes that meditative techniques, such as mantras and visualizations, may create a kind of resonance with parts of the brain (particularly the pineal gland) that produce DMT, causing them to naturally release it, thereby inducing mystical experiences.[58]

Interestingly, it's stress that triggers the pineal gland's defensive shield, which may be connected to the importance of relaxation as a prerequisite for mystical practice and experience. Also interesting is that constant darkness has been found to stimulate pineal growth,[59] which could explain why "dark retreats" were developed in Buddhism, in which practitioners stay in complete darkness for days, years, and even decades at a time.

The composers of the Pyramid Texts may well have understood the mechanism that affects our connection to higher dimensions through spiritual means permanently. There is evidence there were those among the ancient Egyptians who knew about the brain's connection to other dimensions. They symbolically depicted parts of the brain in relation to the journey consciousness makes in the fifth dimension after death, and as part of the process of spiritual transformation on the path of the Spiritual Sun.[60 61 62] This likely has a scientific basis, as a recent study suggests the brain produces DMT and speculates it plays a role in NDEs.[63] The pineal gland is situated very close to the spine, with direct access to the cerebrospinal fluid that surrounds the brain and spinal cord. Perhaps when the inner energy called the kundalini rises up the spine it stimulates the pineal gland (and other relevant parts of the brain), which the Egyptians symbolically depicted as the eye of the sun god Ra, causing it to resonate at a higher frequency permanently so that it naturally produces more DMT (among other things), thereby "opening" it. This would come as a righteous reward for those who have developed love and overcome evil within themselves through the tests on the path of the Spiritual Sun.

An ancient Egyptian illustrated disk that was placed under the head of the deceased and may represent parts of the brain in relation to the journey of consciousness into the afterlife and rising of the kundalini. For example, the crown on the central four-headed figure may represent the part of the brain called the gyrus rectus, within which is the pituitary gland (shown as the small circle of the sun).[64] The disk symbolized the sun and was believed to aid in the transformation of the deceased into a divine being in the afterlife.[65] A disk won't do this however; it takes a long spiritual work.

Yet despite DMT's seemingly significant role in mystical experience, I think there's an important distinction to make between potentially naturally activating it through mystical practice and positive inner change vs. ingesting/injecting/smoking it. The body is an incredibly complex system, and the natural release of DMT within the body is likely to be part of a concert of mechanisms (with physical, psychological, and spiritual components) that prevent any harm being done to it. Forcing DMT into the body is to take it in isolation of all this, and I'd say that's when it causes damage.

As well as inducing mystical experiences, the kinds of effects created by spiritual practices in the Religion of the Sun are spiritually beneficial overall, whereas psychedelics can create harmful spiritual, psychological, and physical effects that hamper long-term spiritual development.

Ultimately, it's by incarnating the parts of one's higher Being, the Spiritual Son, Mother, and Father, that one's perceptions are spiritually enhanced (raising the kundalini is a part of this process). The higher energies of the Being manifesting within one's psyche and body may cause it to resonate at a higher level, thereby enabling a finer perception. I'm sure this acts on more than just the pineal gland, but on other spiritual centers in the body as well, like the heart.

The big difference is that by merging with these parts of our Being, it's not just our perceptions that are transformed, but our multidimensional psyche is fundamentally transformed also—and not just in this life, but beyond death, long after the passing chemical effect of a psychedelic has worn off.

This fundamental transformation that alters our future in the afterlife was the ultimate pursuit of ancient Egyptian religion, as it was of all those traditions of the ancient Religion of the Sun.

THE ANCIENT USE OF PSYCHEDELICS (by Lara)

As already mentioned, the use of psychedelics is common in Shamanism, a tradition we're not part of. However, there is also evidence in texts and artwork that their use was widespread across the ancient world and that they were used by some in traditions of the ancient Religion of the Sun.

In these traditions, they seem to have been used as part of a blend of substances given in a ritual drink either once or rarely, like in the Eleusinian Mysteries of Greece, and the initiatory rites of the Celts and Norse. The evidence points to this drink being given in controlled environments to create a one-off life-altering experience for prepared initiates.

A ritual drink appears in the many branches of Indo-European tradition—as awen to the Celts, mead to the Norse, haoma to the Indo-Iranians, and soma to the Indo-Aryans of India, and each had been associated with the sun (it also appears to have been used in ancient Egypt as described in the Kolbrin). This has led scholars to believe that it must have derived from a very ancient Indo-European religious tradition, before that tradition split into different branches with the migrations of Indo-European peoples to Europe, Iran, India, and elsewhere.[66] For example, it's widely believed that the Indo-Iranian haoma (of Zoroastrian religion), and the Indo-Aryan soma (of Vedic/Hindu religion) are based on the same ritual drink, which is described in some places in their texts as the juice of a plant that altered one's perception. In both traditions the knowledge of this plant was lost (or withdrawn), and a non-intoxicating plant was substituted in its place in the ritual in which it had been used. It's argued this cannot be coincidence, and that for essentially the same thing to have happened in both traditions the original plant must have been lost before they diverged. One explanation of what happened comes from the Vedic priests themselves who said the original soma wasn't lost, but that the gods had taken it with them when they had withdrawn from this wicked world at the end of the golden age,[67] and stories in the Norse and Vedic traditions tell of people trying to steal it from them.[68]

What this sounds like is that the Children of the Sun may have been the original source of the blend of ingredients that was used to induce an NDE, which they shared with initiated humans to allow them to have an experience of the otherworlds, but that they withdrew it when they saw how people had become too degenerate and would abuse it—though some knowledge of it survived in different places, perhaps for a time among the Twice Born, among the giants of Norse tradition, and in ancient stories. It's also likely that over time with the movements of people and the availability of specific plants, the ingredients of the blend changed, later incorporating more hallucinogenic ingredients, rather than those that induced an NDE. For example, soma and haoma are described as being consumed regularly in ceremonies where they produced altered perceptions. The Zoroastrian priests said the haoma intoxicant they took "goes lightly" unlike all others that "are accompanied by the Violence of the Bloody Club,"[69] though in Vedic texts the offering of soma to the gods became accompanied by animal sacrifice[70] (something the wisdom bringers of the ancient Religion of the Sun were completely opposed to[71]).

It's possible that initiates didn't even know they were taking a psychoactive substance, and that it was a strictly guarded secret held by a certain class of priests/priestesses—for example, in Norse tradition the ritual mead was guarded by the Dísir goddesses (and also by female giants), while in India the soma drink was guarded by the Dhisana goddesses, both likely deriving from the same ancient tradition of initiatic priestesses.[72] This would have given the initiate the impression they were having a real divine experience as a result of the initiatory process, when they probably weren't. It also seems that they were enacting the initiations of the path of the Spiritual Sun in the physical world without necessarily having met the grade to go through the real initiations that take place out of the body, where they are administered by divine beings.

Image next page top: What appears to be an *amanita muscaria* mushroom below three priestesses (in the top left of the image, with an arrow drawn pointing at it) on the Oseberg tapestry, which was found in a high-status Viking burial in Norway dated to AD 834. This tapestry portrays various scenes of Viking life at the time. The placement of the mushroom near the priestesses connects them to its ritual use, however, ritual serving spoons and drinking vessels found in burials have never been found to contain traces of *amanita muscaria*. The priestesses on the tapestry appear as part of a wider ritual scene; though hard to make out, a tree rises from the center of the image, and a number of men hang from it. The tree is the Norse world tree Yggdrasil, and the men are likely going through an initiation in which they are emulating Odin's hanging. As part of this, they may have been served a ritual drink of mead, which the tapestry indicates possibly contained *amanita muscaria*.[73] At some point this degenerated into human sacrifice, as there is an account of men and animals being ritually killed and hung in trees every nine years at the Temple of Uppsala in Sweden.[74]

Osiris (right) is often portrayed with his arms in this awkward position, instead of crossed over his chest (right arm over left). When I came across this photo of a cross section of the *amanita muscaria* mushroom, I found the similarities between these two images striking. People have noticed other similarities like this between psychoactive mushrooms and some ancient Egyptian art. While most are unconvincing, and there is no direct evidence for the use of psychoactive mushrooms in ancient Egypt, there's enough to suggest that at some stage psychedelics were used by some people in ancient Egyptian religious ritual.

In other traditions their use was regular and widespread. For example, the priestly class of the Maya were recorded as ingesting an intoxicating (and believed to be hallucinogenic) drink at every ritual, and using mushrooms during their gruesome rituals of bloodletting, while the general population of the Aztecs were recorded as eating wild mushrooms together en masse; they were described as going "out of their minds," and the resulting activities were an absolute horror show of extreme mass violence, cruelty, and barbarism.

Maya sculptures of psilocybin mushrooms found in Guatemala that are approximately one foot tall and date from between 1000 BC to AD 500.

The use of psychedelics appears in the archaeological record in Central America at around 1000 BC, along with the introduction of ritual decapitation, a deadly ballgame, and human sacrifice.[75] Mushrooms are found painted in scenes alongside human sacrifice,[76] and the "gods" being sacrificed to are usually depicted as monstrous looking human-animal hybrids. The crazed orgiastic festivals of the Greek god Dionysus are also believed to have been fueled by the consumption of psychoactive mushrooms mixed with wine.[77]

Image from a fourteenth-century codex belonging to the Mixtec civilization of Mexico, showing the ritual use of mushrooms, which the participant holds in their hand while crying before a monstrous deity holding a severed head.

To me this says it all. Of course, psychedelic drug use may start with what seem to be good intentions, and most casual, recreational users consider them to be harmless enough—it's a slippery slope though and even a small amount will adversely affect a person's spiritual abilities. History tells us what happens when their use becomes regular and widespread, which is when their true nature and effect becomes more apparent. One of these effects is that they can connect people to demons, and these demons then have a channel of communication open to them to start influencing people and their religion directly, leading to the adoption of demonic practices, like human sacrifice, and the depiction of gods as frightful animals, monsters, and demons.

Yet there is an idea today that the civilizations of the past with their monumental pyramids and temples and great spiritual wisdom were somehow a product of Shamanism and of taking psychedelics. However, I think the evidence presented in this book clearly demonstrates that the knowledge of the other dimensions and the afterlife found in the ancient Religion of the Sun, in places like Egypt and India, largely came from OBEs, not from psychedelic experiences, and that these OBEs were mostly due to an adherence to spiritual disciplines and from inner spiritual development.

Having OBEs in the Religion of the Sun was part of a wider knowledge, which had been inherited from a far older lost civilization that had belonged to the Children of the Sun—those who had been more psychic and seem like they had OBEs easily. The great knowledge, civilization, and monumental architecture of the past had its origin in this civilization, not in psychedelics and shamans, whose own societies have not produced the knowledge of civilization, monumental architecture, or texts of profound wisdom. The building of ancient pyramids and other megalithic structures aligned to the sun, for example, spread as part of the diffusion of the Religion of the Sun across large parts of the world by way of what we call the wisdom bringers and the Lost Civilization of the Sun. There is ample evidence to show that the major ancient civilizations arose by way of diffusion, and were not originated by local shamans, as I explain in my book *The Ancient Religion of the Sun*.

There were different kinds of OBEs people had in the ancient Religion of the Sun, as we detailed in chapter 3. We've found no evidence that they were due to psychedelics. Although there were cases in which some ingested substances, these were not originally intended to induce psychedelic experiences, but to put someone into a near-death state to enable certain kinds of OBEs (which we completely recommend against). Even the Great Pyramid appears to have been used to induce OBEs to heaven, and I don't believe anyone would have created or used such a structure if it were possible to get the same experience simply by ingesting a psychedelic (or by doing an OBE practice at home for that matter). I wonder the same about the ancient megalithic chambers in the British Isles that used huge, carefully placed stones to create the resonance of specific frequencies that help induce mystical states and experiences; why would they have gone to such lengths, if these kinds of experiences could simply be induced by psychedelics?

Looking back now, it's very difficult to piece together what happened, but based on what we've seen so far, it seems as though the Children of the Sun had greater psychic abilities and a connection to heaven which allowed them to have OBEs easily without the use of substances, particularly to higher realms. However, this connection was lost, largely it seems after interbreeding with humans. At some distant time in the past, ancient sites were built utilizing a form of technology which appears to have involved acoustics and electromagnetic energy to help induce OBEs particularly to heaven—the Great Pyramid being the greatest and probably oldest surviving example. Yet at some point it seems this technology was lost or alone wasn't enough, and a blend of substances was used to induce NDEs to heaven instead. Additionally, these ancient portal sites became used and built for the dead. Then the knowledge of the blend of substances was lost, and seems to have been substituted with psychedelics. Then, even the knowledge of what these psychedelics were, or that they had been used, was lost in most places, as they had been kept secret as part of a long tradition of initiation that was mostly destroyed or died out. However, in some places where psychedelics had been used regularly by the populace at large, as with the Aztecs and Maya, a record of them did survive, along with the absolutely heinous behavior that accompanied their use. This is a very oversimplified timeline of events, but over the course of the long history of the Religion of the Sun there does seem to have been an overall downward trend that led to psychedelics use in some cases.

Yet the wisdom bringers and great teachers that appeared at different times in the history of the Religion of the Sun such as Jesus, Osiris, and Thoth/Hermes, didn't use or advocate for the use of psychedelics, and had OBEs and mystical experiences without the use of substances—rather they taught about spiritual, inner change as the means to learn about reality and connect with the divine. And they left behind enough information to allow us to learn to travel naturally to the otherworlds, as they once did and taught.

CHAPTER TWENTY-NINE

Spiritual Practice and the Misconception of Supernatural Powers

Some might have the idea that the more OBEs someone has, the more spiritually advanced they are, and that the ability to astral project is a kind of special, supernatural ability.

Belief in the connection between spiritual progress and the ability to have OBEs may have originated in Hinduism, where lists of supernatural powers, called *siddhis*, are said to naturally arise in those who become proficient in forms of yogic practice. The ability to have OBEs is not mentioned explicitly as one of them, but some *siddhis* can be interpreted as referring to it—particularly one of the eight classical *siddhis* called *prapti*, which is "the ability to access any place in the world," and another called *manojavah*, which is "moving the body wherever thought goes." Some of the other *siddhis* sound more like things one can do while out of their body in the astral plane.[1]

One of the oldest lists of *siddhis* comes from the Yoga Sutras of Patanjali—a Hindu text I discussed in more detail in chapter 15. It describes how they are gained, saying:

> "Siddhis (extraordinary powers) are either revealed at birth, or acquired through drugs, repeating a mantra, or self-discipline, or Samadhi."[2]

That is to say, in their view, someone can be born with certain supernatural abilities, these abilities can be experienced while taking drugs, can be stimulated by repeating mantras, gained temporarily through practice, or experienced while in a certain advanced meditative state.

The text also makes the important point that *siddhis* arise naturally with practice, but are not necessary to achieving liberation, and are even impediments to it, as they can become a source of attachment and pride[3]—and I have seen many fall prey to this.

Those who've taken the way of darkness can also have OBEs through some of these methods—namely through mantras, drugs (and ingesting other substances), and practice—but also with the help of demons in the astral who take them out of their bodies.

In my experience, I've seen that people have OBEs mostly due to two things, which are one, the amount of practice done, and two, help from spiritual beings (or from demons for those aligned with dark forces). Involuntary OBEs can also happen when caused by trauma, such as death or severe illness.

The number of OBEs we have is not an indicator of spiritual progress. It just means that we've practiced more, or have been given more spiritual help. If we do make spiritual progress, it doesn't equate to having more OBEs either—we still need practice and help from spiritual beings to be able to have conscious OBEs. Most people can have OBEs fairly regularly so long as they are dedicated enough in their practices.

We can progress spiritually even if our time is taken with other spiritual related activities that prevent us from spending enough time to have OBEs. We have to live a life in which we learn about ourselves, and that means working, shopping, planning, and all the things life involves—none of which are practicing for OBEs and thus will result in few or no OBEs, but that's how things can be. Spending time helping others usually involves giving up time for nonessential practice, like OBE practice, and this again means we can have less OBEs.

We can however make time for practice and have periods of time, either long or short, that we more or less dedicate to spiritual practice and having OBEs. For example, a short time could be a weekend program, a longer one could be going on a purpose-designed retreat, and longer still could be staying in a retreat-like situation for some time or organizing our life to be like one as much as possible. Once these dedicated times are over, our level of OBEs will usually go back to what it was before we started, as I said, even if we have made inner spiritual progress.

I want to make this clear so that a fantasy is not created where we think we should be having OBEs more than is realistically possible. For those who are interested in spirituality, that idea can lead to misery, as we never reach the number of experiences we think we should have. Having negative feelings like that is far more harmful than not having OBEs, as negative feelings drag our inner level down, making it harder to observe and eliminate our egos, which is far more important to spiritual progress than OBEs. It's also usually harmful for someone's spiritual progress to abandon whatever duties they may have toward helping others spiritually to have OBEs instead, as it then becomes more of a self-gratifying activity. I want to reiterate that not having OBEs does not mean you aren't making spiritual progress; if you're not having OBEs, look into your dreams for indicators of your spiritual state.

The aim of acquiring psychic or supernatural powers can easily be an egocentric activity that can lead to self-deception. A worthy spiritual aim is instead increasing one's true goodness and attaining liberation. Being able to levitate and see things at a distance could be seen as useful tools of spiritual beings, but they are also things that evil people or beings can like to do, whereas attaining goodness and liberation are not.

Demons use people's wishes for powers to entrap them in evil or to use them for evil purposes. A person enabled with dark powers like this can, either unconsciously or consciously, lead others astray. Satanism is awash with acquiring power or powers because of the tendency for people to desire them. Many people are impressed by dark powers, and can be confused or deceived as to their origin. In this way dark forces infiltrate places of light, causing many religious activities to be merged with darkness, ruining them. This has happened a lot in the past, for example with the dark practices in Tibetan Buddhism and Bon, and in Baal worship in the Levant (Baal is a demon).

By aligning ourselves with divine laws and changing inwardly, we make use of OBEs for spiritual purposes, and we discard the darkness and contribute to the light, and so receive its protection.

CHAPTER THIRTY

Having Out-of-Body Experiences for a Spiritual Purpose

I'll finish this book by restating that OBEs and dreams are best used for spiritual purposes. Based on their records and beliefs, it's clear that numerous ancient cultures knew of the existence of the fifth dimension and used it, and they did so not for pleasure or entertainment, but as a means of acquiring spiritual knowledge to assist them in their understanding of the afterlife and their purpose for living, and to bring back knowledge to help people here. I propose a return to this ancient way of learning for everyone interested in discovering profound truths in relation to our existence.

Many of these ancient peoples used OBEs within a similar context, which emerges as we study their writings, traditions, artwork, and sacred sites.

That context had the Spiritual Sun at its center, with the physical sun being a manifestation of a more spiritual one in the higher dimensions, which is why we call it the Religion of the Sun.

It contained a vast cosmology of deities, values, and processes such as karma and reincarnation. The purpose of living was to reach salvation/liberation. This book is really just a beginning in terms of a look into some of the beliefs of that religion and the means it used to explore reality.

In OBEs, knowledge is revealed in stages according to our capacity to understand it and according to our inner spiritual level. This is why although many can learn to travel in the fifth dimension, some on a fairly regular basis, few ever receive profound spiritual knowledge, or receive the kind of knowledge reserved for actual initiates. To do that requires much more than learning how to consciously project out of the body. It requires initiation into the mysteries by spiritual beings in the otherworld, and that's not easy to do.

Yet no matter what level someone is at, as long as they are sincere, they can receive messages and knowledge from spiritual beings and their own Being that can help them enormously. As they were depicted in the ancient Religion of the Sun, spiritual beings fulfill many different roles, and work to maintain the processes of life, death, and learning, giving much help to those who wish to learn and change for the better.

And it's this kind of spiritual knowledge that ultimately matters, as we're only here for a relatively short time and will one day take the results of our lives to the afterlife.

The spiritual is inescapable in near-death experiences, which is when OBEs are at their clearest and most objective. The spiritual is inescapable for everyone, since life here is temporary and everyone passes into the next world. It makes sense then to try to have direct contact with the otherworld, to see that it's there, to know what awaits us, and to find out how to change our course for the better. And, as I hope I've explained clearly enough in this book, it is to a large extent our dreams and OBEs that provide us with the means to do this.

Out-of-body travel helps us to understand our purpose in living and allows us to see that we exist in a phenomenal multidimensional universe. It also provides us with much needed contact with spiritual beings and supports us in so many ways in our spiritual journey.

PUBLISHER'S NOTE

The authors have worked very hard for over two and a half years to put together this book, and the utmost has been done to ensure all sources are fully referenced and credited. It contains unique and original work, which is breaking new ground in its field, and the authors should be properly credited if this work is used elsewhere.

In academia, there are rigorous standards and expectations requiring proper attribution when drawing upon the work of others. Outside this field, however, there often seems to be a "free for all" kind of attitude and plagiarism is rife.

Yet stealing is not ok, whether it is of physical items, a passage of writing, or something more intangible like an idea or a body of research—all of these things have cost their owner in time and effort. It's unethical and intellectually dishonest to present the ideas and research of another as if it were one's own.

If you have seen any work from this book that has been used without proper attribution, please let us know by contacting us, the publisher, through our website suraondrunar.org

HOW TO CITE THIS WORK

If you would like to use this book as a source in your own work, at a minimum please include a reference to the authors' names, the book title, and where applicable, the relevant page number(s) for any content or ideas referred to. In informal internet mediums like blog posts and online videos, a hyperlink back to the original source should also be provided where possible.

In formal publications, full citations should be used that follow any industry-recognized style guide. Here is an example of a formal citation of this book:

Atwood, Mark and Lara Atwood. *The Spiritual Out-of-Body Experience: The Practice of OBEs and Lucid Dreaming in the Ancient Religion of the Sun*. First edition. Sura Ondrunar Publishing, 2024, p. [Insert page number(s) where applicable].

References and Copyright Acknowledgments

TEXT REFERENCES

PREFACE

1. "Plagiarism." Legal Information Institute. Updated August, 2022. https://www.law.cornell.edu/wex/plagiarism.

CHAPTER ONE

1. Blackmore, Susan A. "A Postal Survey of OBEs and Other Experiences." *Journal of the Society for Psychical Research* 52, no. 796 (February 1984): 225. http://www.susanblackmore.uk/wp-content/uploads/2017/05/JSPR-1984.pdf.
2. "Lucid Dream." Wikipedia. https://en.wikipedia.org/wiki/Lucid_dream.
3. Sheils, Dean. "A Cross-Cultural Study of Beliefs in Out-of-the-Body Experiences, Waking and Sleeping." *Journal of the Society for Psychical Research* 49, no. 775 (1978): 697-741. https://psycnet.apa.org/record/1979-27510-001.
4. Tucker, Reed. "5% Have Had a Near-Death Experience—And They Say It Made Life Worth Living." New York Post, Updated February 20, 2021. https://nypost.com/article/five-percent-have-had-near-death-experiences-research.
5. Spink Health. "One in Ten People Have 'Near-Death' Experiences, According to New Study." EurekAlert!, June 28, 2019. https://www.eurekalert.org/news-releases/894649.

CHAPTER TWO

1. Miller, J. Steeve. *Near-Death Experiences as Evidence for the Existence of God and Heaven: A Brief Introduction in Plain Language*. Wisdom Creek Press, LLC, 2012.

CHAPTER THREE

1. Siracusa, Philip. "Fourteen Year Old Crosses Over; Gets Taught about Negative Thoughts during NDE." YouTube, August 13, 2022, 0:40-5:50. https://youtu.be/-h_5uX-Kd2Q&t=40.
2. Atwood, Lara. *The Ancient Religion of the Sun: The Wisdom Bringers and The Lost Civilization of the Sun*. 2nd ed. Sura Ondrunar Publishing, 2021, p. 31-41.
3. Dungen, Wim van den. "Amduat: The Book of the Hidden Chamber - Book of What Is in the Duat." Sofiatopia, 2012. http://www.maat.sofiatopia.org/amduat.htm.
4. "Duat." Wikipedia. https://en.wikipedia.org/wiki/Duat.
5. Ibid.
6. Hancock, Graham, and Robert Bauval. *The Message of the Sphinx: A Quest for the Hidden Legacy of Mankind*. New York: Three Rivers Press, 1996, p. 140.

7. "Pyramid of Djoser—Burial Chamber." Wikipedia. https://en.wikipedia.org/wiki/Pyramid_of_Djoser#Burial_chamber.
8. "Ancient Egyptian Conception of the Soul." Wikipedia. https://en.wikipedia.org/wiki/Ancient_Egyptian_conception_of_the_soul.
9. Allen, James P., trans. *The Ancient Egyptian Pyramid Texts*. 2nd ed. Atlanta, Georgia: SBL Press, 2015, p. 1-2, 5-8, 10-12. https://www.sbl-site.org/assets/pdfs/pubs/061538p-front.pdf.
10. Morrow, Susan Brind. *The Dawning Moon of the Mind: Unlocking the Pyramid Texts*. Farrar, Straus and Giroux, 2015, p. 103, Kindle edition.
11. Ibid., 121.
12. Ibid., 127.
13. Ibid., 122.
14. Ibid., 116.
15. Ibid., 125.
16. Ibid., 136.
17. Ibid., 139-140.
18. Ibid., 117.
19. Whiteman, Yvonne. "Guide to the Kolbrin." GrahamHancock.com, October 17, 2015. https://grahamhancock.com/whitemany1.
20. Atwood, *Ancient Religion of the Sun*, 42-43.
21. "The Scroll of Herakat." In *The Kolbrin*. The Culdian Trust, 2014, p. 229. eBook.
22. Hancock and Bauval, *Message of the Sphinx*, 143.
23. Allen, *The Ancient Egyptian Pyramid Texts*, 4.
24. Atwood, Mark, with Lara Atwood. A*ncient Solstice: Uncovering the Spiritual Meaning of the Solstices and Equinoxes*. Updated 4th ed. Sura Ondrunar Publishing, 2021, p. 89-93.
25. Atwood, *Ancient Religion of the Sun*, 31-38.
26. Hancock and Bauval, *Message of the Sphinx*, 151.
27. *The Kolbrin*, "The Way of Yosira," 127.
28. Ibid., 112.
29. "Aaru." Wikipedia. https://en.wikipedia.org/wiki/Aaru.
30. Allen, *The Ancient Egyptian Pyramid Texts*, 9, 11, 16.
31. Dungen, "Amduat."
32. "Aker (Deity)." Wikipedia. https://en.wikipedia.org/wiki/Aker_(deity).
33. Atwood, *Ancient Religion of the Sun*, 345-349.
34. Morrow, *Dawning Moon of the Mind*, 27-28, 30.
35. Dash, Glen. "Solar Alignments of Giza." *AERAgram* 12, no. 2 (Fall 2011). https://www.academia.edu/10080181/The_Solar_Alignments_of_Giza.
36. Atwood with Atwood, *Ancient Solstice*, 339.
37. Ibid., see chapter 5: "Decoding the Ancient Meaning of the Sphinx and its Origin as Anubis."
38. Gigal, Antoine. "An Undiscovered Sphinx of Giza, Part I." Gigal Research, October 2010. https://gigalresearch.com/uk/publications-sphinx-secret.php.
39. Maged, Ahmed. "There Could Have Been Two Sphinxes, Argues One Researcher." Daily News Egypt, Updated August 7, 2015. https://www.dailynewsegypt.com/2007/08/28/there-could-have-been-two-sphinxes-argues-one-researcher.
40. Atwood with Atwood, *Ancient Solstice*, 93-96.
41. Dungen, "Amduat."
42. Hancock and Bauval, *Message of the Sphinx*, 153.
43. Ibid., 73-74, 88, 144.
44. Ibid., 153.
45. Dungen, "Amduat."
46. Hill, J. "Great Pyramid: 'Air Shafts.'" Ancient Egypt Online, 2010. https://ancientegyptonline.co.uk/pyramid-air-shafts.
47. David, Rosalie. *Religion and Magic in Ancient Egypt*. Penguin UK, 2002, p. 97.

48. Faulkner, R. O., trans. *The Ancient Egyptian Pyramid Texts*. Oxford: Clarendon Press, 1969, line 1657, p. 247. In Hancock and Bauval, *Message of the Sphinx*, 232.
49. Ibid., lines 1713-17. In Hancock and Bauval, *Message of the Sphinx*, 116.
50. Ibid., lines 798-803, p. 144. In Hancock and Bauval, *Message of the Sphinx*, 237.
51. Ibid., utterance 610, p. 279. In Hancock and Bauval, *Message of the Sphinx*, 141.
52. Ibid., line 852. In Hancock and Bauval, *Message of the Sphinx*, 116.
53. Ibid., line 907. In Hancock and Bauval, *Message of the Sphinx*, 116.
54. Hancock and Bauval, *Message of the Sphinx*, 116.
55. Allen, *The Ancient Egyptian Pyramid Texts*, 9-11.
56. Allen, James P., trans. *The Ancient Egyptian Pyramid Texts*. Atlanta, Georgia: Society of Biblical Literature, 2005, recitation 196, p. 80.
57. Hancock and Bauval, *Message of the Sphinx*, 143-145.
58. Allen, *The Ancient Egyptian Pyramid Texts*, 10-11.
59. "Great Sphinx of Giza." Wikipedia. https://en.wikipedia.org/wiki/Great_Sphinx_of_Giza.
60. Temple, Robert, with Olivia Temple. *The Sphinx Mystery*. Inner Traditions, 2009, chapter 4.
61. Ibid., 289-290.
62. Atwood with Atwood, *Ancient Solstice*, 217-219.
63. Allen, *The Ancient Egyptian Pyramid Texts*, 11-12.
64. Hancock and Bauval, *Message of the Sphinx*, 143-145.
65. Allen, *The Ancient Egyptian Pyramid Texts*, 4-5.
66. "Utterance 222." Based on translations by Faulkner, R. O. *The Ancient Egyptian Pyramid Texts*. Oxford University Press, 1969; Piankoff, Alexandre. *The Pyramid of Unas*. Princeton University Press, 1968; Speleers, Louis. *Les Textes des Pyramides Egyptiennes*. Gand: I. Vanderpoorten, 1923. Pyramid Texts Online. http://www.pyramidtextsonline.com/translation.html.
67. Allen, *The Ancient Egyptian Pyramid Texts*, 10-12, 16.
68. Weyburne, Kyle. "An Investigation into the Purpose of the Southern Shaft of the King's Chamber of the Great Pyramid." *Palarch's Journal of Archaeology of Egypt/Egyptology* 18, no. 4 (February 2021). https://archives.palarch.nl/index.php/jae/article/view/6706.
69. Allen, James P. "Why a Pyramid? Pyramid Religion." In *The Treasures of the Pyramids*, edited by Zahi Hawass, Italy: White Star, 2003, p. 27. https://gizamedia.rc.fas.harvard.edu/documents/allen_treasures_022-027.pdf.
70. Hancock and Bauval, *Message of the Sphinx*, 116.
71. Dunn, Christopher. *The Giza Power Plant: Technologies of Ancient Egypt*. Bear & Company, August 1, 1998, chapter 7, Kindle edition.
72. Ibid., chap. 13.
73. Balezin, Mikhail, Kseniia V. Baryshnikova, Polina Kapitanova, and Andrey B. Evlyukhin. "Electromagnetic Properties of the Great Pyramid: First Multipole Resonances and Energy Concentration." *Journal of Applied Physics* 124, no. 3 (July 21, 2018). https://aip.scitation.org/doi/10.1063/1.5026556.
74. Danley, Tom. "The Great Pyramid: Early Reflections and Ancient Echoes." ProSoundWeb, August 4, 2020. https://www.prosoundweb.com/the-great-pyramid-early-reflections-ancient-echoes.
75. Dunn, *Giza Power Plant*, chap. 8.
76. "Coptic Chant." Encyclopedia Britannica. https://www.britannica.com/art/Coptic-chant.
77. Collins, Andrew. *The Cygnus Key: The Denisovan Legacy, Göbekli Tepe, and the Birth of Egypt*. Bear & Company, May 15, 2018, chapter 20, Kindle edition.
78. Ibid., chap. 20-21.
79. Ibid., 176-177.
80. "Gregorian Chant." Wikipedia. https://en.wikipedia.org/wiki/Gregorian_chant.
81. Dunn, Christopher. *Lost Technologies of Ancient Egypt: Advanced Engineering in the Temples of the Pharaohs*. Illustrated ed. Rochester, Vermont: Bear & Company, June 24, 2010, chapter 6 and p. 262-276.
82. Dunn, *Giza Power Plant*, chap. 4.

83. "About Chris Dunn." GIZAPOWER The Official Website of Christopher Dunn. https://www.gizapower.com/CPDBio.htm.
84. Dunn, *Giza Power Plant*, chap. 3.
85. Dunn, *Lost Technologies of Ancient Egypt*, chap. 6 and p. 333-334.
86. UnchartedX. "Astonishing Results! More Ancient Egyptian Granite Vases Analyzed! More STL's Available." YouTube, November 1, 2023. https://youtu.be/QzFMDS6dkWU.
87. UnchartedX. "Scanning a Predynastic Granite Vase to 1000th of an Inch—Changing the Game for Ancient Precision!" YouTube, January 28, 2023. https://youtu.be/WAyQQRNoQaE.
88. Dunn, *Giza Power Plant*, chap. 8.
89. *The Kolbrin*, "The Scroll of Thotis," 421-422.
90. "Electrum." Wikipedia. https://en.wikipedia.org/wiki/Electrum.
91. Conte, Michael. "Pentagon Officially Releases UFO Videos." CNN, Updated April 29, 2020. https://ww.cnn.com/2020/04/27/politics/pentagon-ufo-videos/index.html.
92. See the Disclosure Project led by Dr. Steven Greer, and the latest U.S. government whistleblower testimony from David Grusch.
93. "Great Pyramid of Giza." Wikipedia. https://en.wikipedia.org/wiki/Great_Pyramid_of_Giza.
94. "Earth Mass." Wikipedia. https://en.wikipedia.org/wiki/Earth_mass.
95. Dunn, *Giza Power Plant*, chap. 8.
96. Spivey, Robin. "The Great Pyramid's Conspicuous Speed of Light Latitude Is No Accident." ResearchGate, August, 2016. https://dx.doi.org/10.13140/RG.2.2.10731.36645.
97. Dunn, *Giza Power Plant*, chap. 8.
98. Morrow, *Dawning Moon of the Mind*, 46-47, 127, 282.
99. "Pi." Wikipedia. https://en.wikipedia.org/wiki/Pi.
100. Spivey, "Great Pyramid's Conspicuous Speed of Light Latitude Is No Accident."
101. Proctor, Richard A. *The Great Pyramid: Observatory, Tomb, and Temple*. London: Longmans, Green, and Co., 1888, p. 71-77.
102. Davidson, D., and H. Aldersmith. *The Great Pyramid: Its Divine Message, Vol. I. Pyramid Records*. London: William Rider and Son Limited, 1961, p. 129-137.
103. This study argues that the pyramids were either intended to align to Orion or to Cygnus, but we wonder if they were intended to align to both, and this may explain why neither alignment is exact so that both could be reasonably accurate. The Cygnus alignment as seen from the ground is only explored by the study authors as occurring during the so-called "pyramid age," which is when the Great Pyramids are believed to have been constructed in mainstream Egyptology, at around 2,500 BC. It would have also occurred tens of thousands of years earlier as per precession, but still thousands of years apart from other astronomical alignments to Orion and Leo. And yet all these alignments seem to have been intended, but why so far apart we just don't know. See: Hale, Rodney, and Andrew Collins. "A Study of the Simple Geometrical Relationship of the Main Monuments of Giza and a Possible Connection to Stars." *Archaeological Discovery* 4, no. 2 (April, 2016): 87-102. https://dx.doi.org/10.4236/ad.2016.42007.
104. Collins, Andrew. "The Mystery of Dwn-'Nwy and Its Identification and Role in Ancient Egyptian Astronomy." AndrewCollins.com, April 5, 2007. https://www.andrewcollins.com/page/articles/dwn_nwy.htm.
105. Allen, *The Ancient Egyptian Pyramid Texts*, 12-13.
106. Collins, "The Mystery of Dwn-'Nwy."
107. Dash, Glen. "How the Pyramid Builders May Have Found Their True North." *AERAgram* 14, no. 1 (Spring 2013): 8-14. https://www.academia.edu/4035001/How_the_Pyramid_Builders_May_Have_Found_Their_True_North.
108. "When Was the Giza Complex Constructed—Archaeo-Astronomy at Giza." Ancient-Wisdom. http://www.ancient-wisdom.com/Ghizawhen.htm#6.4.
109. "Egyptian Pyramids." Wikipedia. https://en.wikipedia.org/wiki/Egyptian_pyramids.
110. Elsis, Mark R. "The Great Pyramid of Giza Encodes the Speed of Light at Least Six Different Ways." GreatPyramidofGiza.net, September 11, 2022. https://greatpyramidofgiza.net.
111. Temple with Temple, *The Sphinx Mystery*, 366-380.
112. Temple, Robert. *Egyptian Dawn*. London: Random House, 2010, p. 17-42.
113. Collins, *The Cygnus Key*, chap. 18-19.

114. Creighton, Scott, and Gary Osborn. "The Great Pyramid and the Axis of the Earth – Part 2." GrahamHancock.com, December 5, 2008. https://grahamhancock.com/creightons4.
115. Morrow, *Dawning Moon of the Mind*, 115.
116. For example, see the NDEs of Vincent Colman and Rosemary Thornton: Next Level Soul Podcast. "Clinically Dead Forty-Five Minutes! Meets God, Then Wakes up in a Body Bag—Chilling NDE | Vincent Tolman." YouTube, March 7, 2023, 29:40-31:46. https://youtu.be/CmrWT6D8oNk&t=1780; The Other Side NDE. "Woman Dies and Gets Shown the Power of Intention during Miraculous NDE." YouTube, September 6, 2022, 11:28-13:00. https://youtu.be/6NgAT-QVF-w&t=688.
117. We document numerous sites that were aligned to the sun at the solstices and/or equinoxes in our book *Ancient Solstice*.
118. "Robert Monroe." Wikipedia. https://en.wikipedia.org/wiki/Robert_Monroe.
119. *The Kolbrin*, "The Annexed Scroll - 2," 445.
120. Dunn, *Giza Power Plant*, chap. 12.
121. Atwood, *Ancient Religion of the Sun*, 65-71, 76-78.
122. *The Kolbrin*, "The Rolls of Record - 7," 315-316.
123. Ibid., "The Scroll of Herakat," 229.
124. Ibid., "The Brotherhood," 242.
125. Whiteman, Yvonne. "The Kolbrin on Immortality: How Egypt Regained the Secret of the Ages." GrahamHancock.com, January 29, 2019. https://grahamhancock.com/whitemany9.
126. *The Kolbrin*, "The Hibsathy," 235, 238, 240.
127. Whiteman, "Osiris the Great One."
128. Whiteman, "The Kolbrin on Immortality."
129. See my book *Ancient Solstice*.
130. *The Kolbrin*, "The Hibsathy," 238.
131. Ibid., "Hurmentar Journeys to the Netherworld," 99.
132. See "The Children of the Sun" in Atwood, *Ancient Religion of the Sun*.
133. Eliade, Mircea. *Shamanism – Archaic Techniques of Ecstasy*, translated by Williard R. Trask. Princeton University Press, 1964, p. 130, 133, 250 (in book it appears as 260 because of a typo), 265, 286, 441, 482-486.
134. Mei, Armando. *36.400 A.C.: Il Segreto degli Dèi*. Casa Editrice Amazon, 2018.
135. GeoCosmic REX. "Sphinx Quarry Erosion from Floods? / Durable Civilization? -Cosmography101-32.3 Randall Carlson '08." YouTube, November 2008. https://youtu.be/IwVcNlykoVs.
136. Atwood, *Ancient Religion of the Sun*, 31-35.
137. Cooper, Alan, Chris Turney, Jonathan M. Palmer, et al. "A Global Environmental Crisis Forty-Two Thousand Years Ago." *Science* 371, no. 6531 (February 19, 2021): 811-818. https://science.sciencemag.org/content/371/6531/811.
138. "Hermeticism." Wikipedia. https://en.wikipedia.org/wiki/Hermeticism.
139. Copenhaver, Brian P., trans. *Hermetica: The Greek Corpus Hermeticum and the Latin Asclepius in a New English Translation, with Notes and Introduction*. Reprint ed. Cambridge University Press, October 12, 1995, Kindle edition.
140. Salaman, Clement, Dorine Van Oyen, William D. Wharton, and Jean-Pierre Mahe, trans. *The Way of Hermes: New Translations of The Corpus Hermeticum and The Definitions of Hermes Trismegistus to Asclepius*. Rochester: Inner Traditions, 2004, book 1, p. 17.
141. "Poimandres." Wikipedia. https://en.wikipedia.org/wiki/Poimandres.
142. Hanegraaff, Wouter J. "Hermetic Spirituality." In *Hermetic Spirituality and the Historical Imagination: Altered States of Knowledge in Late Antiquity*. Cambridge: Cambridge University Press, 2022, p. 11–22.
143. Copenhaver, trans., *Hermetica*, 7.
144. Salaman et al., trans., *The Way of Hermes*, book 13, p. 65-66.
145. Ibid., book 13, p. 66.
146. Atwood, *Ancient Religion of the Sun*, 66-67.
147. Ibid., 25-31.
148. Easwaran, Eknath, trans. *The Upanishads*. Tomales: Nilgiri Press, 2007, p. 109.
149. "Kosha." Wikipedia. https://en.wikipedia.org/wiki/Kosha.

150. V, Jayaram. "Hinduism, Life after Death and Planes of Existence." Hinduwebsite.com. https://www.hinduwebsite.com/heavenhell.asp.
151. V, Jayaram. "Akasa, Ether or the Sky and the Fifth Element." Hinduwebsite.com. https://www.hinduwebsite.com/hinduism/concepts/akasa.asp.
152. "Yoga Vasistha." Wikipedia. https://en.wikipedia.org/wiki/Yoga_Vasistha.
153. Aiyer, K. Narayanaswami, trans. *Laghu-Yoga-Vasishta*. Madras, India: The Adyar Library and Research Centre, 1971, p. 68-69.
154. Aiyer, trans., *Laghu-Yoga-Vasishta*, 74-77.
155. "Chapter XXIII. The Aerial Journey of Spiritual Bodies." In Mitra, Vihari-Lala, trans. *The Yoga-Vasishtha Maharamayana of Valmiki, Vol. 1*. Delhi, India: Low Price Publications, 1999, p. 4-16, Kindle locations 7680-7681, Kindle edition. https://www.gutenberg.org/ebooks/71326.
156. "Chapter XL. Reflections on Human Life and Mind." In Ibid., 62-64, Kindle locations 9100-9105.
157. Ibid., 23-24, Kindle locations 9029-9031.
158. "Chapter XXVIII. Section I. Exposition of Lílá's Vision." In Ibid., 1, 2, 9-10, 13-14, Kindle Locations 8070-8091.
159. "Chapter XXI. Guide to Peace." In Ibid., 1-4, Kindle locations 7480-7485.
160. "Yoga Vasistha." Wikipedia.
161. "Mahabharata." Wikipedia. https://en.wikipedia.org/wiki/Mahabharata.
162. "Brahmamuhurta." Wikipedia. https://en.wikipedia.org/wiki/Brahmamuhurta.
163. Ganguli, Kisari Mohan, trans. "Book 7: Sections LXXX and LXXXI" in *The Mahabharata*. Calcutta: Bharata Press (Pratep Chandra Roy), 1883-1896. https://sacred-texts.com/hin/m07/m07077.htm, https://sacred-texts.com/hin/m07/m07078.htm.
164. Nadumuri, Jijith. "Astras." AncientVoice, Updated Dec 10, 2011. http://ancientvoice.wikidot.com/feedbacks:astras.
165. Misra, Bibhu Dev. "The Vimanas and Aerial Cities Described in the Ancient Indian Texts." Ancient Inquiries, September 21, 2022. https://www.bibhudevmisra.com/2022/09/the-vimanas-and-aerial-cities-described.html.
166. Purkayastha, Moushumi, and Kanchan Kumar Mukherjee. "Three Cases of Near-Death Experience: Is It Physiology, Physics, or Philosophy?." *Annals of Neurosciences* 19, no. 3 (July, 2012): 104-106. https://www.ncbi.nlm.nih.gov/pmc/articles/PMC4117086.
167. Rangasthalam. "I Astral Traveled and Met Lord Shiva." Spiritual Forums, March 15, 2018. https://www.spiritualforums.com/vb/showthread.php?t=121350.
168. "Mandukya Upanishad." Wikipedia. https://en.wikipedia.org/wiki/Mandukya_Upanishad.
169. Easwaran, trans., *The Upanishads*, 204.
170. V, Jayaram. "Shiva Sutras, the Aphorisms of Shiva." Hinduwebsite.com. Sections 3-20, 3-38. https://www.hinduwebsite.com/siva/shiva-sutras.asp.
171. V, Jayaram. "Attaining Oneness with Shiva." Hinduwebsite.com. https://www.hinduwebsite.com/siva/attaining-oneness-with-shiva.asp.
172. "Practice in Kashmir Shaivism." Lakshmanjoo Academy. https://www.lakshmanjooacademy.org/practice.
173. Abhinavagupta, *Tantrasara of Abhinavagupta*, translated by H. N. Chakravarty, edited by Boris Marjanovic. Portland, Oregon: Rudra Press, 2012, p. 72, 80-84.
174. "Abhinavagupta." New World Encyclopedia. https://www.newworldencyclopedia.org/entry/Abhinavagupta.
175. Chakravarty, H. N. In Abhinavagupta, *Tantrasara of Abhinavagupta*, 37-38.
176. Das, Tom. "Deep Sleep Is Brahman—The Three States According to the Birhadaranyaka Upanishad with Commentary by Shankara." Tom Das, February 19, 2021. https://tomdas.com/2021/02/19/deep-sleep-is-brahman-the-three-states-according-to-the-birhadaranyaka-upanishad-with-commentary-by-shankara.
177. Easwaran, trans., *The Upanishads*, 111.
178. Ibid., 150.
179. Ibid., 203-204.
180. Ganguli, trans., Book 1: Section XXI in *The Mahabharata*.
181. "Yoga Nidra." Wikipedia. https://en.wikipedia.org/wiki/Yoga_nidra.

182. Parker, Stephen. "Chapter 11—Training Attention for Conscious Non-REM Sleep: The Yogic Practice of Yoga-Nidrā and Its Implications for Neuroscience Research." *Progress in Brain Research* 244 (2019): 255-272. https://doi.org/10.1016/bs.pbr.2018.10.016.
183. Maharshi, Sri Ramana. *Talks with Sri Ramana Maharshi*. Sri Ramanasramam, Tiruvannamalai, 1955. In "Ramana Maharshi: The Method of Wakeful Sleep (Jagrat Sushupti) to Attain Liberation." Tom Das, April 26, 2019. https://tomdas.com/2019/04/26/ramana-maharshi-the-method-of-wakeful-sleep-jagrat-sushupti-to-attain-liberation.
184. Ganguli, trans., Book 12: Section CCLXXV in *The Mahabharata*.
185. "Deep Nidra Experiences?." Reddit, April 28, 2020. https://www.reddit.com/r/YogaNidra/comments/g9oigk/deep_nidra_experiences.
186. "Yoga Nidra Session Experience." Reddit, September 14, 2018. https://www.reddit.com/r/yoga/comments/9ft0gk/yoga_nidra_session_experience.
187. Sioni, Pinelopi. "Confused about Yoga Nidra: A Personal Story." English Yoga Berlin, January 20, 2013. https://www.englishyogaberlin.com/confused-about-yoga-nidra-a-personal-story.
188. For example, see RosalieYoga. "Guided Astral Projection | Yoga Nidra | Mind Awake Body Asleep." YouTube, April 12, 2022. https://youtu.be/ab0vVYerffE.
189. Stumbrys, Tadas, and Daniel Erlacher. "Lucid Dreaming during NREM Sleep: Two Case Reports." *International Journal of Dream Research* 5, no. 2 (2012): 151-155. https://journals.ub.uni-heidelberg.de/index.php/IJoDR/article/download/9483/pdf_30/10929.
190. Aalto University. "Dreaming Also Occurs during Non Rapid Eye Movement Sleep." ScienceDaily, August 9, 2016. https://www.sciencedaily.com/releases/2016/08/160809121817.htm.
191. Yirka, Bob. "New Research Suggests We Also Dream during Non-REM Sleep Cycles." Medical Xpress, April 11, 2017. https://medicalxpress.com/news/2017-04-non-rem.html.
192. Bucklin, Stephanie. "The Mysteries of 'Dreamless Sleep' Come to Light." Live Science, November 8, 2016. https://www.livescience.com/56788-dreamless-sleep-consciousness-states.html.
193. Atwood, *Ancient Religion of the Sun*, 92-93.
194. "Axis Mundi." Wikipedia. https://en.wikipedia.org/wiki/Axis_mundi.
195. Reymond, Eve A. E. *The Mythical Origin of the Egyptian Temple*. Manchester: Manchester University Press, 1969, p. 71, 76, 83, 86.
196. "Ancient Egyptian Creation Myths." Wikipedia. https://en.wikipedia.org/wiki/Ancient_Egyptian_creation_myths.
197. "Benben." Wikipedia. https://en.wikipedia.org/wiki/Benben.
198. Frawley, David. *Gods, Sages and Kings*. Twin Lakes, WI: Lotus Press, 1991, p. 226.
199. "The Bhagavadgita—Cosmogony." Encyclopedia Britannica. https://www.britannica.com/topic/Hinduism/The-Bhagavadgita#ref405106.
200. "Egyptian Pyramids." Wikipedia. https://en.wikipedia.org/wiki/Egyptian_pyramids.
201. "Benben." Wikipedia.
202. "Egyptian Pyramids." Wikipedia.
203. "Bennu." Wikipedia. https://en.wikipedia.org/wiki/Bennu.
204. Mark, Joshua J. "Egyptian Obelisk." World History Encyclopedia, November 6, 2016. https://www.worldhistory.org/Egyptian_Obelisk.
205. "Obelisk." Encyclopedia Britannica. https://www.britannica.com/technology/obelisk.
206. Temple, Robert. "Lost Technology of the Ancients: The Crystal Sun." *New Dawn* 65 (March-April, 2001). https://www.newdawnmagazine.com/articles/lost-technology-of-the-ancients-the-crystal-sun.
207. Temple with Temple, *The Sphinx Mystery*, 367.
208. Ibid., 142, 395-401.
209. Ibid., 397, 398, 408.
210. Wilkinson, Richard H. *Symbol & Magic in Egyptian Art*. New York: Thames & Hudson, 1994, p. 66, quoted in Mark, "Egyptian Obelisk."
211. "Djed." Wikipedia. https://en.wikipedia.org/wiki/Djed.
212. Hancock and Bauval, *Message of the Sphinx*, 151.
213. "Kesh Temple Hymn." Wikipedia. https://en.wikipedia.org/wiki/Kesh_temple_hymn.
214. Atwood, *Ancient Religion of the Sun*, 303.

215. Joe, Jimmy. "Abzu God: The Mysterious Ancient Deity That Resided beneath the Earth." Timeless Myths. https://www.timelessmyths.com/mythology/abzu-god.
216. *The Kesh Temple Hymn: Translation*. The Electronic Text Corpus of Sumerian Literature, February 27, 1999, Lines 31-43, 45-57, 58A-58-Q. https://etcsl.orinst.ox.ac.uk/section4/tr4802.htm.
217. "Tablet IX. The Wanderings of Gilgamesh." In George, Andrew, trans. *The Epic of Gilgamesh*. Penguin Books, 1999, IX 38-40, IX-80-85, IX 135, p. 71, 73.
218. "The Bon Religion – An Introduction," and "Olmo Lungring: The Imperishable Sacred Land." In Dhundup, Tsering, Per Kvaerne, and John Myrdhin Reynolds. *A Collection of Studies on the Tibetan Bon Tradition*. Holybooks.com, p. 11, 21-24. https://holybooks.com/studies-tibetan-bon-tradition.
219. Hancock and Bauval, *Message of the Sphinx*.
220. Reynolds, "Olmo Lungring: The Imperishable Sacred Land," 21. In *A Collection of Studies on the Tibetan Bon Tradition*.
221. Kvaerne, "The Bon Religion – An Introduction," and Reynolds, "Olmo Lungring: The Imperishable Sacred Land," 11, 21-24. In *A Collection of Studies on the Tibetan Bon Tradition*.
222. Nampak, Lonpon Tenzin, and Vajranātha (John Myrdhin Reynolds), editor. *Practices from the Zhang-Zhung Nyan Gyud*. San Francisco/Oregon: Bonpo Translation Project, 1989, p. 59.
223. See Atwood, *Ancient Religion of the Sun*, chap. 5.
224. "Vidyadhara." Wikipedia. https://en.wikipedia.org/wiki/Vidyadhara.
225. Reynolds, "Olmo Lungring: The Imperishable Sacred Land," 20, 23. In *A Collection of Studies on the Tibetan Bon Tradition*.
226. "Mount Kailash." Wikipedia. https://en.wikipedia.org/wiki/Mount_Kailash.
227. Ibid.
228. Atwood, *Ancient Religion of the Sun*, 125-126.
229. Kamalakaran, Ajay. "When a Russian Doctor Tried to Crack the Mystery of the Abode of Lord Shiva." Russia Beyond, Feb 24, 2017. https://www.rbth.com/blogs/tatar_straits/2017/02/24/when-a-russian-doctor-tried-to-crack-the-mystery-of-the-abode-of-lord-shiva_707558.
230. "Churning of the Ocean of Milk." Encyclopedia Britannica. https://www.britannica.com/topic/churning-of-the-ocean-of-milk.
231. Newell, Zo. "Discover the Foundation of Dandasana." Yoga International. https://yogainternational.com/article/view/discover-the-foundation-of-dandasana.
232. Gray, Martin. "Mt. Kailash." World Pilgrimage Guide. https://sacredsites.com/asia/tibet/mt_kailash.html.
233. "Mount Meru." Encyclopedia Britannica. https://www.britannica.com/topic/Mount-Meru-mythology.
234. Misra, Bibhu Dev. "The Turtle Supporting Mount Meru in Asian and Mesoamerican Art." Ancient Inquiries, November 22, 2016. https://www.bibhudevmisra.com/2016/11/the-turtle-supporting-mount-meru-in.html.
235. Freidel, David, Linda Schele, and Joy Parker. *Maya Cosmos: Three Thousand Years on the Shaman's Path*. New York: William Morrow and Company, Inc., 1993, p. 82-83, 146.
236. Hamsanandi. "Where in the World Is Mount Meru?." Medium, December 29, 2014. https://hamsanandi.medium.com/where-in-the-world-is-mount-meru-41556dfc4178.
237. See Ganguli, trans., Book 17: Mahaprasthanika Parva in *The Mahabharata*.
238. "Mount Meru." Wikipedia. https://en.wikipedia.org/wiki/Mount_Meru.
239. "Angkor Wat." Wikipedia. https://en.wikipedia.org/wiki/Angkor_Wat.
240. Shelby, Dr. Karen. "The Great Stupa at Sanchi." Khan Academy. https://www.khanacademy.org/humanities/ap-art-history/introduction-cultures-religions-apah/buddhism-apah/a/the-stupa.
241. "Stupa." Encyclopedia Britannica. https://www.britannica.com/topic/stupa.
242. Sokolov, Tolek. "Buddhist Stupas: Their History and Purpose." Buddhism Today Magazine, Spring-Summer, 2011. https://buddhism-today.org/buddhist-stupas-history-purpose.
243. "Stupa." Wikipedia. https://en.wikipedia.org/wiki/Stupa.
244. Shelby, "The Great Stupa at Sanchi."
245. "Pagoda." Encyclopedia Britannica. https://www.britannica.com/technology/pagoda.
246. "Kunlun (Mythology)." Wikipedia. https://en.wikipedia.org/wiki/Kunlun_(mythology).
247. Robinet, Isabelle. *Taoist Meditation: The Mao-Shan Tradition of Great Purity*, translated by Julian F. Pas and Norman J. Girardot. State University of New York Press, 1993, p. 179-180.

248. Holden, Kevin. "Rediscovering China's 'Son of Heaven.'" Al Jazeera, June 2, 2013. https://www.aljazeera.com/features/2013/6/2/re-discovering-chinas-son-of-heaven.
249. Rogers, James. "China's Ancient 'Pyramids' Reveal Their Stunning Secrets." FOX News, December 6, 2018. https://www.foxnews.com/science/chinas-ancient-pyramids-reveal-their-stunning-secrets.
250. Freidel et al., *Maya Cosmos*, 31, 41-43, 48, 51, 55, 115, 127.
251. Ibid., 134-135, 139-156.
252. The Temple of the Inscriptions at Palenque, the Temple of the Grand Jaguar at Tikal, and the Pyramid of Kukulcán (El Castillo) at Chichen Itza each have nine terraces. See Cartwright, Mark. "Xibalba." World History Encyclopedia. October 21, 2014. https://www.worldhistory.org/Xibalba.
253. Nyman, Whitney. "Mayan Architecture & Pyramids | History, Facts & Examples." Study.com, Updated October 8, 2022. https://study.com/academy/lesson/mayan-architecture-pyramids-history-facts-achievements.html.
254. Freidel et al., *Maya Cosmos*, 75-76.
255. Minster, Christopher. "The Wonders of the Sarcophagus of Pakal." ThoughtCo., Updated January 18, 2020. https://www.thoughtco.com/the-sarcophagus-of-pakal-2136165.
256. Freidel et al., *Maya Cosmos*, 155-156.
257. Cassaro, Richard. "Research—The Triptych Temples of Atlantis." RichardCassaro.com. https://www.richardcassaro.com/research; Cassaro, Richard. "The Secrets of Asia's Pyramid Temples." RichardCassaro.com, February 16, 2017. https://www.richardcassaro.com/secrets-asias-pyramid-temples; Cassaro, Richard. "Suppressed by Scholars: The Mystery of Twin Cultures on Opposite Sides of the Atlantic." RichardCassaro.com, November 5, 2012. https://www.richardcassaro.com/suppressed-by-scholars-twin-ancient-cultures-on-opposite-sides-of-the-pacific.
258. Misra, Bibhu Dev. "Olmec Yogis with Hindu Beliefs: Did They Migrate from Ancient China?." Ancient Inquiries, August 31, 2016. https://www.bibhudevmisra.com/2016/08/olmec-yogis-with-hindu-beliefs-did-they.html.
259. Freidel et al., *Maya Cosmos*, 138-139.
260. Heyworth, Robin. "Teotihuacan: Pyramid of the Sun & the Orion Mystery." Uncovered History, November 11, 2014. https://uncoveredhistory.com/mexico/teotihuacan-pyramid-of-the-sun.
261. Fagan, Brian. "The City at the Center of the Cosmos." Nautilus, February 15, 2018. https://nautil.us/the-city-at-the-center-of-the-cosmos-236988.
262. Maestri, Nicoletta. "Ceiba Pentandra: The Sacred Tree of the Maya." ThoughtCo., Updated March 28, 2019. https://www.thoughtco.com/ceiba-pentandra-sacred-tree-maya-171615.
263. Freidel et al., *Maya Cosmos*, 39, 53, 73, 76, 79, 82, 88-89.
264. Devereaux, Kathryn, PhD. "The Moche, Maya and Pueblo Visual Programs of Connections: The Water Ritualist as Magician." Visual Program of the First Civilizations in the Americas. https://thetinkuy.wordpress.com/tinkuy-twisted-gourd-chaco-pueblo-bonito-devereaux.
265. "Yggdrasil." Wikipedia. https://en.wikipedia.org/wiki/Yggdrasil.
266. "Irminsul." Wikipedia. https://en.wikipedia.org/wiki/Irminsul. (The term "Irmin" is believed to be a name used for Odin, and in an account of an ancient Germanic ritual, the Irminsul pillar was said to represent the body of the god they associated with the sun, who is possibly referred to as "Hirmin," thus suggesting the god of the Irminsul was Odin.)
267. Collins, *The Cygnus Key*, 277.
268. Eliade, *Shamanism – Archaic Techniques of Ecstasy*, 266-270.
269. Wong, Eva. *Taoism: An Essential Guide*. Boston, Massachusetts: Shambhala Publications, Inc., 1997, p. 98, 100.
270. Nampak and Vajranātha, ed., *Practices from the Zhang-Zhung Nyan Gyud*, 60.
271. Natawidjaja, Danny H., Andang Bachtiar, Bagus Endar B. Nurhandoko, et al. "Geo-Archaeological Prospecting of Gunung Padang Buried Prehistoric Pyramid in West Java, Indonesia." *Archaeological Prospection* (October 20, 2023): 1-25. https://onlinelibrary.wiley.com/doi/10.1002/arp.1912.
272. Atwood, *Ancient Religion of the Sun*, 132-136.
273. "The Ynglinga Saga—7. Of Odin's Feats" In Sturlson, Snorri. *Heimskringla or The Chronicle of the Kings of Norway*, translated by Samuel Laing, 1844. https://sacred-texts.com/neu/heim/02ynglga.htm.
274. "Nordic Concepts of Soul." The Bone Kindred. http://bonekindred.weebly.com/nordic-soul-concepts.html.

275. Paxson, Diana L. "Hyge-Cræft: Working with the Soul in the Northern Tradition." *Idunna* 28 (Autumn, 1995). https://hrafnar.org/articles/dpaxson/norse/hyge-craeft.
276. Agrippa, Henry Cornelius of Nettesheim. *Three Books of Occult Philosophy*, translated by James Freake, edited and annotated by Donald Tyson. Woodbury, Minnesota: Llewellyn Publications, 2009, p. 629.
277. Kvilhaug, Maria. *The Seed of Yggdrasill: Deciphering the Hidden Messages in Old Norse Myths*. Whyte Tracks, 2016, section 3: The Maiden with the Mead, Kindle edition.
278. Ibid., Introduction Notes, section 10.3: The Vision Quest.
279. Ibid., section 9.3: Odinn and the Goddess.
280. Ibid., section 10.2: The Ritual Behind the Myth.
281. Ibid., section 1.1: The Forgotten Manuscript – Poetic Edda, Heroic Poems, The First Song of Helgi Hunding's Bane.
282. Ibid., section 2.12: Odinn – Uprooting the Runes, chap. 3: The Maiden with the Mead, section 3.1: The Mead of Poetry, section 3.7: The Bride of the Burial Mound, section 3.17: Not Quite the Christian Poem After All. Sólarljóð (The Song of the Sun), section 10.2: The Ritual Behind the Myth.
283. McCoy, Daniel. "The Mead of Poetry." Norse Mythology for Smart People, November 14, 2012. https://norse-mythology.org/tales/the-mead-of-poetry.
284. Kvilhaug, *Seed of Yggdrasill*, section 2.4: Evil Giants – Or the Guardians of Wisdom?.
285. Ibid., section 3.16: The Mead and the Sun Goddess, section 3.17: Not Quite the Christian Poem After All. Sólarljóð (The Song of the Sun).
286. "Dvija." Wikipedia. https://en.wikipedia.org/wiki/Dvija.
287. Samuel, Geoffrey. *The Origins of Yoga and Tantra: Indic Religions to the Thirteenth Century*. Cambridge: Cambridge University Press, 2008, p. 86-87, Kindle edition.
288. Atwood, *Ancient Religion of the Sun*, 123, 145-146.
289. Kvilhaug, *Seed of Yggdrasill*, section 3.17: Not Quite the Christian Poem After All. Sólarljóð (The Song of the Sun).
290. Ibid., section 2.12: Odinn – Uprooting the Runes, section 3: The Maiden with the Mead, section 3.1: The Mead of Poetry.
291. "Stone Ship." Wikipedia. https://en.wikipedia.org/wiki/Stone_ship.
292. Söderberg, Bengt, and Annika Knarrström. "New Light on Ale's Stones." *Lund Archaeological Review* 21 (2015): 96. https://journals.lub.lu.se/lar/article/view/21629.
293. "Solar Barque." Wikipedia. https://en.wikipedia.org/wiki/Solar_barque.
294. "Experiences with Odin." Sakro Sawel, August 25, 2020. Updated April 19, 2023. https://sakrosawel.com/experiences-with-odin.
295. Evans-Wentz, W.Y. *The Fairy-Faith in Celtic Countries*. London and New York: H. Froude, 1911. https://www.sacred-texts.com/neu/celt/ffcc/ffcc260.htm.
296. Kvilhaug, *Seed of Yggdrasill*, section 3: The Maiden with the Mead, section 3.14: The Book of Taliesin.
297. *The Kolbrin*, "The Hibsathy," 235.
298. Evans-Wentz, *Fairy-Faith in Celtic Countries*.
299. *The Kolbrin*, "The Teachings of Elidor 1," 634-635.
300. Murphy, Anthony. "101 Facts about Newgrange." Mythical Ireland, November 8, 2017. https://mythicalireland.com/ancient-sites/101-facts-about-newgrange.
301. Shaw, Judith. "Boann, Celtic Goddess of Inspiration and Creativity." Feminism & Religion, July 27, 2016. https://feminismandreligion.com/2016/07/27/boann-celtic-goddess-of-inspiration-and-creativity-by-judith-shaw.
302. Atwood with Atwood, *Ancient Solstice*, 196.
303. *The Kolbrin*, "The Sacred Registers – part 7," 173.
304. Ibid., "Shards of Wisdom," 816.
305. Atwood with Atwood, *Ancient Solstice*, 150-152.
306. Ibid., 162, 340.
307. Carlson, Randall. "Stonehenge and the Squaring of the Circle." YouTube, August 27, 2018. https://youtu.be/cKXDWy_zXzI?t=371.
308. Atwood with Atwood, *Ancient Solstice*, 291-292.
309. Ibid., 194-197.

310. Ibid., 270.
311. Ibid., 341.
312. Muckerman, Anna. "What Did Stonehenge Sound Like?." BBC, June 2, 2023. https://www.bbc.com/travel/article/20230601-what-did-stonehenge-sound-like.
313. Owen, James. "Stonehenge 'Hedge' Found, Shielded Secret Rituals?." National Geographic, February 12, 2010. https://www.nationalgeographic.com/adventure/article/100211-stonehenge-stonehedge-secret-rituals.
314. "Celtic Otherworld." Wikipedia. https://en.wikipedia.org/wiki/Celtic_Otherworld.
315. Freeman, Mara. "Cauldron of Changes: The Birth of Taliesin." Chalice Centre. http://www.chalicecentre.net/cauldron-of-changes.html.
316. Kvilhaug, *Seed of Yggdrasill*, section 3: The Maiden with the Mead, section 3.14: The Book of Taliesin.
317. Lewis, Gwyneth, and Rowan Williams, trans. *The Book of Taliesin*. Penguin, June 27, 2019, p. 76, Kindle edition.
318. NicGrioghair, Branfionn. "Who is Brigid?." Mythical Ireland, 1997. https://mythicalireland.com/blogs/myths-legends/bridget-bright-goddess-of-the-gael.
319. Atwood with Atwood, *Ancient Solstice*, 260-264.
320. Lewis and Williams, trans., *The Book of Taliesin*, 99.
321. "Annwn." Wikipedia. https://en.wikipedia.org/wiki/Annwn.
322. "Pair Dadeni." Wikipedia. https://en.wikipedia.org/wiki/Pair_Dadeni.
323. Smithers, Lorna. "Gwyn AP Nudd and the Spirits of Annwn: Remembering the Underworld Gods." The Cell of Sister Patience, July 31, 2014. https://lornasmithers.com/2014/07/31/gwyn-ap-nudd-and-the-spirits-of-annwn-remembering-the-underworld-gods.
324. Comment by "pixelobservations." On Sakro Sawel. "Who is Odin/Wotan? [An Alternative Perspective]." YouTube, August 3, 2017. https://youtu.be/rnN5upwW84s.
325. "Annwn." Wikipedia.
326. "Glastonbury Tor." Wikipedia. https://en.wikipedia.org/wiki/Glastonbury_Tor.
327. "History and Legends of Glastonbury Tor." National Trust. https://www.nationaltrust.org.uk/visit/somerset/glastonbury-tor/history-of-glastonbury-tor.
328. "Glastonbury Tor." Wikipedia.
329. Ibid.
330. Mann, Nicholas. "Nicholas Mann: Avebury Cosmos: Our Ancestors and the Stars." YouTube, April 4, 2014. https://youtu.be/6uixeGHmK4g?t=406.
331. "History of Silbury Hill." English Heritage. https://www.english-heritage.org.uk/visit/places/silbury-hill/history.
332. "Silbury Hill." Wikipedia. https://en.wikipedia.org/wiki/Silbury_Hill.
333. Marshall, Steve. "Acoustics of the West Kennet Long Barrow, Avebury, Wiltshire." *Time and Mind* 9, no. 1 (2016): 43-56. https://doi.org/10.1080/1751696X.2016.1142292. Article can be read on Marshall's website at https://exploringavebury.com/assets/uploads/long-barrows/Acoustics of the West Kennet Long Barrow Avebury Wiltshire.pdf.
334. Larson, Jennifer. "What Is the Purpose of Theta Brain Waves?." Healthline, October 9, 2019. https://www.healthline.com/health/theta-waves?c=1547701501337.
335. "Alpha Wave." Wikipedia. https://en.wikipedia.org/wiki/Alpha_wave.
336. Marshall, "Acoustics of the West Kennet Long Barrow." p. 54
337. Ibid., 53.
338. Ibid., 52.
339. Jahn, Robert G., Paul Devereux, and Michael Ibison. "Acoustical Resonances of Assorted Ancient Structures." *Journal of the Acoustical Society of America* 99, no. 2 (February, 1996): 649-658. https://doi.org/10.1121/1.414642.
340. Cook, Ian A., Sarah K. Pajot, and Andrew F. Leuchter. "Ancient Architectural Acoustic Resonance Patterns and Regional Brain Activity." *Time and Mind* 1, no. 1 (November, 2013): 95-104. https://www.researchgate.net/figure/Changes-in-Regional-Brain-Activity-at-90-110-and-130-Hz-Tones-Changes-from-baseline_fig1_233638157.
341. "Awen—The Holy Spirit of Druidry." The British Druid Order. https://www.druidry.co.uk/awen-the-holy-spirit-of-druidry.

342. Ibid.
343. *The Kolbrin*, "Sacred Registers—Part 9," 177.
344. "Awen." Wikipedia. https://en.wikipedia.org/wiki/Awen.
345. Ibid.
346. *The Kolbrin*, "The Hibsathy," 236.
347. Lewis and Williams, trans., *The Book of Taliesin*, xxv, xxvi.
348. See Atwood with Atwood, *Ancient Solstice*, particularly chapters 3 and 4.
349. "Ġgantija." Wikipedia. https://en.wikipedia.org/wiki/Ġgantija.
350. "Mnajdra." Wikipedia. https://en.wikipedia.org/wiki/Mnajdra.
351. The temples in Malta have many solar and stellar alignments. Someone from our publisher who visited the sites of Malta has provided this list of alignments based on information at the sites and local museums and his own observations. At Ħaġar Qim the winter solstice sunrise shines through an "oracle hole" into one of its inner chambers. At the Mnajdra South Temple the rising equinox sun shines down the central passageway into the temple (it also has solstice alignments into the central passage), and like at Ħaġar Qim the winter solstice sunrise shines through an "oracle hole" into an inner chamber. At Ta' Ħaġrat the winter solstice sunrise shines down its central passage into a back, inner chamber. At Ġgantija the winter solstice sunrise shines down one of its central passages into a back, inner chamber. At Borġ in-Nadur the equinox sunrise shines down its central passage, but the temple is now too dilapidated to tell where it was directed.
352. Reedijk, Lenie. "Sirius and the Maltese Temples: A Tale of Two Revelations." GrahamHancock.com, February 6, 2019. https://grahamhancock.com/reedijkl1.
353. Toffetti, Rudi. "Hypogeum Ħal Saflieni, Island of Malta—Historical Notes, Geobiological Surveys, and Perceptions." Rudi Toffetti, May 10, 2018, p. 31, 56. http://www.ruditoffetti.it/articoli/Hypogeum-Hal-Saflieni-by-Rudi-Toffetti-ENGLISH-VERSION.pdf.
354. Debertolis, Prof.agg. Paolo, Dr. Fernando Coimbra, and Linda Eneix. "Archaeoacoustic Analysis of the Hal Saflieni Hypogeum in Malta." *Journal of Anthropology and Archaeology* 3, no. 1 (June, 2015): 59-79. https://www.researchgate.net/publication/282480957_Archaeoacoustic_Analysis_of_the_Hal_Saflieni_Hypogeum_in_Malta.
355. Toffetti, "Hypogeum Ħal Saflieni," 12, 14, 15, 20-21, 46.
356. "Ħal Saflieni Hypogeum." Wikipedia. https://en.wikipedia.org/wiki/Ħal_Saflieni_Hypogeum.
357. Collins, *The Cygnus Key*, 11.
358. "Göbekli Tepe." Wikipedia. https://en.wikipedia.org/wiki/Göbekli_Tepe.
359. Collins, *The Cygnus Key*, 23, 26-27.
360. Ibid., 18-20.
361. Ibid., 20.
362. Ibid., 37-51.
363. Ibid., 132-134.
364. Ibid., 141.
365. George, trans., *Epic of Gilgamesh*, tablet IX, 71.
366. Collins, *The Cygnus Key*, 133.
367. Ibid., 60.
368. Ibid., 13-16.
369. Ibid., 16.
370. "Mên-an-Tol." Wikipedia. https://en.wikipedia.org/wiki/Mên-an-Tol.
371. "Men-An-Tol Holed Stone." The Cornwall Guide, Updated Jan 13, 2022. https://www.cornwalls.co.uk/history/sites/men_an_tol.htm.
372. Collins, *The Cygnus Key*, 56.
373. Ibid., chap. 23.
374. "Zoroastrianism." Wikipedia. https://en.wikipedia.org/wiki/Zoroastrianism.
375. Eduljee, E. E. "Composition and Transmission of the Avesta—Compilation and Destruction of the Avesta." Zoroastrianism Heritage. https://www.heritageinstitute.com/zoroastrianism/scriptures/history.htm#complilation.
376. Eduljee, E. E. "Zoroastrianism Overview Expanded." Zoroastrianism Heritage, https://www.heritageinstitute.com/zoroastrianism/overview/index.htm.

377. Shaked, Shaul. "Gētīg and Mēnōg." Encyclopædia Iranica, December 15, 2001. Updated February 7, 2012. https://iranicaonline.org/articles/getig-and-menog.
378. Eduljee, "Zoroastrianism Overview Expanded: The Soul, Urvan - Fate of the Soul."
379. Karanjia, Ramiyar P. "Human Being—Concept and Composition." Ramiyar Karanjia. https://ramiyarkaranjia.com/human-being-concept-and-composition.
380. Eduljee, "Zoroastrianism Overview Expanded: United Fravashi."
381. "Fravashi." Wikipedia. https://en.wikipedia.org/wiki/Fravashi.
382. Kvilhaug, Maria. "The Sacred Drink and Other Links between Indian, Iranian, Greek, Celtic and Norse Mythology." Blade Honer, January 29, 2020. https://bladehoner.wordpress.com/2020/01/29/the-sacred-drink-and-other-links-between-indian-iranian-greek-celtic-and-norse-mythology.
383. Haug, Martin, trans., with Edward William West. *The Book of Arda Viraf*. Bombay: Government Central Book Depot, 1872, chapter 3, verses 1-6, p. 152. https://archive.org/details/bookofardaviraf00haug. Note: I have slightly modernized the language of the translation.
384. Ibid., chap. 4, verses 2-4, p. 154.
385. Ibid., chap. 4, verse 7, p. 154.
386. Ibid., chap. 5, verses 6-8, p. 156.
387. Peterson, Joseph H., trans. *Zand-i Vohuman Yasht*. 1995, Updated May 8, 2022, chapter 3: 6-16. Digital edition and translation from Anklesaria, Behramgore Tehmurasp. *Zand-I Vohuman Yasn and Two Pahlavi Fragments*. Bombay: Mrs. B. T. Anklesaria, 1957. http://www.avesta.org/mp/vohuman.html.
388. Flattery, David Stophlet, and Martin Schwartz. *Haoma and Harmaline*. University of California Press, 1989, p. 14-23.
389. Ibid., 17-19.
390. "Vishtaspa." Wikipedia. https://en.wikipedia.org/wiki/Vishtaspa.
391. "Kartir's Inscription at Naqsh-e Rajab." Wikipedia. https://en.wikipedia.org/wiki/Kartir's_inscription_at_Naqsh-e_Rajab.
392. Skjaervo, Prods Oktor. "Kartīr." Encyclopædia Iranica, December 15, 2011. Updated April 24, 2012. https://iranicaonline.org/articles/kartir.
393. Flattery and Schwartz, *Haoma and Harmaline*, 20.
394. Atwood, *Ancient Religion of the Sun*, chap. 6.
395. Mead, G. R. S., trans. *Pistis Sophia*. London: J. M. Watkins, 1921, book one, chapters 10-11, 14, 17, 19.
396. "Pistis Sophia." Wikipedia. https://en.wikipedia.org/wiki/Pistis_Sophia.
397. "Gnosticism." Wikipedia. https://en.wikipedia.org/wiki/Gnosticism.
398. "Gospel of Judas." Wikipedia. https://en.wikipedia.org/wiki/Gospel_of_Judas.
399. Kasser, Rodolphe, Marvin Meyer, and Gregor Wurst, trans., in collaboration with François Gaudard. *The Gospel of Judas*. Washington: National Geographic Society, 2006, p. 2.
400. Emmel, Stephen, trans. "The Dialogue of the Savior." In *The Nag Hammadi Library in English*, edited by James M. Robinson. San Francisco: HarperCollins, 1990, p. 250-251.
401. "Edmond Bordeaux Szekely." Wikipedia. https://en.wikipedia.org/wiki/Edmond_Bordeaux_Szekely.
402. Szekely, Edmond Bordeaux, trans. *The Essene Gospel of Peace: Book Four*. USA: International Biogenic Society, 1981, p. 15.
403. Ibid., 43.
404. Morrow, *Dawning Moon of the Mind*, 124.
405. Ibid., 125.
406. Ibid., 128.
407. Ibid., 103.
408. Ibid., 148.
409. Ibid., 158.
410. "Harrowing of Hell." Wikipedia. https://en.m.wikipedia.org/wiki/Harrowing_of_Hell.
411. Drower, E. S. *The Mandaeans of Iraq and Iran: Their Cults, Customs, Magic, Legends, and Folklore*. Leiden: Brill, 1962. The Gnostic Society Library. http://gnosis.org/library/manda-dower-1937.html.
412. "Gospel of Judas." Wikipedia.

413. See "Matthew 27:34" and "Mark 15:23" in *The Holy Bible*, New International Version (NIV). Biblica, 2011.
414. *The Holy Bible*, NIV, "John 19:28-30."
415. *The Kolbrin*, "Sacred Registers—Part 9," 177.
416. Whiteman, "Guide to the Kolbrin."
417. "The Kolbrin—The Culdian Trust Kolbrin Manuscripts." TheKolbrin.com. https://thekolbrin.com.
418. *The Holy Bible*, NIV, "John 19:33-34."
419. *The Gospel of the Kailedy*. The Culdian Trust, 1998, p. 174.
420. "Healing the Centurion's Servant." Wikipedia. https://en.wikipedia.org/wiki/Healing_the_centurion's_servant; *The Holy Bible*, NIV, "Matthew 27:54."
421. *The Holy Bible*, NIV, "John 19:38," "Matthew 27:57," "Luke 23:50-52."
422. Keyser, John D. "Joseph of Arimathea and David's Throne in Britain!." Hope of Israel Ministries. https://www.hope-of-israel.org/i000111a.htm.
423. *The Holy Bible*, NIV, "Matthew 27:59-60," "Luke 23:54."
424. Ibid., "Luke 23:56."
425. *The Gospel of the Kailedy*, 175.
426. Ibid.
427. *The Holy Bible*, NIV, "Luke 24:9-12," "John 20:2-10."
428. Ibid., "Mark 16:4-7," "Luke 24:4-7."
429. Ibid., "Mark 16:4-8."
430. Ibid., "John 19:19, 26."
431. Ibid., "John 19:14-16."
432. *The Gospel of the Kailedy*, 175-176.
433. *The Holy Bible*, NIV, "Matthew 27:2-3."
434. "Scorpius." Wikipedia. https://en.wikipedia.org/wiki/Scorpius.
435. *The Holy Bible*, NIV, "2 Corinthians 12:2."
436. Ibid., "Revelation 1:10-11."
437. Wiese, Bill. "23 Minutes in Hell (Original) - Bill Wiese, 'The Man Who Went to Hell' Author '23 Minutes in Hell.'" YouTube, January 16, 2013, 4:38-5.07, 14:46-15:05. https://youtu.be/AYxKRoONrfY&t=278.
438. Robinet, Isabelle. *Taoist Meditation: The Mao-Shan Tradition of Great Purity*, translated by Julian F. Pas and Norman J. Girardot. Albany: State University of New York Press, 1993, p. 171, 175.
439. Ibid., 172.
440. Erzeng, Yang. *The Story of Han Xiangzi*, translated by Philip Clart. Seattle: University of Washington Press, 2007, p. 166. https://uw.manifoldapp.org/projects/story-of-han-xiangzi.
441. Ibid., 218, 222-223.
442. Ibid., 218, 207-209.
443. Esposito, Monica. "Sun-Worship in China – The Roots of Shangqing Taoist Practices of Light." *Cahiers d'Extrême-Asie* 14 (2004): 349-353. https://www.persee.fr/doc/asie_0766-1177_2004_num_14_1_1212.
444. Shizhong, Lu. *The Incomparable Mysterious, Original Great Methods of the Jade Hall of the Three Celestial Realms*. Chinese Text Project. Chapter 4. https://ctext.org/wiki.pl?if=en&res=648420&remap=gb. Note: This text has not been translated into English, but is available in Simplified Chinese only. We have used ChatGPT version 3.5 to translate the text, so the translation is approximate.
445. Ibid., chap. 4.
446. Ibid., chap. 2.
447. Ibid.
448. Ibid., chap. 4.
449. Wong, *Taoism: An Essential Guide*, 101-105, 290-291.
450. Shizhong, *Original Great Methods*, chap. 4. Translation by Pavlin Boev using a translation by ChatGPT as a basis.
451. Robinet, *Taoist Meditation*, 214-215.

452. Shizhong, *Original Great Methods*, chap. 5. Boev, trans.
453. Ibid., chap. 5. ChatGPT version 3.5, trans.
454. Ibid., chap. 5. ChatGPT version 4 and Boev, trans.
455. Robinet, *Taoist Meditation*, 209, 222.
456. Morrow, *Dawning Moon of the Mind*, 115.
457. Padmasambhava. *The Tibetan Book of the Dead*, translated by Lama Kazi Dawa-Samdup. Holybooks.com, p. 31, 35. https://holybooks.com/the-tibetan-book-of-the-dead-2. Note: I have modernized the English in the translation without changing the meaning.
458. Ibid., 55.
459. "Dream Yoga." Wikipedia. https://en.wikipedia.org/wiki/Dream_yoga.
460. "What Is Vajrayana Buddhism?." Tricycle: Buddhism for Beginners. https://tricycle.org/beginners/buddhism/what-is-vajrayana-buddhism.
461. "Oddiyana." Wikipedia. https://en.wikipedia.org/wiki/Oddiyana.
462. Norbu, Chögyal Namkhai. *Dream Yoga and the Practice of Natural Light*. USA: Snow Lion Boulder, 2002, p. 131.
463. Wallis, Christopher, PhD. "The Tantric Age: A Comparison of Shaiva and Buddhist Tantra." Sutra Journal, February 2016. http://www.sutrajournal.com/the-tantric-age-a-comparison-of-shaiva-and-buddhist-tantra-by-christopher-wallis.
464. Browne, Y. Y. "Shaivism and Dzogchen: Hinduism and Buddhism—The Bonds, the Tantras, the View." Accidental Hindu, December 11, 2014. https://accidentalhindu.blogspot.com/2014/12/shaivism-and-dzogchen-hinduism-and.html.
465. "What Is Buddhist Tantra?." Tricycle: Buddhism for Beginners. https://tricycle.org/beginners/buddhism/what-is-buddhist-tantra.
466. Mark, Joshua J. "Esoteric Buddhism." World History Encyclopedia, July 20, 2021. https://www.worldhistory.org/Esoteric_Buddhism.
467. Drakpa, Je Tsongkhapa Lobsang. *Brilliant Illumination of the Lamp of Five Stages*. Introduction and Translation by Robert A. F. Thurman. New York: The American Institute of Buddhist Studies, Columbia University Center for Buddhist Studies, Tibet House US, 2010, Letter of Support from the Dalai Lama, Introduction, p. 23-24.
468. "Dream Yoga." Wikipedia.
469. Holecek, Andrew. "What Is Dream Yoga?." Kripalu Center for Yoga and Health. https://kripalu.org/resources/what-dream-yoga.
470. Norbu, *Dream Yoga and the Practice of Natural Light*, 131.
471. "Mahāmāyā Tantra." Wikipedia. https://en.wikipedia.org/wiki/Mahamaya_Tantra.
472. Jinavara, and Gö Lhetsé, trans. *The Mahāmāyā Tantra*. Translated into English by the Dharmachakra Translation Committee, 2013, verses 1.12, 3.13. https://read.84000.co/translation/toh425.html.
473. Ibid., section i.15, verses 1.29-1.32.
474. Ibid., section i.7.
475. Ibid., verses 1.12-1.14.
476. Ibid., verse 2.17.
477. Ibid., verse 1.17.
478. Wangyal Rinpoche, Tenzin. *The Tibetan Yogas of Dream and Sleep*. Shambhala, August 30, 2022, p. 13, Kindle edition.
479. Chaoul, Alejandro. "The Most Generous Cut." Tricycle Magazine: The Buddhist Review, Summer 2008. https://tricycle.org/magazine/the-most-generous-cut.
480. Chaoul, Marco Alejandro. "The Mother Tantras." ИщущЕму. https://www.surajamrita.com/bon/MotherTantra.html.
481. "Chöd–Indian Antecedents." Wikipedia. https://en.wikipedia.org/wiki/Chöd#Indian_antecedents.
482. For example, *The Instructions on the Primordial A* and *The Quintessential Instruction on the Illusory Body of Dream* (which is the earliest known Chinese translation of a Tibetan Tantric Buddhist text).
483. As found in Gyaltsen, Shardza Tashi. *Self-Arising Three-Fold Embodiment of Enlightenment*; *Guhyasamāja Tantra*; and *Hevajra Tantra*.
484. Wangyal Rinpoche, *Tibetan Yogas of Dream and Sleep*, 129, 132-133, 136, 143, 152, 167, 171, 189, 223-225.

485. Ibid., 328.
486. Quote from Sravakabhumi in Shukla, K., ed. *Sravakabhumi of Acarya Asanga*. 1973. Revised Sanskrit Text and Japanese Translation, Sbh Studying Group, Taisho University, 1998. In Abe, Takako. "Practice of Wakefulness." *Journal of Indian and Buddhist Studies* 53, no. 1 (December, 2004): 478-480.
487. Wangyal Rinpoche, *Tibetan Yogas of Dream and Sleep*, 258-260.
488. Ibid., 269-270.
489. "Aether (Classical Element)." Wikipedia. https://en.wikipedia.org/wiki/Aether_(classical_element).
490. "Astral Body." Wikipedia. https://en.wikipedia.org/wiki/Astral_body.
491. "Okhema." Wikipedia. https://en.wikipedia.org/wiki/Okhema.
492. "Astral Plane." Wikipedia. https://en.wikipedia.org/wiki/Astral_plane.
493. Pliny the Elder. *The Natural History of Pliny, 6 Volumes*, translated by John Bostock and H. T. Riley. London: Henry G. Bohn, 1855-7, 7.53, 2:210. In Agrippa, *Three Books of Occult Philosophy*, 631.
494. Ibid.
495. Plutarch, *Moralia*, translated by Philip H. De Lacy and Benedict Einarson. Loeb Classical Library edition, 1959, part 2, 22.1. https://penelope.uchicago.edu/Thayer/E/Roman/Texts/Plutarch/Moralia/De_genio_Socratis*/B.html.
496. Ibid.
497. Ibid.
498. Ibid.
499. Eliade, Mercia, and Vilmos Diószegi. "Shamanism." Encyclopedia Britannica. https://www.britannica.com/topic/shamanism.
500. Ibid.
501. Eliade, *Shamanism – Archaic Techniques of Ecstasy*, 259-279.
502. Siikala, Anna-Leena. "The Siberian Shaman's Technique of Ecstasy." *Scripta Instituti Donneriani Aboensis* 11 (1982): 103.
503. Ibid., 112.
504. Eliade and Diószegi, "Shamanism—Selection."
505. Siikala, "Siberian Shaman's Technique of Ecstasy," 109.
506. Ibid.
507. Ibid., 110.
508. Ibid., 111.
509. Eliade and Diószegi, "Shamanism."
510. Siikala, "Siberian Shaman's Technique of Ecstasy," 111.
511. Ibid., 113-114.
512. "Hamat´Sa Fact Sheet." Living Tradition, The Kwakwaka'wakw Potlatch on the Northwest Coast. https://umistapotlatch.ca/enseignants-education/cours_5_partie_3-lesson_5_part_3-eng.php.
513. "Nagual." Wikipedia. https://en.wikipedia.org/wiki/Nagual.
514. Makra, László. "Chapter 3. Anthropogenic Air Pollution in Ancient Times." In Wexler, Philip. *History of Toxicology and Environmental Health. Toxicology in Antiquity II*. Elsevier Inc., December, 2015. https://www.researchgate.net/figure/Hidden-in-plain-sight-the-ceramic-pre-Columbian-mask-depicts-the-transformation-of-a_fig3_285657093.
515. Flor-Henry, Pierre, Yakov Shapiro, and Corine Sombrun. "Brain Changes during a Shamanic Trance: Altered Modes of Consciousness, Hemispheric Laterality, and Systemic Psychobiology." *Cogent Psychology* 4, no. 1 (2017). https://www.tandfonline.com/doi/full/10.1080/23311908.2017.1313522.
516. Eliade and Diószegi, "Shamanism."
517. Little, Gregory. *Path of Souls: The Native American Death Journey: Cygnus, Orion, the Milky Way, Giant Skeletons in Mounds, & the Smithsonian*. ATA-Archetype Books, July, 2014, p. 148, 201, Kindle edition.
518. Boas, Gary. "The Neuroscience of Trance." Athinoula A. Martinos Center for Biomedical Imaging, July 10, 2015. https://www.nmr.mgh.harvard.edu/news/20150710/neuroscience-trance.
519. Flor-Henry et al., "Brain Changes during a Shamanic Trance."
520. Little, *Path of Souls*, 152.

521. Ibid., 140.
522. Romain, William F. *Mysteries of the Hopewell: Astronomers, Geometers, and Magicians of the Eastern Woodlands*. The University of Akron Press, October 2010, chapter 5, section "Azimuths to the Otherworld," Kindle edition.
523. Little, *Path of Souls*, 153-155.
524. Ibid., 2-4.
525. Ibid., 141-142.
526. Morrow, *Dawning Moon of the Mind*, 82.
527. "Mound Builders." Wikipedia. https://en.wikipedia.org/wiki/Mound_Builders.
528. Hancock, Graham. *America Before: The Key to Earth's Lost Civilization*. St. Martin's Press, 2019, chapter 21, Kindle edition.
529. Ibid., chap. 21, sections "Triangulation," "The Directors."
530. Ibid., chap. 21, section "Reincarnation."
531. Ibid., chap. 1, section "The Serpent and the Egg," chap. 15, sections "Curiosities," "A Global Legacy?," chap. 16.
532. Boutet, Michel-Gérald. "On the Origins of the Oghamic Writing System." Academia.edu, February 2, 2008, p. 3. https://www.academia.edu/4134903/Proto-Ogham.
533. Keys, David. "Found: Europe's Oldest Civilisation." The Independent, June 11, 2005. https://www.independent.co.uk/news/world/europe/found-europes-oldest-civilisation-5345769.html.
534. "Newark Earthworks." Wikipedia. https://en.wikipedia.org/wiki/Newark_Earthworks.
535. Little, *Path of Souls*, 38.
536. Romain, *Mysteries of the Hopewell*, chap. 6, section "Introduction."
537. Ibid., chap. 6, section "The Earth Diver."
538. Ibid., chap. 6, section "Circular Enclosures."
539. Ibid., chap. 7, section "Burials."
540. Little, *Path of Souls*, 199.
541. Romain, *Mysteries of the Hopewell*, chap. 7, section "Burials."
542. Little, *Path of Souls*, 11.
543. Ibid., 11-12.
544. Romain, *Mysteries of the Hopewell*, chap. 7, sections "Altered States of Consciousness," "Shamans and Shape-Shifters," "Magic Mushrooms," "Smoking Pipes."
545. See footnote 23: "Kunio Yanagita" in "Ikiryō." Wikipedia. https://en.wikipedia.org/wiki/Ikiryo.
546. "Astral." Merriam-Webster. https://www.merriam-webster.com/dictionary/astral.
547. Mark, Joshua J. "Field of Reeds (Aaru)." World History Encyclopedia, August 20, 2019. https://www.worldhistory.org/Field_of_Reeds.
548. "Aaru." Wikipedia. https://en.wikipedia.org/wiki/Aaru.
549. "Did you go to Heaven?." International Association for Near-Death Studies, April 25, 2015. https://iands.org/ndes/nde-stories/iands-nde-accounts/961-did-you-go-to-heaven.html.
550. "Kayak Spill Gives Teen Visit with Her Angel Plus New Psychic Abilities and New Purpose." International Association for Near-Death Studies, November 30, 2021. https://iands.org/research/nde-research/nde-archives31/newest-accounts/1595-kayak-spill-gives-teen-visit-with-her-angel-plus-new-psychic-abilities-and-new-purpose.html.
551. Samuel, Geoffrey. *The Origins of Yoga and Tantra*. Cambridge University Press, 2011, p. 221, Kindle edition.
552. "Yoga." Wikipedia. https://en.wikipedia.org/wiki/Yoga.
553. Misra, Bibhu Dev. "The Egyptian Ankh and the Hindu Pasha Are Equivalent Symbols." Ancient Inquiries, May 9, 2019. https://www.bibhudevmisra.com/2019/05/the-egyptian-ankh-and-hindu-pasha-are.html.
554. Easwaran, trans., *The Upanishads*, 91.
555. Ibid., 159, 167, 175-176.
556. Ibid., 284.
557. Ibid., 178.
558. *Rigveda* I.67.2-4, IV.58.11, I.146.4. In Frawley, David. *Vedic Yoga: The Path of the Rishi*. Lotus Press, 2014, p. 193, Kindle edition.

559. Atwood, *Ancient Religion of the Sun*, 271-272.

560. Frawley, *Vedic Yoga*, 234.

561. Easwaran, trans., *The Upanishads*, 141-142.

562. "Buddhism and Hinduism." Wikipedia. https://en.wikipedia.org/wiki/Buddhism_and_Hinduism.

563. Ganguli, trans., Book 3: Section CCXII in *The Mahabharata*.

564. Saradananda, Swami, Swami Jagadananda, trans. *Sri Ramakrishna The Great Master*. Sri Ramakrishna Math, 1952. In "Ramakrishna." Wikipedia. https://en.wikipedia.org/wiki/Ramakrishna.

565. *The Kolbrin*, "The Annexed Scroll 1," 435.

566. "The Milky Way in Irish Mythology and Folklore." Mythical Ireland, October 10, 2016. https://mythicalireland.com/blogs/news/the-milky-way-in-irish-mythology-and-folklore.

567. "Boann." Wikipedia. https://en.wikipedia.org/wiki/Boann.

568. Atwood with Atwood, *Ancient Solstice*, 214, 219.

569. The stepped pyramid known as the Temple of Inscriptions at the ancient Maya site of Palenque in Mexico was aligned to the summer solstice, and there is reason to believe it was used for initiations of death and rebirth in its underground chambers, sharing many similarities with the pyramids of Egypt and their associated beliefs. At the ancient Maya site of Tulum there are similar themes of underworld, death, and resurrection, and we suspect similar initiations were conducted there too, as they probably were at other Maya sites. See Atwood with Atwood, *Ancient Solstice*, 258, 352.

570. Swanson, Todd. "Womb of Fire: Crisis and Transformation." Eleusinian Mysteries, May 1993. https://eleusinianmysteries.org/WombOfFire.html.

571. I explain the meaning behind the symbols used in the ancient initiatory rituals of death, rebirth, and resurrection in my book *Ancient Solstice*.

572. *The Kolbrin*, "The Annexed Scroll 2," 445.

CHAPTER FOUR

1. Hughes, J. Donald. "Dream Interpretation in Ancient Civilizations." *Dreaming* 10, no. 1 (March 2000): 7-18. https://www.researchgate.net/publication/227247381_Dream_Interpretation_in_Ancient_Civilizations.

2. "Epic of Gilgamesh." Wikipedia. https://en.wikipedia.org/wiki/Epic_of_Gilgamesh.

3. Atwood, Lara. *The Ancient Religion of the Sun: The Wisdom Bringers and The Lost Civilization of the Sun*. 2nd ed. Sura Ondrunar Publishing, 2021, p. 94-97.

4. "Epic of Gilgamesh." Wikipedia.

5. George, Andrew, trans. *The Epic of Gilgamesh*. Penguin Books, 1999, IV 5-15, 25-30, p. 30-31.

6. "The Epic Adventures of the Gilgamesh Dream Tablet." BBC, September 23, 2021. https://www.bbc.com/news/world-middle-east-58662893.

7. "Lugalbanda in the Mountain Cave." Wikipedia. https://en.wikipedia.org/wiki/Lugalbanda_in_the_Mountain_Cave.

8. Black, J. A., G. Cunningham, E. Fluckiger-Hawker, E. Robson, and G. Zólyomi. *The Electronic Text Corpus of Sumerian Literature*. University of Oxford, 1998, "Lugalbanda in the Mountain Cave," Segment A, lines 326-350. https://etcsl.orinst.ox.ac.uk/section1/tr1821.htm.

9. Szpakowska, Kasia. "Through the Looking Glass: Dreams and Nightmares in Pharaonic Egypt." In *Dreams: A Reader on the Religious, Cultural, and Psychological Dimensions of Dreaming*, edited by Kelly Bulkeley. New York: Palgrave Macmillan, 2001, p. 31-32. https://www.academia.edu/20309065/Through_the_Looking_Glass_Dreams_and_Nightmares_in_Pharaonic_Egypt.

10. "Dream Stele." Wikipedia. https://en.wikipedia.org/wiki/Dream_Stele.

11. Szpakowska, "Through the Looking Glass," 34-35.

12. "Mysteries of Isis." Wikipedia. https://en.wikipedia.org/wiki/Mysteries_of_Isis.

13. Apuleius, Lucius. *The Golden Ass, Book XI*, translated by A. S. Kline. Poetry in Translation, 2013. https://www.poetryintranslation.com/PITBR/Latin/TheGoldenAssXI.php.

14. Ibid.

15. Ibid.

16. Ibid.

17. "Mysteries of Isis." Wikipedia.

18. Apuleius, *The Golden Ass, Book XI*.
19. Ibid.
20. Ibid.
21. Ibid.
22. Prada, Luigi. "Dreambooks, Ancient Egypt." In *The Encyclopedia of Ancient History*, edited by Andrew Erskine, David B. Hollander, and Arietta Papaconstantinou. John Wiley & Sons, Ltd., 2019. https://www.academia.edu/41658242/Dream_Books_Ancient_Egypt.
23. Szpakowska, "Through the Looking Glass."
24. "Ashurbanipal Library." The Assyrian Cultural Foundation. https://www.auaf.us/library.
25. "Ashur (God)." Wikipedia. https://en.wikipedia.org/wiki/Ashur_(god).
26. Oppenheim, A. Leo. "The Interpretation of Dreams in the Ancient Near East. With a Translation of an Assyrian Dream Book." *Transactions of the American Philosophical Society* 46, no. 3 (1956): 179-373. https://www.jstor.org/stable/1005761.
27. Hughes, "Dream Interpretation in Ancient Civilizations."
28. "Dream Incubation." Wikipedia. https://en.wikipedia.org/wiki/Dream_incubation.
29. Puhle, Annekatrin. "Dream Incubation." Psi Encyclopedia, May 18, 2020, Updated August 17, 2023. https://psi-encyclopedia.spr.ac.uk/articles/dream-incubation.
30. Van Hove, Rebecca. "Where Dreams May Come: Incubation Sanctuaries in the Greco-Roman World." *Kernos* 32 (2019): 347-350. https://journals.openedition.org/kernos/3213.
31. Puhle, "Dream Incubation."
32. Renberg, Gil. *Where Dreams May Come: Incubation Sanctuaries in the Greco-Roman World. Volume 1*. Leiden, The Netherlands: Brill, January 2017, chapter 7, p. 394-414.
33. Ibid., 392-393.
34. Baer, Jeremy J. "The History of Serapis." Neos Alexandria. https://neosalexandria.org/syncrestism/the-history-of-serapis.
35. Van de Castle, Robert L. "Psychology of Dreaming." In *Dreams and Dreaming*, edited by S. G. M. Lee and A. R. Mayes. Baltimore, Maryland: Penguin Books, 1973, p. 17, 19. Cited in Ong, Robert Keh. "The Interpretation of Dreams in Ancient China." Retrospective Theses and Dissertations, 1919-2007, University of British Columbia, 1981, p. 45. https://open.library.ubc.ca/soa/cIRcle/collections/ubctheses/831/items/1.0095113.
36. "Asclepieion." Wikipedia. https://en.wikipedia.org/wiki/Asclepeion.
37. "Greek Magical Papyri." Wikipedia. https://en.wikipedia.org/wiki/Greek_Magical_Papyri.
38. Puhle, "Dream Incubation."
39. Byrd, Andrew Miles. "Deriving Dreams from the Divine." Academia.edu, p. 8. https://www.academia.edu/345147/Deriving_Dreams_from_the_Divine.
40. Ibid.
41. Harrisson, Juliette. "The Classical Greek Practice of Incubation and Some Near Eastern Predecessors." Academia.edu, p. 5. https://www.academia.edu/277934/The_Classical_Greek_Practice_of_Incubation_and_some_Near_Eastern_Predecessors.
42. Ong, "The Interpretation of Dreams in Ancient China," 48-49.
43. Griffith, Ralph T. H., trans. *The Hymns of the Rigveda*. 2nd ed. Kotagiri, 1896, Hymn LXXXII Savitar 4, Hymn XLVII Adityas 18, Hymn XXXVII Surya 4.
44. Prabhavananda, Swami, and Frederick Manchester, trans. *The Upanishads: Breath from the Eternal*. New York: New American Library, 2002, p. 121.
45. Ganguli, Kisari Mohan, trans. "Book 12: Santi Parva: Mokshadharma Parva: Section CCLXXV" in *The Mahabharata*. Calcutta: Bharata Press (Pratep Chandra Roy), 1883-1896. https://sacred-texts.com/hin/m12/m12b102.htm.
46. Ibid., "Book 3: Vana Parva. Section CCLVI."
47. Rajendran, Abhilash. "Dream of Trijata in the Ramayana." Hindu Blog, April 27, 2018. https://www.hindu-blog.com/2018/04/dream-of-trijata-in-ramayana.html.
48. "Auspicious Dreams in Jainism." Wikipedia. https://www.wikipedia.org/wiki/Auspicious_dreams_in_Jainism.
49. Atwood, *Ancient Religion of the Sun*, 142-144.
50. Ong, "The Interpretation of Dreams in Ancient China," 8-13.

51. "Late Shang Divination and Religion." Encyclopedia Britannica. https://www.britannica.com/place/China/Late-Shang-divination-and-religion.
52. Jiang, Fercility. "Dream Meanings (Chinese Theory) – How to Interpret Dreams." China Highlights, Updated December 7, 2023. https://www.chinahighlights.com/travelguide/culture/dream-meanings.htm.
53. "The Secret of the Golden Flower." New World Encyclopedia. https://www.newworldencyclopedia.org/entry/The_Secret_of_the_Golden_Flower.
54. Wilhelm, Richard, trans. *Secret of the Golden Flower*. Translated from German to English by Cary F. Baynes. Kegan Paul, Trench and Trubner, 1931, Routledge and Kegan Paul Ltd, 1965.
55. Yutang, Lin, trans. "Chuangtse." In *The Wisdom of China*, edited by Lin Yutang. London: Michael Joseph, 1954, p. 83.
56. Lin, Fu-shih. "Religious Taoism and Dreams: An Analysis of the Dream-Data Collected in the Yün-chi ch'i-ch'ien." *Cahiers d'Extrême-Asie Année* 8 (1995): 95-112. https://www.jstor.org/stable/44171430.
57. Crumm, David. "The Importance of Dreams in American Indian Tradition." Read the Spirit, January 27, 2009. https://readthespirit.com/explore/the-importance-of-dreams-in-american-indian-tradition.
58. "An Ojibway Legend—The Dream Fast." Native Languages of the Americas. https://www.native-languages.org/ojibwestory2.htm.
59. Levi, E., El Mundo Maya, and Jay Levi. "Dreams in Mayan Spirituality: Concepts of Dreaming from the Ancient Mayans to the Contemporary Mayans around Lake Atitlán." Semantic Scholar, 2010, p. 8, 13-14. https://www.semanticscholar.org/paper/Dreams-in-Mayan-Spirituality:-Concepts-of-Dreaming-Levi-Maya/bf0582681cb012636837daaaac5ff708763e6ba2.
60. Cecconi, Arianna. "Dreams, Memory, and War: An Ethnography of Night in the Peruvian Andes." *The Journal of Latin American and Caribbean Anthropology* 16, no. 2 (2011): 404.
61. Mannheim, Bruce. "After Dreaming: Image and Interpretation in Southern Peruvian Quechua." *Etnofoor* 4, no. 2 (1991): 43. https://www.jstor.org/stable/25757758.
62. Atwood, *Ancient Religion of the Sun*, 109-117.
63. See the dreams of Pachacuti Yupanque, the ninth king of the Inca Empire recorded in De Betanzos, Juan. *Narrative of the Incas*, edited and translated by Roland Hamilton and Dana Buchanan. Austin: University of Texas Press, 1996, p. 29, 46; The dream of Pachacuti Yupanque's father, the eighth king Hatun Topac later called Viracocha Inca ("Huiracocha Inca." Wikipedia. https://es.wikipedia.org/wiki/Huiracocha_Inca).
64. Cecconi, "Dreams, Memory, and War," 405.
65. Gregory, Lady Augusta. *Gods and Fighting Men*. London: J. Murray, 1904. https://www.sacred-texts.com/neu/celt/gafm/gafm03.htm.
66. Weir-Wakely, Nathanael. "The Path of Cúchulainn." The Incredibly Long Journey, April 28, 2014. https://theincrediblylongjourney.com/2014/04/28/the-path-of-cuchulainn.
67. Ettlinger, E. "Precognitive Dreams in Celtic Legend." *Folklore* 59, no. 3 (September 1948): 97-117. https://www.jstor.org/stable/1257283.
68. King, Anthony. *Roman Gaul and Germany*. University of California Press, 1990, p. 143.
69. McCoy, Daniel. "Dreams." Norse Mythology for Smart People. https://norse-mythology.org/dreams.
70. "Alfar." Odin's Volk. http://odinsvolk.ca/new/gods-goddesses/alfar.
71. Guerber, H. A. *Myths of the Norsemen. From the Eddas and Sagas*. Project Gutenberg EBook, 2009 (EBook #28497). https://www.gutenberg.org/files/28497/28497-h/28497-h.htm.
72. Hippocrates of Cos, *Regimen 4, or Dreams*. Loeb Classical Library, p. 421. https://www.loebclassics.com/view/hippocrates_cos-regimen_iv_dream/1931/pb_LCL150.421.xml.
73. "Separating the Fiction from Reality in Aeneid." Literature Essay Samples, December 9, 2020. https://literatureessaysamples.com/separating-the-fiction-from-reality-in-aeneid.
74. Kasser, Rodolphe, Marvin Meyer, and Gregor Wurst, trans., in collaboration with François Gaudard. *The Gospel of Judas*. Washington: National Geographic Society, 2006, p. 2.
75. Ibid., 4.
76. King, Karen L., George W. MacRae, R. McL. Wilson, and Douglas M. Parrott, trans. "The Gospel of Mary." In *The Nag Hammadi Library in English*, edited by James M. Robinson. San Francisco: HarperCollins, 1990, p. 525-526.

77. James, M. R., trans. "The Acts of Thomas." In *The Apocryphal New Testament*. Oxford: Clarendon Press, 1924. http://www.gnosis.org/library/actthom.htm.
78. "Matthew 1:20-21" in *The Holy Bible*, New International Version (NIV). Biblica, 2011.
79. Ibid., "Matthew 27:19."

CHAPTER FIVE

1. Greyson, Bruce. "Near-Death Experiences and Spirituality." *Zygon Journal of Religion & Science* 41, no. 2 (2006): 394. https://doi.org/10.1111/j.1467-9744.2005.00745.x.
2. Shushan, Gregory. *Conceptions of the Afterlife in Early Civilizations: Universalism, Constructivism, and Near-Death Experience*. London: Continuum, 2009.
3. IanRamseyCentre. "Gregory Shushan – 'Near-Death Experience and the Origins of Afterlife Beliefs.'" YouTube, November 19, 2012. https://youtu.be/QVeoV14J2dY.
4. Atwood, Lara. *The Ancient Religion of the Sun: The Wisdom Bringers and The Lost Civilization of the Sun*. 2nd ed. Sura Ondrunar Publishing, 2021.
5. "Myth of Er." Wikipedia. https://en.wikipedia.org/wiki/Myth_of_Er..
6. Plutarch. *On the Delay of Divine Justice*, translated by Andrew P. Peabody. Boston: Little, Brown, 1885, p. 61. https://archive.org/details/plutarchondelay00plut/page/n9/mode/2up.
7. Ibid., 63-74.
8. Ibid., 74.
9. George, Andrew, trans. *The Epic of Gilgamesh*. Penguin Books, 1999, IX 135-145, IX 170-175, p. 73-75.
10. Scher, Dr. Sarahh. "City of Cusco." Khan Academy. https://www.khanacademy.org/humanities/ap-art-history/indigenous-americas-apah/south-america-apah/a/city-of-cusco.
11. Ziółkowski, Mariusz, and Jacek Kościuk. "Astronomical Observations in the Inca Temple of Coricancha." Arqueología del Perú, September 11, 2021. https://arqueologiadelperu.com/astronomical-observations-in-the-inca-temple-of-coricancha.
12. "Coricancha." Wikipedia. https://en.wikipedia.org/wiki/Coricancha.
13. Cartwright, Mark. "Coricancha." World History Encyclopedia, March 9, 2014. https://www.worldhistory.org/Coricancha.
14. Atwood, *Ancient Religion of the Sun*, 234-237.
15. Milbrath, Susan. *Star Gods of the Maya: Astronomy in Art, Folklore, and Calendars*. Austin: University of Texas Press, 1999, p. 274, 282-284. https://www.academia.edu/2762803/Star_Gods_of_the_Maya_Astronomy_in_Art_Folklore_and_Calendars.
16. "Vision Serpent." Wikipedia. https://en.wikipedia.org/wiki/Vision_Serpent.
17. Virgil. *The Aeneid*, translated by A. S. Kline. Poetry in Translation, 2002, Book VI: The Sibyl Describes Tartarus. https://www.poetryintranslation.com/PITBR/Latin/VirgilAeneidVI.php#anchor_Toc2242935.
18. Ibid., Book VI: The Fields of Elysium.
19. Ibid., Book VI: The Souls Due for Rebirth.
20. "What Does It Mean That Paul Went to the Third Heaven?." Got Questions, September 11, 2023. https://www.gotquestions.org/Paul-third-heaven.html.
21. "2 Corinthians 12:1-5" in *The Holy Bible*, New International Version (NIV). Biblica, 2011.
22. "Apocalypse of Paul." Wikipedia. https://en.wikipedia.org/wiki/Apocalypse_of_Paul.
23. "The Vision of Paul the Apostle." In *The Ante-Nicene Fathers, Vol X*. The Gnostic Society Library. http://www.gnosis.org/library/visionpaul.htm.
24. Ward, Benedicta, trans. *The Sayings of the Desert Fathers: The Alphabetical Collection Paperback*. Liturgical Press, January 1, 1984.
25. "Book I" in *The Evergetinos, A Complete Text*, translated and edited by Archbishop Chrysostomos, Hieromonk Patapios, Bishop Ambrose, Bishop Auxentios, et al. The Center for Traditionalist Orthodox Studies, July 1, 2008. https://www.ctosonline.org/patristic/EvCT.html.
26. Stockton, Shona Nichole. "Near-Death Experience in Indian Religions. Encountering Yama." Dissertation, University of Chester, September 2017. https://chesterrep.openrepository.com/bitstream/handle/10034/621026/S Stockton.pdf.
27. Ibid., 31-33.
28. Ibid., 50.

29. Ibid., 36.
30. "Garuda Purana." Wikipedia. https://en.wikipedia.org/wiki/Garuda_Purana.
31. Stockton, "Near-Death Experience in Indian Religions," 36-37.
32. Ibid., 43.
33. "Ajamila." Wikipedia. https://en.wikipedia.org/wiki/Ajamila.
34. Tagare, Dr. G. V., trans. *The Bhagavata Purana*, Motilal Banarsidass, 1950, book 6, chapters 1 and 2. https://www.wisdomlib.org/hinduism/book/the-bhagavata-purana/d/doc1127145.html, https://www.wisdomlib.org/hinduism/book/the-bhagavata-purana/d/doc1127146.html.
35. See the NDE of Kathy McDaniel in Oaks, Shaman. "Good Catholic Goes to Hell; Says Religion Is to Blame (Shocking NDE!)." YouTube, June 7, 2023. https://youtu.be/MfOAvfwEMVs.
36. De Groot, J. J. M., PhD. *The Religious System of China, Its Ancient Forms, Evolution, History and Present Aspect, Manners, Customs and Social Institutions Connected Therewith*. Leyden, E. J. Brill, 1892-1910.
37. Richardson, Matthew, BA, LLB. "Revelations from Near-Death Experiences of Two Ancient Chinese Coma Patients." *Journal of Near-Death Studies* 37, no. 1 (Spring 2019): 5-26.
38. Stefon, Matt. "Bardo Thödol." Encyclopedia Britannica. https://www.britannica.com/topic/Bardo-Thodol.
39. Padmasambhava. *The Tibetan Book of the Dead*, translated by Lama Kazi Dawa-Samdup. Holybooks.com, p. 13. https://holybooks.com/the-tibetan-book-of-the-dead-2. Note: I have modernized the English in the translation without changing the meaning.
40. "Mahavairocana." Tibetan Buddhist Encyclopedia, February 9, 2016. http://tibetanbuddhistencyclopedia.com/en/index.php?title=Mahavairocana.

CHAPTER SIX

1. Parnia, Sam, et al. "AWARE—AWAreness during REsuscitation—A prospective study." *Resuscitation* 85, no. 12 (December 2014): 1799-1805. https://www.resuscitationjournal.com/article/S0300-9572(14)00739-4/abstract.
2. Lichfield, Gideon. "The Science of Near-Death Experiences." The Atlantic, April 2015. https://www.theatlantic.com/magazine/archive/2015/04/the-science-of-near-death-experiences/386231.
3. Eulitt, May, and Dr. Stephen Hoyer. *Fireweaver: The Story of a Life, a Near-Death, and Beyond*. Xlibris, September, 2001.
4. Williams, Kevin. "A Group of Firefighters Near-Death Experience." NDE, September 20, 2019. https://near-death.com/firefighters-nde.
5. Corliss, William R. "Precognitive Dreams." *Science Frontiers* 120 (Nov-Dec 1998). https://www.science-frontiers.com/sf120/sf120p00.htm.
6. Ryback, David, PhD. *Dreams That Came True*. New York: Bantam Doubleday Dell Publishing Group, 1988.
7. Ring, Kenneth, PhD, and Sharon Cooper, MA. "Near-Death and Out-of-Body Experiences in the Blind: A Study of Apparent Eyeless Vision." *Journal of Near-Death Studies* 16, no. 2 (Winter 1997): 101-147.
8. Ring, Kenneth, and Sharon Cooper. *Mindsight: Near-Death and Out-of-Body Experiences in the Blind*. 2nd ed. iUniverse, 2008.
9. Sunfellow, David. "Vicki Noratuk – NDE." NDE Stories, November 20, 2022. https://ndestories.org/vicki-noratuk.
10. Sabom, Michael, M.D. *Light and Death: One Doctor's Fascinating Account of Near-Death Experiences*. Zondervan, November 1998.
11. Parnia, Sam, M.D. *What Happens When We Die: A Groundbreaking Study into the Nature of Life and Death*. Hay House Inc., February 2007.
12. Carter, Chris. *Science and the Near-Death Experience: How Consciousness Survives Death*. Inner Traditions, August 2010.
13. "Can Reincarnation Be Proven? How Researchers Have Investigated Claims of Past Lives." Beliefnet, February 2003. https://www.beliefnet.com/wellness/2003/02/can-reincarnation-be-proven.aspx.
14. Stevenson, Ian. "Birthmarks and Birth Defects Corresponding to Wounds on Deceased Persons." *Journal of Scientific Exploration* 7, no. 4 (1993): 403-410. https://med.virginia.edu/perceptual-studies/wp-content/uploads/sites/360/2016/12/STE39stevenson-1.pdf.
15. See Michael Nahm's website: www.michaelnahm.com/terminal-lucidity.

16. Nahm, Michael. *Wenn die Dunkelheit ein Ende findet: Terminale Geistesklarheit und andere Phänomene in Todesnähe*. Amerang: Crotona, February 2012, p. 286.
17. Haig, Scott, M.D. "The Brain: The Power of Hope." Time, January 29, 2007. https://content.time.com/time/magazine/article/0,9171,1580392,00.html.
18. Chiriboga-Oleszczak, Boris Alejandro. "Review Paper. Terminal Lucidity." Current Problems of Psychiatry 18, no. 1 (2017): 34-46. https://doi.org/10.1515/cpp-2017-0003.
19. Sunfellow, David. "Miraculous NDE Healings." The Formula for Creating Heaven on Earth, May 5, 2022. https://theformulaforcreatingheavenonearth.com/near-death-experiences-miraculous-healings.
20. Sunfellow, David. "Anita Moorjani." The Formula for Creating Heaven on Earth, December 3, 2021. https://theformulaforcreatingheavenonearth.com/anita-moorjani.
21. Sartori, Dr. Penny. *Wisdom of Near-Death Experiences: How Understanding NDEs Can Help Us Live More Fully*. Watkins Publishing, February 2014.
22. "At Heaven's Door by William Peters." Life After Life, February 8, 2022. https://www.lifeafterlife.com/blog/at-heavens-door-by-william-peters.
23. Moody, Raymond. *Glimpses of Eternity: An Investigation into Shared Death Experiences*. Rider, 2011.
24. Moody, Raymond. "An Experience of My Own." Guideposts. https://guideposts.org/angels-and-miracles/life-after-death/an-experience-of-my-own.
25. Alvarado, C. "Neglected Near-Death Phenomena." *Journal of Near-Death Studies* 24 (2006): 131-151; Crookall, R. *Events on the Threshold of the Afterlife*. Moradabad, India: Darshana International, 1967; Fenwick, P., and E. Fenwick. *The Art of Dying*. London, England, and New York, NY: Continuum, 2008; Fenwick, P., H. Lovelace, and S. Brayne. "End of Life Experiences and Their Implications for Palliative Care." *International Journal of Environmental Studies* 64 (2007): 315-323; Martensen-Larsen, H. *Ein Schimmer durch den Vorhang*. Berlin, Germany: Furche, ca. 1927; O'Connor, D. "Palliative Care Nurse's Experiences of Paranormal Phenomena and Their Influence on Nursing Practice." Paper presented at the Second Global Making Sense of Dying and Death Interdisciplinary Conference, Paris, France, November 21-23, 2003; Roesermueller, W. O. *Um die Todesstunde*. Nurnberg, Germany: Selbstverlag, 1957.
26. Kerr, Christopher W., James P. Donnelly, Scott T. Wright, Sarah M. Kuszczak, et al. "End-of-Life Dreams and Visions: A Longitudinal Study of Hospice Patients' Experiences." *Journal of Palliative Medicine* 17, no. 3 (2014): 296-303. https://pubmed.ncbi.nlm.nih.gov/24410369.
27. Podmore, Frank. *Studies in Psychical Research*. London: Kegan Paul, Trench, Trubner & Company, 1897, p. 281-285. https://www.google.com/books/edition/Studies_in_Psychical_Research/V10AAAAAMAAJ.
28. Guggenheim, Bill, and Judy Guggenheim. *Hello from Heaven: A New Field of Research—After-Death Communication—Confirms That Life and Love Are Eternal*. Random House Publishing Group, 1997, chapter 10.
29. Osis, Karlis, PhD, and Erlendur Haraldsson, PhD. *At the Hour of Death*. Avon, January 1977.
30. Williams, Kevin. "Scientific Evidence Supporting Near-Death Experiences and the Afterlife." NDE, September 16, 2019. https://near-death.com/afterlife-evidence.
31. International Association for Near-Death Studies (IANDS) website: https://iands.org/research/publications/journal-of-near-death-studies/basic-information.html.
32. Near-Death Experience Research Foundation (NDERF) website: https://www.nderf.org.
33. Morse, Melvin. "Kim Clark Finds the Tennis Shoe and Proves Near Death Experiences Are Real." YouTube, March 2, 2011. https://youtu.be/WPXK2Ls-xzQ.
34. Walker, Evan Harris. *The Physics of Consciousness: The Quantum Mind and the Meaning of Life*. Basic Books, December 2000.
35. Selbie, Joseph. *The Physics of God: Unifying Quantum Physics, Consciousness, M-Theory, Heaven, Neuroscience and Transcendence*. New Page Books, September 2017.
36. Fenwick, Peter. "Non-Local Effects in the Process of Dying: Can Quantum Mechanics Help?." *Neuroquantology* 8, no. 2 (2010): 143-154. https://eprints.soton.ac.uk/162391.
37. Dobrijevic, Daisy, and Vicky Stein. "Do Parallel Universes Exist? We Might Live in a Multiverse." Space.com, November 3, 2021. https://www.space.com/32728-parallel-universes.html.
38. Fenwick, Peter, M.D., F.R.C. Psych. "Science and Spirituality: A Challenge for the Twenty First Century." International Association for Near-Death Studies, Updated June 11, 2022. https://iands.org/research/nde-research/important-research-articles/42-dr-peter-fenwick-md-science-and-spirituality.html?start=2.

39. Morse, Melvin, M.D., with Paul Perry. *Transformed by the Light: The Powerful Effect of Near-Death Experiences on People's Lives*. Villard, August 1992.
40. Gresham College. "The Man with No Brain: Brain Adaptation and Self-Repair - By Professor Keith Kendrick." YouTube, March 29, 2011. https://youtu.be/v8R71Q8_0y0.
41. Society for Scientific Exploration. "SSE Talks - Science and Postmortem Survival - Bruce Greyson -3/5." YouTube, May 16, 2010. https://youtu.be/ARjtHrqbqu4.
42. "Man with Tiny Brain Shocks Doctors." New Scientist, July 20, 2007. https://www.newscientist.com/article/dn12301-man-with-tiny-brain-shocks-doctors.
43. Noë, Alva. *Out of Our Heads: Why You Are Not Your Brain, and Other Lessons from the Biology of Consciousness*. New York: Hill and Wang, 2009, p. xi.

CHAPTER SEVEN

1. Sylvia, Claire, with William Novak. *A Change of Heart: A Memoir*. Little, Brown and Company, May 1997.

CHAPTER EIGHT

1. V, Jayaram. "Hinduism, Life after Death and Planes of Existence." Hinduwebsite.com. https://www.hinduwebsite.com/heavenhell.asp.
2. Vega, Garcilaso de la. *Royal Commentaries of the Incas and General History of Peru*, translated by Harold V. Livermore. University of Texas Press, 2014, Part One, book 2, chapter 7, Kindle edition.
3. "Pacha (Inca Mythology)." Wikipedia. https://en.wikipedia.org/wiki/Pacha_(Inca_mythology).
4. "Celtic Otherworld." Wikipedia. https://en.wikipedia.org/wiki/Celtic_Otherworld.
5. "Chinese Mythology." Wikipedia. https://en.wikipedia.org/wiki/Chinese_mythology.
6. "Tian." Wikipedia. https://en.wikipedia.org/wiki/Tian.
7. "Diyu." Wikipedia. https://en.wikipedia.org/wiki/Diyu.
8. McCoy, Daniel. "The Nine Worlds." Norse Mythology for Smart People. https://norse-mythology.org/cosmology/the-nine-worlds.
9. Mursell, Ian. "The Thirteen Mexica Heavens and Nine Underworlds." Mexicolore. https://www.mexicolore.co.uk/aztecs/ask-us/13-heavens-and-9-underworlds.
10. Hall, Manly P. *The Secret Teachings of All Ages*. San Francisco: H.S. Crocker Company, 1928, https://www.sacred-texts.com/eso/sta/sta06.htm.
11. See the ancient Gnostic text *Pistis Sophia* (Mead, G. R. S., trans. *Pistis Sophia*. London: J. M. Watkins, 1921).
12. See the texts "2 Corinthians" in *The Holy Bible*, New International Version (NIV). Biblica, 2011; "The Vision of Paul the Apostle" in *The Ante-Nicene Fathers, Vol X*. The Gnostic Society Library. http://www.gnosis.org/library/visionpaul.htm; and "The Apocalypse of Paul" in *The Nag Hammadi Library in English*, edited by James M. Robinson. San Francisco: HarperCollins, 1990.
13. Halpern, Paul. "Spiritual Hyperplane," edited by Corey S. Powell. Aeon, January 18, 2018. https://aeon.co/essays/the-occult-roots-of-higher-dimensional-research-in-physics.
14. Blacklock, Matt. "Chapter 5—Through: The Theosophical Society, Authority, and Mediation." In *The Emergence of the Fourth Dimension: Higher Spatial Thinking in the Fin de Siècle*. Oxford University Press, 2018. https://academic.oup.com/book/6631/chapter-abstract/150656864.
15. "The Time Machine." Wikipedia. https://en.wikipedia.org/wiki/The_Time_Machine.
16. "The Plattner Story." Wikipedia. https://en.wikipedia.org/wiki/The_Plattner_Story.
17. Tietz, Tabea. "Hermann Minkowski and the Four-Dimensional Space-Time." SciHi Blog, June 22, 2021. http://scihi.org/hermann-minkowski-space-time.
18. "Five-Dimensional Space." Wikipedia. https://en.wikipedia.org/wiki/Five-dimensional_space.
19. Chown, Marcus. "Our Universe May Have a Fifth Dimension That Would Change Everything We Know about Physics." BBC Science Focus, September 25, 2023. https://www.sciencefocus.com/space/fifth-dimension.
20. Wertheim, Margaret. "Radical Dimensions," edited by Marina Benjamin. Aeon, January 10, 2018. https://aeon.co/essays/how-many-dimensions-are-there-and-what-do-they-do-to-reality.
21. Chown, "Our Universe May Have a Fifth Dimension."
22. Coming Home. "Teacher Drowns: Meets Creator of the Universe (Near-Death Experience)." YouTube, May 5, 2023, 7:23-7:29. https://youtu.be/gsq72npuxFs&t=443.
23. "Visible Spectrum." Wikipedia. https://en.wikipedia.org/wiki/Visible_spectrum.

24. Science Mission Directorate. "Visible Light." NASA Science, 2010. https://science.nasa.gov/ems/09_visiblelight.
25. "Is the Electromagnetic Spectrum Infinite?." Quora. https://www.quora.com/Is-the-electromagnetic-spectrum-infinite.
26. "Dark Matter." Wikipedia. https://en.wikipedia.org/wiki/Dark_matter.
27. Sundermier, Ali. "99.9999999% of Your Body Is Empty Space." ScienceAlert, September 23, 2016. https://www.sciencealert.com/99-9999999-of-your-body-is-empty-space.
28. Secondbase17. "What Is the 'Empty Space' in an Atom?." Reddit, January 2, 2014. https://www.reddit.com/r/askscience/comments/1u8ood/what_is_the_empty_space_in_an_atom.
29. "Emotional Plane." Theosophy Wiki, Edited May 1, 2013. https://theosophy.wiki/en/Emotional_Plane.
30. "Plane (Esotericism)—Mental Plane." Wikipedia. https://en.wikipedia.org/wiki/Plane_(esotericism)#Mental_plane.
31. "Plane." The Britannica Dictionary. https://www.britannica.com/dictionary/plane.
32. The Other Side NDE. "Man Is Shown the Future During NDE; Taught the Meaning of Life (Near-Death Experience)." YouTube, August 20, 2022, 3:45-4:44 (Jeff Tobey). https://youtu.be/-DbqXXF_88Q&t=225.
33. The Institute of Art and Ideas. "Will We Ever Grasp the Nature of the Mind? | Rupert Sheldrake, David Chalmers, Philip Goff..." YouTube, April 28, 2022, 4:55 (Rubert Sheldrake). https://youtu.be/UWjh0TVywow&t=295.
34. Hanegraaff, Wouter J. "Chapter 1—Hermetic Spirituality." In *Hermetic Spirituality and the Historical Imagination: Altered States of Knowledge in Late Antiquity*. Cambridge: Cambridge University Press, 2022. https://www.cambridge.org/core/books/hermetic-spirituality-and-the-historical-imagination/hermetic-spirituality/54B16F545D3B0F5C671AFE1841798B75.
35. Copenhaver, Brian P., trans. *Hermetica: The Greek Corpus Hermeticum and the Latin Asclepius in a New English Translation, with Notes and Introduction*. Reprint ed. Cambridge University Press, October 12, 1995, p. 32, 43-44, Kindle edition.
36. "Manas." Veda. http://veda.wikidot.com/manas.
37. "Buddhi." Veda. http://veda.wikidot.com/buddhi.
38. "Buddhi." Wikipedia. https://en.wikipedia.org/wiki/Buddhi.
39. Dunn, Jimmy. "The Ancient Egyptian Ka." Tour Egypt. https://www.touregypt.net/featurestories/ka.htm.
40. "Pranamaya Kosha." Yogapedia, Updated December 21, 2023. https://www.yogapedia.com/definition/7764/pranamaya-kosha.
41. Beguin, Sylvie, Interview with Dr. Pasang Y. Arya. "*La* and *La* Ceremony." TME – Tibetan Medicine Education Center. https://tibetanmedicine-edu.org/tmm/tm/psychology-and-psychiatry/la-and-la-ceremony.
42. Parrott, Douglas M., trans., "Sophia of Jesus Christ." In *The Nag Hammadi Library*, 234-235.
43. Easwaran, Eknath, trans. *The Upanishads*. Tomales: Nilgiri Press, 2007, p. 188.
44. "Chit (Consciousness)." Wikipedia. https://en.wikipedia.org/wiki/Chit_(consciousness).
45. "Jiva." Encyclopedia Britannica. https://www.britannica.com/topic/jiva.
46. Sovik, Rolf. "Gayatri Mantra: History, Meaning, & Benefits." Yoga International. https://yogainternational.com/article/view/the-gayatri-mantra-awakening-to-the-sun.
47. See my book on self-knowledge for a history and modern reconstruction of this practice.

CHAPTER NINE

1. "Sam Parnia." Wikipedia. https://en.wikipedia.org/wiki/Sam_Parnia.
2. Moody Jr., Raymond A., MD. *Life After Life: The Bestselling Original Investigation That Revealed "Near-Death Experiences."* HarperOne, September 2015.
3. Lundahl, Craig R., PhD. "The Near-Death Experience: A Theoretical Summarization." *Journal of Near-Death Studies* 12 (1993): 105-118. https://digital.library.unt.edu/ark:/67531/metadc799141/m2/1/high_res_d/vol12-no2-105.pdf.
4. Next Level Soul Podcast. "ER Doctor has NDLE; Is TAKEN to HEAVEN & Shown the SECRETS of Healing the HUMAN BODY! | Anoop Kumar." YouTube, December 26, 2023, 11:17-11:25. https://youtu.be/uZvWJdcRtOQ&t=677.

5. The Other Side NDE. "Professor Studied NDE's for 30 Years; What She Discovers Is Incredible (Near Death Experiences)." YouTube, February 13, 2024, 8:51-11.43. https://youtu.be/QQWoQFtxYsM&t=531.
6. Shaman Oaks. "Non-Christian Sees Jesus During Near-Death Experience (NDE)." YouTube, May 18, 2021. https://youtu.be/5nJz8I7Nhbk.
7. Williams, Kevin. "Carl G. Jung's Near-Death Experience." Near-Death Experiences and the Afterlife, September 23, 2019. https://near-death.com/carl-jung-nde.
8. Greyson, Bruce, MD, and Nancy Evans Bush, MA. "Distressing Near-Death Experiences." In *The Near-Death Experience: A Reader*, edited by Lee W. Bailey and Jenny Yates. New York: Routledge, 1996.
9. Botsford, Nancy. *A Day in Hell*. Tate Publishing, July 2010.

CHAPTER TEN

1. Twemlow, Stuart W., Glen O. Gabbard, and F. C. Jones. "The Out-of-Body Experience: A Phenomenological Typology Based on Questionnaire Responses." *The American Journal of Psychiatry* 139, no. 4 (1982): 452-454. https://api.semanticscholar.org/CorpusID:42318966.
2. Tart, Charles. T., PhD. "Six Studies of Out-of-Body Experiences." *Journal of Near-Death Studies* 17, no. 2 (Winter 1998): 79-81. https://digital.library.unt.edu/ark:/67531/metadc799368/m2/1/high_res_d/vol17-no2-73.pdf.
3. "Charles Tart." Wikipedia. https://en.wikipedia.org/wiki/Charles_Tart.
4. Tart, "Six Studies of Out-of-Body Experiences," 81-82.
5. Ibid., 82-91.
6. Chasing Consciousness Podcast. "#27 Thomas Campbell - Testing Out-of-Body Experiences." YouTube, August 31, 2022, 36:20-37:01. https://youtu.be/5d3B0cxcllA&t=2180.
7. Parker, Vince. "Paranormal: What Evidence Exists for Out-of-Body Experiences? (Answer)." Quora. https://www.quora.com/Paranormal-What-evidence-exists-for-out-of-body-experiences/answer/Vince-Parker.
8. "Form Constant." Wikipedia. https://en.wikipedia.org/wiki/Form_constant.
9. "Temporoparietal Junction." Wikipedia. https://en.wikipedia.org/wiki/Temporoparietal_junction.
10. Blackmore, Susan, PhD. "Out-of-Body Experiences: A Neuroscientific Explanation." Psychology Today, August 23, 2019. https://www.psychologytoday.com/us/blog/ten-zen-questions/201908/out-body-experiences-neuroscientific-explanation.
11. The Other Side NDE. "Man Dies in Surgery; Shown Truth about Black Holes, Other Dimensions during Shocking NDE." YouTube, April 15, 2023, 5:20-6:36. https://youtu.be/zQTgiXdFZrw&t=320.
12. The Afterlife Files. "Eight Lessons Learned through NDEs with Dr. Bruce Greyson | Episode 3." YouTube, Mach 9, 2022, 36:09-36:48. https://youtu.be/xjlk3aDcSDA&t=2169.
13. Greyson, Bruce, MD. *After: A Doctor Explores What Near-Death Experiences Reveal about Life and Beyond*. St. Martin's Publishing Group, p. 125, Kindle edition.
14. The Afterlife Files. "Eight Lessons Learned through NDEs," 36:95-37:13.
15. Greyson, *After*, 126-127.
16. Zyga, Lisa. "CRO Magnon Skull Shows That Our Brains Have Shrunk." Phys.org, March 15, 2010. https://phys.org/news/2010-03-cro-magnon-skull-brains-shrunk.html.
17. "Our Brains Are Shrinking. Are We Getting Dumber?." NPR, January 22, 2011. https://www.npr.org/2011/01/02/132591244/our-brains-are-shrinking-are-we-getting-dumber.
18. Chasing Consciousness Podcast, "#27 Thomas Campbell," 15:23-16:20.
19. Blanke, Olaf, Stephanie Ortigue, Theodor Landis, and Margitta Seeck. "Stimulating Illusory Own-Body Perceptions." *Nature* 419 (2002): 269–270. https://doi.org/10.1038/419269a.
20. De Ridder, Dirk, Koen Van Laere, Patrick Dupont, et al. "Visualizing Out-of-Body Experience in the Brain." *The New England Journal of Medicine* 357 (Nov 1, 2007): 1829-33. https://www.nejm.org/doi/full/10.1056/NEJMoa070010.
21. Heydrich, Lukas, Christophe Lopez, Margitta Seeck, and Olaf Blanke. "Partial and Full Own-Body Illusions of Epileptic Origin in a Child with Right Temporoparietal Epilepsy." *Epilepsy & Behavior* 20, no. 3 (March 2011): 583-586. https://www.sciencedirect.com/science/article/pii/S1525505011000114.
22. Blanke, Olaf, Theodor Landis, Laurent Spinelli, and Margitta Seeck. "Out-of-Body Experience and Autoscopy of Neurological Origin." *Brain* 127, no. 2 (February 2004): 243-258. https://academic.oup.com/brain/article/127/2/243/347826.

23. The Weekend University. "The Science of Out-of-Body Experiences – Dr. Susan Blackmore." YouTube, November 12, 2019. https://youtu.be/3VoixOyTPwg.
24. Bülow, Pernille, PhD. "Dissociation as Self-Defense in Childhood Sexual Abuse." Psychology Today, December 30, 2022. https://www.psychologytoday.com/us/blog/your-brain-on-body-dysmorphia/202212/dissociation-as-self-defense-in-childhood-sexual-abuse.
25. Blanke, Olaf, and Christine Mohr. "Out-of-Body Experience, Heautoscopy, and Autoscopic Hallucination of Neurological Origin: Implications for Neurocognitive Mechanisms of Corporeal Awareness and Self-Consciousness." *Brain Research Reviews* 50, no. 1 (December 2005): 184-199. https://www.sciencedirect.com/science/article/abs/pii/S0165017305000792.
26. "Autoscopy." Wikipedia. https://en.wikipedia.org/wiki/Autoscopy.
27. Dening, T. R., and G. E. Berrios. "Autoscopic Phenomena." *British Journal of Psychiatry* 165, no. 6 (1994): 808–817. https://doi.org/10.1192/bjp.165.6.808.
28. Blanke, et al., "Out-of-Body Experience and Autoscopy of Neurological Origin."
29. Braithwaite, Jason J., Dana Samson, Ian Apperly, et al. "Cognitive Correlates of the Spontaneous Out-of-Body Experience (OBE) in the Psychologically Normal Population: Evidence for an Increased Role of Temporal-Lobe Instability, Body-Distortion Processing, and Impairments in Own-Body Transformations." *Cortex* 47, no. 7 (July-August 2011): 839-853. https://www.sciencedirect.com/science/article/abs/pii/S0010945210001486.
30. Welsh, Jennifer. "Out-of-Body Hallucinations Linked to Brain Glitch." Live Science, July 12, 2011. https://www.livescience.com/15005-normal-body-experience.html.
31. Lopez, Christophe, and Maya Elzière. "Out-of-Body Experience in Vestibular Disorders - A Prospective Study of 210 Patients with Dizziness." *Cortex* 104 (2018): 193-206. https://pubmed.ncbi.nlm.nih.gov/28669509.
32. Ehrsson, H. Henrik. "The Experimental Induction of Out-of-Body Experiences." *Science* 317 (2007): 1048. https://doi.org/10.1126/science.1142175.
33. Ibid., "Supplementary Material." https://www.science.org/doi/10.1126/science.1142175#supplementary-materials.
34. Lewis, Tanya. "Out-of-Body Experience Is Traced in the Brain." Live Science, April 30, 2015. https://www.livescience.com/50683-out-of-body-illusion.html.
35. "Visualized Heartbeat Can Trigger 'Out-of-Body Experience.'" Association for Psychological Science, August 14, 2013. https://www.psychologicalscience.org/news/releases/visualized-heartbeat-can-trigger-out-of-body-experience.html.
36. University College London. "First Out-of-Body Experience Induced in Laboratory Setting." ScienceDaily, August 24, 2007. https://www.sciencedaily.com/releases/2007/08/070823141057.htm.
37. Tart, "Six Studies of Out-of-Body Experiences," 76.
38. De Ridder, et al., "Visualizing Out-of-Body Experience in the Brain."
39. Shaman Oaks. "Atheist Dies; Shocked by What She Saw on the Other Side (Powerful NDE)." YouTube, May 2, 2023, 22:07-22:15, 21:24-21:34. https://youtu.be/w65SNVpmuR8&t=1327.

CHAPTER ELEVEN

No references.

CHAPTER TWELVE

No references.

CHAPTER THIRTEEN

1. Reed, Henry, PhD. "Incubating Dreams Solves Problems: A Description of Two Studies." Intuitive Connections Network, Updated February 17, 2003. http://intuitive-connections.net/2003/dreamincubation.htm.
2. Delaney, Gayle. "Dream Incubation, Targeting Dreaming to Focus on Particular Details." In *Dream Research: Contributions to Clinical Practice*, edited by Milton Kramer and Myron L. Glucksman. New York: Routledge, 2015.
3. Barrett, Deirdre. "The 'Committee of Sleep:' A Study of Dream Incubation for Problem Solving." *Dreaming* 3, no. 2 (1993). https://asdreams.org/journal/articles/barrett3-2.htm.

4. Winkler, Brian, PhD. "Dream Incubation: An Experimental Inquiry into the Process of Petitioning Dreams for Guidance, Healing and Problem Solving." Doctoral Dissertation, Institute of Transpersonal Psychology, 1990.
5. Forti, Kathy J., PhD. "Healing through Dream Incubation." Trinfinity8, September 23, 2014. https://trinfinity8.com/healing-through-dream-incubation.
6. Puhle, Annekatrin. "Dream Incubation." Psi Encyclopedia, May 18, 2020, Updated August 17, 2023. https://psi-encyclopedia.spr.ac.uk/articles/dream-incubation.
7. Betz, Hans Deiter, editor. *The Greek Magical Papyri in Translation*. London: The University of Chicago Press, 1986. PGM VII. 664-685, PGM VII. 359-369, PGM VII. 740-755, PGM VII. 795-845, PDM lxi. 63-78, PDM lxi. 63-78.
8. Puhle, "Dream Incubation."
9. Betz, ed., *Greek Magical Papyri*, PGM VII. 359-69.
10. Ibid., PDM lxi. 63-78.
11. Ibid., PDM Suppl. 130-138.
12. Ibid., PGM VII. 664-685.
13. Ibid., PGM VII. 1009-1016.
14. Ibid., PGM VIII. 64-110.
15. Ibid., PGM V. 370-446.
16. Ibid., PGM VI. 1-47.
17. Ibid., PGM IV. 3172-3208.
18. Ibid., PDM xiv. 117-149.
19. "Papyrus Chester-Beatty 3, known as the 'Dream Book.'" In Puhle, "Dream Incubation."
20. Betz, ed., *Greek Magical Papyri*, PGM VII. 359-69.
21. Atwood, Mark, with Lara Atwood. *Ancient Solstice: Uncovering the Spiritual Meaning of the Solstices and Equinoxes*. Updated 4th ed. Sura Ondrunar Publishing, 2021, p. 31-38.
22. Betz, ed., *Greek Magical Papyri*, PGM VII. 740-55.
23. Puhle, "Dream Incubation."
24. Nielsen, T. "Dream Incubation: Ancient Techniques of Dream Influence." Dream and Nightmare Laboratory, 2012, p. 4-6. https://www.dreamscience.ca/en/documents/New content/incubation/Incubation overview for website updated.pdf.
25. Betz, ed., *Greek Magical Papyri*, PGM V. 447-458.
26. Ibid., PGM VII. 795-845.
27. Ibid., PGM V. 447-458, PGM VII 664-685, PGM VIII. 64-110, PGM XII. 190-192.
28. Ibid., PDM Suppl. 130-138.
29. Ibid., PGM VIII. 64-110.
30. Nielsen, "Dream Incubation," 5-7.
31. El-Kilany, Engy, and Islam Elgammal. "Dream Incubation Tourism: The Resurrection of Ancient Egyptian Heritage of Sleep Temples." *International Journal of Heritage and Museum Studies* 1, no. 1 (October 2019): 93-106. https://journals.ekb.eg/article_118759.html.
32. Janes, Sarah. "Sleeping in Sacred Space." https://themysteries.org/dream-pilgrimage.
33. "Lindisfarne Dream Incubation and Pilgrimage Workshop." The British Pilgrimage Trust. https://britishpilgrimage.org/events-new/lindisfarne-dream-incubation-and-pilgrimage-workshop.

CHAPTER FOURTEEN

No references.

CHAPTER FIFTEEN

1. Frawley, David. *Vedic Yoga: The Path of the Rishi*. Lotus Press, 2014, p. 117, Kindle edition.
2. Patañjali, *Yoga Sutras of Patanjali, Samadhi Pada*. Stillnessinyoga, 2020, Sutra I.2-I.4. https://www.stillnessinyoga.com/wp-content/uploads/2020/10/01.samadhi_pada-1.pdf. Note: I have omitted the Sanskrit terms to make it more readable.
3. *Rigveda* V.82.1. In Frawley, David. *Textual Evidence in the Vedas: Cultural and Historical Implications*. Indian Council of Historical Research, March 2015.

4. Patañjali, *Yoga Sutras of Patanjali, Samadhi Pada*, Sutra I.2-I.4.
5. Ibid., Sutra I.13, I.30-32.
6. Ibid., Sutra I.35; Patañjali, *Yoga Sutras of Patanjali, Vibhuti Pada*. Stillnessinyoga, 2020, Sutra III.1. https://www.stillnessinyoga.com/wp-content/uploads/2020/10/03.vibuti_pada.pdf.
7. Chitrabhanu, Shree. *Realize What You Are: The Dynamics of Meditation*, edited by Leonard M. Marks. New York: Jain Meditation International Center, 1978. p. 16-17.
8. "Kammaṭṭhāna." Wikipedia. https://en.wikipedia.org/wiki/Kammatthana.
9. Nanamoli, Bhikkhu, trans. *Visuddhimagga: The Path of Purification*. Sri Lanka: Buddhist Publication Society, 2010, p. 119-120.
10. "Kasiṇa." Encyclopedia of Buddhism. https://encyclopediaofbuddhism.org/wiki/Kasina.
11. Patañjali, *Yoga Sutras of Patanjali, Vibhuti Pada*, Sutra III.1-5, III.27.
12. Satchidananda, Sri Swami, trans. *The Yoga Sutras of Patanjali*. Pocket ed. Integral Yoga Publications, July 2002, Sutra I.40.
13. Patañjali, *Yoga Sutras of Patanjali, Samadhi Pada*, Sutra I.39
14. Patañjali, *Yoga Sutras of Patanjali, Vibhuti Pada*, Sutra III.26

CHAPTER SIXTEEN

No references.

CHAPTER SEVENTEEN

1. Milazzo, Nick, MSc, MPH. "Research Breakdown on Binaural Beats." Examine, Updated September 28, 2022. https://examine.com/other/binauralbeats/research.
2. Society for Neuroscience. "Binaural Beats Synchronize Brain Activity, Don't Affect Mood." ScienceDaily, February 17, 2020. https://www.sciencedaily.com/releases/2020/02/200217143447.htm.
3. Nantawachara, Jirakittayakorn, and Wongsawat Yodchanan. "Brain Responses to a 6-Hz Binaural Beat: Effects on General Theta Rhythm and Frontal Midline Theta Activity." *Frontiers in Neuroscience* 11 (June 2017). https://www.frontiersin.org/articles/10.3389/fnins.2017.00365/full.
4. Chasing Consciousness Podcast. "#27 Thomas Campbell – Testing Out-of-Body Experiences." YouTube, Aug 31, 2022, 1:05:04-1:23:17. https://youtu.be/5d3B0cxcllA&t=3904.
5. Alexandru, Bogdan V., Balázsi Róbert, Lupu Viorel, and Bogdan Vasile. "Treating Primary Insomnia: A Comparative Study of Self-Help Methods and Progressive Muscle Relaxation." *Journal of Cognitive and Behavioral Psychotherapies* 9, no. 1 (March 2009): 67-82. https://www.researchgate.net/publication/286004425_Treating_primary_insomnia_A_comparative_study_of_self-help_methods_and_progressive_muscle_relaxation.
6. Lavallee, Christina F., Stanley A. Koren, and Michael A. Persinger. "A Quantitative Electroencephalographic Study of Meditation and Binaural Beat Entrainment." *Journal of Alternative and Complementary Medicine* 17, no.4 (April 2011): 351–355. https://pubmed.ncbi.nlm.nih.gov/21480784.
7. Chaieb, Leila, Elke Caroline Wilpert, Thomas P. Reber, and Juergen Fell. "Auditory Beat Stimulation and Its Effects on Cognition and Mood States." *Frontiers in Psychiatry* 6, article 70 (May 2015). https://www.ncbi.nlm.nih.gov/pmc/articles/PMC4428073.
8. Danley, Tom. "The Great Pyramid: Early Reflections and Ancient Echoes." ProSoundWeb, August 4, 2020. https://www.prosoundweb.com/the-great-pyramid-early-reflections-ancient-echoes/6.
9. Kvilhaug, Maria. *The Seed of Yggdrasill: Deciphering the Hidden Messages in Old Norse Myths*. Whyte Tracks, 2016, Introduction Notes, section 10.3: The Vision Quest, Kindle edition.

CHAPTER EIGHTEEN

1. "Chapter XXIII. The Aerial Journey of Spiritual Bodies." In Mitra, Vihari-Lala, trans. *The Yoga-Vasishtha Maharamayana of Valmiki, Vol.* 1. Delhi, India: Low Price Publications, 1999, p. 4-16, Kindle locations 7680-7681, Kindle edition. https://www.gutenberg.org/ebooks/71326.
2. "Rishabhanatha." Wikipedia. https://en.wikipedia.org/wiki/Rishabhanatha.
3. Sangave, Dr. Vilas. "Antiquity of Jaina Tradition." Encyclopedia of Jainism, March 28, 2023. https://encyclopediaofjainism.com/antiquity-of-jaina-tradition.

4. "In Jainism, what is the difference between Kayotsarga and Samayik?." Quora. https://www.quora.com/In-Jainism-what-is-the-difference-between-Kayotsarga-and-Samayik.
5. Kothari, Dhara. "Kayotsarg." The Jain Universe, September 24, 2012. https://jaincosmos.blogspot.com/2012/09/kayotsarg.html.
6. Mahendra Kumar, Muni. "Kayotsarga." Jain World, September 2, 2022. https://jainworld.com/philosophy/others/preksha-dhayan/a-handbook-of-preksha-meditation-for-the-trainers/13-kayotsarga.
7. "Kayotsarga." Preksha International, October 31, 2009. https://www.preksha.com/preksha/kayotsarga.
8. Atwood, Mark, with Lara Atwood. *Ancient Solstice: Uncovering the Spiritual Meaning of the Solstices and Equinoxes*. Updated 4th ed. Sura Ondrunar Publishing, 2021, p. 31-38.

CHAPTER NINETEEN

1. Patañjali, *Yoga Sutras of Patanjali, Samadhi Pada*. Stillnessinyoga, 2020, Sutra I.36. https://www.stillnessinyoga.com/wp-content/uploads/2020/10/01.samadhi_pada-1.pdf.

CHAPTER TWENTY

1. Morrow, Susan Brind. *The Dawning Moon of the Mind: Unlocking the Pyramid Texts*. Farrar, Straus and Giroux, 2015, p. 129, 132, 136, Kindle edition.
2. Allen, James P., trans. *The Ancient Egyptian Pyramid Texts*, edited by Peter Der Manuelian. Atlanta, Georgia: Society of Biblical Literature, 2005, p. 16.
3. "Amun." Wikipedia. https://en.wikipedia.org/wiki/Amun.
4. Atwood, Lara. *The Ancient Religion of the Sun: The Wisdom Bringers and The Lost Civilization of the Sun*. 2nd ed. Sura Ondrunar Publishing, 2021, p. 260-261.
5. "Atum." Wikipedia. https://en.wikipedia.org/wiki/Atum.
6. "Soham (Sanskrit)." Wikipedia. https://en.wikipedia.org/wiki/Soham_(Sanskrit). The phrase originates from verse 16 of the Isha Upanishad.
7. Holistic Yoga. "How Do You Pronounce Aum (Is It Aum or Om)." YouTube, September 21, 2018. https://youtu.be/XxzLm4hypp4.
8. "What Is the Meaning of Om Tat Sat?." Stack Exchange, January 17, 2015. https://hinduism.stackexchange.com/questions/5206/what-is-the-meaning-of-om-tat-sat.
9. Frawley, David. *Vedic Yoga: The Path of the Rishi*. Lotus Press, 2014, p. 164, Kindle edition.
10. "Hari Om." Yogapedia, Updated December 21, 2023. https://www.yogapedia.com/definition/7560/hari-om.

CHAPTER TWENTY-ONE

1. Buhlman, William. "Early Morning Technique." Astralinfo.org. https://astralinfo.org/early-morning-technique.

CHAPTER TWENTY-TWO

No references.

CHAPTER TWENTY-THREE

1. Abhinavagupta, *Tantrasara of Abhinavagupta*, translated by H. N. Chakravarty, edited by Boris Marjanovic. Portland, Oregon: Rudra Press, 2012, p. 83.
2. "Jain Meditation." Wikipedia. https://en.wikipedia.org/wiki/Jain_meditation.
3. Shizhong, Lu. *The Incomparable Mysterious, Original Great Methods of the Jade Hall of the Three Celestial Realms*. Chinese Text Project. Chapter 5. https://ctext.org/wiki.pl?if=en&res=648420&remap=gb. Note: This text has not been translated into English, but is available in Simplified Chinese only. We have used ChatGPT version 3.5 to translate the text, so the translation is approximate.
4. Morrow, Susan Brind. *The Dawning Moon of the Mind: Unlocking the Pyramid Texts*. Farrar, Straus and Giroux, 2015, p. 115, Kindle edition.

5. Szekely, Edmond Bordeaux, trans. *The Essene Gospel of Peace: Book Four*. USA: International Biogenic Society, 1981, p. 43.
6. Shizhong, *Original Great Methods*, chap. 4. Translation by Pavlin Boev using a translation by ChatGPT as a basis.
7. Ibid., chap. 1. ChatGPT version 3.5, trans.
8. Takehiro, Teri. "Translation: The Twelve Sleep Exercises of Mount Hua." *Taoist Resources* 2, no. 1 (June 1990): 83. https://scholarworks.iu.edu/iuswrrest/api/core/bitstreams/fa5d38ec-23fa-4516-aa7a-ef3fd9732635/content.
9. Pregadio, Fabrizio, editor. *The Encyclopedia of Taoism: A-Z, Volume 1 & 2*. London: Routledge, 2008, p. 1027.
10. Esposito, Monica. "Sun-Worship in China – The Roots of Shangqing Taoist Practices of Light." *Cahiers d'Extrême-Asie* 14 (2004): 379. https://www.persee.fr/doc/asie_0766-1177_2004_num_14_1_1212.
11. "Jain Relaxation and Meditation." JAINA: Federation of Jain Associations in North America. https://www.jaina.org/resource/resmgr/jwol_jain_relaxation_and_med.pdf.
12. Ibid.
13. Shizhong, *Original Great Methods*, chap. 4. Boev, trans.
14. "Jain Meditation." Wikipedia.
15. Giri, Swami Nirmalananda (Abbot George Burke). "Podcast: How to Pronounce the Soham Mantra in Meditation." OCOY.org, September 28, 2021. https://ocoy.org/podcast-how-to-pronounce-the-soham-mantra-in-meditation.
16. Chakravarty, Hemendra Nath. In Abhinavagupta. *Tantrasara*, translated by Hemendra Nath Chakravarty. Varanasi, 1986, p. lv-lvi.
17. Abhinavagupta, *Tantrasara of Abhinavagupta*, 72, 80-84.
18. "Abhinavagupta." New World Encyclopedia. https://www.newworldencyclopedia.org/entry/Abhinavagupta.
19. Wangyal Rinpoche, Tenzin. *The Tibetan Yogas of Dream and Sleep*. Shambhala, August 30, 2022, p. 274-275, Kindle edition.
20. Abhinavagupta, *Tantrasara of Abhinavagupta*, 80, 83, 85.
21. "Svaha." Wikipedia. https://en.wikipedia.org/wiki/Svaha.
22. Abhinavagupta, *Tantrasara of Abhinavagupta*, 72.
23. Ibid., 83, 84.
24. Ibid., 81.

CHAPTER TWENTY-FOUR

No references.

CHAPTER TWENTY-FIVE

1. The Other Side NDE. "Girl Drowns; Shown The Power of Instinct and Intuition While In Heaven (NDE)." YouTube, July 15, 2023. https://youtu.be/Bj5dWGx2smg.
2. Tevington, Patricia, and Manolo Corichi. "Many Americans Report Interacting with Dead Relatives in Dreams or Other Ways." Pew Research Center, August 23, 2023. https://www.pewresearch.org/short-reads/2023/08/23/many-americans-report-interacting-with-dead-relatives-in-dreams-or-other-ways.
3. "Ghosts, Fortunetellers, and Communicating with the Dead." In Pew Forum on Religion & Public Life. "Many Americans Mix Multiple Faiths." Pew Research Center, December 9, 2009. https://www.pewforum.org/2009/12/09/many-americans-mix-multiple-faiths/#ghosts-fortunetellers-and-communicating-with-the-dead.
4. Schott, Ben, and Ipsos. "Survey on Beliefs." Ipsos, October 31, 2007. https://www.ipsos.com/en-uk/survey-beliefs.
5. Dewi Rees, W. "The Hallucinations of Widowhood." *British Medical Journal* 4, no. 5778 (1971): 37-41. https://www.bmj.com/content/4/5778/37.
6. "An Investigation into the Alleged Haunting of Hampton Court Palace: Psychological Variables and Magnetic Fields." In Wiseman, Richard, Caroline Watt, Emma Greening, Paul Stevens, and Ciarán O'Keeffe. "An Investigation into Alleged 'Hauntings.'" *British Journal of Psychology* 94, pt. 2 (2002): 66. https://pubmed.ncbi.nlm.nih.gov/12803815.

7. "List of Reportedly Haunted Locations." Wikipedia. https://en.wikipedia.org/wiki/List_of_reportedly_haunted_locations.
8. "Experiences with Odin." Sakro Sawel, August 25, 2020. Updated April 19, 2023. https://sakrosawel.com/experiences-with-odin.
9. "Kayak Spill Gives Teen Visit with Her Angel Plus New Psychic Abilities and New Purpose." International Association for Near-Death Studies, November 30, 2021. https://iands.org/research/nde-research/nde-archives31/newest-accounts/1595-kayak-spill-gives-teen-visit-with-her-angel-plus-new-psychic-abilities-and-new-purpose.html.
10. "Ten-Year-Old Boy Is Thrown from Car and Is Saved by Light Being." International Association for Near-Death Studies, September 26, 2023. https://iands.org/research/nde-research/nde-archives31/newest-accounts/1752-ten-year-old-boy-is-thrown-from-car-and-is-saved-by-light-being.html.
11. Hammad, Manal B. "Demonic Beings in Ancient Egypt." *International Academic Journal Faculty of Tourism and Hotel Management* 4, no. 1 (October 2018): 15. https://www.researchgate.net/publication/342292821_Demonic_Beings_in_Ancient_Egypt.
12. "Naraka (Hinduism)." Wikipedia. https://en.wikipedia.org/wiki/Naraka_(Hinduism).
13. "Diyu." Wikipedia. https://en.wikipedia.org/wiki/Diyu.
14. "Demon." Wikipedia. https://en.wikipedia.org/wiki/Demon.
15. "Xibalba." Wikipedia. https://en.wikipedia.org/wiki/Xibalba.
16. Greyson, Bruce, MD, and Nancy Evans Bush, MA. "Distressing Near-Death Experiences." In *The Near-Death Experience: A Reader*, edited by Lee W. Bailey and Jenny Yates. New York: Routledge, 1996.
17. Botsford, Nancy. *A Day in Hell*. Tate Publishing, July 2010.
18. Williams, Kevin. "Howard Storm's Near-Death Experience." Near-Death Experiences and the Afterlife, September 26, 2019. https://near-death.com/howard-storm-nde.
19. "Two Demons Appear to Woman during Physical Attack." International Association for Near-Death Studies, Updated January 13, 2020. https://iands.org/ndes/nde-stories/nde-like-accounts/1427-two-demons-appear-to-woman-during-physical-attack.html.
20. "Man Visits Hell Hole after Dying of Sepsis." International Association for Near-Death Studies, June 15, 2019. https://iands.org/research/nde-research/nde-archives31/newest-accounts/1357-man-visits-hell-hole-after-dying-of-sepsis.html.
21. The Fight of Faith - Bible Teaching & Testimonies. "Jim Woodford Died and Spent 11 Hours in Heaven! Find Out What He Saw." YouTube, January 12, 2023, 34:58-39:31. https://youtu.be/AE903nhtZi8&t=2098.
22. This Celtic demon is described in the poem "The Battle of the Trees" from *The Book of Taliesin*, along with another in which souls are also tortured within different parts of its body. See "Annwn." Wikipedia. https://en.wikipedia.org/wiki/Annwn.
23. "Wicker Man." Wikipedia. https://en.wikipedia.org/wiki/Wicker_man.
24. "The Brightest of Lights." International Association for Near-Death Studies, Updated April 25, 2015. https://iands.org/ndes/nde-stories/iands-nde-accounts/198-the-brightest-of-lights.html.
25. "Fairy." Wikipedia. https://en.wikipedia.org/wiki/Fairy.
26. "Peri." Wikipedia. https://en.wikipedia.org/wiki/Peri.
27. "The Writings of Abaris." In *The Kolbrin*. The Culdian Trust, 2014, p. 791, eBook.
28. "Fairy." Wikipedia.
29. See the NDE of Tyler Deal as an example (The Other Side NDE. "Man Dies and Is Shown Our True Connection to Nature during Incredible Nde." YouTube, July 9, 2022. https://youtu.be/e07Gcat79sM) and this woman (Destination America. "Fairies on the Operating Table." YouTube, September 6, 2015. https://youtu.be/C6CHrtRnxBc).
30. Atwood, Lara. "Extraterrestrial Contact Experience with Dr. Steven Greer." Sakro Sawel, August 21, 2013. https://sakrosawel.com/extraterrestrial-contact-experience-with-dr-steven-greer.
31. Atwood, Lara. "Making Contact with Extraterrestrials through Other Dimensions." Sakro Sawel, August 17. 2013. https://sakrosawel.com/making-contact-with-extraterrestrials-through-other-dimensions.
32. See the experience of Aaron Green (Love Covered Life Podcast. "Most Detailed Pre-Birth Memory EVER RECORDED! I Chose Every Detail of My Body, Parents, and Life!." YouTube, August 4, 2023. 18:02-18:35. https://youtu.be/4HvCz4ql1XE&t=1082).

33. "Teen Commits Suicide but Is Taken by God and Feels Pure Love before Being Returned to His Body." International Association for Near-Death Studies, September 26, 2023. https://iands.org/research/nde-research/nde-archives31/newest-accounts/1750-teen-commits-suicide-but-is-taken-by-god-and-feels-pure-love-before-being-returned-to-his-body.html.
34. Magic Is Real. "A Six-Year-Old Boy Has a Near-Death Experience & Is Shown How We Choose Our Lives before Birth." YouTube, August 21, 2023, 12:30-13:09. https://youtu.be/72MpA2jhPG8&t=750.
35. The Other Side NDE. "Man Dies in Surgery; Shown Truth about Black Holes, Other Dimensions during Shocking Nde." YouTube, April 15, 2023. 4:20-5:02. https://youtu.be/zQTgiXdFZrw&t=260.
36. Coming Home. "Teacher Drowns: Meets Creator of the Universe (Near-Death Experience)." YouTube, May 5, 2023, 8:17-11:51. https://youtu.be/gsq72npuxFs&t=497.
37. Coming Home. "Life after Suicide: Given a Message for Humanity (Near-Death Experience)." YouTube, December 30, 2022, 8:46-11:47. https://youtu.be/JPN58pveqlc&t=526.
38. Mauro Biglino Official Channel. "ELOHIM Are Not GOD | Paul Wallis & Mauro Biglino. Ep 1." YouTube, June 26, 2022. https://youtu.be/WijP_yczjbE.
39. Wallis, Paul. "Did Jesus Worship Yahweh? | ET Contact Vs. Religion | Paul Wallis." YouTube, June 22, 2023. https://youtu.be/WZg6_eqczMI.

CHAPTER TWENTY-SIX

1. Sadlier, Allison. "This Is the Average Age That Americans Are Old Enough to Watch Scary Movies." SWNS Digital, September 6, 2021. https://swnsdigital.com/us/2019/10/this-is-the-average-age-that-americans-are-old-enough-to-watch-scary-movies.
2. Suni, Eric. "Nightmares." Medically reviewed by Dr. Abhinav Singh. Sleep Foundation, Updated December 8, 2023. https://www.sleepfoundation.org/nightmares.
3. Parker, Hilary. "Nightmares in Adults." Medically reviewed by Melinda Ratini, DO. WebMD, May 30, 2023. https://www.webmd.com/sleep-disorders/nightmares-in-adults.
4. Esposito, Karin, Amparo Benitez, Lydia Barza, and Thomas Mellman "Evaluation of Dream Content in Combat-Related PTSD." *Journal of Traumatic Stress* 12, no. 4 (October 1999): 681-687. https://pubmed.ncbi.nlm.nih.gov/10646186.
5. Atwood, Mark, with Lara Atwood. *Ancient Solstice: Uncovering the Spiritual Meaning of the Solstices and Equinoxes*. Updated 4th ed. Sura Ondrunar Publishing, 2021, p. 108-109.
6. Coleman, Kali. "17 Signs Your Bad Dreams Could Mean Something Worse." Best Life, February 13, 2019. https://bestlifeonline.com/bad-dreams-symptoms.
7. "Sleep Paralysis." Wikipedia. https://en.wikipedia.org/wiki/Sleep_paralysis.
8. Farooq, Maheen, and Fatima Anjum. "Sleep Paralysis." National Center for Biotechnology Information, Updated September 4, 2023. https://www.ncbi.nlm.nih.gov/books/NBK562322.
9. Denis, Dan. "Relationships between Sleep Paralysis and Sleep Quality: Current Insights." *Nature and Science of Sleep* 10 (November 2018): 355-367. https://www.ncbi.nlm.nih.gov/pmc/articles/PMC6220434.
10. "Sleep Paralysis Demons & Demonic Attacks." MentalHealthDaily.com, May 11, 2015. https://mentalhealthdaily.com/2015/05/11/sleep-paralysis-demons-demonic-attacks.
11. "Night Hag." Wikipedia. https://en.wikipedia.org/wiki/Night_hag.
12. "Sleep Paralysis." Wikipedia.
13. Newsom, Rob. "Sleep Demon." Medically reviewed by Dr. Kara Bagot. Sleep Foundation, Updated December 8, 2023. https://www.sleepfoundation.org/parasomnias/sleep-demon.
14. "Incubus." Wikipedia. https://en.wikipedia.org/wiki/Incubus.
15. "Succubus." Wikipedia. https://en.wikipedia.org/wiki/Succubus.
16. Perina, Kaja. "Alien Abductions: The Real Deal?." Psychology Today, March 1, 2003. Last Reviewed June 9, 2016. https://www.psychologytoday.com/us/articles/200303/alien-abductions-the-real-deal.
17. "Abducted by Aliens: Believers Tell Their Stories." ABC News, August 14, 2009. https://abcnews.go.com/Primetime/story?id=8330290.
18. "Invaders from Mars (1953 Film)." Wikipedia. https://en.wikipedia.org/wiki/Invaders_from_Mars_(1953_film).

19. Purtill, Corinne. "A Stressed, Sleep-Deprived Couple Accidentally Invented the Modern Alien Abduction Phenomenon." Quartz, July 2, 2017. https://qz.com/1019806/a-stressed-sleep-deprived-couple-accidentally-invented-the-modern-alien-abduction-phenomenon.
20. Perina, "Alien Abductions: The Real Deal?."
21. Blackmore, Susan, and Marcus Cox. "Alien Abductions, Sleep Paralysis and the Temporal Lobe." *European Journal of UFO and Abduction Studies* 1 (2000): 113-118, https://www.susanblackmore.uk/articles/alien-abductions-sleep-paralysis-and-the-temporal-lobe.
22. McNally, Richard J. "Explaining 'Memories' of Space Alien Abduction and Past Lives: An Experimental Psychopathology Approach." *Journal of Experimental Psychopathology* 3, no. 1 (2012): 2-16. https://dash.harvard.edu/bitstream/handle/1/8862147/alien_abduction.pdf.
23. Potier, Beth. "Starship Memories." The Harvard Gazette, October 31, 2002. https://news.harvard.edu/gazette/story/2002/10/starship-memories-2.
24. Microsoft Research. "Abducted: How People Come to Believe They Were Kidnapped by Aliens [1/11]." YouTube, Sep 5, 2016. https://youtu.be/Yx8zGRUjf8Y.
25. "Alien Abduction." Wikipedia. https://en.wikipedia.org/wiki/Alien_abduction.
26. Alien Resistance. "Unholy Communion: The Fourth Kind Unveiled - Joseph Jordan and Guy Malone." YouTube, June 21, 2013, 1:02:27-1:03:12, 1:15:53-1:16:01. https://youtu.be/f7qy9oY0cRw&t=3747.
27. Ibid.
28. "Frequently Asked Questions." CE4 Research. http://www.alienresistance.org/ce4faq.htm.
29. Greer, Steven M., MD. *Hidden Truth: Forbidden Knowledge*. Crossing Point, Inc., chapter 3, chapter 18, Kindle edition.
30. Hoax Alien Attack Coming! "Dr. Steven Greer: Alien Abductions Are All Staged." YouTube, July 4, 2013. https://youtu.be/f_eM7GSgCs4.
31. "Evidence." Sirius Disclosure. https://siriusdisclosure.com/evidence.
32. Andrew, Scottie. "The US Navy Just Confirmed These UFO Videos Are the Real Deal." CNN, September 18, 2019. https://www.cnn.com/2019/09/18/politics/navy-confirms-ufo-videos-trnd/index.html.
33. Conte, Michael. "Pentagon Officially Releases UFO Videos." CNN, April 29, 2020. https://www.cnn.com/2020/04/27/politics/pentagon-ufo-videos/index.html.
34. Greyson, Bruce, MD, and Nancy Evans Bush, MA. "Distressing Near-Death Experiences: The Basics." *Missouri Medicine* 111, no. 6 (2014): 486-490. https://www.ncbi.nlm.nih.gov/pmc/articles/PMC6173534.
35. "Distressing Near-Death Experiences." International Association for Near-Death Studies, Updated December 14, 2017. https://iands.org/distressing-near-death-experiences.html.
36. Bush, Nancy Evans. *Dancing Past the Dark: Distressing Near-Death Experiences*. Nancy Evans Bush, 2012.
37. Pickens, Rod. "Urgent Warning!! God Showed This Man the Judgment Day." YouTube, August 27, 2015. https://youtu.be/1sd3C9dkjjQ.
38. Freidel, David, Linda Schele, and Joy Parker. *Maya Cosmos: Three Thousand Years on the Shaman's Path*. New York: William Morrow and Company, Inc., 1993, p. 149-151, 269-270.
39. Mead, G. R. S., trans. *Pistis Sophia*. London: J. M. Watkins, 1921, book 4, chapters 126 and 127.

CHAPTER TWENTY-SEVEN

1. Brown, William. "Arslan Tash Amulet." World History Encyclopedia, February 26, 2019. https://www.worldhistory.org/Arslan_Tash_Amulet.
2. Ibid.
3. The Babylonian deity Adad, the Canaanite deity Hadad, the Sumerian deity Ishkur, and the Hurrian deity Teshub are considered equivalent storm and warrior gods, and were depicted holding lightning bolts.
4. "Flying Broomstick." Come Home, Witch, November 17, 2021. https://web.archive.org/web/20211202003413/https://comehomewitch.com/flying-broomstick.
5. "Helgakviða Hjorvarþssonar (The First Lay of Helgi Hjorvarthsson)." In Hollander, Lee M., trans. *The Poetic Edda*. University of Texas Press, January 1, 1962, stanza 15.
6. "The Rule of Yosira." In *The Kolbrin*. The Culdian Trust, 2014, p. 126, eBook.

7. Ibid., 118.
8. Lightbody, David Ian. "The Encircling Protection of Horus." In El Gawad, Heba Abd, Nathalie Andrews, Maria Correas-Amador, Veronica Tamorri, and James Taylor. *Current Research in Egyptology 2011: Proceedings of the Twelfth Annual Symposium*. Oxford: Oxbow Books, 2012, p. 134, 136. https://www.academia.edu/1061206/The_Encircling_Protection_of_Horus_in_Proceedings_of_the_XIIthe_Current_Resarches_in_Egyptology_Conference_University_of_Durham.
9. Pinch, Dr. Geraldine. "Ancient Egyptian Magic." BBC, Updated February 17, 2011. https://www.bbc.co.uk/history/ancient/egyptians/magic_01.shtml.
10. Mironova, Alexandra V. "Festival of Sokar (Egypt)." Calendars and Festivals of the Ancient Near East, July 14, 2020. https://anefest.spbu.ru/en/articles/ancient-minor-asia/157-festival-of-sokar-egypt.html.
11. Lightbody, "The Encircling Protection of Horus," 133, 138.
12. "Zisurrû." Wikipedia. https://en.wikipedia.org/wiki/Zisurru.
13. "Tablet IV. The Journey to the Forest of Cedar." In George, Andrew, trans. *The Epic of Gilgamesh*. Penguin Books, 1999, IV 10, p. 30.
14. Carmichael, Alexander. *Carmina Gadelica: Hymns and Incantations, Volume III*. Edinburgh: Oliver and Boyd, 1940, p. 102.
15. Ibid., 103.
16. Garcia Martinez, Florentino. *The Dead Sea Scrolls Translated. The Qumran Texts in English*, translated by Wilfred G. E. Watson. Leiden: Brill, 1994, p. 371.
17. Schwemer, David. "Maqlû." Corpus of Mesopotamian Anti-Witchcraft Rituals Online, 2014. https://www.phil.uni-wuerzburg.de/cmawro/magic-witchcraft/maqlu.
18. Abusch, Tzvi. *The Witchcraft Series Maqlu*, edited by Theodore J. Lewis. Atlanta, Georgia: SBL Press, 2015, p. 8. https://www.sbl-site.org/assets/pdfs/pubs/061537P-front.pdf.
19. Ibid., 6-7, incantation 1:95, 110-117.
20. Ibid., 9.
21. "Nuska." Wikipedia. https://en.wikipedia.org/wiki/Nuska.
22. "Nusku." Encyclopedia Britannica. https://www.britannica.com/topic/Nusku.
23. Abusch, *The Witchcraft Series Maqlu*, 12, 26.
24. Pfanku, Kristin, MA, SRC. "Ancient Magic: A Survey of the Technical Hermetica." *Rosicrucian Digest* 1 (2011): 46-53. https://1bd9723bc8b0724b89d9-3657cf458561592fd0c7e3ec3895a19d.ssl.cf5.rackcdn.com/11_ancient_magic_052411.pdf.
25. Betz, Hans Deiter, editor. *The Greek Magical Papyri in Translation*. London: The University of Chicago Press, 1986. PGM VII. 490-504, p. 131. Note: I have slightly modified the translation to make it more comprehensible. In the line "I am the one established in Pelusium," I have changed "Pelusium" to "the Temple of the Sun" as Pelusium is the Roman name for the Egyptian city Per-Amun, which means house or temple of the sun god Amun, and this religious meaning is no doubt what was intended, rather than indicating someone actually lived in that city (see "Pelusium." Wikipedia. https://en.wikipedia.org/wiki/Pelusium.).
26. Bloomfield, Maurice, trans. "Hymns of the Atharva-Veda." In Muller, F. Max, editor. *Sacred Books of the East, Volume 42*. Oxford: The Clarendon Press, 1897. https://www.sacred-texts.com/hin/av.htm.
27. Balaram, Dr. Padmini Tolat. "Swastika: A Sacred Symbol Of Hinduism, Jainism and Buddhism." Indica Today, December 24, 2021. https://www.indica.today/research/conference/swastika-a-sacred-symbol-of-hinduism-jainism-and-buddhism.
28. "Swastika." Wikipedia. https://en.wikipedia.org/wiki/Swastika.
29. McCoy, Daniel. "The Swastika – Its Ancient Origins and Modern (Mis)Use." Norse Mythology for Smart People. https://norse-mythology.org/symbols/swastika-ancient-origins-modern-misuse.
30. "Swastika." Wikipedia.
31. "Pentagram." Wikipedia. https://en.wikipedia.org/wiki/Pentagram.
32. Ibid.
33. "Ankh—Christianity." Wikipedia. https://en.wikipedia.org/wiki/Ankh#Christianity.
34. Hill, J. "Ankh." Ancient Egypt Online, 2010. https://ancientegyptonline.co.uk/ankh.
35. "Shen-Ring." The Global Egyptian Museum. https://globalegyptianmuseum.org/glossary.aspx?id=348.

36. Hill, J. "Horus of Behdet (Edfu)." Ancient Egypt Online, 2010. https://ancientegyptonline.co.uk/horusbehedet.
37. "John 1:1-5." in *The Holy Bible,* New International Version (NIV). Biblica, 2011.

CHAPTER TWENTY-EIGHT

1. Strassman, Rick, MD. *DMT: The Spirit Molecule: A Doctor's Revolutionary Research into the Biology of Near-Death and Mystical Experiences.* Park Street Press, December 1, 2000, p. 146-147, Kindle edition.
2. Ibid., 182.
3. O'Hare, Ryan. "Ayahuasca Compound Changes Brainwaves to Vivid 'Waking-Dream' State." Imperial News, November 19, 2019. https://www.imperial.ac.uk/news/193993/ayahuasca-compound-changes-brainwaves-vivid-waking-dream.
4. De Araujo, Draulio B., Sidarta Ribeiro, Guillermo A. Cecchi, et al. "Seeing with the Eyes Shut: Neural Basis of Enhanced Imagery Following Ayahuasca Ingestion." *Human Brain Mapping* 33, no. 11 (2012): 2550-2560. https://www.ncbi.nlm.nih.gov/pmc/articles/PMC6870240.
5. Strassman, *DMT: The Spirit Molecule,* 146, 148, 191, 194, 196, 204, 208-209, 212, 230.
6. Ibid., 315, 327.
7. Ibid., 5.
8. Ibid., 71-72.
9. Kent, James. "The Case Against DMT Elves." Tripzine.com, May 4, 2004. https://tripzine.com/listing.php?id=dmt_pickover.
10. "DeepDream." Wikipedia. https://en.wikipedia.org/wiki/DeepDream.
11. Strassman, *DMT: The Spirit Molecule,* 212.
12. Ibid., 183-184.
13. De Araujo et al., "Seeing with the Eyes Shut."
14. Strassman, *DMT: The Spirit Molecule,* 31.
15. This study gives some idea of the kinds of entities people describe seeing: Davis, Alan K., John M. Clifton, Eric G. Weaver, et al. "Survey of Entity Encounter Experiences Occasioned by Inhaled *N,N*-Dimethyltryptamine: Phenomenology, Interpretation, and Enduring Effects." *Journal of Psychopharmacology* 34, no. 9 (2020): 1008-1020. https://journals.sagepub.com/doi/full/10.1177/0269881120916143.
16. Strassman, *DMT: The Spirit Molecule,* 248.
17. Ibid., 216-219.
18. Ibid., 252.
19. Redwendigo. "My Experience with Being Possessed by an Evil Entity." Reddit, September 4, 2017. https://www.reddit.com/r/Paranormal/comments/6y34ux/my_experience_with_being_possessed_by_an_evil/?rdt=39137.
20. For example, see the experiences of A'zariYahion (A'zariYahion. "Died and Went to Hell and Was Given into the Hands of the Devil/Ha Satan (Testimony)." YouTube, January 8, 2023. https://youtu.be/x9B9RXOyLEs) and Myles B (Myles B. "Smoking Weed Seeing the Devil in Jay-Z on My Way to Hell!!!." YouTube, February 3, 2021. https://youtu.be/F5iimPUv8kM).
21. Strassman, *DMT: The Spirit Molecule,* 292.
22. Ibid., 189.
23. Delafé Testimonies. "I Took Psychedelics as a Christian, What I Saw Shocked Me... (Testimony)." YouTube, July 7, 2022, 33:21-34:21. https://youtu.be/-BmqCZMLjEE&t=2001.
24. Leptourgos, Pantelis, Martin Fortier-Davy, Robin Carhart-Harris, et al. "Hallucinations Under Psychedelics and in the Schizophrenia Spectrum: An Interdisciplinary and Multiscale Comparison." *Schizophrenia Bulletin* 46, no. 6 (November 2020): 1396-1408. https://academic.oup.com/schizophreniabulletin/article/46/6/1396/5908041.
25. Vardy, Michael M., PhD, and Stanley R. Kay, PhD. "LSD Psychosis or LSD-Induced Schizophrenia? A Multimethod Inquiry." *Archives of General Psychiatry* 40, no. 8 (August 1983): 877-883. https://pubmed.ncbi.nlm.nih.gov/6870484.
26. "Mental Disorders." World Health Organization, June 8, 2022. https://www.who.int/news-room/fact-sheets/detail/mental-disorders.
27. "LSD Art." Wikipedia. https://en.wikipedia.org/wiki/LSD_art.

28. "About Jerry Marzinsky." Jerry Marzinsky: Engineering Mental and Spiritual Sanity, Updated January 8, 2023. https://www.jerrymarzinsky.com/about.
29. The James Delingpole Channel. "Jerry Marzinsky | The Delingpod." YouTube, April 28, 2021. https://youtu.be/64uyYw2jywA.
30. Marzinsky, Jerry. "Demons Are for Real." Keyhole Journey, March 11, 2016. http://www.keyholejourney.com/article-demons-are-for-real.html.
31. Marzinsky, Jerry. "List of Lies." Keyhole Journey, April 8, 2016. http://www.keyholejourney.com/list-of-lies.html.
32. Irmak, M. Kemal. "Schizophrenia or Possession?." *Journal of Religion and Health* 53, no. 3 (2014): 773-777. https://pubmed.ncbi.nlm.nih.gov/23269538.
33. The James Delingpole Channel, "Jerry Marzinsky | The Delingpod."
34. Marzinsky, "List of Lies."
35. Marzinsky, "Demons Are for Real."
36. Gray, Benjamin. "Hidden Demons: A Personal Account of Hearing Voices and the Alternative of the Hearing Voices Movement." *Schizophrenia Bulletin* 34, no. 6 (November 2008): 1006-1007. https://doi.org/10.1093/schbul/sbn099.
37. Quote is from here, and this case also serves as an example of a schizophrenic who can see a demon: ErosPram. "I Am a Schizophrenic Female with One Visible Hallucination and Two Inner Voices. AMA." Reddit, December 5, 2013. https://www.reddit.com/r/AMA/comments/1s6se3/comment/cdukszz.
38. Another example of a schizophrenic who can see a demon: Letzter, Rafi. "A Woman with Schizophrenia Told Us What It's Really like to Live with Incurable Hallucinations." Business Insider, August 30, 2016. https://www.businessinsider.com/living-with-schizophrenia-2016-8.
39. Marzinsky, "Demons Are for Real."
40. Cagliostro, Dina, PhD. "Signs and Causes of Schizophrenia." Psycom, Updated September 30, 2020. https://www.psycom.net/schizophrenia-signs-causes.
41. Murray, Robin M., MD MRCPsych, and Michael C. H. Oon, BSC. "The Excretion of Dimethyltryptamine in Psychiatric Patients." *Proceedings of the Royal Society of Medicine* 69, no. 11 (December 1976): 831-832. https://www.researchgate.net/publication/22085117_The_Excretion_of_Dimethyltryptamine_in_Psychiatric_Patients.
42. Strassman, *DMT: The Spirit Molecule*, 72.
43. Marzinsky, "Demons Are for Real."
44. Miller, Brian, MD, PhD, MPH. "Drug Psychosis May Pull the Schizophrenia Trigger." Psychiatric Times, February 4, 2020. https://www.psychiatrictimes.com/view/drug-psychosis-may-pull-schizophrenia-trigger.
45. White, Mark. "When Hallucinations Persist after the Party Drugs Have Worn Off." January 22, 2016. Updated September 6, 2017. https://web.archive.org/web/20210920150536/https://www.sbs.com.au/topics/voices/health/article/2016/01/22/when-hallucinations-persist-after-party-drugs-have-worn.
46. Strassman, *DMT: The Spirit Molecule*, 270.
47. Ibid., 247, 276-277, 280.
48. Ibid., 291.
49. Ibid., 282.
50. Morrow, Susan Brind. *The Dawning Moon of the Mind: Unlocking the Pyramid Texts*. Farrar, Straus and Giroux, 2015, p. 134, Kindle edition.
51. Ibid., 114.
52. Ibid., 136.
53. Ibid., 157.
54. Ibid., 124.
55. Ibid., 132.
56. Ibid., 131.
57. Atwood, Lara. *The Ancient Religion of the Sun: The Wisdom Bringers and The Lost Civilization of the Sun*. 2nd ed. Sura Ondrunar Publishing, 2021, p. 309-311.
58. Strassman, *DMT: The Spirit Molecule*, 74-75.
59. Ibid., 62.

60. Colmer, James. "Ancient Brain Mapping: The Hypocephalus and the Symbolism of the Egyptian Atef Crown." Egypt Mysteries. https://web.archive.org/web/20131112073416/http://www.antigravitymovie.com:80/hypocephalus.html.
61. Colmer, James. "Origins of the Eye of Horus." Egypt Mysteries. https://web.archive.org/web/20131011032720/http://www.antigravitymovie.com:80/eyeofhorus.html.
62. ChaosandOrder. "Egyptian Winged Disk Represents the Pituitary Gland." EncompassingChaos, June 18, 2016. https://encompassingchaos.wordpress.com/2016/06/18/egyptian-winged-disk-represents-the-pituitary-gland.
63. Dolan, Eric W. "Study Provides Evidence That DMR Is Produced Naturally from Neurons in the Mammalian Brain." PsyPost, July 15, 2019. https://www.psypost.org/2019/07/study-provides-evidence-that-dmt-is-produced-naturally-from-neurons-in-the-mammalian-brain-54051.
64. Colmer, "Ancient Brain Mapping."
65. Smoot, Stephen O., John Gee, Kerry Muhlestein, and John S. Thompson. "The Purpose and Function of the Egyptian Hypocephalus." *BYU Studies Quarterly* 61, no. 4 (2022): 234. https://byustudies.byu.edu/article/the-purpose-and-function-of-the-egyptian-hypocephalus.
66. Kvilhaug, Maria. "The Sacred Drink and Other Links between Indian, Iranian, Greek, Celtic and Norse Mythology." Blade Honer, January 29, 2020. https://bladehoner.wordpress.com/2020/01/29/the-sacred-drink-and-other-links-between-indian-iranian-greek-celtic-and-norse-mythology.
67. Flattery, David Stophlet, and Martin Schwartz. *Haoma and Harmaline*. University of California Press, 1989, p. 7-8.
68. Kvilhaug, "The Sacred Drink."
69. Flattery and Schwartz, *Haoma and Harmaline*, 13.
70. Knipe, David M. "Soma." Encyclopedia.com, Updated June 27, 2018. https://www.encyclopedia.com/philosophy-and-religion/eastern-religions/hinduism/soma.
71. Atwood, *Ancient Religion of the Sun*, 153-158.
72. Kvilhaug, Maria. *The Seed of Yggdrasill: Deciphering the Hidden Messages in Old Norse Myths*. Whyte Tracks, 2016, section 3.1: The Mead of Poetry, Kindle edition.
73. Kvilhaug, "The Sacred Drink."
74. "The Oseberg Tapestry: Selected Images." Germanic Mythology: Texts, Translations, Scholarship, July 23, 2017. https://www.germanicmythology.com/works/OsebergTapestry.html.
75. De Borhegyi, Carl. "Soma in the Americas." Hidden in Plain Sight, 2010. https://web.archive.org/web/20230506165411/https://www.mushroomstone.com/sointheamericas.htm. Note: The Spanish chroniclers recorded their observations of the use of hallucinogens among the natives of Central America. Friar Diego de Landa recorded that the Maya drank intoxicating beverages at every ritual occasion, and Friar Diego Duran records the mass eating of wild mushrooms by the Aztecs accompanied by mass sacrifice, suicide, and cannibalism. Stephan F. de Borhegyi identified the emergence of mushroom use along with human sacrifice at around 1000 BC in Central America.
76. "Entheogenics and the Maya." Wikipedia. https://en.wikipedia.org/wiki/Entheogenics_and_the_Maya.
77. De Borhegyi, Carl. "The Secret of Secrets." Hidden in Plain Sight, 2017. https://web.archive.org/web/20230608043543/https://www.mushroomstone.com/secret-of-secrets.

CHAPTER TWENTY-NINE

1. "Siddhi." Wikipedia. https://en.wikipedia.org/wiki/Siddhi.
2. Patañjali, *Yoga Sutras of Patanjali, Kaivalya Pada*. Stillnessinyoga, 2020, Sutra IV.1. https://www.stillnessinyoga.com/wp-content/uploads/2020/10/04.kaivalya_pada-1.pdf.
3. Patañjali, *Yoga Sutras of Patanjali, Vibhuti Pada*. Stillnessinyoga, 2020, Sutra III.38, III.50. https://www.stillnessinyoga.com/wp-content/uploads/2020/10/03.vibuti_pada.pdf; Patañjali, *Yoga Sutras of Patanjali, Kaivalya Pada*, Sutra IV.3.

CHAPTER THIRTY

No references.

TEXT COPYRIGHT ACKNOWLEDGMENTS

Where works under a Creative Commons license have been used, an abbreviated form of the license name is listed. Full details of the Creative Commons (CC) licenses may be viewed here https://creativecommons.org licenses.

Copyrighted texts quoted in this book are listed alphabetically by title of work.

"23 Minutes in Hell (Original) - Bill Wiese, 'The Man Who Went to Hell' Author '23 Minutes in Hell,'" © 2013 Bill Wiese, YouTube, https://youtu.be/AYxKRoONrfY&t=278.

"A Six-Year-Old Boy Has a Near-Death Experience & Is Shown How We Choose Our Lives before Birth," © 2023, Aaron Thomas Green, Magic Is Real, YouTube, https://youtu.be/72MpA2jhPG8&t=750.

"Acoustics of the West Kennet Long Barrow, Avebury, Wiltshire," © 2015 Steve Marshall, *Time and Mind* 9, no. 1 (2016): 43-56. https://doi.org/10.1080/1751696X.2016.1142292. Article can be read on Marshall's website at https://exploringavebury.com/assets/uploads/long-barrows/Acoustics of the West Kennet Long Barrow Avebury Wiltshire.pdf.

After: A Doctor Explores What Near-Death Experiences Reveal about Life and Beyond, © 2021 Bruce Greyson, St. Martin's Publishing Group, Kindle edition.

"Amduat: The Book of the Hidden Chamber - Book of What Is in the Duat," © 2012 Wim van den Dungen, Sofiatopia, http://www.maat.sofiatopia.org/amduat.htm.

America Before: The Key to Earth's Lost Civilization, © 2019 Graham Hancock, St. Martin's Press, Kindle edition.

"Arslan Tash Amulet," © 2019 William Brown, World History Encyclopedia, CC BY-NC-SA 4.0, https://www.worldhistory.org/Arslan_Tash_Amulet.

"Atheist Dies; Shocked by What She Saw on the Other Side (Powerful NDE)," © 2023, Nancy Rynes, Shaman Oaks, YouTube, https://youtu.be/w65SNVpmuR8&t=1327.

"AWARE—AWAreness during REsuscitation—A prospective study" by Sam Parnia, et al, *Resuscitation* 85, no. 12 (December 2014): 1799-1805, © 2014 Elsevier Ireland Ltd, published by Elsevier Inc, https://www.resuscitationjournal.com/article/S0300-9572(14)00739-4/abstract.

"Ayahuasca Compound Changes Brainwaves to Vivid 'Waking-Dream' State," by Ryan O'Hare, © 2019 Imperial College London, Imperial News, https://www.imperial.ac.uk/news/193993/ayahuasca-compound-changes-brainwaves-vivid-waking-dream.

"Brain Changes during a Shamanic Trance: Altered Modes of Consciousness, Hemispheric Laterality, and Systemic Psychobiology," © 2017 Pierre Flor-Henry, Yakov Shapiro, Corine Sombrun, and Peter Walla, *Cogent Psychology* 4, no. 1, CC-BY 4.0, https://www.tandfonline.com/doi/full/10.1080/23311908.2017.1313522.

"Cognitive Correlates of the Spontaneous Out-of-Body Experience (OBE) in the Psychologically Normal Population: Evidence for an Increased Role of Temporal-Lobe Instability, Body-Distortion Processing, and Impairments in Own-Body Transformations," by Jason J. Braithwaite, Dana Samson, Ian Apperly, Emma Broglia, Johan Hulleman, © 2010 Elsevier, *Cortex* 47, no. 7 (July-August 2011), https://www.sciencedirect.com/science/article/abs/pii/S0010945210001486.

Comment by "pixelobservations," On Sakro Sawel, "Who is Odin/Wotan? [An Alternative Perspective]," YouTube, August 3, 2017, https://youtu.be/rnN5upwW84s.

"Deriving Dreams from the Divine," © Andrew Miles Byrd, Academia.edu, https://www.academia.edu/345147/Deriving_Dreams_from_the_Divine.

"Did you go to Heaven?," © 2015, International Association for Near-Death Studies, https://iands.org/ndes/nde-stories/iands-nde-accounts/961-did-you-go-to-heaven.html.

DMT: The Spirit Molecule: A Doctor's Revolutionary Research into the Biology of Near-Death and Mystical Experiences, © 2001 Rick J. Strassman, M.D., Park Street Press, Kindle edition.

"Dream Interpretation in Ancient Civilizations," by J. Donald Hughes, © 2000, American Psychological Association, *Dreaming* 10, no. 1 (March 2000): 7-18, https://www.researchgate.net/publication/227247381_Dream_Interpretation_in_Ancient_Civilizations.

"Eight Lessons Learned through NDEs with Dr. Bruce Greyson | Episode 3," © 2022, The Afterlife Files, YouTube, Mach 9, 2022, 36:09-36:48. https://youtu.be/xjlk3aDcSDA&t=2169.

"First Out-of-Body Experience Induced in Laboratory Setting," © 2007, University College London, ScienceDaily, https://www.sciencedaily.com/releases/2007/08/070823141057.htm.

"Fourteen Year Old Crosses Over; Gets Taught about Negative Thoughts during NDE," © 2022, Philip Siracusa, The Other Side NDE, YouTube, https://youtu.be/-h_5uX-Kd2Q&t=40.

Haoma and Harmaline, David Stophlet Flattery and Martin Schwartz, ©1989 The Regents of the University of California, University of California Press.

Hermetica: The Greek Corpus Hermeticum and the Latin Asclepius in a New English Translation, with Notes and Introduction, Brian P. Copenhaver, translator, © 1992 Cambridge University Press, Cambridge University Press, Kindle edition.

"Hidden Demons: A Personal Account of Hearing Voices and the Alternative of the Hearing Voices Movement," © 2008 Benjamin Gray, *Schizophrenia Bulletin* 34, no. 6 (November 2008): 1006-1007, Oxford University Press, https://doi.org/10.1093/schbul/sbn099.

"Hippocrates of Cos, Regimen 4, or Dreams" in *Nature of Man. Regimen in Health. Humours. Aphorisms. Regimen 1-3. Dreams. Heracleitus: On the Universe,* by Hippocrates, Heracleitus, translated by W. H. S. Jones, ©1931, Loeb Classical Library, https://www.loebclassics.com/view/hippocrates_cos-regimen_iv_dream/1931/pb_LCL150.421.xml.

"I Took Psychedelics as a Christian, What I Saw Shocked Me... (Testimony)," © 2022, Delafé Testimonies, YouTube, https://youtu.be/-BmqCZMLjEE&t=2001.

"Jim Woodford Died and Spent 11 Hours in Heaven! Find Out What He Saw," © 2023, Jim Woodford, The Fight of Faith - Bible Teaching & Testimonies, YouTube, https://youtu.be/AE903nhtZi8&t=2098.

"Kayak Spill Gives Teen Visit with Her Angel Plus New Psychic Abilities and New Purpose," © 2021, International Association for Near-Death Studies, https://iands.org/research/nde-research/nde-archives31/newest-accounts/1595-kayak-spill-gives-teen-visit-with-her-angel-plus-new-psychic-abilities-and-new-purpose.html.

Laghu-Yoga-Vasishta, K. Narayanaswami Aiyer, Madras, India: The Adyar Library and Research Centre, 1971.

"Life after Suicide: Given a Message for Humanity (Near-Death Experience)," © 2022, Chris Batts, Coming Home, YouTube, https://youtu.be/JPN58pveqlc&t=526.

"Man Dies in Surgery; Shown Truth about Black Holes, Other Dimensions during Shocking NDE," © 2023, Mark Hodges, The Other Side NDE, YouTube, https://youtu.be/zQTgiXdFZrw&t=320.

"Man Is Shown the Future During NDE; Taught the Meaning of Life (Near-Death Experience)," © 2022, Jeff Tolley, The Other Side NDE, YouTube, https://youtu.be/-DbqXXF_88Q&t=225.

"Man Visits Hell Hole after Dying of Sepsis," © 2019, International Association for Near-Death Studies, https://iands.org/research/nde-research/nde-archives31/newest-accounts/1357-man-visits-hell-hole-after-dying-of-sepsis.html.

Moralia by Plutarch, translated by Philip H. De Lacy and Benedict Einarson, ©1959 The President and Fellows of Harvard College, Loeb Classical Library edition.

"Mt. Kailash," © Martin Gray, World Pilgrimage Guide, https://sacredsites.com/asia/tibet/mt_kailash.html.

"My Experience with Being Possessed by an Evil Entity," © 2017 Redwendigo, Reddit, https://www.reddit.com/r/Paranormal/comments/6y34ux/my_experience_with_being_possessed_by_an_evil/?rdt=39137.

Mysteries of the Hopewell: Astronomers, Geometers, and Magicians of the Eastern Woodlands, © 2000 William F. Romain, The University of Akron Press, 2010, Kindle edition.

"Near-Death Experience in Indian Religions. Encountering Yama," by Shona Nichole Stockton, dissertation, University of Chester, © 2017, CC BY-NC-ND 4.0, https://chesterrep.openrepository.com/handle/10034/621026.

"Non-Christian Sees Jesus During Near-Death Experience (NDE)," © 2021, Robin Landsong, Shaman Oaks, YouTube, https://youtu.be/5nJz8I7Nhbk.

"Osiris the Great One," © 2022 Yvonne Whiteman, GrahamHancock.com, https://grahamhancock.com/whitemany16.

"Out-of-Body Experiences: A Neuroscientific Explanation," © 2019 Susan Blackmore, PhD, *Psychology Today*, https://www.psychologytoday.com/us/blog/ten-zen-questions/201908/out-body-experiences-neuroscientific-explanation.

"Out-of-Body Experience and Autoscopy of Neurological Origin," by Olaf Blanke, Theodor Landis, Laurent Spinelli, and Margitta Seeck, © 2004 The Guarantors of Brain, *Brain* 127, no. 2 (February 2004): 243-258, https://academic.oup.com/brain/article/127/2/243/347826.

Out of Our Heads: Why You Are Not Your Brain, and Other Lessons from the Biology of Consciousness, ©2009 Alva Noë, Hill and Wang.

Path of Souls: The Native American Death Journey: Cygnus, Orion, the Milky Way, Giant Skeletons in Mounds, & the Smithsonian, foreword and afterword © 2014 Andrew Collins, © 2014 Gregory Little, ATA-Archetype Books, Kindle edition.

"Professor Studied NDE's for 30 Years; What She Discovers Is Incredible (Near Death Experiences)," © 2024, Janice Holden, The Other Side NDE, YouTube, https://youtu.be/QQWoQFtxYsM&t=531.

Pyramid Texts Online, by Vincent Brown, based on translations by Faulkner, R. O. *The Ancient Egyptian Pyramid Texts,* Oxford University Press, 1969; Piankoff, Alexandre, *The Pyramid of Unas,* Princeton University Press, 1968; Speleers, Louis, *Les Textes des Pyramides Egyptiennes,* Gand: I. Vanderpoorten, 1923, Pyramid Texts Online, http://www.pyramidtextsonline.com/translation.html.

Rigveda V.82.1, in *Textual Evidence in the Vedas: Cultural and Historical Implications,* by David Frawley, © 2015, published by the Indian Council of Historical Research.

"Science and Spirituality: A Challenge for the Twenty First Century," © 2004 Peter Fenwick, M.D., F.R.C. Psych, International Association for Near-Death Studies, updated June 11, 2022, https://iands.org/research/nde-research/important-research-articles/42-dr-peter-fenwick-md-science-and-spirituality.html?start=2.

Secret of the Golden Flower, Richard Wilhelm, translator, translated from German to English by Cary F. Baynes, © 1931, 1962, Harvest/HBJ Book.

"Seeing with the Eyes Shut: Neural Basis of Enhanced Imagery Following Ayahuasca Ingestion," by Draulio B.De Araujo, Sidarta Ribeiro, Guillermo A. Cecchi, et al, © 2011 Wiley Periodicals, Inc., *Human Brain Mapping* 33, no. 11 (2012): 2550-2560. https://www.ncbi.nlm.nih.gov/pmc/articles/PMC6870240.

"Shiva Sutras, the Aphorisms of Shiva," © 2020 Jayaram V, Hinduwebsite.com, Pure Life Vision Book, https://www.hinduwebsite.com/siva/shiva-sutras.asp.

"Six Studies of Out-of-Body Experiences," by Charles. T. Tart, PhD, © 1998 Human Sciences Press, Inc. *Journal of Near-Death Studies* 17, no. 2 (Winter 1998), https://digital.library.unt.edu/ark:/67531/metadc799368/m2/1/high_res_d/vol17-no2-73.pdf.

Sri Ramakrishna The Great Master, by Swami Saradananda, translated by Swami Jagadananda, © 1952, Sri Ramakrishna Math, https://en.wikipedia.org/wiki/Ramakrishna.

"Stimulating Illusory Own-Body Perceptions," by Olaf Blanke, Stephanie Ortigue, Theodor Landis, and Margitta Seeck, © 2002 Springer Nature Limited, *Nature* 419 (2002): 269-270. https://doi.org/10.1038/419269a.

Talks with Sri Ramana Maharshi, Sri Ramana Maharshi, © 1955 Ramanasramam, Tiruvannamalai, published by Sri Ramanasramam, Tiruvannamalai.

Tantrasara of Abhinavagupta, translated by H. N. Chakravarty, edited by Boris Marjanovic, © 2012 H. N. Chakravarty, Rudra Press.

Taoist Meditation: The Mao-Shan Tradition of Great Purity, by Isabelle Robinet, 1979, translated by Julian F. Pas and Norman J. Girardot from French into English, © 1993 State University of New York, State University of New York Press.

"Teacher Drowns: Meets Creator of the Universe (Near-Death Experience)," © 2023 Donna Rebadow, Coming Home, YouTube, https://youtu.be/gsq72npuxFs&t=443.

"Teen Commits Suicide but Is Taken by God and Feels Pure Love before Being Returned to His Body," ©2023, International Association for Near-Death Studies, https://iands.org/research/nde-research/nde-archives31/newest-accounts/1750-teen-commits-suicide-but-is-taken-by-god-and-feels-pure-love-before-being-returned-to-his-body.html.

"Ten-Year-Old Boy Is Thrown from Car and Is Saved by Light Being," © 2023, International Association for Near-Death Studies, https://iands.org/research/nde-research/nde-archives31/newest-accounts/1752-ten-year-old-boy-is-thrown-from-car-and-is-saved-by-light-being.html.

The Aeneid, by Virgil, translated by A. S. Kline, © 2002 A.S. Kline, Poetry in Translation, Book VI: The Sibyl Describes Tartarus, https://www.poetryintranslation.com/PITBR/Latin/VirgilAeneidVI.php#anchor_Toc2242935.

The Ancient Egyptian Pyramid Texts, James P. Allen, translator, © 2005, 2015 SBL Society of Biblical Literature.

The Ancient Egyptian Pyramid Texts, R.O. Faulkner, translator, © 1969 Oxford University Press.

The Book of Taliesin, translation and editorial material © Gwyneth Lewis and Rowan Williams, Penguin, 2019, Kindle edition.

"The Bon Religion – An Introduction," and "Olmo Lungring: The Imperishable Sacred Land," in Dhundup, Tsering, Per Kvaerne, and John Myrdhin Reynolds, *A Collection of Studies on the Tibetan Bon Tradition,* Holybooks.com, p. 11, 21–24, https://holybooks.com/studies-tibetan-bon-tradition.

"The Case Against DMT Elves," © 2004 James Kent, Tripzine.com, https://tripzine.com/listing.php?id=dmt_pickover.

"The Classical Greek Practice of Incubation and Some Near Eastern Predecessors," © 2009 Juliette Harrisson, Academia.edu, https://www.academia.edu/277934/The_Classical_Greek_Practice_of_Incubation_and_some_Near_Eastern_Predecessors.

The Cygnus Key: The Denisovan Legacy, Göbekli Tepe, and the Birth of Egypt, © 2018 Andrew Colins, Bear & Company, Kindle edition.

The Dawning Moon of the Mind: Unlocking the Pyramid Texts, © 2015 Susan Brind Morrow, Farrar, Straus and Giroux, Kindle edition.

The Dead Sea Scrolls Translated: The Qumran Texts in English, edited by Florentino Garcia Martinez, 1992, translated to Engligh by Wilfred G. E. Watson, English edition © 1994 E.J. Brill.

The Electronic Text Corpus of Sumerian Literature, © J.A. Black, G. Cunningham, E. Robson, and G. Zólyomi 1998, 1999, 2000; J.A. Black, G. Cunningham, E. Flückiger-hawker, E. Robson, J. Taylor, and G. Zólyomi 2001, the authors have asserted their moral rights, University of Oxford, https://etcsl.orinst.ox.ac.uk/section1/tr1821.htm.

The Epic of Gilgamesh, translated by Andrew George, © 1999, 2003, 2020 Andrew George, Penguin Books.

The Essene Gospel of Peace: Book Four, Edmond Bordeaux, Szekely, translator, © 1981 International Biogenic Society.

The Evergetinos, A Complete Text, translated and edited by Archbishop Chrysostomos, Hieromonk Patapios, Bishop Ambrose, Bishop Auxentios, et al. The Center for Traditionalist Orthodox Studies, 2008. https://www.ctosonline.org/patristic/EvCT.html.

"The Experimental Induction of Out-of-Body Experiences," by H. Henrik Ehrsson, © 2007 American Association for the Advancement of Science, *Science* 317 (2007): 1048, https://doi.org/10.1126/science.1142275, https://www.science.org/doi/10.1126/science.1142275#supplementary-materials.

The Giza Power Plant: Technologies of Ancient Egypt, © 1998 Christopher P Dunn, Bear & Company, Kindle edition.

The Golden Ass, Book XI, by Lucius Apuleius, translated by A. S. Kline, © 2013 A.S. Kiline, Poetry in Translation, https://www.poetryintranslation.com/PITBR/Latin/TheGoldenAssXI.php.

The Gospel of Judas, edited by Rodolphe Kasser, Marvin Meyer, and Gregor Wurst in collaboration with François Gaudard, © 2006 National Geographic Society.

"The Great Pyramid: Early Reflections and Ancient Echoes," © 2000 Tom Danley, ProSoundWeb, August 4, 2020, https://www.prosoundweb.com/the-great-pyramid-early-reflections-ancient-echoes/6.

The Greek Magical Papyri in Translation, edited by Hans Betz, © 1986, 1992 The University of Chicago Press.

The Holy Bible, New International Version® NIV®, Copyright © 1973, 1978, 1984, 2011 by Biblica, used with permission, all rights reserved worldwide.

The Incomparable Mysterious, Original Great Methods of the Jade Hall of the Three Celestial Realms by Lu Shizhong, 12th century text, Chinese Text Project, https://ctext.org/wiki.pl?if=en&res=648420&remap=gb. Note: this text has not been translated into English, but is available in Simplified Chinese only. Translation by Pavlin Boev using a translation by ChatGPT as a basis.

The Kolbrin, © 2014 The Culdian Trust, eBook.

The Mahāmāyā Tantra, translated into English by the Dharmachakra Translation Committee, © 2013, CC BY-NC-ND 3.0, https://read.84000.co/translation/toh425.html.

The Message of the Sphinx: A Quest for the Hidden Legacy of Mankind, © 1996 Graham Hancock and Robert Bauval, Three Rivers Press.

The Nag Hammadi Library in English, edited by James M. Robinson. © 1978, 1988 E.J. Brill, HarperCollins, 1990.

The Seed of Yggdrasill: Deciphering the Hidden Messages in Old Norse Myths, © 2016 Maria Kvilhaug, Whyte Tracks, Kindle edition.

"The Siberian Shaman's Technique of Ecstasy," © 1982 Anna-Leena Siikala, *Scripta Instituti Donneriani Aboensis* 11 (1982): 103. CC BY-NC-ND 4.0. https://journal.fi/scripta/article/view/67133.

The Story of Han Xiangzi, Yang Erzeng, translated by Philip Clart, © 2007 University of Washington Press, https://uw.manifoldapp.org/projects/story-of-han-xiangzi.

The Upanishads, 2nd ed., translated by Eknath Easwaran, © 1987, 2007 The Blue Mountain Center of Meditation, Nilgiri Press.

The Upanishads: Breath from the Eternal, translated by Swami Prabhavananda and Frederick Manchester, © 1948, 1957, 1975, The Vedanta Society of Southern California, New American Library, 2002.

The Way of Hermes: New Translations of The Corpus Hermeticum and The Definitions of Hermes Trismegistus to Asclepius, © 2004, Clement Salaman, Dorine Van Oyen, William D. Wharton, and Jean-Pierre Mahe, translators, Inner Traditions.

The Wisdom of China, edited by Lin Yutang, © 1942, Michael Joseph, 1954.

The Witchcraft Series Maqlu, by Tzvi Abusch, edited by Theodore J. Lewis, © 2015 SBL Press, https://www.sbl-site.org/assets/pdfs/pubs/061537P-front.pdf.

The Yoga Sutras of Patanjali, translated by Sri Swami Satchidananda, © 1978, 1984, 1990, 2012 by Satchidananda Ashram – Yogaville, Integral Yoga Publications.

The Yoga-Vasishtha Maharamayana of Valmiki, Vol. 1, Vihari-Lala Mitra translator, Delhi, India: Low Price Publications, 1999, Kindle edition.

"Two Demons Appear to Woman during Physical Attack," © 2020, International Association for Near-Death Studies, https://iands.org/ndes/nde-stories/nde-like-accounts/1427-two-demons-appear-to-woman-during-physical-attack.html.

"Unholy Communion: The Fourth Kind Unveiled - Joseph Jordan and Guy Malone," © 2013, Alien Resistance, YouTube, https://youtu.be/f7qy9oY0cRw&t=3747.

"Urgent Warning!! God Showed This Man the Judgment Day," © 2015 Rod Pickens, YouTube, https://youtu.be/1sd3C9dkjjQ.

Vedic Yoga: The Path of the Rishi, © 2014 David Frawley, Lotus Press, 2015, Kindle edition.

"Visualizing Out-of-Body Experience in the Brain," by Dirk De Ridder, Koen Van Laere, Patrick Dupont, et al, Copyright © 2007, Massachusetts Medical Society, *The New England Journal of Medicine* 357 (Nov 1, 2007): 1829-33, https://www.nejm.org/doi/full/10.1056/NEJMoa070010.

Yoga Sutras of Patanjali, Kaivalya Pada, by sage Patañjali, translation © Stillnessinyoga, 2020, Sutra IV.1. https://www.stillnessinyoga.com/wp-content/uploads/2020/10/04.kaivalya_pada-1.pdf.

Yoga Sutras of Patanjali, Samadhi Pada, by sage Patañjali, translation © Stillnessinyoga, 2020, Sutra I.2-I.4. https://www.stillnessinyoga.com/wp-content/uploads/2020/10/01.samadhi_pada-1.pdf.

Yoga Sutras of Patanjali, Vibhuti Pada, by sage Patañjali, translation © Stillnessinyoga, 2020, Sutra III.1. https://www.stillnessinyoga.com/wp-content/uploads/2020/10/03.vibuti_pada.pdf.

Zand-i Vohuman Yasht, © 1995 Joseph H. Peterson, commentary, translator, updated May 8, 2022, digital edition and translation from Anklesaria, Behramgore Tehmurasp, *Zand-I Vohuman Yasn and Two Pahlavi Fragments,* Bombay: Mrs. B. T. Anklesaria, 1957, http://www.avesta.org/mp/vohuman.html.

IMAGE CREDITS
REFERENCES & COPYRIGHT ACKNOWLEDGMENTS

Where works under a Creative Commons license have been used, an abbreviated form of the license name is listed. Full details of the Creative Commons (CC) licenses may be viewed here https://creativecommons.org licenses.

All Creative Commons works in this book are derivatives which have been processed with cropping, rotation, and/or other image adjustments.

Image credits are listed by page number.

PREFACE

No images.

CHAPTER ONE

5. O'Keene, Michael, artist. *Glowing Spirit Angel.* Shutterstock.com. https://www.shutterstock.com/image-photo/glowing-spirit-angel-coming-out-dead-1641487537. Licensed from Shutterstock.com.

6. Domenichino, artist. *The Rapture of St. Paul.* Painting circa 1600s. Louvre Museum. Wikimedia Commons, 2013. https://commons.wikimedia.org/wiki/File:Domenichino,_rapimento_di_san_paolo,_1606-08.JPG. Public domain. Photograph by Sailko, CC BY-SA 3.0.

7. Sahlsten, Anna, artist. *Passage*. Painting circa 1894. Wikimedia Commons, 2020. https://commons.wikimedia.org/wiki/File:Anna_Sahlst%C3%A9n_-_Passage.jpg. Public domain.

CHAPTER TWO

14. Prazeres, R., photographer. *KV9, Tomb of Ramses V-VI*. Ceiling of the burial chamber, Luxor, Egypt, 2019. Wikimedia Commons, 2021. https://commons.wikimedia.org/wiki/File:KV9_Tomb_of_Ramses_V-VI_DSCF2907.jpg. CC BY-SA 4.0.

CHAPTER THREE

18. *Depiction of an Out-of-Body Experience*: Image created by DALL-E 3, an AI by OpenAI, prompted by Sura Ondrunar Publishing.

20. *Illustration of Heaven at end of a Dark Tunnel*: Image created by DALL-E 3, an AI by OpenAI, prompted by Sura Ondrunar Publishing.

21. Bajaj, Rajiv, photographer. *Blue sky with white clouds during daytime*. Unsplash.com, 2020. https://unsplash.com/photos/i4QIqfcTkN8. Licensed from Unsplash.com.

22. Top: Johnson-Roehr, S.N., photographer. *Pyramid Texts*. Tomb of Teti, Egypt. Flickr.com, 2023. https://www.flickr.com/photos/snjr22/53031910886/in/photostream. CC BY-NC 2.0.

22. Bottom: Hamerani, photographer. *Djeser-Djeseru – Hatshepsut' temple*. Luxor, Egypt. Wikimedia Commons, 2016. https://commons.wikimedia.org/wiki/File:Djeser-Djeseru.Hatshepsut%27s_temple_(3).jpg. CC BY-SA 4.0.

23. Artist unknown. *Pyramid of Unas*. Photograph. Burial Chamber, Saqqara, Egypt. Brooklyn Museum circa 1900s. Wikimedia Commons, 2011. https://commons.wikimedia.org/wiki/File:Unas_Pyramidentexte_det1.jpg. Public domain.

25. *Depiction of the King Leaving the Pyramid to Travel to the Stars in his Light Body*: Image created by DALL-E 3, an AI by OpenAI, prompted by Sura Ondrunar Publishing.

27. Left: Frith, Francis, photographer. *View of the pyramids of Saqqara*. Photograph circa 1856-1859. Saqqara, Egypt. Rijksmuseum, Netherlands. Wikimedia Commons, 2020. https://commons.wikimedia.org/wiki/File:The_pyramids_of_Sakkarah._From_the_North-East,_RP-F-F25403-M.jpg. Public domain.

27. Right: AXP Photography, photographer. *Three Pyramids in the Dessert*. Giza, Egypt. Unsplash.com, 2023. https://unsplash.com/photos/three-pyramids-in-the-desert-with-a-blue-sky-in-the-background-MerG8J_79Wc. Licensed from Unsplash.com.

28. Artist unknown. *Osiris detail from the grave of Sennedjem*. Luxor, Egypt. Wikimedia Commons, 2009. https://commons.wikimedia.org/wiki/File:Detail_aus_dem_Grab_des_Sennudjem.jpg. Public domain.

29. Artist unknown. *Book of the Dead of Ani*. Papyrus, frame 17, full colour vignettes. 19th Dynasty, Egypt. British Museum. https://www.britishmuseum.org/collection/object/Y_EA10470-17. Public domain. Photograph: The Trustees of the British Museum, CC BY-NC-SA 4.0.

30. Top: van der Heyden, Pieter and After Pieter Bruegel the Elder, artists. *The Last Judgment*. Engraving/Print, 1558. The Metropolitan Museum of Art, Harris Brisbane Dick Fund, 1928. Wikimedia Commons, 2017. https://commons.wikimedia.org/wiki/File:The_Last_Judgment_MET_DP818258.jpg. Public Domain.

30. Bottom: Artist unknown. *Book of the Dead of Hunefer*. Papyrus of Hunefer, 1275 BCE, 19th Dynasty. British Museum. Wikimedia Commons, 2012. https://commons.wikimedia.org/wiki/File:The_judgement_of_the_dead_in_the_presence_of_Osiris.jpg. Public domain. Photograph: The Trustees of the British Museum, CC BY-NC-SA 4.0.

31. Top: Dahl, Jeff, artist. *Aker*. Digital artwork, 2008. Wikimedia Commons, 2008. https://commons.wikimedia.org/wiki/File:Aker.svg. CC BY-SA 4.0

31. Bottom: *Sphinx Summer Solstice Sunset*, Sura Ondrunar Publishing.

32. Left: *Sphinx as Anubis*, Sura Ondrunar Publishing.

32. Right: Pal1983, photographer. *Small Sphinx with the Head of a Jackal*. https://www.shutterstock.com/image-photo/small-sphinx-head-jackal-ramesseum-memorial-422367220. Licensed from Shutterstock.com.

33. Left: Eichmann, Gerd, photographer. *Valley of the Kings in Egypt, Grave 34*. Luxor, Egypt, 1982. Wikimedia Commons, 2020. https://commons.wikimedia.org/wiki/File:Tal_der_Koenige-48-Grab_34-Fluss_durch_4_Register-1982-gje.jpg. CC BY-SA 4.0.

IMAGE CREDITS

33. Right: Gasparetti, Francesco, photographer. *Valle dei Re: tomba di Thutmosi III*. Valley of the Kings: tomb of Thutmose III, Egypt, 2006. https://commons.wikimedia.org/wiki/File:Flickr_-_Gaspa_-_Valle_dei_Re,_tomba_di_Thutmosi_III_(7).jpg. CC BY 2.0.

33. Bottom: cmglee, artist. *Orion's Belt superimposed on the Giza pyramid complex illustrating the Orion Correlation Theory*. Image, 2012. Wikimedia Commons, 2023. https://commons.wikimedia.org/wiki/File:Orion_belt_vs_giza_pyramid_complex.jpg. CC BY-SA 4.0. Image features: Bernal Andreo, Rogelio, photographer. *An image of the constellation Orion. Photograph*, 2010. Wikimedia Commons, 2012. https://commons.wikimedia.org/wiki/File:Orion_Head_to_Toe.jpg. CC BY-SA 3.0.

35. Artist unknown. *Book of the Dead of Hunefer*. Papyrus of Hunefer, 1275 BCE, 19th Dynasty. British Museum. Wikimedia Commons, 2012. https://commons.wikimedia.org/wiki/File:The_judgement_of_the_dead_in_the_presence_of_Osiris.jpg. Public domain. Photograph: The Trustees of the British Museum, CC BY-NC-SA 4.0

36. Hancock, Luke, artist. *Great Pyramid Star Shafts*. Wikimedia Commons, 2023. https://commons.wikimedia.org/wiki/File:Great_Pyramid_Star_Shafts.svg. CC BY-SA 4.0. Derivative of: Dahl, Jeff, artist. *Diagram of the Great Pyramid*. Wikimedia Commons, 2007. https://commons.wikimedia.org/wiki/File:Great_Pyramid_Diagram.svg. CC BY-SA 4.0.

38. Artist unknown. *Egyptian Representation of the Heavens and Earth*. Uncredited illustration after ancient Egyptian papyrus, for "How the Earth Was Regarded in Old Times," by Camille Flammarion (translator uncredited), The Popular Science Monthly, vol. 10, Mar. 1877, p. 546. Wikimedia Commons, 2019. https://commons.wikimedia.org/wiki/File:Egyptian_Representation_of_the_Heavens_and_Earth_%E2%80%94_The_Popular_Science_Monthly_(mdp).jpg. Public Domain.

39. Stu 10255, artist. *The Orion*. Image, 2011. Wikimedia Commons, 2011. https://commons.wikimedia.org/wiki/File:The_Orion.jpg. CC BY-SA 3.0.

40. Top: Monnier, Franck, artist. *Plan du complexe funéraire d'Ouans à Saqqarah*. Wikimedia Commons, 2007. https://en.wikipedia.org/wiki/File:Unas_Pyramid_Complex.png. Public Domain. Derivative used: by GDK, Wikimedia Commons, 2009. https://en.wikipedia.org/wiki/File:Unas_Pyramid_Complex.png. Public Domain.

40. Left: Mr Rnddude, artist. *Unas' Substructure*. Based on Sethe, Kurt (1922) *Die altaegyptischen Pyramidentexte nach den Papierabdrücken und Photographien des Berliner Museums*, Dritter Band, Leipzig: J. C. Hinrischs'sche Buchhandlung, pp. 116–119 & 164–166. Wikimedia Commons, 2019. https://en.wikipedia.org/wiki/File:Unas%27_Substructure.png. CC BY-SA 4.0.

40. Right: Chipdawes, photographer. *Passageway in the Medium Pyramid*. Wikimedia Commons, 2006. https://commons.wikimedia.org/wiki/File:MeidumPyramidPassage.JPG. Public Domain.

41. *Illustration of the constellation of Leo Superimposed over the Great Sphinx*: Image created by DALL-E 3, an AI by OpenAI, prompted by Sura Ondrunar Publishing, based on the work of Graham Hancock and Robert Bauval.

48. *Illustration of the Great Pyramid covered in White Limestone and Capped*: Image created by DALL-E 3, an AI by OpenAI, prompted by Sura Ondrunar Publishing.

50. Left: Bubeníček, Jiří, artist. *Krušné hory (Ore Mountains): Hora sv. Šebestiána*. Image, 2018. Wikimedia Commons, 2021. https://commons.wikimedia.org/wiki/File:Kru%C5%A1n%C3%A9_hory,_Hora_sv._%C5%A0ebesti%C3%A1na,_imgp0651-71info_(2018-05).jpg. CC BY-SA 4.0.

50. Right: Lepsius, Karl Richard, artist. *Détails des constellations représentées dans la tombe de Séthi Ier dans la vallée des rois*. Illustration between 1849 and 1858. In *Denkmäler aus ägypten und äthiopen*, Vol. III. Wikimedia Commons, 2008. https://commons.wikimedia.org/wiki/File:Seti1-Lepsius-III-137-add%C3%A9tails-constellations.jpg. Public Domain.

54. Artist unknown. *Rite of Sema taouy or meeting of the 2 lands by Horus & Seth*. Wikimedia Commons, 2014. https://en.wikipedia.org/wiki/File:Seth_%2B_horus.jpg. Public domain. Photograph: Soutekh67 CC BY-SA 4.0.

56. Tausch, Olaf, photographer. *Statuen im Tempel von Karnak nördlich Luxor, Ägypten*. Photograph, 2009. Wikimedia Commons, 2010. https://commons.wikimedia.org/wiki/File:Karnak_Tempel_14.jpg. CC BY 3.0.

58. Budge, E.A Wallis, illustrator, author. *The Soul of Osirus on the Erica Tree*. In *Osiris and the Egyptian Resurrection*; Illustrated after drawings from Egyptian Papyri and Monuments by E. A. Wallis Budge. London: P.L. Warner, 1911, pg. 40. Internet Archive, 2006. https://archive.org/details/osirisandtheeg02budguoft/page/n53/mode/2up. Public Domain.

59. Ryckaert, Marc, photographer. *Karnak Ramses III Temple*. Ramses III temple at Karnak. Luxor, Egypt. Photograph, 2018. Wikimedia Commons, 2019. https://commons.wikimedia.org/wiki/File:Karnak_Ramses_III_Temple_R01.jpg. CC BY-SA 4.0.

62. Chernov, Mstyslav, photographer. *Great Sphinx of Giza (foreground) Pyramid of Menkaure (background)*. Cairo, Egypt. Photograph, 2009. Wikimedia Commons, 2013. https://commons.wikimedia.org/wiki/File:Great_Sphinx_of_Giza_(foreground)_Pyramid_of_Menkaure_(background)._Cairo,_Egypt,_North_Africa.jpg. CC BY-SA 3.0.

64. Left: Artist unknown. *Thoth, the Ibis-headed God of Books*. In *The Sacred Books and Early Literature of the East* by Charles F Horne. New York: Parke, Austin and Lipscomb Inc, 1917, vol. 2, pg. 416-417. Wikimedia Commons, 2020. https://commons.wikimedia.org/wiki/File:The_Sacred_Books_and_Early_Literature_of_the_East,_vol._2,_pg._416-417,_Thoth.jpg. Internet Archive, 2007. https://archive.org/details/sacredbooksearly02hornuoft/page/416/mode/2up. Public Domain.

64. Right: Artist unknown. *Marble relief with Hermens*. Marble, 27 B.C.–A.D. 68. Metropolitan Museum of Art. Harris Brisbane Dick Fund, 1991. Wikimedia Commons, 2017. https://commons.wikimedia.org/wiki/File:Marble_relief_with_Hermes_MET_DT6551.jpg. Public domain.

65. *Poimandres inspires Hermes*. From Hermes Trismegistus, Sesthien Boecken, Amsterdam 1643. Public domain.

68. Gita Press, publisher. *King Janaka tells his soldiers about Hell and Heaven*. Illustration in *Mahabharata* by Sriman Maharshi Vedavyasa, translated by Pandit Ramnarayan Dutt Shastri. Gita Press, Vol 5, page 4678. Internet Archive, 2009. https://archive.org/details/mahabharat05ramauoft/page/4678/mode/2up. Digitized by University of Toronto Collection, acquired 1965.

70. *Illustration of Lila and Saraswati traveling out of the body together*: Image created by DALL-E 3, an AI by OpenAI, prompted by Sura Ondrunar Publishing.

75. Gita Press, publisher. *Arjuna's Dream*. Illustration in *Mahabharata,* by Sriman Maharshi Vedavyasa, translated by Pandit Ramnarayan Dutt Shastri. Gita Press, Vol 4, page 243. Internet Archive, 2009. https://archive.org/details/mahabharata04ramauoft/page/243/mode/1up. Digitized by University of Toronto Collection, acquired 1965.

77. Kumar, Kalyan, photographer. *Shiva Bangalore*. Photograph, 2006. Wikimedia Commons, 2008. https://commons.wikimedia.org/wiki/File:Shiva_Bangalore.jpg. CC BY-SA 2.0.

78. *Pushpaka Viman* in *Tulsi Ramayan*, by Tulsidas, published by Tej Kumar Book Depo. Wikimedia Commons, 2018. https://commons.wikimedia.org/wiki/File:Pushpaka_Viman.jpg.

82. King, Bob, photographer. *Vishnu Dreaming*. Statue at Dasavatara Temple, Deogarh, India. Photograph, 2007. Wikimedia Commons, 2010. https://commons.wikimedia.org/wiki/File:Vishnu_Hood2_Deogarh.jpg. CC BY 2.0.

88. Left: Magnússon, Finnur, illustrator. *Yggdrasill, the mundane tree*. Print, 1824. Wikimedia Commons, 2017. https://en.wikipedia.org/wiki/File:Yggdrasill,_the_mundane_tree_(26938965955).jpg. Public Domain.

88. Right: Granpar, photographer. *Maibaum Buchen*. Wikimedia Commons, 2023. https://commons.wikimedia.org/wiki/File:2023er_Maibaum_Buchen_(Odw.)_00.jpg. CC BY 3.0.

88. Bottom: Artist unknown. Illustration from *The Book of the Dead of Khensumose*. Wikimedia Commons, 2015. https://commons.wikimedia.org/wiki/File:Sunrise_at_Creation.jpg. Public domain.

89. Top left: Artist unknown. *Book of the Dead of Ani*. Papyrus of Ani, spell 17, 19th Dynasty. British Museum. https://www.britishmuseum.org/collection/object/Y_EA10470-7. Public domain. Photograph: The Trustees of the British Museum, CC BY-NC-SA 4.0.

89. Top center: *Sphinx Summer Solstice Sunset*, Sura Ondrunar Publishing.

89. Top right: LeMay, Warren, photographer. *Pylon, Temple of Horus at Edfu*. Edfu, Egypt, 2019. Wikimedia Commons, 2019. https://commons.wikimedia.org/wiki/File:Pylon,_Temple_of_Horus_at_Edfu,_Edfu,_AG,_EGY_(48022522446).jpg. Public domain.

89. Bottom left: Smith, G. Elliot, Sir, author. *The Evolution of the Dragon*. Illustration. The University Press, 1919. Wikimedia Commons, 2015. https://commons.wikimedia.org/wiki/File:The_evolution_of_the_dragon_(1919)_(14579308500).jpg. Public domain.

89. Bottom right: Chronikhiles, artist. *Vaikunthanatha - Sri Appan Venkatachalapati Temple, Cheranmahadevi*. Wikimedia Commons, 2023. https://commons.wikimedia.org/wiki/File:Vaikunthanatha_-_Sri_Appan_Venkatachalapati_Temple,_Cheranmahadevi.jpg. CC BY-SA 4.0.

90. Top left: Museo Egizio, photographer. *Pyramidion of Ramose Limestone*. Limestone carving, 1292-1190 BCE. Museo Egizio, Italy. Wikimedia Commons, 2023. https://commons.wikimedia.org/wiki/File:Pyramidion_di_Ramose_PAP8834-HDR.tif. CC BY 2.5.

90. Top right: gjuzi, gerti, photographer. *Close-up photography of brown tower during daytime*. Paris, France. Unsplash.com, 2019. https://unsplash.com/photos/close-up-photography-of-brown-tower-during-daytime-smLvQRHqpIM. Licensed from Unsplash.com.

IMAGE CREDITS

90. Bottom: Parrot, A., derivative work of photograph by Nina Aldin Thune. *Sun over Pyramid*. Wikimedia Commons, 2009. https://commons.wikimedia.org/wiki/File:Sun_Over_Pyramid.jpg. CC BY-SA 3.0.

91. Artist unknown. *Amduat papyrus for Herytubekhet* or Book of the Dead Heruben Papyrus. 21st Dynasty Egypt. Egyptian Museum Cairo. Ushabtis.com, 2021. https://www.ushabtis.com/papyrus-herytubekhet-cairo-89/. Photograph by Dik van Bommel 2021.

92. Top left: Dahl, Jeff, artist. *Diagram of the Great Pyramid*. Wikimedia Commons, 2007. https://commons.wikimedia.org/wiki/File:Great_Pyramid_Diagram.svg. CC BY-SA 4.0.

92. Top right: Russel, C.T., author. *Millennial Dawn*. Illustration. Tower Pub. Co., 1891. Wikimedia Commons, 2015. https://commons.wikimedia.org/wiki/File:Millennial_dawn_(1891)_(14784575922).jpg. Public Domain.

92. Bottom left: Dubois, Leon Jean Joseph, author. *Pantheon Egyptien*. Illustration, 1823. Wikimedia Commons, 2022. https://commons.wikimedia.org/wiki/File:Champollion_-_Panth%C3%A9on_%C3%A9gyptien,_1823_(page_275_crop).jpg. Public Domain.

92. Bottom right: Tausch, Olaf, photographer. *Abydos Telpel Relief Sethos I*. Relief at temple of Seti I, Abydos, Egypt, 2011. Wikimedia Commons, 2011. https://commons.wikimedia.org/wiki/File:Abydos_Tempelrelief_Sethos_I._20.JPG. CC BY 3.0.

93. Collage, top left: Bon, Jerome, photographer. *Great Pyramid of Giza*, Egypt, 2008. Wikimedia Commons, 2015. https://commons.wikimedia.org/wiki/File:Great_Pyramid_of_Giza_(2427530661).jpg. CC BY 2.0.

93. Collage, top center: Skubasteve834, photographer. *Monks Mound*, Collinsville, Illinois, 2007. Wikimedia Commons, 2013. https://commons.wikimedia.org/wiki/File:Monks_ Mound_in_July.JPG. CC BY-SA-3.0.

93. Collage, top right: Brücke-Osteuropa, photographer. *Pingling*, 2011. Wikimedia Commons, 2011. https://de.wikipedia.org/wiki/Datei:Pingling_1.jpg. Public domain.

93. Collage, second left: Schwen, Daniel, photographer. *Chichen Itza*, Mexico, 2009. Wikimedia Commons, 2009. https://commons.wikimedia.org/wiki/File:Chichen_Itza_3.jpg. CC BY-SA 4.0.

93. Collage, second center: Peaceofangkor, photographer. *Prang* (Behind Prasat Thom) Koh Ker, Cambodia, 2006. Wikimedia Commons, 2006. https://commons.wikimedia.org/ wiki/File:0505280017PThompyramid.jpg. Public domain.

93. Collage, second right: Ximenez, Pedro, photographer. *Pyramid Güimar*, Canary Islands, Spain, 1998. Wikimedia Commons, 2009. https://commons.wikimedia.org/wiki/ File:Pyramide Güimar.jpg. CC BY-SA 2.0.

93. Collage, third left: Wilson, W., artist. *Marae Mahaiatea on Tahiti Island*, 1799, British Museum. Wikimedia Commons, 2017. https://commons.wikimedia.org/wiki/ File:Oc,G.T.1663,_ Mana_Expedition_to_Easter_Island,_British_Museum.jpg. Public domain.

93. Collage, third center: Jagadeesan, Madhuranthakan, photographer. *Sri Kanteshwara Temple Gopuram*, Nanjangud, Karnataka, India, 2007. Wikimedia Commons, 2016. https://commons.wikimedia.org/wiki/File:N-KA-B159_Srikanteshwara_Temple_Gopuram_ Nanjangud.jpg. CC BY-SA 4.0.

93. Collage, third right: Neoclassicism Enthusiast, photographer. *Model of a Mesopotamian ziggurat* in the Pergamon Museum. Wikimedia Commons, 2023. https://commons.wikimedia.org/wiki/File:Model_of_a_Mesopotamian_ziggurat_in_the_Pergamon_Museum_(01).jpg. Public domain.

93. Collage bottom left: Torbenbrinker, photographer. *Jardim dos Maroicos park*, Pico island, Azores, 2016. Wikimedia Commons, 2016. https://commons.wikimedia.org/wiki/ File%3AMadalenaJardim.jpg. CC BY-SA 4.0.

93. Collage bottom center: Gianf84 at Italian Wikipedia, photographer. *Monte D' Accoddi*, Sardinia, Italy, 2008. Wikimedia Commons, 2009. https://commons.wikimedia.org/wiki/File:Monted%27accoddisardegna.png. CC BY-SA 3.0.

93. Collage bottom right: Uli sh, photographer. *Mauritius pyramid*, 2014. Wikimedia Commons, 2015. https://commons.wikimedia.org/wiki/File%3AMauritius-Pyramiden-5-4-3.jpg. CC BY-SA 4.0.

94. Neoclassicism Enthusiast, photographer. *Model of a Mesopotamian ziggurat* in the Pergamon Museum. Wikimedia Commons, 2023. https://commons.wikimedia.org/wiki/File:Model_of_a_Mesopotamian_ziggurat_in_the_Pergamon_Museum_(01).jpg. Public domain.

96. Nocera, Cosimo, photographer. *Mandala Olmo Lungring*. Wall painting at the Yung Drung Kundrak Ling Bon Monastery South Sikkim, India. Ususmundi.info, 2015. https://ususmundi.info/2015/06/sikkim-darjiling-impressions-de-linde-himalayenne7/monastere-yung-drung-kundrak-ling-bon-peinture-murale-mandala-olmo-lungring-3-4-15/. Photograph courtesy of Cosimo Nocera.

98. Platonides, photographer. *Kailash south side*. Mount Kailash, Tibet, 1998. Wikimedia Commons, 2006. https://commons.wikimedia.org/wiki/File:Kailash_south_side.jpg. CC BY-SA 3.0.

99. Left: Raja Ravi Varma, publisher. *Sagar Manthan*. Illustration, circa 1920s. Wikimedia Commons, 2019. https://commons.wikimedia.org/wiki/File:Sagar_Manthan.jpg.

99. Center: Heng, Kim, photographer. *Equinox at Angkor 21st March 2012*, Wikimedia Commons, 2012. https:// commons.wikimedia.org/wiki/File:Equinox_at_Angkor_21st_March_2012.JPG. CC BY-SA 3.0.

99. Right: Artist, unknown. *Cosmological Mandala with Mount Meru*. Tapestry, 14th century, China. The Metropolitan Museum of Art. Wikimedia Commons, 2012. https://commons.wikimedia.org/wiki/File:Cosmological_Mandala_with_Mount_Meru.jpg. Public domain.

100. Left: Lambarri, Sebastian Pena, photographer. *Stupa*. Namche Bazaar, Nepal. Unsplash.com, 2018. https://unsplash.com/photos/white-on-rocky-hill-viewing-mountain-VEXstplvBxs. Licensed from Unsplash.com.

100. Right: Ha'Eri, Bobak, photographer. *The Giant Wild Goose Pagoda of Xi'an*. 652 AD, Tang Dynasty, China. Wikimedia Commons, 2006. https://en.wikipedia.org/wiki/File:ChinaTrip2005-110.jpg. CC BY 2.5.

102. Lukiyanova Natalia frenta, photographer. *Ancient Mayan pyramid (Kukulcan Temple)*, Chichen Itza, Yucatan, Mexico. Shutterstock.com. https://www.shutterstock.com/ image-photo/ancient-mayan-pyramid-kukulcan-temple-chichen-699889807. Licensed from Shutterstock.com.

103. Left: Jarvis, Dennis, photographer. *Throne of the Jaguar*. Yucatan, Mexico, 2010. Wikimedia Commons, 2018. https://commons.wikimedia.org/wiki/File:Mexico-6366_-_Throne_of_the_Jaguar_(4691171977).jpg. CC BY-SA 2.0.

103. Right: Waldeck, J.F. artist. *Palenque*, stucco panel in Temple of the Lion, 1838. Wikimedia Commons, 2024. https://commons.wikimedia.org/wiki/File:WaldeckPalenqueLionTablet.jpg. Public domain.

105. Left: Madman2001, artist. *A drawing of the lid of the tomb of Maya ruler Pacal the Great*. Wikimedia Commons, 2008. https://commons.wikimedia.org/wiki/File:Pakal_the_Great_tomb_lid.png. CC BY-SA 3.0.

105. Right: Le Plongeon, Augustus. Illustration in *Sacred Mysteries Among the Mayas and the Quiches*, 1886. Third edition, New York: Macoy Publishing and Masonic Supply Company, 1909, p. 134. Internet Archive, 2017. https://archive.org/details/ PlongeonALeSacredMysteriesAmongTheMayansQuiches1909/page/n179. Public domain.

106. Left: Burger, Ludwig, illustrator. *Die Nornen Urd, Werdanda, Skuld, unter der Welteiche Yggdrasil* in *Nordisch-germanische Götter und Helden* by Wilhelm Wägner Otto Spamer, Leipzig & Berlin, 1882, page 231. Wikimedia Commons, 2008. https://commons.wikimedia.org/wiki/File:Die_Nornen_Urd,_Werdanda,_Skuld,_unter_der_Welteiche_Yggdrasil_by_Ludwig_Burger.jpg. Public domain.

106. Center: RootOfAllLight, artist. *Irminsul*. Illustration, 2019. Wikimedia Commons, 2020. https://commons.wikimedia.org/wiki/File:Irminsul.svg. CC BY-SA 4.0.

106. Right: Laboratories Servier, artist. *Nervous System*. Illustration, 2016. Smart Servier Medical Art. Wikimedia Commons, 2023. https://commons.wikimedia.org/wiki/File:Nervous_system_-_Nervous_system_1_--_Smart-Servier.png. CC BY-SA 3.0.

106. Bottom: Hakhamaneshian, Parthsbod K.A., photographer. *Froohar symbol*. Stone relief. Wikimedia Commons, 2022. https://commons.wikimedia.org/wiki/File:Froohar.jpg. CC BY-SA 4.0.

107. Left: Artist unknown. *Stela of Senu Adoring Osiris*. Limestone relief, Egypt, 18th dynasty. The Metropolitan Museum of Art, Rogers Fund, 1918. Wikimedia Commons, 2017. https://commons.wikimedia.org/wiki/File:Stela_of_Senu_Adoring_Osiris_MET_18.2.5_01.jpg. Public domain.

108. Center: Artist unknown. *Hermes - the Greek god of transitions and boundaries*. Woodcut engraving. Featured in the book *Der Olymp oder die Mythologie der Griechen und Römer (The Olympus or the Mythology of the Greeks and Romans)*, August Heinrich Petiscus in C.F. Amelang's Verlag, Leipzig, 1878, 18th edition. Wikimedia Commons, 2022. https://commons.wikimedia.org/wiki/File:Hermes_-_the_Greek_god_of_transitions_and_boundaries.jpg. Public domain.

108. Right: L.A. Huffman, photographer. *Two Moons, a Cheyenne Chief, in Wearing Feathered Headdress and Wrapped in a Blanket at Fort Keogh*. Little Bighorn Battlefield National Monument, Montana, 1878. Wikimedia Commons, 2019. https://commons.wikimedia.org/wiki/File:Two_Moons,_a_Cheyenne_Chief,_in_Wearing_Feathered_Headdress_and_Wrapped_in_a_Blanket_at_Fort_Keogh_(29ba7247eccd485a8af56f0a37798599).tif. Public domain.

107. Bottom: Carter, John, photographer. *Land of Legends*. Glastonbury Tor, England, UK. iStock.com, 2016. https://www.istockphoto.com/photo/land-of-legends-gm509857264-86001907. Licensed from iStock.com.

IMAGE CREDITS

108. Brücke-Osteuropa, photographer. *Mausoleum of Han Yang Ling near Xian*, model of pyramid, der Han Yang Ling Museum, Xianyang, China, 2008. Wikimedia Commons, 2010. https:// commons.wikimedia.org/wiki/File:Han_Yang_Ling_02.JPG. Public domain.

111. Bauer, John, artist. *Odin and Sleipnir*, illustration. In For Our Fathers' Godsaga by Viktor Rydberg, 1906. Wikimedia Commons, 2006. https://commons.wikimedia.org/wiki/File:Odin_and_Sleipnir_-_John_Bauer.jpg. Public domain.

112. *Depiction of a practice of Utiseta*: Image created by DALL-E 3, an AI by OpenAI, prompted by Sura Ondrunar Publishing.

113. Francis R Niglutsch, publisher. *The Summons to Valhalla*, illustration. In *The Story of the Greatest Nations* by Edward Ellis and Charles Horne. Ney York: F.R. Niglustch, 1900. Wikimedia Commons, 2016. https://commons.wikimedia.org/wiki/File:The_story_of_the_greatest_nations,_from_the_dawn_of_history_to_the_twentieth_century_-_a_comprehensive_history,_founded_upon_the_leading_authorities,_including_a_complete_chronology_of_the_world,_and_(14775193741).jpg. Public domain.

114. Faith-Ell, Harald, photographer. *Odin, Suttungr and Gunnlöd*. Stone relief, Gotlandic image stone Hammars III. Photo in *Gotlands Bildsteine* by Sune Lindquist, 1941. Wikimedia Commons, 2008. https://commons.wikimedia.org/wiki/File:Odin,_Suttungr_and_Gunnl%C3%B6d.jpg. Public domain.

116. Schoppe, Amalia, author. *Norns*, illustration in *Die Helden und Götter des Nordens, oder Das Buch der sagen*, 1832. Wikimedia Commons, 2008. https://commons.wikimedia.org/wiki/File:Norns_(1832)_from_Die_Helden_und_G%C3%B6tter_des_Nordens,_oder_Das_Buch_der_sagen.jpg. Public Domain.

117. Left: Collingwood, W. G. *Odin's Self-Sacrifice*. In T*he Elder or Poetic Edda, Commonly Known as Sæmund's Edda*, edited and translated by Olive Bray, 1908, p. 61. Wikimedia Commons, 2008. https://en.m.wikipedia.org/wiki/File:Odin%27s_Self-sacrifice_by_Collingwood.jpg. Public domain.

117. Right: Barber, John Warner. *The Crucifixion*. In *The life of Our Lord and Savior Jesus Christ* by John Fleetwood, New Haven: Nathan Whiting, 1830, p. 426. Wikimedia Commons, 2015. https://commons.wikimedia.org/wiki/File:The_life_of_our_Lord_and_Savior_Jesus_Christ_-_containing_a_full,_accurate,_and_universal_history_from_his_taking_upon_himself_our_nature_to_his_crucifixion,_resurrection,_and_ascension-_together_with_(14592569250).jpg. Public domain.

118. Left: Bjoertvedt, photographer. *Aaby sotenäs petroglyphs*. The Åby petroglyphs in Sotenäs municipality, western Sweden. Wikimedia Commons, 2016. https://commons.wikimedia.org/wiki/File:Aaby_soten%C3%A4s_petroglyphs_IMG_6445_Tossene_73-1_RA_10161200730001.jpg. CC BY-SA 4.0.

118. Center: John-Eric Gustafsson / Riksantikvarieämbetet, photographer. *Ales Stenar*. Sweden, 1985. Wikimedia Commons, 2017. https://commons.wikimedia.org/wiki/File:Ales_stenar_-_KMB_-_16001000036132.jpg. CC BY 2.5.

118. Right: Artist unknown. *Egyptian god Ra in his solar barque*. Wikimedia Commons, 2005. https://commons.wikimedia.org/wiki/File:Ra_Barque.jpg. Public domain.

119. Top: Reid, Stephen, artist. *They rode up to a stately palace*. Illustration in *The High Deeds of Finn and other Bardic Romances of Ancient Ireland*, by T. W. Rolleston, 1900. Wikimedia Commons, 2013. https://en.wikipedia.org/wiki/File:15_They_rode_up_to_a_stately_palace.jpg. Public Domain.

119. Bottom: Keeshan, Dave, photographer. *Newgrange*. Ireland, 2008. Wikimedia Commons, 2021. https://commons.wikimedia.org/wiki/File:Newgrange_065.jpg. CC BY-SA 2.0.

121. The Discovery Programme, photographer, 3D model. *Decorated Stone Basin, Knowth*. 3D model, Basin stone located in the northern recess of the eastern passage at the megalithic passage tomb at Knowth, Ireland. https://www.europeana.eu/en/item/2048705/object_HA_1327. CC BY-NC-ND 4.0

122. Top: Wakeman, William Frederick. *Sketch of a Cross Section of the Newgrange Passage Grave*, circa 1900. In *Wakeman's Handbook of Irish Antiquities*, Dublin: Hodges, Figgis, 1903, p. 85. Wikimedia Commons, 2010. https://commons.wikimedia.org/wiki/File:Wakeman_Newgrange_tumulus_chamber_cross_section.png. Public domain.

122. Left: Arkyn, Erik, photographer. *Inside Chambered Mound*, Taversöe Tuick, Scotland. Courtesy of Erik Arkyn.

122. Right: lassedesignen, artist. *Light at the end of the tunnel*. Shutterstock.com. https://www.shutterstock.com/image-photo/light-end-tunnel-192906149. Licensed from Shutterstock.com.

123. Left: Artist unknown. *Stonehenge on Midsummer, 1700 BC*. In *Nordisk Familjebok*, vol. 27, 1918, p. 115. Wikimedia Commons, 2006. https://commons.wikimedia.org/wiki/File:Stonehenge_vid_midsommar_1700_f_Kr,_Nordisk_familjebok.png. Public domain.

123. Right: Branley, Stephen, photographer. *Calanais Stones*, 2008. Wikimedia Commons, 2011. https://commons.wikimedia.org/wiki/File:Calanais_Stones_-_geograph.org.uk_-_1236575.jpg. CC BY-SA 2.0.

124. Left: MikPeach, photographer. *Avebury henge and stone circles*, 2009. Wikimedia Commons, 2017. https://commons.wikimedia.org/wiki/File:Wiltshire-Avebury.jpg. CC BY-SA 4.0.

124. Right: Lertola, Joseph, artist. *3D rendering of Stonehenge*. Illustration, 2007. Wikimedia Commons, 2011. https://commons.wikimedia.org/wiki/File:Stonehenge_render.jpg. Public Domain.

126. Valette, Claude, photographer. *Chaudron de Gundestrup*. Gundestrup cauldron, interior plate 2, copy by galvanoplasty, museum of Bibracte, France, 2012. Wikimedia Commons, 2012. https://commons.wikimedia.org/wiki/File:ChaudronDeGunstrup2bis.jpg. CC BY-SA 3.0.

127. Pogány, Willy, illustrator. *Odin*. In *The Children of Odin: The Book of Northern Myths* by Padaric Colum, 1917. Wikimedia Commons, 2013. https://commons.wikimedia.org/wiki/File:The_Children_of_Odin_The_Book_of_Northern_Myths_37.jpg. Public domain

128. johncarter5, photographer. *Sun rising over Glastonbury Tor*. Somerset, UK. iStock.com, 2012. https://www.istockphoto.com/photo/sunrise-over-glastonbury-tor-gm1402927625-455668399 Licensed from iStock.com.

129. Tomw37, photographer. *West Kennet Long Barrow*. England, UK, 2016. Wikimedia Commons, 2017. https://commons.wikimedia.org/wiki/File:West_kennet_long_barrow_interior.jpg. CC BY-SA 4.0.

132. Left: Wikimedia user: MithrandirMage, artist, based on work of Wikimedia user BD2412. *A symbol representing the Awen from Celtic mythology*. Wikimedia Commons, 2007. https://en.wikipedia.org/wiki/File:Awen_symbol_final.svg. Public domain.

132. Right: Arkyn, Erik, photographer. *Egyptian Stele*, British Museum. Courtesy of Erik Arkyn.

133. *Ancient Europe OBE Theory Illustration 1*: Image created by DALL-E 3, an AI by OpenAI, prompted by Sura Ondrunar Publishing.

134. Top: *Ancient Europe OBE Theory Illustration 2*: Image created by DALL-E 3, an AI by OpenAI, prompted by Sura Ondrunar Publishing.

134. Center: *Ancient Europe OBE Theory Illustration 3*: Image created by DALL-E 3, an AI by OpenAI, prompted by Sura Ondrunar Publishing.

134. Bottom: *Ancient Europe OBE Theory Illustration 4*: Image created by DALL-E 3, an AI by OpenAI, prompted by Sura Ondrunar Publishing.

135. Top left: de Guettelet, Hamelin, artist. *Evolution du plan des temples*. Illustrations of Maltese temples. Wikimedia Commons, 2008. https://commons.wikimedia.org/wiki/File:Evolution_du_plan_des_temples_copie.jpg. Public Domain.

135. Top right: Arkyn, Erik, photographer. *Model of the Mnajdra temple complex*, Malta. Courtesy of Erik Arkyn.

135. Bottom left: Arkyn, Erik, photographer. *Trilithon Doorway*, Hal Tarxien Prehistoric Complex in Malta. Courtesy of Erik Arkyn.

135. Bottom right: Arkyn, Erik, photographer. *Stone Bowl*, Hal Tarxien Prehistoric Complex in Malta. Courtesy of Erik Arkyn.

136. Arkyn, Erik, photographer. *Model of the Hal Saflieni Hypogeum*, Malta. Courtesy of Erik Arkyn.

137. Top: Arkyn, Erik, photographer. *Sleeping Goddess Statue*, Malta. Courtesy of Erik Arkyn.

137. Bottom: Teomancimit, photographer. *Göbekli Tepe*. Şanlıurfa, Turkey. Wikimedia Commons, 2011. https://commons.wikimedia.org/wiki/File:G%C3%B6bekli_Tepe,_Urfa.jpg. CC BY-SA 3.0.

138. Göbekli Tepe Project, photographer. *Pillar 43 in Building D*. Pilar with reliefs at Göbekli Tepe. World Heritage Convention Unesco.org, 2010. https://whc.unesco.org/en/documents/165846. © DAI, Göbekli Tepe Project. Used with permission.

140. Left: Koopman, Rob, photographer. *Nut detail coffin Peftjauneith*. Egypt, 2009. Wikimedia Commons, 2017. https://commons.wikimedia.org/wiki/File:Nut_detail_coffin_peftjauneith_(rmo_leiden,_egypt_26d_664-525bc)_(3956335139).jpg. CC BY-SA 2.0. Image edited from original by Sura Ondrunar Publishing.

140. Right: Credner, Till, artist. *Cygnus*. Photography of the constellation Cygnus, the swan, 2014. Wikimedia Commons, 2023. https://commons.wikimedia.org/wiki/File:CygnusCC.jpg. AlltheSky.com. CC BY-SA 3.0.

142. Left: Talskiddy, photographer. *Men-an-Tol*. Cornwall, England, 2008. Wikimedia Commons, 2012. https://commons.wikimedia.org/wiki/File:Cornwall_-_Men-an-Tol.jpg. CC BY 3.0.

142. Right: Steel, Trish, photographer. *Sculptures at Heaven's Gate*. Sculpture garden UK, designed and carved by Paul Norris. Wikimedia Commons, 2011. https://commons.wikimedia.org/wiki/File:Sculptures_at_Heaven%27s_Gate_-_geograph.org.uk_-_445063.jpg. CC BY-SA 2.0.

145. Artist unknown. *Life of Zoroaster*. 19th century. Wikimedia Commons, 2010. https://commons.wikimedia.org/wiki/File:Zoroaster_1.jpg. Public domain.

IMAGE CREDITS

146. Derfash Kaviani, photographer. *Naqsh-e Raja*. Wikimedia Commons, 2014. https://en.wikipedia.org/wiki/File:Naqshe_Rajab_Darafsh_Ordibehesht_93_(1).jpg. CC BY 3.0.

148. Doré, Gustave, artist. *L'Ascension*. Oil on canvas, 1879. Petit Palais, France. Wikimedia Commons, 2016. https://commons.wikimedia.org/wiki/File:Gustave_Dor%C3%A9_-_L%27Ascension.jpg. Public domain.

152. Follower of Hieronymus Bosch. *Christ in Limbo*. Oil on panel, circa 1575. Indianapolis Museum of Art. Wikimedia Commons, 2015. https://commons.wikimedia.org/wiki/File:Follower_of_Jheronimus_Bosch_Christ_in_Limbo.jpg. Public domain.

153. Bolswert, Schelte Adamsz, artist. *Christ on the Cross*. Engraving between 1630-1635. British Museum. https://commons.wikimedia.org/wiki/File:Print_(BM_R,2.27_1).jpg. Public domain. Photograph: The Trustees of the British Museum, CC BY-NC-SA 4.0.

154. Bloch, Carl. *Burial of Christ*, circa 1865-1879. Wikimedia Commons, 2013. https://commons.wikimedia.org/wiki/File:BurialofChrist_CarlBloch.jpg. Public domain.

155. Borchert, Andreas F., photographer. *Detail Women at the Empty Tomb*. St. Peter's Church (Church of Ireland), Peter's Hill, Drogheda, County Louth, Ireland. Wikimedia Commons, 2022. https://commons.wikimedia.org/wiki/File:Drogheda_St._Peter%27s_Church_of_Ireland_W07_Detail_Women_at_the_Empty_Tomb_2022_08_26.jpg. CC BY-SA 3.0.

156. Rivalz, Antoine, artist. *Jesus appearing to Madeleine*. Oil on canvas, before 1735. Musée Ingres Bourdelle. Wikimedia Commons, 2020. https://commons.wikimedia.org/wiki/File:Mus%C3%A9e_Ingres-Bourdelle_-_Noli_me_tangere_ou_J%C3%A9sus_apparaissant_%C3%A0_Madeleine_-_Antoine_Rivalz_-_Joconde06070000238.jpg. Public domain. Photograph by: Didier Descouens, CC BY-SA 4.0.

158. Bathas, Thomas, artist. *Vision of the Apocalypse*. Egg tempera on wood, 1596. Monastery of Saint John the Theologian. Wikimedia Commons, 2021. https://commons.wikimedia.org/wiki/File:Thomas_Bathas_Revelation_of_Saint_John_the_Divine.png. Public domain. Photograph by Tzim78, CC BY-SA 4.0.

159. Kunitora, Utagawa, artist. *Taoist Immortal Flying through the Air*. Wood block print, early 19th century, Japanese Edo period. On display at MFA Boston, gift of Porter Sargent. https://collections.mfa.org/objects/253681. Public domain.

164. Lu Shizhong, author. Illustration in *The Great Method of the Jade Hall of the Three Heavens of the Supreme Mysterious Origin*. 12th century. https://ctext.org/library.pl?if=en&file=98805&page=31#box(474,532,10,6). Public Domain.

165. Lu Shizhong, author. Illustration in *The Great Method of the Jade Hall of the Three Heavens of the Supreme Mysterious Origin*. 12th century. https://ctext.org/library.pl?if=en&file=98805&page=30#box(586,602,0,2). Public domain.

166. Todd, Gary, photographer. *Bronze Sun-wheel*. Sanxingdui Museum Gallery, China, 2010. Wikimedia Commons, 2020. https://commons.wikimedia.org/wiki/File:Bronze_Sun-wheel,_Sanxingdui.jpg. Public domain.

168. Artist unknown. *Peaceful & Wrathful Deities - of the Bardo*. Tapestry, ground mineral pigment on cotton, Nyingma lineage, 1700-1799, Tibet. Rubin Museum of Art. Wikimedia Commons, 2011. https://en.wikipedia.org/wiki/File:Peaceful_%26_Wrathful_Deities_-_of_the_Bardo.jpg. Public domain.

169. Artist unknown. *Darikapa*. 9th Century Buddhist Mahasiddha. Wikimedia Commons, 2014. https://commons.wikimedia.org/wiki/File:Darikapa.jpg. Public domain.

171. Artist unknown. *Yama Dharmaraja*. Painting on cloth, 19th century, Mongolia. The Rubin Museum of Art. Wikimedia Commons, 2022. https://commons.wikimedia.org/wiki/File:Yama_Dharmaraja_-_19th_century_Mongolian_painting_(thangka).jpg. Public domain.

174. Left: Artist unknown. *Plato*. Luni marble, copy of the portrait made by Silanion ca. 370 BC for the Academia in Athens, 370 BC, Capitoline Museums. Wikimedia Commons 2009. https://en.wikipedia.org/wiki/File:Plato_Silanion_Musei_Capitolini_MC1377.jpg. Photograph © Marie-Lan Nguyen, CC BY 2.5.

174. Right: After Lysippos, sculptor. *Bust of Aristotle*. Marble, roman copy after a Greek bronze original by Lysippos from 330 BC. Museo nazionale romano di palazzo Altemps. Wikimedia Commons, 2006. https://commons.wikimedia.org/wiki/File:Aristotle_Altemps_Inv8575.jpg. Public domain.

175. Messier, C, photographer. Μαντείο Τροφωνίου. Trofonios oracle, at the springs of River Herkyna, Greece, 2020. Wikimeida Commons, 2021. https://commons.wikimedia.org/wiki/ File:Μαντείο_Τροφωνίου_1771.jpg. CC BY-SA 4.0.

177. Borisov, Sergei Ivanovich, photographer. *An Altai shaman (sorcerer)*, 1908. Postcard made in the Russian empire. Wikimedia Commons, 2010. https://commons.wikimedia.org/wiki/File:SB_-_Altay_shaman_with_drum.jpg. Public domain.

178. Carpenter, Frank G. (Frank George), 1855-1924, photographer, collector. *Yup'ik shaman exorcising evil spirits*. Nushagak, Alaska, 1890s. Library of Congress. Wikimedia Commons, 2007. https://commons.wikimedia.org/wiki/File:Yupik_shaman_Nushagak.jpg. Public domain.

180. Top: Curtis, Edward S, photographer. *Hamasta Shaman*, 1914. Library of Congress. Wikimedia Commons, 2009. https://commons.wikimedia.org/wiki/File:Hamatsa_shaman2.jpg. Public domain.

180. Left: *Jaguar Nagual*. From Zapotec culture Stela 1 from Cerro del Rey, Río Grande, coast of Oaxaca. Adapted from an illustration of the Stela 1 by Javier Urcid https://en.wikipedia.org/wiki/File:Jaguarnagual.jpg.

180. Right: International Museum of Ceramics, photographer. *Pre-Columbian Mask*. International Museum of Ceramics in Faenza, Italy. Featured in https://www.researchgate.net/figure/Hidden-in-plain-sight-the-ceramic-pre-Columbian-mask-depicts-the-transformation-of-a_fig3_285657093. https://www.micfaenza.org. Courtesy of the International Museum of Ceramics.

183. Dr. Alexey Yakovlev, photographer. *Shaman*. Jama-Coaque Culture (350 BC – 1530 AD). Quito, Ecuador, Casa del Alabado Museum of Pre-Columbian Art. Wikimedia Comons, 2021. https://commons.wikimedia.org/wiki/File:Shaman,_Jama-Coaque_Culture_(350_BC_%E2%80%94_1530_AD)_(32550974268).jpg. CC BY-SA 2.0.

185. Left: Moore, Clarence Bloomfield, artist. *Figures on Vessel No. 4, Decoration, Mound D*. In *Certain aboriginal remains of the Black Warrior River. Certain aboriginal remains of the lower Tombigbee River. Certain aboriginal remains of Mobile Bay and Mississippi Sound. Miscellaneous investigation in Florida* by Clarence Bloomfield Moore. Philadelphia: P.C. Stockhausen, 1908, page 174. Archive.org, 2006. https://archive.org/details/blackwarriorriver00moorrich/page/174/mode/2up. Public domain.

185. Right: Artwork from Mississippian culture artifact, found in Clarence Bloomfield Moore book circa 1894-1922, referenced in Little, Gregory. *Path of Souls: The Native American Death Journey: Cygnus, Orion, the Milky Way, Giant Skeletons in Mounds, & the Smithsonian*, ATA-Archetype Books, page 164.

185. Bottom: Moore, Clarence Bloomfield, artist. *Engraved Stone Disc*, Carthage Alabama. In *The antiquities of Tennessee and the adjacent states, and the state of aboriginal society in the scale of civilization represented by them; a series of historical and ethnological studies* by Clarence Bloomfield Moore. Cincinnati: The R. Clarke Company, 1897, page 332. Archive.org, 2006. https://archive.org/details/antiquitiestenn00thurrich/page/332/mode/2up. Public domain.

186. Roe, Herb, artist. *Mississippian Cultures*. Wikimedia Commons, 2010. https://commons.wikimedia.org/wiki/File:Mississippian_cultures_HRoe_2010.jpg. CC BY-SA 3.0.

187. Collage, top left: Kvaran, Einar E (Carptrash), photographer. *Newark Mounds*, Newark, Ohio, USA, 1980s. Wikimedia Commons, 2017. https://commons.wikimedia.org/wiki/ File:Newark_Mounds,_Newark,_Ohio,_USA.jpg. CC BY-SA 4.0.

187. Collage, top center: Saunaluoma, Sanna, photographer. *Fazenda Colorada*, Rio Branco, Acre, Brazil, 2012. Wikimedia Commons, 2012. https://en.wikipedia.org/wiki/File:Fazenda_ Colorada.jpg. CC BY-SA 3.0.

187. Collage, top right: Google Maps. 2018. *Goseck Circle*. Imagery ©2018 Google, Map data ©2018 GeoBasis-DE/BKG (©2009), Google.

187. Collage, bottom left: MikPeach, photographer. Avebury henge and stone circles, 2009. Wikimedia Commons, 2017. https://commons.wikimedia.org/wiki/File:Wiltshire-Avebury. jpg. CC BY-SA 4.0.

187. Collage, bottom right: 4Kclips, photographer. *Fantastic view over Stonehenge in England*, Brighton, UK, 2019. Shutterstock.com. https://www.shutterstock.com/image- photo/fantastic-view-over-stonehenge-england-brighton-1648235137. Licensed from Shutterstock.com.

188. Roe, Herb, photographer. *Cox Style Gorget*. Mississippian Culture. Wikimedia Commons, 2012. https:// commons.wikimedia.org/wiki/File:Cox_style_gorget_HRoe_2012.jpg. CC BY-SA 3.0.

189. Roe, Herb, photographer. *Craig style shell gorget Spiro Raccoon dancers*. Engraved shell, Spiro Mounds, Oklahoma. Wikimedia Commons, 2012. https://commons.wikimedia.org/wiki/File:Craig_style_shell_gorget_Spiro_Raccoon_dancers_HRoe_2012.jpg. CC BY-SA 3.0.

191. Roe, Herb, artist. *Winterville Aerial View*. Wikimedia Commons, 2016. https://en.wikipedia.org/wiki/File:Winterville_Aerial_View_HRoe_2016.jpg. CC BY-SA 4.0.

192. Roe, Herb, artist. *S.E.C.C. shaman dancing*. Wikimedia Commons, 2008. https://commons.wikimedia.org/wiki/File:S.E.C.C._shaman_dancing_HRoe_2008.jpg. CC BY-SA 3.0.

194. Artist unknown. *Laru, the rush realm of the blessed*. Painting on the east wall of the tomb of Sennedjem in Deir el Medineh, Thebes-West, Egypt, ca. 1775 BC. Wikimedia Commons, 2020. https://en.wikipedia.org/wiki/File:27.1_Iaru.tif. Public domain. Photograph from Shedid, Abdel Ghaffar *The Tomb of Sennedjem / An artist grave of the 19th century Dynasty in Deir el Medineh*, Philipp von Zabern, Mainz, 1994.

196. Gita Press, publisher. *The chanting Brahmin and the ascension of Maharaja Ikshvaku*. Illustration in *Mahabharata*, by Sriman Maharshi Vedavyasa, translated by Pandit Ramnarayan Dutt Shastri. Gita Press, Vol 5, Page 567. https://archive.org/details/mahabharat05ramauoft/page/n567/mode/2up. Digitized by University of Toronto Collection, acquired 1965.

197. Left: Artist unknown. *The God Re-Harakhty and Amentit, the goddess of the West*. Painting, burial chamber of Nefertari, circa 1298-1235 BCE. The Yorck Project 2002. https://commons.wikimedia.org/wiki/File:Maler_der_Grabkammer_der_Nefertari_001.jpg. Public domain.

197. Right: Artist unknown. *Yama on Buffalo*. Painting, circa 1820. British Museum. Wikimedia Commons, 2020. https://commons.wikimedia.org/wiki/File:Yama_on_buffalo.jpg. Public domain. Photograph: The Trustees of the British Museum, CC BY-NC-SA 4.0.

197. Bottom: Artist unknown. *Dendera Hathor Temple Complex*, stone relief, Egypt. Photographed by JMCC1, retouched by Csorfoly Daniel. Wikimedia Commons, 2011. https://commons.wikimedia.org/wiki/File:DenderaHathorTempleComplexQenaEgypt548-2007feb10_CsorfolyDaniel_c.jpg. Public Domain.

198. Left: Artist unknown. *Pharaoh and two heads*, two-sided relief, Egypt, 664-32 BCE. Nelson-Atkins Museum of Art. Photographed by Daderot. Wikimedia Commons, 2011. https://commons.wikimedia.org/wiki/File:Pharaoh_and_two_heads,_two-sided_relief,_Egypt,_Late_Period_to_Ptolemaic_Period,_26th_Dynasty_to_Ptolemaic_Dynasty,_664-32_BCE_-_Nelson-Atkins_Museum_of_Art_-_DSC08138.JPG. Public domain.

198. Right: Artist unknown. *Gilded shrine from the tomb treasure of the ancient Egyptian king Tutankhamun*, 18th dynasty, ca. 1336-1327 BC. Egyptian Museum, Cairo. Wikimedia Commons, 2020. https://commons.wikimedia.org/wiki/File:%C3%84gyptisches_Museum_Kairo_2019-11-09_Tutanchamun_Grabschatz_24.jpg. Public domain. Photograph by Djehouty, 2020. CC BY-SA 4.0.

199. Belnos, S.C. artist. *Gayatri, The Secret Prayer*. Color lithograph, 1851. New York Public Library. Wikimedia Commons, 2019. https://commons.wikimedia.org/wiki/File:Gayatri_japa.jpg. Public Domain.

202. Left: Photographer of Pixabay, 16944022. *Sacred Lotus, Laxmi Lotus*. https://pixabay.com/photos/lotus-sacred-lotus-laxmi-lotus-7477666. Licensed from Pixabay.com

202. Center: Sriyanto, Leonita Yuliana, photographer. *Purple Flower on Green Leaves*. Unsplash.com, 2021. https://unsplash.com/photos/purple-flower-on-green-leaves--DR_T4oBZG8. Licensed from Unsplash.com.

202. Right: Denisa, Beata, artist. *Lord Vishnu*. Oil painting on canvas. Wikimedia Commons, 2018. https://commons.wikimedia.org/wiki/File:Lord_Vishnu_Narayana.jpg. CC BY-SA 4.0.

203. Marfurt, Nadine, photographer. *Tian Tan Buddha*, Hong Kong. Unsplash.com, 2021. https://unsplash.com/photos/gray-concrete-statue-under-blue-sky-during-daytime-QaYUfFohygc. Licensed from Unsplash.com

205. Left: Budge, E.A Wallis, author. *Isis suckling Horus*. In *The Gods of the Egyptians* Vol. II, 1904, page 208. Wikimedia Commons, 2010. https://commons.wikimedia.org/wiki/File:Isis_suckling_Horus.png. Public Domain.

205. Right: Becquet frères, artist. *Histoire Sainte*. Lithographs, 1850-1880. British Museum. Wikimedia Commons, 2020. https://commons.wikimedia.org/wiki/File:Histoire_Sainte_(BM_1981,U.56-134_26).jpg. Public domain. Photograph: The Trustees of the British Museum, CC BY-NC-SA 4.0.

206. Left: Popo le Chien, photographer. *Tomb in Cheops pyramid*, King's room, Giza, Egypt. Wikimedia Commons, 2011. https://commons.wikimedia.org/wiki/File:Kheops_Kings_tomb.JPG. Public domain.

206. Center: Arkyn, Erik, photographer. *Stone Bowl*, Hal Tarxien, Malta. Courtesy of Erik Arkyn.

206. Right: The Discovery Programme, photographer, 3D model creator. *Decorated Stone Basin*, Knowth, 3D Model. https://www.europeana.eu/en/item/2048705/object_HA_1327. CC BY-NC-ND.

207. Top left: Arkyn, Erik, photographer. *Grey Cairns of Camster*, Scotland. Courtesy of Erik Arkyn.

207. Top center: Fran_Kie, artist. *Man Getting of a Dark Tunnel Toward Light*. Shutterstock.com. https://www.shutterstock.com/image-photo/man-getting-out-dark-tunnel-toward-1044915097. Licensed from Shutterstock.com.

207. Top right: Tcherkasski, Evgeni, photographer. *Milky Way on Forest*. Unsplash.com, 2019. https://unsplash.com/photos/devkd2d69Tw. Licensed from Unsplash.com.

207. Center left: Budge, E.A. Wallis, author. *Section of the Pyramid of Cheops at Gizeh*. In *The Nile. Notes for Travelers in Egypt*, 1893. Wikimedia Commons, 2015. https://commons.wikimedia.org/wiki/File:The_Nile._Notes_for_travellers_in_Egypt_(1893)_(14760158691).jpg. Public Domain.

207. Center right: Artist unknown. *Stonehenge on Midsummer, 1700 BC*. In *Nordisk Familjebok*, edited by Theodor Westrin, vol. 27, 1918, p. 115. Wikimedia Commons, 2006. https://commons.wikimedia.org/wiki/File:Stonehenge_vid_midsommar_1700_f_Kr,_Nordisk_familjebok.png. Public domain.

207. Bottom: Wakeman, William Frederick, artist. *Sketch of a Cross Section of the Newgrange Passage Grave*, circa 1900. In *Wakeman's Handbook of Irish Antiquities*, Dublin: Hodges, Figgis, 1903, p. 85. Wikimedia Commons, 2010. https://commons.wikimedia.org/wiki/File:Wakeman_Newgrange_tumulus_ chamber_cross_section.png. Public domain.

208. Left: Eternal Space, artist. *A representation of the Egyptian Goddess Nut*. Wikimedia Commons, 2023. https://commons.wikimedia.org/wiki/File:Goddess_Nut.png. CC BY-SA 4.0.

208. Right: Sewell, Jesse, photographer. *Milky Way Panorama*, in Big Bend National Park, USA. Unsplash.com, 2015. https://unsplash.com/photos/q75_AMCgsZU. Licensed from Unsplash.com.

209. Left: Carlota O, photographer. *Great Pyramid of Giza*, Cairo Egypt. Unsplash.com, 2023. https://unsplash.com/photos/a-group-of-people-standing-in-front-of-a-large-pyramid-hq6hwCQ3u4U. Licensed from Unsplash.com.

209. Center: Superchilum, photographer. *Knowth*, Ireland. Wikimedia Commons, 2013. https://commons.wikimedia.org/wiki/File:Knowth_Ireland_02.JPG. CC BY-SA 3.0.

209. Right: MikPeach, photographer. *Avenbury Henge and Stone Circles*, Avenbury, UK, 2009. Wikimedia Commons, 2017. https://commons.wikimedia.org/wiki/File:Wiltshire-Avebury.jpg. CC BY-SA 4.0.

209. Bottom: Roe, Herb, artist. *Ogee Motif, from Southeastern Ceremonial Complex*, Lake Jackson Mounds, Florida. Wikimedia Commons, 2012. https://commons.wikimedia.org/wiki/File:S.E.C.C._Ogee_Motif_HRoe_2012.jpg. CC BY-SA 3.0.

210. *Ancient Sites Align* composite by Sura Ondrunar Publishing featuring:

IR Stone, photographer. *Mayan pyramid of Kukulkan*, Chichen Itzá, Yucatán. https://www.shutterstock.com/image-photo/mexico-chichen-mayan-pyramid-kukulcan-el-1070680868. Licensed from Shutterstock.com.

Kooanantkul, Chuta, photographer. *Stonehenge during sunset Winter Solstice*. https://www.shutterstock.com/image-photo/stonehenge-during-sunset-winter-solstice-1601037709. Licensed from Shutterstock.com.

Nadja1, photographer. *Pyramids and Sphinx in Giza*. https://www.shutterstock.com/image-photo/pyramids-sphinx-giza-36214633. Licensed from Shutterstock.com.

Yukinobu N, photographer. *Angkor Wat Sunrise*. https://www.shutterstock.com/image-photo/angkor-wat-sunrise-338949902. Licensed from Shutterstock.com.

Marfin, Artur, photographer. *Sunset behind the Sea*. https://www.shutterstock.com/image-photo/sun-set-behind-sea-139890292. Licensed from Shutterstock.com.

Dascal, Adrian, photographer. *Giza Plateau, Cairo, Egypt*. Unsplash.com, 2019. https://unsplash.com/photos/brown-pyramid-during-daytime-FXXuJ9S-KkQ. Licensed from Unsplash.com.

211. Left: Käyttäjä:Kompak, artist. Derivative by Perhelion. *Ra-Horakhty Based on Nefertari's Tomb*, 2010. Wikimedia Commons, 2016. https://commons.wikimedia.org/wiki/File:Sun_god_Ra.svg. CC BY-SA 3.0.

211. Center: Putsykovich, Feofil Feofilovich, author. *Illustration of Jesus* in *Life of the Saviour of the World*, sixth reprint 1905. Wikimedia Commons, 2009. https://commons.wikimedia.org/wiki/File:F.F._Putsykovich_-_Life_of_the_Saviour_of_the_World_155.png. Public domain.

211. Right: Gita Press, publisher. *Lord of Gods Vishnu*. Illustration in *Shrimad Bhagavata Mahapurana*, Gita Press. Wikimedia Commons, 2018. https://commons.wikimedia.org/wiki/File:Lord_of_ Gods_Vishnu.jpg.

211. Bottom: *Illustration of the Great Sphinx with the Sun forming a Halo*: Image created by DALL-E 3, an AI by OpenAI, prompted by Sura Ondrunar Publishing.

212. Bodsworth, Jon, photographer. *House of the King of the Great Pyramid of Khufu*. Egyptarchive.co.uk. Wikimedia Commons, 2007. https://en.wikipedia.org/wiki/File:Chambre-roi-grande-pyramide.jpg. Photo copyright Jon Bodsworth.

213. Artist unknown. *Votive plaque depicting elements of the Eleusinian Mysteries*, discovered in the sanctuary at Eleusis, mid-4th century BC. Wikimedia Commons, 2015. https://commons.wikimedia.org/wiki/File:Votive_plaque_depicting_elements_of_the_Eleusinian_Mysteries,_discovered_in_the_sanctuary_at_Eleusis_(mid-4th_century_BC)_(13931872424).jpg. Photograph by Carole Raddato, 2014. CC BY-SA 2.0.

217. Left: Brown, Vincent, photographer. *Great Pyramid Air Shaft*, pyramid of Khufu, 2019. Wikimedia Commons, 2020. https://commons.wikimedia.org/wiki/File:Great_Pyramid_Air_Shaft_(39752498153).jpg. CC BY 2.0.

217. Right: Row17, photographer. *Men-an-Tol - an hedgehog's viewpoint*. Mên-an-Tol standing stones, Cornwall, UK, 2007. Wikimedia Commons, 2011. https://commons.wikimedia.org/wiki/File:Men-an-Tol_-_an_hedgehog%27s_viewpoint_-_geograph.org.uk_-_765327.jpg. CC BY-SA 2.0.

IMAGE CREDITS

CHAPTER FOUR

220. Artist unknown. *Gilgamesh Dream Tablet*. 1500 BCE. Wikimedia Commons, 2020. https://commons.wikimedia.org/wiki/File:Gilgamesh_Dream_Tablet.png. Photograph by District Court for the Eastern District of New York. Public domain.

222. Top: Guignet, Adrien, artist. *Joseph explains Pharaoh's Dream*. 19th century. Musée des Beaux-Arts de Rouen, France. Wikimedia Commons, 2009. https://commons.wikimedia.org/wiki/File:Adrien_Guignet_Joseph_et_Pharaon.jpg. Public Domain.

222. Bottom: Wheeler, Chanel, photographer. *Great Sphinx with Stelae*. Wikimedia Commons, 2009. https://commons.wikimedia.org/wiki/File:Great_Sphinx_with_Stelae.jpg. CC BY-SA 2.0.

223. Artist unknown. *Roman Statue of Isis*, 2nd century, marble. Kunsthistorisches Museum, Vienna. Wikimedia Commons, 2009. https://commons.wikimedia.org/wiki/File:Isis_-_Vienna.jpg. Photograph by Gryffindor, 2006, CC BY-SA 3.0.

224. Bridgman, Frederick Arthur, artist. *Procession in Honor of Isis*, painting, 1902. Wikimedia Commons, 2011. https://commons.wikimedia.org/wiki/File:NavigiumIsidis.jpg. Public Domain.

225. Artist unknown. *Bas-relief, mortuary temple of Ramesses III*. Wikimedia Commons, 2007. https://commons.wikimedia.org/wiki/File:Bas-relief_at_the_mortuary_temple_of_Ramesses_III_9.jpg. Photograph by Asta, Public domain.

227. Todd, Gary, photographer. *Library of Ashurbanipal Mesopotamia*, 1500-539 BC Gallery, British Museum, London, England, UK. Wikimedia Commons, 2020. https://commons.wikimedia.org/wiki/File:Library_of_Ashurbanipal.jpg. Public domain.

228. Weatherstone, A.C., artist. *The famous library of Ashurbanipal at Nineveh*, illustration in *Hutchinson's History of the Nations*. London: Hutchinson and Co, 1915. Wikimedia Commons, 2022. https://commons.wikimedia.org/wiki/File:The_famous_library_of_Ashurbanipal_at_Nineveh.png. Public domain.

229. Left: Petrosyan, Leon, photographer. *The main tunnel in serapeum of Saccara*. Wikimedia Commons, 2021. https://commons.wikimedia.org/wiki/File:The_main_tunel_in_serapeum_of_Saccara.jpg. CC BY-SA 4.0.

229. Right: Artist, unknown. *Bust of Serapis*. Marble, Roman copy after a Greek original from the 4th century BC, stored in the Serapaeum of Alexandria. Museo Pio-Clementino, Sala Rotonda, Vatican Museums. Wikimedia Commons, 2010. https://commons.wikimedia.org/wiki/File:Serapis_Pio-Clementino_Inv689_n2.jpg. Photograph by Jastrow, 2003. Public domain.

230. Top left: Horokos, photographer. *Asklepiio Kos*. Wikimedia Commons, 2016. https://commons.wikimedia.org/wiki/File:Horokos_Wiki-1-17.jpg. CC BY-SA 4.0.

230. Top center: Gorski, Heiko, photographer. *Kos*, Asklepeion, Greece, 2003. Wikimedia Commons, 2005. https://commons.wikimedia.org/wiki/File:Kos_Asklepeion.jpg. CC BY-SA 3.0.

230. Top right: Koronaios, George E., photographer. *The stoa of Abaton or Enkoimeterion at the Sanctuary of Asclepius in Epidaurus*. Argolis, Greece. Wikimedia Commons, 2019. https://commons.wikimedia.org/wiki/File:The_stoa_of_Abaton_or_Enkoimeterion_at_the_Sanctuary_of_Asclepius_in_Epidaurus.jpg. Public domain.

230. Middle: Wellcome Images. *Model of the Asklepion at Epidaurus*, Greece, 1936. Science Museum. Wikimedia Commons, 2014. https://commons.wikimedia.org/wiki/File:Model_of_the_Asklepion_at_Epidaurus,_Greece,_1936_Wellcome_L0058351.jpg. CC BY 4.0.

230. Bottom left: Artist unknown. *Abaton of Epidaurus*. Plaque with an example of the healing procedure. Wikimedia Commons, 2021. https://commons.wikimedia.org/wiki/File:Abaton_of_Epidaurus,_202470.jpg. Photograph by Zde, 2020, CC BY-SA 4.0.

230. Bottom right: Artist unknown. *Abaton of Epidaurus*. Plaque with an example of the healing procedure. Wikimedia Commons, 2021. https://commons.wikimedia.org/wiki/File:Abaton_of_Epidaurus,_202471.jpg. Photograph by Zde, 2020, CC BY-SA 4.0.

231. *Depiction of People Practicing Dream Incubation in Ancient Greece*: Image created by DALL-E 3, an AI by OpenAI, prompted by Sura Ondrunar Publishing.

234. Goble, Warwick, artist. *Rama Spurns the Demon Lover*. Illustration in *Indian Myth and Legend* by Donald Mackenzie, London: Gresham, 1913. Wikimedia Commons, 2023. https://commons.wikimedia.org/wiki/File:Rama_spurns_the_demon_lover.jpg. Public domain.

235. Ike no Taiga, artist. *Zhuangzi dreaming of a butterfly*, circa 1747-1776. Wiki Art, 2013. https://www.wikiart.org/en/ike-no-taiga/zhuangzi-dreaming-of-a-butterfly-or-a-butterfly-dreaming-of-zhuangzi. Public domain.

237. Millais, John Everett, artist. *Pizarro Seizing the Inca of Peru*, 1845. Victoria and Albert Museum, UK. Wikimedia Commons, 2010. https://en.wikipedia.org/wiki/File:John_Everett_Millais_-_Pizarro_seizing_the_Inca_of_Peru.jpg. Public domain.

238. Griffiths, Moses, artist. *The Chief Druid*. Illustration in *A Tour in Wales* by Thomas Pennant, 1781. Wikimedia Commons, 2016. https://commons.wikimedia.org/wiki/File:The_chief_Druid,_engraving.jpg. Public domain.

239. Lehle, Dr. Eugen, photographer. *Apollo-Grannus Temple* (partial reconstruction) in Lauingen-Faimingen in the district of Dillingen. Wikimedia Commons, 2009. https://commons.wikimedia.org/wiki/File:Lauingen_Apollo-Grannus-Tempel.jpg. CC BY-SA 3.0.

240. Tiepolo, Giovanni Battista, artist. *Mercury Appearing to the Aeneas*, 1757. Villa Valmarana ai Nani, Italy. Wikimedia Commons, 2011. https://commons.wikimedia.org/wiki/File:Giovanni_Battista_Tiepolo_-_Mercury_Appearing_to_Aeneas_-_WGA22338.jpg. Public domain.

241. Kirke, Trinitatis, artist. *Velsignelsen, The Blessing*, 1873. Wikimedia Commons, 2007. https://commons.wikimedia.org/wiki/File:Trinitatis_Kirke_Copenhagen_painting1.jpg. Public domain.

242. Giordano, Luca, artist. *Dream of Saint Joseph*, 1696. Kunsthistorisches Museum, Austria. Wikimedia Commons, 2020. https://commons.wikimedia.org/wiki/File:Luca_Giordano_-_Traum_des_Hl._Joseph_-_GG_1626_-_Kunsthistorisches_Museum.jpg. Public domain.

243. François, Alphonse, artist. *The dream of Pilate's wife*, circa 1879. United States Library of Congress's Prints and Photographs division. Wikimedia Commons, 2007. https://commons.wikimedia.org/wiki/File:The_dream_of_Pilate%27s_wife_by_Alphonse_Fran%C3%A7ois.jpg. Public domain.

CHAPTER FIVE

248. Left: Doré, Gustave, artist. *Inferno* Canto 15 verses 28-29. Illustration in *The Vision of Hell* by Dante Alighieri, 1866. Wikimedia Commons, 2005. https://commons.wikimedia.org/wiki/File:Inferno_Canto_15_verses_28-29.jpg. Public domain.

248. Right: Doré, Gustave, artist. *Paradisio*, illustration in *The Divine Comedy* by Dante Alighieri, published by Paris: L. Hachette et Cie, 1868. Wikimedia Commons, 2007. https://commons.wikimedia.org/wiki/File:Par_18_dore.jpg. Public domain.

249. Artist unknown. *The judgment of the dead in the presence of Osiris* from *the Book of the Dead of Hunefer*, 1275 BCE. British Museum, Wikimedia Commons, 2012. https://commons.wikimedia.org/wiki/File:The_judgement_of_the_dead_in_the_presence_of_Osiris.jpg. Public domain. Photograph: The Trustees of the British Museum, CC BY-NC-SA 4.0.

251. Martín de Murúa, artist. *Illustration showing the Inca Pachacútec in the Coricancha*. In *Crónicas de Martín de Murúa*, 17th century. https://en.wikipedia.org/wiki/File:Pachacuteckoricancha.jpg. Public domain.

252. Guereta, Paulo, photographer. *Cusco*, Peru, 2015. Wikimedia Commons, 2020. https://commons.wikimedia.org/wiki/File:Cusco_-_Peru_(20137940794).jpg. CC BY 2.0.

253. Artist unknown. *Aeneas and the Sibyl*, oil on canvas, circa 1800. Yale Center for British Art. https://commons.wikimedia.org/wiki/File:Aeneas_and_the_Sibyl_-_Google_Art_Project.jpg. Public domain.

254. Vrancx, Sebastiaen, artist. *Aeneas meeting with his father in the Elysium*, painting, 1597. Museum of Fine Arts of Lyon, France. Wikimedia Commons, 2017. https://commons.wikimedia.org/wiki/File:Enee_meeting_with_his_father_in_the_Elysium-Sebastien_Vrancx-MBA_Lyon_H1153-IMG_0415.jpg. Public domain.

255. Honthorst Gerrit Van Detto Gherardo Delle Notti, artist. *Rapture of Saint Paul to the Third Heaven*, Santa Maria della Vittoria in Rome, before 1656. Wikimedia Commons, 2017. https://commons.wikimedia.org/wiki/File:Gherardo_delle_notti,_rapimento_di_san_paolo_al_terzo_cielo,_1620,_00.jpg. Public domain. Photograph by Sailko, 2016, CC BY 3.0.

256. Varma, Raja Ravi, artist. *Savitri and Satyavan*, Chromolithograph, before 1906. Wikimedia Commons, 2012. https://commons.wikimedia.org/wiki/File:Savitri_and_Satyavan.jpg. Public domain.

258. Gita Press, publisher. *Vishnu rescues Azamila*, in *Shrimad Bhagavata Mahapurana* published by Gita Press, Wikimedia Commons, 2018. https://commons.wikimedia.org/wiki/File:Nam_Mahatya_-_Vishnu_rescues_Azamila.jpg.

259. Nyx, Ning, photographer. *Spring Temple Buddha*, Giant Buddha in Central Plains, Henan, 2013. Wikimedia Commons, 2019. https://commons.wikimedia.org/wiki/File:Spring_Temple_Buddha_1.jpg. CC BY-SA 3.0.

CHAPTER SIX

264. Vasarhelyi, Paul, artist. *Near Death Out-of-Body Experience*. https://www.shutterstock.com/image-photo/near-death-out-body-experience-77003539 Licensed from Shutterstock.com

IMAGE CREDITS

266. *Depiction of a Person Sensing the Presence of the Deceased*: Image created by DALL-E 3, an AI by OpenAI, prompted by Sura Ondrunar Publishing.

267. Spiegler, Franz Joseph, artist. *St. Benedict as patron of the dying*, Parish Church of St. Peter, 1727. Wikimedia Commons, 2008. https://commons.wikimedia.org/wiki/File:St_Peter_Fresko_Seitenkapelle_Benedikt_als_Patron_der_Sterbenden.jpg. Public domain.

CHAPTER SEVEN

275. *Illustration of an Out-of-Body experience*: Image created by DALL-E 3, an AI by OpenAI, prompted by Sura Ondrunar Publishing.

276. Schneider, Sascha, artist. *About a soul*. Wood engraving. From the series Masterpieces of the Art of Wood Cutting, Verlag J. J. Weber, Leipzig, circa 1896. Wikimedia Commons, 2011. https://commons.wikimedia.org/wiki/File:Sascha_Schneider_Um_eine_Seele.jpg. Public domain.

277. Tissot, James, artist. *The Vision of Saint Joseph*, painting, between 1886-1894. Brooklyn Museum. Wikimedia Commons, 2010. https://commons.wikimedia.org/wiki/File:Brooklyn_Museum_-_The_Vision_of_Saint_Joseph_(Vision_de_Saint_Joseph)_-_James_Tissot_-_overall.jpg. Public domain.

281. Duquefer, Dany, artist. *Hallucinations of the Quixote*, illustration, 2005. Wikimedia Commons, 2012. https://commons.wikimedia.org/wiki/File:ALUCINACIONES_DEL_QUIJOTE.jpg. CC BY-SA 3.0. Modern interpretation of *A world of disorderly notions, picked out of his books, crowded into his imagination* in *The History of Don Quixote by Cervantes*, illustrated by Gustave Doré, 1863.

CHAPTER EIGHT

284. Top left: Elangovan, Suresh, artist. *Jain Universe*, illustration. Wikimedia Commons, 2010. https://en.wikipedia.org/wiki/File:Jain_Universe.jpg. Public domain. Illustration recreated for book production by Sura Ondruar Publishing.

284. Top right: Pratyk321, photographer. *Trilok Teerth Dham*. Wikimedia Commons, 2021. https://en.wikipedia.org/wiki/File:Trilok_Teerth_Dham_(cropped).jpg. CC BY-SA 4.0.

284. Bottom left: Lds, photographer. *Entrance of the Ten Courts of Hell attraction at Haw Par Villa*, Singapore. Wikimedia Commons, 2014. https://commons.wikimedia.org/wiki/File:Haw_Par_Villa_7,_Dec_14.jpg. CC BY-SA 4.0.

284. Bottom right: Doctorow, Cory, photographer. *Sufferers in Buddhist Hell*, Haw Par Villa (Tiger Balm Theme Park), Singapore, 2005. Wikimedia Commons, 2020. https://commons.wikimedia.org/wiki/File:Sufferers_in_Buddhist_Hell,_Haw_Par_Villa_(Tiger_Balm_Theme_Park),_Singapore_(41367724).jpg. CC BY-SA 2.0.

285. Paiore, artist. *Drawing made by Paiore, a man from the Paumotu Group*, in 1869, representing the world, and the heavens above as conceived of by the branch of the Polynesians to which Paiore belonged. Reproduced in the *Journal of the Polynesian Society* 28 (1919), p. 210. Wikimedia Commons 2006. https://en.wikipedia.org/wiki/File:Paumotuheavens.gif. Public domain.

287. Rogilbert, artist. *Two D-branes connected by an open string*. Wikimedia Commons, 2007. https://en.wikipedia.org/wiki/File:D3-brane_et_D2-brane.PNG. Public domain.

289. United States, Division of Radiological Health, author. *The electromagnetic spectrum*, extracted from Radiological health for nurses, 1962. Wikimedia Commons, 2020. https://commons.wikimedia.org/wiki/File:The_electromagnetic_spectrum,_extracted_from_Radiological_health_for_nurses_(1962).png. Public domain.

291. Artist unknown. *Man Between Righteousness and Materialism*, Print, India, circa 1940s. Wikimedia Commons, 2020. https://commons.wikimedia.org/wiki/File:India_40%27s_Print_MAN_BETWEEN_RIGHTEOUSNESS_AND_MATERIALISM.jpg.

294. Zalewski, Nikki, artist. *Astral Body Rising Up*. https://www.shutterstock.com/image-photo/female-lying-supine-eyes-closed-experiencing-222292144. Licensed from Shutterstock.com.

298. Top: Voinescu, Eugeniu, artist. *Apparition*, painting, early 19th century. Wikimedia Commons, 2019. https://commons.wikimedia.org/wiki/File:Apparition_by_Eugeniu_Voinescu.jpg. Public domain. Photograph by Ruth Tillman, CC BY-SA 4.0.

298. Bottom: Marmion, Simon, artist. *The soul of Saint Bertin raised towards God*, painting, circa 1425-1489. Wikimedia Commons, 2019. https://commons.wikimedia.org/wiki/File:Volet_%C3%A2me_Retable_de_Saint_Bertin.jpg. Public domain. Photograph by Octave 444, CC BY-SA 4.0.

299. Artist unknown, *Kali*, Dutch Bengal School, circa late 19th - early 20th century, oil on canvas, Wikimedia Commons, 2021. https://commons.wikimedia.org/wiki/File:Kali_-_Dutch_Bengal_School.jpg. Public domain.

CHAPTER NINE

302. Bosch, Hieronymus, artist. *Ascent of the Blessed*. Oil painting, circa 1504. Doge's Palace, Italy. Wikimedia Commons, 2017. https://commons.wikimedia.org/wiki/File:Hieronymus_Bosch_013.jpg. Public domain.

304. Cole, Herbert, artist. *Then he became aware that there was One who stood beside him*. Illustration in *A Child's Book of Warriors*, by William Canton, 1907. Wikimedia Commons, 2015. https://commons.wikimedia.org/wiki/File:A_child%27s_book_of_warriors_(1907)_(14752805552).jpg. Public domain.

306. Toyokuni I, Utagawa, artist. *Onoe Matsusuke I (later Onoe Shōroku I) as the Ghost of the Murdered Wife Oiwa*, in *A Tale of Horror from the Yotsuya Station on the Tōkaidō Road*, 1812. Metropolitan Museum of Art. Wikimedia Commons, 2017. https://commons.wikimedia.org/wiki/File:Tokaido_Yotsuya_Kaidan-Onoe_Matsusuke_as_the_Ghost_of_the_Murdered_Wife_Oiwa,_in_%22A_Tale_of_Horror_from_the_Yotsuya_Station_on_the_Tokaido_Road%22_MET_DP136979.jpg. Public domain.

CHAPTER TEN

312. Intraversato, Anthony, photographer. *Person Holding Ace of Heart Playing Card*. Unsplash.com, 2017. https://unsplash.com/photos/person-holding-ace-of-heart-playing-card-hIMvMIu-HGY. Licensed from Unsplash.com. Modified by Sura Ondrunar Publishing.

313. Diez, Lisa, artist. *Klüver's Form Constants*. Wikimedia Commons, 2020. https://commons.wikimedia.org/wiki/File:Kl%C3%BCver%27s_Form_Constants.jpg. CC BY-SA 4.0.

315. Left: Sransom2, artist. *Temporoparietal Junction*. Illustration, 2013. Wikimedia Commons, 2014. https://commons.wikimedia.org/wiki/File:Temporoparietal_junction_diagram.jpg. CC BY-SA 3.0.

315. Right: Was a Bee, artist. *Temporoparietal Junction*. Wikimedia Commons, 2013. https://commons.wikimedia.org/wiki/File:Temporoparietal_junction.png. CC BY-SA 2.1 Japan.

CHAPTER ELEVEN

334. Baocheng, artist. *Dream of Queen Maya*, before 1487. Wikimedia Commons, 2022. https://commons.wikimedia.org/wiki/File:Baocheng_Dream_of_Maya.jpg. Public domain.

335. Puvis de Chavannes, Pierre, artist. *The Dream*, painting, 1883. Walters Art Museum, Baltimore, Maryland. Wikimedia Commons, 2005. https://commons.wikimedia.org/wiki/File:Pierre-C%C3%A9cile_Puvis_de_Chavannes_003.jpg. Public domain. Photograph by The Yorck Project, 2002.

336. Goya, Francisco, artist. *The Sleep of Reason Produces Monsters*, etching, circa 1797. Museo del Prado, Spain. Wikimedia Commons, 2015. https://commons.wikimedia.org/wiki/File:Museo_del_Prado_-_Goya_-_Caprichos_-_No._43_-_El_sue%C3%B1o_de_la_razon_produce_monstruos.jpg. Public domain.

338. Buss, Robert W. artist. *Dickens' Dream*, unfinished painting, 1875. Wikimedia Commons, 2020. https://commons.wikimedia.org/wiki/File:Dickensdream.jpg. Public domain.

339. Artist unknown. *Book of Revelation Illustration*, in 1583 edition of the *Leuven Vulgate*. Wikimedia Commons, 2020. https://commons.wikimedia.org/wiki/File:1583_edition_of_the_Leuven_Vulgate_-_Book_of_Revelation,_illustration.jpg. Public domain.

342. Morales, Nick, photographer. *United Airlines 737-900 taking off*. Unsplash.com, 2019. https://unsplash.com/photos/BwYcH78rcpI. Licensed Unsplash.com. Modified by Sura Ondrunar Publishing.

CHAPTER TWELVE

No images.

CHAPTER THIRTEEN

350. Board, Ernest, artist. *Patients sleeping in the temple of Aesculapius at Epidaurus*. Oil painting, before 1934. Wikimedia Commons, 2014. https://commons.wikimedia.org/wiki/File:Patients_sleeping_in_the_temple_of_Aesculapius_at_Epidaurus._Wellcome_M0000141.jpg. Public domain. Photograph by Wellcome Collection, CC BY 4.0. Modified by Sura Ondrunar Publishing.

351. Artist unknown. *The Asclepion in the Hellenistic period, from east*. Wikimedia Commons, 2014. https://commons.wikimedia.org/wiki/File:The_Asclepion_in_the_Hellenistic_period,_from_east._Wellcome_M0009520.jpg. Photograph by Wellcome Collection, CC BY 4.0.

355. Left: Artist unknown. *Lapis lazuli intaglio: Serapis enthroned*, 2nd century. Metropolitan Museum of Art. Wikimedia Commons, 2022. https://commons.wikimedia.org/wiki/File:Detail,_Lapis_lazuli_intaglio-_Serapis_enthroned_MET_DP280448_(cropped).jpg. Public domain.

355. Right: Artist unknown. *Hellenistic art, Isis and Serapis*, 3rd century. Wikimedia Commons, 2011. https://commons.wikimedia.org/wiki/File:Arte_ellenistica,_iside_e_serapide,_3_sec._ac.,_corniola.JPG. Public domain. Photograph by Sailko, CC BY-SA 3.0.

CHAPTER FOURTEEN

364. Top: *Astral Jump Illustration*. Sura Ondrunar Publishing.

364. Bottom left: *Checking Dimensions by Pulling Finger Illustration*. Sura Ondrunar Publishing.

364. Bottom right: *Pulling a Finger and it Stretches Illustration*. Sura Ondrunar Publishing.

368. Photo courtesy of Mark Atwood, 1993.

CHAPTER FIFTEEN

374. *Relaxation Illustration*: Image created by DALL-E 3, an AI by OpenAI, prompted by Sura Ondrunar Publishing.

375. Chus, Igor, photographer. *Yogi on the Bank of the Ganges,* Varanasi, India. https://www.shutterstock.com/image-photo/yogi-on-bank-ganges-varanasi-india-1019440771. Licensed from Shutterstock.com.

377. Left: *Teacup Illustration*: Image created by DALL-E 3, an AI by OpenAI, prompted by Sura Ondrunar Publishing.

377. Right: *Teacup Floating Illustration*: Image created by DALL-E 3, an AI by OpenAI, prompted by Sura Ondrunar Publishing.

378. 1st image (left to right): Anklekar, Kiran, photographer. *Man Sitting on Brown Sand Near Body of Water During Daytime*. Unsplash.com, 2021. https://unsplash.com/photos/topless-man-sitting-on-brown-sand-near-body-of-water-during-daytime-_wOgy5M2y9g. Licensed from Unsplash.com.

378. 2nd image: Renault, Claude, photographer. *Jain Sadhvis meditating in Brindavan*. Wikimedia Commons, 2006. https://commons.wikimedia.org/wiki/File:Jain_meditation.jpg. CC BY 2.0.

378. 3rd image: Wihelm, Richard. *Meditation, Stage 1: Gathering the Light*. In *The Secret of the Golden Flower*, 1931. https://commons.wikimedia.org/wiki/File:Stage1.gif.

378. 4th image: Tong KBP, photographer. *Buddhist Monk sitting meditation*. Unsplash.com, 2022. https://unsplash.com/photos/a-man-sitting-on-a-rock-by-a-river-_brhl3cAfB4. Licensed from Unsplash.com.

379. Yocham, Carter, photographer. *Leather making in Montour*. Unsplash.com, 2020. https://unsplash.com/photos/man-in-black-and-white-plaid-dress-shirt-wearing-black-framed-eyeglasses-tnYWFvk-frU. Licensed from Unsplash.com.

383. Left: *Concentrating on a Lit Candle Illustration*: Image created by DALL-E 3, an AI by OpenAI, prompted by Sura Ondrunar Publishing.

383. Right: *Visualizing Lit Candle Illustration*: Image created by DALL-E 3, an AI by OpenAI, prompted by Sura Ondrunar Publishing.

384. *Visualizing Flame at Center of Brow Illustration:* Image created by DALL-E 3, an AI by OpenAI, prompted by Sura Ondrunar Publishing.

387. *Visualizing the Pyramids of Giza Illustration:* Image created by DALL-E 3, an AI by OpenAI, prompted by Sura Ondrunar Publishing.

CHAPTER SIXTEEN

390. Giordano, Luca, artist. *Dream of Solomon*. Painting, circa 1694-1695. Museo del Prado, Spain. Wikimedia Commons, 2016. https://commons.wikimedia.org/wiki/File:Giordano_Le_R%C3%AAve_de_Salomon_Prado.jpg. Public domain.

391. *The Process of Astral Projection Illustration:* Image created by DALL-E 3, an AI by OpenAI, prompted by Sura Ondrunar Publishing.

392. Top: *The Astral Split Illustration:* Image created by DALL-E 3, an AI by OpenAI, prompted by Sura Ondrunar Publishing.

392. Bottom: *Getting up in the Astral Illustration:* Image created by DALL-E 3, an AI by OpenAI, prompted by Sura Ondrunar Publishing.

CHAPTER SEVENTEEN

No images.

CHAPTER EIGHTEEN

407. Artist unknown. *Tirthankara Rishabhanatha, the first mystical savior of the Jains*. India, Rajasthan, Chandravati, 11th- 12th century. Rietberg Museum, Zurich, Germany. Wikimedia Commons, 2011. https://commons.wikimedia.org/wiki/File:Tirthankara_Rishabhanatha_Rietberg_RVI_213.jpg. Photographed by Andreas Praefcke, public domain.

CHAPTER NINETEEN

413. *Visualization of the Heart Illustration:* Image created by DALL-E 3, an AI by OpenAI, prompted by Sura Ondrunar Publishing.

414. *Visualization of a Spiritual Place in the Heart Illustration:* Image created by DALL-E 3, an AI by OpenAI, prompted by Sura Ondrunar Publishing.

CHAPTER TWENTY

418. Mahendra, Parikh, photographer. *Tamil Brahmin Students Studying Vedas and Sanskrit in a Traditional Brahmin School*, Thiruparankundram Murugan temple, Madurai, India. https://www.shutterstock.com/image-photo/maduraitamilnaduindia-ocotber-072022-tamil-brahmin-students-2293999469. Licensed from Shutterstock.com.

419. Artist unknown. *The Ba or soul bird*, from the Book of the Dead of Tehenena, 18th dynasty (ca. 1550-1295 B.C.E.) Egypt, on display Louvre, Paris. https://commons.wikimedia.org/wiki/File:Book_of_the_Dead_of_Tchenena.jpg. https://collections.louvre.fr/en/ark:/53355/cl010003212. Photograph by Musée du Louvre.

CHAPTER TWENTY-ONE

426. *Traveling in Space Illustration:* Image created by DALL-E 3, an AI by OpenAI, prompted by Sura Ondrunar Publishing.

CHAPTER TWENTY-TWO

434. *Visualizing Nature Illustration:* Image created by DALL-E 3, an AI by OpenAI, prompted by Sura Ondrunar Publishing.

436. *Projecting to a Sacred Place Illustration:* Image created by DALL-E 3, an AI by OpenAI, prompted by Sura Ondrunar Publishing.

437. *Meeting others at a Sacred Place Illustration:* Image created by DALL-E 3, an AI by OpenAI, prompted by Sura Ondrunar Publishing.

CHAPTER TWENTY-THREE

441. *Starlight Energy Visualization Illustration:* Image created by DALL-E 3, an AI by OpenAI, prompted by Sura Ondrunar Publishing.

444. *Sun Heart Visualization Illustration:* Image created by DALL-E 3, an AI by OpenAI, prompted by Sura Ondrunar Publishing.

445. *Star Travel Visualization Illustration:* Image created by DALL-E 3, an AI by OpenAI, prompted by Sura Ondrunar Publishing.

448. Top left: *Mountain Peak Energy Visualization Illustration 1*: Image created by DALL-E 3, an AI by OpenAI, prompted by Sura Ondrunar Publishing.

448. Top right: *Mountain Peak Energy Visualization Illustration 2*: Image created by DALL-E 3, an AI by OpenAI, prompted by Sura Ondrunar Publishing.

448. Bottom left: *Mountain Peak Energy Visualization Illustration 3*: Image created by DALL-E 3, an AI by OpenAI, prompted by Sura Ondrunar Publishing.

448. Bottom right: *Mountain Peak Energy Visualization Illustration 4*: Image created by DALL-E 3, an AI by OpenAI, prompted by Sura Ondrunar Publishing.

450. Image 1 (top to bottom): *Fire in the Lotus Visualization Illustration 1*: Image created by DALL-E 3, an AI by OpenAI, prompted by Sura Ondrunar Publishing.

450. Image 2: *Fire in the Lotus Visualization Illustration 2*: Image created by DALL-E 3, an AI by OpenAI, prompted by Sura Ondrunar Publishing.

450. Image 3: *Fire in the Lotus Visualization Illustration 3:* Image created by DALL-E 3, an AI by OpenAI, prompted by Sura Ondrunar Publishing.

450. Image 4: *Fire in the Lotus Visualization Illustration 4*: Image created by DALL-E 3, an AI by OpenAI, prompted by Sura Ondrunar Publishing.

451. *Fire in the Lotus Visualization Illustration 5*: Image created by DALL-E 3, an AI by OpenAI, prompted by Sura Ondrunar Publishing.

453. *Complete Light Visualization Illustration*: Image created by DALL-E 3, an AI by OpenAI, prompted by Sura Ondrunar Publishing.

CHAPTER TWENTY-FOUR

No images.

CHAPTER TWENTY-FIVE

467. Memling, Hans, artist. *The Last Judgment Triptych*. Painting, between 1467-1471. National Museum in Gdańsk, Poland. Wikimedia Commons, 2010. https://commons.wikimedia.org/wiki/File:Memling,_giudizio_universale_01.jpg. Public domain.

468. Sir Jon Gilbert, illustrator. *Hamlet in the Presence of His Father's Ghost*. In *An art edition of Shakespeare* by Charles and Mary Lamb and Mary Seymor. U.S. Publishing House, 1889. https://commons.wikimedia.org/wiki/File:An_art_edition_of_Shakespeare,_classified_as_comedies,_tragedies,_histories_and_sonnets,_each_part_arranged_in_chronological_order,_including_also_a_list_of_familiar_quotations_(1889)_(14759974806).jpg. Public domain.

471. Top: Botticini, Francesco, artist. *The Assumption of the Virgin*. Painting, circa 1475. National Gallery, London. Wikimedia Commons, 2022. https://en.wikipedia.org/wiki/File:Francesco_Botticini_-_The_Assumption_of_the_Virgin.jpg. Public domain.

471. Center left: Collingwood, W.G., artist. *The Northern Gods Descending*. Painting, 1890. Wikimedia Commons, 2019. https://commons.wikimedia.org/wiki/File:The_Northern_Gods_Descending_by_William_Gersham_Collingwood,_1890.jpg. Public domain.

471. Center right: Artist unknown. *Dendera Hathor Temple Complex*, Egypt. Wikimedia Commons, 2007. https://commons.wikimedia.org/wiki/File:DenderaHathorTempleComplexQenaEgypt540-2007feb10PhotoByCsorfolyDaniel.JPG. Public domain.

471. Bottom left: Artist unknown. *Devas in Hevan*. Mural in Wat Bowonniwet, Bangkok. Wikimedia Commons, 2016. https://commons.wikimedia.org/wiki/File:018_Devas_in_Heaven_(9174314518)_(2).jpg. Photograph by Anandajoti Bhikkhu, CC BY 2.0.

471. Bottom right: Gita Press, publisher. *Indra and Gods giving boons to Arjuna and Krishna*. Illustration in *Mahabharata*, by Sriman Maharshi Vedavyasa, translated by Pandit Ramnarayan Dutt Shastri. Gita Press, Vol 1, page 725. https://archive.org/details/mahabharata01ramauoft/page/n725/mode/2up. Digitized by University of Toronto Collection, acquired 1965.

472. Gita Press, publisher. *Goddess Saraswati appears before Yajnavalkya*. Illustration in *Mahabharata*, by Sriman Maharshi Vedavyasa, translated by Pandit Ramnarayan Dutt Shastri. Gita Press, Vol 5, page 5268. https://archive.org/details/mahabharat05ramauoft/page/5268/mode/2up Digitized by University of Toronto Collection, acquired 1965.

474. Top left: Hokusai, Katsushika, artist. *The Laughing Demoness*. Painting, 1831. Wikimedia Commons, 2022. https://commons.wikimedia.org/wiki/File:The_Laughing_Demon_by_Hokusai.jpg. Public domain.

474. Top center: Artist unknown. *Ah Puch* from Dresden Codex. Wikimedia Commons, 2006. https://commons.wikimedia.org/wiki/File:AhPuch.jpg. Public domain.

474. Top right: Artist unknown. *Stirrup Spout Bottle with Figure and Demon*, Moche; Bottle, Ceramics Containers, 1st-4th century. Metropolitan Museum of Art. Wikimedia Commons, 2017. https://commons.wikimedia.org/wiki/File:Stirrup_Spout_Bottle_with_Figure_and_Demon_MET_vs1979_206_412.jpg. Public domain.

474. Bottom left: Artist unknown. *Cylinder seal and modern impression: winged demon*, circa 8th-7th century BC. Metropolitan Museum of Art. Wikimedia Commons, 2017. https://commons.wikimedia.org/wiki/File:Cylinder_seal_and_modern_impression-_winged_demon_MET_ss1986_311_55.jpg. Public domain.

474. Bottom right: Artist unknown. *Sambara*. Painting, illustration to the Bhagavata Purana, circa 1760-1765. Victoria and Albert Museum. Wikimedia Commons, 2014. https://commons.wikimedia.org/wiki/File:Sambara.jpg. Public domain.

475. Artist unknown. *Demons practicing cannibalism*. Painting, circa 1450-1470. Livre de la Vigne nostre Seigneur, France. Wikimedia Commons, 2015. https://commons.wikimedia.org/wiki/File:Demons_Canibalism_Livre_de_la_Vigne_nostre_Seigneur_f._100r_1450-1470.JPG. Public domain.

477. Martin, John, artist. *Satan Presiding at the Infernal Council*. Engraving, 1824. Victoria and Albert Museum, London. Wikimedia Commons, 2015. https://commons.wikimedia.org/wiki/File:Martin,_John_-_Satan_presiding_at_the_Infernal_Council_-_1824.JPG. Public domain.

478. Top left: Fuzhou, author. *Yu li chao chuan jing shi (Jade Calendar Notes are a Warning to the World)*, Chen fengming ke zi pu, Xianfeng ren zi (Chen Fengming Engraving Shop, Xianfeng Renzi), 1852, image 17. National Library of Australia. https://nla.gov.au/nla.obj-48188008/view?partId=nla.obj-48189612#page/n16/mode/1up image 17. Public domain.

478. Top center: Herrad of Landsberg, artist. *Hortus Deliciarum – Hell*. Painting, 1180. Wikimedia Commons, 2018. https://en.wikipedia.org/wiki/File:Hortus_Deliciarum_-_Hell.jpg. Public domain.

478. Top right: Chore Bagan Art Studio. *Yama the god of death*. Color lithograph, circa 1895. British Museum. Wikimedia Commons, 2020. https://commons.wikimedia.org/wiki/File:Hindu_hell.jpg. Public domain.

478. Bottom left: Artist unknown. *Dumuzi compelled to enter the Underworld*. Sumerian cylindrical seal, rom 2600 until 2300 BC. British Museum. Wikimedia Commons, 2016. https://commons.wikimedia.org/wiki/File:Dumuzi_aux_enfers.jpg. Public domain. Photograph: The Trustees of the British Museum, CC BY-NC-SA 4.0.

478. Bottom right: Artist unknown. *Buddhist Hell*. Burmese temple painting, 19th century. Wikimedia Commons, 2011. https://commons.wikimedia.org/wiki/File:Buddhist_hell.jpg. Public domain.

479. Utamaro, Kitagawa, artist. *One Hundred Stories of Demons and Spirits*. Painting, early 19th century. Wikimedia Commons, 2006. https://commons.wikimedia.org/wiki/File:Kitagawa_One_Hundred_Stories_of_Demons_and_Spirits.jpg. Public domain.

480. Benois, A., artist. *Petrouchka*. Painting, 1911. Wikimedia Commons, 2011. https://commons.wikimedia.org/wiki/File:Petrouchka_by_A._Benois_02.jpg. Public domain.

481. Left: Warwick, Goble, illustrator. *Fairies dangling on and frolicking around flowers*. In *The Book of Fairy Poetry* by Dora Owen, 1920. Wikimedia Commons, 2020. https://commons.wikimedia.org/wiki/File:Goble-Book_of_Fairy_Poetry062Fairy-revel.jpg. Public domain.

481. Center: Hughes, Edward Robert, artist. *Midsummer Eve*. Painting, 1908. Wikimedia Commons, 2015. https://commons.wikimedia.org/wiki/File:Edward_Robert_Hughes_-_Midsummer_Eve_(1908c).jpg. Public domain.

481. Right: Warwick, Goble, illustrator. *Fairies around a child in a rocking crib*. In *The Book of Fairy Poetry* by Dora Owen, 1920. Wikimedia Commons, 2020. https://commons.wikimedia.org/wiki/File:Goble-Book_of_Fairy_Poetry000frontispiece.jpg. Public domain.

482. Top: *Illustration of Meeting with an Extraterrestrial*: Image created by DALL-E 3, an AI by OpenAI, prompted by Sura Ondrunar Publishing.

482. Bottom: *Photo of Lara Atwood and Dr. Steven Greer*, taken by Sura Ondrunar Publications.

485. Left: Baedeker, Karl, author. *The ancient Egyptian mythological Trinity or Triad: Osiris, Horus and Isis*. Illustration in *Handbook for Traveling, pt.1 Lower Egypt, with the Fayum and the peninsula of Sinai*, 1885. Wikimedia Commons, 2007. https://commons.wikimedia.org/wiki/File:The_mythological_Trinity_or_Triad_Osiris_Horus_Isis.jpg. Public domain.

485. Right: Collinson, James. *The Holy Family*. Painting, 1878. Wikimedia Commons, 2007. https://commons.wikimedia.org/wiki/File:Collinson,_Holy_Family.jpg. Public domain.

CHAPTER TWENTY-SIX

493. Artist unknown. *Man Being Attacked by Demons and Devils*. Painting, 1500s. Wikimedia Commons, 2010. https://commons.wikimedia.org/wiki/File:Man_with_7_Devils_from_book_of_7_Deadly_Sins_(582x800).jpg. Public domain.

494. Fuseli, Henry, artist. *The Nightmare*. Painting, 1781. Detroit Institute of Arts. Wikimedia Commons, 2011. https://commons.wikimedia.org/wiki/File:Johann_Heinrich_F%C3%BCssli_-_The_Nightmare_-_WGA08332.jpg. Public domain.

497. Top: Schwimbeck, Fritz, artist. *My Dream, Bad Dream*. Painting, 1909. Wikimedia Commons, 2015. https://commons.wikimedia.org/wiki/File:Fritz_Schwimbeck_-_My_Dream,_My_Bad_Dream._1915.jpg. Public domain.

IMAGE CREDITS

497. Bottom: Kinninger, Vincenz Georg, artist. *The dream of Countess Marguerite of Flanders*. Illustration, 1795. Wikimedia Commons, 2022. https://commons.wikimedia.org/wiki/File:Incubus.jpg. Public domain.

498. Top: Gregory, Fer, artist. *Young man getting abducted by an UFO*. https://www.shutterstock.com/image-photo/young-man-getting-abducted-by-ufo-794631268 Licensed from Shutterstock.com.

498. Bottom: Kay Von Drive-In theater, artist. *Kay Von Drive-In theater advertisement for the sci-fi film, Invaders from Mars*. 20 June 1953. Napa Valley Register. Wikimedia Commons, 2023. https://commons.wikimedia.org/wiki/File:Kay_Von_Drive-In_Ad_-_20_June_1953,_Napa,_CA.jpg.

501. Hancock, Luke, artist. *POV of and Alien Abduction Experience*. Wikimedia Commons, 2022. https://commons.wikimedia.org/wiki/File:Alien_Abduction_Perspective.jpg. Public domain.

502. United States Navy, photographer. *Gimbal The First Official UAP Footage from the USG for Public Release, 2015*. Gimbal is one of three US military videos of unidentified aerial phenomenon (UAP) that has been through the official declassification review process of the United States government and has been approved for public release. Wikimedia Commons, 2020. https://commons.wikimedia.org/wiki/File:Gimbal_The_First_Official_UAP_Footage_ from_the_USG_for_Public_Release.webm. Public domain.

503. Boilly, Louis-Léopold, artist. *Tartini's Dream*. Illustration of the legend behind Giuseppe Tartini's Devil's Trill Sonata, 1824. Wikimedia Commons, 2014. https://commons.wikimedia.org/wiki/File:Le_Songe_de_Tartini_par_Louis-L%C3%A9opold_Boilly_1824.jpg. Public domain.

504. Artist unknown. *Night Before the Exam*. Cartoon in University of Leiden student Almanac, 1844. Wikimedia Commons, 2020. https://commons.wikimedia.org/wiki/File:Spotprent_in_Leidse_studentenalmanak,_1844_Nacht_voor_het_examen_(titel_op_object),_BI-B-FM-154.jpg. Public domain.

506. Bosch, Hieronymus, artist. *The Garden of Earthly Delights*. Painting, circa 1480-1505. Museo del Prado, Spain. Wikimedia Commons, 2011. https://commons.wikimedia.org/wiki/File:Hieronymus_Bosch_-_Triptych_of_Garden_of_Earthly_Delights_(right_wing)_-_WGA2523.jpg. Public domain.

507. Pinelli, Luca, author. *Vision of Hell*. Illustration in Libretto d'imagini e di brevi meditationi sopra i quattro nouissimi dell'huomo by Luca Pinelli, 1594. Wikimedia Commons, 2020. https://commons.wikimedia.org/wiki/File:6._La_Seconda_Meditatione_dell%E2%80%99Inferno.jpg. Public domain.

508. Top: Klontzas, Georgios, artist. *The Second Coming*. Painting, late 16th century. Wikimedia Commons, 2009. https://commons.wikimedia.org/wiki/File:KLONTZAS_GEORGIOS_End_of_16th_cent_The_Second_Coming_detail_The_Hell.png. Public domain. Photograph by P. Vasiliadis, CC BY-SA 3.0.

508. Bottom: Artist unknown. *Ammit*. In The Book of the Dead of Ani. British Museum. https://commons.wikimedia.org/wiki/File:Ammit_BD.jpg. Public domain. Photograph: The Trustees of the British Museum, CC BY-NC-SA 4.0.

CHAPTER TWENTY-SEVEN

511. Artist unknown. *Assyrian demon Pazuzu*, 1st millennium BCE. Louvre Museum. https://en.wikipedia.org/wiki/File:PazuzuDemonAssyria1stMil_2.jpg. Photograph by PHGCOM, CC BY-SA 3.0.

512. Artist unknown. *Krishna Killing the Horse Demon Keshi*. Relief, sculpture, 5th century, India. Metropolitan Museum of Art. Wikimedia Commons, 2020. https://commons.wikimedia.org/wiki/File:MET_DT5237_(cropped).jpg. Public domain.

513. Artist unknown. *Arslan Tash amulet*. Stone carving, 7th century BCE. National Museum of Aleppo. Wikimedia Commons, 2020. https://commons.wikimedia.org/wiki/File:Arslan_Tash_amulet.png. Public domain.

514. Goya, Francisco, artist. *A couple hovering off the ground being observed by a huge goat with two cats*. Etching, 1796-1798. Wikimedia Commons, 2014. https://commons.wikimedia.org/wiki/File:A_couple_hovering_off_the_ground_being_observed_by_a_huge_go_Wellcome_V0025835.jpg. Public domain. Photograph by Wellcome Collection Gallery, CC BY 4.0.

515. Beard, William Holbrook. *Lightning Struck a Flock of Witches*. Painting, 1850. Smithsonian American Art Museum. Wikimedia Commons, 2023. https://commons.wikimedia.org/wiki/File:SAAM-2020.20.12_1.jpg. Public domain.

517. Left: Artist unknown. *Cartouche with the name of Pharaoh Chabaka from a door jamb*, with the 3 hieroglyphs: Sha-Ba-Ka. 25th dynasty. Limestone. Chapel of Ptah in Memphis. Egyptian Museum Berlin. Wikimedia Commons, 2022. https://commons.wikimedia.org/wiki/File:Cartouche_au_nom_du_pharaon_Chabaka_(%C3%84gyptisches_Museum_Berlin_AM_31235).jpg. Public domain.

517. Right: Wilkinson, Charles, artist. *Facsimile of a falcon protecting the king*, Hatshepsut's Temple, circa 1479–1458 B.C. Metropolitan Museum of Art. Wikimedia Commons, 2017. https://commons.wikimedia.org/wiki/File:Facsimile_of_a_falcon_protecting_the_king_MET_30.4.139_EGDP012971.jpg. Public domain.

519. Downman, John, artist. *The Apparition*. Painting between 1749-1824. Grosvenor Museum. Wikimedia Commons, 2022. https://commons.wikimedia.org/wiki/File:John_Downman,_The_Apparition_(with_Elizabeth_Inchbald).jpg. Public domain. Photograph by Furius, CC BY-SA 4.0.

520. Schneider, Sascha, artist. *To a Soul*. Artwork between 1870-1927. Wikimedia Commons, 2019. https://commons.wikimedia.org/wiki/File:Sascha_Schneider_-_To_A_Soul.jpg. Public domain.

521. Artist unknown. *Mesopotamian Sun God Shamash*; Assyrian Relief, North-West Palace of Nimrud (room B, panel 23); 865–860 BC. British Museum. Wikimedia Commons, 2008. https://commons.wikimedia.org/wiki/File:Shamash.jpg. Public domain.

523. Top: *Solar Cross Symbol*. Wikimedia Commons, 2021. https://en.wikipedia.org/wiki/File:Crossed_circle.svg. Public domain.

523. Bottom: Artist unknown. *Thorsberg Swastika Mounting*. Illustration in *The Industrial Arts of Denmark* by J.J.A. Worsaae, 1883. Wikimedia Commons, 2010. https://commons.wikimedia.org/wiki/File:Thorsberg_Swastika_Mounting.jpg. Public domain.

524. Emsworth, Aethelwolf, artist. *Current processional north celestial pole centered in Ursae Minoris*. Wikimedia Commons, 2018. https://en.m.wikipedia.org/wiki/File:Precessional_north_pole_(B%C4%9Bij%C3%AD_%E5%8C%97%E6%9E%81)_in_%CE%B1_Ursae_Minoris,_drawing_a_w%C3%A0n_%E5%8D%8D_in_the_four_phases_of_time.svg. Public domain.

525. Left: KovacsUr, artist. *Pentagram (endless knot)*. Wikimedia Commons, 2005. https://commons.wikimedia.org/wiki/File:Pentagram_(endless_knot).png. CC BY-SA 3.0.

525. Right: da Vinci, Leonardo, artist. *Vitruvian Man*, 1492. Gallerie dell'Accademia, Italy. Wikimedia Commons, 2010. https://commons.wikimedia.org/wiki/File:Vitruvian.jpg. Public domain.

525. Bottom: *Triquetra symbol*. Wikimedia Commons, 2005. https://commons.wikimedia.org/wiki/File:Triquetra-Vesica.png. Public domain.

526. Top: Artist unknown. *Ankh Symbols*. Textile fragment, circa 400-600 AD. Victoria and Albert Museum, London. Wikimedia Commons, 2019. https://commons.wikimedia.org/wiki/File:Ankh_symbols_(on_a_fragment_of_cloth).jpg. Public domain. Photograph by Amitchell125, CC BY-SA 4.0.

526. Center: Elwood at Danish Wikipedia, artist. *The Classic Ankh Symbol*. Wikimedia Commons, 2006. https://commons.wikimedia.org/wiki/File:Ankh1.png. CC BY-SA 3.0.

526. Bottom: Artist unknown. *Detail of a sarcophagus from the Ptolemaic period*. Musée de Grenoble, France. Wikimedia Commons, 2017. https://commons.wikimedia.org/wiki/File:Sarcophage_ptol%C3%A9ma%C3%AFque_Grenoble_06082017_13.jpg. Public domain.

528. de Montalegre, Johann Daniel, artist. *Christ heals a demoniac; a demon is expelled into the air*. Etching, circa 1689-1768. Wellcome Collection. https://wellcomecollection.org/works/mpjya76e/items. Public domain.

529. Harunobu, Suzuki, artist. *Spring: Demon-Chasing Ceremony*. Woodblock print, circa 1766. Honolulu Museum of Art. Wikimedia Commons, 2014. https://commons.wikimedia.org/wiki/File:%27Spring,_Demon-Chasing_Ceremony%27_by_Suzuki_Harunobu,_Honolulu_Museum_of_Art,_15553.JPG. Public domain.

532. Waterhouse, John William, artist. *The Magic Circle*. Painting, 1886. Tate Britain, London. https://commons.wikimedia.org/wiki/File:John_William_Waterhouse_-_Magic_Circle.JPG. Public domain. Photograph by Tate Britain, CC BY-NC-ND 4.0.

533. *Circle of Protection Illustration*: Image created by DALL-E 3, an AI by OpenAI, prompted by Sura Ondrunar Publishing.

534. Duncan, John, artist. *Yorinda and Yoringel in the Witch's Wood*. Painting, 1909. https://www.flickr.com/photos/sofi01/6525898317. Public domain. Photograph by Sofi, CC BY-NC 2.0.

535. Artist unknown. *Magic Ceremonies*. Illustration published by William Charlton Wright. In *The Astrologer of the Nineteenth Century* by Raphael, edited by Merlinus Anglicus, 1825, page 28. https://archive.org/details/astrologerofnine00raph/page/n27/mode/2up. Public domain. Illustration edited for use in this book by Sura Ondrunar Publishing.

537. Le Breton, Louis, artist. *Démon D'Assassinat*. An illustration for the article *Assassination in the Dictionnaire Infernal* by Collin de Plancy, 1863. Wikimedia Commons, 2015. https://commons.wikimedia.org/wiki/File:D%C3%A9mon_d%27assassinat.png. Public domain.

IMAGE CREDITS

CHAPTER TWENTY-EIGHT

541. Johnson, Matthew W., photographer. *Johns Hopkins psilocybin session room*. Wikimedia Commons, 2011. https://en.wikipedia.org/wiki/File:Johns_Hopkins_psilocybin_session_room-SessionRm_2176x.jpg. CC BY-SA 3.0.

543. Darinzo, Nicholas, artist. *Hello*. Wikimedia Commons, 2016. https://commons.wikimedia.org/wiki/File:Hell0_Darinzo.jpg. CC BY 2.0.

546. DoctorWho42, artist. *Deep Dream Toast Sandwich*. Wikimedia Commons, 2015. https://en.wikipedia.org/wiki/File:Deep_Dream_Toast_Sandwich.jpg. CC BY-SA 3.0.

551. Bisams, artist. *Ayahuasca experience*. https://www.shutterstock.com/image-illustration/ayahuasca-experience-holistic-healing-spiritual-insight-2200965045 Licensed from Shutterstock.com.

553. Dalemundi, artist. *LSD Face Coloured*. Wikimedia Commons, 2006. https://commons.wikimedia.org/wiki/File:Lsdfacecoloured.jpg. CC BY-SA 3.0.

556. Khurd, Kesu, artist. *Nath yogis on Babur's 1519 visit to Gorkhatri*. One yogi is using a strap to support his pose. Mughal Dynasty, India, 1590-92. British Library. Wikimedia Commons, 2021. https://commons.wikimedia.org/wiki/File:Nath_yogis_on_Babur%27s_1519_visit_to_Gorkhatri_(detail_of_yoga_using_strap).png. Public domain.

558. Top left: Artist Unknown. *Tomb KV34 (Thutmose III) 11.th hour Amduat*, Valley of the Kings, Luxor, Egypt. Wikimedia Commons, 2005. https://commons.wikimedia.org/wiki/File:Egypt. KV34.07.jpg. Public domain. Photograph by Hajor, 2002, CC BY-SA 3.0.

558. Top right: Artist unknown. *Osiris detail from the grave of Sennedjem*, 2009. Wikimedia Commons, 2009. https://commons.wikimedia.org/wiki/File:Detail_aus_dem_Grab_des_Sennudjem. jpg. Photographed by Ignati, Public domain.

558. Bottom left: Life Science Databases, author. *Pineal gland*. Images are from Anatomography maintained by Life Science Databases (LSDB). Wikimedia Commons, 2009. https://commons.wikimedia.org/wiki/File:Pineal_gland.png. CC BY-SA 2.1 Japan.

558. Bottom right: Artist unknown. *Pharaoh Seti I, detail of a wall painting of a pillar at the Tomb of Seti I*, Valley of the Kings, Western Thebes, Egypt. New Kingdom, 19th Dynasty, 1290-1279 BCE. Neues Museum, Berlin, German. Wikimedia Commons, 2019. https://commons.wikimedia.org/wiki/File:Pharaoh_Seti_I,_detail_of_a_wall_painting_from_the_Tomb_of_Seti_I_at_the_Valley_of_the_Kings,_Western_Thebes,_Egypt._Neues_Museum.jpg. Public domain. Photograph by Osama Shukir Muhammed Amin, CC BY-SA 4.0.

559. Klavins, Raimond, photographer. *Swayambhunath Stupa Eye Buddha* in Kathmandu, Nepal. Unsplash.com, 2021. https://unsplash.com/photos/gold-and-white-concrete-building-B7Z9-vb664Q. Licensed from Unsplash.com.

560. Artist unknown. *Hypocephalus of Tasheritkhons*. British Museum. Wikimedia Commons, 2008. https://commons.wikimedia.org/wiki/File:Hypocephalus_of_Tasheritkhons_(c._305%E2%80%9330_BCE),_British_Museum,_London_-_20080821.jpg. Public domain. Photographed by Captmondo, CC BY-SA 3.0.

563. Top: Kulturhistorisk Museum, artist. *Reconstruction drawing of an Oseberg tapestry*. Wikimedia Commons, 2016. https://commons.wikimedia.org/wiki/File:Oseberg_offerhenging_tegning.jpg. CC BY-SA 4.0.

563. Bottom left: Casliber, photographer. *Cross section of Amanita muscaria fruiting body*. Wikimedia Commons, 2016. https://commons.wikimedia.org/wiki/File:Amanita_muscaria_section_1_WF_orig.jpg. CC BY-SA 3.0.

563. Bottom right: Artist unknown. *Papyrus with the Book of the Dead of ancient Egyptian*, Yuya, 14th century BC. Egyptian Museum, Cairo. Wikimedia Commons, 2020. https://commons.wikimedia.org/wiki/File:%C3%84gyptisches_Museum_Kairo_2019-11-09_Totenbuch_des_Juja_08.jpg. Public domain. Photograph by Djehouty, CC BY-SA 4.0.

564. Top: Artist unknown. *Psilocybe Mushrooms statues*. Featured in US gov website on drug abuse, National Institute of Drug Abuse. Wikimedia Commons, 2010. https://commons.wikimedia.org/wiki/File:Psilocybe_Mushrooms_statues.jpg. Public domain.

564. Bottom: Artist unknown. *Codex Vindobonensis Mexicanus 1*, a Mexican pictorial manuscript; ritual-calendrical also contains mythological genealogies. British Museum. https://www.britishmuseum.org/collection/image/560918001. Public domain. Photograph: The Trustees of the British Museum, CC BY-NC-SA 4.0.

CHAPTER TWENTY-NINE

No images.

CHAPTER THIRTY

No Images.

COVER

Front: *Woman Traveling in Space Illustration:* Image created by DALL-E 3, an AI by OpenAI, prompted by Sura Ondrunar Publishing.

Back: Artist unknown. *Scene from the Rectangular Zodiac of Denderah.* Egyptian bas-relief in temple at Dendera, Egypt. Drawn by Faucher-Gudin, from a photograph taken with magnesium light by Ddmichen, Resultate. In *The Dawn of Civilization: Egypt and Chaldaea* by Gaston Maspero, 1894, fifth edition, 1910, page 97. https://archive.org/details/dawnofcivilizati00masp/page/96/mode/2up. Public Domain. Image recreated for use by Sura Ondrunar Publishing.

PART SECTIONS

Background: mohamed1, artist. *Ancient Egyptian Ceiling Stars Pattern.* IStock.com, 2013. https://www.istockphoto.com/vector/ancient-egyptian-ceiling-stars-pattern-background-gm1495036296-518184659. Licensed from IStock.com.

SŪRA ONDRÚNAR
PUBLISHING

suraondrunar.org

For More Information Visit

SAKROSAWEL.COM

www.ingramcontent.com/pod-product-compliance
Lightning Source LLC
Chambersburg PA
CBHW060256240426
43661CB00060B/2803